The Quilting Book

The Quilting Book

A step-by-step guide to patchwork and quilting

Christina West
Kacey Crutchfield

CONTENTS

06	**INTRODUCTION**	74	Using a needle and thread
08	What is quilting?	78	Pinning and seam ripping
10	How to use this book	80	Pressing seams
12	**TOOLS**	**82**	**Traditional piecing**
14	Basic quilting supplies	83	Patchwork
16	Cutting tools	86	Common angles
18	Measuring tools	96	Irregular angles
20	Pressing tools	104	Curves
22	Other useful tools		
24	Threads	**108**	**Improv piecing**
28	Needles and pins	109	Improv guidelines
30	Domestic sewing machine	110	Improv techniques
34	**MATERIALS**	**114**	**Foundation paper piecing**
36	Fabrics	115	Preparing FPP templates
40	Standard cuts of fabric	116	Piecing sections
42	Wadding	118	Joining templates
45	Interfacing and binding		
		120	**Hand piecing**
46	**TECHNIQUES**	121	Preparing for hand piecing
48	**Getting started**	122	Joining pieces
49	Choosing a quilt size		
50	Five components of a quilt	**124**	**English paper piecing**
52	Understanding quilt patterns	125	Common EPP shapes
54	Quilt maths	126	Preparing paper pieces
60	Choosing fabrics	128	Basting English paper piecing
62	Understanding scale	130	Joining pieces
64	Selecting fabric designs		
66	Preparing fabrics	**134**	**Appliqué**
68	Measuring and cutting fabrics	135	Preparing for appliqué
70	Cutting fabric accurately	136	Types of appliqué
72	Preparing machine settings		

140	**Quilt top construction**	186	**PROJECTS**
141	Matching points and seams	188	**Building blocks sampler**
144	Assembling a quilt top	196	**Cascading cabin**
		204	**Stellar prism**
148	**FINISHING**	212	**Nexus shift**
150	Assembling a quilt sandwich	220	**Happy patch**
151	Preparing a quilt top	226	**Primrose crown**
152	Preparing wadding and backing	234	**Papered blooms**
156	Layering	240	**Off script**
157	Basting	250	**Iridian puff**
160	**Quilting**	256	**Quilts to go:** pillow cover, wall hanging, back patch, and tote bag
161	Preparing for quilting		
164	Machine quilting	264	**BLOCK GALLERY**
168	Hand quilting	266	Classic quilt block gallery
172	**Binding**	278	**RESOURCES**
173	Preparing for binding	280	Quilting charts
174	Making binding	292	Glossary
176	Attaching binding	296	Index
178	Finishing binding	302	Acknowledgments
180	Facing		
182	**Caring for quilts**		
183	Labelling quilts		
184	Quilt maintenance		

Introduction

Welcome to *The Quilting Book*! Quilting has brought us so much joy and purpose: it has served as a much-needed creative outlet in good times and bad, helped us find community (including each other!), and taught us crucial lessons about ourselves, making us more patient and less stressed about perfection. Our 20-plus years of combined experience with sewing and quilting, including designing and technical editing quilt patterns, and teaching has equipped us with knowledge we are thrilled to impart to you in these pages.

This book will walk you through the entire quilting process, from choosing and cutting fabrics, to piecing units, and finally assembling, layering, quilting, and binding a quilt. Whether making your first quilt or building upon your existing quilting skills, the techniques included here have something for everyone. Keep in mind that quilting is a limitless journey: you can pick up the basics quickly, and then, with practice, hone your skills and expand your abilities further than you thought possible.

We want to stress that there is no "right way" to quilt – there is only the way that works best for you. Ultimately, what matters is that you made a quilt and hopefully enjoyed the process! The skills in this book build upon each other, utilizing comprehensive step-by-step instructions, photographs, and illustrations, and by the end we hope you will be confident in producing beautiful quilts of your own.

Christina West
Kacey Crutchfield

Iridian puff (top left) See p.250
Nexus shift (top right) See p.212
Stellar prism (bottom left) See p.204
Happy patch (bottom right) See p.220

What is quilting?

A quilt is defined as three layers of cloth joined together with stitches. The entire process of cutting, piecing, layering, basting, quilting, and binding a quilt is called quilting, but it can also refer to the act of stitching together the quilt layers.

The art of quilting has served both functional and creative purposes for as long as people have needed to keep warm, with the styles and techniques changing as technology progresses. Quilts were pieced and quilted solely by hand for centuries until the mid-1800s when sewing machines became available, which helped to popularize and eventually commercialize the craft. Quilting is now a billion dollar industry, with endless fabrics, tools, and advanced machines at our fingertips to efficiently produce quilts. One tradition carries through: preserving the legacy of quilts by adding labels to include the date and maker's name (see p.183).

The act of quilting has always been a communal tradition. Early quilting bees were originally formed to efficiently complete hand quilted projects while providing a safe space for quilters to convene and share skills and stories. Quilting bees have transformed into quilting guilds and online communities, with quilters still gathering to collaborate, inspire, and support each other across cultures and generations.

Quilts have long served multiple purposes depending on the intention behind their creation: they may be produced to provide comfort, fill a creative outlet, serve as a means of protest and activism, or pass down as an heirloom for future generations.

Functional quilts are made for practicality, warmth, and comfort and are commonly used on beds or as throws for couches. They prioritize functionality over artistic expression, although creativity is still conveyed through fabric and design choices. More recently, the tradition of quilting has expanded to wearable quilts, such as quilt coats, giving older quilts new life as fashion statements or functional clothing.

Art quilts are intended to serve solely as pieces of art. They often blend traditional and modern techniques, sometimes incorporating non-traditional materials and methods, such as improvisational piecing. These quilts range from abstract to detailed realistic designs, and can be found displayed as wall hangings or exhibited in galleries.

Activist quilts are quilts used to raise awareness about social or political issues, honor historical events, or express personal beliefs. Activist quilts may incorporate symbolism, text, imagery, or recycled personal materials to effectively convey their message. They can be displayed in private or public spaces, used for advocacy work or protests, or exhibited in galleries to spark dialogue and provoke thought.

Heirloom quilts are cherished for their sentimental or historical value, such as those intended to be passed down through generations. Heirloom quilts include friendship quilts, memory quilts, and those presented as gifts for milestone events such as graduations, weddings, and childbirth, and may be used, displayed, or carefully stored for preservation.

How to use this book

Begin or advance your quilting journey, learning fundamental knowledge and skills and over 200 piecing and finishing techniques. The resources in this book serve as a reference you can always return to.

TECHNIQUES

GETTING STARTED PP.48–81

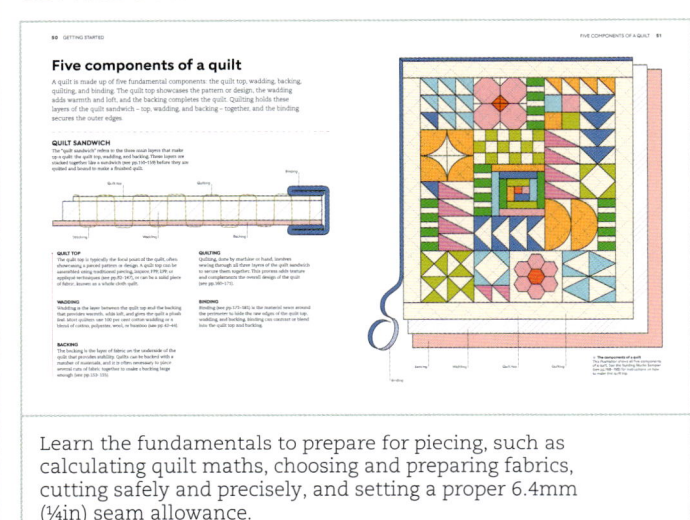

Learn the fundamentals to prepare for piecing, such as calculating quilt maths, choosing and preparing fabrics, cutting safely and precisely, and setting a proper 6.4mm (¼in) seam allowance.

TRADITIONAL PIECING PP.82–107

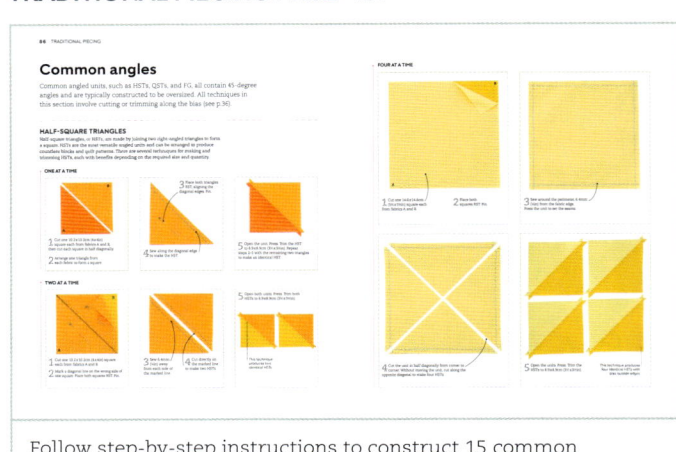

Follow step-by-step instructions to construct 15 common units, covering over 40 piecing and trimming techniques, which can be applied to construct any traditionally pieced quilt top.

IMPROV AND OTHER PIECING TECHNIQUES PP.108–147

These five sections contain alternative piecing techniques, such as improv, foundation paper piecing, hand piecing, English paper piecing, and appliqué, that can be used alone or with others to complete a quilt top.

FINISHING PP.148–185

Learn the steps to prepare, assemble, and baste a quilt sandwich, as well as techniques for binding and quilting by machine or hand and caring for your completed quilts.

HOW TO USE THIS BOOK   11

PROJECTS PP.186–263

Fully illustrated patterns include step-by-step cutting and piecing instructions that guide you through the process of making nine modern quilts and one collection of mini quilt projects containing four alternative finishing options. Refer to the first page of each project for a detailed list of materials and fabric requirements, as well as a colour reference diagram and tips for choosing fabrics.

TEMPLATES AND ONLINE RESOURCES

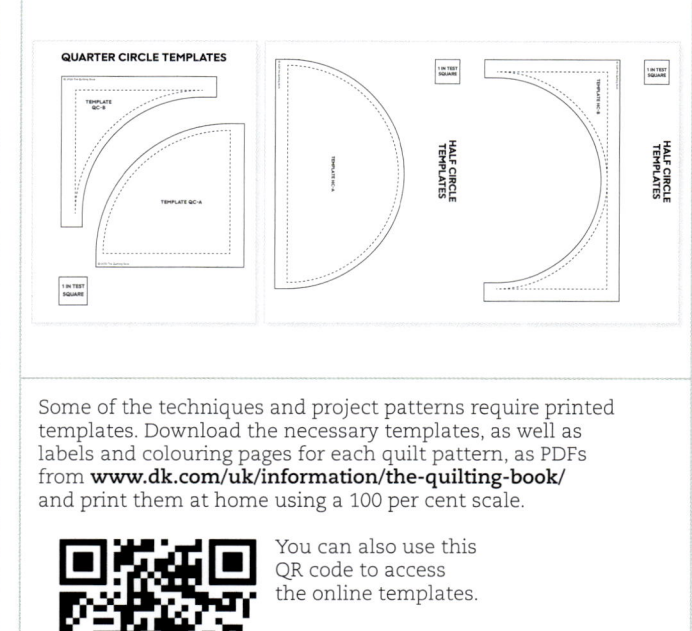

Some of the techniques and project patterns require printed templates. Download the necessary templates, as well as labels and colouring pages for each quilt pattern, as PDFs from **www.dk.com/uk/information/the-quilting-book/** and print them at home using a 100 per cent scale.

You can also use this QR code to access the online templates.

OTHER USEFUL SECTIONS

TOOLS AND MATERIALS PP.12–45

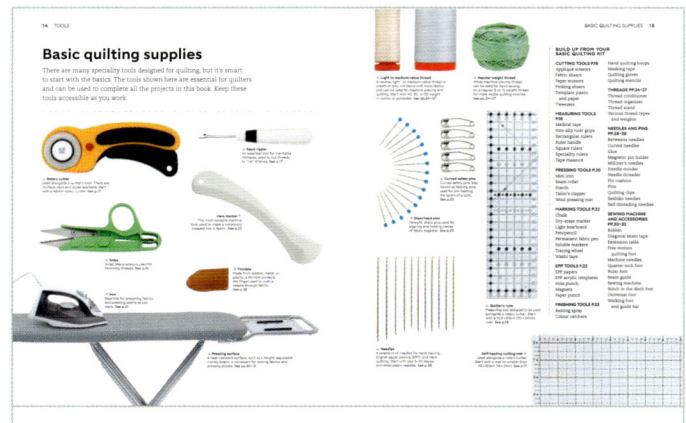

These two chapters contain information about all of the essential, and some additional, tools and materials needed to follow any technique taught in this book. From cutting and measuring tools to fabric, thread, and wadding, each item is described to help you choose the right supplies for any project.

BLOCK GALLERY AND RESOURCES PP.264–295

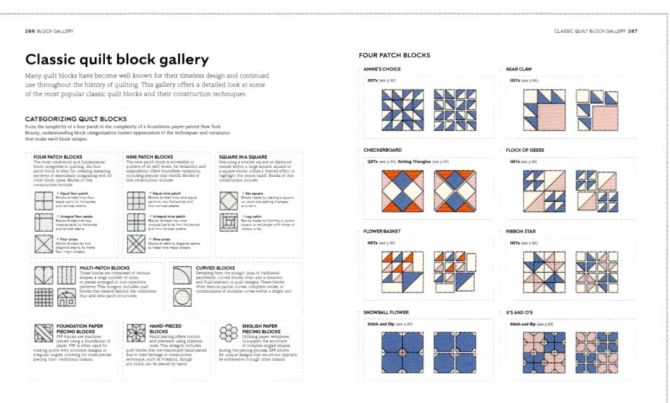

This chapter includes a gallery of 85 classic quilt block designs. It also features 18 charts with metric and imperial measurements needed to make the common units from the traditional piecing section, as well as a glossary to serve as a quick reference for the quilting-specific vocabulary used throughout the book.

TOOLS

Basic quilting supplies

There are many speciality tools designed for quilting, but it's smart to start with the basics. The tools shown here are essential for quilters and can be used to complete all the projects in this book. Keep these tools accessible as you work.

Rotary cutter
Used alongside a quilter's ruler. There are multiple sizes and styles available; start with a 45mm rotary cutter. See p.17

Seam ripper
An essential tool for inevitable mistakes; used to cut threads to "rip" stitches. See p.17

Hera marker
The most versatile marking tool; used to make a temporary creased line in fabric. See p.22

Snips
Small, sharp scissors used for trimming threads. See p.16

Thimble
Made from leather, metal, or plastic, a thimble protects the finger used to push a needle through fabric. See p.29

Iron
Essential for preparing fabrics and pressing seams as you work. See p.21

Pressing surface
A heat-resistant surface, such as a height-adjustable ironing board, is necessary for ironing fabrics and pressing blocks. See pp.20–21

BASIC QUILTING SUPPLIES

▲ **Light to medium-value thread**
A neutral, light- to medium-value thread in cream or grey will blend with most fabrics and can be used for machine piecing and quilting. Start with 40, 50, or 60 weight in cotton or polyester. See pp.24–27

▲ **Heavier weight thread**
While machine piecing thread can be used for hand sewing, try a heavier 8 or 12 weight thread for more visible quilting stitches. See pp.24–27

BUILD UP FROM YOUR BASIC QUILTING KIT

CUTTING TOOLS P.16
Appliqué scissors
Fabric shears
Paper scissors
Pinking shears
Template plastic and paper
Tweezers

MEASURING TOOLS P.18
Medical tape
Non-slip ruler grips
Rectangular rulers
Ruler handle
Square rulers
Speciality rulers
Tape measure

PRESSING TOOLS P.20
Mini iron
Seam roller
Starch
Tailor's clapper
Wool pressing mat

MARKING TOOLS P.22
Chalk
Dry-erase marker
Light box/board
Pen/pencil
Permanent fabric pen
Soluble markers
Tracing wheel
Washi tape

EPP TOOLS P.23
EPP papers
EPP acrylic templates
Hole punch
Magnets
Paper punch

FINISHING TOOLS P.23
Basting spray
Colour catchers

Hand quilting hoops
Masking tape
Quilting gloves
Quilting stencils

THREADS PP.24–27
Thread conditioner
Thread organizer
Thread stand
Various thread types and weights

NEEDLES AND PINS PP.28–29
Betweens needles
Curved needles
Glue
Magnetic pin holder
Milliner's needles
Needle minder
Needle threader
Pin cushion
Pins
Quilting clips
Sashiko needles
Self-threading needles

SEWING MACHINE AND ACCESSORIES PP.30–33
Bobbin
Diagonal seam tape
Extension table
Free motion quilting foot
Machine needles
Quarter inch foot
Ruler foot
Seam guide
Sewing machine
Stitch in the ditch foot
Universal foot
Walking foot and guide bar

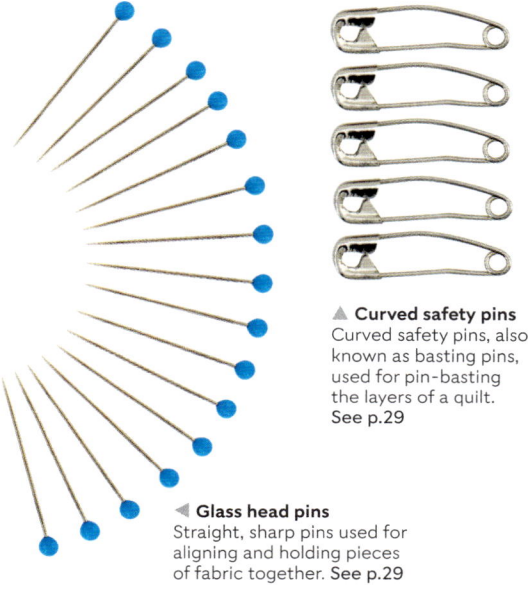

▲ **Curved safety pins**
Curved safety pins, also known as basting pins, used for pin-basting the layers of a quilt. See p.29

◀ **Glass head pins**
Straight, sharp pins used for aligning and holding pieces of fabric together. See p.29

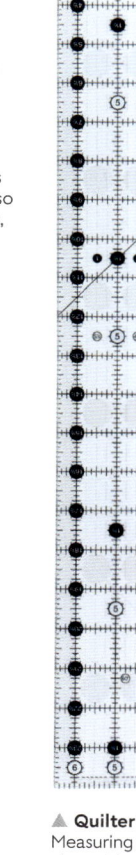

▲ **Quilter's ruler**
Measuring tool designed to be used alongside a rotary cutter. Start with a 16.5 x 62cm (6½ x 24½in) ruler. See p.18

▲ **Needles**
A selection of needles for hand piecing, English paper piecing (EPP), and hand quilting. Start with size 8–10 sharps and embroidery needles. See p.28

Self-healing cutting mat ▶
Used alongside a rotary cutter. Start with a mat no smaller than 45 x 60cm (18 x 24in). See p.17

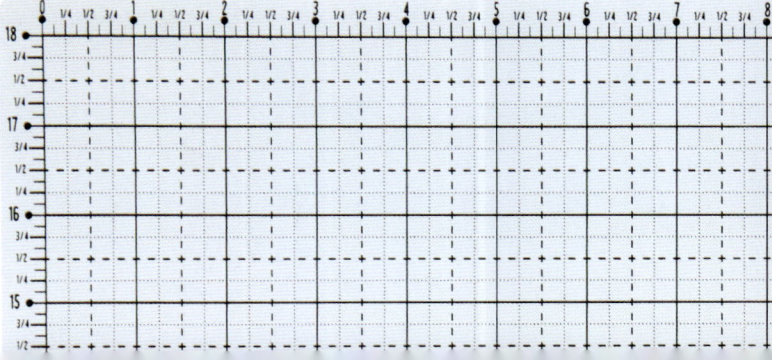

Cutting tools

One of the most crucial steps in quilting is accurately and efficiently cutting fabric (see pp.68–71) using a rotary cutter and ruler. Choose the tool that best fits the task at hand.

SCISSORS
Pair scissors with their appropriate use, whether it is for cutting threads, fabric, or paper. Scissors are available in right- and left-handed designs.

Snips ▶
Small, sharp scissors used for trimming threads.

▲ Fabric shears
Full-size scissors used for cutting fabric or wadding.

▲ Pinking shears
The saw-toothed blades cut a zigzag pattern; used for cutting fabric that will otherwise fray.

▼ Paper scissors
Reserved for cutting paper, such as templates pieces, as paper may dull fabric shears.

Appliqué scissors ▶
Used for trimming fabric layers or threads close to fabric; the duckbill style prevents unwanted cutting into other fabric layers.

CUTTING TOOLS

ROTARY CUTTERS

Efficient and accurate, rotary cutters are the primary tool used for cutting fabrics in quilting. Always use rotary cutters alongside a cutting mat, and make sure to close the blade after use. Many rotary cutters can be used interchangeably for right- or left-handedness.

◀ **28mm rotary cutter**
The small blade allows for precise cutting around curves and template pieces.

◀ **45mm rotary cutter**
This cutter is the most common size; universal for all cutting applications.

◀ **60mm rotary cutter**
This larger blade allows for cutting multiple layers of fabric at once.

▲ **Rotary blades**
Interchangeable round blades made specifically for use with rotary cutters. Be sure to change regularly as they will become blunted with use.

OTHER CUTTING TOOLS

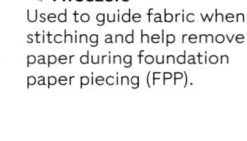

◀ **Tweezers**
Used to guide fabric when stitching and help remove paper during foundation paper piecing (FPP).

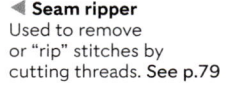

◀ **Seam ripper**
Used to remove or "rip" stitches by cutting threads. See p.79

▲ **Template plastic and paper** Used to make pattern template pieces to make cutting easier. Trace or cut around the template with a rotary cutter or pair of scissors. See p.71

Cutting mat ▶
Cutting mats are typically printed with a 1cm or 1in grid and are used alongside rotary cutters. Mats are available in a variety of sizes and colours, as well as in standard or self-healing styles.

Measuring tools

Quilter's rulers, made out of translucent acrylic, are used alongside a rotary cutter and cutting mat. Various sizes and styles are available for each type of ruler; choose one that best fits the pattern or see below for commonly used sizes. Most rulers show imperial measurements, but some are available in metric or a combination of both.

STANDARD RULERS

Used for accurately measuring and cutting fabric, quilter's rulers are marked with gridded measurements in inches or centimeters.

◀ **Tape measure**
Made of flexible fabric or plastic, this is used for measuring fabric or quilt sizes.

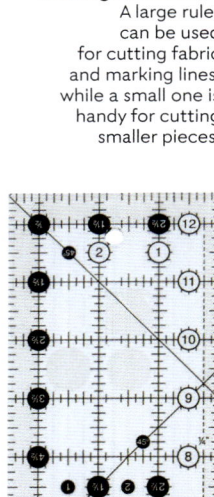
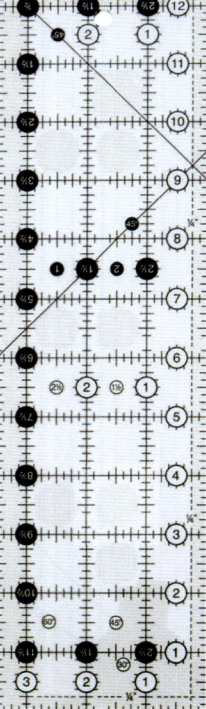
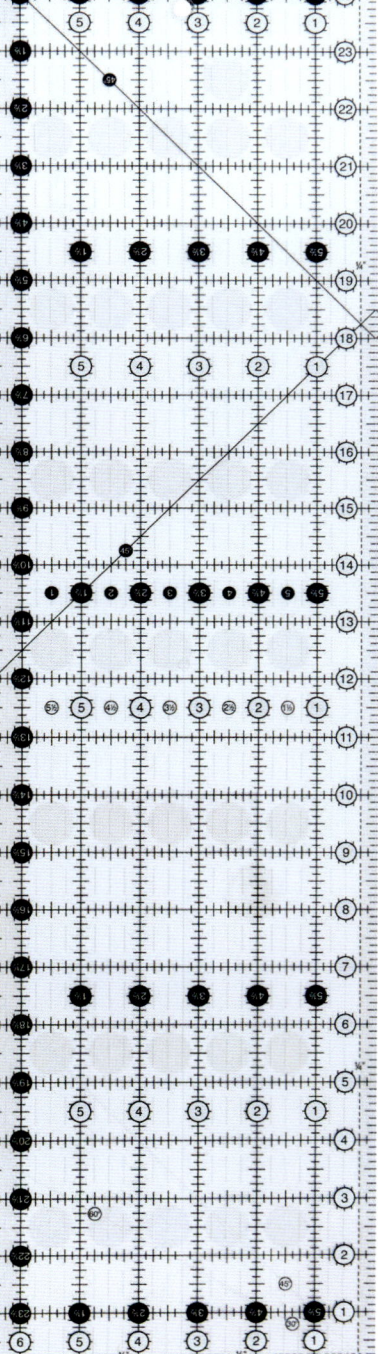

Rectangular rulers ▶
A large ruler can be used for cutting fabric and marking lines, while a small one is handy for cutting smaller pieces.

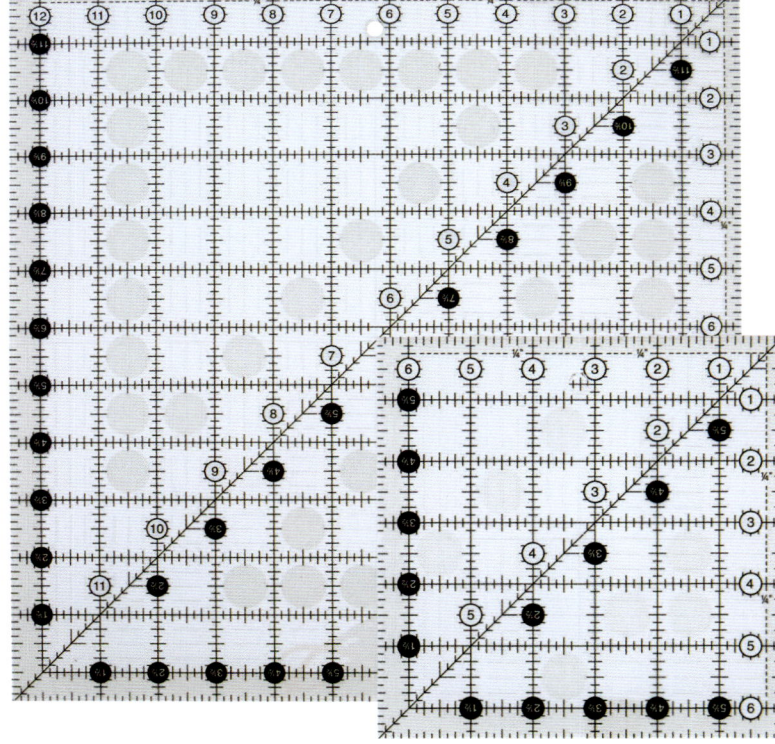

▲ **Square rulers**
Used for cutting small pieces and trimming units. Look for a 31.5cm (12½in) or a 16.5cm (6½in) square.

MEASURING TOOLS 19

SPECIALITY RULERS

Used for cutting pieces of fabric and trimming units to size, speciality quilter's rulers are usually marked with seam allowance guidelines.

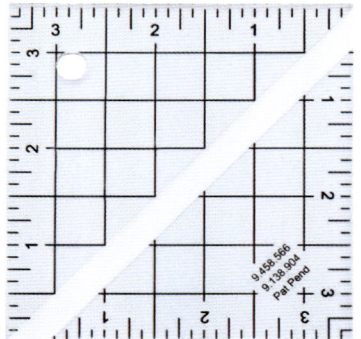

▲ **HST trimming ruler**
Used for trimming half-square triangles; marked with guidelines for aligning seams.

▲ **Flying geese ruler**
Used for trimming flying geese; marked with guidelines for aligning points and seam allowances.

▲ ▶ **Miscellaneous rulers**
Rulers are available for many applications, such as ruler work quilting, foundation paper piecing, and marking registration lines.

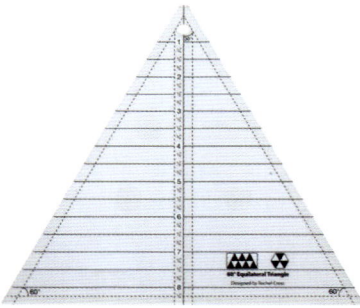

▲ **Triangle ruler**
Used for cutting triangle pieces from fabric.

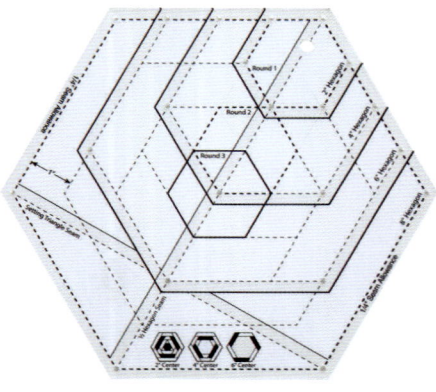

▲ **Hexagon ruler**
Used for cutting hexagon pieces from fabric.

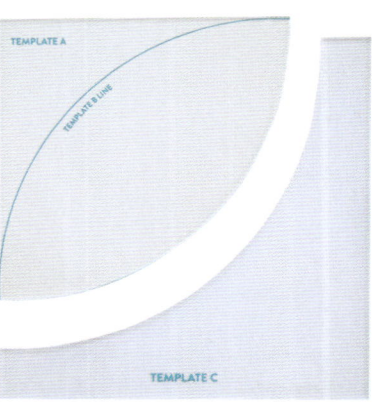

▲ **Acrylic templates**
Available in various shapes and sizes, often designed to be used alongside specific patterns to cut pieces or trim units.

RULER ACCESSORIES

These accessories are all designed to make cutting safer by preventing rulers from slipping on fabric.

Medical tape ▶
An alternative to ruler grips, textured medical tape can be applied to the underside of a ruler to prevent slipping.

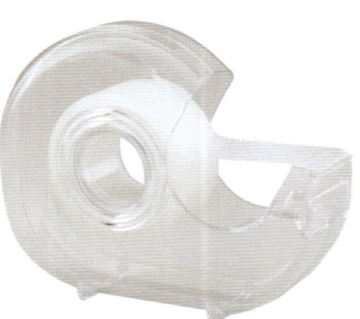

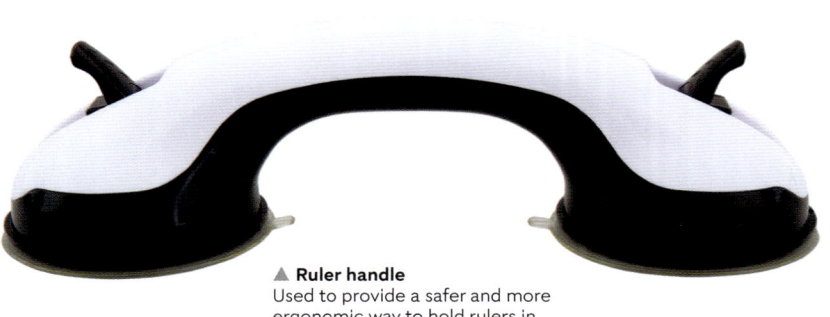

▲ **Ruler handle**
Used to provide a safer and more ergonomic way to hold rulers in place, typically attached to the top side of a ruler using suction.

Non-slip ruler grips ▶
Made of textured material with adhesive on one side, designed to be applied to the underside of a ruler to prevent slipping.

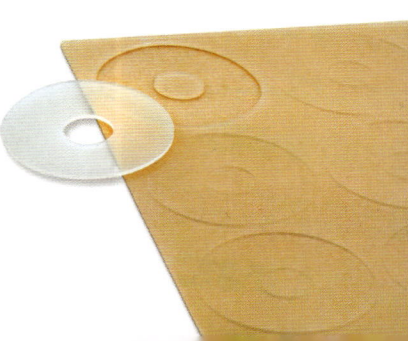

Pressing tools

Pressing is an essential – but often overlooked – step in the quilting process. Press fabric (see p.80) before cutting, all seams during piecing, and finally, the quilt top after assembly.

Seam roller ▶
Typically made of wood or plastic, used as an alternative for pressing with an iron.

Tailor's clapper ▶
A heavy block of wood used to set pressed seams while they cool, resulting in flatter seams.

▲ **Ironing board**
A staple, used for pressing larger cuts of fabric and quilt tops.

PRESSING TOOLS 21

◄ Starch
A liquid used to stabilize fabrics before cutting and after quilt assembly. Starch may cause shrinkage, so avoid using it during the piecing process. Recommended to use before cutting fabric or piecing curves, and when working with bias edges.

◄ Mini iron
Useful for pressing small units and seams between piecing steps. Keep at a pressing station close to your machine for convenience.

Iron ►
Used for all pressing steps; be sure to use an iron with a cotton setting.

Wool pressing mat ►
Made of compressed wool to absorb and reflect heat while pressing.

Other useful tools

Various tools are used for specific applications throughout the quilting process, from marking individual pieces or entire quilt tops, preparing for English paper piecing (EPP), to layering and finishing a quilt.

MARKING TOOLS

Choose the marking tool most appropriate for the task at hand. Keep in mind the permanency and removal process for each tool.

▲ **Hera**
A smooth plastic or wooden tool used to crease fabric for marking lines without ink or chalk.

▲ **Washi tape**
Temporary tape that can be affixed to a ruler for precise alignment or to a needle plate for accurate seams while sewing.

▲ **Light box/board**
Used primarily to see template lines through fabric, such as for foundation paper piecing (FPP).

◀ **Tracing wheel**
Used for perforating foundation paper piecing (FPP) paper.

Pen/pencil ▶
Used for marking on the wrong side of fabric, marking labels, or making notes on patterns.

◀ **Water-/air-soluble marker**
A water-soluble marker is a temporary marking aid that is removed with water, while an air-soluble marker is a temporary marking aid that disappears with exposure to air.

◀ **Permanent fabric pen**
Used for writing labels on quilts.

◀ **Dry-erase marker**
A dry-erase marker is used for making temporary marks on top of rulers to assist with cutting and trimming.

Chalk ▶
A temporary marking aid that brushes or washes away.

ENGLISH PAPER PIECING TOOLS

These tools are essential for EPP (see pp.124–133) and help with precise cutting, basting, and assembling.

◀ **EPP papers**
Provide a base for fabric pieces; these papers are sturdy and reusable. A variety of shapes can be purchased pre-cut or made at home.

◀ **Hole punch**
Used for punching small holes in the centres of EPP papers to prepare for later paper removal.

◀ **EPP acrylic templates**
Used for cutting shapes from fabric, these are available with and without included seam allowance.

◀ **Paper punch**
Used to cut a specific shape out of paper. Paper punches are available in limited sizes and shapes.

Magnets ▶
Used for temporarily holding fabric to its corresponding paper piece while basting and for securely holding pieces together while stitching to avoid shifting.

FINISHING TOOLS

From basting, to quilting, and finally washing a finished quilt, these tools are useful during the quilt finishing process (see pp.150–185).

◀ **Colour catchers**
Small sheets used to prevent colours from running or bleeding by trapping loose dye when washing fabric and quilts.

Masking tape ▶
Used for many applications, such as marking lines for quilting and adhering quilt backing to a hard surface during the basting process.

◀ **Quilting templates and stencils**
Used to mark or guide designs and motifs for quilting.

▲ **Basting spray**
Washable spray adhesive used for temporarily adhering pieces together, such as for appliqué or basting a quilt sandwich.

▲ **Quilting gloves**
Non-slip gloves used to increase grip while machine quilting.

Hand quilting hoops ▶
Used for creating and holding tension in a quilt sandwich, a hoop is made of interlocking 2.5cm (1in) solid and split rings.

Threads

Threads are available in a variety of fibres, sizes, and weights. Some thread is universal and can be used for all piecing and quilting applications. Thread can also be chosen intentionally for each project based on the stitching method, the fabrics, and the desired look of the completed quilt.

THREAD TYPES

The most commonly used threads for quilting are made of cotton, polyester, or a blend of cotton/polyester fibres. Choose the thread type that best fits the project at hand.

Cotton
100 per cent cotton thread is universal and can be used for all piecing and quilting. Available in a range of colours and weights.

Polyester
Commonly used for machine piecing and quilting and sometimes used for EPP. Most long-arm machines use polyester or a polyester/cotton blend thread. Available in a large range of colours and weights.

Monofilament
Used for quilting, EPP, and appliqué to achieve inconspicuous stitches that do not distract from the overall design. Made of clear or coloured translucent nylon or polyester fibre.

Variegated
Characterized by a dye pattern of gradual colour shifts along the length of thread, variegated thread is designed to add depth and variation. It is available in cotton and polyester.

Metallic
Used for machine or hand quilting and is typically made of polyester in a limited range of colours and weights.

SPOOL SIZES

Thread is sold on a spool, cone, or ball, either stacked or cross wound, and available in multiple types and weights. Check which style works best with your machine.

Small spool
Contains approximately 90–200m (100–225yds) of thread. Used for smaller projects or trying new weights or colours.

Large spool
The most common spool size contains approximately 500–1,500m (550–1,600yds) of thread. Used for piecing and quilting projects of various sizes.

Cone
Contains approximately 2,300–6,000m (2,500–6,500yds) of thread. Used for larger or dense quilting projects.

Ball
Contains approximately 70–100m (75–110yds) of thread. Available in thicker weights, such as 12 or 8, which are typically used for hand quilting.

THREAD ACCESSORIES

Various thread accessories are available to help manage and organize thread. Most are universal to be used alongside all thread types and spool sizes.

Thread conditioner
Typically made of beeswax and available in scented or unscented variations, thread conditioner, or gloss, is used to coat thread to prevent fraying, tangling, and knotting when hand piecing or hand quilting.

Thread stand
Most often used to hold cones of thread for domestic sewing machines, these stands act as a spool holder and thread guide. They can also be used to provide support for using cross wound spools with machines that have horizontal spool holders for stacked thread spools.

Thread organizer
Available in various styles, from peg boards to plastic organizers with individual compartments for each spool, organizers keep thread from unraveling.

26 TOOLS

THREAD WEIGHTS

Threads are available in many weights that are designed and suited for various applications. Remember to match thread weight to needle size (p.28). Stitch length may vary based on thread and fabric weight (see p.36).

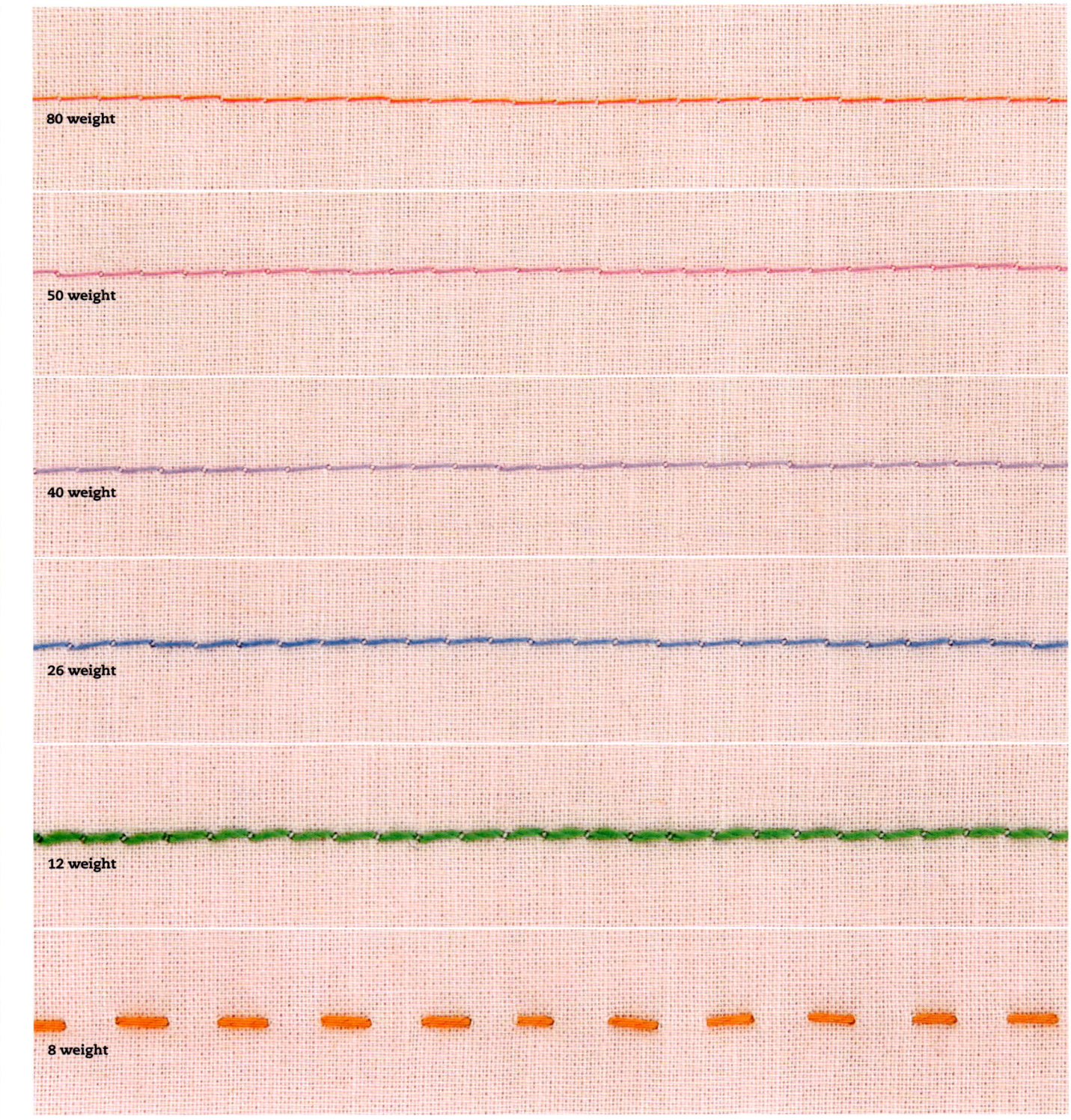

80 weight

50 weight

40 weight

26 weight

12 weight

8 weight

100 WEIGHT AND 80 WEIGHT

Fine threads used in machine or hand piecing and quilting. They are used to achieve a balance between strong and lightweight subtle stitches, such as in EPP, appliqué, and intricate quilting. Pair with light- to medium-weight fabrics.

60 WEIGHT AND 50 WEIGHT

Universal, medium threads used in machine or hand piecing and quilting. They are used for all piecing and quilting applications for visible stitches; the most common thread weight in quilting. Pair with light- to medium-weight fabrics.

40 WEIGHT

A slightly heavier medium thread used in machine or hand quilting. It is used for all quilting applications, producing a durable, visible stitch that holds up well through repeated washings. Pair with medium- to heavy-weight fabrics.

28 WEIGHT

A heavier thread used in machine or hand quilting. It is used to achieve more visible stitches for all-over or accent quilting. Pair with medium- to heavy-weight fabrics.

12 WEIGHT

A heavier thread used in machine quilting. It is used primarily in hand quilting to achieve highly visible stitches for all-over or accent quilting. Pair with medium- to heavy-weight fabrics.

8 WEIGHT

A heavy thread used in hand quilting. It is used to achieve bold stitches, such as in big stitch quilting and binding. Pair with medium- to heavy-weight fabrics.

Needles and pins

Sharp, high-quality needles and pins are used to achieve consistent stitches and precise fabric alignment.

HAND NEEDLES

These needles are used for piecing, appliqué, and quilting by hand, and are available in a variety of sizes and styles. Needle sizes are typically numbered, with smaller numbers indicating larger, thicker needles and larger numbers indicating finer, thinner needles. Choose an appropriate needle based on technique, fabrics, and thread weight.

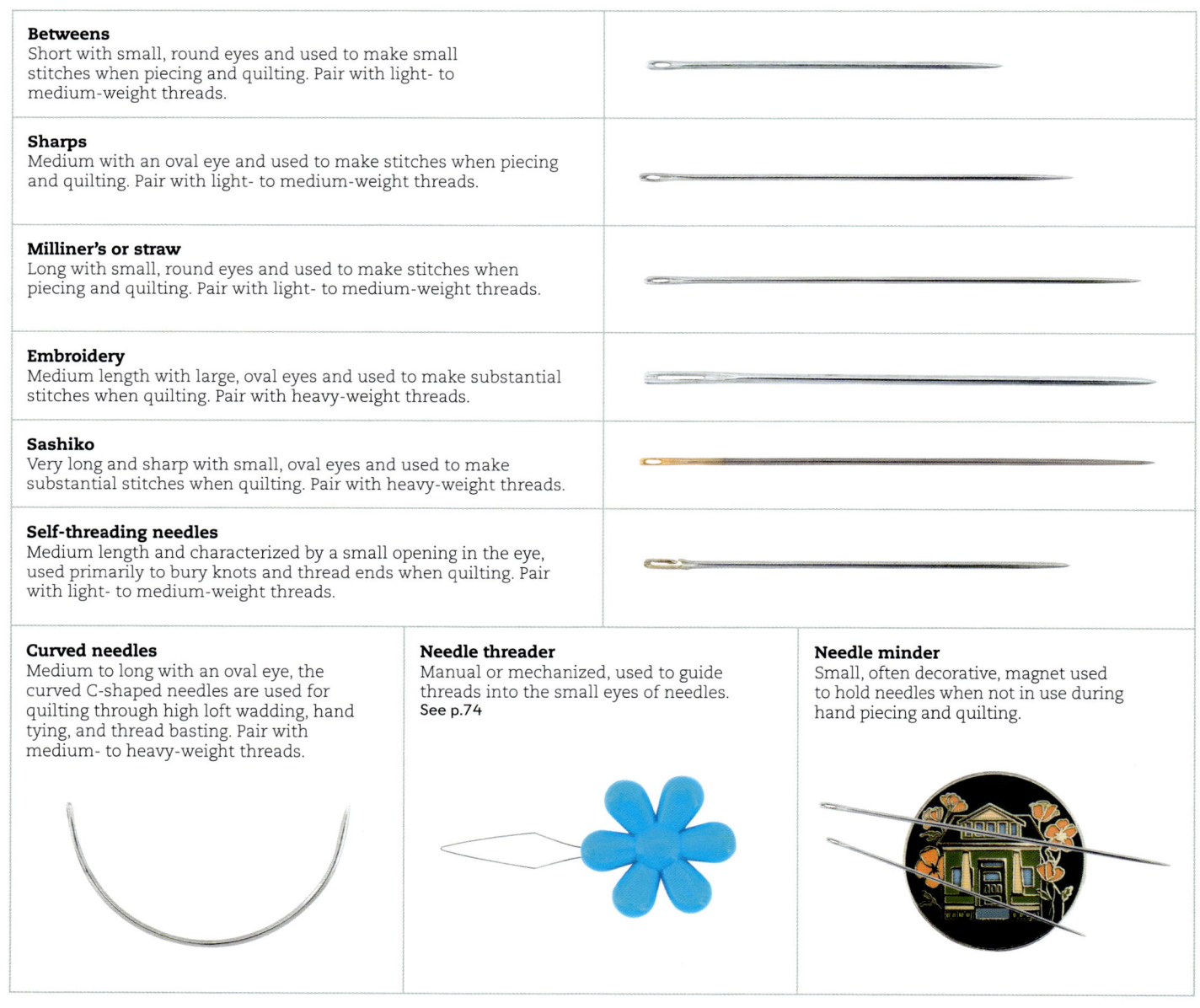

Betweens
Short with small, round eyes and used to make small stitches when piecing and quilting. Pair with light- to medium-weight threads.

Sharps
Medium with an oval eye and used to make stitches when piecing and quilting. Pair with light- to medium-weight threads.

Milliner's or straw
Long with small, round eyes and used to make stitches when piecing and quilting. Pair with light- to medium-weight threads.

Embroidery
Medium length with large, oval eyes and used to make substantial stitches when quilting. Pair with heavy-weight threads.

Sashiko
Very long and sharp with small, oval eyes and used to make substantial stitches when quilting. Pair with heavy-weight threads.

Self-threading needles
Medium length and characterized by a small opening in the eye, used primarily to bury knots and thread ends when quilting. Pair with light- to medium-weight threads.

Curved needles
Medium to long with an oval eye, the curved C-shaped needles are used for quilting through high loft wadding, hand tying, and thread basting. Pair with medium- to heavy-weight threads.

Needle threader
Manual or mechanized, used to guide threads into the small eyes of needles.
See p.74

Needle minder
Small, often decorative, magnet used to hold needles when not in use during hand piecing and quilting.

PINS AND NEEDLE ACCESSORIES

Pins are essential tools available in various styles. They are designed to hold fabric layers in place during piecing and quilting, assisting with precise alignment and preventing shifting (see p.78).

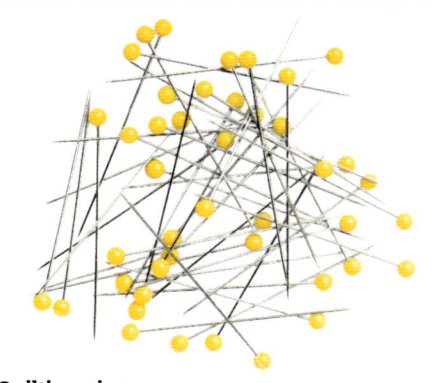

Quilting pins
Thin, sharp, and strong to secure multiple layers of fabric without snagging. Used universally for piecing and appliqué.

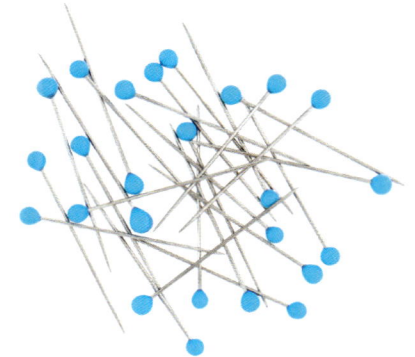

Glass head pins
Similar to quilting pins, featuring a heat-resistant glass head.

Flower head pins
Flat, flower-shaped heads are convenient for FPP.

Curved safety pins
Designed to easily push through multiple layers of fabric without getting caught. Used to temporarily hold fabric while pin-basting the layers of a quilt. See p.157

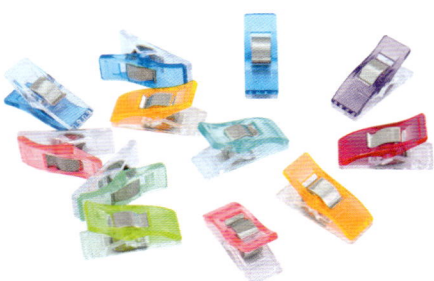

Quilting clips
An alternative to using pins, small quilting clips pinch fabric together. Used primarily for piecing and binding.

Glue
An alternative to pins, liquid washable glue is used to hold fabric together during piecing and basting. Stick glue is used for basting fabric to paper in FPP and EPP.

Magnetic pin holder
Small dishes used to hold pins when not in use; the magnetic base keeps pins in place.

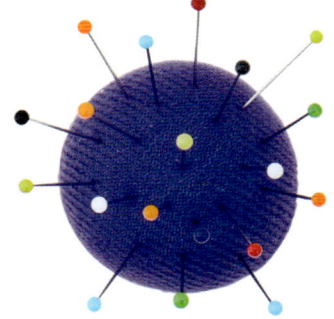

Pin cushion
Used to hold pins when not in use, typically stuffed with fibre or specialized filling intended to keep points sharp.

Thimble
Made of leather, metal, or plastic, these small sheaths cover and protect fingertips from sharp pins and needles when hand piecing or quilting. See p.77

Domestic sewing machine

Sewing machines make piecing and quilting much faster than hand quilting. Modern sewing machines are often computer-based to provide a variety of options and automations, though not all machines have all features shown here. Before investing in a used or new machine, spend time testing the features to make sure it is a good fit for you.

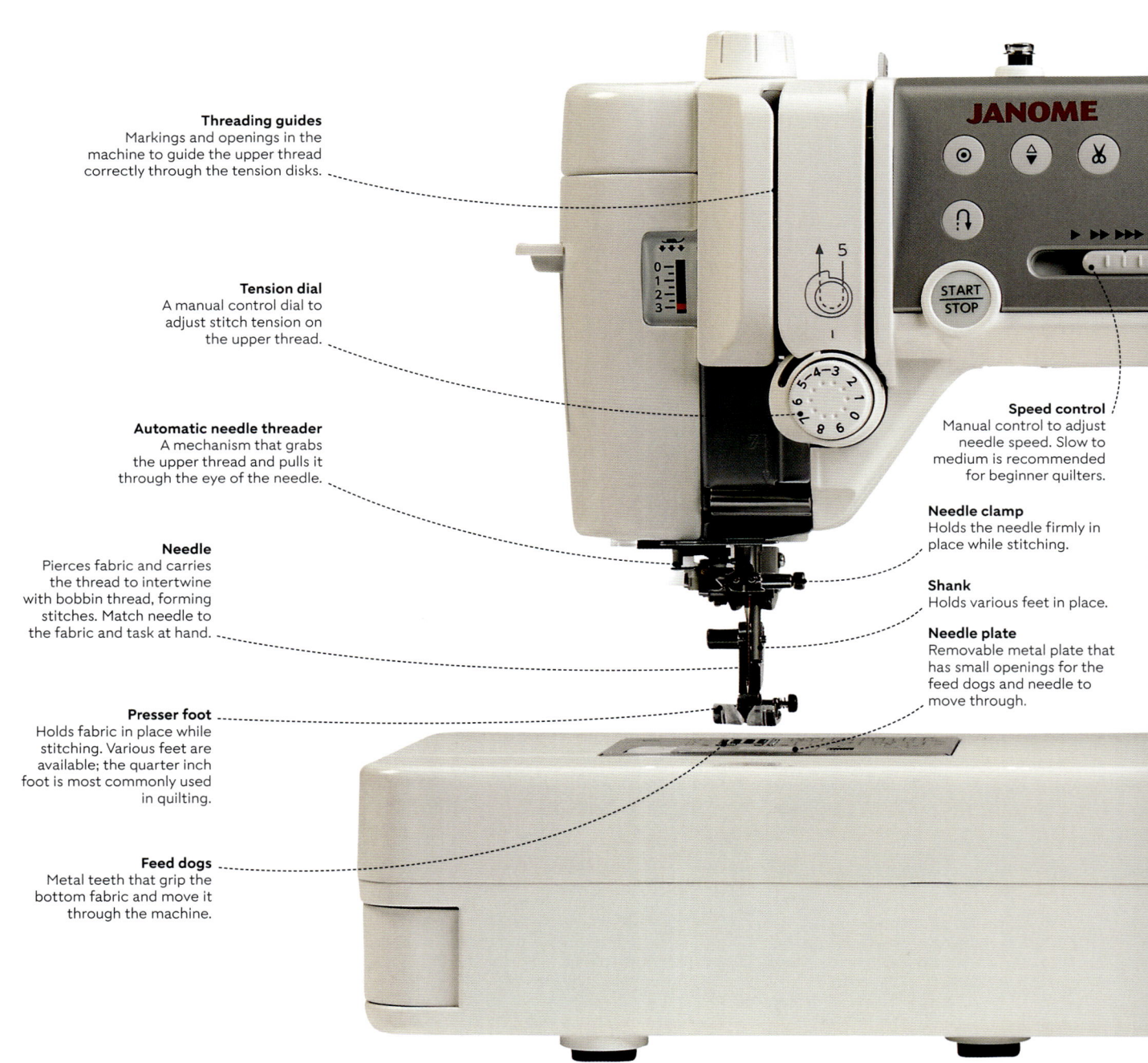

Threading guides
Markings and openings in the machine to guide the upper thread correctly through the tension disks.

Tension dial
A manual control dial to adjust stitch tension on the upper thread.

Automatic needle threader
A mechanism that grabs the upper thread and pulls it through the eye of the needle.

Needle
Pierces fabric and carries the thread to intertwine with bobbin thread, forming stitches. Match needle to the fabric and task at hand.

Presser foot
Holds fabric in place while stitching. Various feet are available; the quarter inch foot is most commonly used in quilting.

Feed dogs
Metal teeth that grip the bottom fabric and move it through the machine.

Speed control
Manual control to adjust needle speed. Slow to medium is recommended for beginner quilters.

Needle clamp
Holds the needle firmly in place while stitching.

Shank
Holds various feet in place.

Needle plate
Removable metal plate that has small openings for the feed dogs and needle to move through.

DOMESTIC SEWING MACHINE **31**

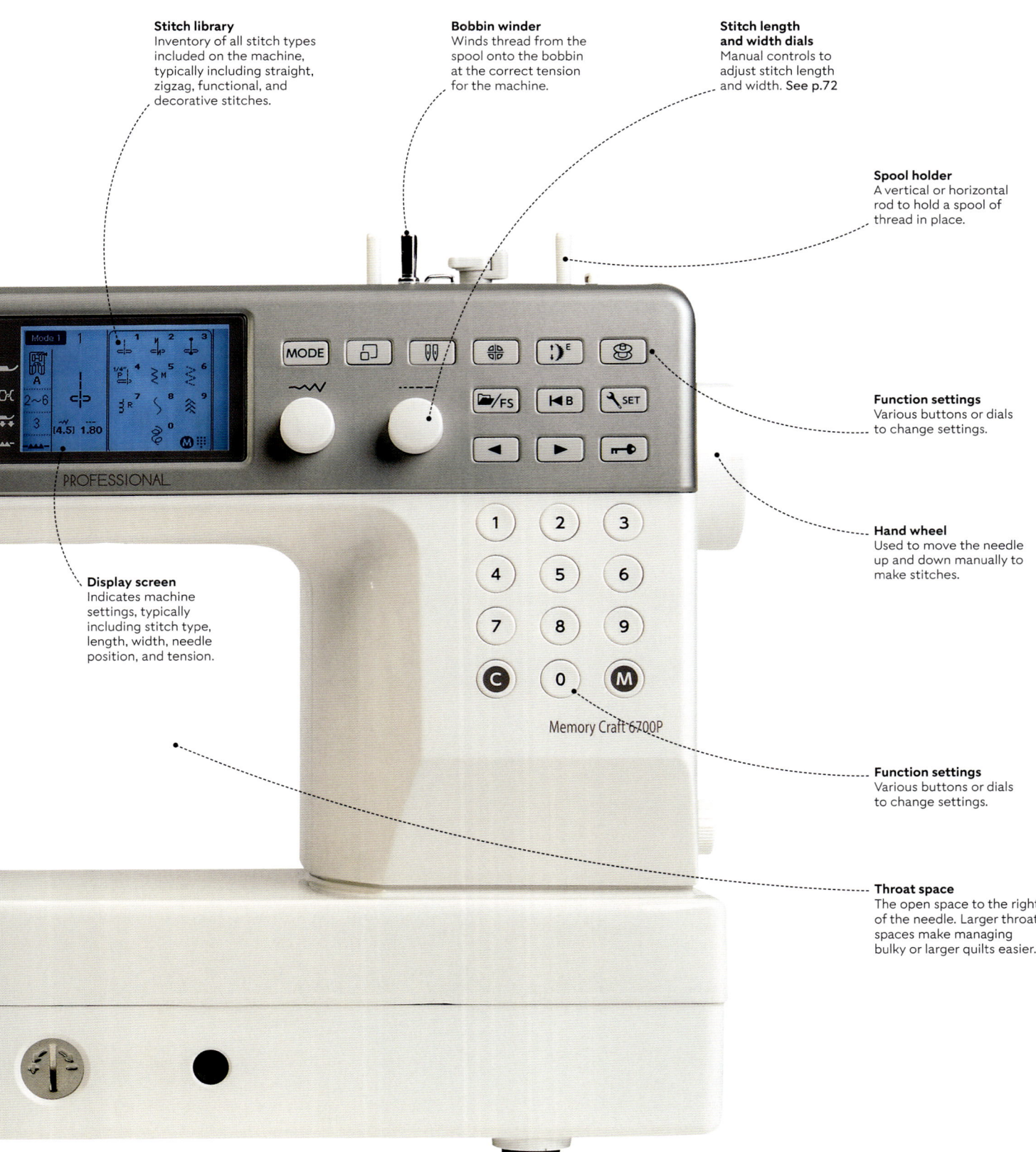

Stitch library
Inventory of all stitch types included on the machine, typically including straight, zigzag, functional, and decorative stitches.

Bobbin winder
Winds thread from the spool onto the bobbin at the correct tension for the machine.

Stitch length and width dials
Manual controls to adjust stitch length and width. See p.72

Spool holder
A vertical or horizontal rod to hold a spool of thread in place.

Function settings
Various buttons or dials to change settings.

Hand wheel
Used to move the needle up and down manually to make stitches.

Display screen
Indicates machine settings, typically including stitch type, length, width, needle position, and tension.

Function settings
Various buttons or dials to change settings.

Throat space
The open space to the right of the needle. Larger throat spaces make managing bulky or larger quilts easier.

MACHINE ACCESSORIES

Many quilting accessories will come with a new sewing machine, while others are available for purchase separately. Each of these accessories is designed for a specific task throughout the quilting process.

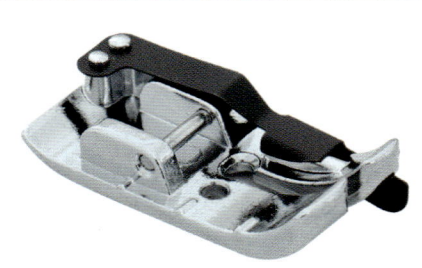

Quarter inch foot
Used to assist with sewing precise 6.4mm (¼in) seams while piecing; position the fabric edge with the right edge of the foot. Quarter inch feet are available with or without a guide. See p.73

Ruler foot
Typically a circular foot, open in the middle, with 6.4mm (¼in) high "walls" to protect the needle; used to safely butt against machine quilting rulers. See p.167

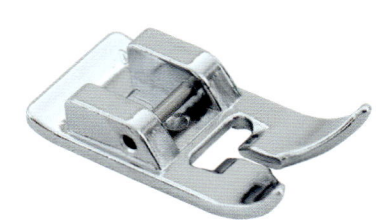

Universal foot
With a wide opening for the needle to pass through and markings for common seam allowances, this foot can be used for many sewing applications.

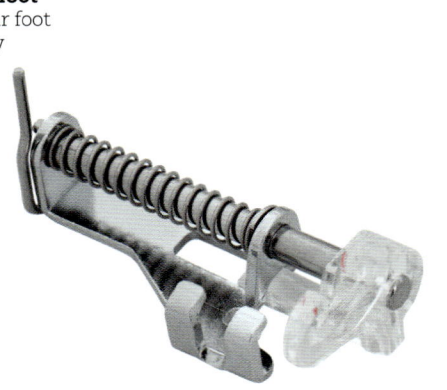

Free motion quilting foot
An open oval or circular foot that allows for visibility while stitching in any direction. Also known as a "darning" or "hopping foot." See p.166

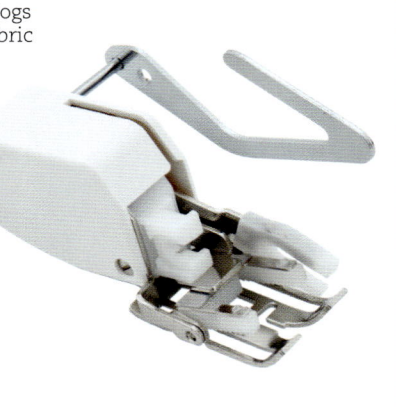

Walking foot and guide bar
Equipped with a set of feed dogs to guide, or "walk," the top fabric through the machine, working in tandem with the lower feed dogs. Use with an adjustable guide bar for spacing quilting lines. See p.164

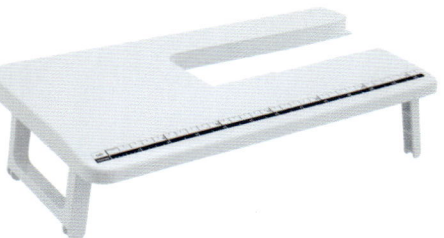

Extension table
Typically made of plastic; a table that is level with the machine bed to provide a larger surface for fabric while piecing or quilting.

Bobbin
Holds the lower thread that becomes the stitches on the bottom of fabric. Match bobbin type to machine specifications.

Seam guide
Provides an edge to keep fabric aligned while piecing; available as a magnet or with the option to screw into the machine bed.

Washi tape
Temporary tape that can be affixed to a needle plate and/or machine bed to guide and aid in achieving accurate 6.4mm (¼in) seams while stitching.

MACHINE NEEDLES

Available in various styles, such as ballpoint or sharp, the size of the needle determines its main use in piecing and quilting. Needle sizes use two numbers, both referring to the diameter of the shaft. Change the needle often as they blunt easily.

70/10 needles Use with 80 and 100 weight threads and lightweight fabrics. Commonly used for piecing.	
80/12 needles Use with 40, 50, and 60 weight thread and light- to medium-weight fabrics. Commonly used for piecing and quilting.	
90/14 needles Use for quilting with medium- to heavy-weight threads, as the needle is sturdy enough to travel through the three layers of a quilt sandwich.	

LONGARM QUILTING MACHINE

Longarm machines have a larger throat space to accommodate quilting large areas at one time and are guided by hand or computer. Rather than traditionally basting a quilt sandwich, the quilt top, wadding, and backing are attached separately to a series of bars on the longarm frame. Many quilters send their quilt tops out to professional longarm quilters for quilting services.

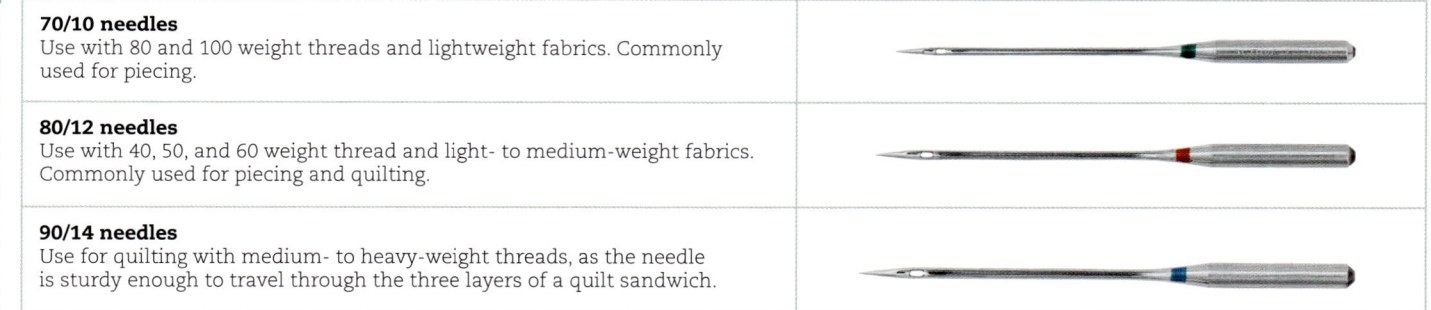

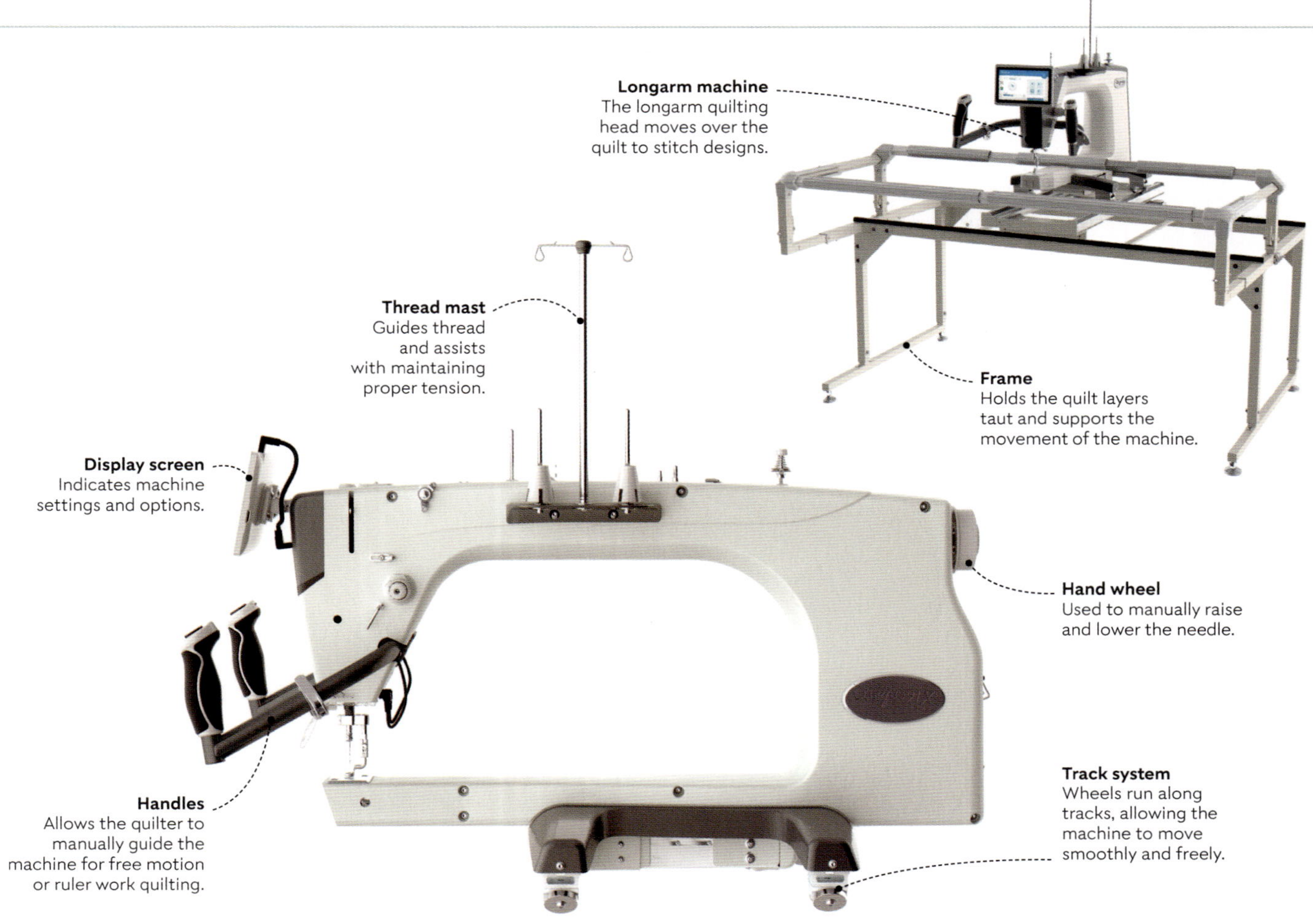

Longarm machine — The longarm quilting head moves over the quilt to stitch designs.

Thread mast — Guides thread and assists with maintaining proper tension.

Frame — Holds the quilt layers taut and supports the movement of the machine.

Display screen — Indicates machine settings and options.

Hand wheel — Used to manually raise and lower the needle.

Handles — Allows the quilter to manually guide the machine for free motion or ruler work quilting.

Track system — Wheels run along tracks, allowing the machine to move smoothly and freely.

MATERIALS

Fabrics

The characteristics of fabric provide information about how and when to use them. Grain and bias apply most when cutting fabric, and thread count and weight are important when choosing threads (see p.24) and needles (see p.28).

GRAIN

The direction of the weave in fabric is called the grain line. Warp threads, creating the straight grain, run parallel to the selvedge and are stronger; weft threads, creating the cross grain, are woven perpendicular to the selvedge. Cutting on the grain means cutting along either of these grain lines.

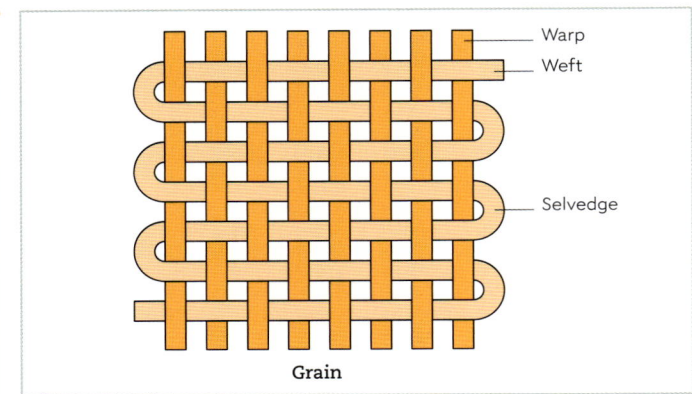

BIAS

The bias line of fabric runs diagonally to the grain lines and is quite stretchy. Some pieces, such as curves (see p.104) and setting triangles (see p.95), have bias edges. It is undesirable for fabrics to stretch during piecing and quilting; starch when preparing fabric (see p.67) and sew a stay stitch (see p.151) to prevent bias edges from stretching.

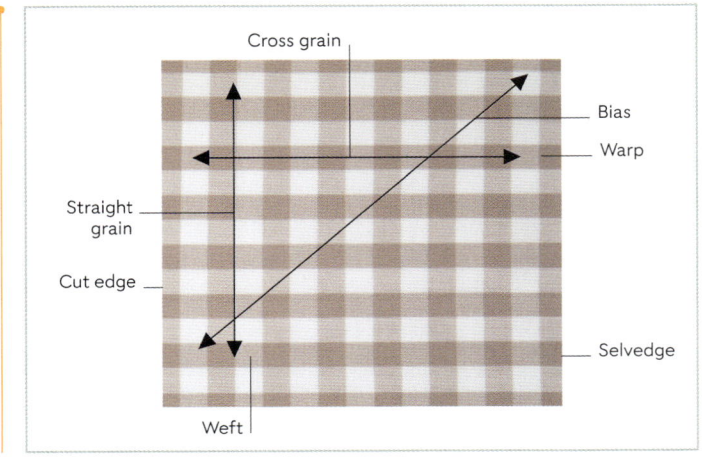

THREAD COUNT AND WEIGHT

The thread count is determined by the number of warp and weft threads per square inch of fabric, which varies based on thread weight and fibre. Fabric weight is determined by how heavy or light a fabric is when measured in ounces per square yard or grams per square meter. The weight affects durability and determines what threads and needles to use.

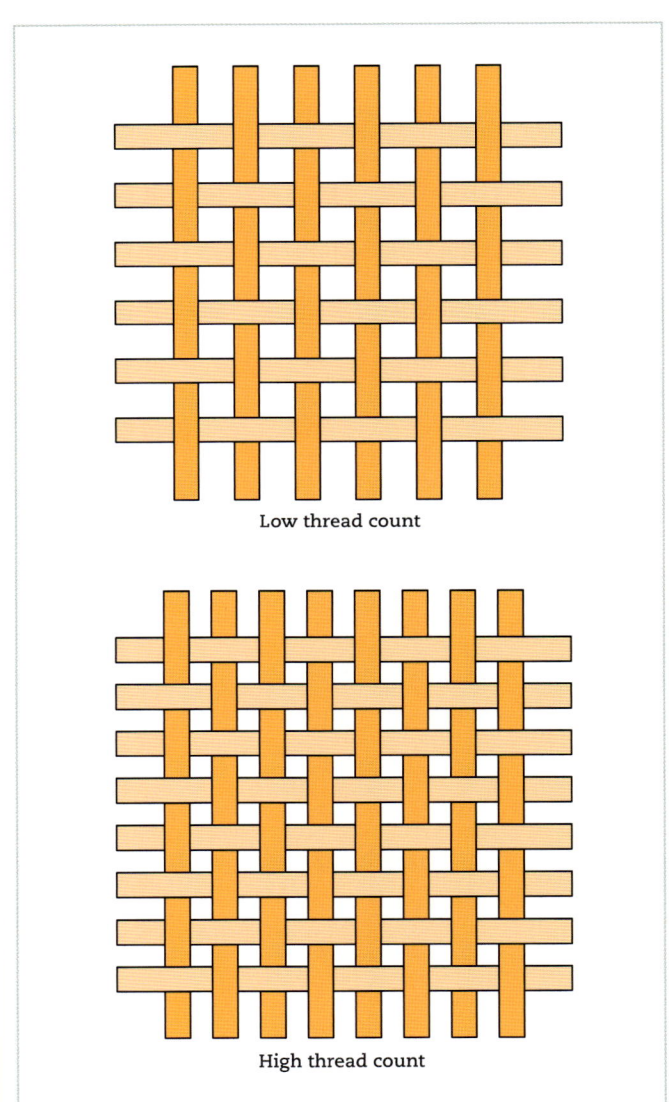

COMMON QUILTING FABRICS

While almost any fabric can be used for quilting, the fabrics listed below are the most common. They are all versatile, light- to medium-weight, non-stretch fabrics that can be used in all quilting applications.

QUILTING COTTON

A crisp, tightly woven fabric made from 100 per cent cotton and specifically designed for quilting. It is stable enough to hold its structure when cut into small pieces, but light enough to keep seams manageable.

Width of fabric:	101.6–111.8cm (40–44in); standard WOF is 106.7cm (42in)
Weight:	light to medium
Used for:	all quilting applications
Special notes:	weight and feel vary greatly by manufacturer; try a variety to find your preference

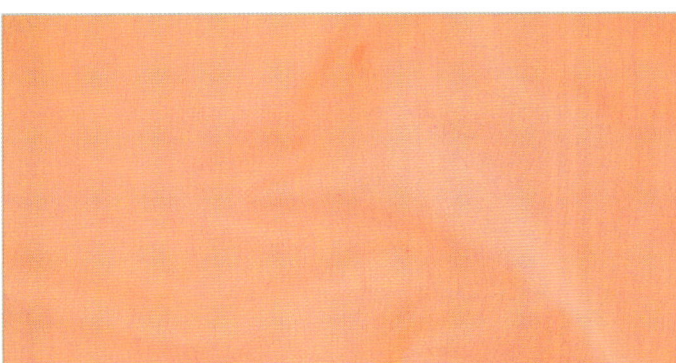

SHOT COTTON

A fabric woven out of two different colours, with one colour running along the warp and the other along the weft, which combine to make what appears to be a new colour. The weave is typically looser than quilting cotton, and it is often chosen to add depth and texture in place of a solid.

Width of fabric:	101.6–121.9cm (40–48in)
Weight:	light to medium
Used for:	all quilting applications
Special notes:	frays; use a shorter stitch length; appearance may be directional due to different warp and weft thread colours

LINEN

Made from 100 per cent linen or a blend of linen and cotton, this fabric has a loose, textured weave, which adds interest and softness. Available in solids, prints, and hand-dyed varieties.

Width of fabric:	101.6–228.6cm (40–90in)
Weight:	light to medium
Used for:	all quilting applications
Special notes:	known to fray; use a shorter stitch length; be mindful of heavy shrinkage

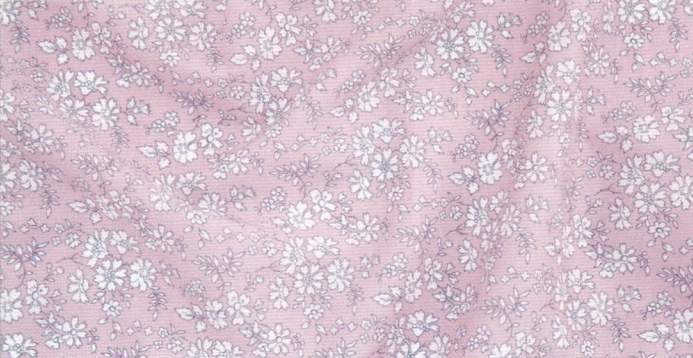

LAWN

A luxurious option, lawn is made with a very fine, high thread count and a tight weave, typically from 100 per cent cotton. The lightweight fabric is semi-transparent with a silky feel due to the fine fibres.

Width of fabric:	101.6–152.4cm (40–60in)
Weight:	light
Used for:	all quilting applications; quite popular for EPP (see p.124)
Special notes:	consider using starch to add stability; use a finer, sharper needle to avoid damaging the fabric

UNCOMMON QUILTING FABRICS

Quilters have always used what they have, and sometimes what they have is not standard quilting cotton. This resourcefulness leads to unique, unexpected fabric choices that add character and interest to each quilt. Be mindful when working with a variety of fabric types, as each one may require different preparations before use (see pp.66–67).

DOUBLE GAUZE

An airy, loosely woven fabric made of two layers of thin gauze that can produce a luscious, cosy quilt. Pre-wash to shrink before use.

Width of fabric:	101.6–152.4cm (40–60in)
Weight:	light
Used for:	quilt backings and baby quilts
Special notes:	not forgiving; use quilting clips instead of pins (see p.78) and try to avoid seam ripping (see p.79); iron and use starch

DOBBY

A soft, woven fabric characterized by small, often geometric, raised shapes that create a pattern. These fabrics add texture, while often still reading as a solid colour.

Width of fabric:	101.6–152.4cm (40–60in)
Weight:	light to medium
Used for:	all quilting applications
Special notes:	consider using starch to add stability; use a shorter stitch length

CHAMBRAY

A woven fabric, typically made of 100 per cent cotton, characterized by coloured warp threads and white weft threads. While it looks much like denim, the weave and lighter weight make chambray a good choice for adding texture to quilts.

Width of fabric:	101.6–152.4cm (40–60in)
Weight:	light to medium
Used for:	all quilting applications
Special notes:	known to bleed; consider pre-washing

FLANNEL

Made from cotton, wool, or synthetic fibres and very soft, flannel is available in solids or prints, often in a tartan motif. Flannel is thicker than other quilting fabrics, and it is often used to add warmth and cosiness to quilts.

Width of fabric:	101.6–274.3cm (40–108in)
Weight:	medium to heavy
Used for:	quilt backings and whole cloth quilts
Special notes:	known to bleed and shrink heavily; consider pre-washing

BATIK

Batik refers to the fabric dying process, which uses dye-resistant wax to create vivid, often intricate designs. Batik fabrics have a tighter weave and stiffer feel than quilting cotton.

Width of fabric:	101.6–304.8cm (40–120in)
Weight:	medium
Used for:	all quilting applications
Special notes:	known to bleed; difficult to work with by hand

HAND DYED

Often using a base of quilting cotton or linen, some quilters choose to dye their own fabrics using synthetic or natural dyes. Fabrics can be dyed with one colour to produce a solid colour or with a variety of colours and other techniques, such as ice-dying, to produce patterns.

Width of fabric:	101.6–111.8cm (40–44in)
Weight:	light to medium
Used for:	all quilting applications
Special notes:	pre-wash to set dye and avoid bleeding

RECLAIMED

Whether reclaimed from another blanket, a closet, or the thrift store, a variety of fabrics can be upcycled and used to make new quilts. Poplin dress shirts, vintage sheets, and denim are some of the most popular fabric types to repurpose into quilts.

Width of fabric:	varies by fabric type
Weight:	varies by fabric type
Used for:	all quilting applications
Special notes:	keep in mind that fabrics behave differently and some may stretch, shrink, or bleed

MUSLIN

A versatile, medium to loosely woven fabric available in a variety of types and weights, most commonly as unbleached, natural cotton. A plain lightweight muslin, similar to linen, is often affordable and used for practising piecing and for quilt backings.

Width of fabric:	101.6–304.8cm (40–120in)
Weight:	light to medium
Used for:	practice and quilt backings
Special notes:	in lower to medium grades, the texture is rough; known to shrink; consider pre-washing

Standard cuts of fabric

Quilt patterns typically list the amount of fabric needed. Fabric is often sold in quarter metre or yard increments, as well as in standard pre-cut sizes. While the width of fabric varies, the standard width of fabric, or WOF, in quilting is 106.7cm (42in). Some fabrics are available as a wide back, which typically measures 274cm (108in) from selvedge to selvedge and is primarily used for quilt backings.

YARDAGE AND METERAGE

When purchasing online or in person, decide how much fabric you need. Fabric cut from a bolt is called yardage or meterage, depending on whether it is measured in yards or metres. Both terms are used as such throughout this book. Yardage or meterage is measured along the selvedge edge, while the WOF, which is measured from selvedge to selvedge, does not vary within a piece of fabric. Quilting patterns typically assume WOF is 106.7cm (42in).

- ▶ **0.25 metre or ¼ yard**
  Measures 25cm (9in) x WOF
- ▶ **0.5 metre or ½ yard**
  Measures 50cm (18in) x WOF
- ▶ **By the metre or yard**
  Measures 100cm (36in) x WOF
- ▶ **Wide back (not included in illustration)**
  Used primarily for quilt backings, wide back fabric typically measures 274cm (108in) from selvedge to selvedge and is also sold by the metre or yard

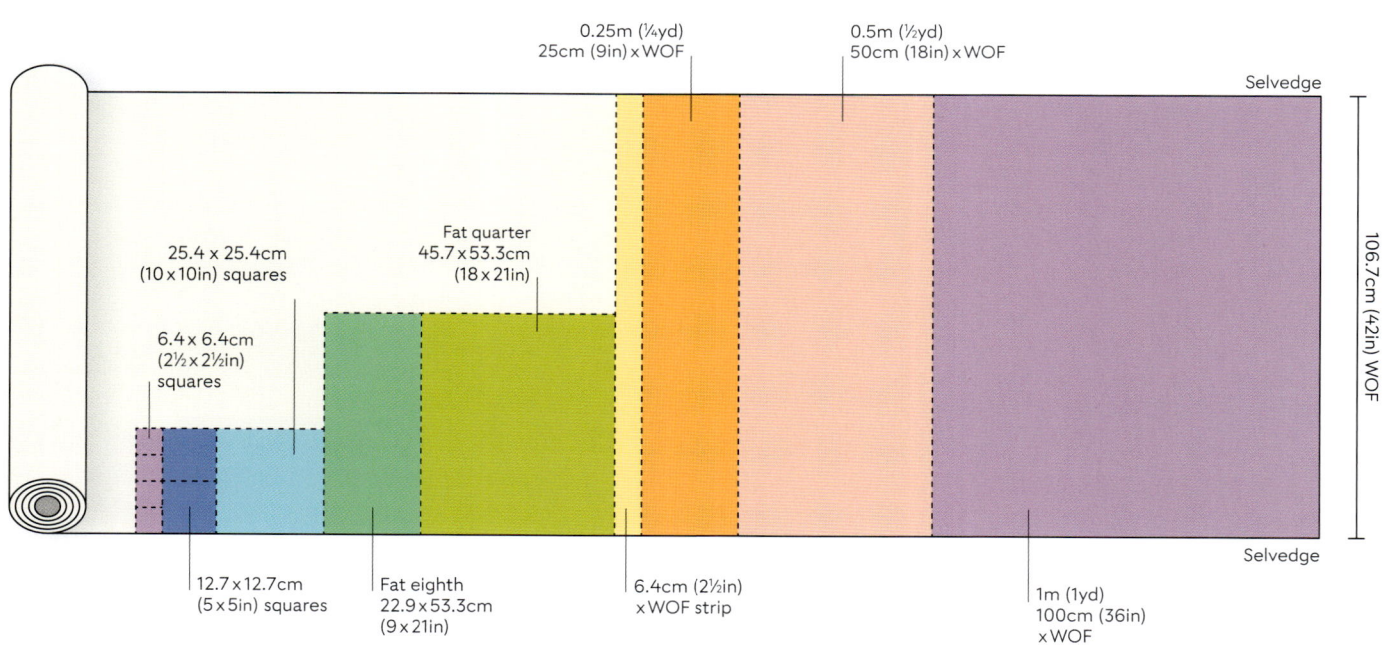

PRE-CUTS

Versatile and convenient, pre-cuts are pieces of fabric that have been cut into standard sizes by the manufacturer or fabric store and sold as a packaged set, typically containing a variety of fabrics within a collection. Some are finished with a pinked (zigzag) edge to reduce fraying. The name of each type of pre-cut and number of pieces in each set varies, but the sizes of the pieces remain the same.

▶ SCRAPS

Any fabric remaining after cutting all the pieces for a quilt is called a scrap. These leftovers can often be used by repurposing them for other projects. Some quilters prefer to cut down their scrap pieces of fabric into standard pre-cut sizes to stay organized, while others use scraps as they need them (see p.65).

Fat quarters 45.7 x 53.3cm (18 x 21in)

25.4 x 25.4cm (10 x 10in) squares

Laser cut

12.7 x 12.7cm (5 x 5in) squares

Fat eighths 22.9 x 53.3cm (9 x 21in)

6.4 x 6.4cm (2½ x 2½in) squares

6.4cm (2½in) x WOF strips

Wadding

Wadding is the inner layer of a quilt sandwich, resting between the quilt top and backing to provide cushion, weight, and warmth. There are many types of wadding made of different fibres and featuring different properties. Quilt wadding is sold in pre-cut, packaged sizes that correspond with standard bed and quilt sizes (see p.49) or by the roll, which allows you to cut wadding to size.

PROPERTIES OF WADDING

The properties of wadding determine how a finished quilt will look and feel, from soft and fluffy to dense and warm. Pay attention to the instructions listed on the wadding packaging for wadding preparation, quilting, and care.

LOFT
Loft is determined by the thickness of wadding. High loft refers to thick and fluffy wadding, which adds dimension and definition to quilting, while low loft refers to thinner, sometimes denser wadding, which appears flatter.

NEEDLE-PUNCHED
Some wadding has been punched through with thousands of needles to help the fibres interlock and add stability. It is recommended to quilt from the same side of the wadding that the needles entered, which is visible as indentations.

SCRIM
A thin layer of stabilizer, known as scrim, is needle-punched to one side of the wadding to add strength and stability. The scrim allows for quilting lines to be spaced further apart. This is not recommended for hand quilting, as the layer of scrim is difficult to push a needle through.

WADDING DIMENSIONS
Choose a packaged wadding in a standard size or cut your own wadding from a roll. Packaged wadding is more accessible, but purchasing rolls of wadding ends up more cost effective over time. Always allow for 15.2cm (6in) larger than your quilt top to account for overage. Refer to p.281 for a review of wadding sizes.

TYPES OF WADDING

Wadding is available in various types of fibres. When choosing wadding, consider how the quilt will be used and cared for.

100 PER CENT COTTON

Cotton wadding is the most common type of wadding. Available in natural, which is cream and typically contains flecks of cotton seeds, and bleached, which is white.

Properties:	warm and breathable; often low or medium loft and light to medium weight
Advantages:	natural fibres; typically machine washable and dryable
Disadvantages:	shrinks; holds creases; natural options may contain seeds

100 PER CENT POLYESTER

Polyester wadding is made of synthetic fibres, making it resistant to mould and mildew. It is a good choice for people with allergies.

Properties:	warm and durable; medium to high loft and lightweight
Advantages:	does not shrink; resistant to creasing; affordable; typically machine washable and dryable
Disadvantages:	no natural fibres; does not breathe well

COTTON/POLYESTER BLEND

A popular choice for its availability and affordability, this blend has the best features of both cotton and polyester waddings.

Properties:	warm and durable; medium to high loft and light to medium weight
Advantages:	mostly resistant to creasing; good for machine and hand quilting; typically machine washable and dryable
Disadvantages:	not natural fibre; slight shrinkage

BLACK

Available in cotton/polyester blends or 100 per cent polyester, black wadding is recommended for high-contrast or dark quilt tops.

Properties:	warm and durable; medium to high loft and light to medium weight
Advantages:	mostly resistant to creasing; good for machine and hand quilting; typically machine washable and dryable
Disadvantages:	slight shrinkage

WOOL

Wool wadding is made from natural wool fibres bonded together. It is available in 100 per cent wool or blended with other fibres.

Properties:	very soft and warm; medium to high loft and light to medium weight
Advantages:	natural fibres; resistant to creasing; great for hand quilting and providing definition for quilting stitches
Disadvantages:	shrinks; loft may be inconsistent; expensive; may not be machine washable depending on manufacturing

BAMBOO

Bamboo wadding is a natural, allergen-friendly choice. It is available in 100 per cent bamboo or blended with other fibres.

Properties:	soft and breathable; low to medium loft and light weight
Advantages:	natural fibres; great for machine and hand quilting; typically machine washable and dryable
Disadvantages:	slight shrinkage; limited availability and expensive

LOOSE POLYESTER FILLING

Loose filling is typically made of polyester fibre and is used for filling pillows and puff quilts (see pp.250–255). It is not recommended to use in place of wadding for typical quilts.

Properties:	puffy; very high loft and light to medium weight
Advantages:	does not shrink; affordable; typically machine washable and dryable
Disadvantages:	not natural fibre; prone to clumping

FUSIBLE WADDING

Fusible wadding has a thin layer of glue, allowing it to temporarily adhere to fabric by applying heat. It is often used for smaller projects. It is not recommended for hand quilting.

Properties:	available in cotton or cotton/polyester blends; low to medium loft and light to medium weight
Advantages:	eliminates the need for basting; good for machine quilting; typically machine washable and dryable
Disadvantages:	limited wadding types and sizes available

Interfacing and binding

While interfacing and binding serve distinct roles in quilting, they both add stability and longevity to projects. Interfacing is a material used to provide support or structure to fabric, and binding finishes the edges of a quilt sandwich and frames the quilt.

INTERFACING

Interfacing is most commonly used for appliqué (see p.134) and quilt repair (see p.184). Though there are many types of interfacing available, woven interfacing is preferred in quilting, as it matches the woven nature of common quilting fabrics. Choose an interfacing lighter than the fabric it will be attached to.

FUSIBLE

Fusible, or iron-on, interfacing is adhered to fabric by applying heat. It is useful for basting appliqué pieces.

SEW-IN

Sew-in interfacing must be sewn to fabric, either with a temporary basting stitch or as part of the seams. It is useful for lining appliqué and small projects.

BINDING

Binding is a continuous, pieced strip of fabric that measures the length of the perimeter of the quilt and is typically 5.1–6.4cm (2–2½in) wide. Folded in half lengthways and pressed before attaching, binding fully encloses all raw edges of a quilt (see pp.172–182).

STRAIGHT AND BIAS

Straight grain binding: continuous binding made from strips cut on the cross grain

Bias binding: continuous binding made from strips cut on the bias designed to stretch around curved edges

TECHNIQUES

Getting started

This section includes the background information you need to set yourself up for success as you begin your quilting journey. Learn about what makes a quilt and how to choose fabrics, then progress to preparing, measuring, and cutting fabrics safely and accurately. Prepare your tools for machine or hand piecing and practice pinning, ripping, and pressing seams. Work through this entire section to build basic skills before advancing to other techniques.

Choosing a quilt size

Quilts can be any shape or size and vary based on personal preference, but standard measurements typically align with mattress and pre-packaged wadding sizes (see p.281).

COMPARING QUILT SIZES

When making a quilt for a specific mattress, measure the bed first, allowing for extra length for the quilt to hang over the edges, then consider adding borders to adjust the size as needed (see p.147). Refer to the illustration below to determine which size best fits your needs, whether making a quilt for a bed or to use for lounging.

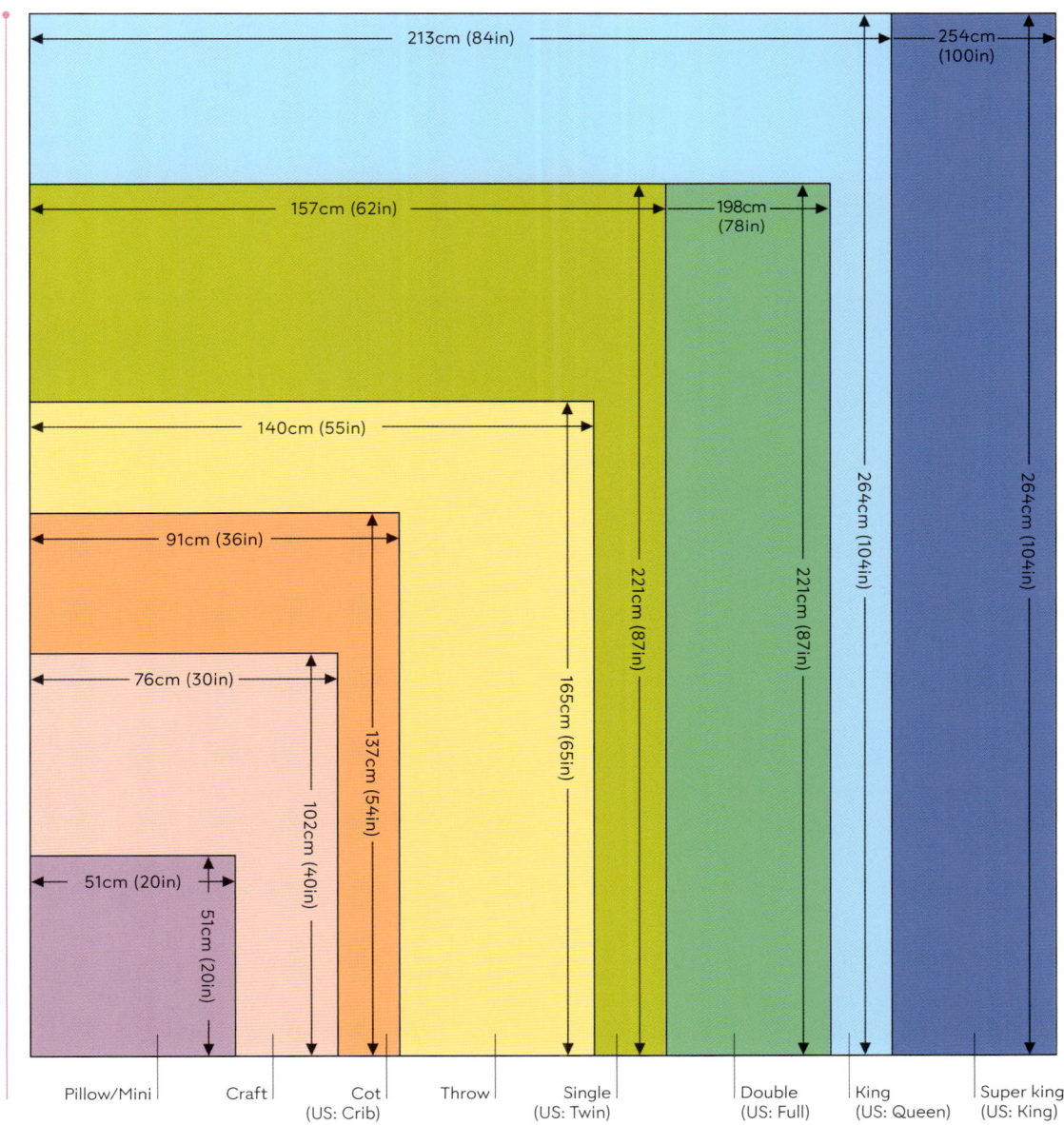

Five components of a quilt

A quilt is made up of five fundamental components: the quilt top, wadding, backing, quilting, and binding. The quilt top showcases the pattern or design, the wadding adds warmth and loft, and the backing completes the quilt. Quilting holds these layers of the quilt sandwich – top, wadding, and backing – together, and the binding secures the outer edges.

QUILT SANDWICH

The "quilt sandwich" refers to the three main layers that make up a quilt: the quilt top, wadding, and backing. These layers are stacked together like a sandwich (see pp.150–159) before they are quilted and bound to make a finished quilt.

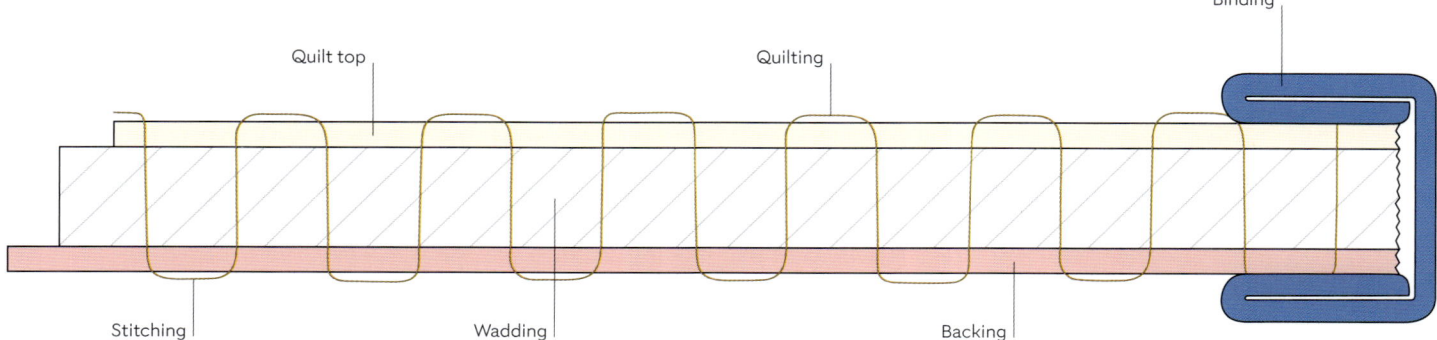

QUILT TOP
The quilt top is typically the focal point of the quilt, often showcasing a pieced pattern or design. A quilt top can be assembled using traditional piecing, improv, FPP, EPP, or appliqué techniques (see pp.82–147), or can be a solid piece of fabric, known as a whole cloth quilt.

WADDING
Wadding is the layer between the quilt top and the backing that provides warmth, adds loft, and gives the quilt a plush feel. Most quilters use 100 per cent cotton wadding or a blend of cotton, polyester, wool, or bamboo (see pp.42–44).

BACKING
The backing is the layer of fabric on the underside of the quilt that provides stability. Quilts can be backed with a number of materials, and it is often necessary to piece several cuts of fabric together to make a backing large enough (see pp.153–155).

QUILTING
Quilting, done by machine or hand, involves sewing through all three layers of the quilt sandwich to secure them together. This process adds texture and complements the overall design of the quilt (see pp.160–171).

BINDING
Binding (see pp.172–181) is the material sewn around the perimeter to hide the raw edges of the quilt top, wadding, and backing. Binding can contrast or blend into the quilt top and backing.

FIVE COMPONENTS OF A QUILT   51

Binding   Backing   Wadding   Quilt top   Quilting

▲ **The components of a quilt**
This illustration shows all five components of a quilt. See the Building Blocks Sampler (see pp.188–195) for instructions on how to make this quilt top.

Understanding quilt patterns

Quilt patterns provide a guide for making a quilt from beginning to end, and while the content may vary, many contain similar elements and follow a standard structure. Read patterns thoroughly before beginning.

COVER PAGE

The cover page highlights the pattern name, a photo, or illustration of the finished quilt, and details such as the finished size(s), designer information, and experience level. If the pattern is designed for pre-cuts (see p.41), the type maybe listed here.

FABRIC REQUIREMENTS

The amounts of fabrics required are displayed in a table so quilters can gather materials in advance. The table includes meterage or yardage for quilt sizes and design options. A fabric reference diagram is typically included here. Overage amounts or other notes may be noted under the table.

	COT (US: CRIB) 114 x 152cm (45 x 60in)	**THROW** 163 x 203cm (64 x 80in)
FQ VERSION		
BACKGROUND (BG)	1.5m (1½yds)	2.75m (3yds)
FLOWERS	6 FQs	8 FQs
STEMS*	3 FQs	4 FQs
CENTRES**	1 FQ	1 FQ
METERAGE OR YARDAGE VERSION		
FABRIC A (BG)	1.5m (1½yds)	2.75m (3yds)
FABRIC B	1.5m (1½yds)	2m (2yds)
FABRIC C	0.75m (¾yd)	1m (1yd)
FABRIC D**	0.25m (¼yd)	0.25m (¼yd)
BINDING	0.5m (½yd)	0.75m (¾yd)
BACKING**	3.75m (4yds)	4.75m (5yds)

*0.25 metre (¼ yard) can be used.
**Exact amounts needed.
***Backing amounts account for 7.6cm (3in) overage on all sides.

GETTING STARTED

This section provides background information and lists skills and materials needed to complete the quilt, as well as pattern-specific definitions and assumptions. Links to digital resources, such as templates, are typically included here.

Common assumptions:

- **WOF:** 106.7cm (42in)
- **Seam allowance:** 6.4mm (¼in), unless otherwise specified.
- **Pressing instructions:** "press seams open" or "press seams to the side;" may include "unless otherwise instructed." Press after sewing each seam, even if not specified in the instructions.

Common definitions:

- **WOF:** Width of fabric
- **FQ:** Fat quarter
- **BG:** Background fabric
- **RST:** Right sides together
- **WST:** Wrong sides together
- **Right side:** The side meant to be visible
- **Wrong side:** The side meant to be hidden
- **Subcut:** Cutting smaller pieces from larger; typically WOF strips
- **HST:** Half-square triangle
- **QST:** Quarter-square triangle
- **FG:** Flying geese
- **HRT:** Half-rectangle triangle
- **QC:** Quarter circle
- **HC:** Half circle

CUTTING INSTRUCTIONS

Cutting instructions are organized in a table by fabric and quilt size. The table typically lists WOF strips from largest to smallest, with sub-cuts (see p.70) nested underneath each strip, to ensure all pieces fit within the fabric requirements. The number of pieces to cut are often indicated by parentheses or bold formatting, and specific pieces may be labelled with letters and/or numbers. Cutting diagrams may illustrate how to arrange cuts on a WOF strip or pre-cut.

	COT (US: CRIB) SIZE 45 x 60in (114 x 152cm)
FABRIC A	Cut (2) 15.2cm (6in) x WOF strips; sub-cut: **A1**: (8) 15.2 x 15.2cm (6 x 6in) **A2**: (12) 15.2 x 7.6cm (6 x 3in) Cut (1) 7.6cm (3in) x WOF strip; sub-cut: **A2**: (4) 7.6 x 15.2cm (3 x 6in) (16 total)
FABRIC B	Cut (1) 7.6cm (3in) x WOF strip; sub-cut: **B1**: (4) 7.6 x 14cm (3 x 5½in) **B2**: (4) template A
BACKGROUND (BG)	Cut (4) 6.4cm (2½in) x WOF strips; set (3) aside (**BG1**) and sub-cut (1) into: **BG2**: (16) 6.4 x 6.4cm (2½ x 2½in)

To cut fabrics using the included table, follow these instructions:

1. From fabric A, cut two WOF strips that are 15.2cm (6in) wide. Sub-cut these strips into eight 15.2 x 15.2cm (6 x 6in) squares (A1) and twelve 15.2 x 7.6cm (6 x 3in) rectangles (A2). Then cut one WOF strip that is 7.6cm (3in) wide. Sub-cut this strip into four 7.6 x 15.2cm (3 x 6in) rectangles for a total of 16 A2.

2. From fabric B, cut one WOF strip that is 7.6cm (3in) wide. Sub-cut this strip into four 7.6 x 14cm (3 x 5½in) rectangles (B1) and four pieces (B2) using template A.

3. From background (BG), cut four WOF strips that are 6.4cm (2½in) wide. Label three of these WOF strips as BG1 and set aside to be used later. Sub-cut the remaining WOF strip into sixteen 6.4 x 6.4cm (2½ x 2½in) squares (BG2).

ASSEMBLY INSTRUCTIONS

The assembly instructions describe piecing techniques step-by-step for pieces, units, and blocks, including specific pressing and trimming instructions. Figures and diagrams illustrate the progression of steps and where to mark, sew, and trim.

1. Mark a diagonal line from corner to corner on the wrong side of one BG1 using a marking tool.

2. Place the marked BG1 square on one A1 RST.

3. Sew 6.4mm (¼in) away from each side of the marked diagonal line.

4. Cut along the marked diagonal line to make two HSTs. Press the seams toward the darker fabric.

5. Repeat for all BG1 and A1. Trim all HSTs to 8.9 x 8.9cm (3½ x 3½in).

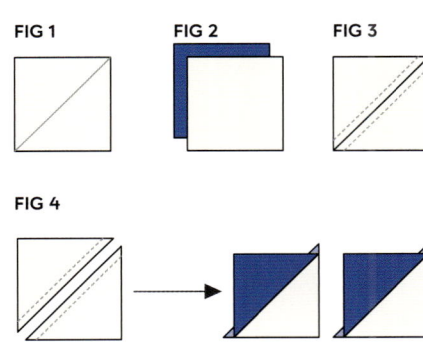

FINISHING INSTRUCTIONS AND RESOURCES

The instructions here are brief and generalized, as finishing options vary based on personal preferences. Specific finishing techniques (see p.150) may be referenced but not explained. Labels, which assist with organization, and colouring pages, which can be coloured digitally or by hand, are often included here as additional resources.

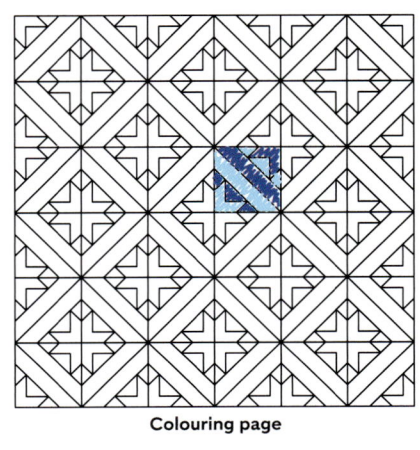

Colouring page

Quilt maths

The maths involved in quilting, such as accounting for seam allowances, often seems intimidating. However, you can follow standard formulas to calculate how fabric pieces fit together, determine fabric requirements, and scale blocks and patterns. In this section, the horizontal measurement of a piece is referred to as *width* and the vertical measurement is referred to as *length*.

ACCOUNTING FOR SEAM ALLOWANCE

Unfinished size refers to the measurements of a piece, unit, block, or quilt top before the outside edges have been sewn, and finished size refers to the final measurement after all seams, including the outside edges, have been sewn.

UNFINISHED VS. FINISHED SIZES

1 The unfinished size of a piece is the size that is initially cut. Each seam where pieces of fabric are joined takes up 6.4mm (¼in) of seam allowance from the edge of each piece, for a total of 1.3cm (½in) per seam. This 1.3cm (½in) must be accounted for when calculating unfinished and finished sizes. To calculate the unfinished size of a single piece, add 1.3cm (½in) to both the finished width and length.

unfinished size (cm) = (finished width + 1.3cm) by (finished length + 1.3cm)
unfinished size (in) = (finished width + ½in) by (finished length + ½in)
EXAMPLE = (3½in + ½in) by (3½in + ½in)
= 4in by 4in

2 To calculate the finished size of a single piece, subtract 1.3cm (½in) from both the unfinished width and length.

finished size (cm) = (unfinished width − 1.3cm) by (unfinished length − 1.3cm)
finished size (in) = (unfinished width − ½in) by (unfinished length − ½in)
EXAMPLE = (4in − ½in) by (4in − ½in)
= 3½in by 3½in

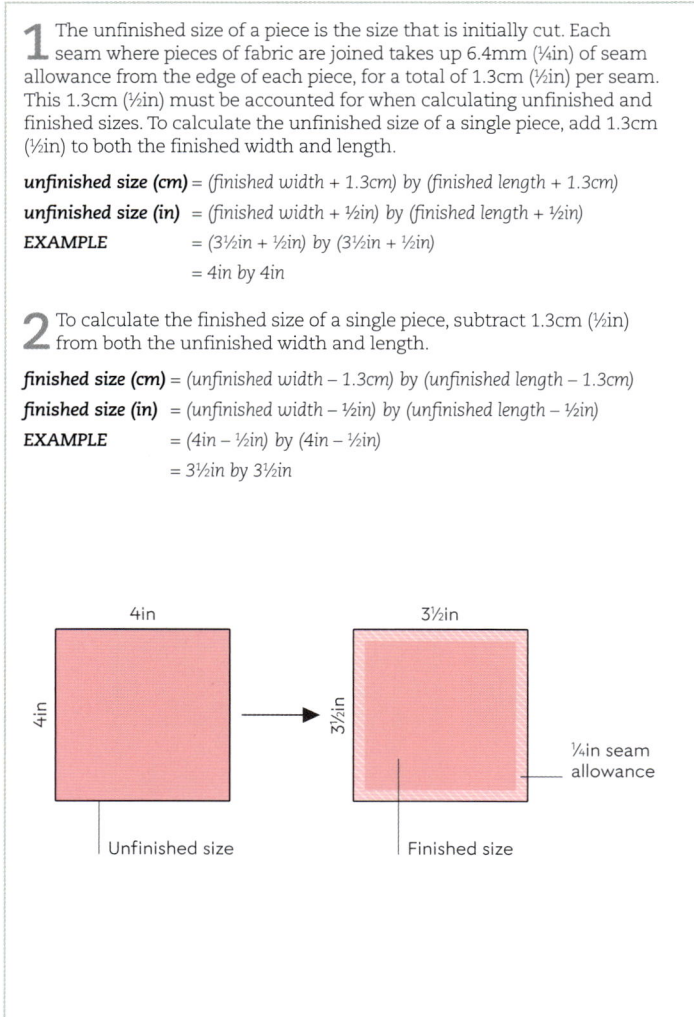

3 To calculate the unfinished width of two pieces joined into a unit, add together the unfinished width of each piece, then subtract 1.3cm (½in) to account for the fabric taken up by the seam allowance. Use the same formula to calculate the unfinished length of two pieces joined along their length, substituting length for width.

unfinished unit width (cm) = (unfinished width + unfinished width) − 1.3cm
unfinished unit width (in) = (unfinished width + unfinished width) − ½in
EXAMPLE = (4in + 4in) − ½in
= 8in − ½in
= 7½in

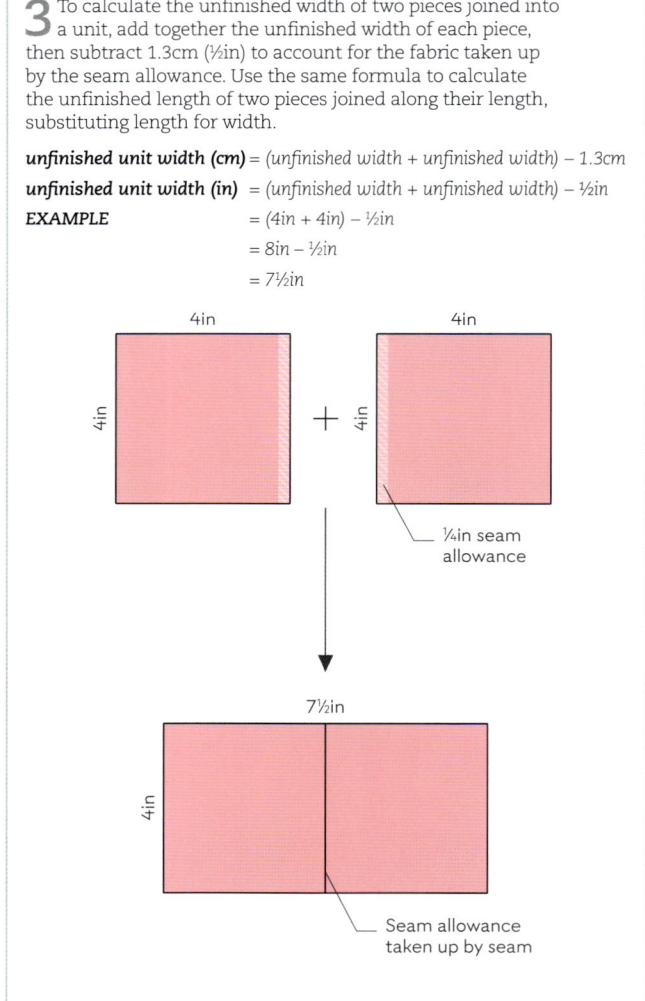

CALCULATING BLOCK OR QUILT SIZES

1 To calculate the unfinished width of a completed block, add together the width of each piece in a row. Subtract 1.3cm (½in) for each seam. Repeat for each row.

unfinished block width (cm) = (piece width + piece width + ... piece width) − (# of seams x 1.3cm)
unfinished block width (in) = (piece width + piece width + ... piece width) − (# of seams x ½in)
EXAMPLE = (3½in + 6½in + 3½in) − (2 x ½in)
= 13½in − 1in
= 12½in

2 To calculate the unfinished length of a completed block, add together the length of each piece in a column. Subtract 1.3cm (½in) for each seam. Repeat for each column.

unfinished block length (cm) = (piece length + piece length + ... piece length) − (# of seams x 1.3cm)
unfinished block length (in) = (piece length + piece length + ... piece length) − (# of seams x ½in)
EXAMPLE = (3½in + 6½in + 3½in) − (2 x ½in)
= 13½in − 1in
= 12½in

3 The unfinished size of the completed block is the unfinished block width by the unfinished block length.

unfinished block size = unfinished width by unfinished length
EXAMPLE = 12½in by 12½in

4 To calculate the finished size of a completed block, subtract 1.3cm (½in) from both the unfinished width and unfinished length.

finished block size (cm) = (unfinished block width − 1.3cm) by (unfinished block length − 1.3cm)
finished block size (in) = (unfinished block width − ½in) by (unfinished block length − ½in)
EXAMPLE = (12½in − ½in) by (12½in − ½in)
= 12in by 12in

5 To calculate the unfinished and finished sizes of a completed quilt top, follow steps 1–4, adding the unfinished measurements of each completed block and sashing if applicable.

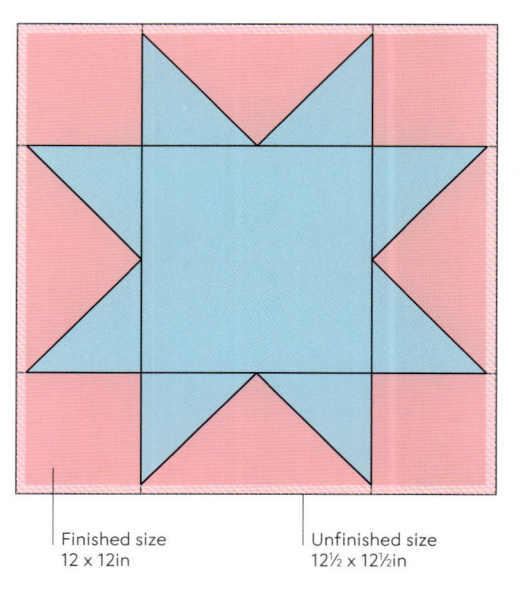

Finished size 12 x 12in
Unfinished size 12½ x 12½in

CALCULATING FABRIC REQUIREMENTS

Quilters may need to calculate fabric requirements when altering patterns or drafting their own. This section provides instructions for determining the amount needed for a single fabric. Refer to the charts section (pp.280–291) to quickly reference fabric requirements for various WOF strips, backing, and binding.

GROUPING PIECES INTO WOF STRIPS

1 Determine all pieces needed from one fabric. Organize and group the pieces by similar widths. Use these widths to estimate the size of WOF strips needed.

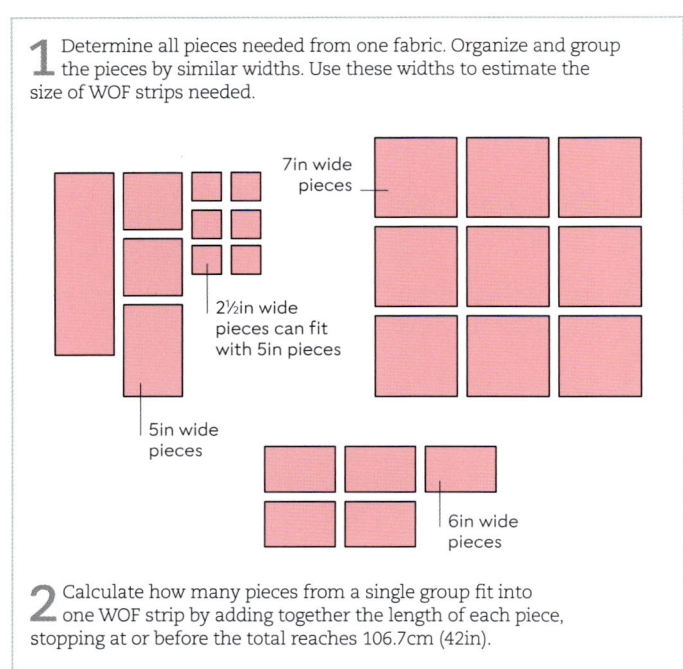

2 Calculate how many pieces from a single group fit into one WOF strip by adding together the length of each piece, stopping at or before the total reaches 106.7cm (42in).

3 Grouped pieces may fit exactly within a WOF strip, span multiple strips, or leave unused space that can be filled with pieces from other groups. Experiment with groupings to maximize the use of each WOF strip and minimize waste.

4 In the example diagram, the 17.8cm (7in) pieces fit across two WOF strips, and the 15.2cm (6in) pieces fit within the leftover space in the second strip. The 12.7cm (5in) pieces fit within one WOF strip, and the 6.4cm (2½in) pieces fit side by side within the same strip.

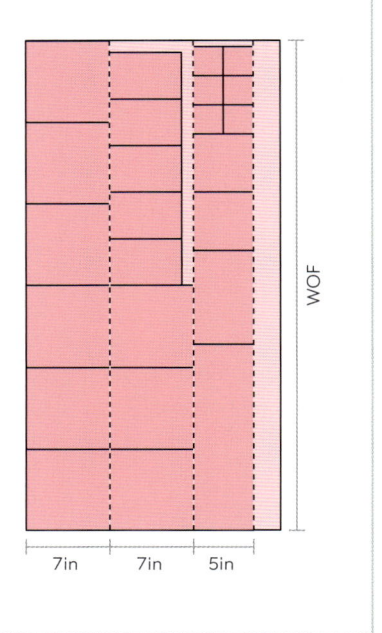

CALCULATING YARDAGE AND METERAGE

1 To calculate the yardage needed, add together all of the WOF strips, then divide the total by 36in.

yardage needed = [WOF strip (in) + WOF strip (in) + ... WOF strip (in)] ÷ 36in

EXAMPLE = (7in + 7in + 5in + 3in + 3in + 3in + 3in) ÷ 36in

= 31in ÷ 36in

= 0.86yd

2 To calculate the meterage needed, add together all of the WOF strips, then divide the total by 100cm.

meterage needed = [WOF strip (cm) + WOF strip (cm) + ... WOF strip (cm)] ÷ 100cm

EXAMPLE = (17.8cm + 17.8cm + 12.7cm + 7.6cm + 7.6cm + 7.6cm + 7.6cm) ÷ 100cm

= (78.7cm) ÷ 100cm

= 0.78m

3 Include overage to account for shrinkage during fabric preparation, potential miscuts, and rounding errors. To calculate the amount of fabric needed with overage, add 10% to the amount of fabric needed. Round up to the nearest ¼ yard or 0.25 metre increment.

amount needed with overage = (amount needed x 0.10) + amount needed

EXAMPLE = (0.86yd x 0.10) + 0.86yd

= 0.086yd + 0.86yd

= 0.95yd; rounded up to 1yd

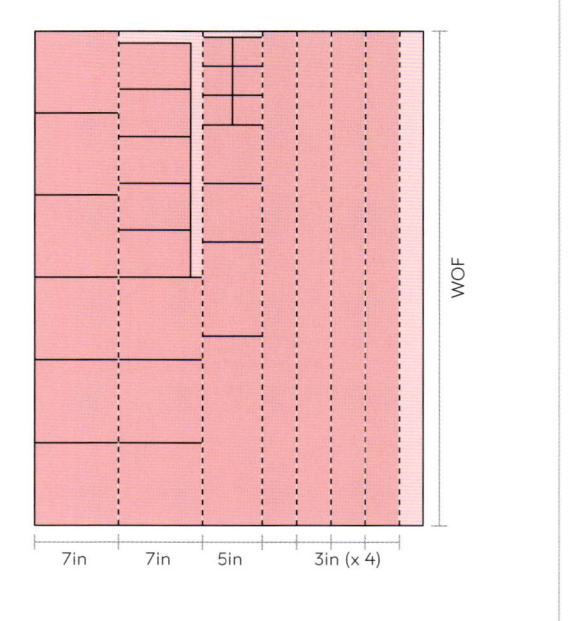

CALCULATING BACKING

1 Quilt backings (see p.153) should include overage to account for fabric shifting during quilting. For domestic machine or hand quilting, add 15.2cm (6in) to both the width and length of the quilt top to account for overage; for longarm quilting, consult your quilter for recommendations. To calculate the required backing dimensions, measure the width and length of the quilt top, then add 15.2cm (6in) overage to each measurement.

quilt backing (cm) = *(quilt top width + 15.2cm) by (quilt top length + 15.2cm)*
quilt backing (in) = *(quilt top width + 6in) by (quilt top length + 6in)*
EXAMPLE = *(52in + 6in) by (60in + 6in)*
= *58in by 66in*

2 A single backing piece may be wide enough for some quilt tops smaller than a WOF, but multiple backing pieces must often be joined together to make the required backing width (see p.290). Always use a 1.3cm (½in) seam allowance when piecing backing. To calculate the number of backing pieces needed, divide the quilt backing width by the WOF. Round up to the nearest whole number.

# of backing pieces (cm) = *quilt backing width ÷ (WOF − 1.3cm)*
# of backing pieces (in) = *quilt backing width ÷ (WOF − ½in)*
EXAMPLE = *58in ÷ (42in − ½in)*
= *1.40, rounded up to 2*

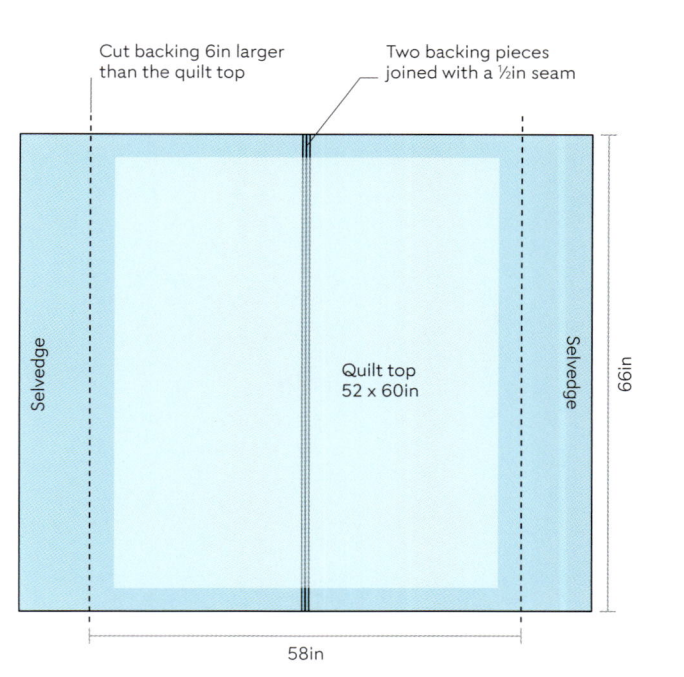

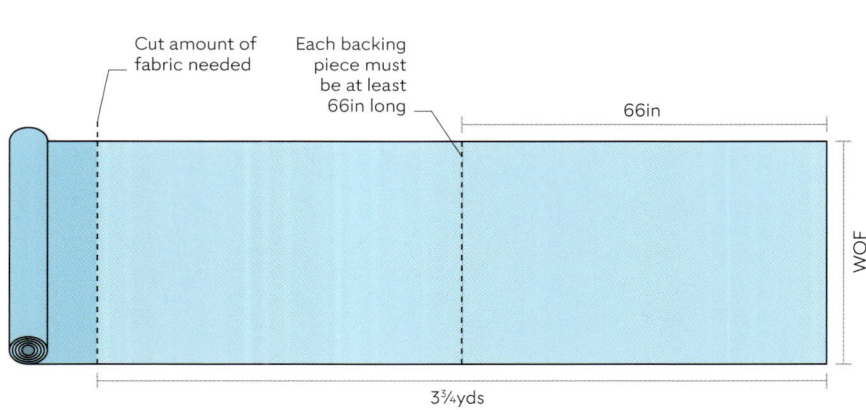

3 To calculate the amount of yardage needed, multiply the number of backing pieces by the quilt backing *length*, then divide this total by 36in. Round up to the nearest ¼ yard increment.

backing yardage = *[# of backing pieces x quilt backing length (in)] ÷ 36in*
EXAMPLE = *(2 x 66in) ÷ 36in*
= *132in ÷ 36in*
= *3.66yds, rounded up to 3.75yds*

4 To calculate the amount of meterage needed, multiply the number of backing pieces by the quilt backing length, then divide this total by 100cm. Round up to the nearest 0.25 metre increment.

backing meterage = *[# of backing pieces x quilt backing length (cm)] ÷ 100cm*
EXAMPLE = *(2 x 167.6cm) ÷ 100cm*
= *335.2cm ÷ 100cm*
= *3.35m, rounded up to 3.5m*

CALCULATING BINDING

1 Binding amounts are calculated using the perimeter of the quilt and overage to account for seam allowances, corners, and joining ends. To calculate the perimeter of the quilt, add the measurements of all sides together.

perimeter = (width + width + length + length)
EXAMPLE = (52in + 52in + 60in + 60in)
= 224in

2 To calculate the length of binding needed, add 38.1cm (15in) to the perimeter measurement to account for overage.

length of binding needed (cm) = perimeter + 38.1cm
length of binding needed (in) = perimeter + 15in
EXAMPLE = 224in + 15in
= 239in

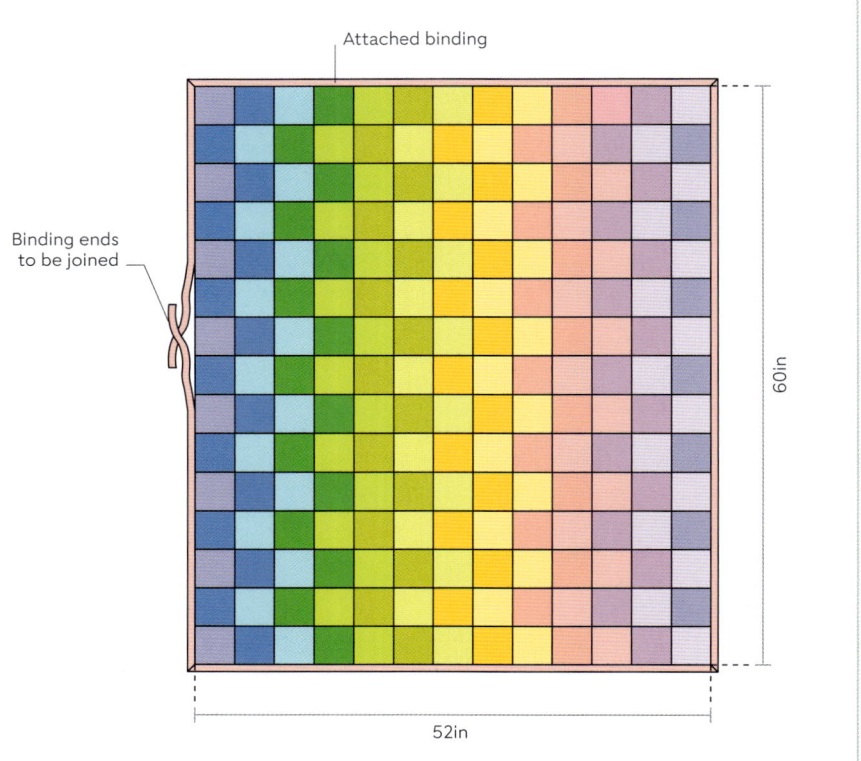

3 To determine the total number of WOF strips needed, divide the length of binding needed by the WOF, typically 106.7cm (42in). Round up to the nearest whole number.

# of WOF strips = length of binding needed ÷ WOF
EXAMPLE = 239in ÷ 42in
= 5.69, rounded up to 6

4 A popular binding width is 6.4cm (2½in), which is used throughout this book. To calculate the total yardage needed, multiply the number of WOF strips needed by the desired binding strip width. Round up to the nearest ¼ yard increment.

binding yardage = # of WOF strips x binding width
EXAMPLE = 6 x 2½in
= 15in, rounded up to ½yd

5 To calculate the total meterage needed, multiply the number of WOF strips needed by the desired binding strip width. Round up to the nearest 0.25 metre increment.

binding meterage = # of WOF strips x binding width
EXAMPLE = 6 x 6.4cm
= 38.4cm, rounded up to 0.5m

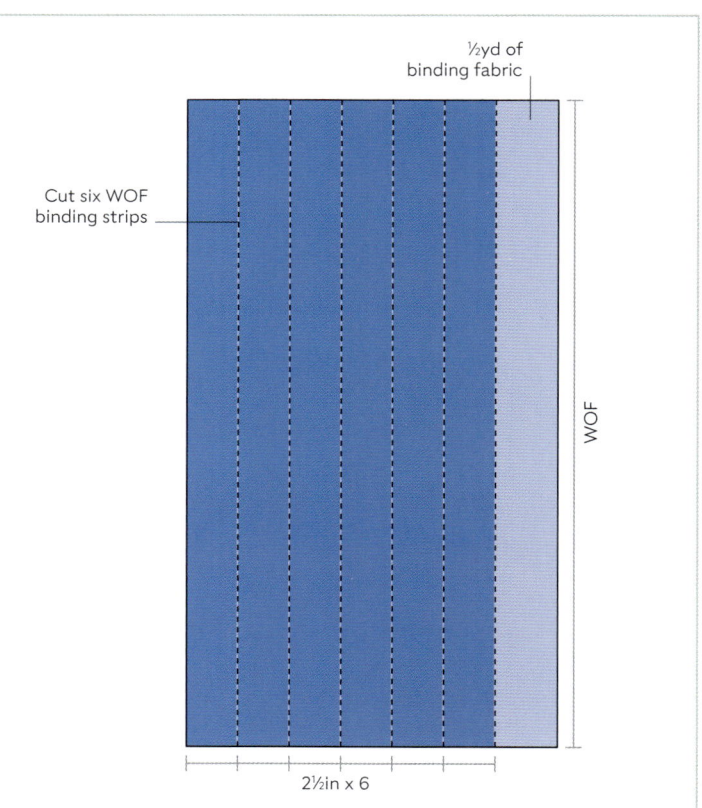

ALTERING QUILT PATTERNS

Though quilt patterns often include instructions for variations of the same design, a pattern may not offer the sizes or fabric options you are looking for. Patterns can be modified by adjusting fabric requirements or scaling block sizes.

ADJUSTING FABRIC REQUIREMENTS

1 Reduce the number of fabrics by combining the fabric requirements and cutting instructions. In the example diagram, the original design uses 18 feature fabrics. The adjusted design has combined cutting instructions to use only four feature fabrics.

2 To use pre-cuts, such as fat quarters or 25cm (10in) squares (see p.41), in place of yardage or meterage, experiment with organizing the pieces listed in the cutting instructions into the size of the desired pre-cut.

3 To use scraps, review the quantity and sizes of pieces in the cutting instructions, then evaluate your scraps to find or cut similarly sized pieces.

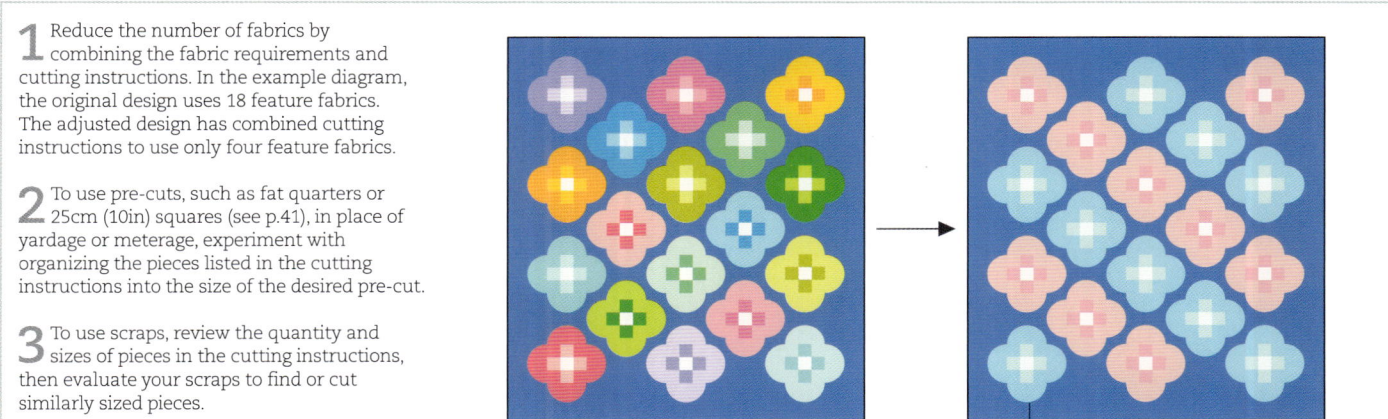

Use a pattern colouring page to visualize fabric choices

SCALING BLOCK SIZES

1 Quilt blocks can be scaled, or resized, to achieve a different finished size. Keep in mind that scaling may result in uncommon or unmanageably sized pieces. Determine the finished measurements of the original block and the desired finished size of the scaled block.

2 To calculate the scaling ratio, divide the desired finished block size by the original finished block size.

scaling ratio = *(desired block width by length) ÷ (original block width by length)*

EXAMPLE = *(18in by 18in) ÷ (12in by 12in)*

= 18 ÷ 12

= 1.5

3 To calculate the finished size of each piece in the scaled block, multiply the original finished piece size by the scaling ratio. Repeat for each piece in the block.

scaled finished piece size = *(original piece width by length) x scaling ratio*

EXAMPLE = *(6in by 6in) x 1.5*

= *9in by 9in*

4 To calculate the unfinished size of each piece in the scaled block, add 1.3cm (½in) to both the finished width and length. Repeat for each piece in the block.

scaled unfinished piece size (cm) = *(scaled piece width + 1.3cm) by (scaled piece length + 1.3cm)*

scaled unfinished piece size (in) = *(scaled piece width + ½in) by (scaled piece length + ½in)*

EXAMPLE = *(9in + ½in) by (9in + ½in)*

= *9½in by 9½in*

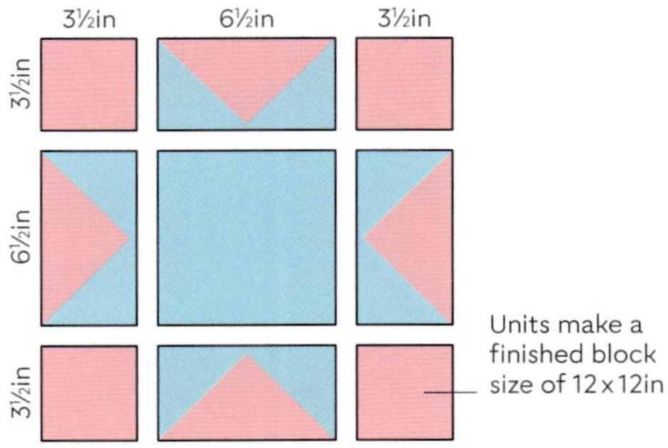
3½in
6½in
3½in
3½in
6½in
3½in
Units make a finished block size of 12 x 12in

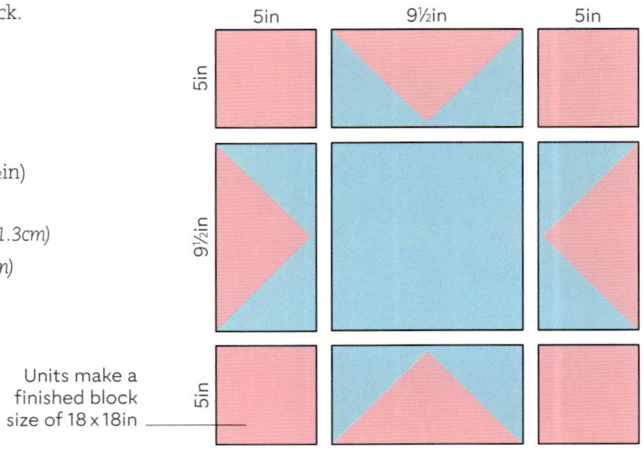
5in
9½in
5in
5in
9½in
5in
Units make a finished block size of 18 x 18in

Choosing fabrics

There are many considerations when choosing fabric for a quilt, like which colour combinations, fabric designs, and scales to use, all of which can feel overwhelming. Use helpful tools such as colouring pages, digital mockups, or fabric swatches, along with this guide, to plan before choosing your fabric and set yourself up for success.

UNDERSTANDING COLOUR THEORY

The colour wheel demonstrates how colours relate to each other, and it consists of three primary colours – red, yellow, and blue. The primary colours combine to make secondary colours: red and yellow make orange, yellow and blue make green, and blue and red make violet. Tertiary colours result from mixing secondary colours with their nearest primary.

THE COLOUR WHEEL

Hue classifies colour by its purest form. Variations occur by adding white to make tints, grey to make tones, or black to make shades. In the example colour wheel, all tints, tones, and shades of yellow fall under the yellow hue.

Value describes how light or dark a colour appears, and saturation measures the intensity of a colour relative to grey. Highly saturated colours are vivid, while desaturated colours are muted. Select fabrics with a range of values – light, medium, and dark – to create dimension. Fabrics with similar saturation levels, whether light or dark, work well together in a quilt.

Temperature divides the colour wheel into warm and cool hues, with cool colours like blue and green creating calmness and warm colours like red and orange adding warmth and energy. Use temperature intentionally when choosing fabrics to add balance or contrast to a design.

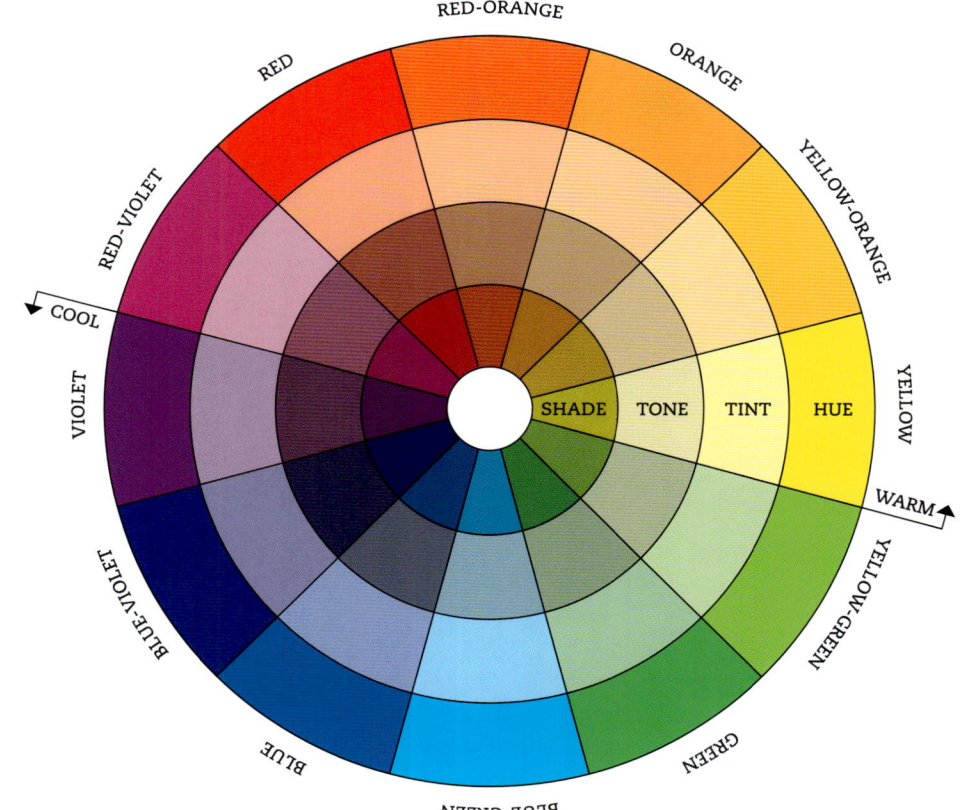

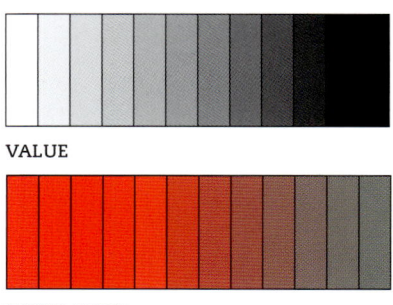

VALUE

SATURATION

COLOUR SCHEMES AND CONTRAST

A colour scheme defines how colours interact with each other on the colour wheel, while a colour palette is a specific selection of colours that fall within a scheme. Contrast is the difference between colours, such as light and dark, warm and cool, or bright and muted. In quilting, use contrasting fabrics to make parts of a quilt stand out, draw focus, and add balance or tension.

Monochromatic colour schemes use a single hue on the colour wheel. Varying light and dark values adds to a sense of depth and creates **light-dark contrast**.

This block uses a variety of light and dark pinks.

Analogous colour schemes use hues next to each other on the colour wheel. Placing muted and vibrant tones together makes one stand out and creates **saturation contrast**.

This block uses muted tones of green and blue with a vibrant yellow-green.

Complementary colour schemes pair opposite hues on the colour wheel, which creates the strongest colour contrast, or **complementary contrast**.

This block uses various tints and shades of violet and yellow.

Split-complementary colour schemes include one hue matched with the two adjacent to its complementary. Pairing warm and cool colours, within or across hues, creates **warm-cold contrast**.

This block uses blue-green with pink and orange.

Triadic colour schemes use three evenly spaced hues on the colour wheel. A small amount of one colour with a large amount of another creates **quantity contrast**.

This block uses a small amount of yellow with larger amounts of red and blue.

Tetradic colour schemes include two complementary pairs for a total of four hues. Use a variety of hues, further apart on the colour wheel for greater contrast, to create **hue contrast**.

This block uses pink and yellow-green with blue and orange.

Understanding scale

Scale refers to the size of designs or motifs on fabric. Solids have no scale, while the designs on printed fabrics range from mini to large scale. Sometimes these designs are a part of a larger motif, which can repeat across the fabric. Understanding scale and repeat can be helpful when selecting fabrics for your quilt.

USING SCALE

Use small-scale prints throughout to create a textured look or large-scale prints to create a bold, maximalist look. Larger scales stand out when placed next to smaller ones. Before cutting, consider how the scales of your chosen fabrics correspond to the pieces in the pattern. Some quilters use a technique called fussy cutting to feature specific fabric designs in quilt pieces by meticulously centring and cutting out motifs.

FABRIC SCALE SIZES

Mini: Very small designs measuring less than 1.3cm (½in) across, such as micro florals or pin dots.

Small: Designs measuring 1.3–2.5cm (½–1in), including small geometric shapes or florals.

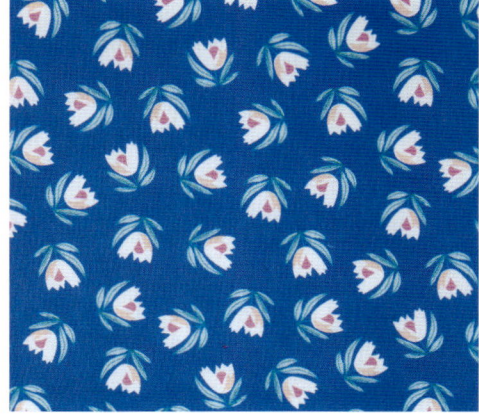

Medium: Designs or motifs measuring 2.5–7.6cm (1–3in), such as scattered objects, geometric shapes, and tartans.

Large: Designs or motifs measuring over 7.6cm (3in), such as large floral patterns or illustrated scenes.

Panels: Large-scale designs, such as landscapes, abstract motifs, or block-sized illustrations, often span the entire WOF and are typically used for large sections or whole cloth quilts and backings.

MEASURING SCALE AND REPEAT

1. To determine scale, use a ruler to measure the width and length of individual designs on the fabric. If the design is part of a group of design elements, measure the size of the complete motif.

2. Identify where, if at all, the design or motif repeats on the fabric.

3. To determine the size of a repeat, measure the distance from the beginning of one motif to the beginning of the next identical motif.

UNDERSTANDING DIRECTIONALITY

Directionality refers to the orientation of designs on fabric, so some prints need careful planning when piecing.

▶ TIPS FOR USING DIRECTIONAL PRINTS

Decide on the orientation of the fabric design before cutting, especially when the direction may impact the final look of the block, such as when using striped fabric. You may choose to disregard directionality; inconsistency can be consistent when intentional.

TYPES OF DIRECTIONAL PRINTS

One-way: Designs that only look correct in a specific orientation. The print has a clear "top" and "bottom," such as prints with text, trees, or landscapes.

Two-way: Designs that can be oriented in two directions, either vertically *or* horizontally. For example, stripes look the same when rotated 180 degrees, but not when turned 90 degrees.

Four-way: Designs that can be oriented vertically and horizontally and still appear consistent. Most tartan and gingham designs fall into this category, as the pattern looks the same whether turned up, down, right, or left.

Non-directional: Designs that can be oriented in any direction, including diagonally, without changing the overall look. Examples include scattered designs like polka dots, florals, and even solids.

Selecting fabric designs

Designs on fabric range from plain solids to intricate prints, textures, and blenders. The unique characteristics of various designs play a role in how they interact in a quilt.

SOLIDS

Solid fabrics are typically single colours without patterns or designs. Available in a variety of hues, solids are simple to use, versatile, and timeless.

- Use solids to practise applying colour theory and contrast (see p.60). They work well for sashing, borders, and backgrounds to provide clean lines and areas of rest.
- Most printed fabrics have colour indicators on the selvedges, useful for matching solids to prints. If you like the colour palette in a print, it will likely work well using solids in a quilt.
- Fabric manufacturers have swatches available for purchase, which can help you test and select a colour palette before committing to it.

TEXTURES

Textured fabrics have either physical textures, such as linen or dobby, or printed designs made to mimic physical textures such as crosshatch or brushstroke.

- Use textures in place of solids or prints to add dimension and an extra sense of cosiness.
- Textured fabrics like linen and flannel can affect the weight and drape of a quilt and may be trickier to work with. Printed textures provide simpler advantages of physically textured fabrics without the added challenge.

SELECTING FABRIC DESIGNS **65**

PRINTS

Printed fabrics have shapes, designs, or motifs printed onto the surface in varying colours, scales, and directionalities.

▶ Use a designer-curated fabric collection as a starting point. These collections are designed with coordinating prints of varied colours, scales, and contrasts.

▶ Choose prints with diverse colours, values, scales, and designs. While digital swatches are useful when purchasing fabric, viewing them in person is ideal. Narrow your selection by choosing prints that fit a theme, as prints come in a wide range of design options.

BLENDERS

Fabrics designed to read as near solid from a distance with subtle, smaller scale patterns are known as blenders. They are typically limited to two or three colours and combine the simplicity of solids with the interest of prints.

▶ When using multiple prints, choose blenders that match colours in the main fabrics to reduce visual clutter. The smaller scale of blenders adds balance to designs of varying scale.

▶ Blenders can replace or be used alongside solids to bridge differences between colours without adding distraction. The subtle designs of blenders make them an ideal choice for adding interest to binding.

LOW VOLUMES

Low-volume prints have negative space, light or neutral backgrounds, and designs of varying scale. They range from quiet, near-white fabrics that read like blenders to loud ones with unexpected designs or pops of colour.

▶ Choose quiet low volumes to add texture without competing for attention or loud low volumes to add complexity and interesting details.

▶ Use low volumes in place of solid background fabrics to add subtle texture and interest to the overall quilt. Some quilters choose to use only low volumes for all the fabrics in a quilt, creating what is known as a low-volume quilt.

SCRAPS

Deciding how and when to use scraps can feel overwhelming, but they can offer low-stakes opportunities to play and experiment with unique fabric combinations.

▶ Organize and store scraps by colour or size to make choosing fabrics more approachable.

▶ Consider the scale, design, and size of your scraps when choosing a scrappy quilt pattern.

▶ Some quilt patterns can be adapted to use scraps in place of fabric requirements (see p.59).

Preparing fabrics

Fabric preparation includes pre-washing to prevent shrinkage, pressing to smooth wrinkles, starching to add stability and to make the fabric easier to handle, and squaring to ensure straight, even edges for accurate cuts.

PRE-WASHING

Some quilters recommend washing fabric before use to prevent bleeding, manage shrinkage, and remove chemicals. However, pre-washing adds time and effort, removes the crispness of new fabric, and may cause damage.

▸ **Skip pre-washing fabric pieces** smaller than a fat quarter.
▸ **Wash fabrics with similar colours,** use a gentle detergent to prevent colour bleeding, and include a colour catcher sheet (see p.23) to capture excess dye.
▸ **For delicate, loose-weave, or small fabric pieces,** prepare edges and wash in a mesh laundry bag to minimize damage.
▸ **Air or tumble dry fabrics** on low heat and remove from the dryer promptly to avoid creases. Refrain from wringing fabrics to prevent stretching.

PREPARING EDGES FOR PRE-WASHING

1 Carefully trim loose or frayed threads along the raw edges to prevent tangling during washing.

2 Snip off a small triangle from each corner of the fabric to prevent the fabric from warping.

3 Sew a straight or zigzag stitch 3.2mm (⅛in) inside the raw edges of the fabric to prevent further unravelling.

4 Alternatively, use pinking shears (see p.16) to trim the edges into a zigzag pattern to minimize fraying. Do not trim the selvedges.

PREPARING FABRICS **67**

PRESSING FABRIC

Pressing involves placing an iron on the fabric, holding it in place, and then lifting it before moving on to the next area. Ironing, in contrast, involves gliding the iron across the fabric, which can cause distortion. Whether preparing fabrics or pressing seams while piecing (see p.80), always press, never iron.

1 Select the appropriate heat setting for your fabric type.

2 Lay the fabric flat on an ironing board or wool mat (see p.21) and smooth by hand.

3 Press the iron down onto the fabric for a few seconds, then lift and move the iron to the next section. Continue pressing, section by section, until the fabric is smooth.

STARCHING

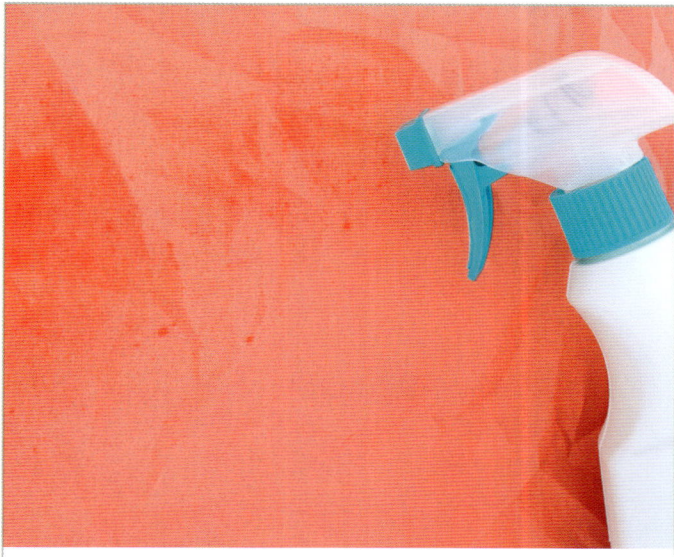

1 Spray a thin, even layer of starch, holding the bottle 15–20cm (6–8in) from the fabric. Allow to dry and set for a few seconds.

2 Press the fabric with the iron at a lower heat setting to avoid scorching. For a crisper feel, repeat steps 1–2.

SQUARING

1 Fold the fabric in half, selvedge to selvedge, ignoring the raw edges. Slide the selvedges along each other until the fabric hangs flat, with no warping along the fold.

2 If necessary, fold the fabric again to fit on the cutting mat.

3 Lay the fabric flat on a cutting mat and position a ruler on top. Align the horizontal lines of the ruler with the fold and selvedges to ensure they are parallel. Use the cutting mat lines as a reference to double check alignment.

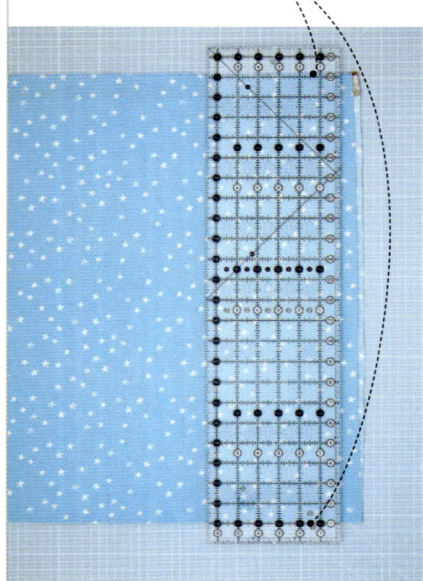

4 Trim the raw edge of the fabric along the ruler, creating a straight edge perpendicular to the fold and selvedges.

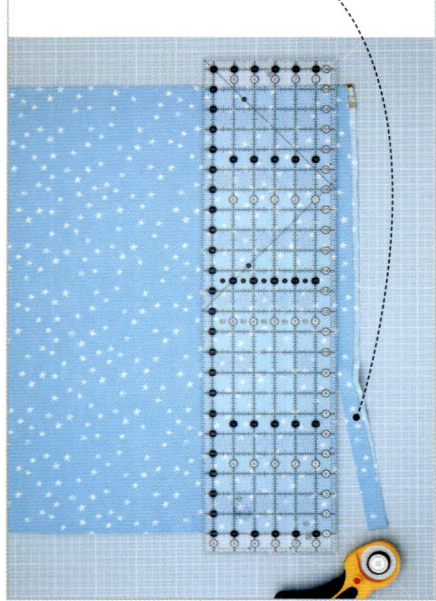

Measuring and cutting fabrics

Accurately measuring and cutting fabric sets the foundation for the entire quilting process. Small errors at this stage accumulate and create a chain reaction of issues that are increasingly difficult to correct, such as fabric shortages, uneven seams, and warped quilt tops. Instructions are written for both right- and left-handed quilters unless otherwise specified.

MEASURING YARDAGE OR METERAGE

When measuring fabric, use the largest cutting mat you have on a large, flat surface. A 61 x 91.4cm (24 x 36in) mat (see p.17) is ideal for accurately measuring up to 1 yard or 1 metre. For fabric longer than the mat, mark the measured section along the selvedge. Shift the fabric to align the mark with the end of the mat and repeat until the entire fabric length is measured.

1 Fold the fabric in half, aligning the selvedge edges.

2 Lay the fabric flat on a cutting mat, aligning the fold and selvedges with the horizontal grid lines. Allow any excess fabric to hang off the edge of the mat.

3 Measure the length of the fabric using the grid lines.

Selvedge

USING A ROTARY CUTTER AND RULER

Before cutting fabric, have a cutting mat, ruler, and a rotary cutter ready (see pp.14–15).

ANATOMY OF A ROTARY CUTTER

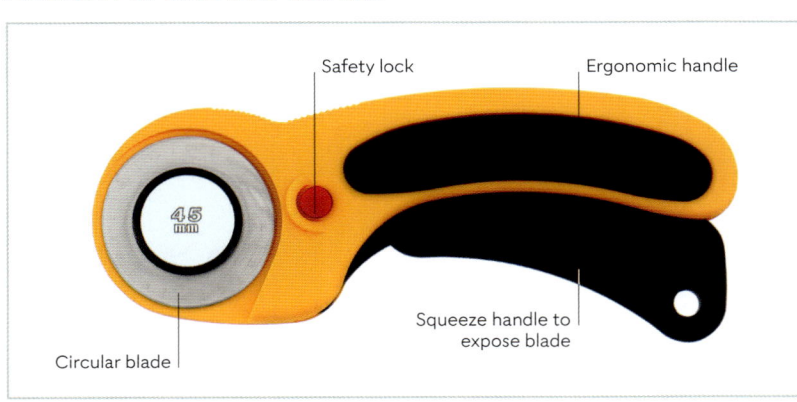

Safety lock
Ergonomic handle
Squeeze handle to expose blade
Circular blade

▶ ROTARY CUTTER SAFETY TIPS

Rotary cutters are extremely sharp tools that require caution. Keep the safety lock engaged when not in use, and store out of reach from children and pets.

Keep fingers at least 2.5cm (1in) away from the blade at all times to avoid accidents. Use a ruler handle and grips for added safety (see p.19), and always push the rotary cutter forward and away from your body.

Replace blades regularly, opting for a fresh blade as often as possible. Dull blades are more dangerous, as they require more force to cut and increase the risk of slipping.

MEASURING AND CUTTING FABRICS **69**

HOLDING A ROTARY CUTTER

1 With the safety lock engaged, hold the rotary cutter in your dominant hand.

2 Position your thumb on the side of the handle, index finger on top, and remaining fingers around the bottom.

3 Your arm, wrist, hand, and rotary cutter should all align for proper form, which provides the most stability and control.

4 When cutting, hold the rotary cutter at a 45-degree angle to the cutting mat, keeping the blade upright.

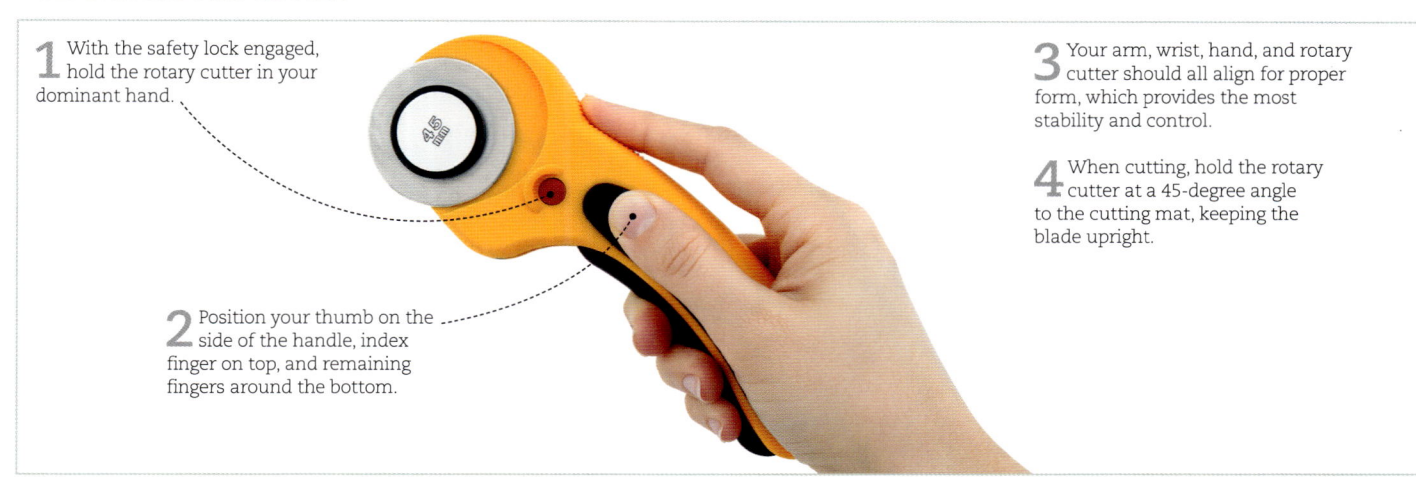

HOLDING A RULER

1 Use your non-dominant hand to press the ruler firmly onto the fabric. Spread your fingers out evenly across the ruler with your palm off the surface.

2 If possible, place your little finger off the edge of the ruler to act as an anchor.

3 Always keep your ruler hand aligned with the rotary cutter. For longer cuts, work in sections and "walk" your hand up the ruler, keeping consistent pressure to avoid shifting.

CUTTING AGAINST A RULER

1 While holding the ruler securely in place, retract the rotary cutter safety lock and align the blade along the right edge of the ruler (left edge for left-handed quilters).

2 Push the rotary cutter down and forward using consistent pressure. Roll the blade smoothly along the ruler edge. Avoid pressing too hard; let the blade do the work.

3 Complete the cut, stopping as needed to reposition your ruler hand for larger cuts. Check that the cut is straight and complete. Trim any skipped threads with another pass.

Cutting fabric accurately

When cutting fabric, width of fabric (WOF) strips, or sub-cuts, always begin with a squared fabric edge. While cutting mat guidelines are helpful for checking ruler and fabric placement, rely on the ruler for precise measurements. Instructions are written for right-handed quilters; mirror these steps if left-handed.

WIDTH OF FABRIC STRIPS

Cutting WOF strips entails cutting fabric into long strips. This is done before sub-cutting smaller pieces or when cutting sashing, borders, and binding. Fold the fabric in half, aligning the selvedges, to manageably cut the full width.

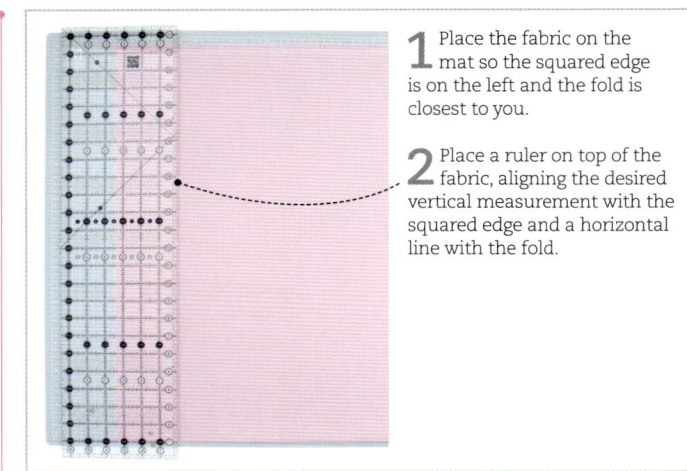

1 Place the fabric on the mat so the squared edge is on the left and the fold is closest to you.

2 Place a ruler on top of the fabric, aligning the desired vertical measurement with the squared edge and a horizontal line with the fold.

3 Cut the fabric along the right edge of the ruler to make the first WOF strip.

4 Shift the ruler to the right by the measurement of the next WOF strip, aligning the desired vertical measurement with the freshly cut edge.

5 Repeat to cut all WOF strips. Occasionally check to ensure the fabric remains square and has not shifted.

SUB-CUTTING

Sub-cutting is cutting smaller pieces from WOF strips (see p.281) or larger pieces. Use the same techniques as when cutting WOF strips, such as ruler alignment, to sub-cut smaller pieces.

1 Remove selvedges before subcutting WOF strips; avoid removing usable fabric.

2 Rotate a ruler vertically or horizontally to find the orientation that best fits the needed measurement.

3 Fold or stack up to four layers of fabric to sub-cut multiple pieces at once.

4 Label sub-cut pieces as you go to stay organized.

CUTTING FABRIC ACCURATELY   71

LARGE PIECES

When a piece of fabric is larger than your ruler, two rulers can be used as long as the combined width is greater than the width of the needed piece.

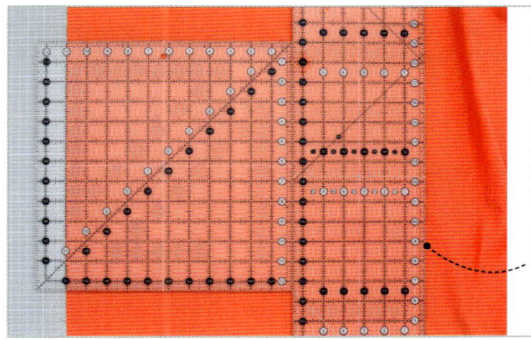

1 Place two rulers side by side on the fabric so the combined width covers the entire piece to be cut.

2 Move the rulers as one, aligning the vertical measurement on the left ruler with the squared edge, and a horizontal line on the right ruler with the horizontal fabric edge.

3 Hold the rightmost ruler in place and cut along the right edge.

USING TEMPLATES

Some patterns require using templates, such as when cutting curves (see p.104), EPP (see p.127), or appliqué (see p.135). They are available in acrylic or can be printed on paper or template plastic.

PREPARING PAPER TEMPLATES

Adjust printer settings to print templates at actual size (100 per cent). Measure the "test square," typically 2.5cm (1in), to check printed templates for accuracy.

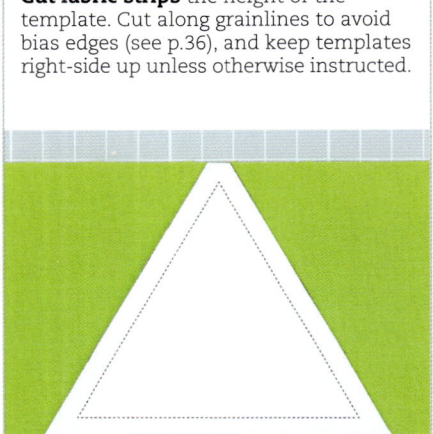

Using paper scissors, carefully cut out templates along the designated lines. For multipage templates, tape sections together as instructed before cutting.

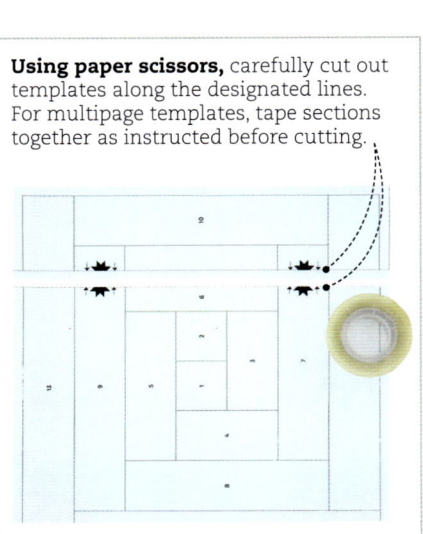

CUTTING

Cut fabric strips the height of the template. Cut along grainlines to avoid bias edges (see p.36), and keep templates right-side up unless otherwise instructed.

Trace detailed shapes and sharp curves using a fabric-safe marking tool (see p.22). Cut along the traced lines with fabric scissors or a rotary cutter.

Cut against large acrylic or paper templates using a rotary cutter.

Curved acrylic template

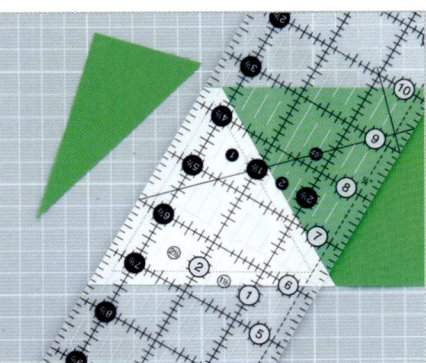

Use a ruler as a guide when using paper templates by aligning the ruler edge with a straight template edge.

Preparing machine settings

This guide outlines the basic machine setup for piecing and quilting. Refer to your sewing machine manual to adjust tension, stitch length, and needle position. Choose the correct thread (see p.24), needle (see p.33), and foot (see p.32) for your project.

TENSION

Tension balances the top and bobbin threads as they interlock to form stitches. If tension is too loose or tight, stitches will look uneven and cause puckering or thread breakage. Test for balanced tension on fabric scraps.

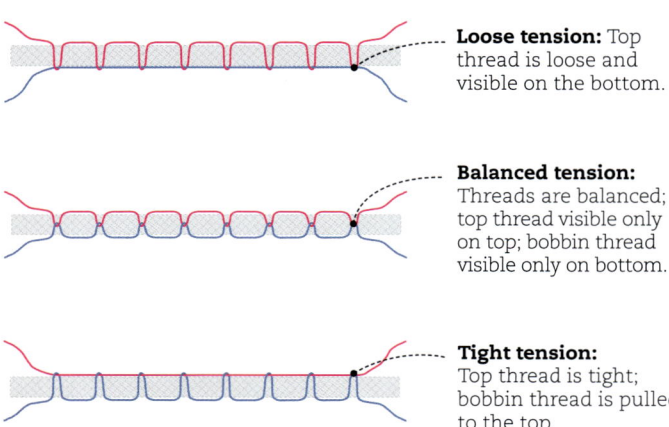

Loose tension: Top thread is loose and visible on the bottom.

Balanced tension: Threads are balanced; top thread visible only on top; bobbin thread visible only on bottom.

Tight tension: Top thread is tight; bobbin thread is pulled to the top.

STITCH LENGTH

Consider thread thickness, fabric type, and number of fabric layers when setting stitch length, as all require different stitch lengths to produce a well-balanced stitch.

Standard piecing: 2.0–2.5mm stitch suits most piecing tasks

Curves: 1.5–2.0mm for a shorter stitch that produces smooth curves

Foundation paper piecing (FPP): 1.5mm for a stitch that secures seams and perforates paper

Basting: 5.0–6.0mm for extra-long stitches to hold layers together

Quilting: 3.0–4.0mm for visible, even stitches; reduces puckering

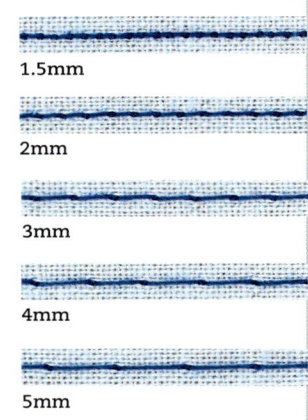

POSITIONING FABRIC

Fabric should be positioned properly to ensure a consistent seam allowance and protect your machine and fabric.

Fabric alignment: Place fabric on the machine bed under the foot, aligning the right fabric edge with the right foot edge. Let the machine feed the fabric.

Right sides together (RST): Fabric should be placed RST with the edges to be joined aligned.

Leaders and enders: Use a small scrap of fabric when starting and finishing sewing pieces together. Leaders and enders can be reused.

SETTING AN ACCURATE SEAM ALLOWANCE

Seam allowance is the space between the seam and fabric edge that provides enough room to hold pieces together without unravelling. In quilting, the standard seam allowance is 6.4mm (¼in). Factors such as the presser foot and needle position may contribute to inconsistencies in the width of the seam allowance.

FOOT

1. Sew a straight line on a fabric scrap, aligning the fabric edge with the right edge of the presser foot. Measure the distance from the seam to the fabric edge.
2. The seam line should be just inside the 6.4mm (¼in) mark on the ruler. Adjust needle position or use a seam guide as needed.

NEEDLE POSITION

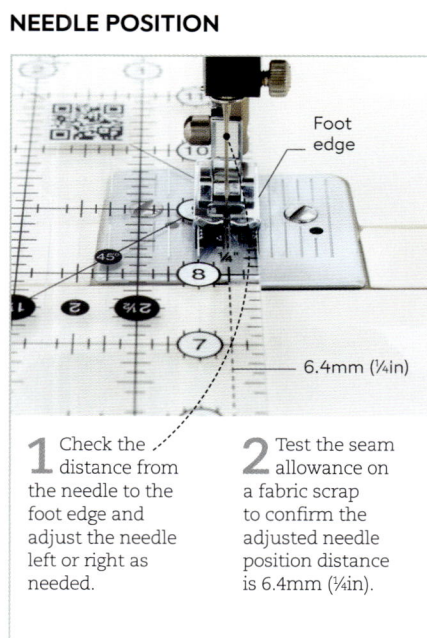

1. Check the distance from the needle to the foot edge and adjust the needle left or right as needed.
2. Test the seam allowance on a fabric scrap to confirm the adjusted needle position distance is 6.4mm (¼in).

SEAM GUIDE

1. If the needle cannot be repositioned, measure 6.4mm (¼in) from the needle, and mark with a seam guide or washi tape (see p.32).
2. Align the fabric with the seam guide or washi tape rather than the edge of the foot.

TESTING SEAM ALLOWANCE

A proper 6.4mm (¼in) seam is a single thread width less than a 6.4mm (¼in) to account for fabric loss during pressing. Variations in thread and fabric thickness can affect how much fabric is lost. Over many seams, these inconsistencies impact fabric alignment, so always test seam allowance.

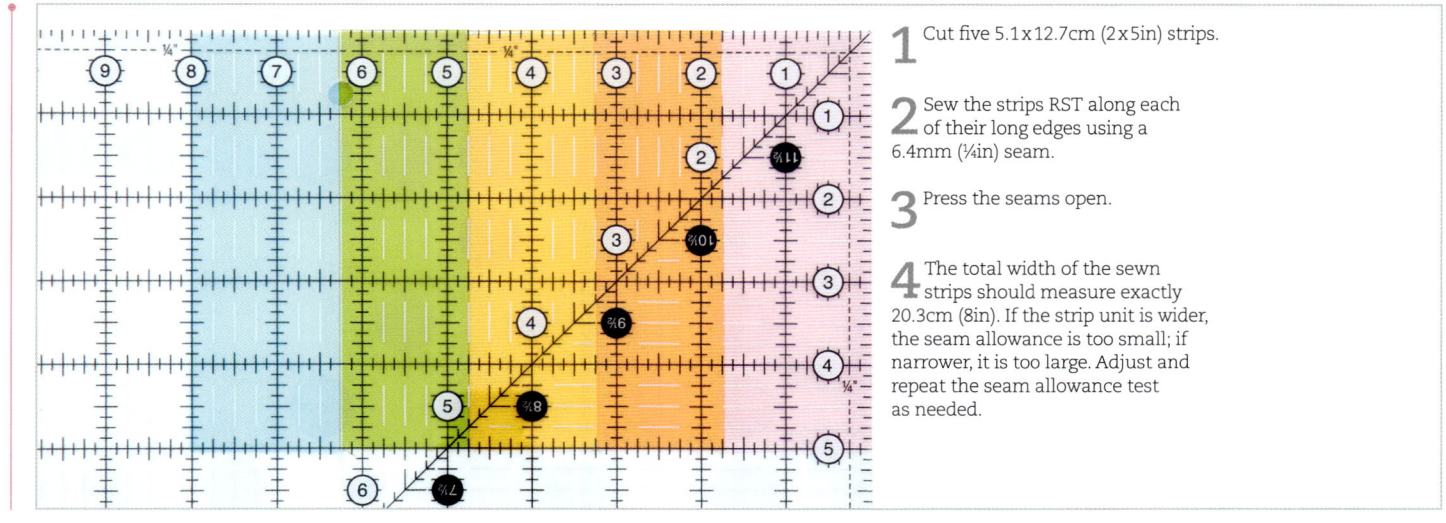

1. Cut five 5.1 x 12.7cm (2 x 5in) strips.
2. Sew the strips RST along each of their long edges using a 6.4mm (¼in) seam.
3. Press the seams open.
4. The total width of the sewn strips should measure exactly 20.3cm (8in). If the strip unit is wider, the seam allowance is too small; if narrower, it is too large. Adjust and repeat the seam allowance test as needed.

Using a needle and thread

Whether hand piecing (see p.120), English paper piecing (EPP) (see p.124), or hand quilting (see p.168), using a needle and thread becomes easier with practice. Choose the appropriate needle (see p.28) and thread (see p.24) for the project at hand.

HOLDING A NEEDLE

Use a firm but relaxed grip to hold a needle between the thumb and index finger. Proper form reduces hand fatigue and produces more accurate, even stitches.

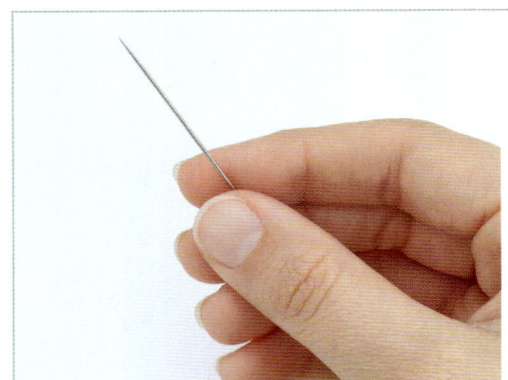

1 Hold the needle in your dominant hand between your thumb and index finger, with the needle eye toward your palm and the pointed tip extending outward.

2 Use firm pressure to hold the needle securely, but not so tightly that it causes discomfort.

3 While piecing or quilting, rest your middle finger against the eye to help push the needle through fabric layers.

THREADING A NEEDLE

Thread needles by hand or use a needle threader (see p.28). Use a self-threading needle when stitching a small section or burying knots (see p.76).

BY HAND

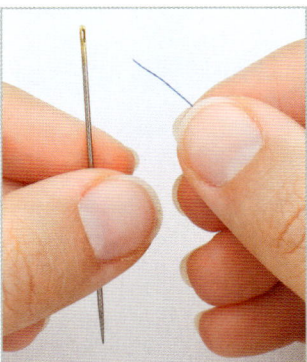

1 Hold the needle in your non-dominant hand, with the eye of the needle exposed.

2 Hold the thread in your dominant hand, with approximately 6.4mm (¼in) extending from your fingertips.

3 Guide the needle and thread toward each other until the thread inserts through the needle eye.

4 Pull a length of thread through the eye, leaving a tail to ensure the thread does not fall out.

NEEDLE THREADER

1 Hold the needle with your non-dominant hand and insert the wire end of the needle threader through the needle eye.

2 Insert the thread through the wire loop.

3 Pull the needle threader and thread back through the needle eye.

4 Continue pulling thread through the needle eye to leave a tail.

MAKING A QUILTER'S KNOT

The multi-purpose quilter's knot is strong and ideal for securing and burying thread ends when beginning a hand quilting section.

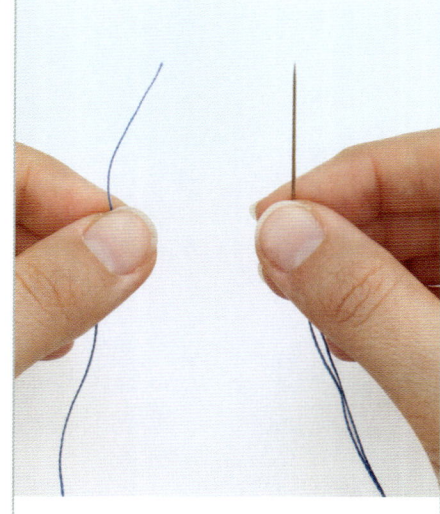

1 Hold a threaded needle in your dominant hand between your thumb and index finger, with the tip pointing upward. Hold the thread end in your non-dominant hand, with the tail extending just beyond your fingertips.

2 Align the thread end beside the needle eye so the thread is perpendicular to the needle. Pinch both needle and thread end in place with your dominant hand. Hold the remaining thread with your non-dominant hand.

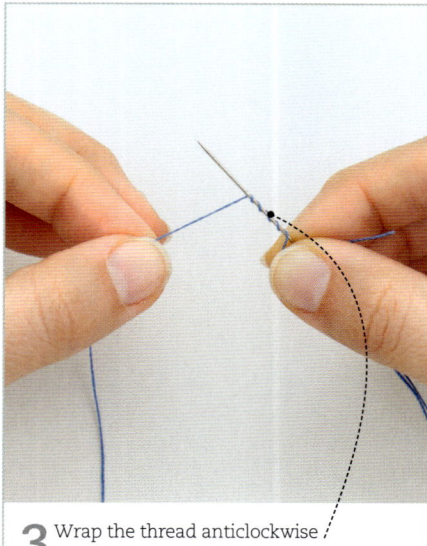

3 Wrap the thread anticlockwise around the needle five times.

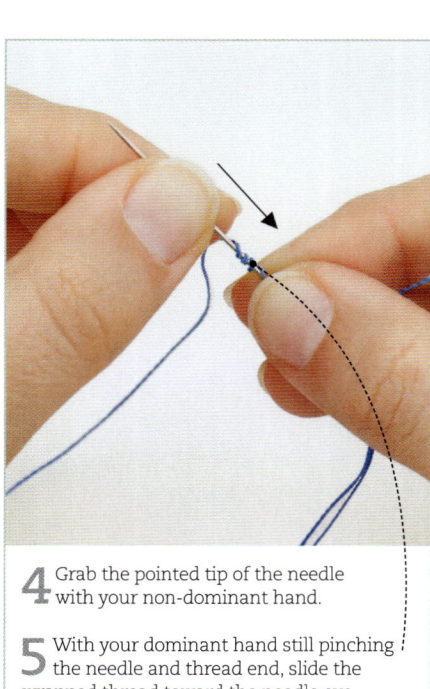

4 Grab the pointed tip of the needle with your non-dominant hand.

5 With your dominant hand still pinching the needle and thread end, slide the wrapped thread toward the needle eye, and firmly hold everything in place.

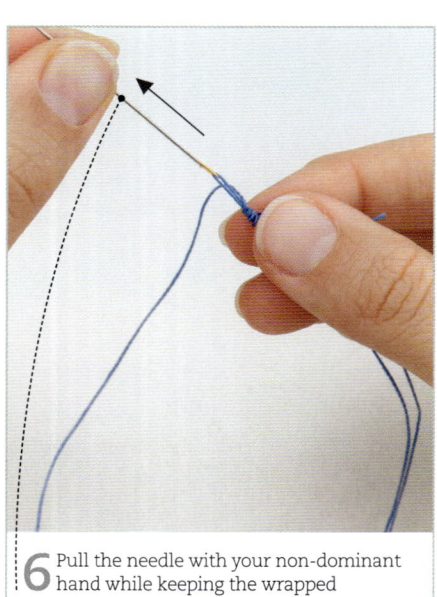

6 Pull the needle with your non-dominant hand while keeping the wrapped thread and thread end pinched between your fingers.

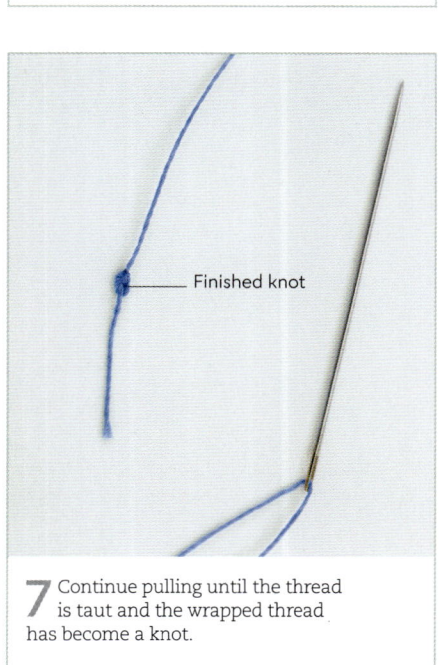

Finished knot

7 Continue pulling until the thread is taut and the wrapped thread has become a knot.

76 GETTING STARTED

BURYING KNOTS

When beginning or finishing a section of hand or machine quilting, knot and bury thread ends inside the quilt sandwich. Bury the end of a single length of thread, such as when hand quilting, using a quilter's knot at the beginning and an overhead knot at the end. When burying machine quilting thread ends, where a top and bobbin thread are present, use a square knot.

QUILTER'S KNOT

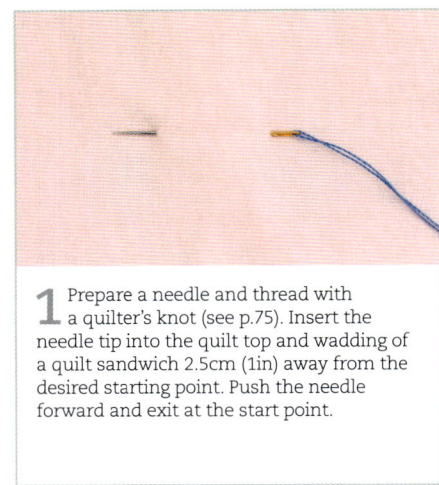

1 Prepare a needle and thread with a quilter's knot (see p.75). Insert the needle tip into the quilt top and wadding of a quilt sandwich 2.5cm (1in) away from the desired starting point. Push the needle forward and exit at the start point.

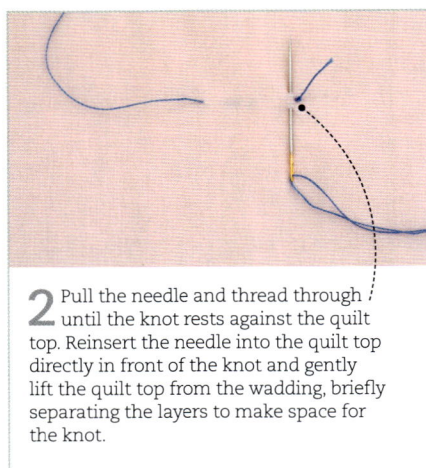

2 Pull the needle and thread through until the knot rests against the quilt top. Reinsert the needle into the quilt top directly in front of the knot and gently lift the quilt top from the wadding, briefly separating the layers to make space for the knot.

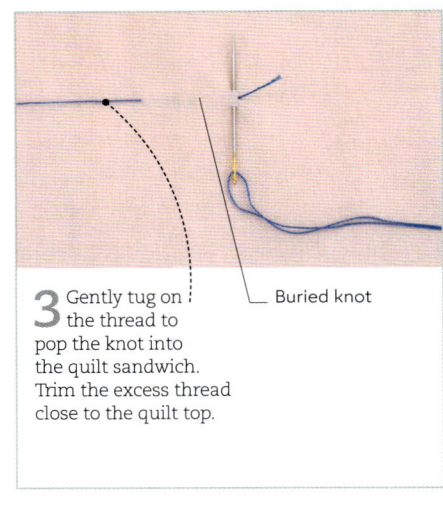

3 Gently tug on the thread to pop the knot into the quilt sandwich. Trim the excess thread close to the quilt top.

Buried knot

OVERHAND KNOT

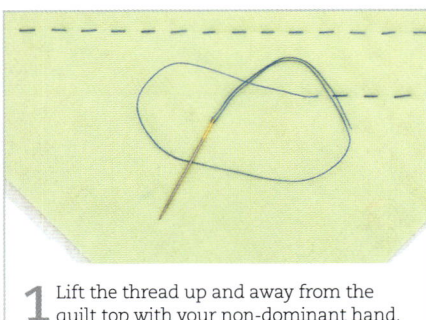

1 Lift the thread up and away from the quilt top with your non-dominant hand. With your dominant hand, place the needle under the thread to form a loop.

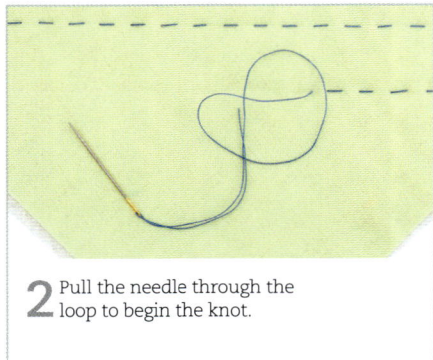

2 Pull the needle through the loop to begin the knot.

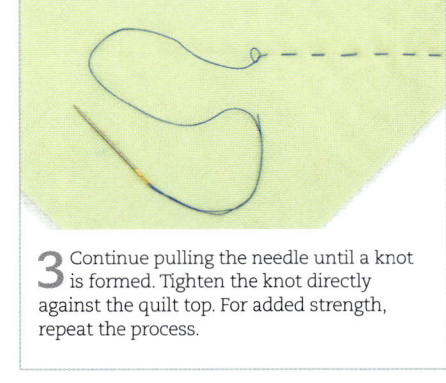

3 Continue pulling the needle until a knot is formed. Tighten the knot directly against the quilt top. For added strength, repeat the process.

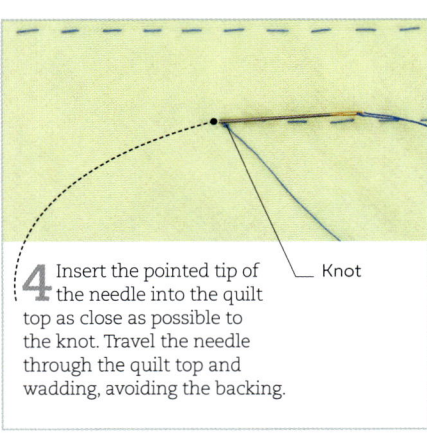

4 Insert the pointed tip of the needle into the quilt top as close as possible to the knot. Travel the needle through the quilt top and wadding, avoiding the backing.

Knot

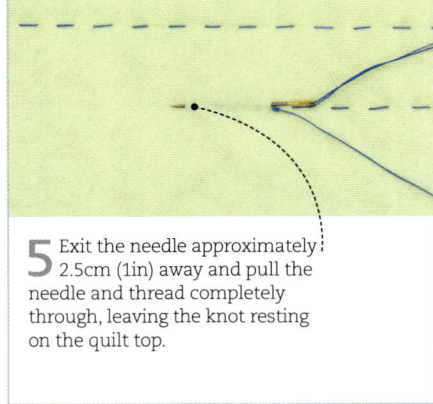

5 Exit the needle approximately 2.5cm (1in) away and pull the needle and thread completely through, leaving the knot resting on the quilt top.

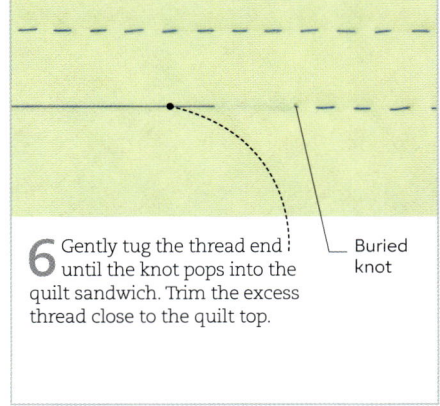

6 Gently tug the thread end until the knot pops into the quilt sandwich. Trim the excess thread close to the quilt top.

Buried knot

USING A NEEDLE AND THREAD   77

SQUARE KNOT

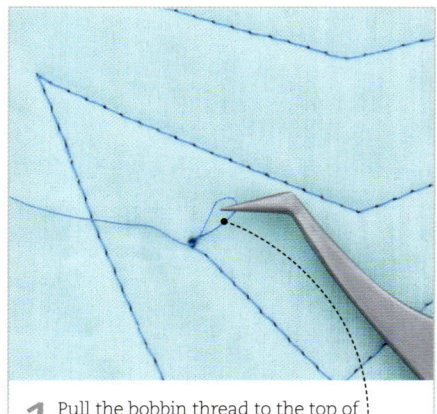

1 Pull the bobbin thread to the top of the quilt using tweezers or the tip of a needle. Pick out stitches as needed to have two thread tails at least 10cm (4in) long.

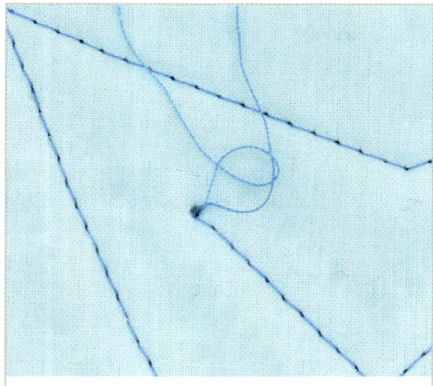

2 Cross the threads to form a loop. Bring one thread down and through the loop to form a knot against the quilt top. Repeat, crossing opposite threads, and tighten to complete a square knot.

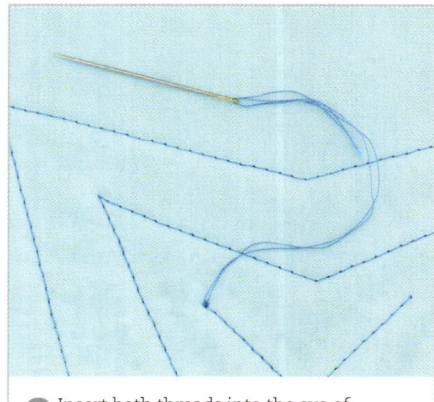

3 Insert both threads into the eye of a self-threading needle (see p.28).

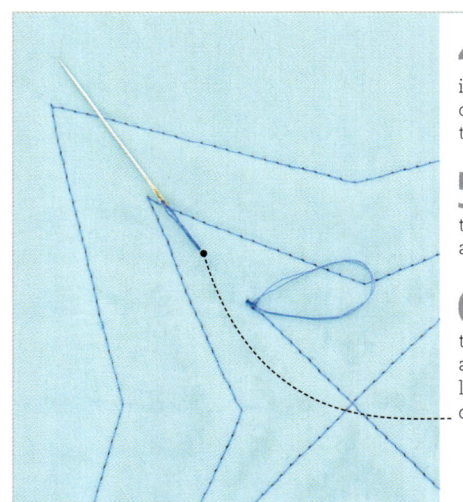

4 Insert the pointed tip of the needle into the quilt top, as close as possible to the knot.

5 Travel the needle through the quilt top and wadding, avoiding the backing.

6 Exit the needle 2.5cm (1in) away then pull the needle and threads through, leaving the knot resting on the quilt top.

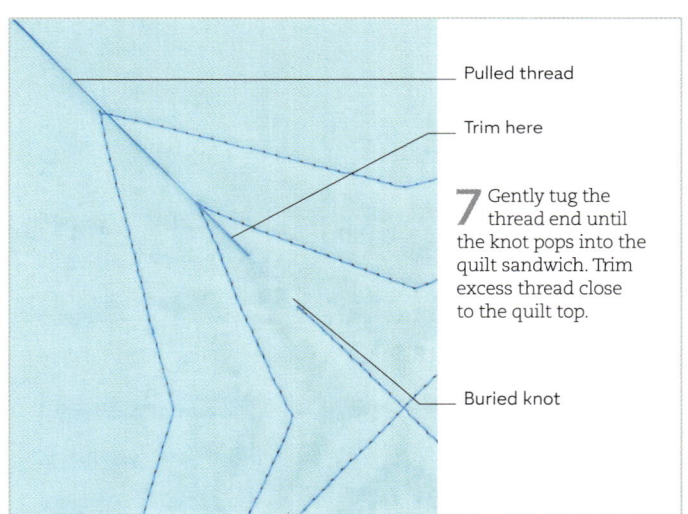

Pulled thread

Trim here

7 Gently tug the thread end until the knot pops into the quilt sandwich. Trim excess thread close to the quilt top.

Buried knot

WEARING A THIMBLE

Wear a thimble to protect your fingertips when pushing the end of a needle while hand piecing or quilting. Thimbles are available in a variety of sizes in metal, plastic, or leather; choose what feels secure and comfortable.

1 Position the thimble so the thickest side covers the pad of your finger.

2 Use the side or top of the thimble to push the needle while stitching. Some thimbles have dimples to provide a place for the needle eye to push against.

Pinning and seam ripping

Pinning and seam ripping highlight contrasting processes of quilting: pinning secures pieces when matching points and seams (see p.141), while seam ripping removes inevitable mistakes, allowing for adjustments and refinement along the way.

USING PINS

Proper pinning ensures seams stay aligned and prevents shifting during piecing, resulting in precise, well-matched points. Be sure to avoid sewing over pins to avoid causing damage to your machine.

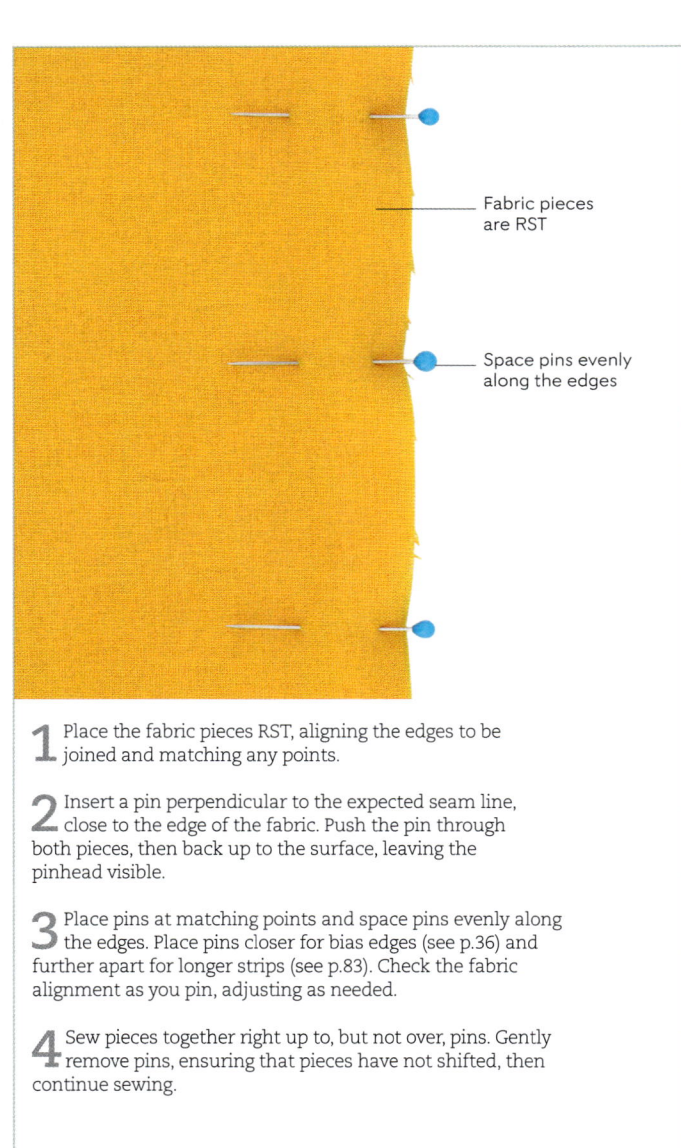

Fabric pieces are RST

Space pins evenly along the edges

1 Place the fabric pieces RST, aligning the edges to be joined and matching any points.

2 Insert a pin perpendicular to the expected seam line, close to the edge of the fabric. Push the pin through both pieces, then back up to the surface, leaving the pinhead visible.

3 Place pins at matching points and space pins evenly along the edges. Place pins closer for bias edges (see p.36) and further apart for longer strips (see p.83). Check the fabric alignment as you pin, adjusting as needed.

4 Sew pieces together right up to, but not over, pins. Gently remove pins, ensuring that pieces have not shifted, then continue sewing.

USING QUILTING CLIPS

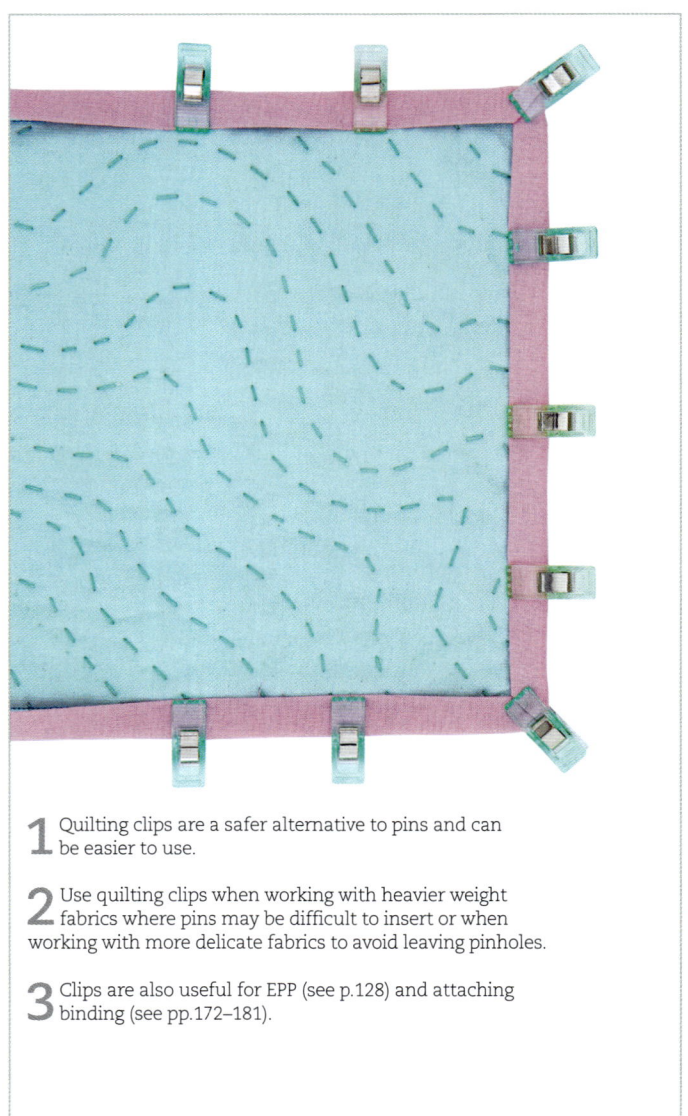

1 Quilting clips are a safer alternative to pins and can be easier to use.

2 Use quilting clips when working with heavier weight fabrics where pins may be difficult to insert or when working with more delicate fabrics to avoid leaving pinholes.

3 Clips are also useful for EPP (see p.128) and attaching binding (see pp.172–181).

SEAM RIPPING

There are two seam ripping techniques, both requiring delicately removing stitches to avoid damaging fabrics. Picking is the process of removing a single stitch at a time and is used to remove stitches from a seam or section of quilting. Ripping is the process of efficiently removing many stitches from a seam and requires more care.

ANATOMY OF A SEAM RIPPER

Seam rippers are available in various styles, but they all have a handle and a metal head. The metal forked head features a curved blade positioned between a sharp, pointed tip and a red ballpoint tip.

- Ballpoint tip
- Curved blade for cutting through the stitch
- Pointed tip
- Handle

PICKING

1. Place the pointed tip of a seam ripper under a stitch, with the ballpoint tip facing up, taking care not to snag the fabric.

2. Carefully lift the stitch from the fabric to form a small gap, then push the seam ripper forward to allow the curved blade to cut through the stitch.

3. Repeat steps 1–2 every few stitches, working slowly to avoid damaging the fabric.

RIPPING

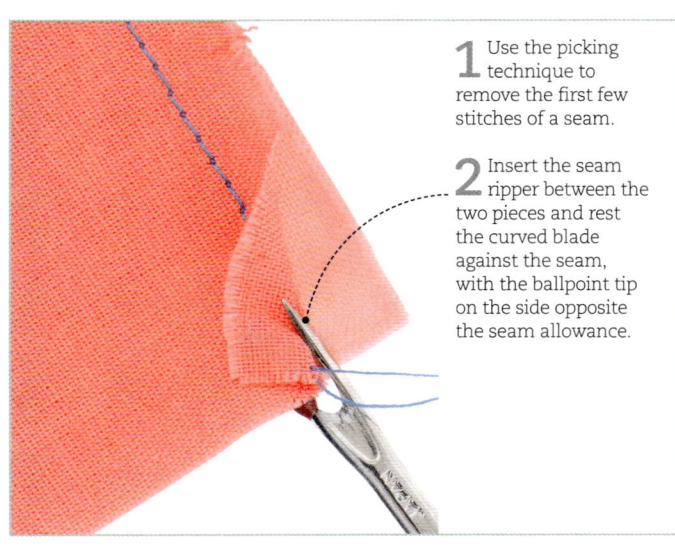

1. Use the picking technique to remove the first few stitches of a seam.

2. Insert the seam ripper between the two pieces and rest the curved blade against the seam, with the ballpoint tip on the side opposite the seam allowance.

3. Hold the fabric steady in one hand while using the other to push the seam ripper forward. Glide the curved blade along the seam, cutting through the stitches and keeping the ballpoint tip under the seam.

4. Continue this motion slowly, working in small sections to avoid damaging the fabrics.

Pressing seams

Press after joining every seam to reduce bulk at seam intersections, make piecing more accurate, and produce flatter blocks. Use a wool mat (see p.21) for smaller units and an ironing board (see p.20) for larger blocks and quilt tops.

SETTING SEAMS

Set seams to relax the fabric and thread fibres, melding stitches in place, to produce a stronger, flatter seam.

1 Before opening a unit, press directly on the sewn seam.

2 Allow the unit to fully cool before pressing the seam open or to the side.

▶ PRESSING TIPS

Make a pressing plan by reviewing how seams will intersect within units, blocks, and the completed quilt top and determining which combination of pressing techniques will produce the best results.

Place a tailor's clapper (see p.20) on a seam directly after pressing to flatten the seam, slow the cooling process, and absorb the moisture naturally produced by rapid cooling.

Use starch (see p.67) to prepare fabric or when pressing a completed quilt top. Always press seams using a dry iron.

PRESSING SEAMS TO THE SIDE

Direct seam allowances to one side to hide seams that would otherwise show through lighter fabrics or to assist with matching points by nesting seams.

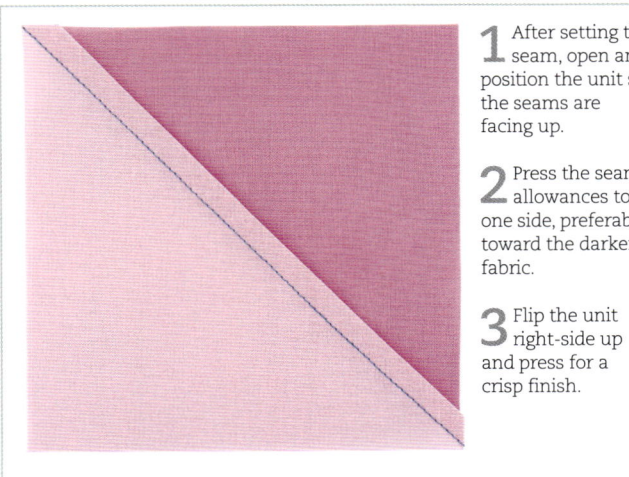

1 After setting the seam, open and position the unit so the seams are facing up.

2 Press the seam allowances to one side, preferably toward the darker fabric.

3 Flip the unit right-side up and press for a crisp finish.

PRESSING SEAMS OPEN

Open seam allowances to reduce bulk and produce flatter units and blocks.

1 After setting the seam, open and position the unit so the seams are facing up.

2 Use your finger to open the seam allowances, then press open.

3 Flip the unit right-side up and press for a crisp finish.

NESTING SEAMS

Nested seams, or alternating seams that rest against each other, are used to reduce bulk and assist with matching points.

1. Press the seams to the side in alternating directions.
2. Align the seams so they lock together.
3. Pinning may not be necessary when nesting seams.

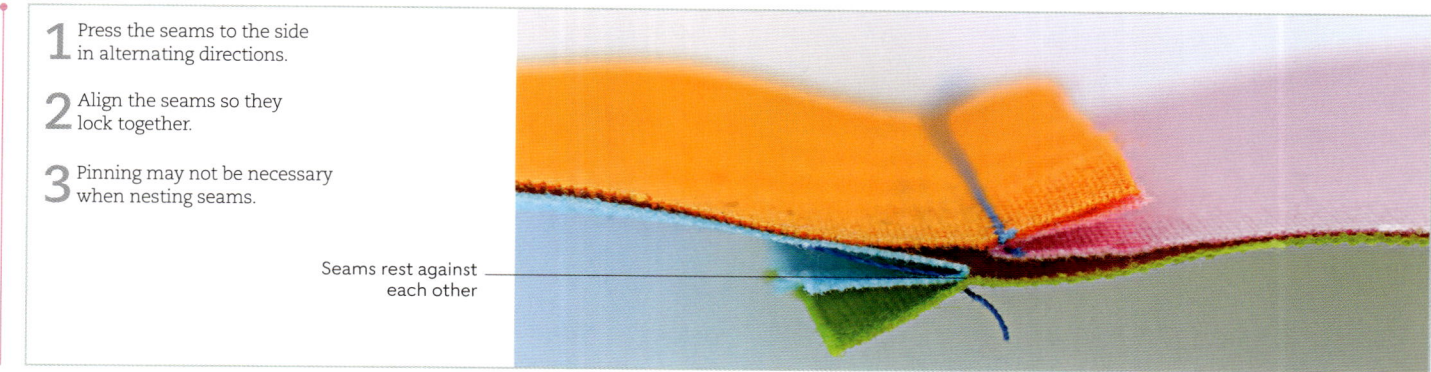

Seams rest against each other

SPINNING SEAMS

Press seams in a circular or "spun" direction to distribute the fabric layers evenly at the centre of multiple intersecting seams.

1. Position a unit as shown. Carefully pick (see p.79) the first few vertical stitches within the horizontal seam allowance. Do not pick any stitches past the horizontal seam. Repeat on the other side of the unit.

2. Open and position the unit so all seams are facing up.
3. Guide the nested seam intersection open with your finger so the seams fall in a circular pattern.

4. Press each seam to the side, following the circular pattern of the seam intersection.
5. Flip the unit right-side up and press for a crisp finish.

PRESSING BLOCKS

A combination of pressing techniques can be used within a single block. Take care not to accidentally flip seams in the wrong direction when pressing. Press a completed block right-side down, then right-side up. Allow the block to cool completely.

Plan pressing techniques before beginning to reduce bulk

Traditional piecing

Piecing is the process of sewing fabric together to make units, blocks, and quilt tops. This section includes the techniques used to piece strip sets, simple patchwork, angled units, and curves. Use a proper 6.4mm (¼in) seam allowance (see p.73) and press after every seam (see p.80) to ensure accuracy. Refer to Charts (see pp.283–289) for specific measurements needed to make various sizes of all included units. This section uses example measurements throughout and assumes right-handedness; if left-handed, mirror the steps.

Patchwork

Patchwork is a piecing style in which individual pieces, typically strips, squares, or rectangles, are sewn together in a simple geometric layout. Patchwork techniques are fundamental in all areas of quilting.

STRIP PIECING

Strip piecing refers to sewing two or more strips together. When joining three or more strips, sew strips in pairs, then join the pairs to make a strip set. For sets with an odd number of strips, sew the odd strip last after making pairs. Alternate the direction in which strips are sewn to prevent warping.

STRIP SETS

1. Cut four 5.1x38.1cm (2x15in) strips from fabric A and three 3.5x38.1cm (1½x15in) strips from fabric B.

Sew strips in pairs

2. Place one fabric A strip RST with one fabric B strip, aligning the long edges. Pin at the centre and either end of the strips, spacing additional pins evenly along the edges.

3. Sew the strips together to make a pair. Open the unit and press.

4. Repeat steps 2–3 to make three pairs. Sew the three pairs together, alternating the fabrics.

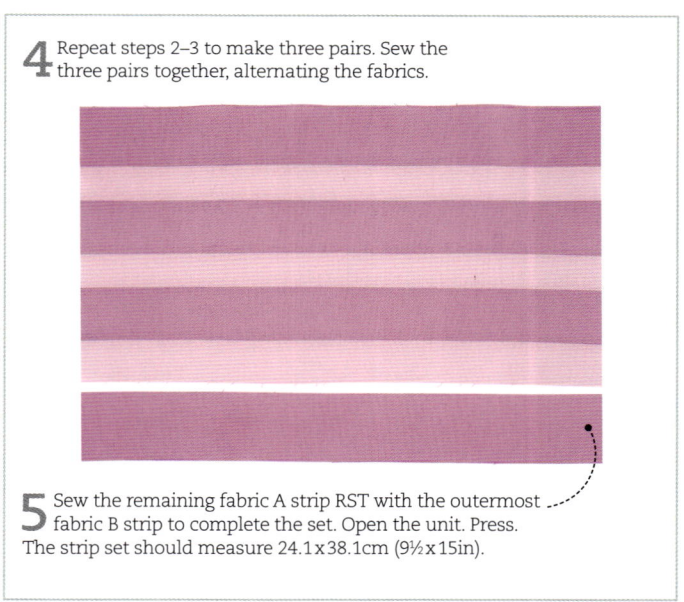

5. Sew the remaining fabric A strip RST with the outermost fabric B strip to complete the set. Open the unit. Press. The strip set should measure 24.1x38.1cm (9½x15in).

SUB-CUTTING STRIP SETS

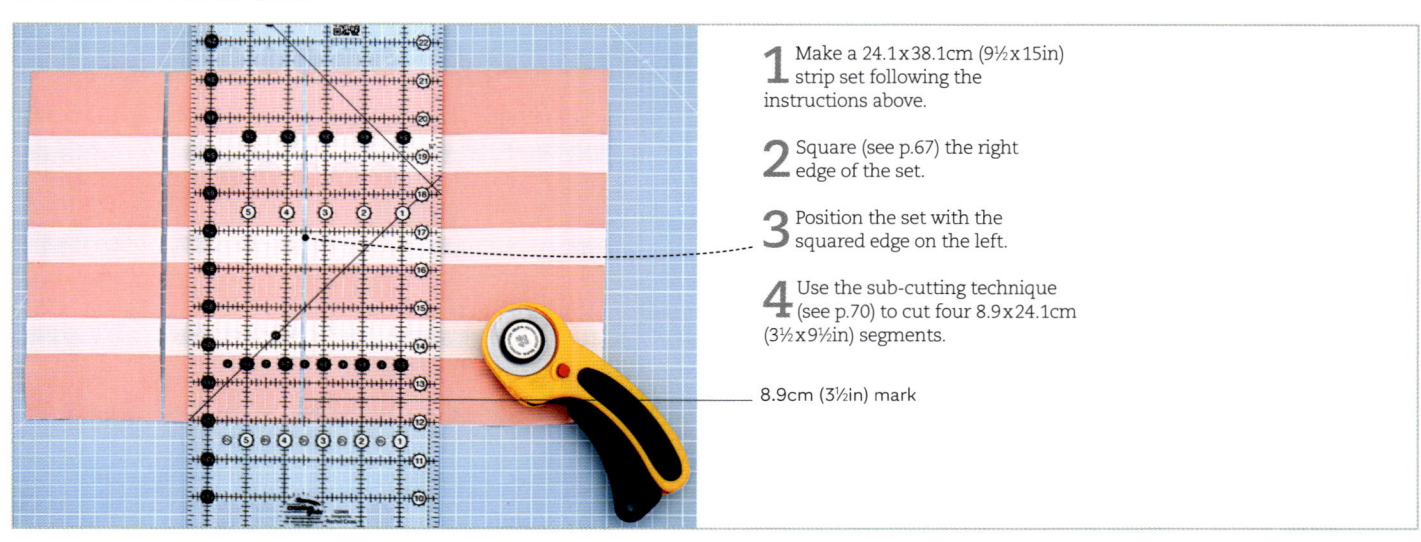

1. Make a 24.1x38.1cm (9½x15in) strip set following the instructions above.

2. Square (see p.67) the right edge of the set.

3. Position the set with the squared edge on the left.

4. Use the sub-cutting technique (see p.70) to cut four 8.9x24.1cm (3½x9½in) segments.

8.9cm (3½in) mark

FOUR AND NINE PATCHES

Four patches consist of four pieces arranged in a grid, and nine patches consist of nine pieces arranged in a grid; both are often combined with other units to make many classic quilt blocks (see pp.264–277). Sew pieces one by one to make four, nine, sixteen, or larger patches, or use the strip-piecing technique (see p.83) to make multiple patches efficiently.

PIECE-BY-PIECE

1 Cut four 8.9x8.9cm (3½x3½in) squares and arrange them to form a grid. Sew squares RST into rows. Press.

2 Sew rows RST to make a four patch, aligning seams at the centre (see p.81). Press. To make a larger patch, cut, arrange, and join the desired number of pieces.

EVEN STRIP-PIECING

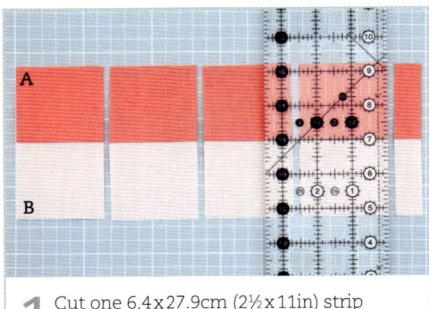

1 Cut one 6.4x27.9cm (2½x11in) strip each from fabrics A and B. Sew strips RST. Press.

2 Sub-cut the strip set into four 6.4x11.4cm (2½x4½in) segments.

3 Arrange two segments to form a grid, alternating the fabrics.

4 Sew the segments RST to make a four patch. Press. Repeat steps 3–4 with the remaining two segments to make an additional four patch. To make a larger even-numbered patch, repeat steps 1–4 using any even number of strips.

ODD STRIP-PIECING

1 Cut three 6.4x21.6in (2½x8½in) strips each from fabrics A and B. Sew strips RST into two sets, alternating the fabrics: ABA and BAB. Press.

2 Sub-cut each strip set into three 6.4x16.5cm (2½x6½in) segments.

3 Arrange three segments to form a grid, alternating fabrics: BAB, ABA, BAB.

4 Sew segments RST to make a nine patch. Press. Repeat steps 3–4 with the remaining three segments to make an additional nine patch with opposite fabric placements. To make a larger odd-numbered patch, repeat steps 1–4 using any odd number of strips.

LOG CABIN

A traditional log cabin features a centre square, often red to symbolize the heart of the home, with light and dark fabrics placed on opposite sides in a spiralling pattern.

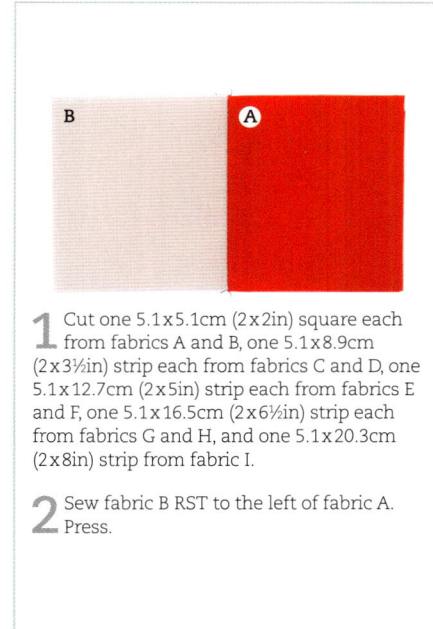

1 Cut one 5.1 x 5.1cm (2 x 2in) square each from fabrics A and B, one 5.1 x 8.9cm (2 x 3½in) strip each from fabrics C and D, one 5.1 x 12.7cm (2 x 5in) strip each from fabrics E and F, one 5.1 x 16.5cm (2 x 6½in) strip each from fabrics G and H, and one 5.1 x 20.3cm (2 x 8in) strip from fabric I.

2 Sew fabric B RST to the left of fabric A. Press.

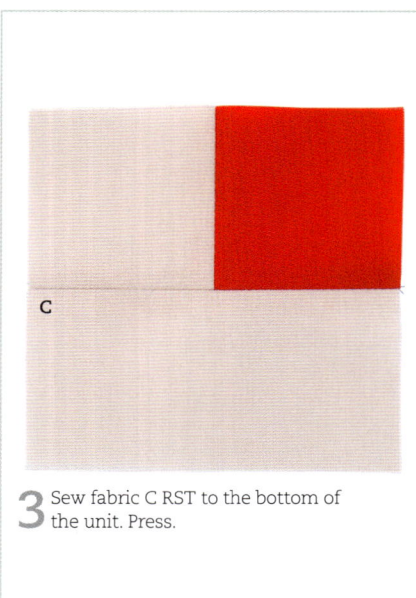

3 Sew fabric C RST to the bottom of the unit. Press.

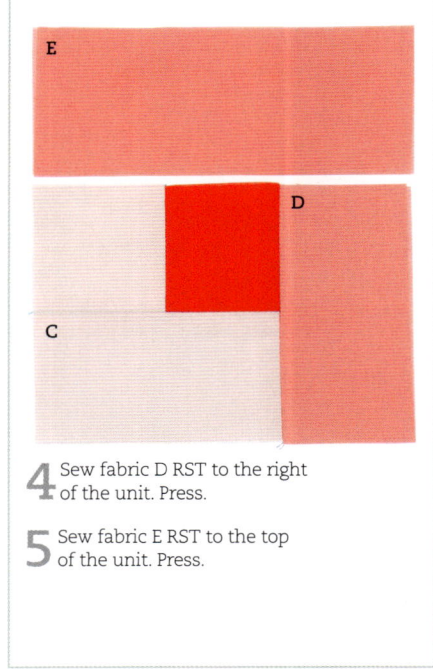

4 Sew fabric D RST to the right of the unit. Press.

5 Sew fabric E RST to the top of the unit. Press.

6 Sew fabric F RST to the left of the unit. Press.

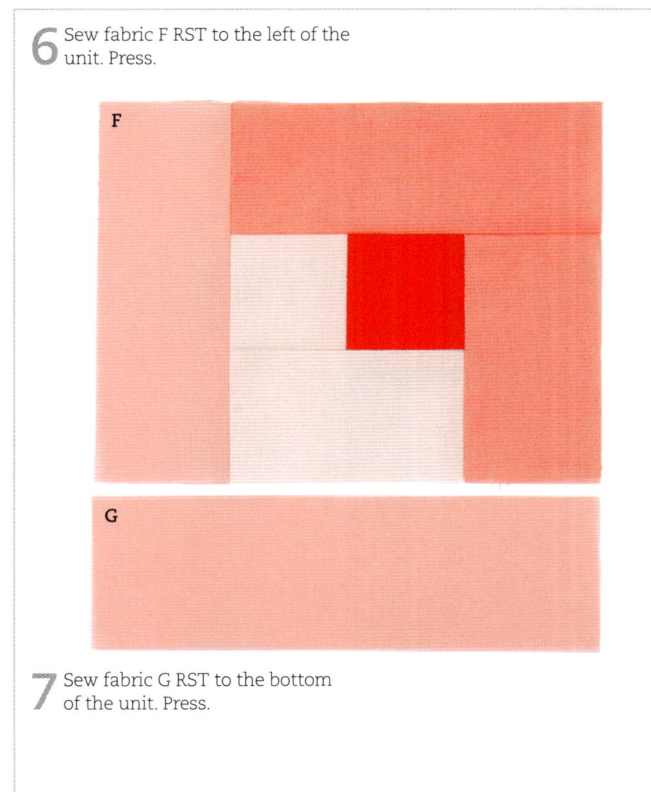

7 Sew fabric G RST to the bottom of the unit. Press.

8 Continue sewing the remaining fabric H and I strips to the unit, working anticlockwise, to complete the log cabin block.

Common angles

Common angled units, such as HSTs, QSTs, and FG, all contain 45-degree angles and are typically constructed to be oversized. All techniques in this section involve cutting or trimming along the bias (see p.36).

HALF-SQUARE TRIANGLES

Half-square triangles, or HSTs, are made by joining two right-angled triangles to form a square. HSTs are the most versatile angled units and can be arranged to produce countless blocks and quilt patterns. There are several techniques for making and trimming HSTs, each with benefits depending on the required size and quantity.

ONE AT A TIME

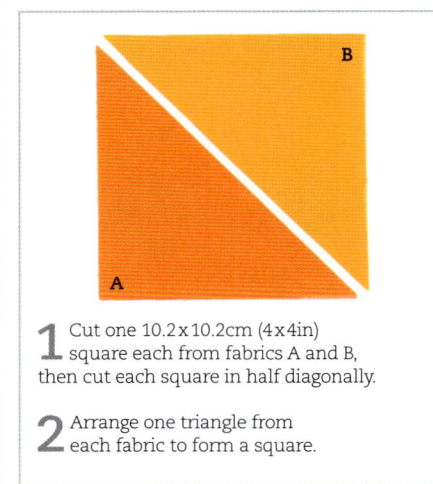

1 Cut one 10.2 x 10.2cm (4 x 4in) square each from fabrics A and B, then cut each square in half diagonally.

2 Arrange one triangle from each fabric to form a square.

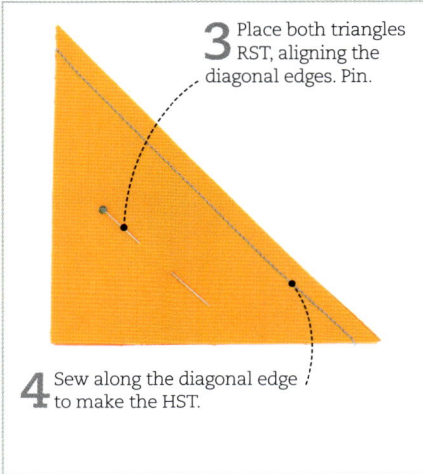

3 Place both triangles RST, aligning the diagonal edges. Pin.

4 Sew along the diagonal edge to make the HST.

5 Open the unit. Press. Trim the HST to 8.9 x 8.9cm (3½ x 3½in). Repeat steps 2–5 with the remaining two triangles to make an identical HST.

TWO AT A TIME

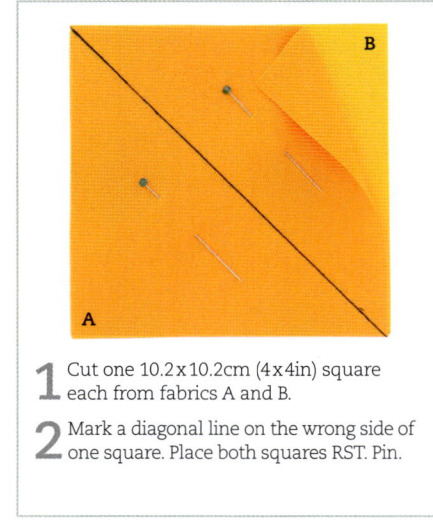

1 Cut one 10.2 x 10.2cm (4 x 4in) square each from fabrics A and B.

2 Mark a diagonal line on the wrong side of one square. Place both squares RST. Pin.

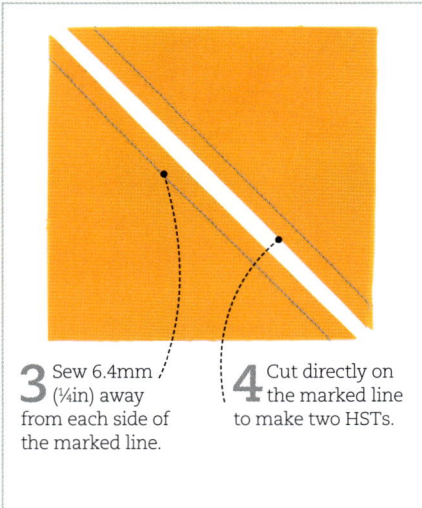

3 Sew 6.4mm (¼in) away from each side of the marked line.

4 Cut directly on the marked line to make two HSTs.

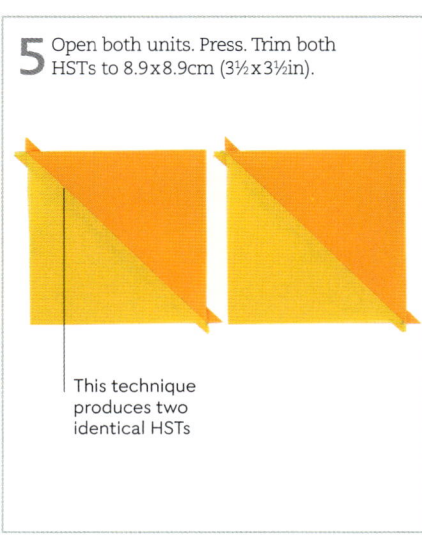

5 Open both units. Press. Trim both HSTs to 8.9 x 8.9cm (3½ x 3½in).

This technique produces two identical HSTs

FOUR AT A TIME

1 Cut one 14.6 x 14.6cm (5¾ x 5¾in) square each from fabrics A and B.

2 Place both squares RST. Pin.

3 Sew around the perimeter, 6.4mm (¼in) from the fabric edge. Press the unit to set the seams.

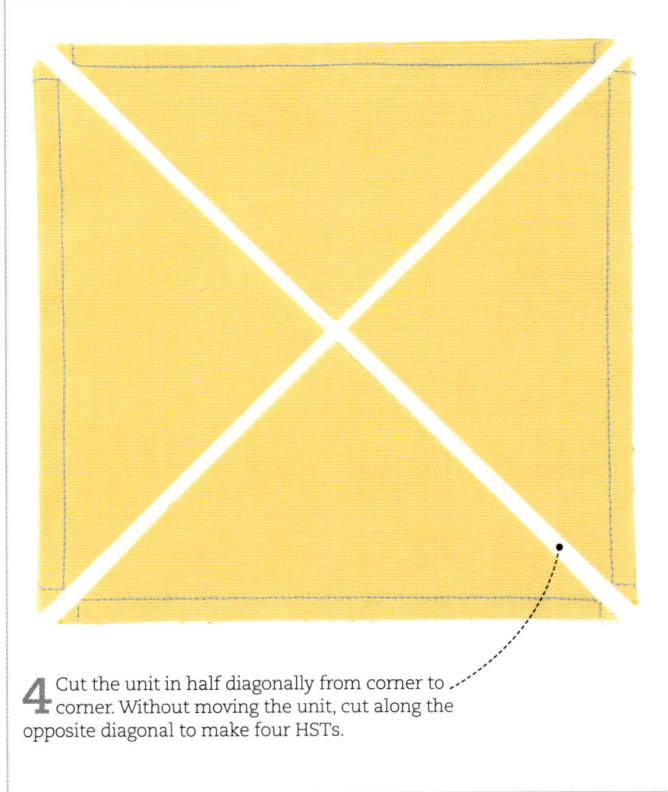

4 Cut the unit in half diagonally from corner to corner. Without moving the unit, cut along the opposite diagonal to make four HSTs.

5 Open the units. Press. Trim the HSTs to 8.9 x 8.9cm (3½ x 3½in).

This technique produces four identical HSTs with bias outside edges

EIGHT AT A TIME

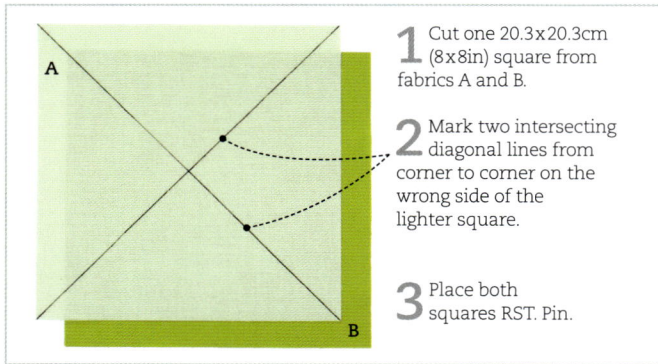

1 Cut one 20.3 x 20.3cm (8 x 8in) square from fabrics A and B.

2 Mark two intersecting diagonal lines from corner to corner on the wrong side of the lighter square.

3 Place both squares RST. Pin.

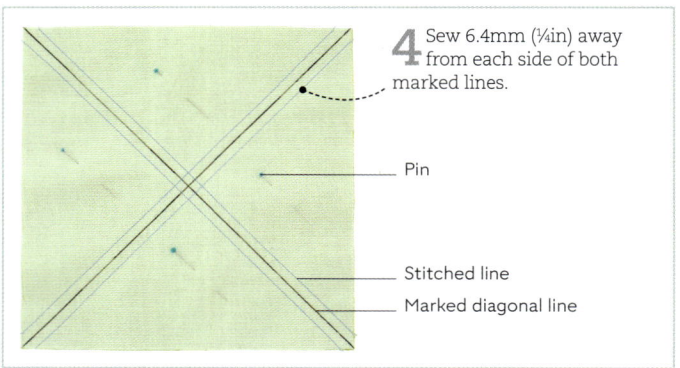

4 Sew 6.4mm (¼in) away from each side of both marked lines.

Pin

Stitched line

Marked diagonal line

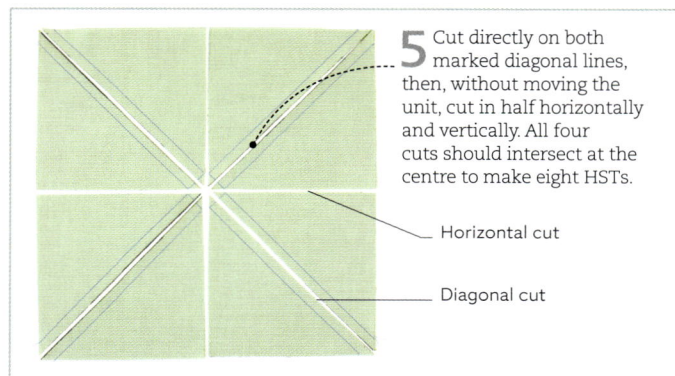

5 Cut directly on both marked diagonal lines, then, without moving the unit, cut in half horizontally and vertically. All four cuts should intersect at the centre to make eight HSTs.

Horizontal cut

Diagonal cut

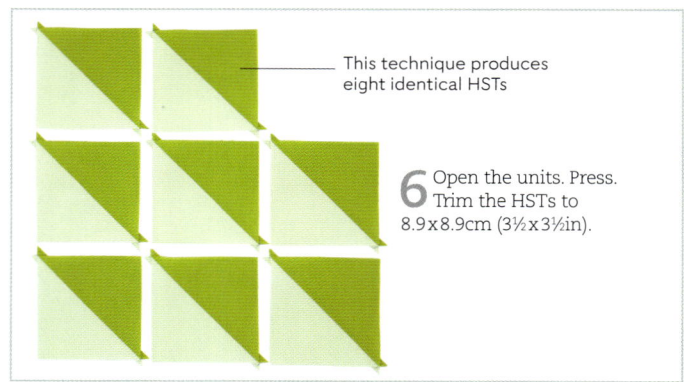

This technique produces eight identical HSTs

6 Open the units. Press. Trim the HSTs to 8.9 x 8.9cm (3½ x 3½in).

STRIP TUBE TECHNIQUE

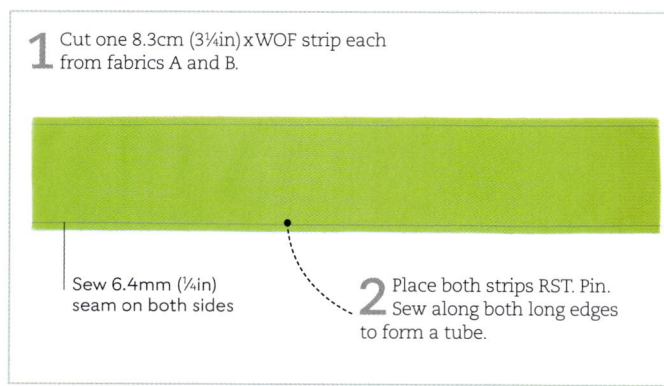

1 Cut one 8.3cm (3¼in) x WOF strip each from fabrics A and B.

Sew 6.4mm (¼in) seam on both sides

2 Place both strips RST. Pin. Sew along both long edges to form a tube.

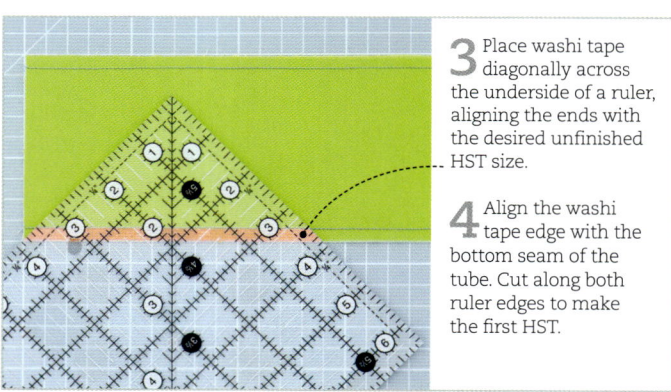

3 Place washi tape diagonally across the underside of a ruler, aligning the ends with the desired unfinished HST size.

4 Align the washi tape edge with the bottom seam of the tube. Cut along both ruler edges to make the first HST.

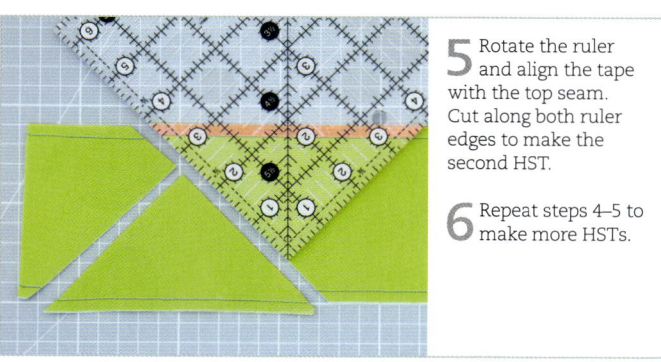

5 Rotate the ruler and align the tape with the top seam. Cut along both ruler edges to make the second HST.

6 Repeat steps 4–5 to make more HSTs.

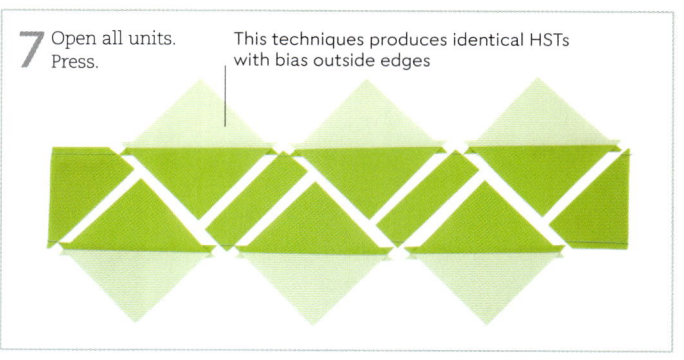

7 Open all units. Press.

This techniques produces identical HSTs with bias outside edges

TRIMMING HSTS

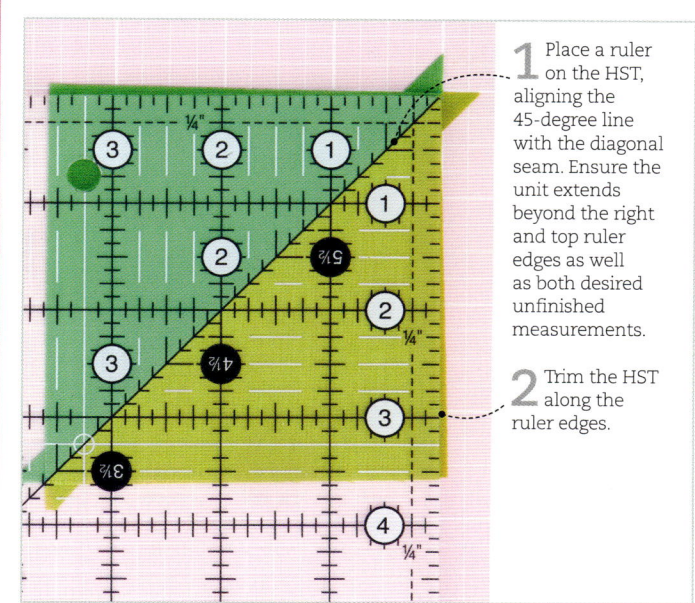

1. Place a ruler on the HST, aligning the 45-degree line with the diagonal seam. Ensure the unit extends beyond the right and top ruler edges as well as both desired unfinished measurements.

2. Trim the HST along the ruler edges.

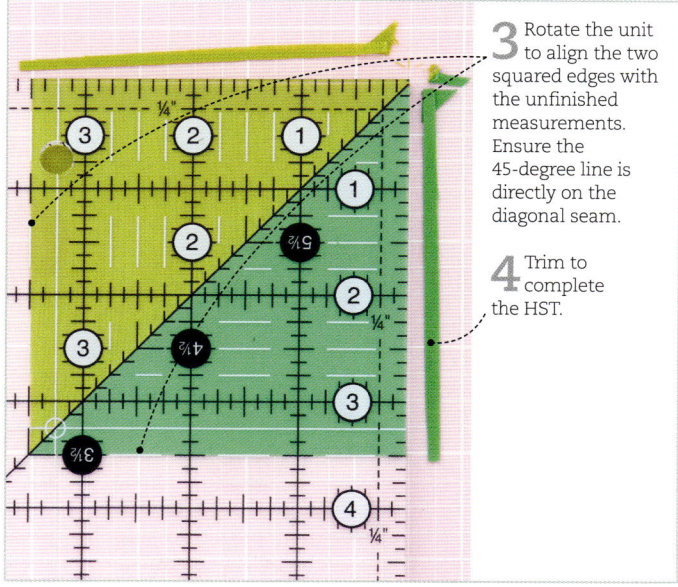

3. Rotate the unit to align the two squared edges with the unfinished measurements. Ensure the 45-degree line is directly on the diagonal seam.

4. Trim to complete the HST.

STITCH AND FLIP UNITS

The stitch and flip technique involves sewing a square diagonally onto the corner of a larger piece, then trimming and pressing the square over to fill the corner. Stitch and flip all four corners of a square to make a snowball unit.

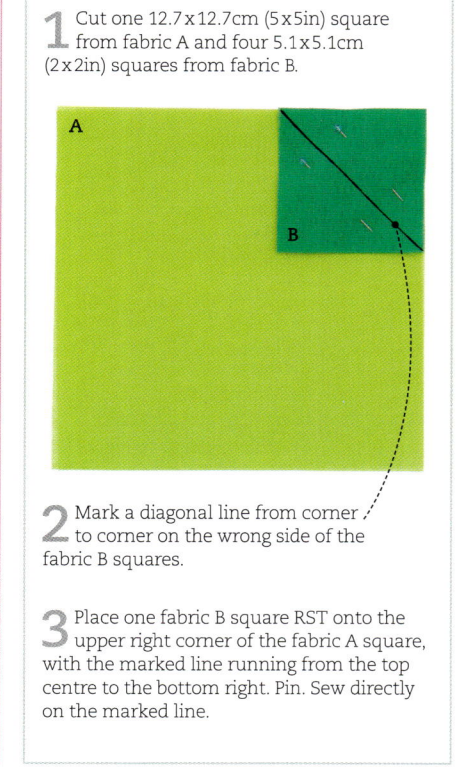

1. Cut one 12.7 x 12.7cm (5 x 5in) square from fabric A and four 5.1 x 5.1cm (2 x 2in) squares from fabric B.

2. Mark a diagonal line from corner to corner on the wrong side of the fabric B squares.

3. Place one fabric B square RST onto the upper right corner of the fabric A square, with the marked line running from the top centre to the bottom right. Pin. Sew directly on the marked line.

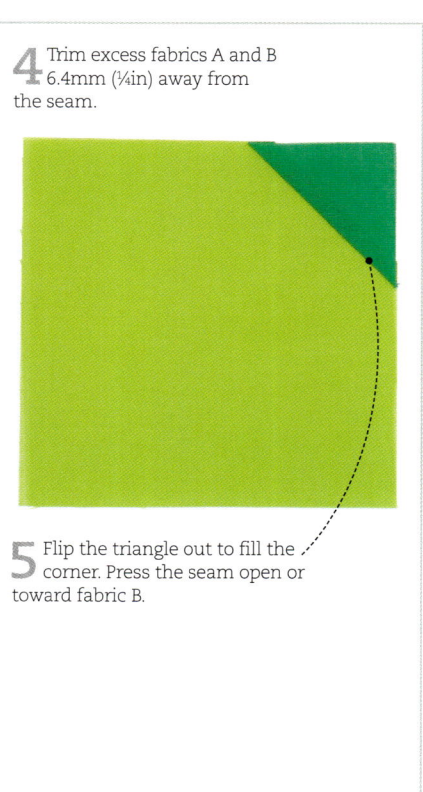

4. Trim excess fabrics A and B 6.4mm (¼in) away from the seam.

5. Flip the triangle out to fill the corner. Press the seam open or toward fabric B.

Stitch and flip units do not typically require trimming

6. Repeat steps 3–5 with the remaining three fabric B squares to make a snowball unit.

QUARTER-SQUARE TRIANGLES

A quarter-square triangle, or QST, consists of four right-angled triangles joined to make a square. Join triangles one at a time for a multicoloured unit, identical HSTs for matching hourglass units, different HSTs for mirrored hourglass units, or one HST with one square for mirrored split units.

ONE AT A TIME

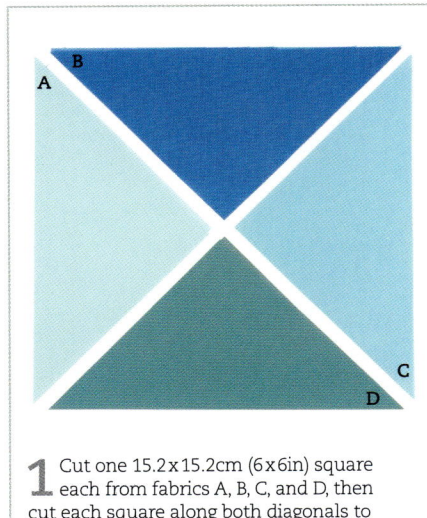

1 Cut one 15.2 x 15.2cm (6 x 6in) square each from fabrics A, B, C, and D, then cut each square along both diagonals to make four triangles of each fabric.

2 Arrange one triangle from each fabric to form a square.

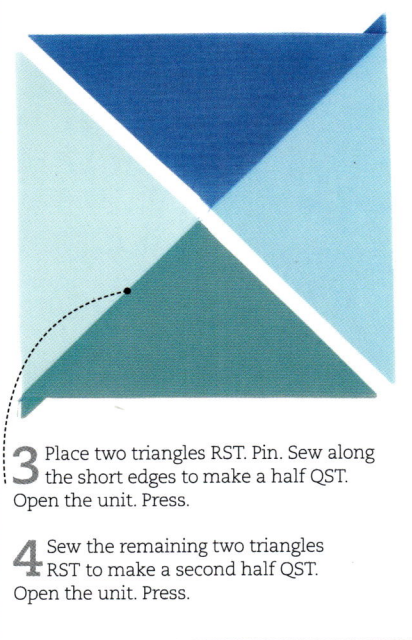

3 Place two triangles RST. Pin. Sew along the short edges to make a half QST. Open the unit. Press.

4 Sew the remaining two triangles RST to make a second half QST. Open the unit. Press.

5 Sew the two half QSTs RST along the long edges, matching the centre seams, to make a QST. Open the unit. Press.

6 Trim the QST to 12.7 x 12.7cm (5 x 5in).

TWO AT A TIME

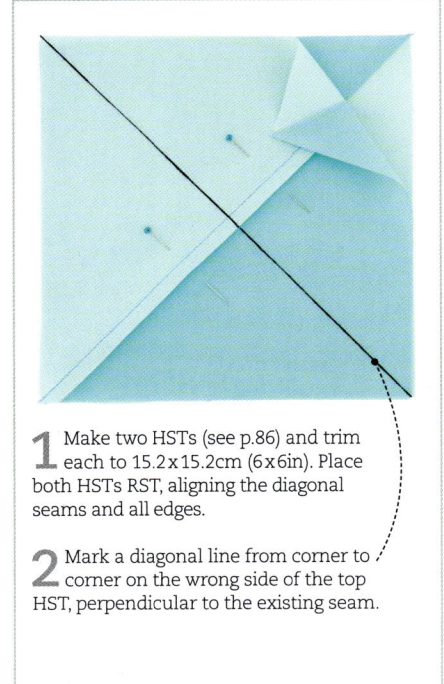

1 Make two HSTs (see p.86) and trim each to 15.2 x 15.2cm (6 x 6in). Place both HSTs RST, aligning the diagonal seams and all edges.

2 Mark a diagonal line from corner to corner on the wrong side of the top HST, perpendicular to the existing seam.

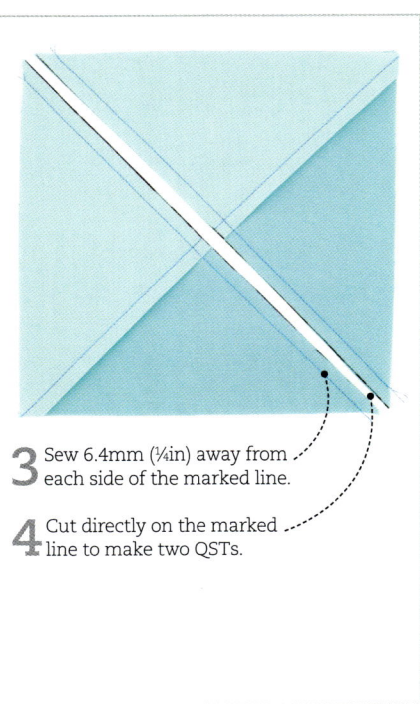

3 Sew 6.4mm (¼in) away from each side of the marked line.

4 Cut directly on the marked line to make two QSTs.

5 Open both units. Press. Trim both QSTs to 12.7 x 12.7cm (5 x 5in).

SPLIT QSTS

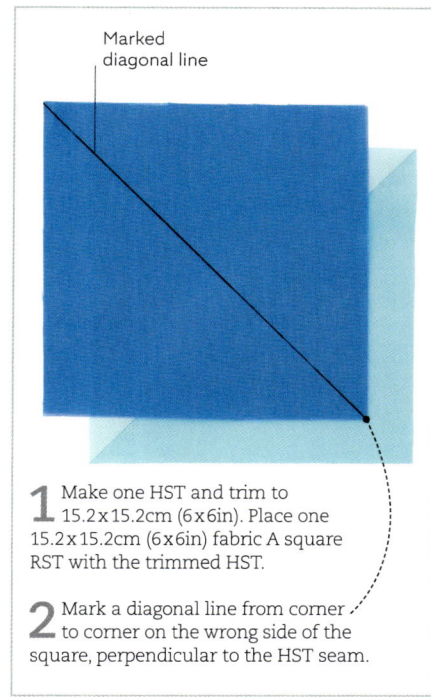

Marked diagonal line

1. Make one HST and trim to 15.2 x 15.2cm (6 x 6in). Place one 15.2 x 15.2cm (6 x 6in) fabric A square RST with the trimmed HST.

2. Mark a diagonal line from corner to corner on the wrong side of the square, perpendicular to the HST seam.

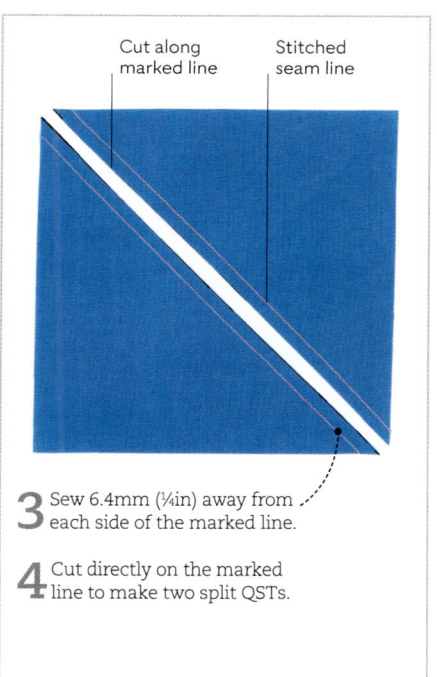

Cut along marked line

Stitched seam line

3. Sew 6.4mm (¼in) away from each side of the marked line.

4. Cut directly on the marked line to make two split QSTs.

5. Open both units. Press the seams open or toward fabric A. Trim both split QSTs to 12.7 x 12.7cm (5 x 5in).

TRIMMING QSTS

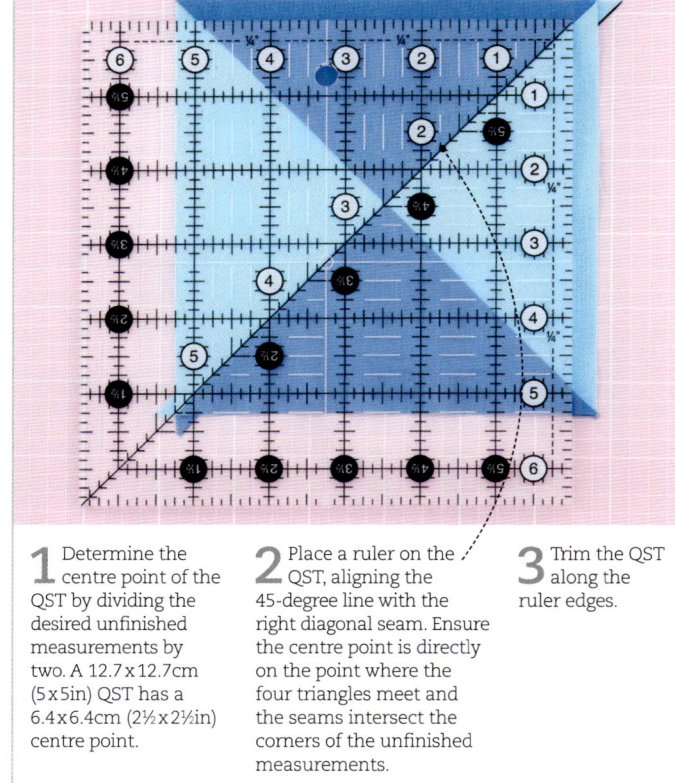

1. Determine the centre point of the QST by dividing the desired unfinished measurements by two. A 12.7 x 12.7cm (5 x 5in) QST has a 6.4 x 6.4cm (2½ x 2½in) centre point.

2. Place a ruler on the QST, aligning the 45-degree line with the right diagonal seam. Ensure the centre point is directly on the point where the four triangles meet and the seams intersect the corners of the unfinished measurements.

3. Trim the QST along the ruler edges.

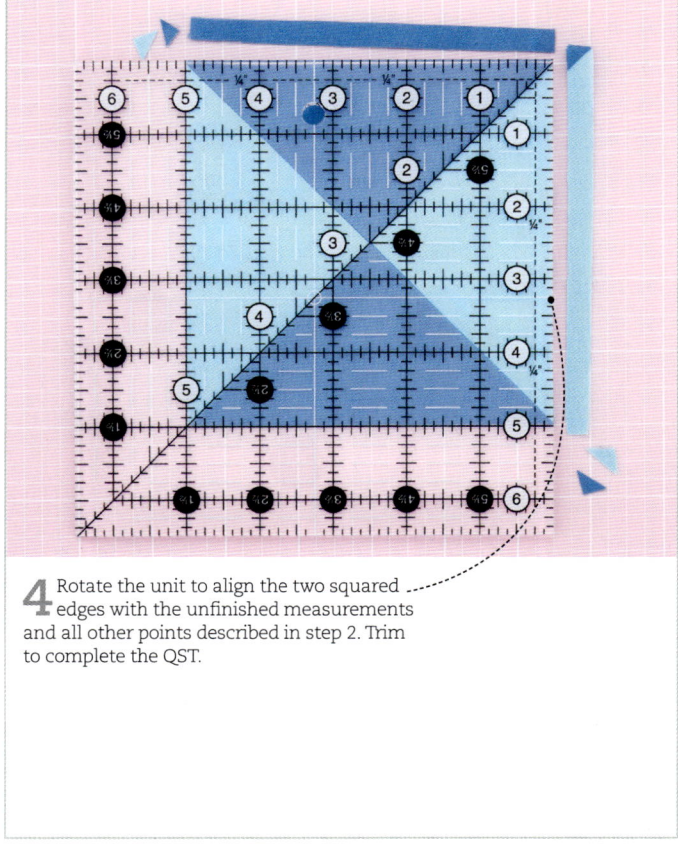

4. Rotate the unit to align the two squared edges with the unfinished measurements and all other points described in step 2. Trim to complete the QST.

FLYING GEESE

Flying geese, or FG, consist of one large triangle and two smaller triangles that join to make a rectangle finishing twice as wide as it is long.

ONE AT A TIME

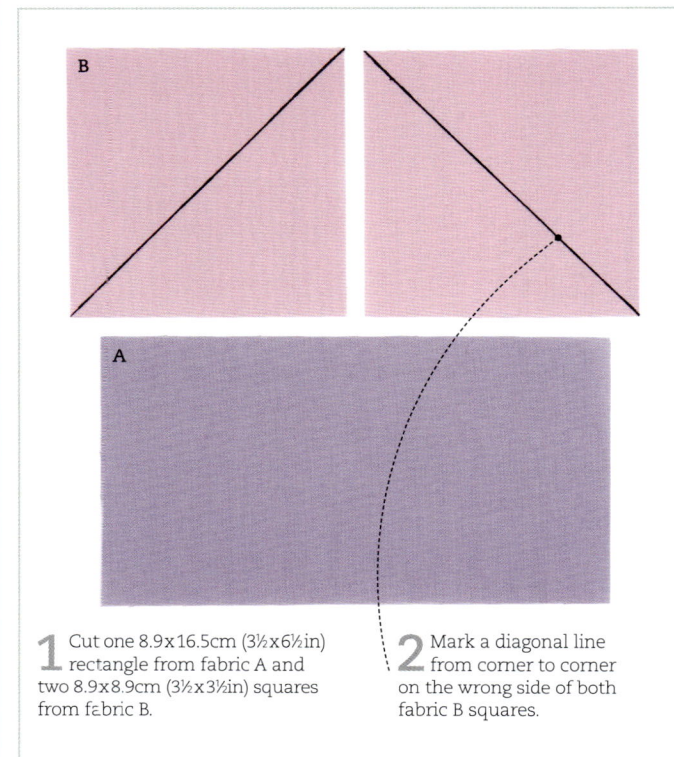

1 Cut one 8.9x16.5cm (3½x6½in) rectangle from fabric A and two 8.9x8.9cm (3½x3½in) squares from fabric B.

2 Mark a diagonal line from corner to corner on the wrong side of both fabric B squares.

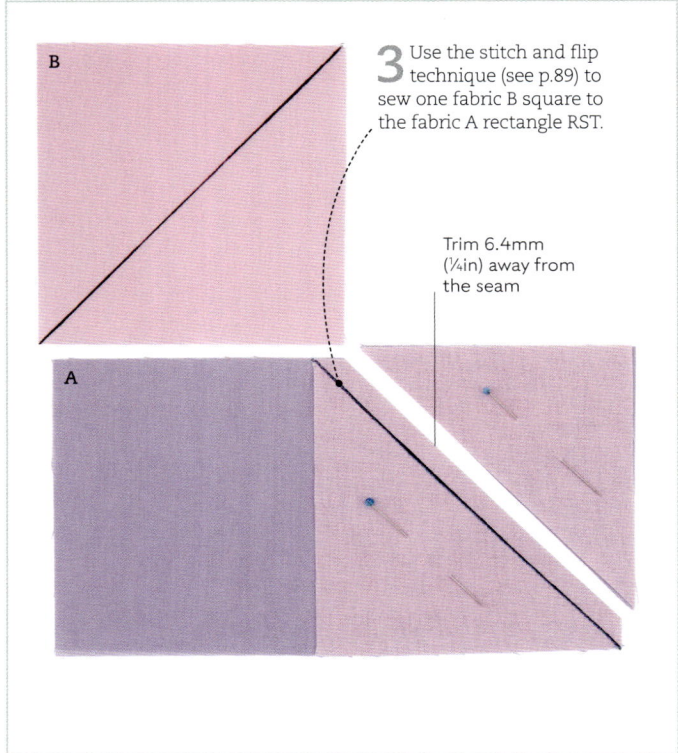

3 Use the stitch and flip technique (see p.89) to sew one fabric B square to the fabric A rectangle RST.

Trim 6.4mm (¼in) away from the seam

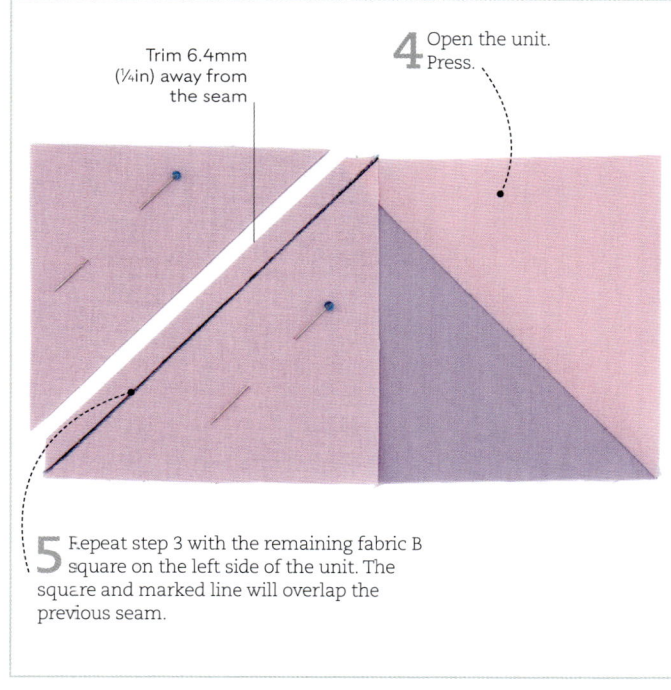

Trim 6.4mm (¼in) away from the seam

4 Open the unit. Press.

5 Repeat step 3 with the remaining fabric B square on the left side of the unit. The square and marked line will overlap the previous seam.

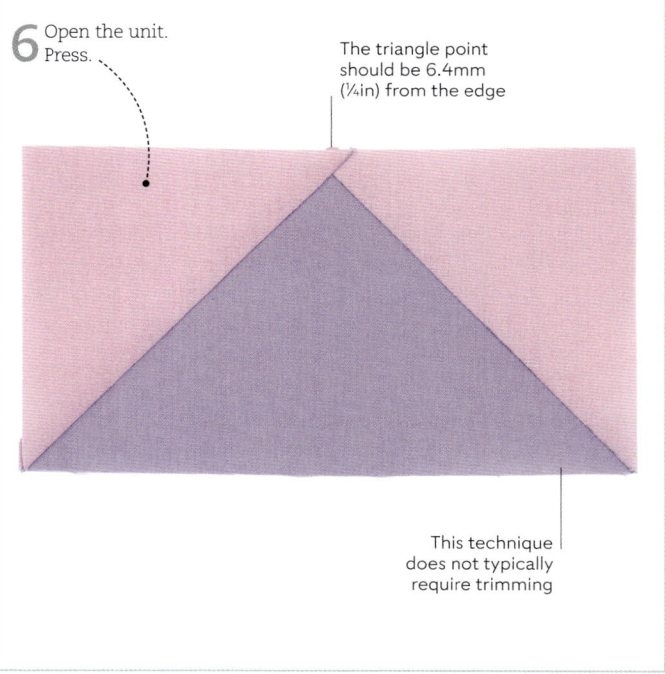

6 Open the unit. Press.

The triangle point should be 6.4mm (¼in) from the edge

This technique does not typically require trimming

FOUR AT A TIME

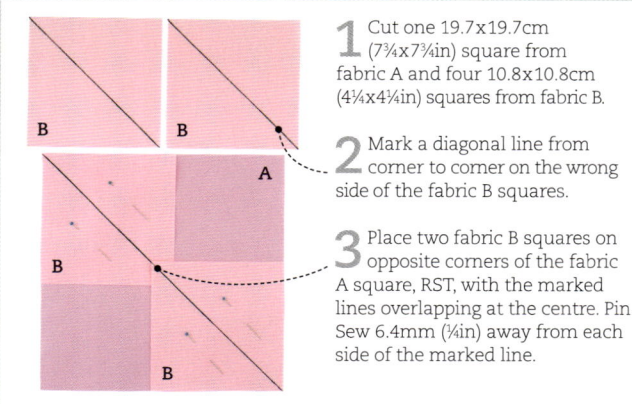

1. Cut one 19.7x19.7cm (7¾x7¾in) square from fabric A and four 10.8x10.8cm (4¼x4¼in) squares from fabric B.

2. Mark a diagonal line from corner to corner on the wrong side of the fabric B squares.

3. Place two fabric B squares on opposite corners of the fabric A square, RST, with the marked lines overlapping at the centre. Pin. Sew 6.4mm (¼in) away from each side of the marked line.

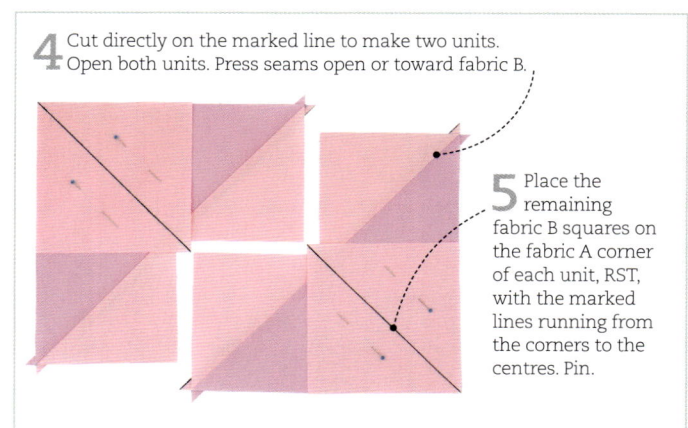

4. Cut directly on the marked line to make two units. Open both units. Press seams open or toward fabric B.

5. Place the remaining fabric B squares on the fabric A corner of each unit, RST, with the marked lines running from the corners to the centres. Pin.

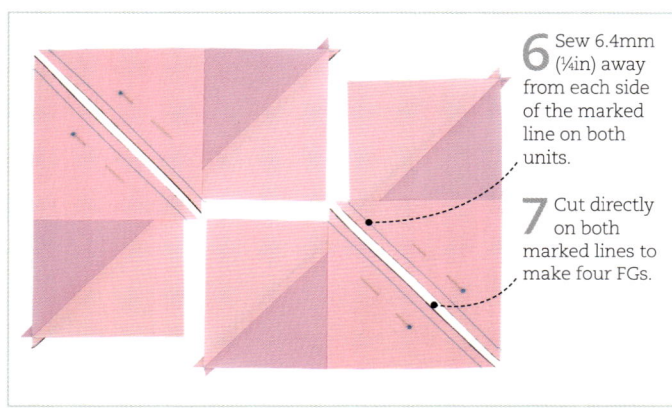

6. Sew 6.4mm (¼in) away from each side of the marked line on both units.

7. Cut directly on both marked lines to make four FGs.

8. Open the units. Press seams open or toward fabric B. Trim the FG to 8.9x16.5cm (3½x6½in).

Sew with a proper 6.4mm (¼in) seam for accurate results

TRIMMING FG

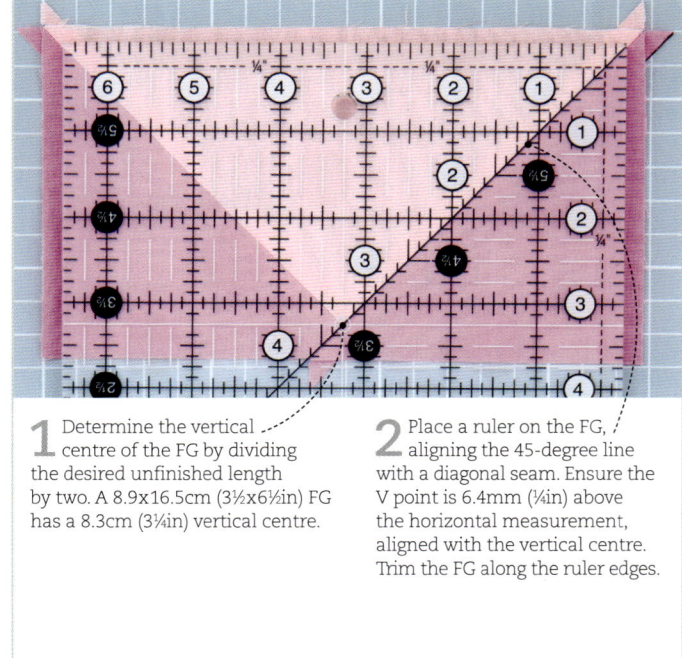

1. Determine the vertical centre of the FG by dividing the desired unfinished length by two. A 8.9x16.5cm (3½x6½in) FG has a 8.3cm (3¼in) vertical centre.

2. Place a ruler on the FG, aligning the 45-degree line with a diagonal seam. Ensure the V point is 6.4mm (¼in) above the horizontal measurement, aligned with the vertical centre. Trim the FG along the ruler edges.

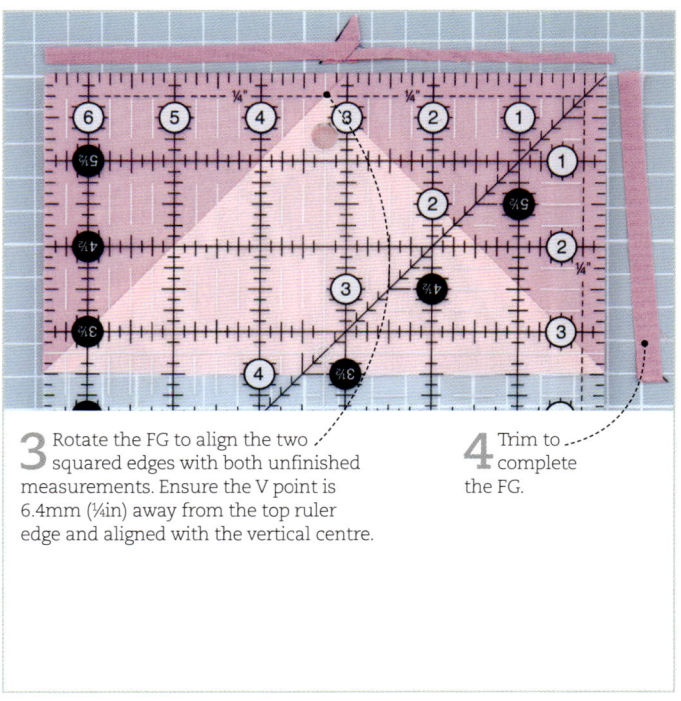

3. Rotate the FG to align the two squared edges with both unfinished measurements. Ensure the V point is 6.4mm (¼in) away from the top ruler edge and aligned with the vertical centre.

4. Trim to complete the FG.

SQUARE IN A SQUARE UNITS

A square in a square unit features a centre square surrounded by four setting triangles to form a larger square. Setting triangles fill gaps on the outer edges of a unit, block, or quilt top oriented at an angle, or "on point". This unit can be constructed using the stitch and flip technique (see p.89), setting triangles, or, for precision, FPP (see p.114).

STITCH AND FLIP TECHNIQUE

1 Cut one 16.5x16.5cm (6½x6½in) square from fabric A and four 8.9x8.9cm (3½x3½in) squares from fabric B.

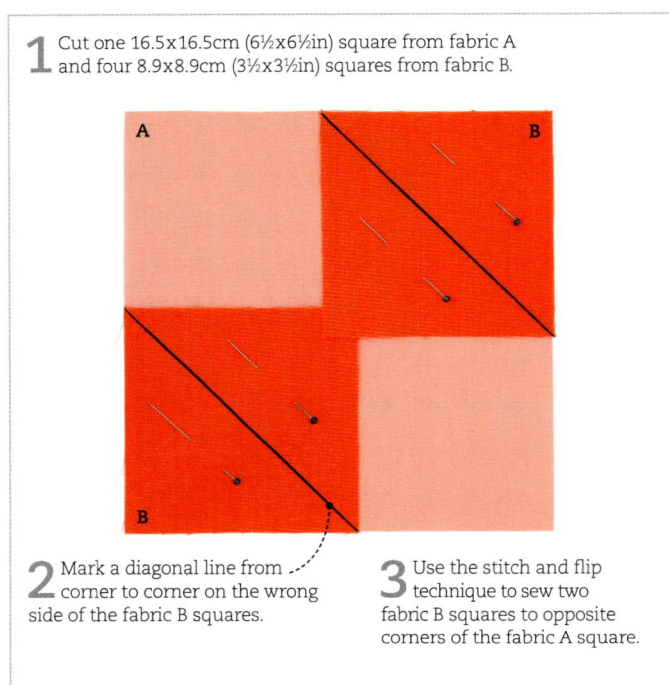

2 Mark a diagonal line from corner to corner on the wrong side of the fabric B squares.

3 Use the stitch and flip technique to sew two fabric B squares to opposite corners of the fabric A square.

4 Open the unit. Press.

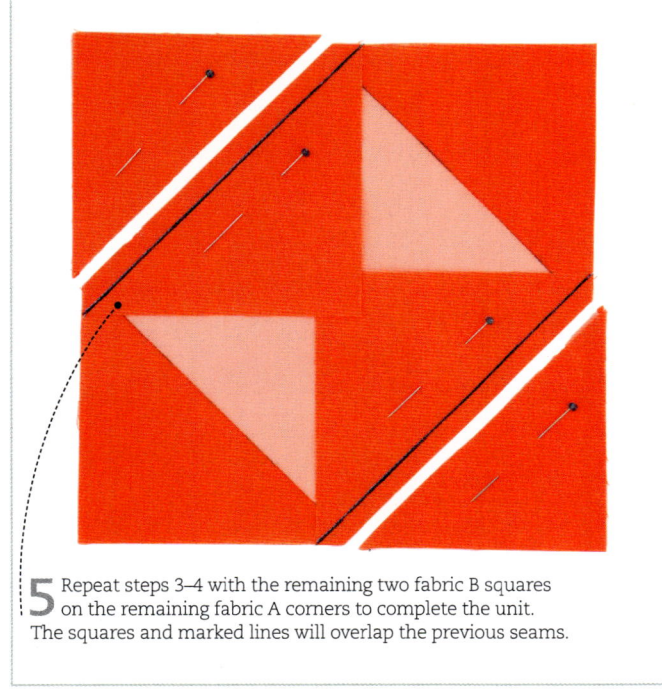

5 Repeat steps 3–4 with the remaining two fabric B squares on the remaining fabric A corners to complete the unit. The squares and marked lines will overlap the previous seams.

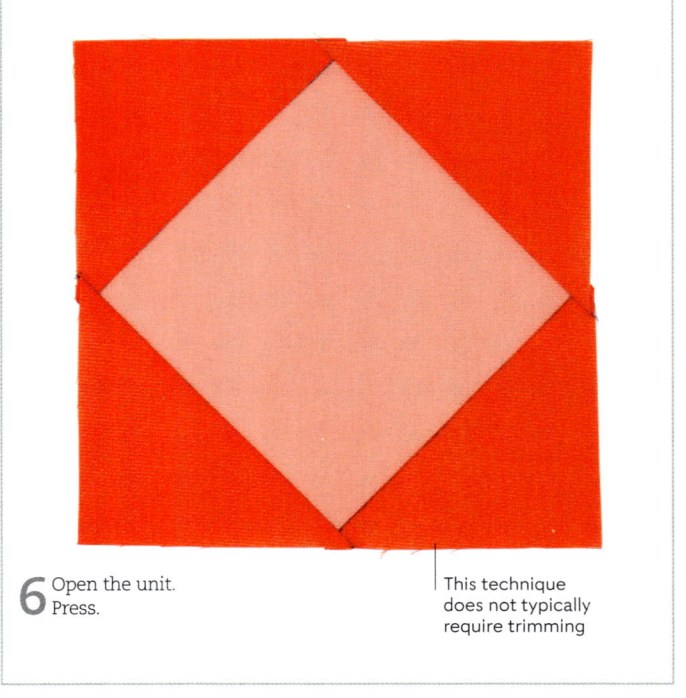

6 Open the unit. Press.

This technique does not typically require trimming

SETTING TRIANGLES TECHNIQUE

1 Cut one 12.1 x 12.1cm (4¾ x 4¾in) square from fabric A and two 10.2 x 10.2cm (4 x 4in) squares from fabric B.

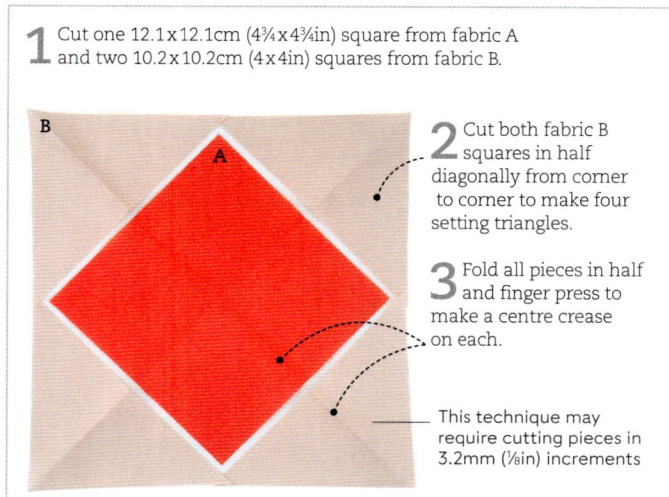

2 Cut both fabric B squares in half diagonally from corner to corner to make four setting triangles.

3 Fold all pieces in half and finger press to make a centre crease on each.

This technique may require cutting pieces in 3.2mm (⅛in) increments

4 Place two triangles on opposite edges of the fabric A square, RST, aligning the centre creases. Pin.

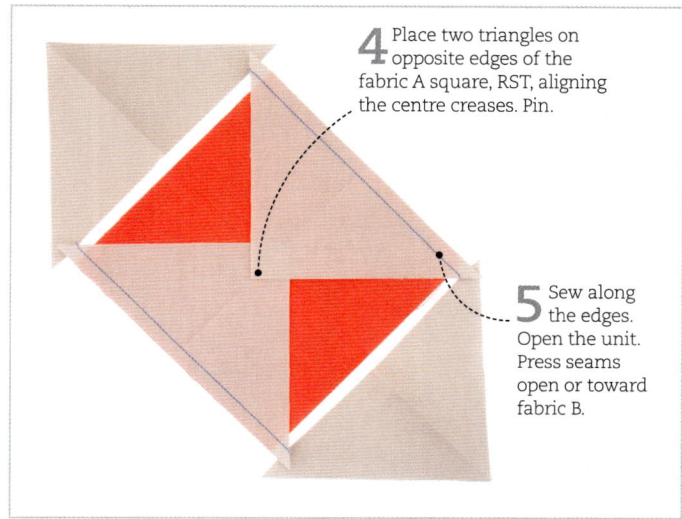

5 Sew along the edges. Open the unit. Press seams open or toward fabric B.

6 Repeat steps 4–5 with the remaining two triangles placed RST on the remaining fabric A edges to complete the unit.

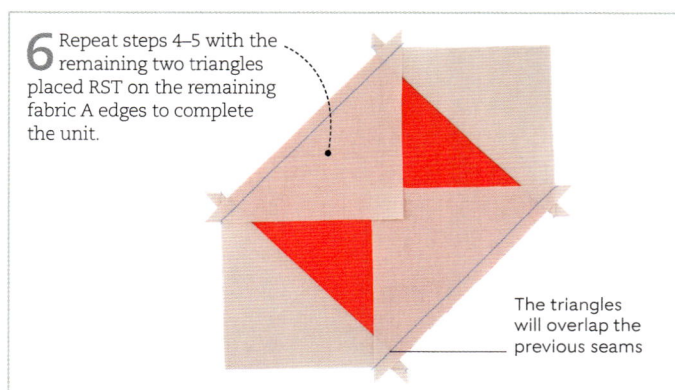

The triangles will overlap the previous seams

7 Trim the unit to 16.5 x 16.5cm (6½ x 6½in).

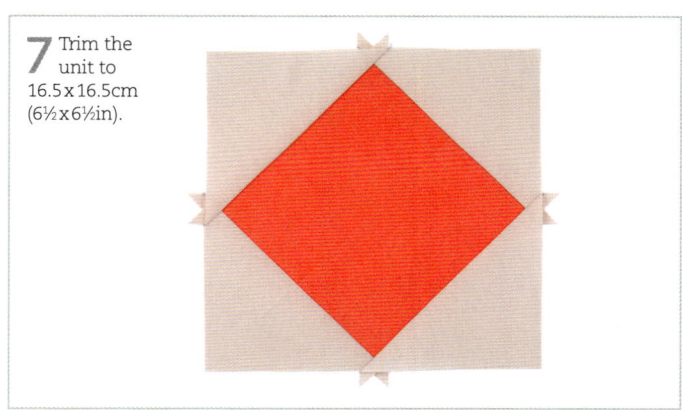

TRIMMING SQUARE IN A SQUARE UNITS

1 Determine the centre measurements of the unit by dividing the desired unfinished width by two. A 16.5 x 16.5cm (6½ x 6½in) square in a square has a 8.3cm (3¼in) vertical and horizontal centre.

2 Place a ruler on the unit, aligning the vertical centrw directly on the top and bottom diamond points and the horizontal centrw on the left and right points. Ensure the four points meet 6.4mm (¼in) inside both unfinished measurements and ruler edges. Trim the unit along the ruler edges.

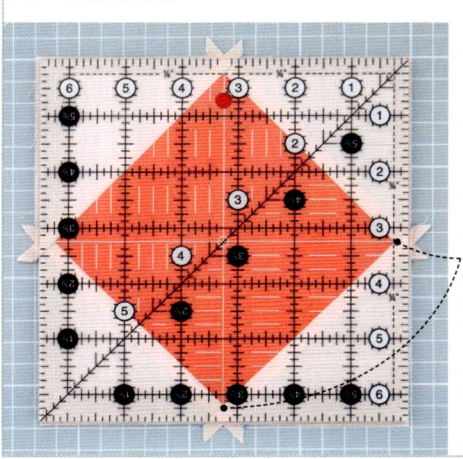

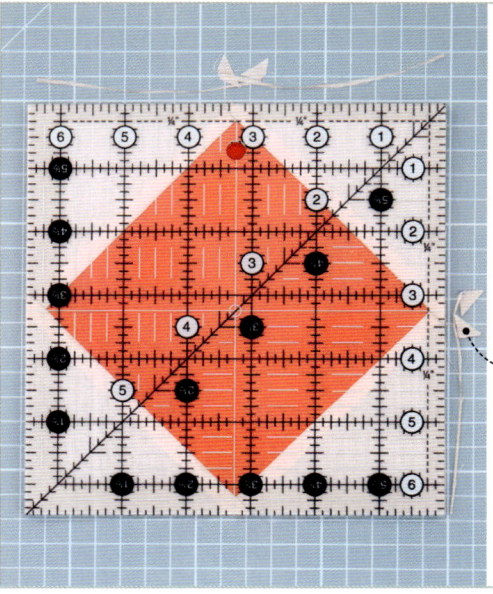

3 Rotate the unit to align the two squared edges with the unfinished measurements and ensure all other points described in step 2 are aligned.

4 Trim to complete the square in a square unit.

Irregular angles

Units with irregular angles, such as HRTs, hexagons, and diamonds, can be cut accurately using standard rulers. All techniques in this section involve sewing along the bias (see p.36) or result in units with bias edges.

OFFSETTING ANGLES

Pieces with irregular angles must be offset to ensure proper alignment when joined. To offset, align the edges of two pieces, then shift the vertices, or where two angled edges meet, slightly beyond each other.

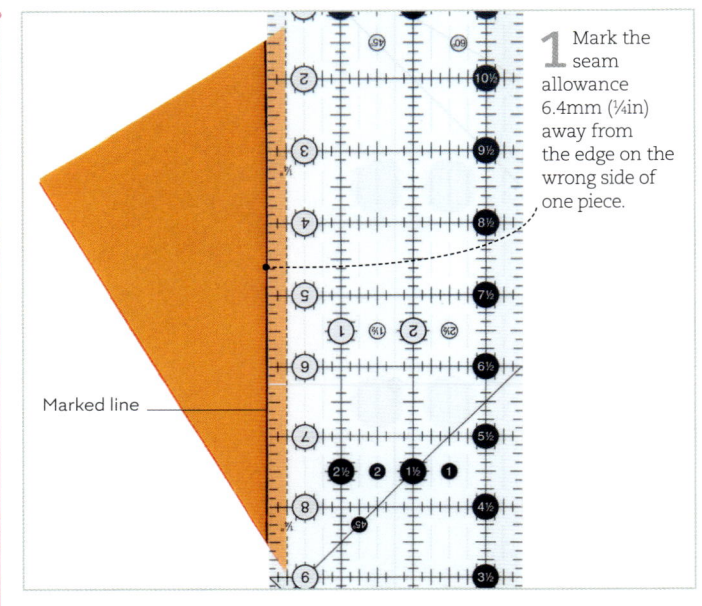

1 Mark the seam allowance 6.4mm (¼in) away from the edge on the wrong side of one piece.

Marked line

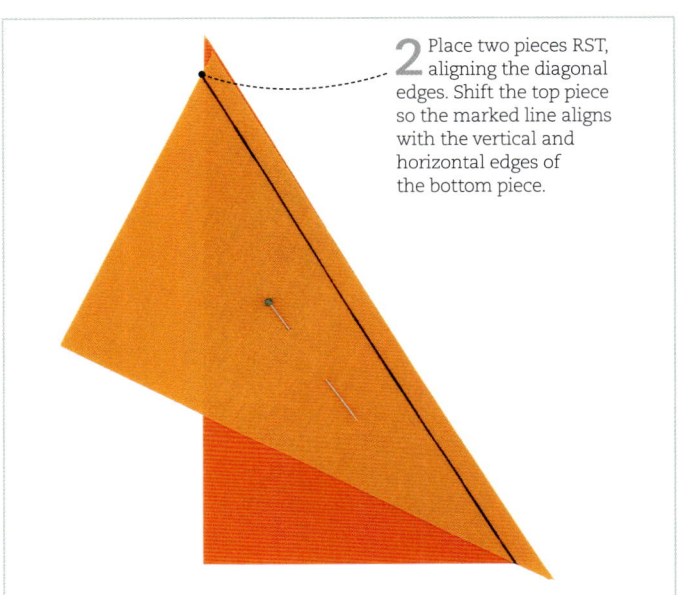

2 Place two pieces RST, aligning the diagonal edges. Shift the top piece so the marked line aligns with the vertical and horizontal edges of the bottom piece.

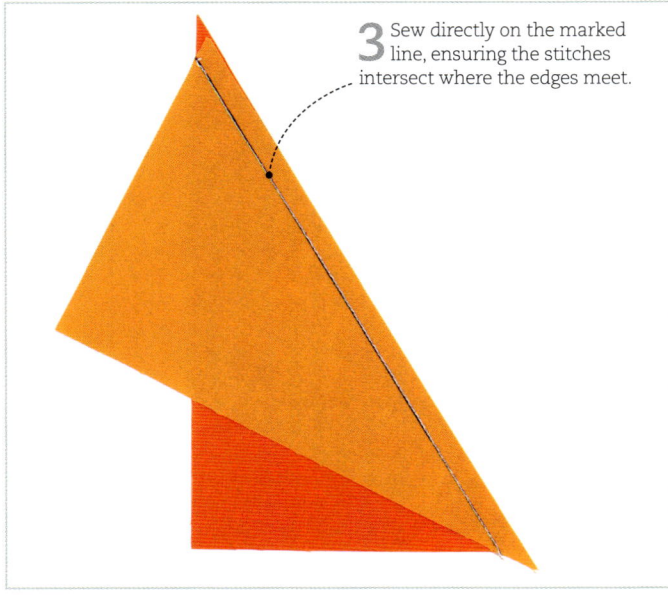

3 Sew directly on the marked line, ensuring the stitches intersect where the edges meet.

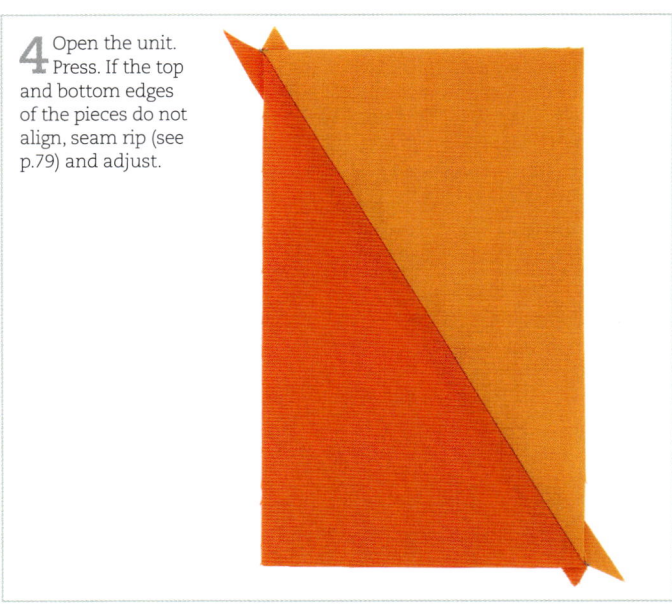

4 Open the unit. Press. If the top and bottom edges of the pieces do not align, seam rip (see p.79) and adjust.

IRREGULAR ANGLES   97

HALF-RECTANGLE TRIANGLES

A half-rectangle triangle, or HRT, is made by joining two elongated triangles to form a rectangle. Mirrored HRTs must be constructed intentionally to produce appropriate diagonal seam placement.

ONE AT A TIME

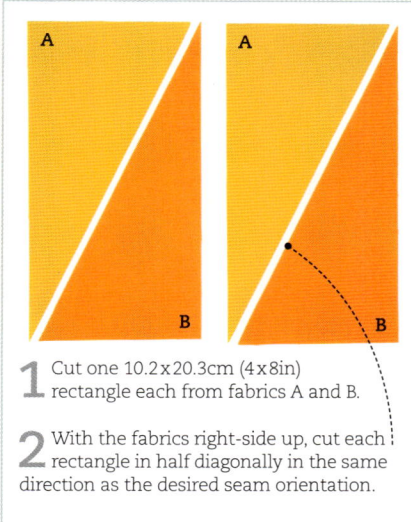

1. Cut one 10.2x20.3cm (4x8in) rectangle each from fabrics A and B.

2. With the fabrics right-side up, cut each rectangle in half diagonally in the same direction as the desired seam orientation.

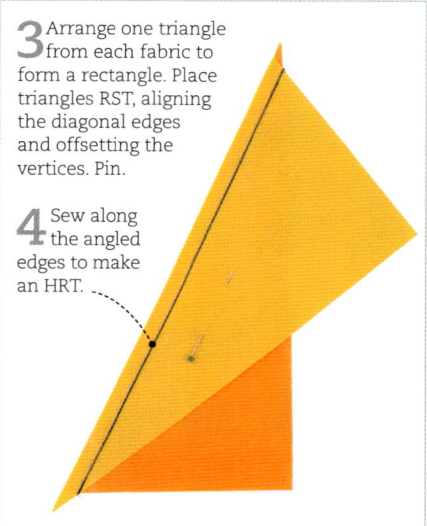

3. Arrange one triangle from each fabric to form a rectangle. Place triangles RST, aligning the diagonal edges and offsetting the vertices. Pin.

4. Sew along the angled edges to make an HRT.

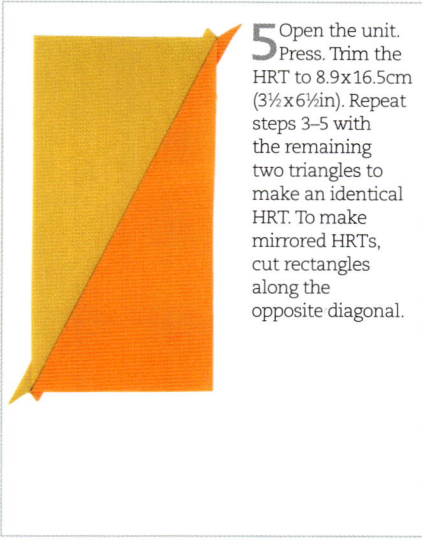

5. Open the unit. Press. Trim the HRT to 8.9x16.5cm (3½x6½in). Repeat steps 3–5 with the remaining two triangles to make an identical HRT. To make mirrored HRTs, cut rectangles along the opposite diagonal.

TWO AT A TIME

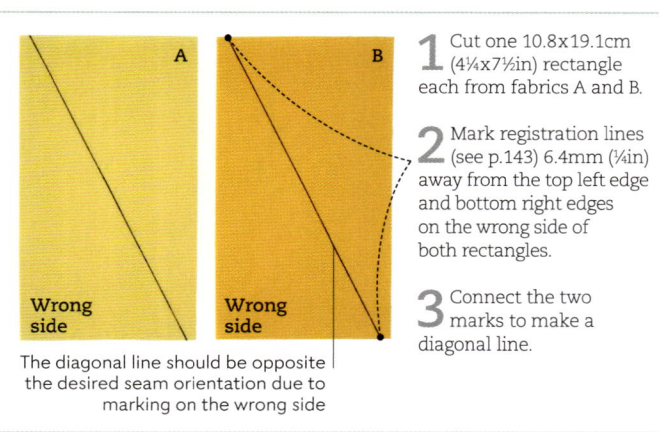

1. Cut one 10.8x19.1cm (4¼x7½in) rectangle each from fabrics A and B.

2. Mark registration lines (see p.143) 6.4mm (¼in) away from the top left edge and bottom right edges on the wrong side of both rectangles.

3. Connect the two marks to make a diagonal line.

The diagonal line should be opposite the desired seam orientation due to marking on the wrong side

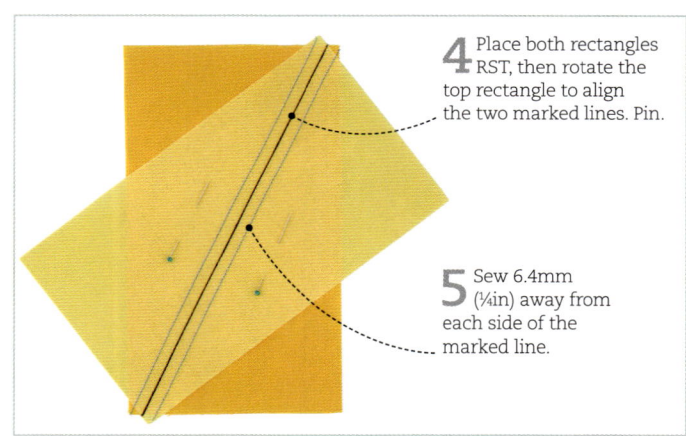

4. Place both rectangles RST, then rotate the top rectangle to align the two marked lines. Pin.

5. Sew 6.4mm (¼in) away from each side of the marked line.

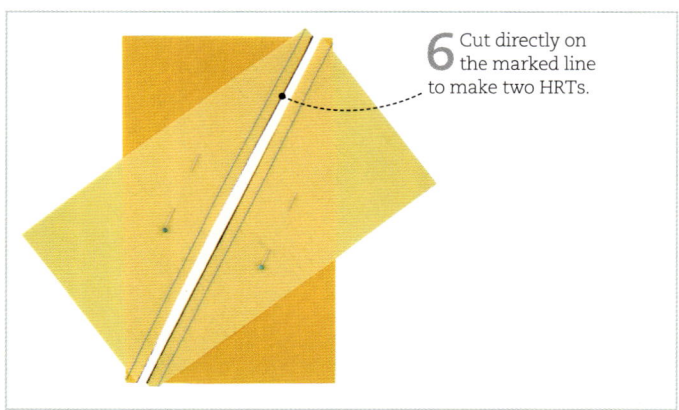

6. Cut directly on the marked line to make two HRTs.

7. Open both units. Press. Trim both HRTs to 8.9x16.5cm (3½x6½in).

8. Make HRTs with mirrored seam orientations by marking the opposite diagonal.

TRIMMING HRTS

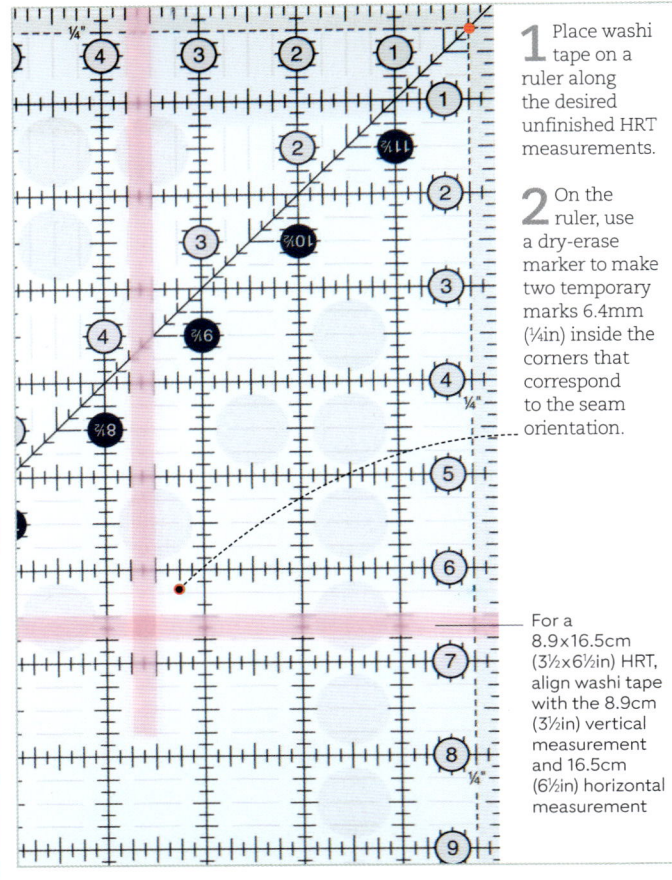

1 Place washi tape on a ruler along the desired unfinished HRT measurements.

2 On the ruler, use a dry-erase marker to make two temporary marks 6.4mm (¼in) inside the corners that correspond to the seam orientation.

For a 8.9x16.5cm (3½x6½in) HRT, align washi tape with the 8.9cm (3½in) vertical measurement and 16.5cm (6½in) horizontal measurement

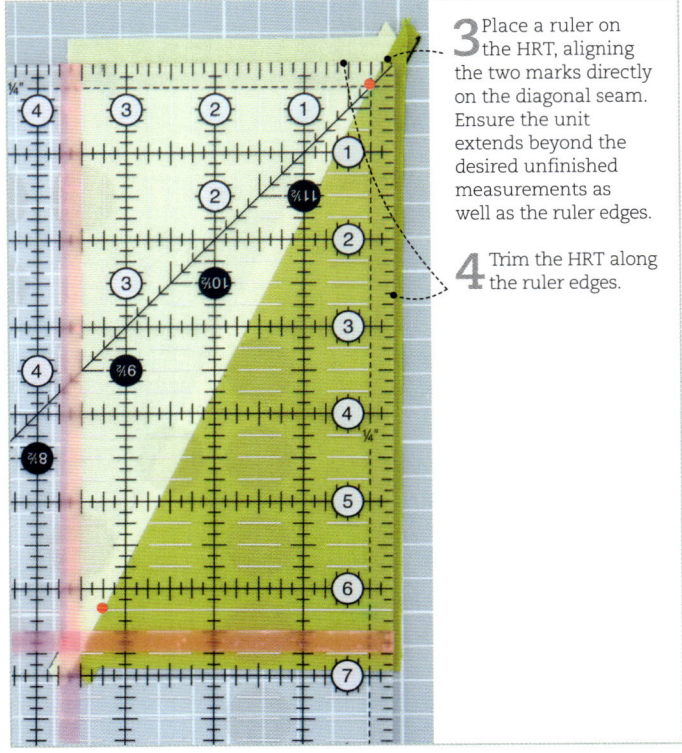

3 Place a ruler on the HRT, aligning the two marks directly on the diagonal seam. Ensure the unit extends beyond the desired unfinished measurements as well as the ruler edges.

4 Trim the HRT along the ruler edges.

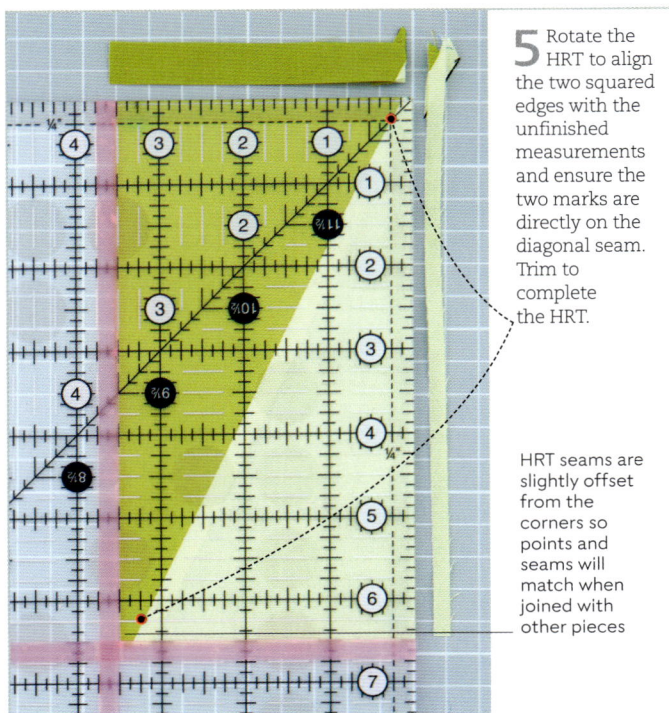

5 Rotate the HRT to align the two squared edges with the unfinished measurements and ensure the two marks are directly on the diagonal seam. Trim to complete the HRT.

HRT seams are slightly offset from the corners so points and seams will match when joined with other pieces

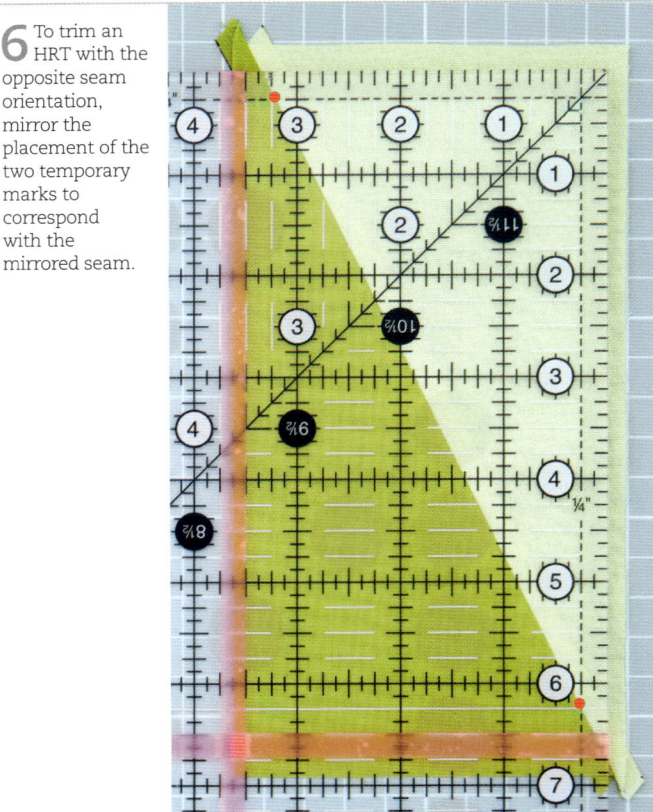

6 To trim an HRT with the opposite seam orientation, mirror the placement of the two temporary marks to correspond with the mirrored seam.

IRREGULAR ANGLES

TRIANGLE IN A SQUARE UNIT
A triangle in a square unit consists of a centre triangle with a setting triangle on either side.

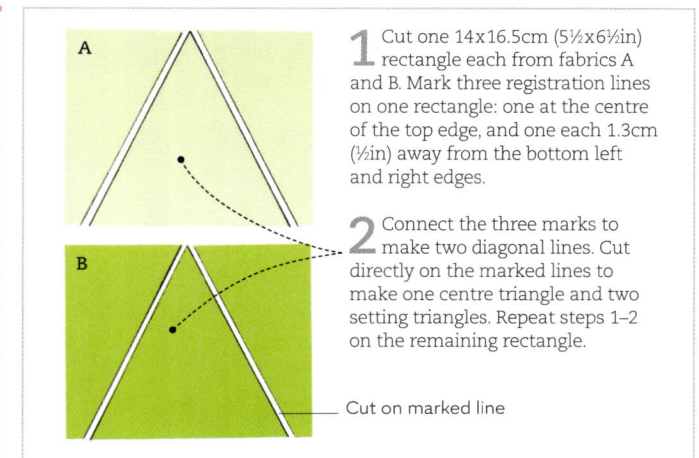

1 Cut one 14x16.5cm (5½x6½in) rectangle each from fabrics A and B. Mark three registration lines on one rectangle: one at the centre of the top edge, and one each 1.3cm (½in) away from the bottom left and right edges.

2 Connect the three marks to make two diagonal lines. Cut directly on the marked lines to make one centre triangle and two setting triangles. Repeat steps 1–2 on the remaining rectangle.

Cut on marked line

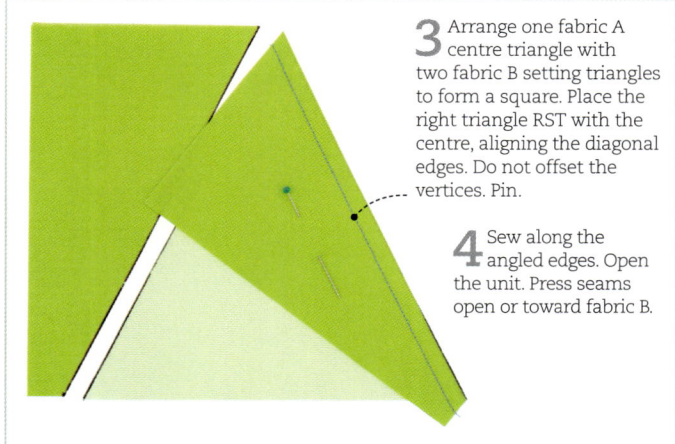

3 Arrange one fabric A centre triangle with two fabric B setting triangles to form a square. Place the right triangle RST with the centre, aligning the diagonal edges. Do not offset the vertices. Pin.

4 Sew along the angled edges. Open the unit. Press seams open or toward fabric B.

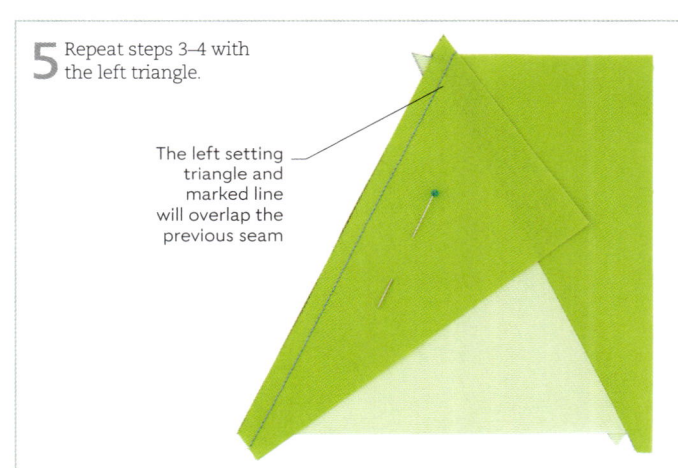

5 Repeat steps 3–4 with the left triangle.

The left setting triangle and marked line will overlap the previous seam

6 Trim the triangle in a square unit to 12.7x12.7cm (5x5in). Repeat steps 3–6 with the remaining triangles to make a second unit with opposite fabric placement.

TRIMMING TRIANGLE IN A SQUARE UNITS

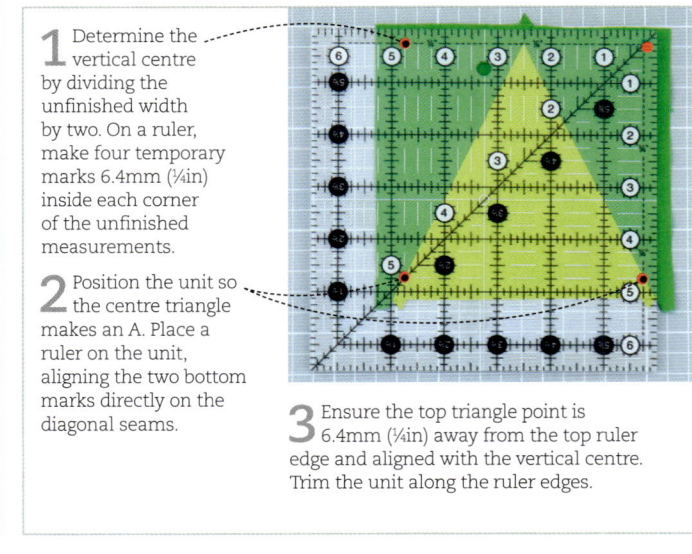

1 Determine the vertical centre by dividing the unfinished width by two. On a ruler, make four temporary marks 6.4mm (¼in) inside each corner of the unfinished measurements.

2 Position the unit so the centre triangle makes an A. Place a ruler on the unit, aligning the two bottom marks directly on the diagonal seams.

3 Ensure the top triangle point is 6.4mm (¼in) away from the top ruler edge and aligned with the vertical centre. Trim the unit along the ruler edges.

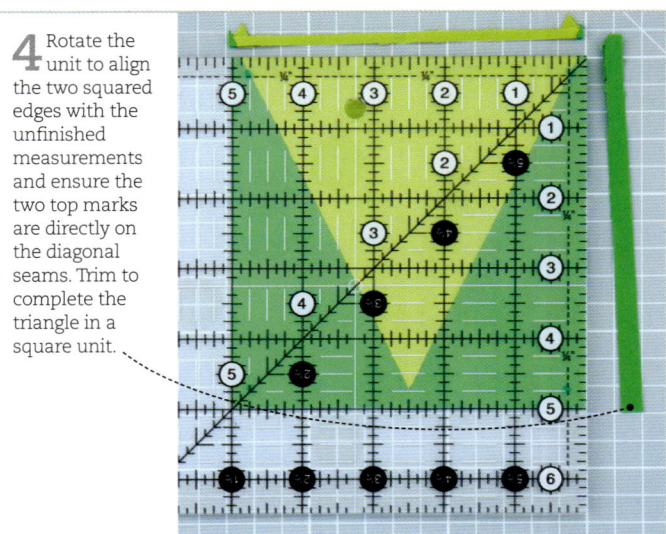

4 Rotate the unit to align the two squared edges with the unfinished measurements and ensure the two top marks are directly on the diagonal seams. Trim to complete the triangle in a square unit.

EQUILATERAL TRIANGLES

Equilateral triangles have equal sides and 60-degree angles, are measured by their height, and are cut from WOF strips 1.3cm (½in) wider than the desired finished height. Cut triangles to produce a single blunted tip to assist with alignment and orientation.

CUTTING EQUILATERAL TRIANGLES

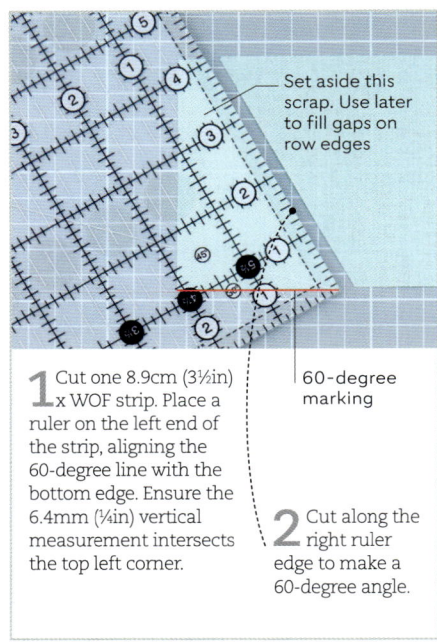

1 Cut one 8.9cm (3½in) x WOF strip. Place a ruler on the left end of the strip, aligning the 60-degree line with the bottom edge. Ensure the 6.4mm (¼in) vertical measurement intersects the top left corner.

2 Cut along the right ruler edge to make a 60-degree angle.

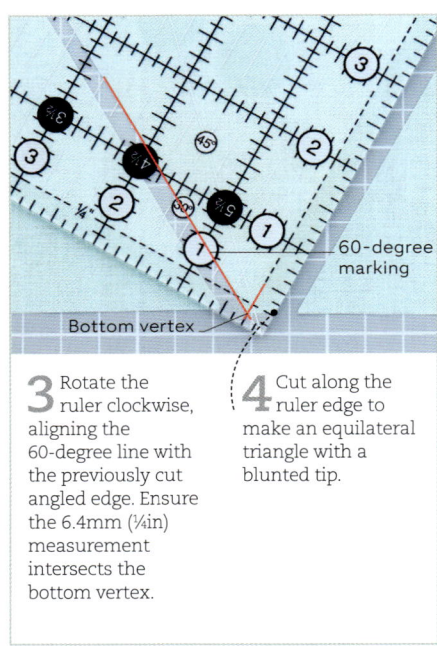

3 Rotate the ruler clockwise, aligning the 60-degree line with the previously cut angled edge. Ensure the 6.4mm (¼in) measurement intersects the bottom vertex.

4 Cut along the ruler edge to make an equilateral triangle with a blunted tip.

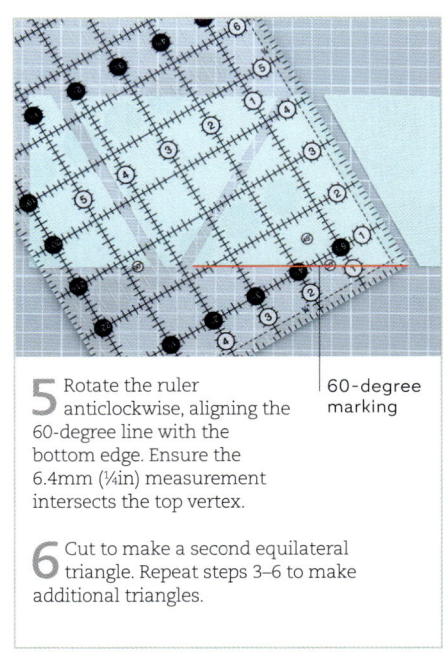

5 Rotate the ruler anticlockwise, aligning the 60-degree line with the bottom edge. Ensure the 6.4mm (¼in) measurement intersects the top vertex.

6 Cut to make a second equilateral triangle. Repeat steps 3–6 to make additional triangles.

PIECING EQUILATERAL TRIANGLE ROWS

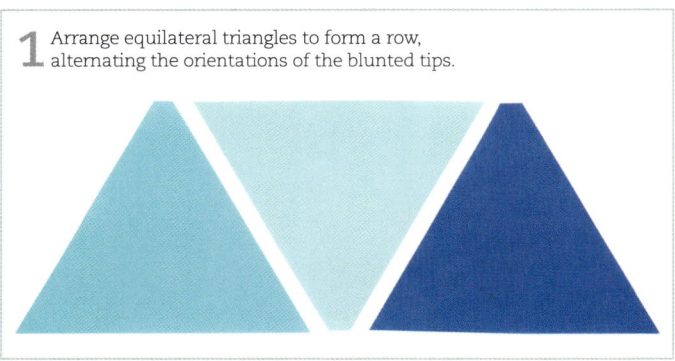

1 Arrange equilateral triangles to form a row, alternating the orientations of the blunted tips.

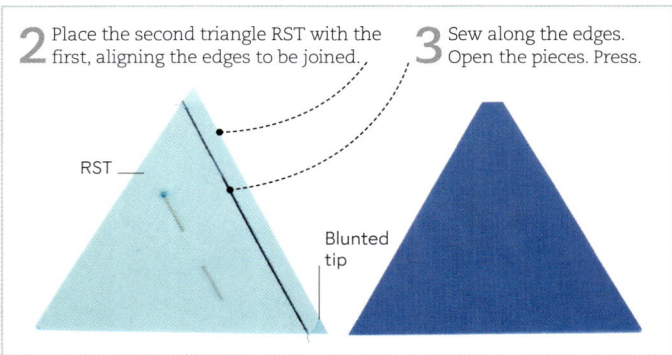

2 Place the second triangle RST with the first, aligning the edges to be joined.

3 Sew along the edges. Open the pieces. Press.

4 Place the third triangle RST with the second, aligning the edges to be joined. Sew along the edges, open the pieces, and press. Seam should hit this point.

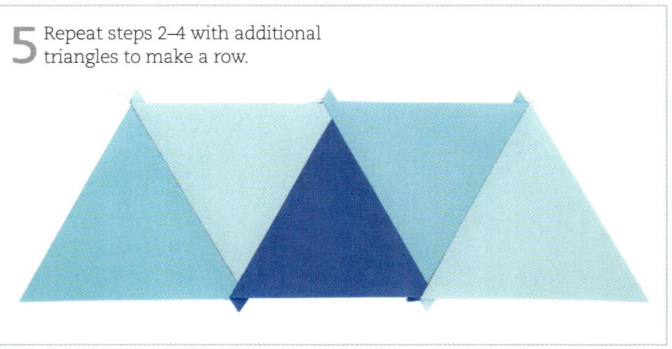

5 Repeat steps 2–4 with additional triangles to make a row.

HALF HEXAGONS

Half hexagons are often joined to form full hexagons and can be combined with other 60-degree angled shapes, such as equilateral triangles and diamonds (see p.102). Half hexagons are measured by their height and cut from WOF strips 1.3cm (½in) wider than the desired finished height.

CUTTING HALF HEXAGONS

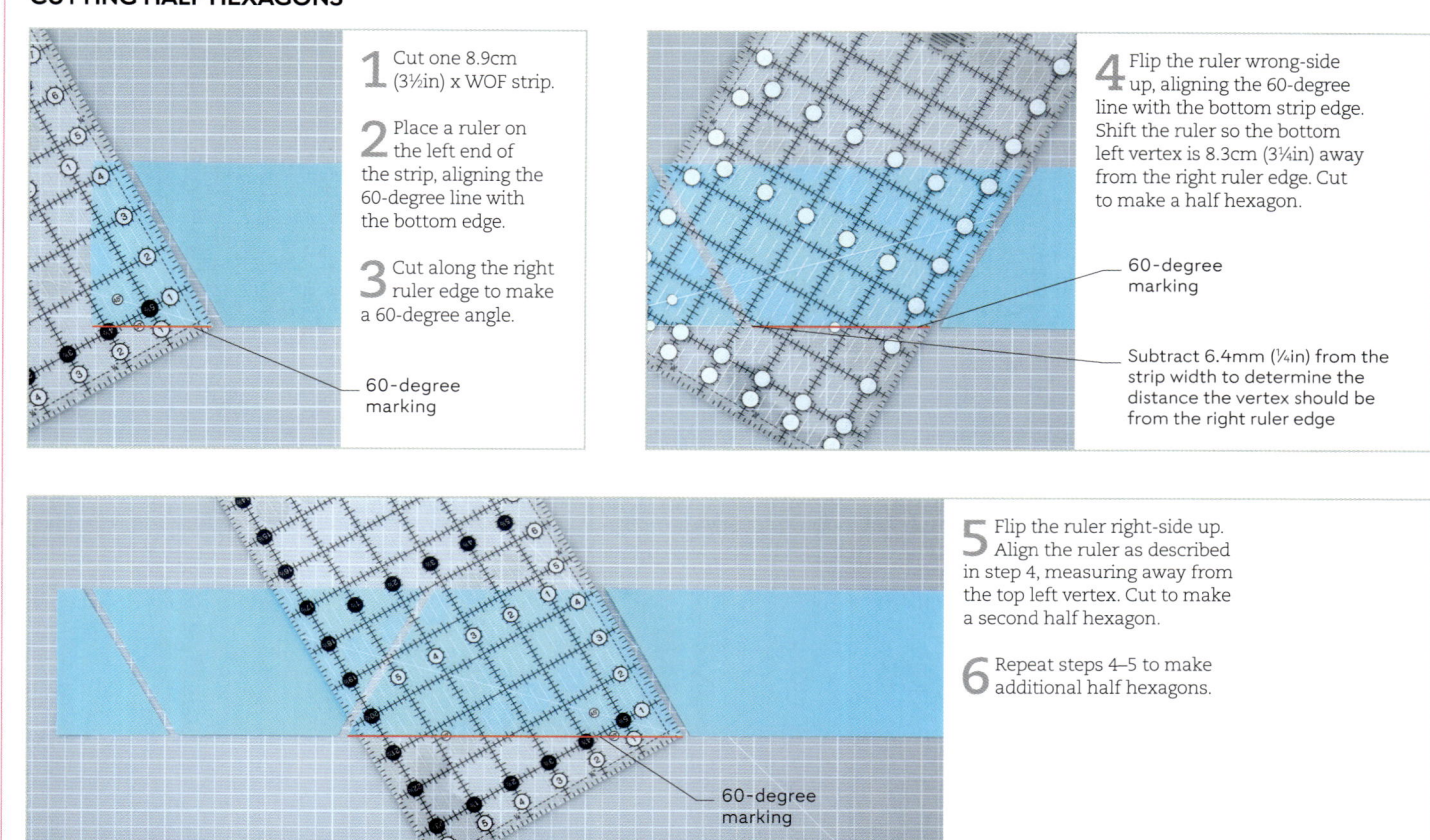

1. Cut one 8.9cm (3½in) x WOF strip.

2. Place a ruler on the left end of the strip, aligning the 60-degree line with the bottom edge.

3. Cut along the right ruler edge to make a 60-degree angle.

60-degree marking

4. Flip the ruler wrong-side up, aligning the 60-degree line with the bottom strip edge. Shift the ruler so the bottom left vertex is 8.3cm (3¼in) away from the right ruler edge. Cut to make a half hexagon.

60-degree marking

Subtract 6.4mm (¼in) from the strip width to determine the distance the vertex should be from the right ruler edge

5. Flip the ruler right-side up. Align the ruler as described in step 4, measuring away from the top left vertex. Cut to make a second half hexagon.

6. Repeat steps 4–5 to make additional half hexagons.

60-degree marking

PIECING HALF HEXAGON ROWS

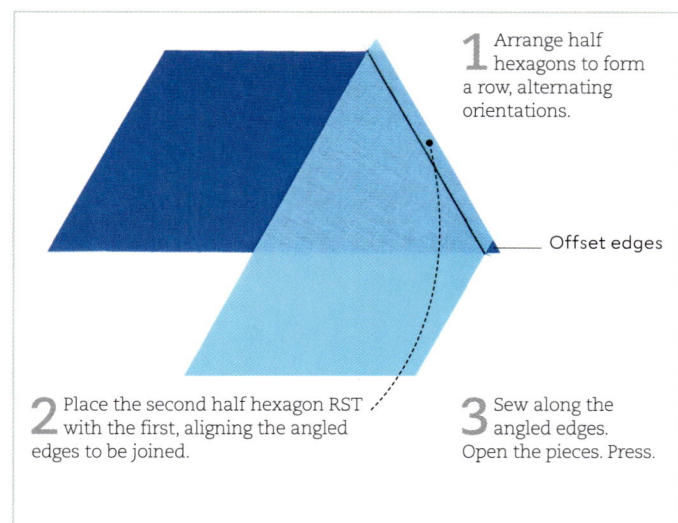

1. Arrange half hexagons to form a row, alternating orientations.

Offset edges

2. Place the second half hexagon RST with the first, aligning the angled edges to be joined.

3. Sew along the angled edges. Open the pieces. Press.

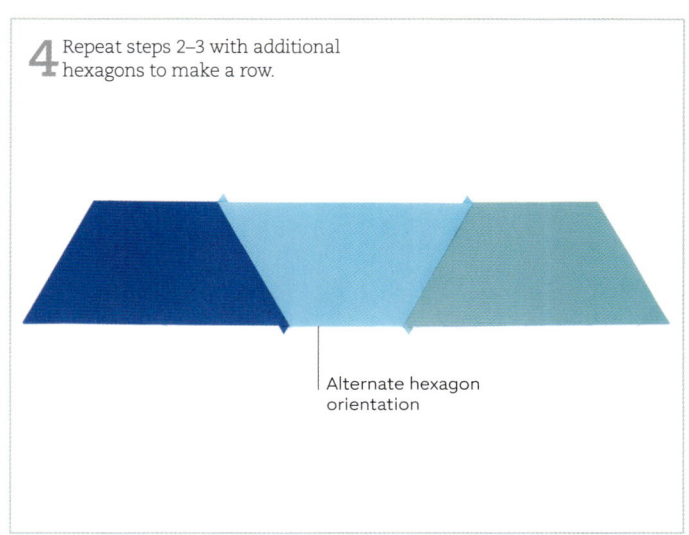

4. Repeat steps 2–3 with additional hexagons to make a row.

Alternate hexagon orientation

DIAMONDS

The most common diamonds are those with 45- or 60-degree angles, which can be joined to form eight- or six-pointed stars, respectively. Diamonds are measured by the distance between two parallel edges and are cut from WOF strips that are 1.3cm (½in) wider than the desired finished width.

CUTTING DIAMONDS

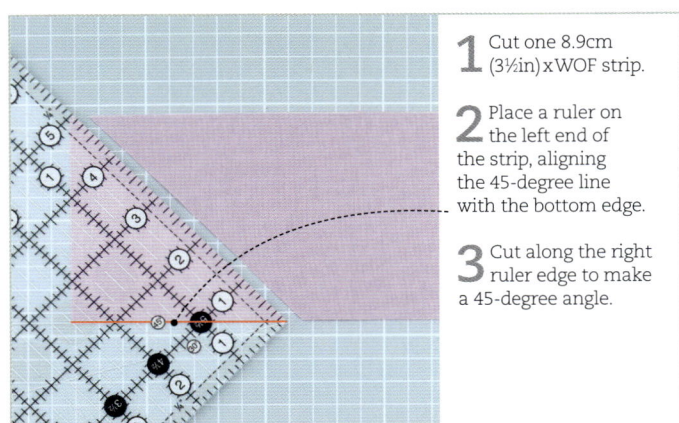

1 Cut one 8.9cm (3½in) x WOF strip.

2 Place a ruler on the left end of the strip, aligning the 45-degree line with the bottom edge.

3 Cut along the right ruler edge to make a 45-degree angle.

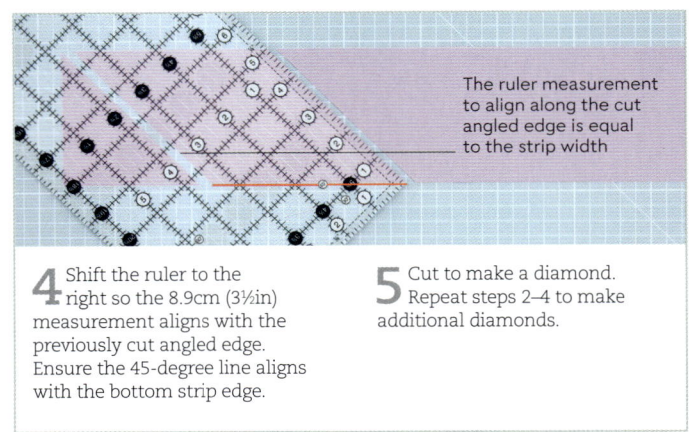

The ruler measurement to align along the cut angled edge is equal to the strip width

4 Shift the ruler to the right so the 8.9cm (3½in) measurement aligns with the previously cut angled edge. Ensure the 45-degree line aligns with the bottom strip edge.

5 Cut to make a diamond. Repeat steps 2–4 to make additional diamonds.

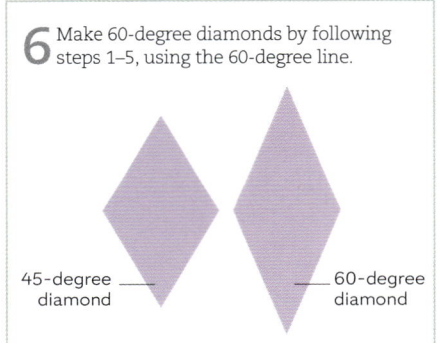

6 Make 60-degree diamonds by following steps 1–5, using the 60-degree line.

45-degree diamond   60-degree diamond

PIECING DIAMONDS INTO ROWS

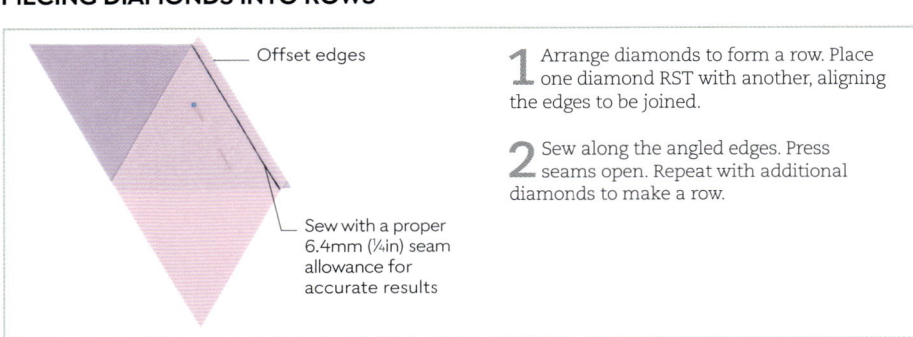

Offset edges

Sew with a proper 6.4mm (¼in) seam allowance for accurate results

1 Arrange diamonds to form a row. Place one diamond RST with another, aligning the edges to be joined.

2 Sew along the angled edges. Press seams open. Repeat with additional diamonds to make a row.

SUB-CUTTING DIAMOND STRIP SETS

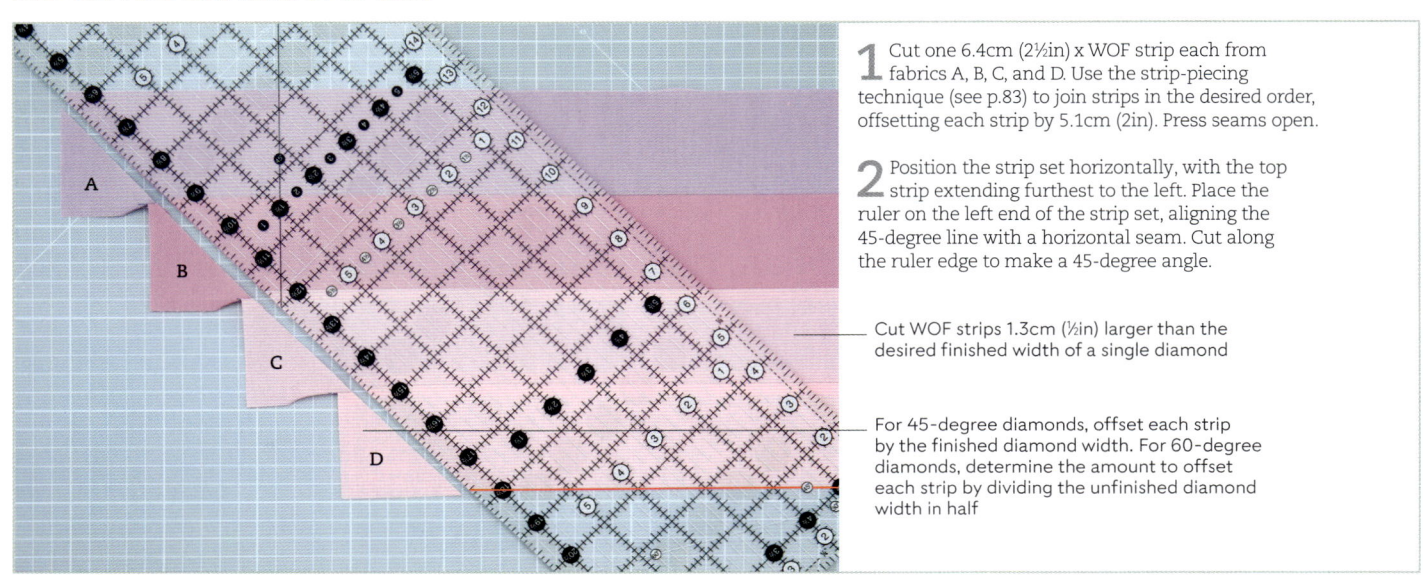

1 Cut one 6.4cm (2½in) x WOF strip each from fabrics A, B, C, and D. Use the strip-piecing technique (see p.83) to join strips in the desired order, offsetting each strip by 5.1cm (2in). Press seams open.

2 Position the strip set horizontally, with the top strip extending furthest to the left. Place the ruler on the left end of the strip set, aligning the 45-degree line with a horizontal seam. Cut along the ruler edge to make a 45-degree angle.

Cut WOF strips 1.3cm (½in) larger than the desired finished width of a single diamond

For 45-degree diamonds, offset each strip by the finished diamond width. For 60-degree diamonds, determine the amount to offset each strip by dividing the unfinished diamond width in half

IRREGULAR ANGLES

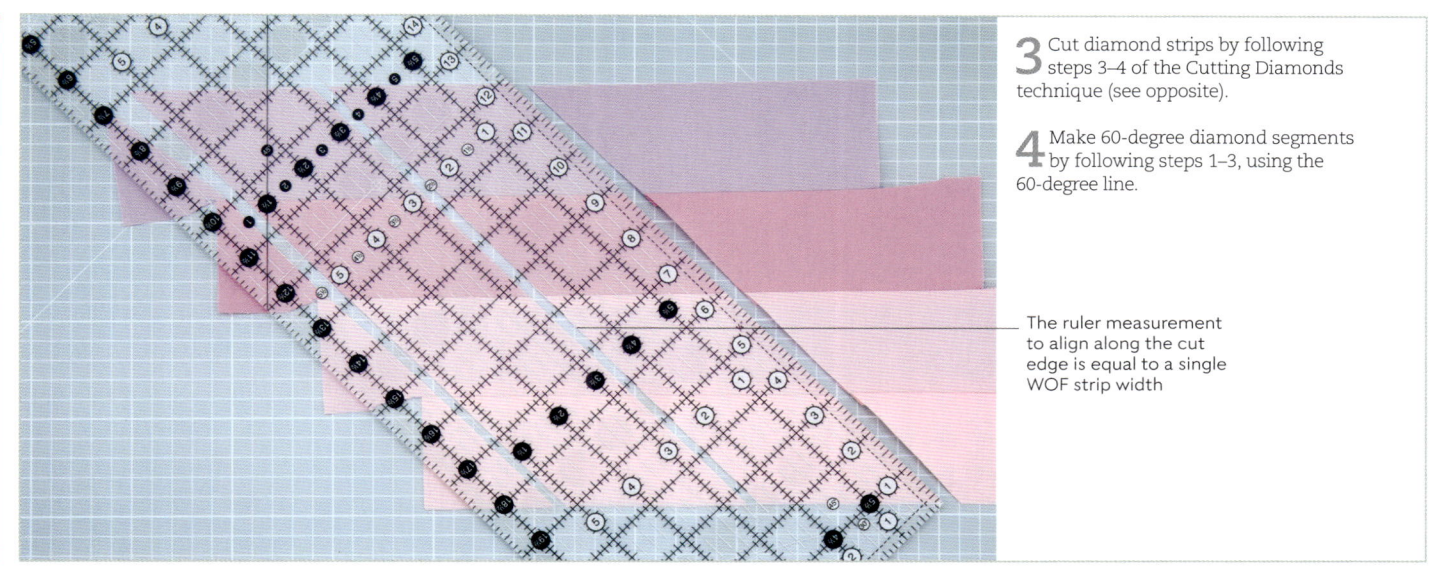

3 Cut diamond strips by following steps 3–4 of the Cutting Diamonds technique (see opposite).

4 Make 60-degree diamond segments by following steps 1–3, using the 60-degree line.

The ruler measurement to align along the cut edge is equal to a single WOF strip width

JOINING DIAMOND SEGMENTS OR ROWS

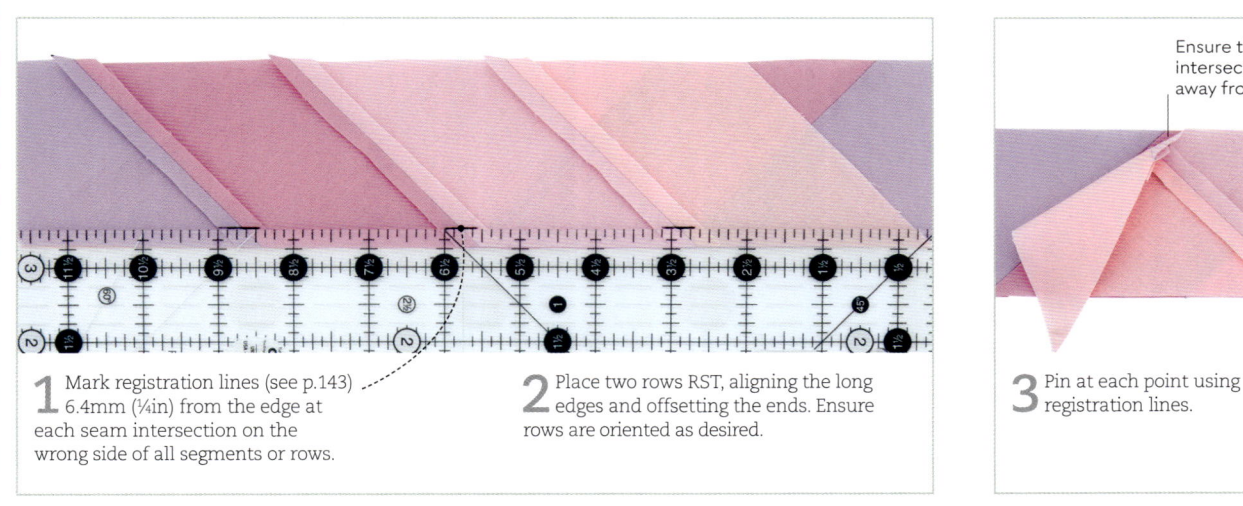

1 Mark registration lines (see p.143) 6.4mm (¼in) from the edge at each seam intersection on the wrong side of all segments or rows.

2 Place two rows RST, aligning the long edges and offsetting the ends. Ensure rows are oriented as desired.

Ensure the seams intersect 6.4cm (¼in) away from the edge

3 Pin at each point using the registration lines.

4 Sew rows RST keeping points aligned. Seam rip (see p.79) and adjust as needed.

5 Press seams open. Repeat steps 1–4 to join additional rows.

Curves

A quarter circle (QC) and a half circle (HC) are made by joining a convex piece, which has an outward curve, with a concave piece, which has an inward curve. All techniques in this section involve cutting and sewing along bias edges (see p.36).

PREPARING CURVES

Curved pieces must be cut using templates (see p.71) that are included with a pattern, speciality rulers, or an improv cutting technique (see p.111). Prepare curved pieces by clipping concave edges and pinning to assist with aligning curves.

CUTTING CURVES

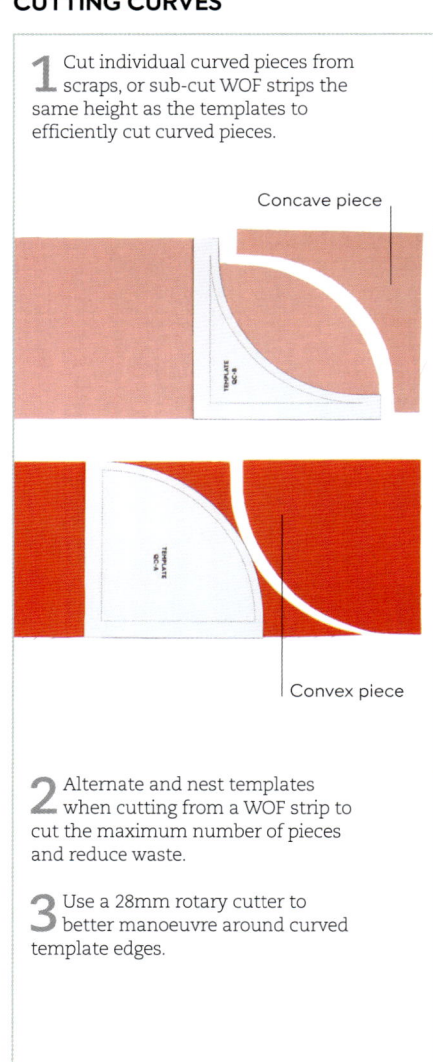

1 Cut individual curved pieces from scraps, or sub-cut WOF strips the same height as the templates to efficiently cut curved pieces.

Concave piece

Convex piece

2 Alternate and nest templates when cutting from a WOF strip to cut the maximum number of pieces and reduce waste.

3 Use a 28mm rotary cutter to better manoeuvre around curved template edges.

CLIPPING CURVES

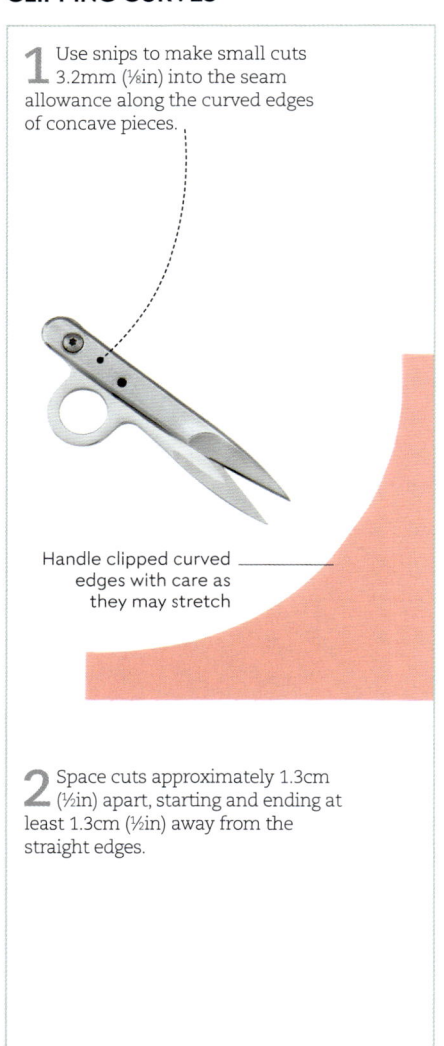

1 Use snips to make small cuts 3.2mm (⅛in) into the seam allowance along the curved edges of concave pieces.

Handle clipped curved edges with care as they may stretch

2 Space cuts approximately 1.3cm (½in) apart, starting and ending at least 1.3cm (½in) away from the straight edges.

PRESSING

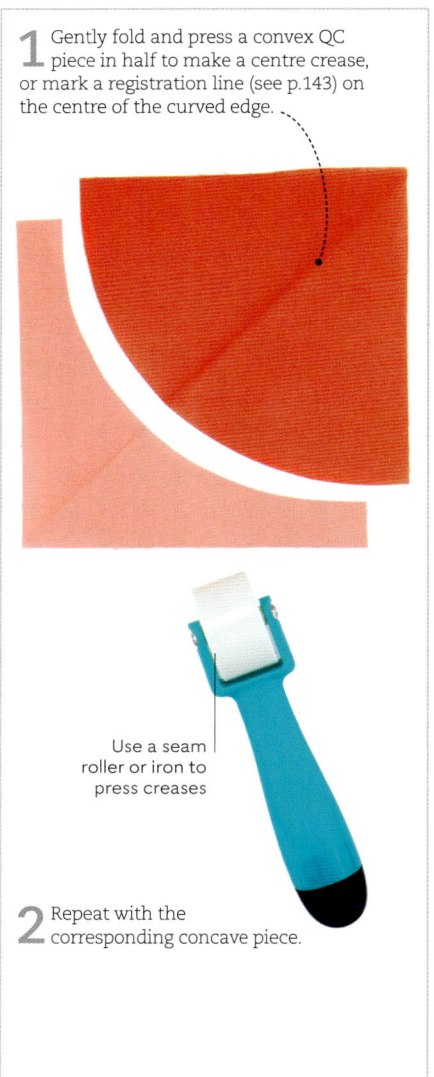

1 Gently fold and press a convex QC piece in half to make a centre crease, or mark a registration line (see p.143) on the centre of the curved edge.

Use a seam roller or iron to press creases

2 Repeat with the corresponding concave piece.

PINNING CURVES

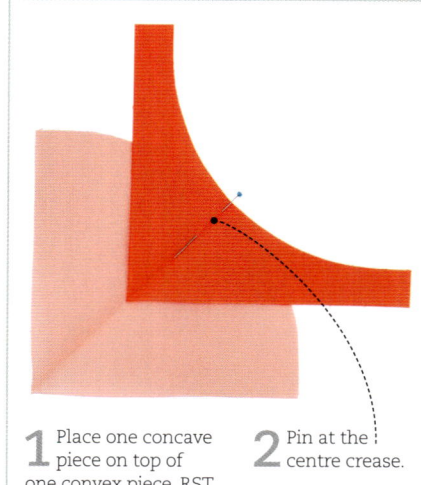
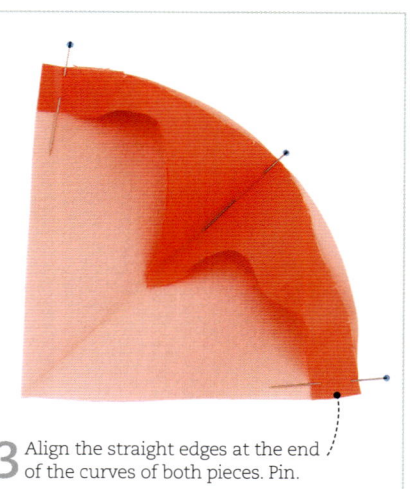
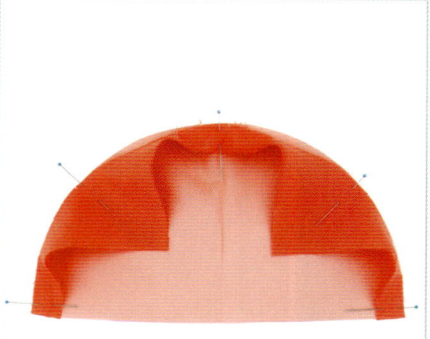

1. Place one concave piece on top of one convex piece, RST, aligning the centre creases.

2. Pin at the centre crease.

3. Align the straight edges at the end of the curves of both pieces. Pin.

4. Place additional pins as needed.

5. Follow steps 1–4 to pin a HC, folding each piece in half twice to make creases at the centre and each quarter of the curved edge. Align and pin at all creases.

GLUEING CURVES

Apply glue on centre crease

1. Position the convex piece right-side up, and apply glue directly on the centre crease within the seam allowance.

2. Place the concave piece on top of the convex piece, RST, aligning the centre creases. Apply glue along the convex curved edge from the centre crease out to a straight edge.

3. Align the concave curved edge with the glued convex edge, ensuring the straight edges of both pieces meet.

4. Apply glue along the remaining curved convex edge and align the pieces. Finger press to secure.

5. Press the seam allowance with a dry iron to set the glue. Follow steps 1–4 to glue a HC.

SEWING CURVES

Use these instructions to piece any curved unit. When sewing along curved edges, lower stitch length (see p.72) and work slowly.

1 Cut one 13.3x13.3cm (5¼x5¼in) convex piece from fabric A using template QC–A and one 14x14cm (5½x5½in) concave piece from fabric B using template QC–B.

2 Place pieces RST with the concave piece on top and pin. Sew around the first half of the curved edge, stopping with the needle down every 3–5 stitches and realigning the edges as needed.

3 Sew up to and remove the centre pin. Check that both centre creases are aligned.

4 Continue sewing around the second half of the curve, realigning as needed. Stop to remove the final pin.

5 Continue sewing, ensuring the straight ends meet, to complete the QC.

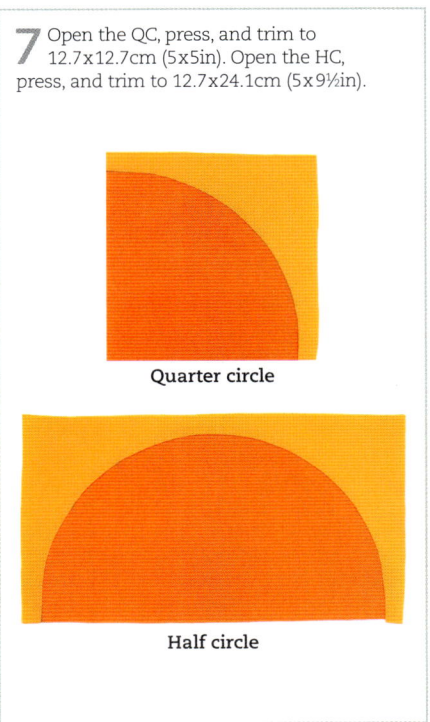

6 To make a HC, follow steps 1–5 using one 13.3x24.1cm (5¼x9½in) convex piece from fabric A using template HC–A and a 14x25.4cm (5½x10in) concave piece from fabric B using template HC–B.

7 Open the QC, press, and trim to 12.7x12.7cm (5x5in). Open the HC, press, and trim to 12.7x24.1cm (5x9½in).

Quarter circle

Half circle

TRIMMING QCS

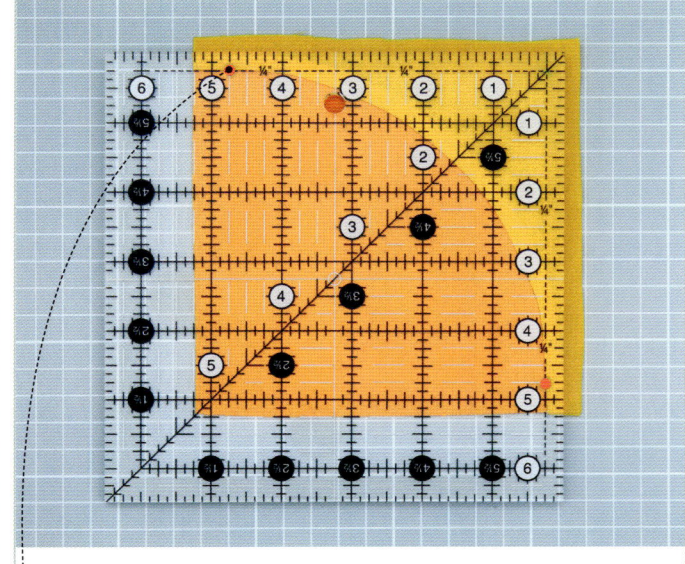
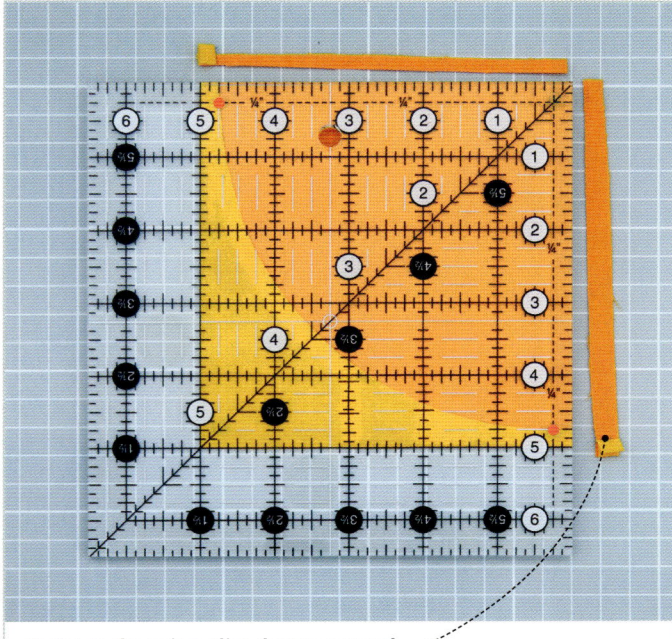

1 Make two temporary marks on a ruler, each 6.4mm (¼in) inside the top left and bottom right corners of the desired unfinished QC measurements.

2 Position the QC so the concave piece is in the upper right corner. Place a ruler on the QC, aligning the two marks directly on the curved seam. Ensure the unit extends beyond the right and top ruler edges. Trim the unit along the ruler edges.

3 Rotate the unit to align the two squared edges with the unfinished measurements and ensure the two marks are directly on the seam. Trim to complete the QC.

TRIMMING HCS

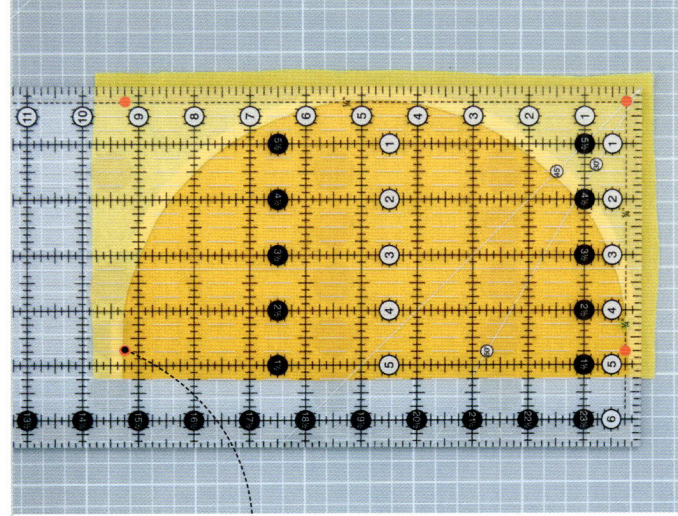
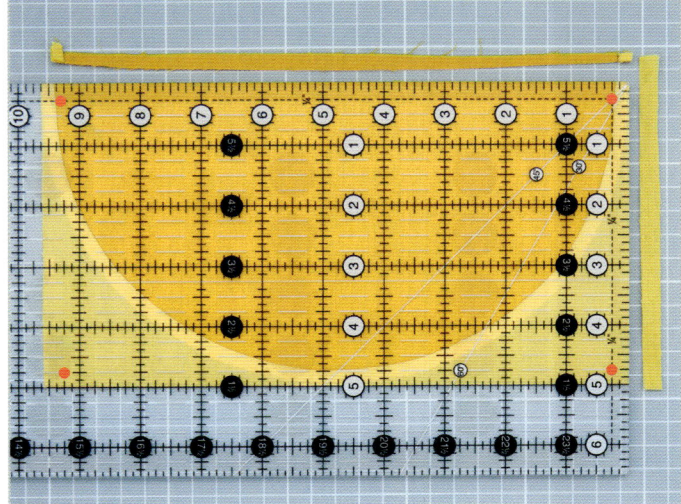

1 Make four temporary marks on a ruler, each 6.4mm (¼in) inside the corners of the desired unfinished measurements.

2 Position the HC so the concave piece is on the top. Place a ruler on the HC, aligning the two bottom marks directly on the seam. Ensure the top seam is 6.4mm (¼in) away from the top ruler edge. Trim the unit along the ruler edges.

3 Rotate the unit to align the two squared edges with the unfinished measurements and ensure the two top marks are directly on the seam. Trim to complete the HC.

Improv piecing

Improv, short for improvisational, is an organic piecing technique that promotes experimentation and creativity and does not rely on traditional quilting rules, precise measurements, or specific pattern instructions. Improv quilts are often made using varied fabric textures, unexpected block shapes, and scraps. Many art quilts are made using improv techniques, allowing quilters to tell stories and convey emotion through abstract designs.

Improv guidelines

Improv involves breaking free from the precise traditional piecing techniques covered in previous sections to encourage creativity and play. However, setting guidelines or limitations for an improv quilt can add structure to a process that otherwise offers limitless possibilities.

GUIDED IMPROV

Colour: Choose a limited set of colours or specific colour schemes (see p.61) to unify elements or establish an overall mood throughout the quilt.

Layout and alignment: Set rules for piecing and aligning elements to create order without compromising the organic feel of improv.

Shape: Experiment with piecing techniques and colour while working within the boundaries of a single shape.

Hierarchy: Establish the most important elements through the use of varying block sizes, colours, and fabric placements.

Repetitiveness: Repeat similar colours, shapes, or patterns throughout the quilt to connect sections and help the viewer's eye move across the design.

Limitless: Work without guidelines, experimenting with fabrics, colours, and piecing techniques. Play with arranging units in unconventional ways.

Improv techniques

While improv techniques are often spontaneous, there are some widely used piecing techniques, shapes, and strategies for joining units. Use these techniques to join pieces into units and blocks and assemble larger sections into quilt tops.

IMPROV PIECING

The main improv piecing techniques involve sewing along straight, curved, or wavy edges. These techniques are similar to traditional piecing techniques, though they do not require the same precision or use of templates.

STRAIGHT EDGE IMPROV

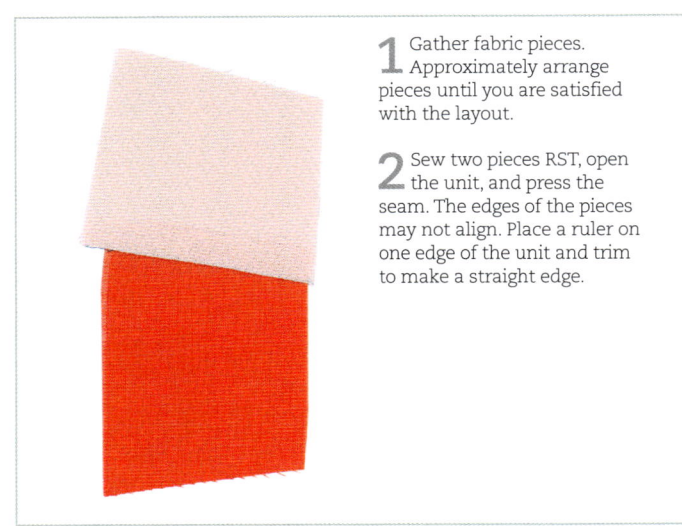

1 Gather fabric pieces. Approximately arrange pieces until you are satisfied with the layout.

2 Sew two pieces RST, open the unit, and press the seam. The edges of the pieces may not align. Place a ruler on one edge of the unit and trim to make a straight edge.

3 Sew another piece to the trimmed edge and press. Place a ruler on the unit and trim to make a straight edge, repeating as necessary.

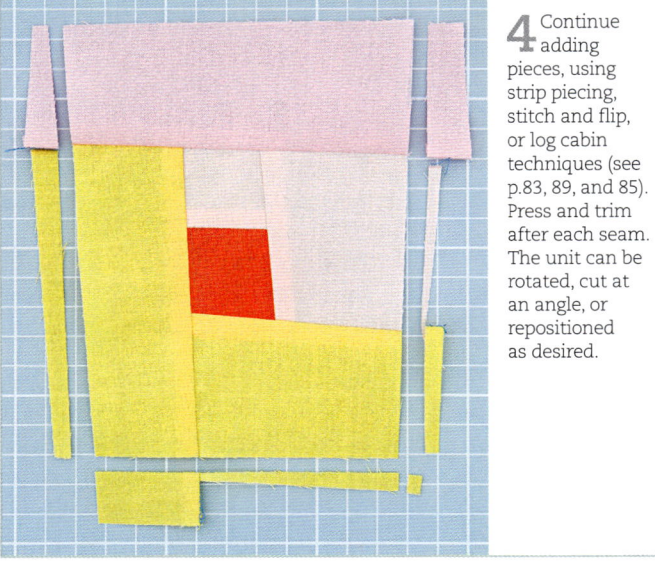

4 Continue adding pieces, using strip piecing, stitch and flip, or log cabin techniques (see p.83, 89, and 85). Press and trim after each seam. The unit can be rotated, cut at an angle, or repositioned as desired.

5 Add the final piece, then trim the finished block to the desired size.

CURVED IMPROV

1. Cut one square each from fabrics A and B. Place the two squares on top of each other with both facing right-side up. Cut a freehand quarter circle from any corner. Mix and match the concave and convex pieces. Mark registration lines (see p.143) across the centre edges of both pieces.

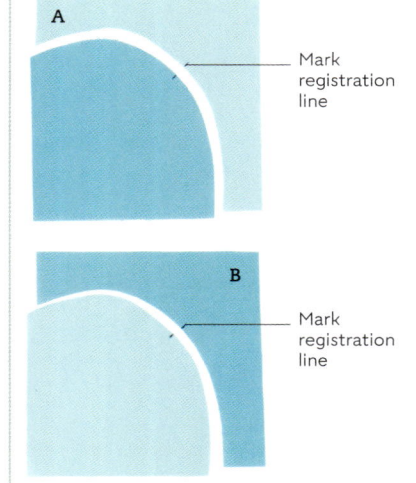

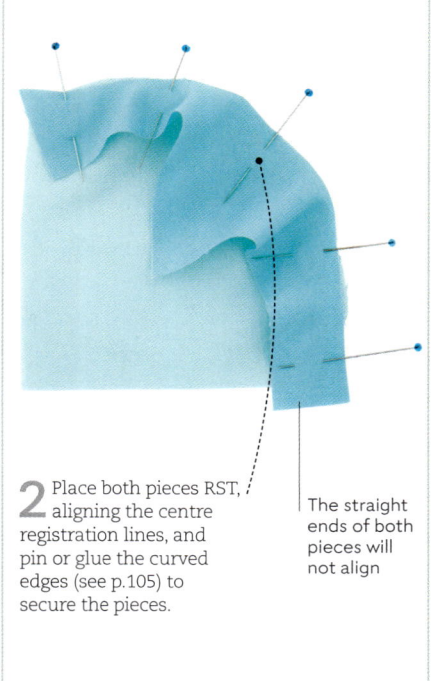

2. Place both pieces RST, aligning the centre registration lines, and pin or glue the curved edges (see p.105) to secure the pieces. The straight ends of both pieces will not align

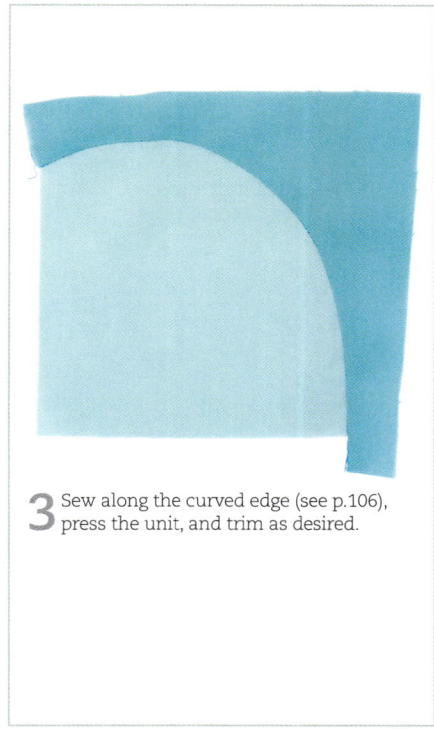

3. Sew along the curved edge (see p.106), press the unit, and trim as desired.

WAVY IMPROV

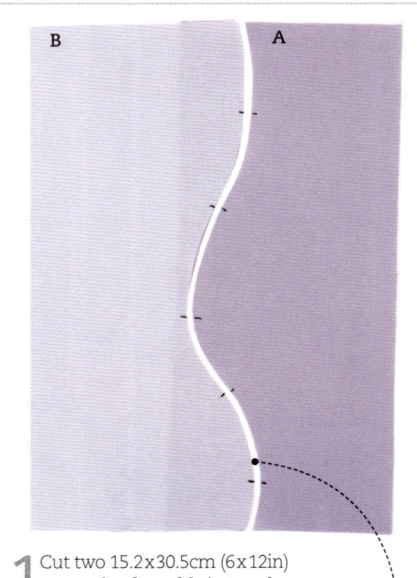

1. Cut two 15.2 x 30.5cm (6 x 12in) rectangles from fabric A and one 15.2 x 30.5cm (6 x 12in) rectangle from B.

2. Overlap one rectangle each from fabrics A and B by approximately 7.6cm (3in), with both pieces right-side up. Cut a gentle wavy line through the overlapping area. Mark registration lines at the peaks and valleys of both pieces.

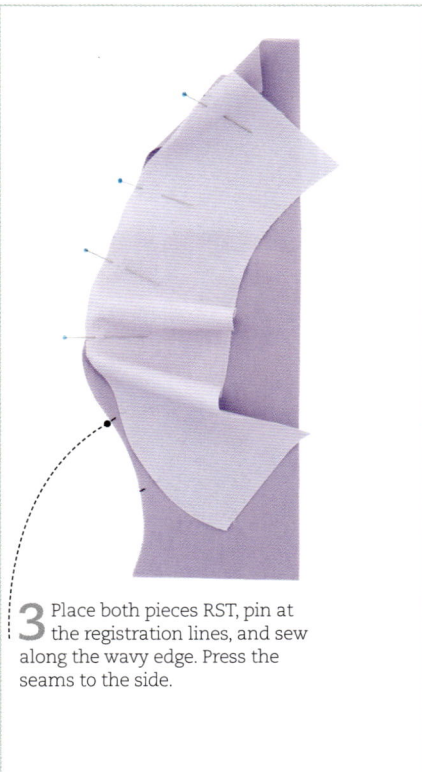

3. Place both pieces RST, pin at the registration lines, and sew along the wavy edge. Press the seams to the side.

4. Overlap the straight edge of fabric B and the remaining fabric A rectangle. Repeat steps 2–3, cutting a second wavy line approximately 6.4cm (2½in) from the first. Press to complete the wavy unit.

COMMON IMPROV SHAPES

While improv piecing can utilize an unlimited number of shapes and sizes, there are basic shapes and units that are commonly used. These units are improv interpretations of classic units covered in the traditional piecing section (see pp.82–107).

Strips: Sew together fabric strips of varied widths and angles. Offset strips to create movement or add strips between units for a sliced or framed effect.

Patchwork: Combine irregularly cut squares and rectangles to form wonky patchwork units. Utilize improv strip piecing and sub-cutting (see p.83) to make multiple units at once.

Log cabin: Start with a central piece and add irregular strips around it, pressing and trimming as you go. Sew strips at slightly angled positions to make a freeform log cabin spiral.

HSTs and HRTs: Roughly cut squares and rectangles in half diagonally, then sew two mismatched triangles along the angled edges. Trim edges as needed.

Square in a square: Use the stitch and flip (see p.89) or setting triangles technique (see p.95) with various sizes of squares to make improv snowball and square in a square units. Position corner pieces at varying angles to produce the desired effect.

QSTs: Make two improv HSTs, then join them to make two improv QSTs (see p.90). Experiment with the sizes, colours, and angles of the HSTs for variety in the improv QSTs.

FG and triangle in a square: Sew two smaller triangles to either side of one centre triangle, or use the stitch and flip technique. Adjust the angle of each piece and square the unit as desired.

QCs and HCs: Use a curved improv piecing technique (see p.111) to make QCs and HCs. Repeat the technique multiple times within a single unit to create concentric improv curves.

Foundation paper piecing

Foundation paper piecing, or FPP, is the process of sewing fabric onto a printed paper foundation, then removing the paper after completing the project. FPP achieves intricate, detailed designs not possible through traditional piecing by using small or irregularly shaped pieces and stitching along straight, printed lines.

Preparing FPP templates

Purchase pre-printed FPP templates or print templates at home on thin, easily tearable paper. Each template section is labelled with a number to indicate the order in which to place and piece fabrics; review before beginning. Templates are mirrored versions of the final design; fabric is placed on the wrong side of the template, while seams are stitched on the right side.

SCORING SEAM LINES

There are two common methods for scoring FPP templates to make handling templates and paper removal easier: using a tracing wheel and folding.

CUTTING FABRICS

Fabrics are not cut into specific shapes, as the pieces within each template section vary. Cut WOF strips and trim pieces as needed or cut fabrics approximately.

Tracing wheel: Roll a tracing wheel (see p.22) along a ruler to perforate the stitch lines. These small holes make it easier to remove the template paper after stitching.

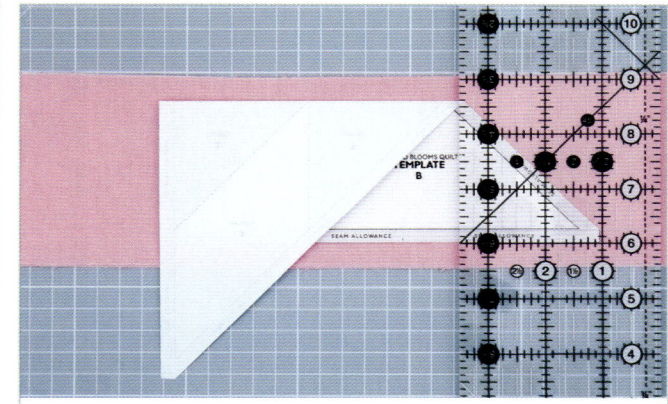

WOF strips: Cut WOF strips based on the widest template section, adding 2.5cm (1in) to accommodate seam allowances and fabric placement. Cut fabric from the WOF strip as you go.

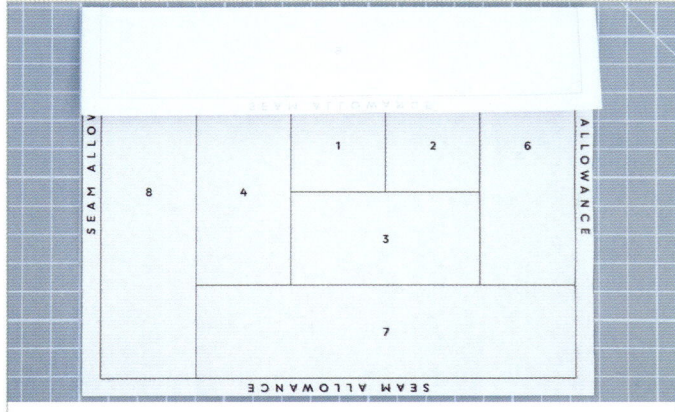

Folding: Prefold all seam lines using a thin ruler or cardstock. These creases assist with folding the fabric and template back when trimming seam allowances.

Rough cutting: Measure or hold a template section over a piece of fabric to estimate the needed fabric size. Be sure to include more than 6.4cm (¼in) seam allowance in the rough cut.

Piecing sections

Sewing FPP sections is like assembling a puzzle – placing each piece of fabric just right to ensure coverage, with frequent flipping, checking, and realigning. Speciality FPP tools, such as lightboards (see p.22) and FPP rulers (see p.19), are desired to assist with fabric placement and trimming seam allowances.

PLACING FABRIC

Each FPP template section is numbered to show the order in which fabric pieces are sewn. Check that fabric pieces completely cover sections and overlap seam lines by at least 6.4mm (¼in).

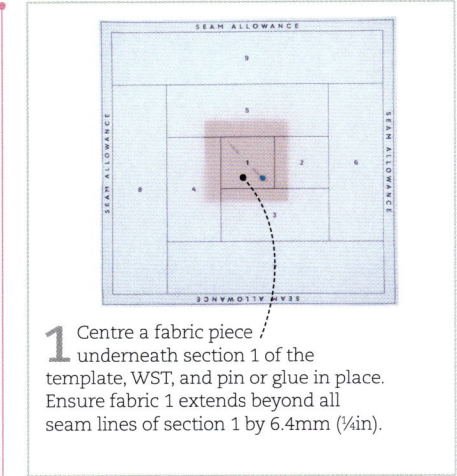

1 Centre a fabric piece underneath section 1 of the template, WST, and pin or glue in place. Ensure fabric 1 extends beyond all seam lines of section 1 by 6.4mm (¼in).

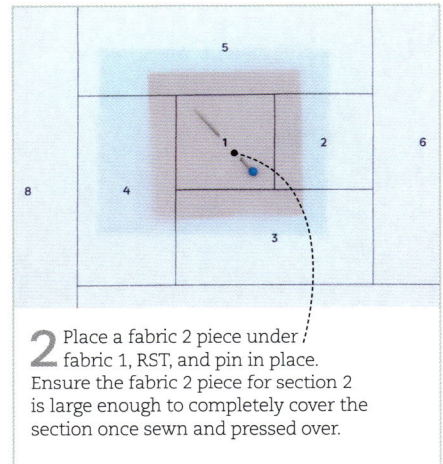

2 Place a fabric 2 piece under fabric 1, RST, and pin in place. Ensure the fabric 2 piece for section 2 is large enough to completely cover the section once sewn and pressed over.

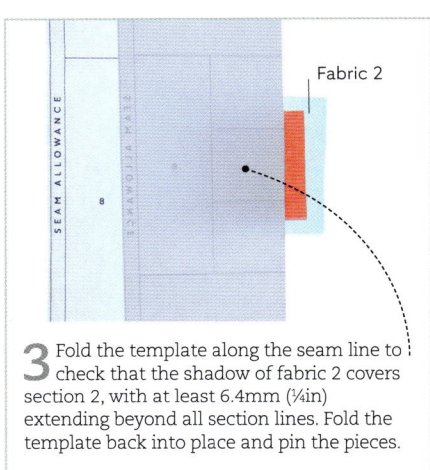

3 Fold the template along the seam line to check that the shadow of fabric 2 covers section 2, with at least 6.4mm (¼in) extending beyond all section lines. Fold the template back into place and pin the pieces.

STITCHING SEAM LINES

Using a short stitch length (see p.72), sew from point to point along the printed seam lines between the two pieces being joined. Backstitch at the beginning and end to provide reinforcement and prevent stitches from unravelling when the paper is removed.

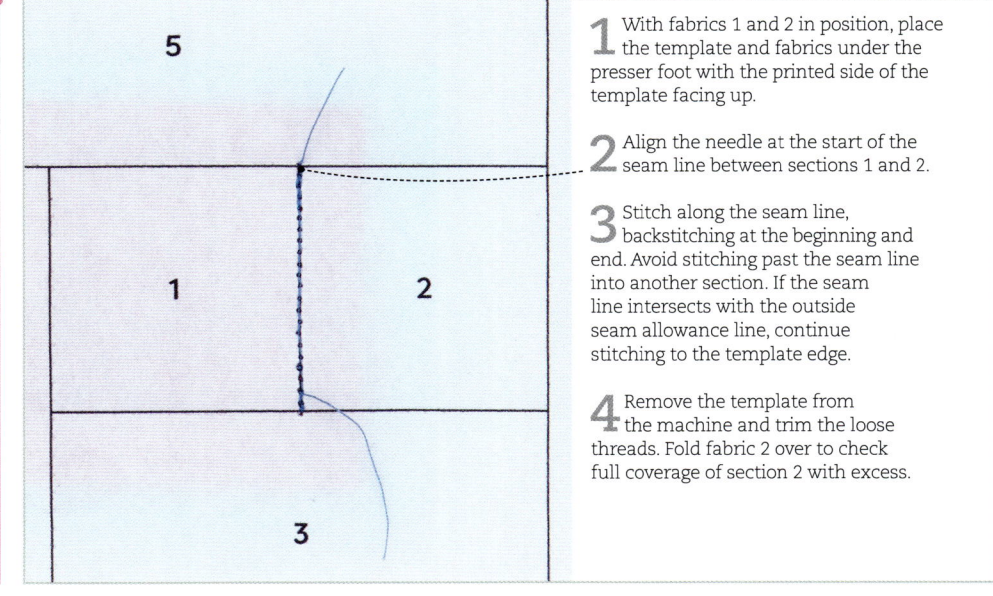

1 With fabrics 1 and 2 in position, place the template and fabrics under the presser foot with the printed side of the template facing up.

2 Align the needle at the start of the seam line between sections 1 and 2.

3 Stitch along the seam line, backstitching at the beginning and end. Avoid stitching past the seam line into another section. If the seam line intersects with the outside seam allowance line, continue stitching to the template edge.

4 Remove the template from the machine and trim the loose threads. Fold fabric 2 over to check full coverage of section 2 with excess.

PIECING SECTIONS 117

FOLDING AND TRIMMING

Trim excess fabric beyond the stitched seam line to make a 6.4mm (¼in) seam allowance and reduce bulk.

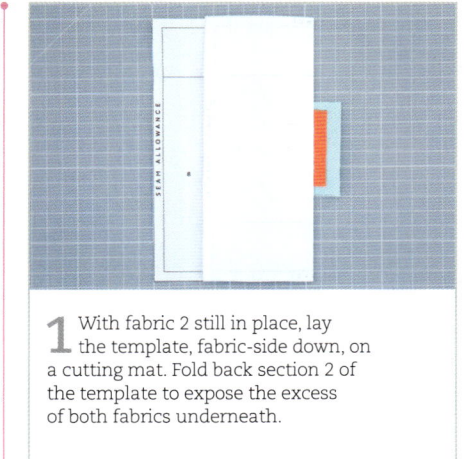

1 With fabric 2 still in place, lay the template, fabric-side down, on a cutting mat. Fold back section 2 of the template to expose the excess of both fabrics underneath.

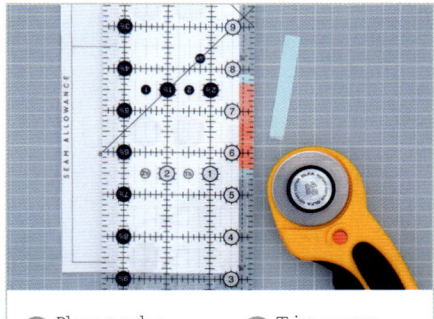

2 Place a ruler on top of the template, aligning the 6.4mm (¼in) measurement with the fold.

3 Trim excess fabric along the ruler edge, leaving a 6.4mm (¼in) seam allowance.

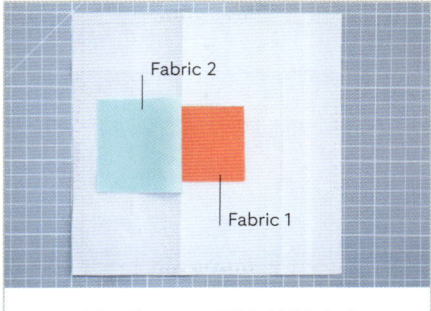

4 Position the template with the fabric right-side up.

5 Fold fabric 2 over to completely cover section 2 of the template.

6 Press the seam using a seam roller or iron.

7 Repeat all steps – placing fabric, stitching, folding, trimming, and pressing – for each section until the entire template is covered.

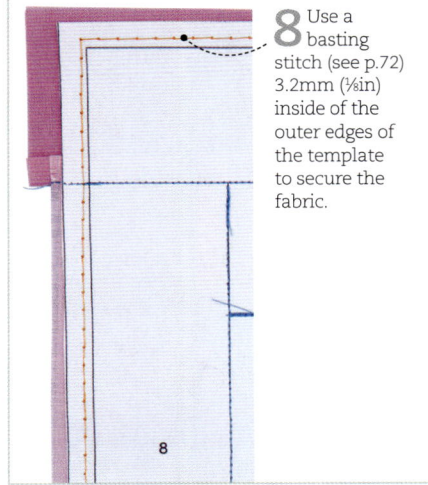

8 Use a basting stitch (see p.72) 3.2mm (⅛in) inside of the outer edges of the template to secure the fabric.

TRIMMING COMPLETED TEMPLATES

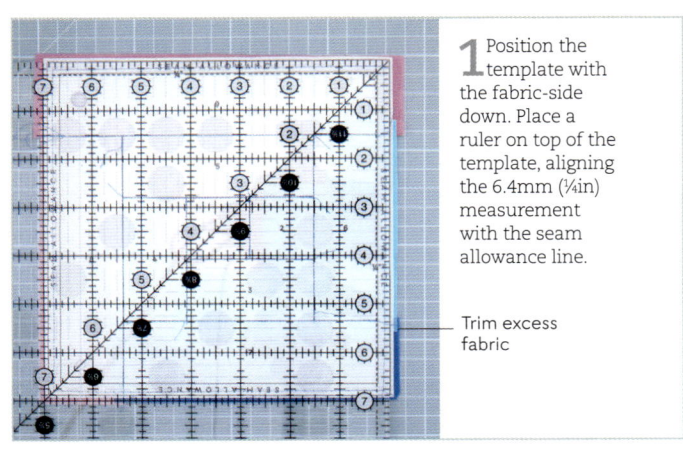

1 Position the template with the fabric-side down. Place a ruler on top of the template, aligning the 6.4mm (¼in) measurement with the seam allowance line.

Trim excess fabric

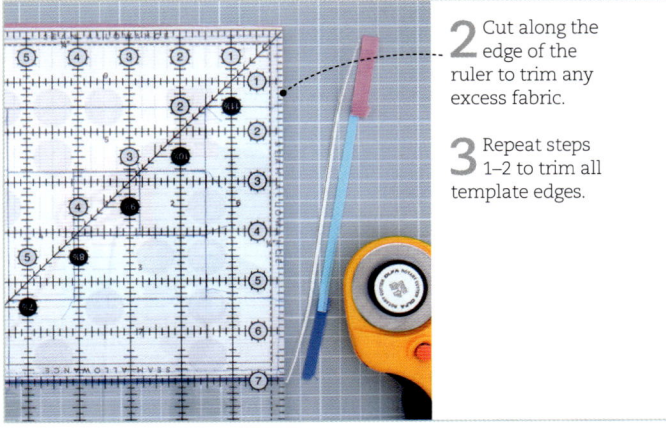

2 Cut along the edge of the ruler to trim any excess fabric.

3 Repeat steps 1–2 to trim all template edges.

Joining templates

FPP often requires joining multiple templates to form a completed quilt block. When sewing templates together, precise alignment is required at seam intersections along template edges to match points (see p.141) and reduce bulk.

MATCHING POINTS

Pinning in FPP is different from pinning in traditional piecing, as the templates have printed seam allowance lines to guide pin placement. It is recommended to use quilting clips (see p.29) along with pins to secure the templates in place while sewing.

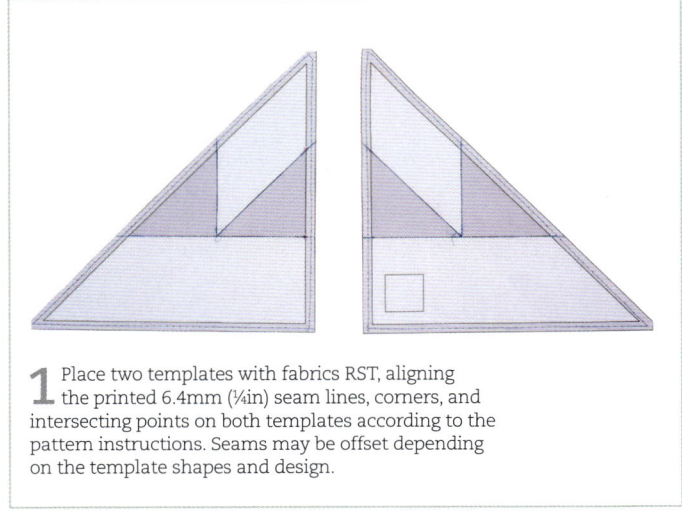

1 Place two templates with fabrics RST, aligning the printed 6.4mm (¼in) seam lines, corners, and intersecting points on both templates according to the pattern instructions. Seams may be offset depending on the template shapes and design.

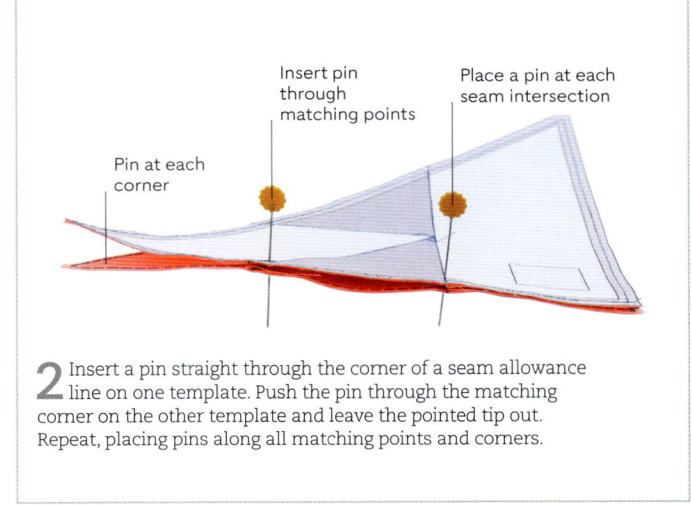

2 Insert a pin straight through the corner of a seam allowance line on one template. Push the pin through the matching corner on the other template and leave the pointed tip out. Repeat, placing pins along all matching points and corners.

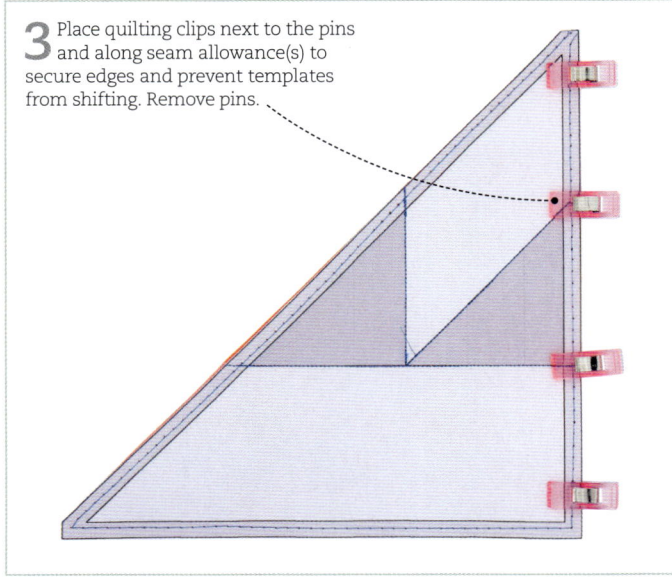

3 Place quilting clips next to the pins and along seam allowance(s) to secure edges and prevent templates from shifting. Remove pins.

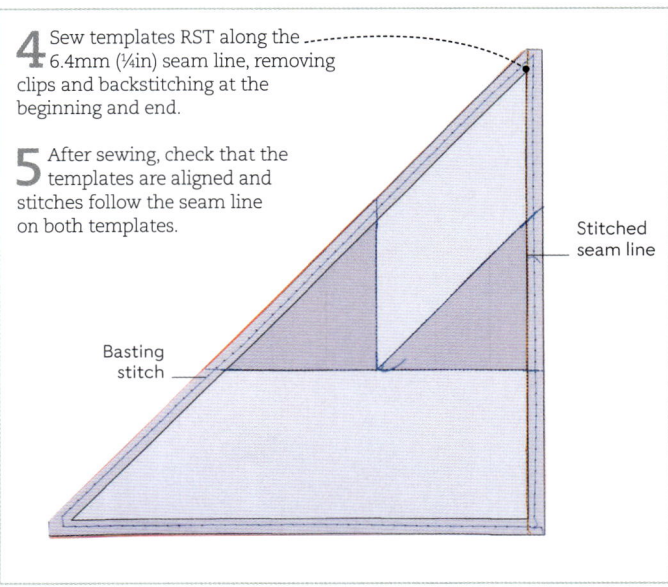

4 Sew templates RST along the 6.4mm (¼in) seam line, removing clips and backstitching at the beginning and end.

5 After sewing, check that the templates are aligned and stitches follow the seam line on both templates.

Stitched seam line

Basting stitch

PRESSING SEAMS

Remove the paper from the seam allowances of two joined pieces and press after each seam is sewn.

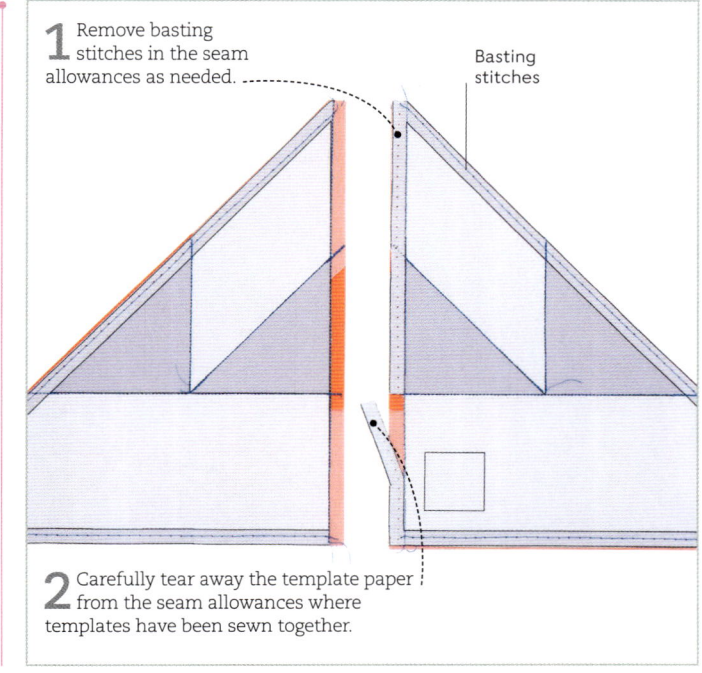

1. Remove basting stitches in the seam allowances as needed.

Basting stitches

2. Carefully tear away the template paper from the seam allowances where templates have been sewn together.

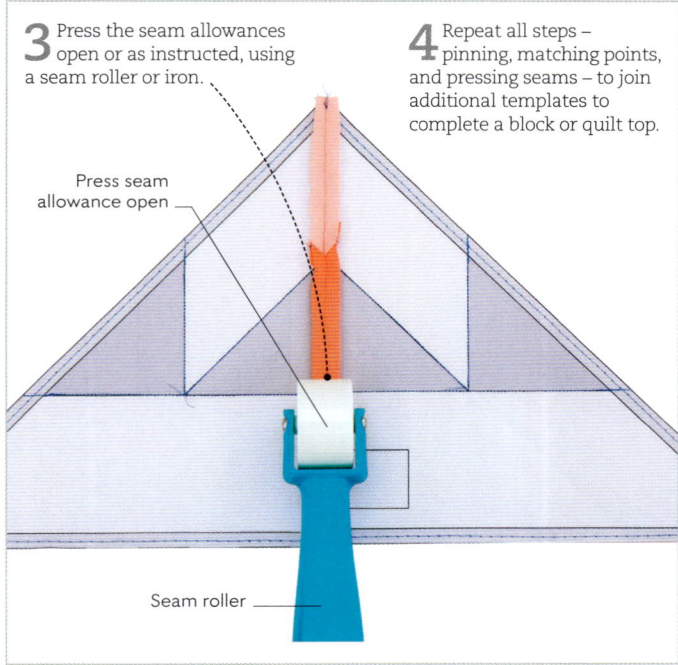

3. Press the seam allowances open or as instructed, using a seam roller or iron.

4. Repeat all steps – pinning, matching points, and pressing seams – to join additional templates to complete a block or quilt top.

Press seam allowance open

Seam roller

REMOVING PAPERS

Template paper can be removed after completing each block or, if the whole top is constructed via FPP, after the quilt top is finished. Use tweezers (see p.17) to assist with removing papers, being careful not to damage seams or fabrics.

1. Carefully tear the paper away from the fabric. Avoid pulling stitches or stretching fabric.

Paper removed   Template

2. Use tweezers to gently remove paper stuck under threads or from smaller sections.

Tweezers

Remove paper

3. Press the completed block using an iron.

Hand piecing

Hand piecing, the oldest sewing method, refers to sewing pieces of fabric together by hand using only a needle and thread. This simple technique allows for joining pieces in ways that might otherwise be difficult, such as when using Y-seams. Use a betweens or milliner's needle (see p.28) and 50 weight or finer thread (see p.26) in a neutral or matching colour for most hand piecing.

Preparing for hand piecing

While piecing by hand requires minimal tools, some preparation is required. Mark seam allowances on fabric pieces to assist with sewing straight and accurate seams. Use pins to mark where to begin and end stitches, as well as to hold pieces together and align points and seams (see p.141).

MARKING SEAM ALLOWANCE

1. Mark a registration line 6.4mm (¼in) away from the edges on the wrong side of the fabric to use as a seam allowance guide.

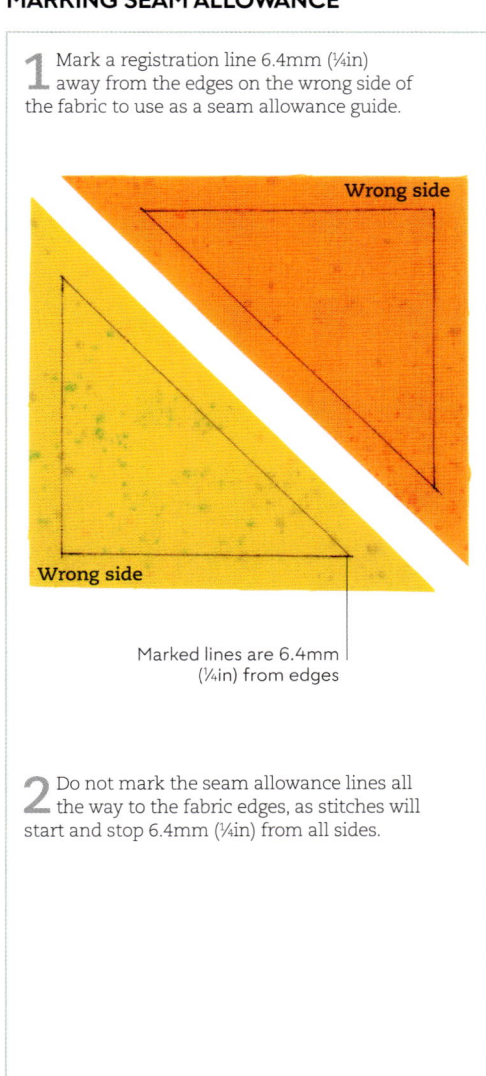

Marked lines are 6.4mm (¼in) from edges

2. Do not mark the seam allowance lines all the way to the fabric edges, as stitches will start and stop 6.4mm (¼in) from all sides.

USING PINS

1. Align the pieces to be joined, RST. Insert a pin through both pieces at the desired ending point, directly through the intersection of the marked seam allowances 6.4mm (¼in) from the corners.

2. Bring the tip of the same pin back through the fabrics to secure the pieces together.

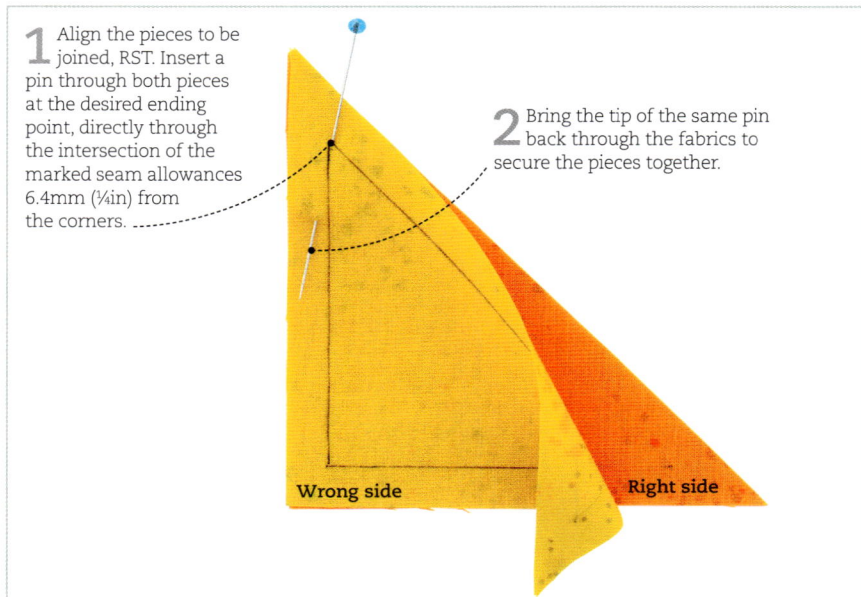

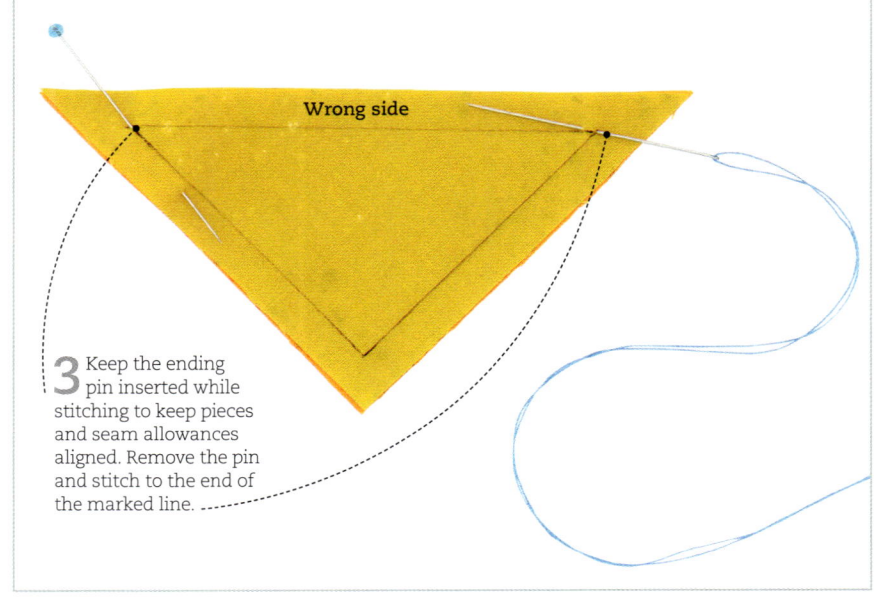

3. Keep the ending pin inserted while stitching to keep pieces and seam allowances aligned. Remove the pin and stitch to the end of the marked line.

Joining pieces

Sew a running stitch on the marked seam allowance lines, starting and stopping 6.4mm (¼in) from the corners of the pieces, to join pieces together.

RUNNING STITCH

Join pieces using a running stitch, which is a line of stitches made using a single length of thread, by weaving stitches back and forth through both fabric pieces.

1 Insert a needle at the desired starting point and pull the needle through until the knot rests against the fabric.

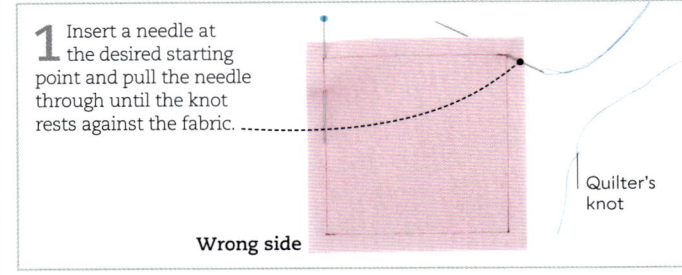

Quilter's knot

Wrong side

2 Insert the needle back through the fabric, approximately 3.2mm (⅛in) from where the thread exits the fabric.

3 Reinsert the needle at the initial entry point and pull through to make a backstitch.

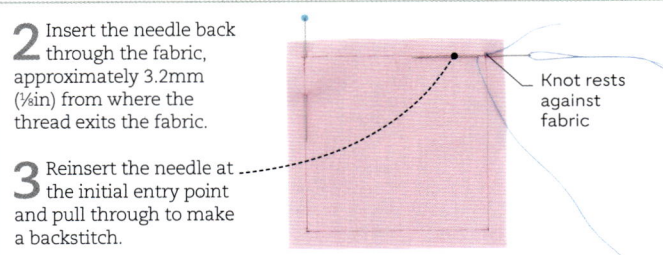

Knot rests against fabric

4 Rock the needle along the marked line 2–6 times, pushing the tip down through both pieces, then back up to the top.

5 Pull the needle and thread completely through both pieces. Backstitch every inch.

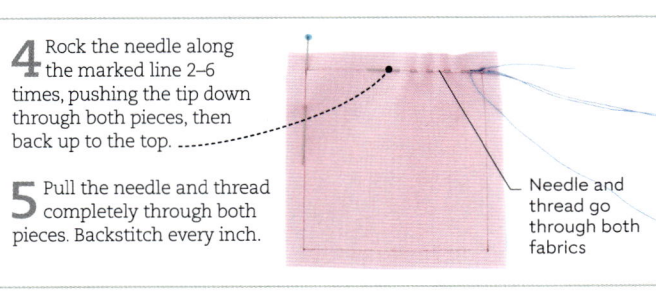

Needle and thread go through both fabrics

6 Repeat steps 4–5, stitching to the end of the seam line; make two backstitches. Secure with a knot (see p.75).

7 Trim the thread, leaving a 1.3cm (½in) thread tail.

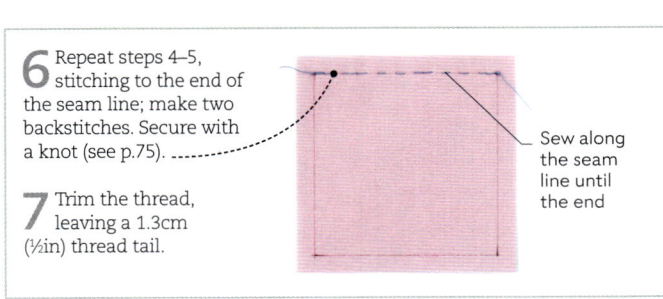

Sew along the seam line until the end

SEAM TYPES

When sewing straight seams, sew through seam intersections rather than over seams. Y-seams are formed where three pieces meet at a single point.

STRAIGHT SEAMS

1 Sew a running stitch on the marked seam line, stopping and backstitching just before the seam intersection.

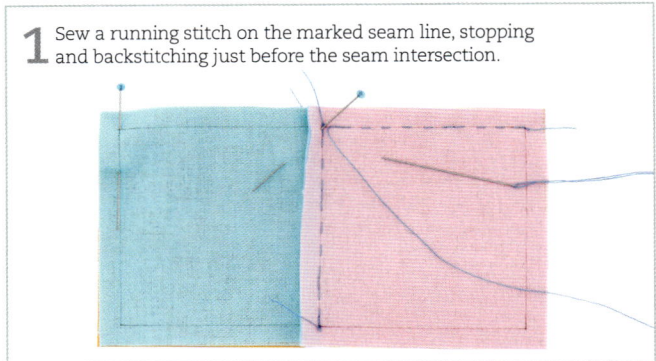

2 Insert the needle at the marked seam intersection, then pull completely through to the other side of the seam.

3 Backstitch, then continue sewing.

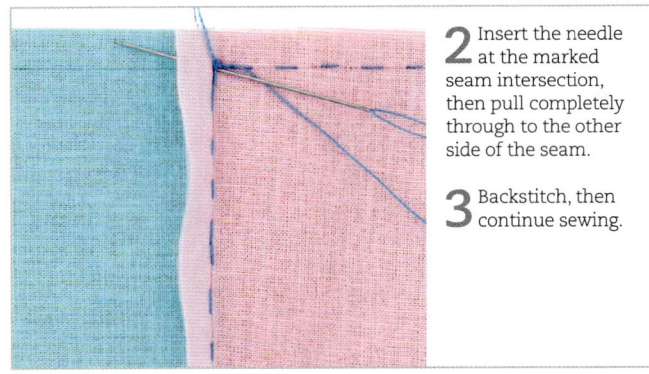

4 Backstitch at the end of the marked seam line and knot the thread. Trim the thread tail. Press.

Wrong side

JOINING PIECES **123**

Y-SEAMS

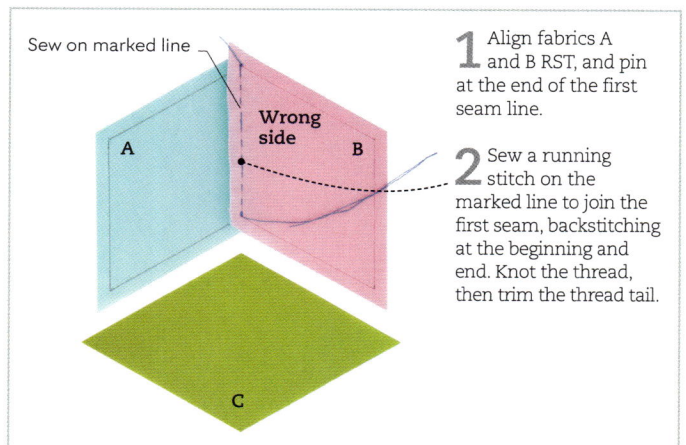

1. Align fabrics A and B RST, and pin at the end of the first seam line.

2. Sew a running stitch on the marked line to join the first seam, backstitching at the beginning and end. Knot the thread, then trim the thread tail.

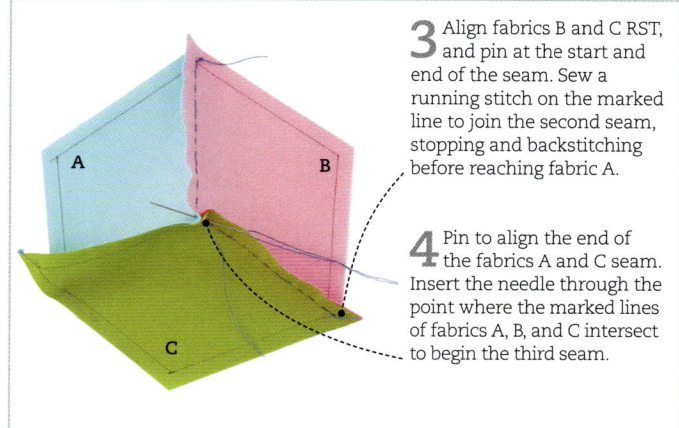

3. Align fabrics B and C RST, and pin at the start and end of the seam. Sew a running stitch on the marked line to join the second seam, stopping and backstitching before reaching fabric A.

4. Pin to align the end of the fabrics A and C seam. Insert the needle through the point where the marked lines of fabrics A, B, and C intersect to begin the third seam.

5. Sew a running stitch on the marked line to join fabrics A and C.

6. Backstitch at the end of the seam line and knot the thread. Trim the thread tail. Press.

CURVED SEAMS

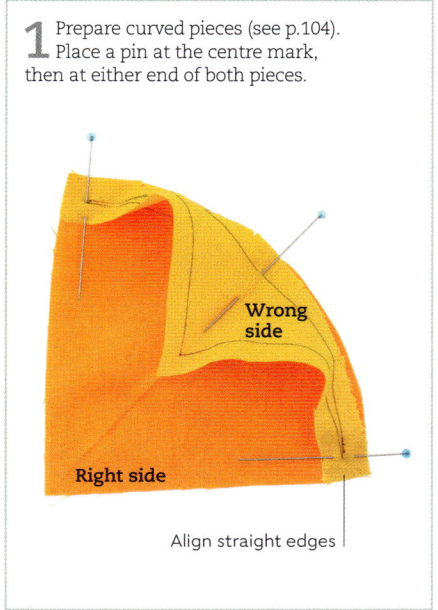

1. Prepare curved pieces (see p.104). Place a pin at the centre mark, then at either end of both pieces.

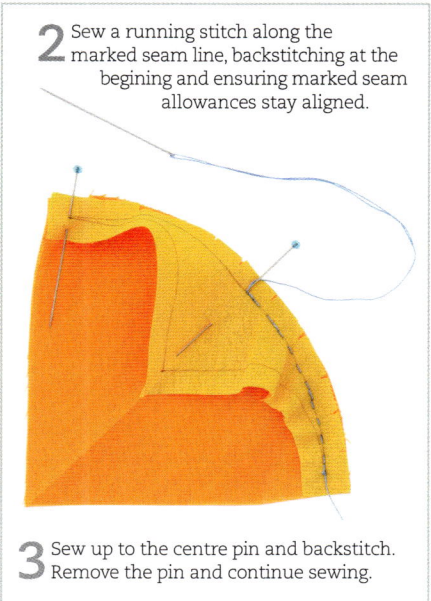

2. Sew a running stitch along the marked seam line, backstitching at the begining and ensuring marked seam allowances stay aligned.

3. Sew up to the centre pin and backstitch. Remove the pin and continue sewing.

4. Backstitch at the end of the marked seam line and knot the thread. Trim the thread tail. Press.

English paper piecing

English paper piecing (EPP) is a hand sewing technique in which fabric pieces are temporarily secured to paper pieces that provide stability while sewing. Once fabric pieces are joined, the paper pieces are removed, and the fabric pieces hold their shapes. EPP is ideal for piecing intricate geometric designs or shapes that are challenging to piece by machine. All techniques in this section assume right-handedness; if left-handed, mirror these steps.

Common EPP shapes

Most EPP shapes have straight edges, such as the classic hexagon. Paper pieces for common EPP shapes are available in standard sizes and do not include seam allowance. Pieces are often joined with pieces of similar sizes and angles to produce tessellating designs.

A hexagon has six equal sides and is measured by the length of one side. Half hexagons and elongated hexagons are common variations.

A diamond has four equal sides and is measured by the length of one side. Diamonds are categorized by their angle, such as 45- or 60-degree diamonds.

A jewel is a combination of a half hexagon and a half diamond. Jewels are measured by the length of one of the short sides.

An equilateral triangle has three equal sides and is measured by the length of one side. Triangles are also available in isosceles and right-angle triangle variations.

A tumbler has one pair of equal sides and one pair of unequal parallel sides. Tumblers are measured by the distance between the two parallel sides.

Curved shapes Apple core and clamshell shapes have convex and concave sides and are both typically measured across the widest point. Joining curved EPP shapes is considered an advanced skill.

Preparing paper pieces

Prepare for EPP by purchasing pre-cut paper pieces, cutting pieces by hand, or using a paper punch to cut pieces. The paper pieces must be cut accurately to ensure they fit together exactly, as they form the shapes that will be joined together.

PRE-CUT PIECES

Purchase pre-cut pieces in standard shapes and sizes or as part of kits. Pre-cut paper pieces are the most accurate templates, as the pieces are cut by machine. They are available cut from cardstock or recycled paper specifcally chosen for its durability and flexibility.

PRINT AND CUT

Download or create printable paper pieces for your desired EPP shape and size. Print the pieces on cardstock or other thick paper, then cut shapes out using paper scissors or a rotary cutter and ruler.

PAPER PUNCH

Punch EPP shapes out of cardstock or recycled thick paper, such as postcards, using a paper punch. Paper punches are only available in some common EPP shapes and sizes, and they may list the shape measurements differently; always check before purchasing.

CENTRE HOLES

Consider using a hole punch to make a hole in the centre of a paper piece to assist with later paper removal. The centre hole can be used when pinning paper pieces to fabric pieces while basting.

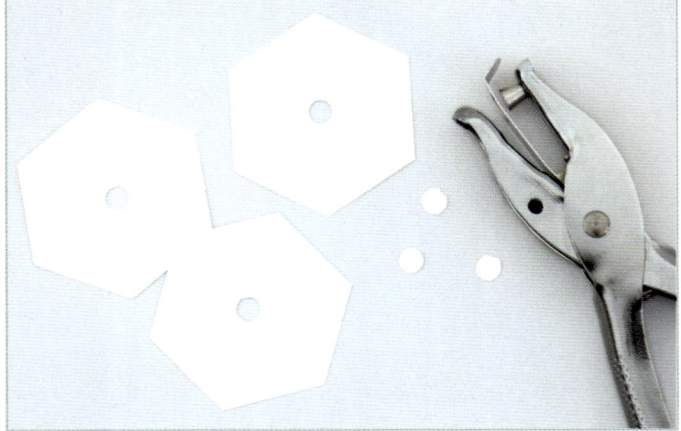

CUTTING FABRIC

When cutting fabric for EPP, use a ruler to add a seam allowance to all sides of a paper piece or use an acrylic template (see p.23) with seam allowance included. A 9.5mm (⅜in) seam allowance is recommended, especially for beginners, as it is easier to handle and creates more stable seams. Fussy cut motifs to achieve specific designs within or across pieces.

USING PAPER PIECES

1 Place a paper piece on top of the fabric to be cut, ensuring fabric extends at least 9.5mm (⅜in) on all sides of the paper piece.

2 Use a rotary cutter and ruler to cut 9.5mm (⅜in) around the outside of the paper piece. For efficiency, cut from WOF strips.

3 Alternatively, use scissors to trim 9.5mm (⅜in) around the outside of all edges of a paper piece.

USING ACRYLIC TEMPLATES

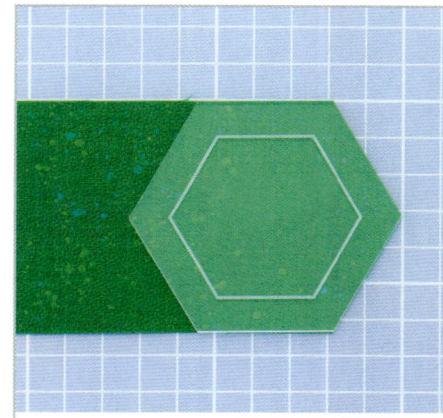

1 Choose an acrylic template with the seam allowance included. Cut pieces from a WOF strip the same width as the acrylic template for efficiency and reduced waste.

2 Alternatively, trace around the acrylic template before cutting.

FUSSY CUTTING

1 Choose the desired motif on a fabric, and use an acrylic template to check how the motif will fit on the paper piece.

2 Mark the motif area with a dry-erase marker (see p.22) to assist with motif alignment when cutting multiple pieces.

3 Carefully cut out fabric pieces, ensuring the motif is centred and aligned within the template.

4 Centre the fabric pieces on the paper pieces and baste (see p.128). Check that motifs align as desired before joining pieces (see p.130).

Basting English paper piecing

In EPP, basting is the process of folding and temporarily securing seam allowances around a paper piece using thread or glue. When basting, start at the widest angle of a piece and work in the same direction.

THREAD BASTING

Make tacking stitches through the seam allowances at each corner. For pieces with sides larger than 3.8cm (1½in), make stitches through the papers along each side. Thread a needle and make a quilter's knot (see p.75) before beginning. After basting all sides, secure with a knot.

TACKING CORNERS

1 Centre a paper piece on the wrong side of a fabric piece. Pin, clip, or glue in place. Fold the seam allowance along one edge of the paper piece, then fold over the adjacent seam allowance, overlapping the fabric at the corner. Insert a needle into the first seam allowance and exit through the second.

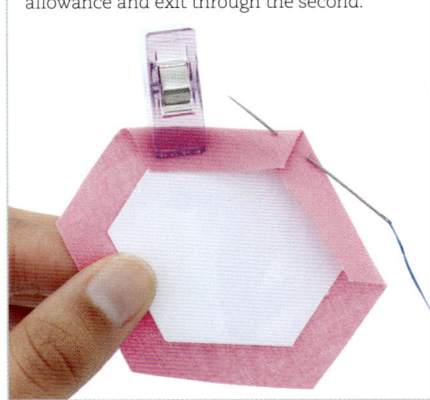

2 Pull the needle and thread through so the knot rests against the fabric. Reinsert the needle beside the knot and exit through the seam allowances to make a tacking stitch.

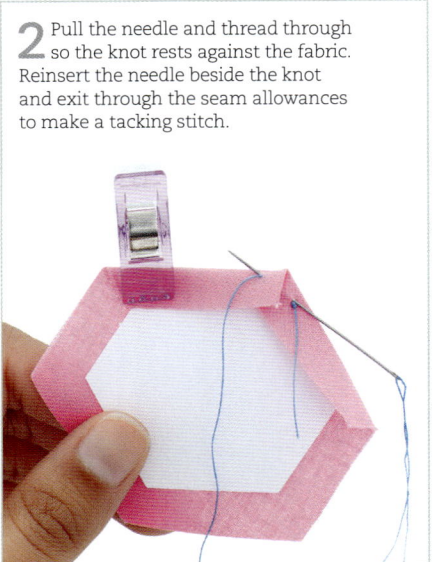

3 Fold over the next adjacent fabric edge and make a tacking stitch, pulling the thread taut.

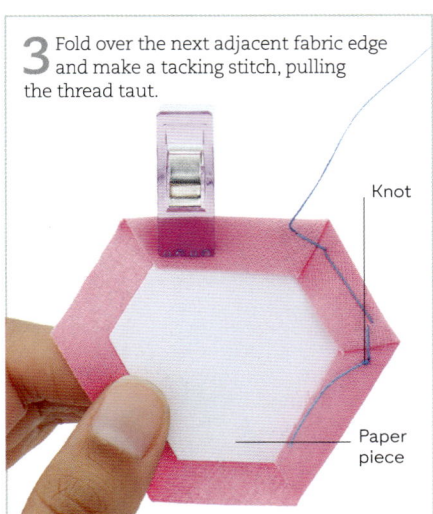

Knot

Paper piece

4 Repeat step 3 to complete thread basting. Tie an overhand knot (see p.76) and trim the thread tail.

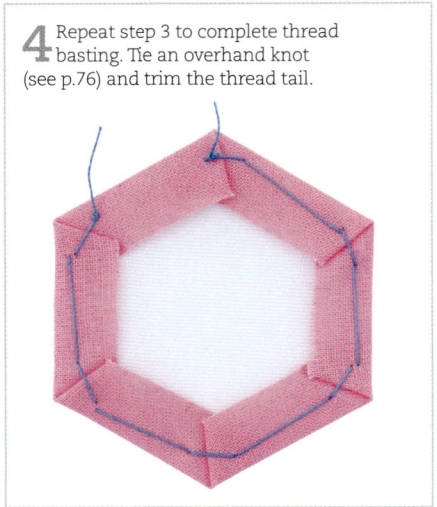

STITCHING THROUGH PAPERS

1 Make a tacking stitch to secure the first corner. Insert the needle through the seam allowance, paper, and front of the fabric, at approximately the centre of the edge.

2 Insert the needle back through all three layers, exiting through the seam allowance. Fold over the next seam allowance and secure the corner with a tacking stitch. Repeat along each edge to complete basting.

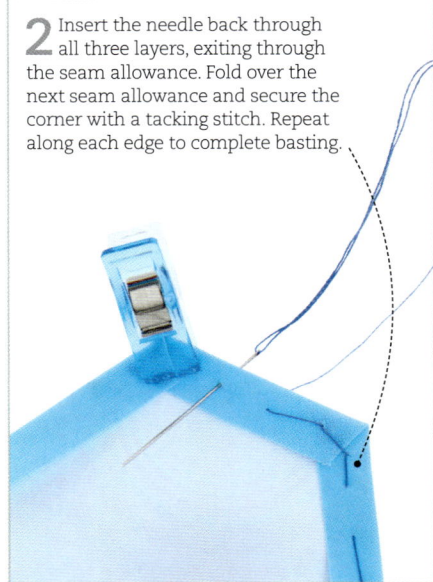

BASTING ENGLISH PAPER PIECING **129**

GLUE BASTING

Secure fabric seam allowances to the edges of paper pieces with a small amount of glue (see p.29). This method is quicker than thread basting, but it may make later paper removal more difficult.

1 Position a fabric piece right-side down. Centre a paper piece on top of the fabric and pin or glue in place.

2 Place a line of glue along one edge of the paper piece. Fold the seam allowance down firmly to adhere.

3 Place a line of glue along the adjacent paper piece edge. Fold and press the seam allowance down.

4 Repeat steps 2–3 to baste all edges.

Final basted seam

ACUTE ANGLES

EPP shapes with narrow (acute) angles produce a fabric tail that extends beyond the paper piece. Begin basting the side below the wider (obtuse) angle and move in a clockwise direction. Baste in the same direction for all pieces so tails nest when pieces are joined.

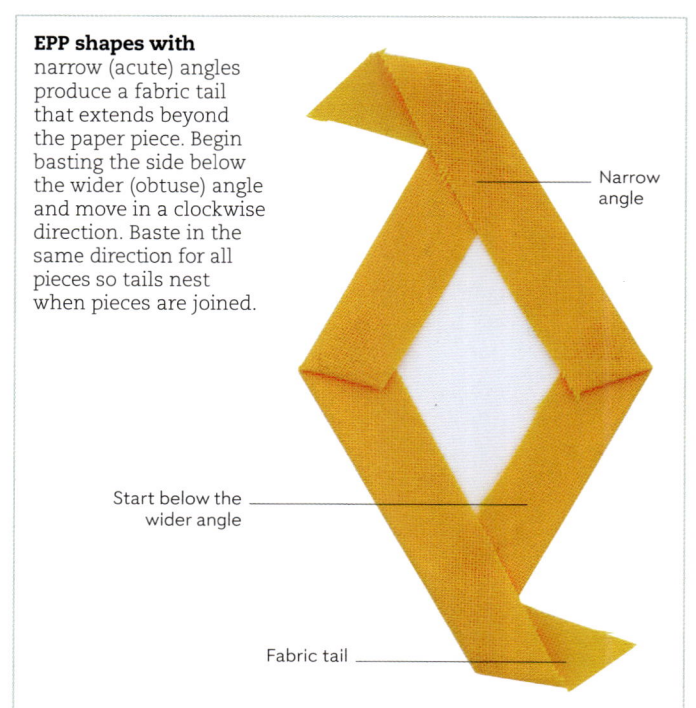

Narrow angle

Start below the wider angle

Fabric tail

CURVED EDGES

Glue curved shapes for accuracy. Seam allowances may pleat along convex curves once basted. Clip concave curves (see p.104) to ensure seam allowances lay flat.

Convex curve

Concave curve

Joining pieces

EPP pieces are commonly joined with whipstitches or flat back stitches. Prepare a needle and thread (see p.74) before beginning. Use quilting clips or magnets to hold pieces together while stitching to reduce hand fatigue.

STITCH TYPES

Whipstitches are strong and ideal for joining straight edges. Flat back stitches are made by holding pieces side-by-side instead of RST, and they are ideal for joining curved edges. To achieve less visible stitches, use a fine needle, such as a betweens or milliner's (see p.28), a neutral or matching lightweight thread (see p.26), and insert the needle as close to the fabric edges as possible. Aim for approximately 12–18 stitches per 2.5cm (1in).

WHIPSTITCH

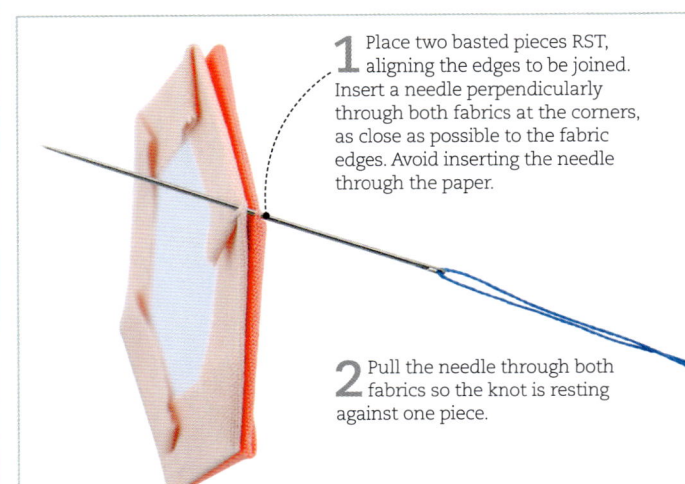

1 Place two basted pieces RST, aligning the edges to be joined. Insert a needle perpendicularly through both fabrics at the corners, as close as possible to the fabric edges. Avoid inserting the needle through the paper.

2 Pull the needle through both fabrics so the knot is resting against one piece.

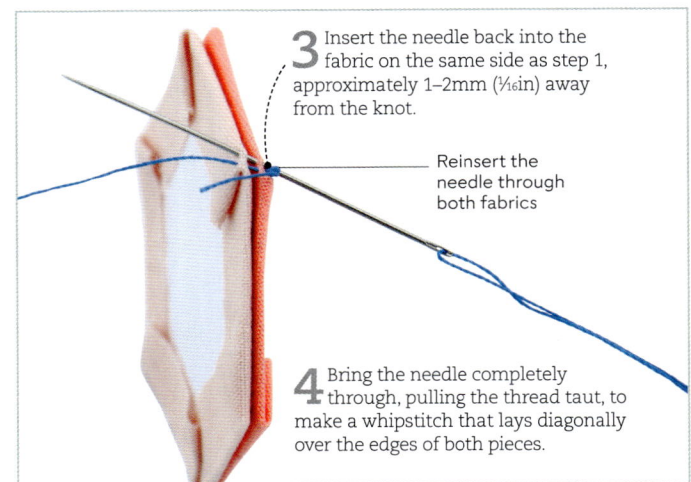

3 Insert the needle back into the fabric on the same side as step 1, approximately 1–2mm (1/16in) away from the knot.

Reinsert the needle through both fabrics

4 Bring the needle completely through, pulling the thread taut, to make a whipstitch that lays diagonally over the edges of both pieces.

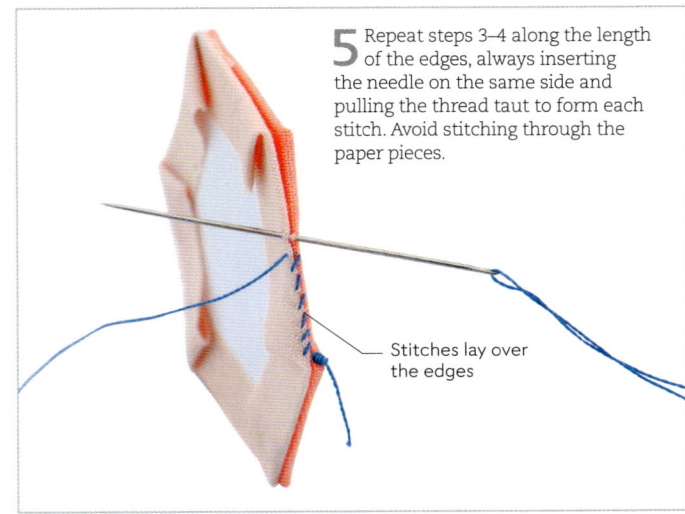

5 Repeat steps 3–4 along the length of the edges, always inserting the needle on the same side and pulling the thread taut to form each stitch. Avoid stitching through the paper pieces.

Stitches lay over the edges

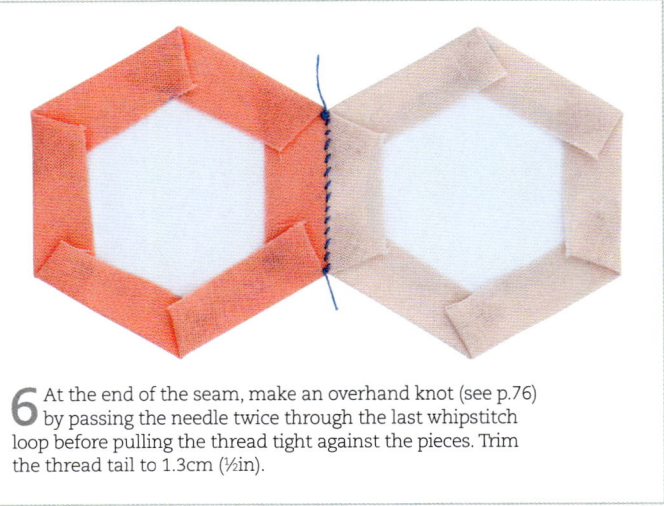

6 At the end of the seam, make an overhand knot (see p.76) by passing the needle twice through the last whipstitch loop before pulling the thread tight against the pieces. Trim the thread tail to 1.3cm (½in).

FLAT BACK STITCH

1 Arrange two pieces, right-sides up, with the edges to be joined aligned. Place masking or washi tape (see p.22) across the seam to temporarily hold the pieces in place.

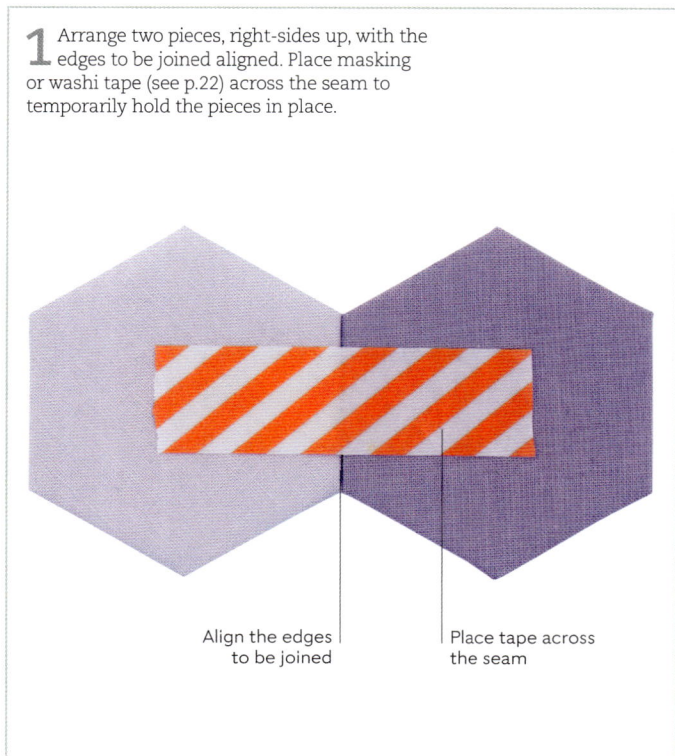

Align the edges to be joined

Place tape across the seam

2 Position the pieces wrong-side up. Insert a threaded needle into the seam allowance at the corner of one piece and exit through the other. Be careful to catch only a bit of fabric, and avoid inserting the needle through the paper. Pull the needle through both fabrics so the knot is resting against one piece.

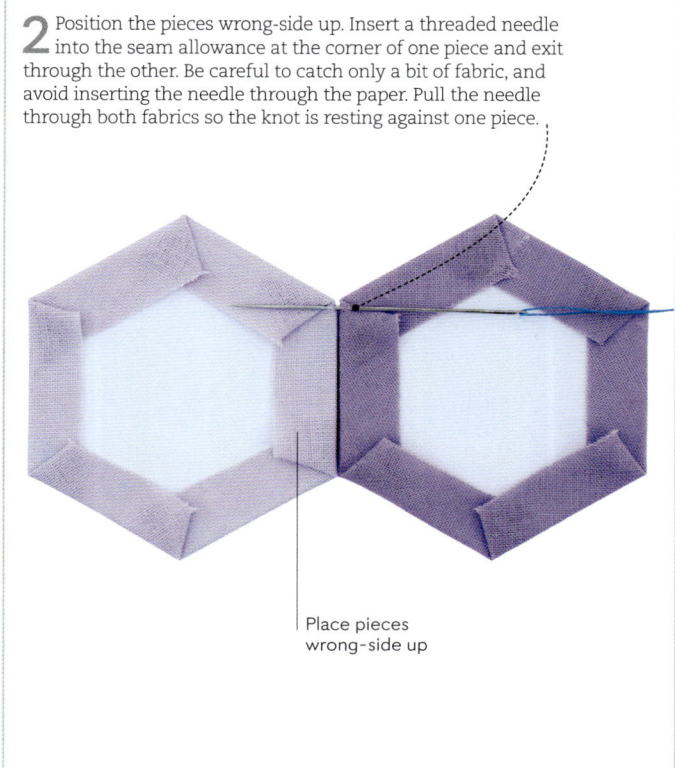

Place pieces wrong-side up

3 Insert the needle back through the seam allowances from the same side as step 2, approximately 1–2mm (1/16in) away from the knot.

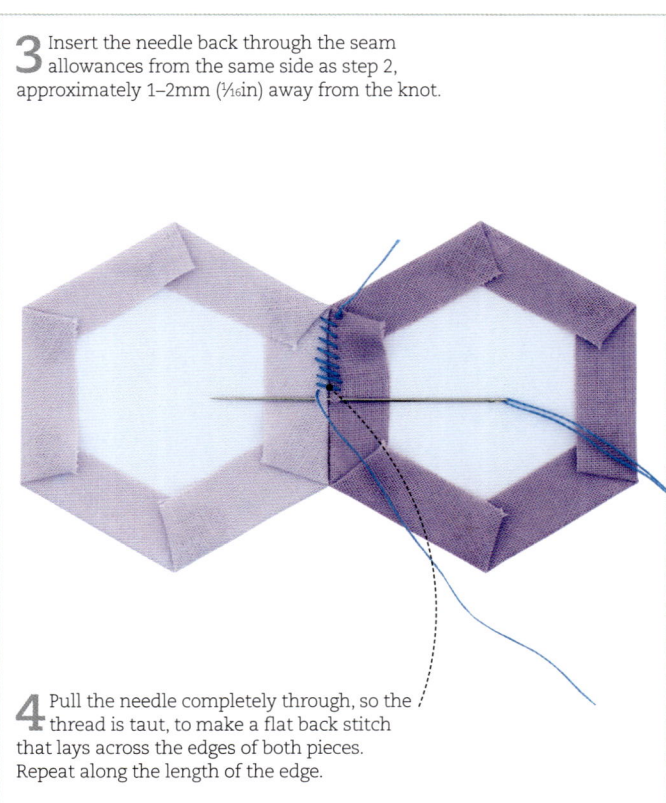

4 Pull the needle completely through, so the thread is taut, to make a flat back stitch that lays across the edges of both pieces. Repeat along the length of the edge.

5 At the end of the seam, make an overhand knot by passing the needle twice through the last flat back loop before pulling the thread tight against the pieces. Trim the thread tail to 1.3cm (½in).

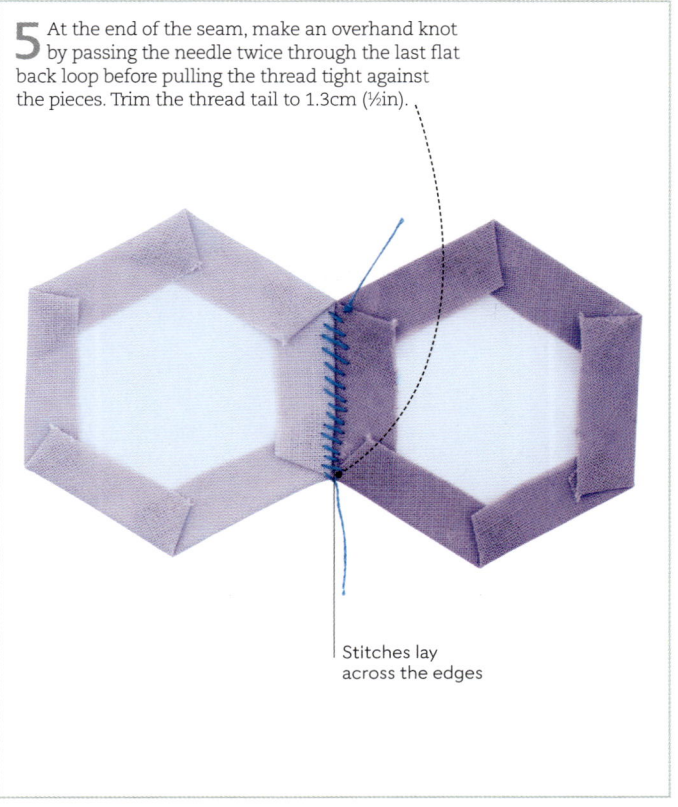

Stitches lay across the edges

JOINING SHAPES

Assemble EPP pieces into blocks or sections one-by-one or join into rows. Determine the most efficient technique by first looking for opportunities to join pieces into rows. Although these examples use hexagon flowers and diamond stars, which are common beginner blocks, the techniques are universal for all EPP applications.

PIECING ONE-BY-ONE

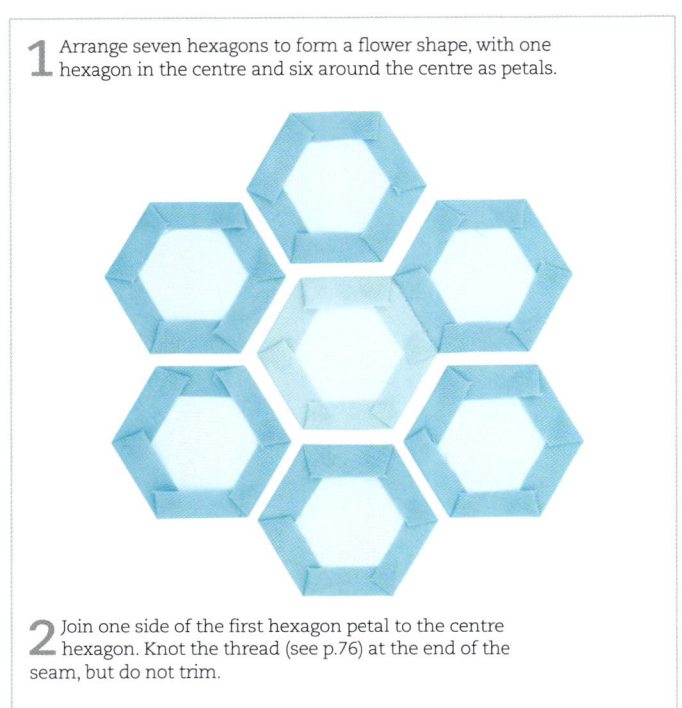

1 Arrange seven hexagons to form a flower shape, with one hexagon in the centre and six around the centre as petals.

2 Join one side of the first hexagon petal to the centre hexagon. Knot the thread (see p.76) at the end of the seam, but do not trim.

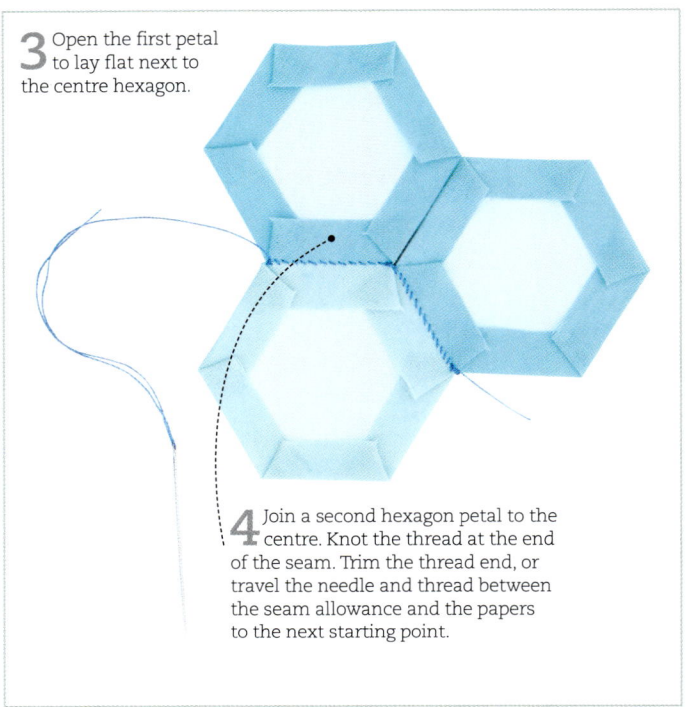

3 Open the first petal to lay flat next to the centre hexagon.

4 Join a second hexagon petal to the centre. Knot the thread at the end of the seam. Trim the thread end, or travel the needle and thread between the seam allowance and the papers to the next starting point.

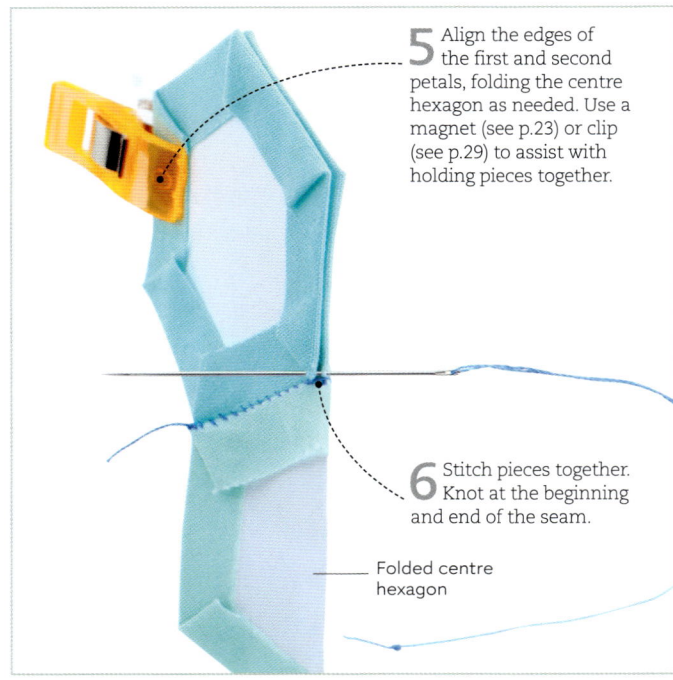

5 Align the edges of the first and second petals, folding the centre hexagon as needed. Use a magnet (see p.23) or clip (see p.29) to assist with holding pieces together.

6 Stitch pieces together. Knot at the beginning and end of the seam.

Folded centre hexagon

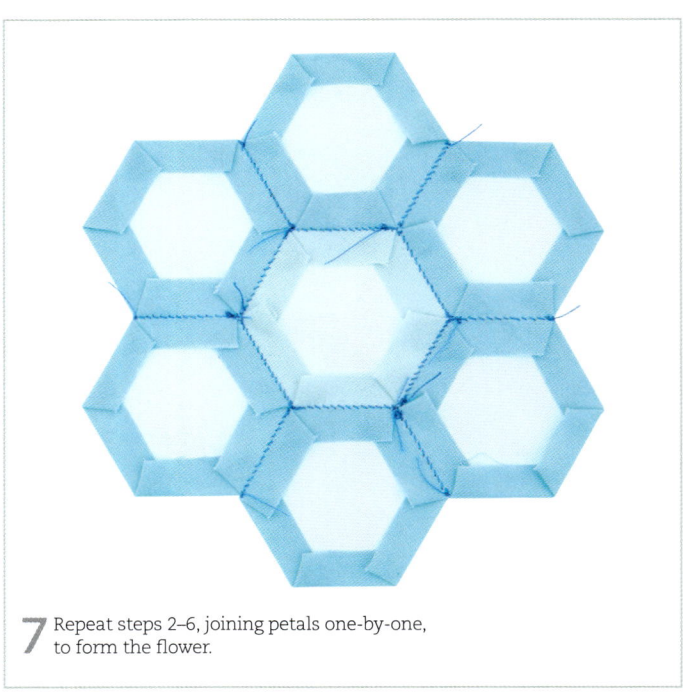

7 Repeat steps 2–6, joining petals one-by-one, to form the flower.

PIECING ROWS

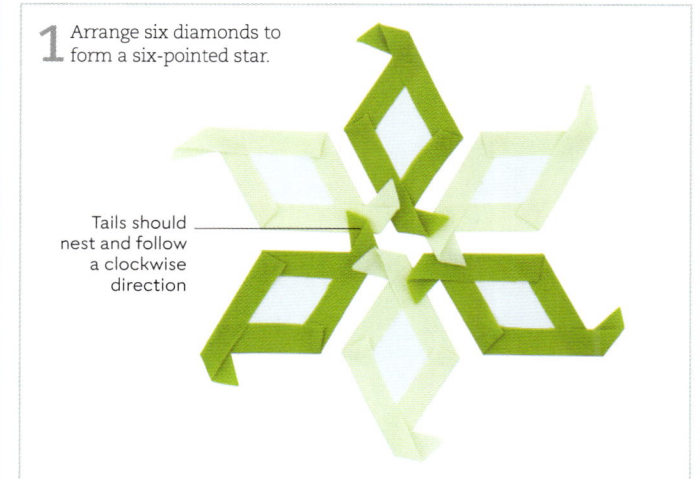

1 Arrange six diamonds to form a six-pointed star.

Tails should nest and follow a clockwise direction

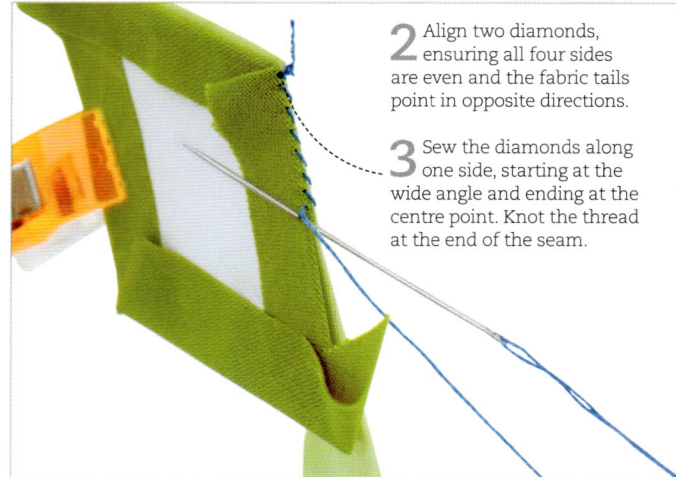

2 Align two diamonds, ensuring all four sides are even and the fabric tails point in opposite directions.

3 Sew the diamonds along one side, starting at the wide angle and ending at the centre point. Knot the thread at the end of the seam.

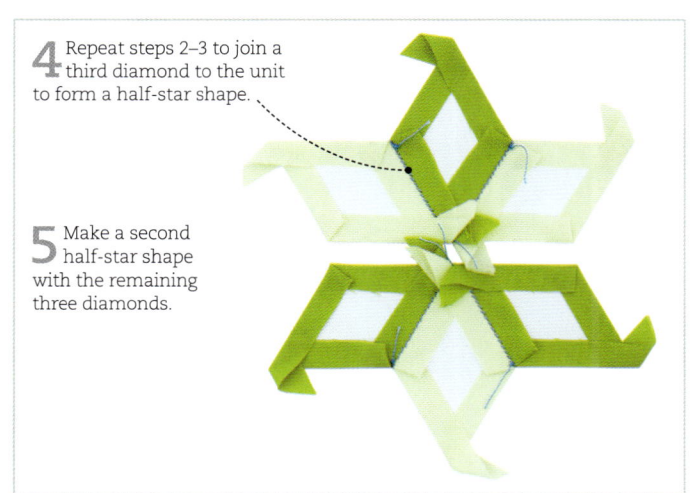

4 Repeat steps 2–3 to join a third diamond to the unit to form a half-star shape.

5 Make a second half-star shape with the remaining three diamonds.

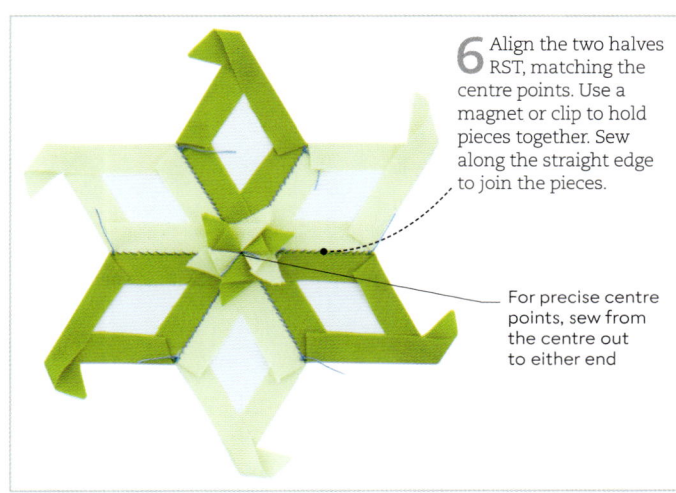

6 Align the two halves RST, matching the centre points. Use a magnet or clip to hold pieces together. Sew along the straight edge to join the pieces.

For precise centre points, sew from the centre out to either end

PIECING CURVED EDGES

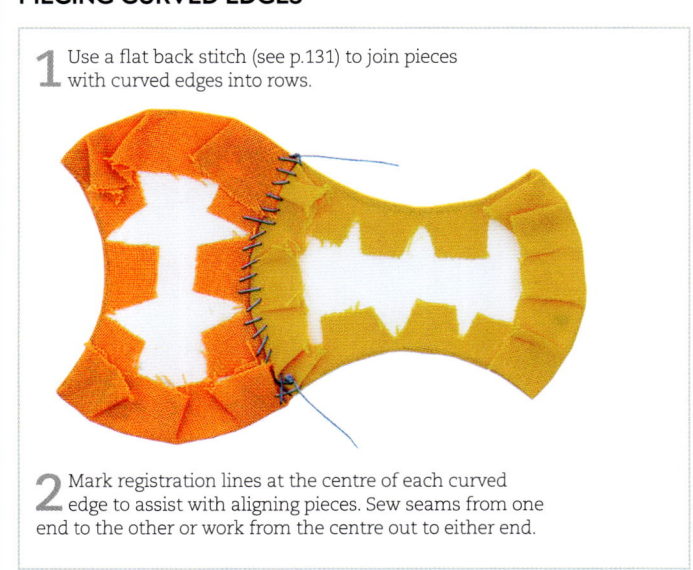

1 Use a flat back stitch (see p.131) to join pieces with curved edges into rows.

2 Mark registration lines at the centre of each curved edge to assist with aligning pieces. Sew seams from one end to the other or work from the centre out to either end.

REMOVING PAPERS

Remove papers before finishing a project, whether during the piecing process or once the project is complete. Save paper pieces to reuse in future projects.

1 Press the completed block or quilt top from the front and back, and remove basting stitches as needed.

2 Remove a paper piece when it is completely surrounded, such as the centre of a hexagon flower, or when the project is complete. Use tweezers to assist with removing papers.

Appliqué

Appliqué is the process of sewing fabric pieces or entire quilt blocks onto a background to create designs, from simple shapes to intricate motifs, not typically achievable through traditional piecing methods. Attach appliqué by machine or hand with various stitch types and techniques.

Preparing for appliqué

Due to the intricate nature of appliqué, carefully cut out shapes and add interfacing (see p.45) as needed to assist with producing smooth and stable edges. Baste shapes before attaching to reduce shifting.

CUTTING SHAPES

Heavily starch fabric before cutting out appliqué shapes using scissors. When tracing or drawing shapes, add 6.4mm (¼in) seam allowance to the outside of a shape unless preparing for raw edge appliqué.

TRANSFERRING TO FABRIC

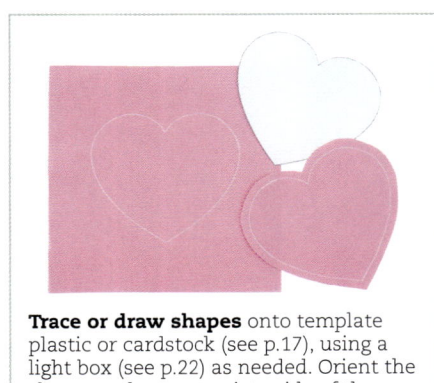

Trace or draw shapes onto template plastic or cardstock (see p.17), using a light box (see p.22) as needed. Orient the shape on the appropriate side of the fabric based on the appliqué technique.

CLIPPING CORNERS

1 Before folding seam allowances under, clip inner corners to allow the seam allowance edges to separate and lay flat. Clip just up to, but not past, the desired seam line.

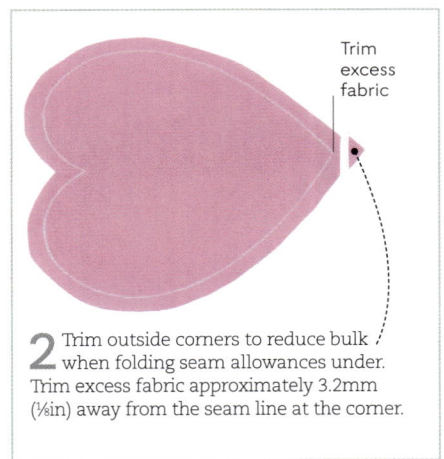

2 Trim outside corners to reduce bulk when folding seam allowances under. Trim excess fabric approximately 3.2mm (⅛in) away from the seam line at the corner.

Trim excess fabric

ATTACHING INTERFACING

Add sew-in or fusible interfacing to provide stability, reduce fraying in raw edge appliqué, and produce smooth edges in prepared edge appliqué. Keep in mind that most interfacing is permanent.

SEW-IN INTERFACING

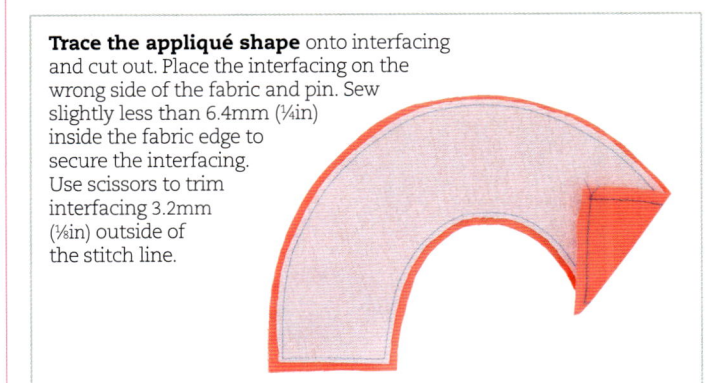

Trace the appliqué shape onto interfacing and cut out. Place the interfacing on the wrong side of the fabric and pin. Sew slightly less than 6.4mm (¼in) inside the fabric edge to secure the interfacing. Use scissors to trim interfacing 3.2mm (⅛in) outside of the stitch line.

FUSIBLE INTERFACING

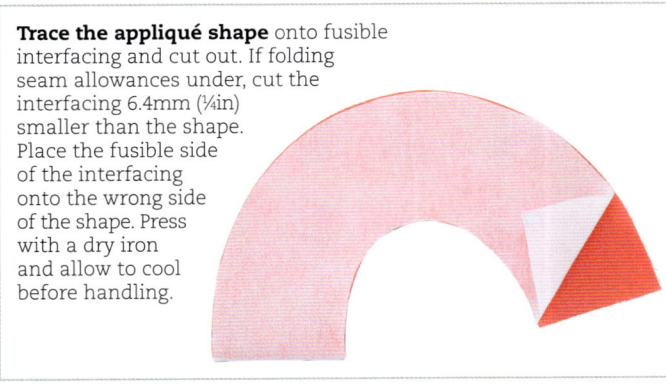

Trace the appliqué shape onto fusible interfacing and cut out. If folding seam allowances under, cut the interfacing 6.4mm (¼in) smaller than the shape. Place the fusible side of the interfacing onto the wrong side of the shape. Press with a dry iron and allow to cool before handling.

Types of appliqué

Choose from a variety of appliqué types to attach shapes using different machine- or hand-stitching techniques. Common appliqué techniques include raw edge, prepared edge, and needle turn appliqué, all of which produce a different finish.

ATTACHING BY MACHINE

Attach appliqué pieces using a machine for efficiency and durability. Use a universal straight stitch, supplied as standard on all machines, or a decorative stitch if it is available to you.

STRAIGHT STITCH

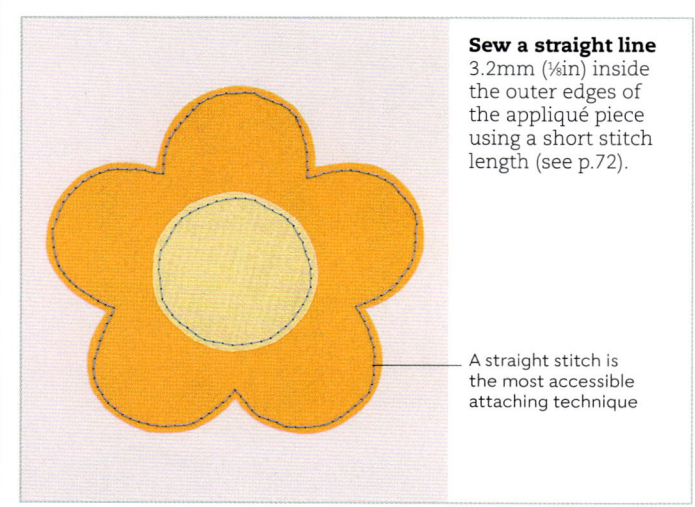

Sew a straight line 3.2mm (⅛in) inside the outer edges of the appliqué piece using a short stitch length (see p.72).

A straight stitch is the most accessible attaching technique

ZIGZAG STITCH

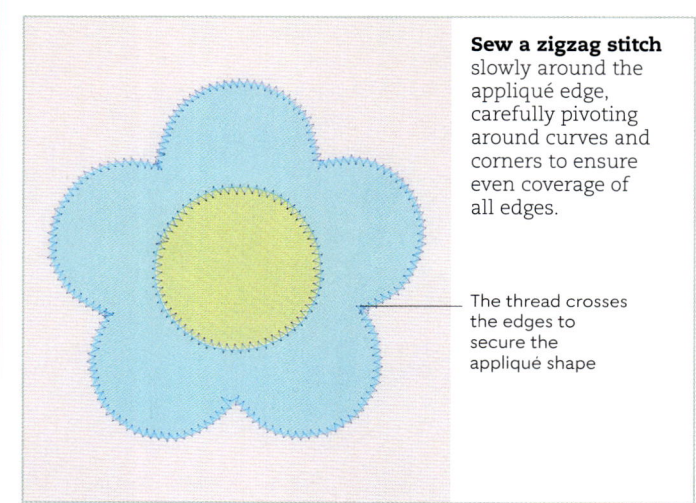

Sew a zigzag stitch slowly around the appliqué edge, carefully pivoting around curves and corners to ensure even coverage of all edges.

The thread crosses the edges to secure the appliqué shape

SATIN STITCH

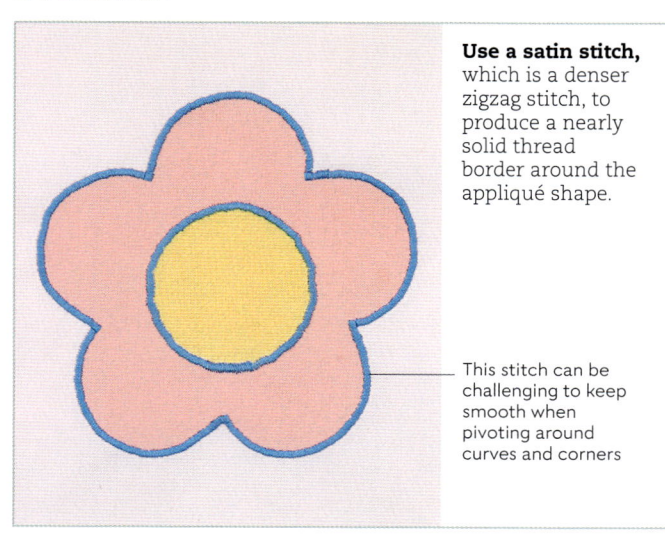

Use a satin stitch, which is a denser zigzag stitch, to produce a nearly solid thread border around the appliqué shape.

This stitch can be challenging to keep smooth when pivoting around curves and corners

BLANKET STITCH

Use a blanket stitch to add a decorative texture while partially enclosing appliqué edges.

The needle pierces the background fabric, while the bite of the stitch pierces the appliqué shape

ATTACHING BY HAND

Attaching appliqué by hand can be nearly invisible when using a ladder stitch, discreet when using a whipstitch, or bold when using a running or blanket stitch. Choose the appropriate needle and thread weight for the intended stitch, and be sure to knot and bury thread ends (see p.76).

RUNNING STITCH

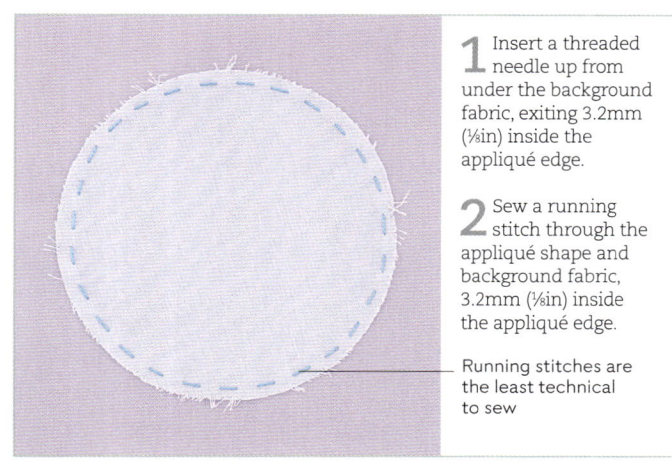

1. Insert a threaded needle up from under the background fabric, exiting 3.2mm (⅛in) inside the appliqué edge.

2. Sew a running stitch through the appliqué shape and background fabric, 3.2mm (⅛in) inside the appliqué edge.

Running stitches are the least technical to sew

WHIPSTITCH

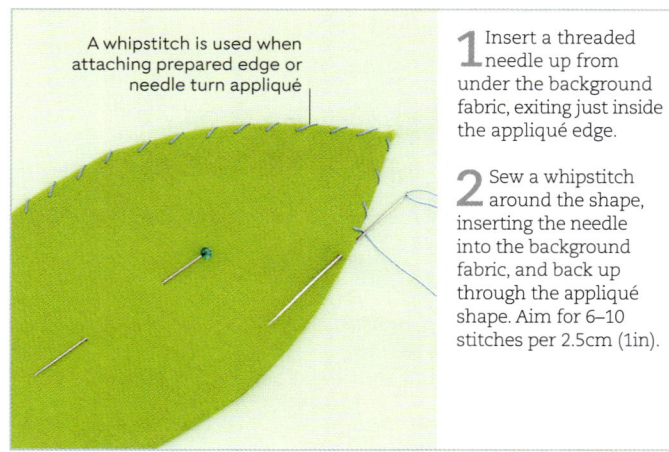

A whipstitch is used when attaching prepared edge or needle turn appliqué

1. Insert a threaded needle up from under the background fabric, exiting just inside the appliqué edge.

2. Sew a whipstitch around the shape, inserting the needle into the background fabric, and back up through the appliqué shape. Aim for 6–10 stitches per 2.5cm (1in).

LADDER STITCH

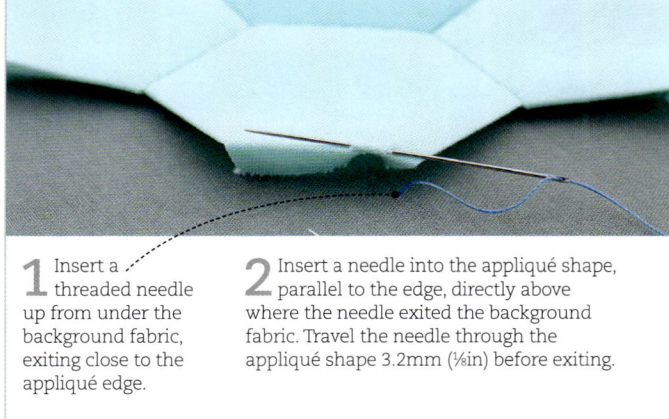

1. Insert a threaded needle up from under the background fabric, exiting close to the appliqué edge.

2. Insert a needle into the appliqué shape, parallel to the edge, directly above where the needle exited the background fabric. Travel the needle through the appliqué shape 3.2mm (⅛in) before exiting.

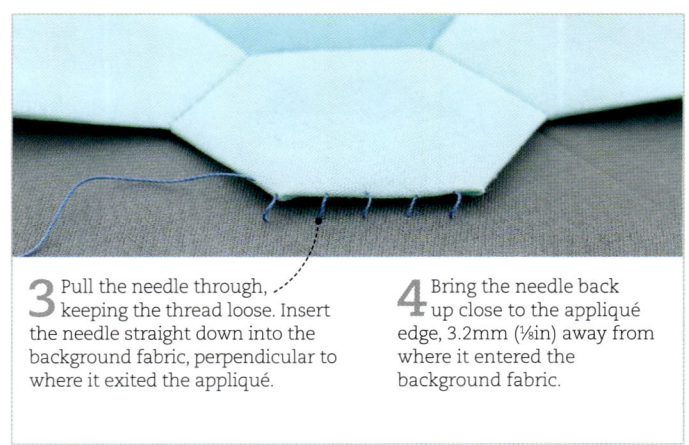

3. Pull the needle through, keeping the thread loose. Insert the needle straight down into the background fabric, perpendicular to where it exited the appliqué.

4. Bring the needle back up close to the appliqué edge, 3.2mm (⅛in) away from where it entered the background fabric.

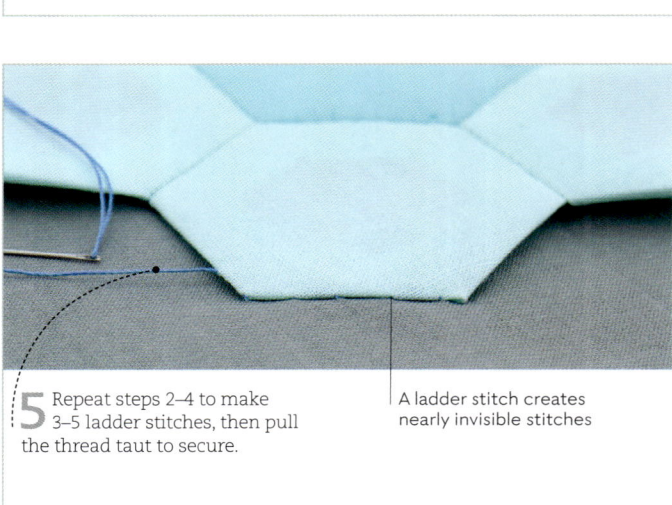

5. Repeat steps 2–4 to make 3–5 ladder stitches, then pull the thread taut to secure.

A ladder stitch creates nearly invisible stitches

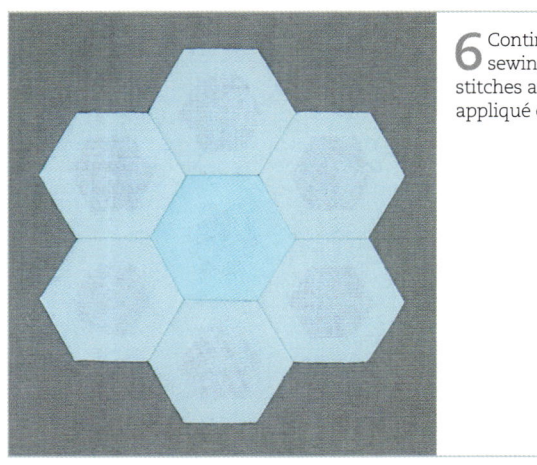

6. Continue sewing ladder stitches around the appliqué edge.

BLANKET STITCH

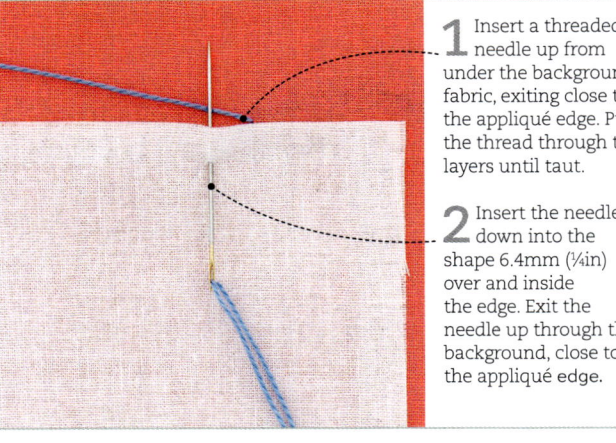

1. Insert a threaded needle up from under the background fabric, exiting close to the appliqué edge. Pull the thread through the layers until taut.

2. Insert the needle down into the shape 6.4mm (¼in) over and inside the edge. Exit the needle up through the background, close to the appliqué edge.

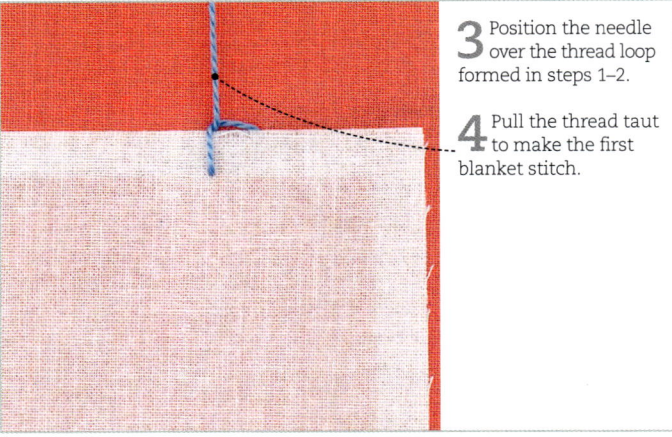

3. Position the needle over the thread loop formed in steps 1–2.

4. Pull the thread taut to make the first blanket stitch.

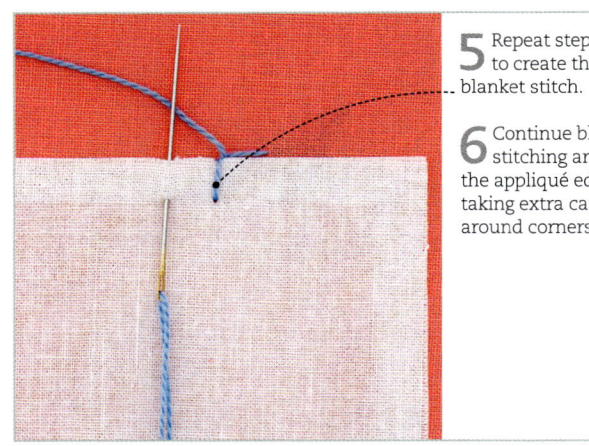

5. Repeat steps 2–4 to create the next blanket stitch.

6. Continue blanket stitching around the appliqué edge, taking extra care around corners.

7. Complete the final blanket stitch by looping the needle under the first stitch, then inserting the tip down into the appliqué piece and pulling the thread taut.

RAW EDGE APPLIQUÉ

Raw edge appliqué uses a double-sided fusible interfacing (see p.45) to adhere appliqué shapes to background fabric and leaves fabric edges exposed to fray over time. Attach by machine using any stitch type or by hand using a running or blanket stitch.

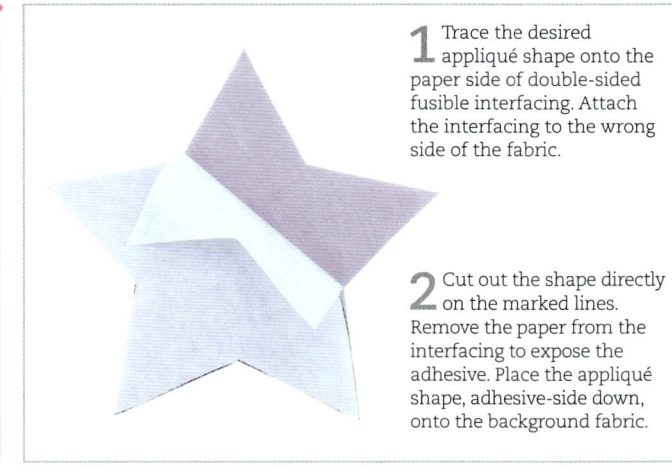

1. Trace the desired appliqué shape onto the paper side of double-sided fusible interfacing. Attach the interfacing to the wrong side of the fabric.

2. Cut out the shape directly on the marked lines. Remove the paper from the interfacing to expose the adhesive. Place the appliqué shape, adhesive-side down, onto the background fabric.

3. Press to fuse the appliqué shape to the background fabric. Stitch around the appliqué edge either by machine or hand.

PREPARED EDGE APPLIQUÉ

Prepared edge appliqué involves folding the appliqué edges under to produce a finished edge, similar to EPP. Attach using any stitch type, except needle turn.

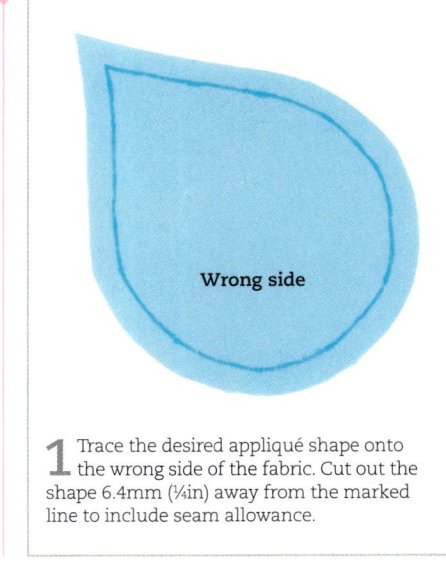

1 Trace the desired appliqué shape onto the wrong side of the fabric. Cut out the shape 6.4mm (¼in) away from the marked line to include seam allowance.

2 Fold the seam allowance toward the wrong side, using the marked line as a guide. Add a small amount of glue (see p.29) as needed to keep edges folded.

3 Pin the appliqué shape to the background fabric and stitch around the appliqué edge.

NEEDLE TURN APPLIQUÉ

Needle turn appliqué is the process of using a needle to gradually turn edges under while stitching using a whipstitch or ladder stitch (see p.137).

1 Trace the desired shape on the right side of the fabric. Cut out the shape 6.4mm (¼in) away from the marked line. Baste the appliqué shape to the background fabric using a long running stitch (see p.137) directly on the marked line.

2 Remove a few running stitches. Use the needle tip to turn the seam allowance under where the stitches were removed, folding along the marked line. Insert a needle up from under the background fabric, catching the very edge of the appliqué shape.

3 Stitch the folded edge to the background fabric. Sew until the end of the folded edge, then stop to remove more running stitches. Use the needle tip to turn under another small section of the seam allowance.

4 Repeat steps 2–3 to complete attaching the appliqué shape.

Quilt top construction

This section provides a guide for assembling units into quilt blocks, and blocks into quilt tops. Learn how to carefully match points and seams, sew units into blocks, and add sashing, then progress to efficient assembly techniques and understanding various quilt top layouts. Use this information to determine your preferred approach to quilt top construction.

Matching points and seams

Many quilt designs require precise points at the intersections of pieced units and blocks to achieve the intended outcome. Carefully match points and align seams, then use pins or glue to secure seams in place while sewing.

PINNING

Place pins to match intersecting points and ensure seams remain aligned while piecing. Insert positioning pins perpendicularly into the exact seam intersection point, then place additional pins to secure units or blocks in place. Always avoid sewing over pins.

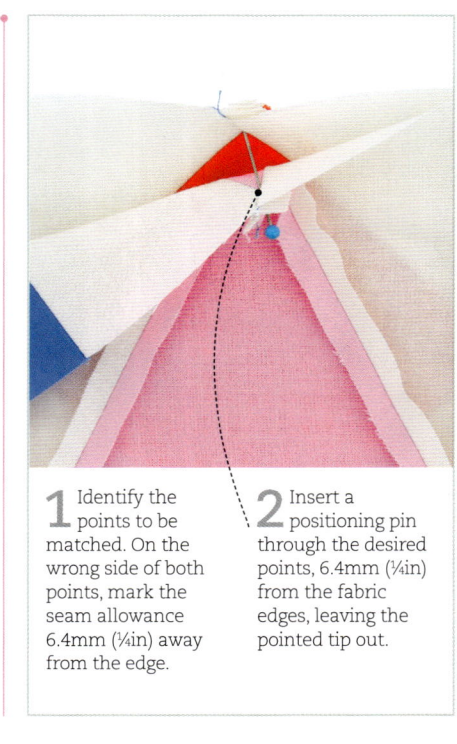

Pin at all seam intersections

1 Identify the points to be matched. On the wrong side of both points, mark the seam allowance 6.4mm (¼in) away from the edge.

2 Insert a positioning pin through the desired points, 6.4mm (¼in) from the fabric edges, leaving the pointed tip out.

3 Insert a pin on either side of the positioning pin, pushing the pointed tip down then back up to the surface, to secure the matched point.

4 Place pins, spaced every few inches, from the matched point out. For multiple points, match and pin all points, then pin along the remaining edges.

5 Sew, stitching through the seam intersections. Remove pins before reaching the needle.

6 Check matched points. If points are not aligned, seam rip (see p.79) and adjust.

GLUEING

Consider using washable glue (see p.29) in place of pins, especially when securing edges likely to stretch or shift, such as bias edges (see p.36) or long seams with many points.

Place a fine line of glue along one fabric edge, within the seam allowance. Apply glue at points or intersecting seams first, similar to pinning, then work outward toward the edges. Set the glue with a dry, hot iron or allow to dry naturally before sewing.

SEWING UNITS INTO BLOCKS

Quilt blocks are composed of pieces and units, such as HSTs or FG, which are traditionally assembled into rows, columns, or quadrants (see p.146). Take care to match points during block assembly.

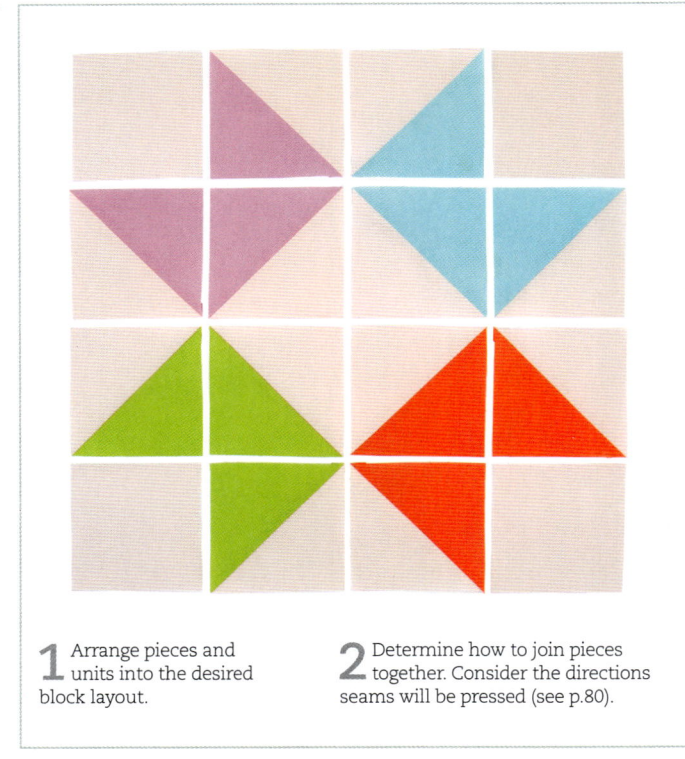

1 Arrange pieces and units into the desired block layout.

2 Determine how to join pieces together. Consider the directions seams will be pressed (see p.80).

3 Chain piece (see p.144) or use the piece-by-piece technique (see p.84) to join pieces to form into rows or columns.

Press seams in alternating directions to nest seams

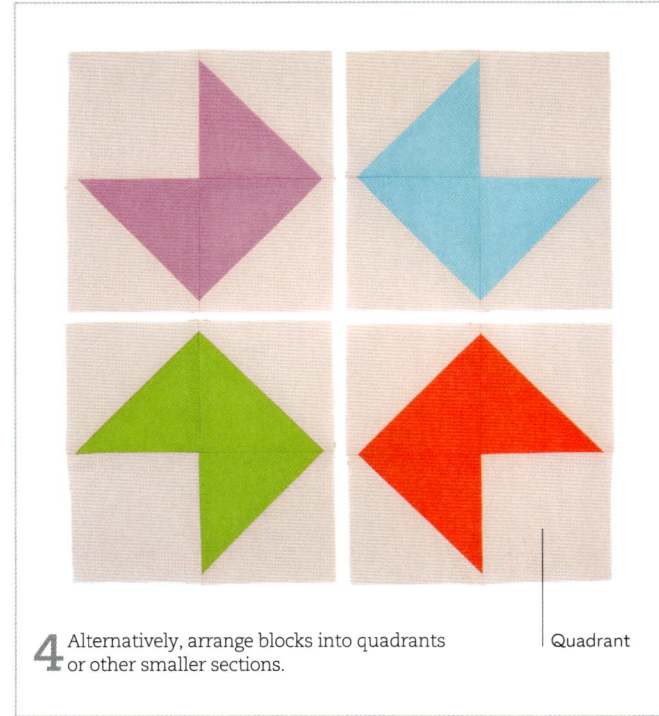

4 Alternatively, arrange blocks into quadrants or other smaller sections.

Quadrant

5 Join rows or sections into a complete block, pressing after each seam.

SASHING

Use sashing strips to separate or frame individual elements within a block or across a quilt, whether short strips between blocks or long strips between rows or columns. Sashing strips may be cut from a single piece of fabric or pieced from multiple fabrics to add to the overall quilt design.

SASHING BETWEEN BLOCKS

1. Cut sashing strips to the same length as the quilt blocks they will be added to.
2. Add sashing to one, two, or all four sides of each block for different effects.
3. Use sashing to increase the size of a quilt without adding or scaling (see p.59) blocks.

SASHING WITH CORNERSTONES

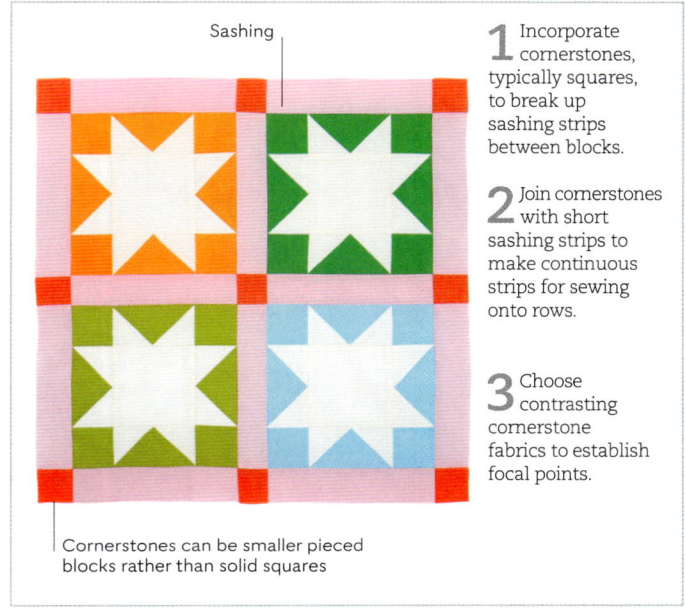

1. Incorporate cornerstones, typically squares, to break up sashing strips between blocks.
2. Join cornerstones with short sashing strips to make continuous strips for sewing onto rows.
3. Choose contrasting cornerstone fabrics to establish focal points.

Cornerstones can be smaller pieced blocks rather than solid squares

REGISTRATION LINES

Registration lines are small marks used to assist with alignment, often made within seam allowances, to align two pieces together. Mark registration lines along fabric edges to evenly align seams when joining pieces, units, or blocks.

1. Sew sashing to one row of blocks. Align sashing with an adjacent row, using a ruler to match seams across the sashing strip. Mark registration lines 3.2mm (⅛in) long within the seam allowance.

2. Align registration lines with seams RST and pin or glue in place. Place additional pins spaced evenly along the remaining sashing.

3. Sew the sashing and row together, checking that seams align across sashing. Seam rip (see p.79) and adjust as needed. Press toward the sashing.

Assembling a quilt top

Join quilt tops block by block, similar to the piece-by-piece technique (see p.84), or in a continuous chain for efficient piecing. Plan ahead to determine the quilt top assembly technique and layout based on the quilt top design.

CHAIN PIECING

Chain piecing, whether continuous or in a web, involves sewing pieces together in pairs without stopping to form a chain of units. Web piecing builds upon continuous piecing, joining all pieces into rows and columns, until all pieces are connected by a web of threads. These assembly style techniques save time and thread.

CONTINUOUS PIECING

1 Arrange pieces in pairs across two columns.

2 Sew the pieces in the first row RST. Instead of stopping after sewing a seam and snipping threads, feed the next pair of pieces, RST, under the foot and continue sewing.

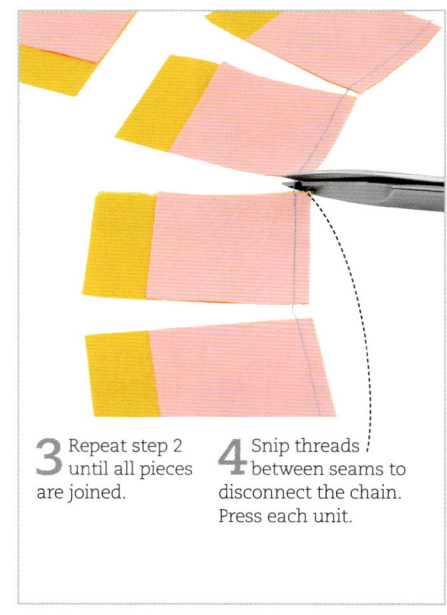

3 Repeat step 2 until all pieces are joined.

4 Snip threads between seams to disconnect the chain. Press each unit.

WEB PIECING

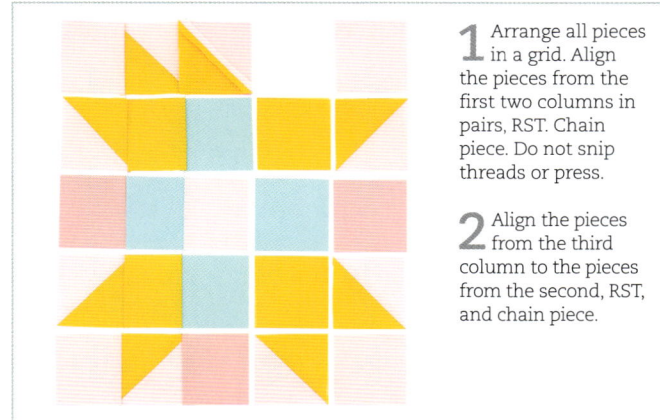

1 Arrange all pieces in a grid. Align the pieces from the first two columns in pairs, RST. Chain piece. Do not snip threads or press.

2 Align the pieces from the third column to the pieces from the second, RST, and chain piece.

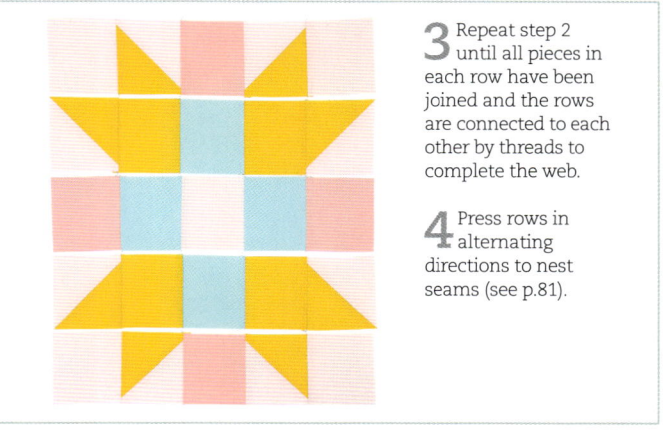

3 Repeat step 2 until all pieces in each row have been joined and the rows are connected to each other by threads to complete the web.

4 Press rows in alternating directions to nest seams (see p.81).

5 Without snipping threads, rotate the web 90 degrees and sew the first two columns RST, nesting the seams.

6 Repeat until all the columns are sewn and the block is complete. Press.

WEB PIECING WITH INTERFACING

1 Arrange all pieces right-side up in the desired layout on top of the fusible interfacing, with the fusible side up. Do not leave space between pieces. Press.

2 Fold the first column of pieces RST with the second column.

3 Sew along the fold using a 6.4mm (¼in) seam allowance. Repeat for all columns.

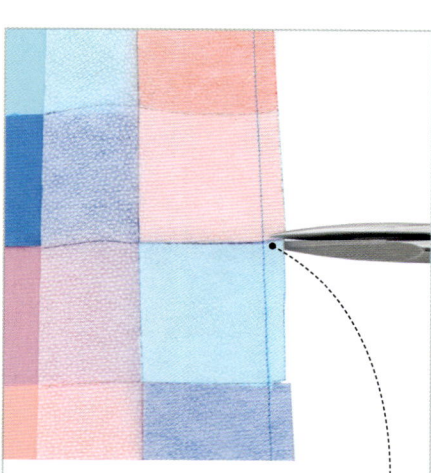

4 Clip the seam allowance at each seam intersection. Do not clip into or past the stitches.

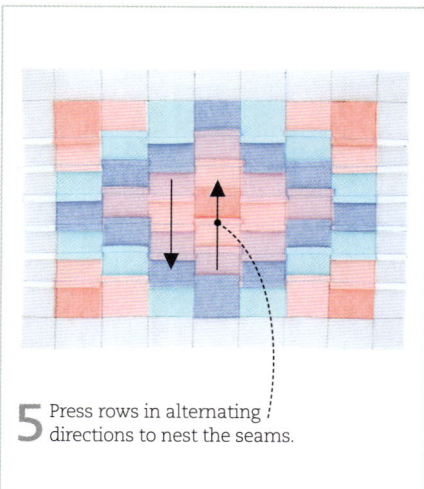

5 Press rows in alternating directions to nest the seams.

6 Repeat steps 2–4, folding the unsewn rows RST, sewing, then clipping the seam intersections to complete the block. Press.

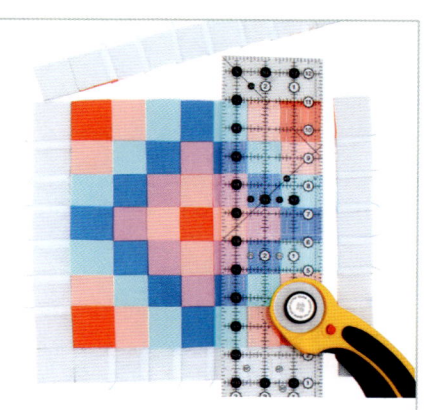

7 Trim the excess interfacing around the outside edges of the completed block.

QUILT TOP LAYOUTS

Quilts can be assembled in any way that pieces and blocks fit together. The following are eight common quilt top layouts that can be mixed and matched depending on block shape, quilt design, and assembly preferences.

ROWS AND COLUMNS

Assemble pieces, units, or blocks into rows or columns to make a quilt top. Chain piece (see p.144) for efficiency and press seams in alternating directions to nest (see p.81).

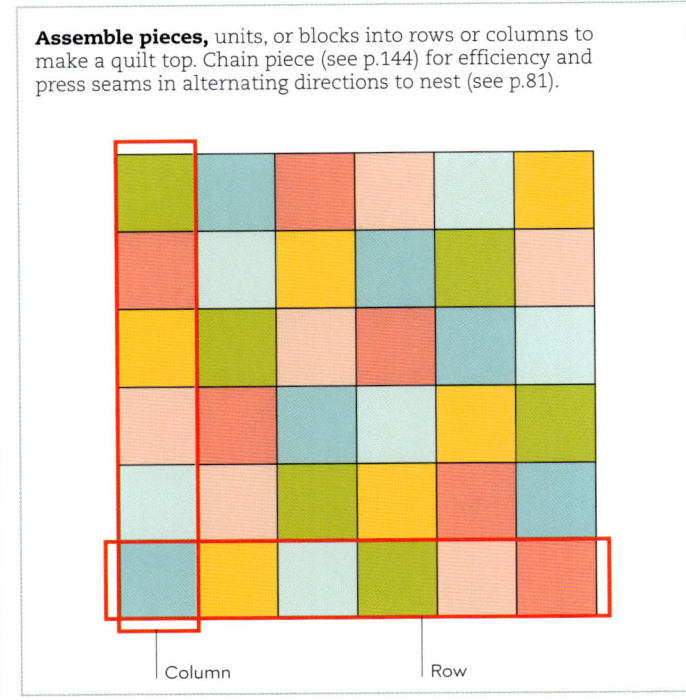

Column | Row

SASHING

Sashing may be short, such as when used between blocks, or long, such as when used between rows or columns. Add cornerstones (see p.143) between sashing strips to create secondary designs.

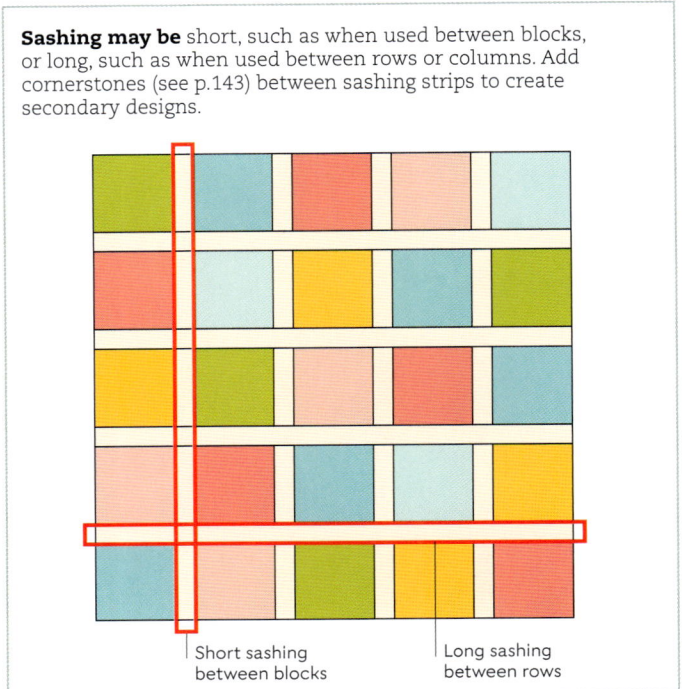

Short sashing between blocks | Long sashing between rows

QUADRANTS

Assemble pieces, units, or blocks into four large sections, or quadrants. Often, the same quadrant is repeated, with each quadrant rotated around the centre to form a larger design.

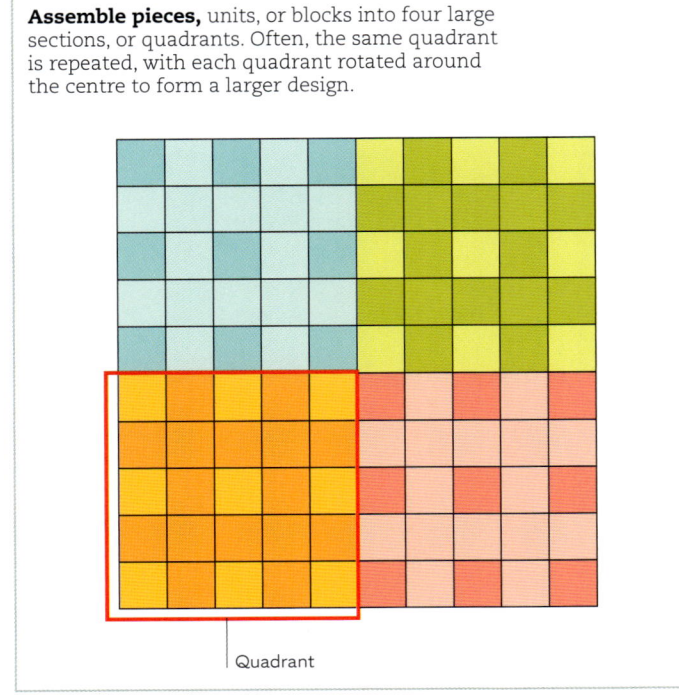

Quadrant

ON POINT

Assemble pieces, units, or blocks at a 45-degree angle, or on point. Setting triangles (see p.95) must be added to fill the outer edges. Sew a stay stitch (see p.151) 3.2mm (⅛in) inside the perimeter of the quilt top to secure the bias edges.

Place pieces at a 45-degree angle | Setting triangle

BORDERS

Add borders to any quilt top to frame the design or increase the quilt size without scaling (see p.59). Use multiple borders for a layered, dimensional effect.

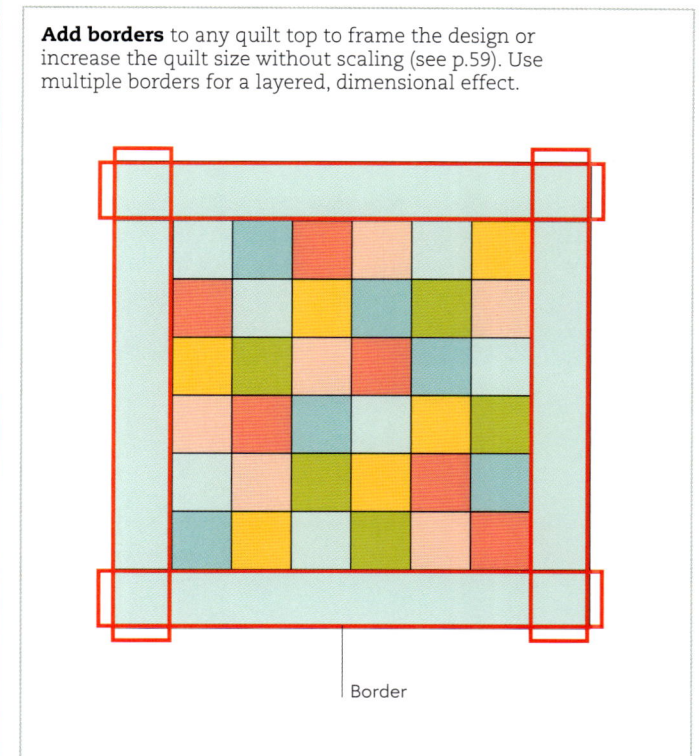

Border

MEDALLION

Medallion quilts are assembled using a log cabin piecing technique (see p.85). Begin with a central block and work outward, adding one "round" of blocks at a time.

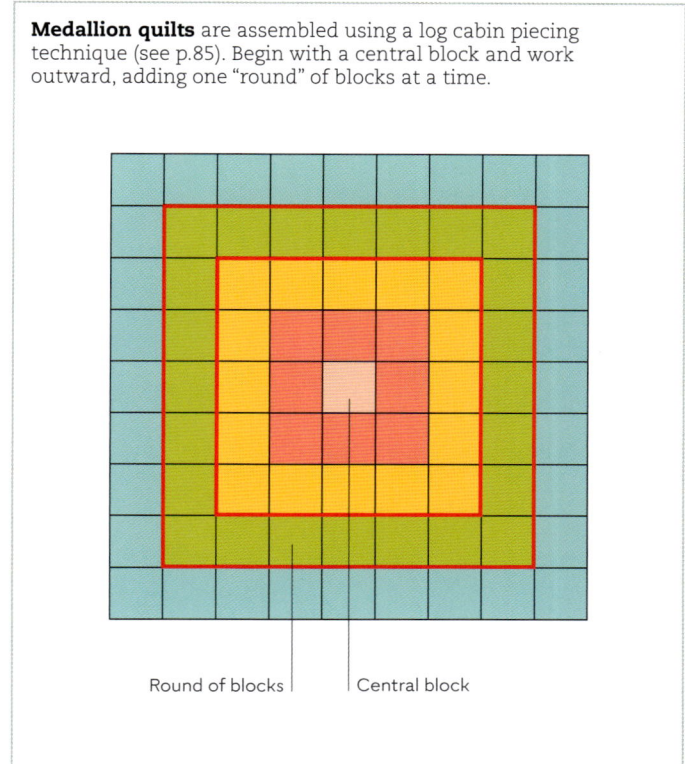

Round of blocks | Central block

IMPROV

Improv quilts use an organic, non-traditional assembly process. Use a straight- or wavy-edge improv technique to join pieces or blocks as they fit together, trimming as needed to remove excess fabric. Improv layouts may require Y-seams.

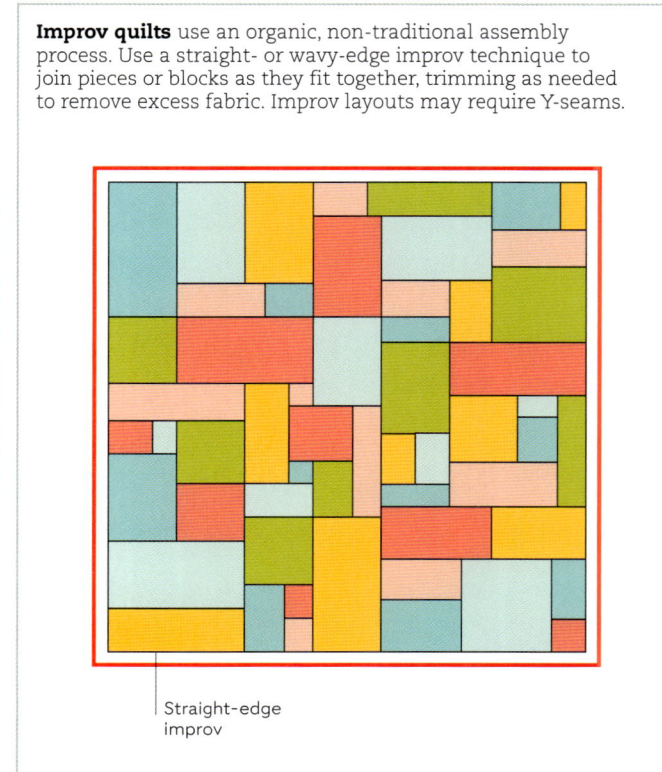

Straight-edge improv

APPLIQUÉ

Appliqué shapes onto individual blocks or a wholecloth background using any appliqué technique (see p.134). Shapes can be arranged in any layout to produce the desired design.

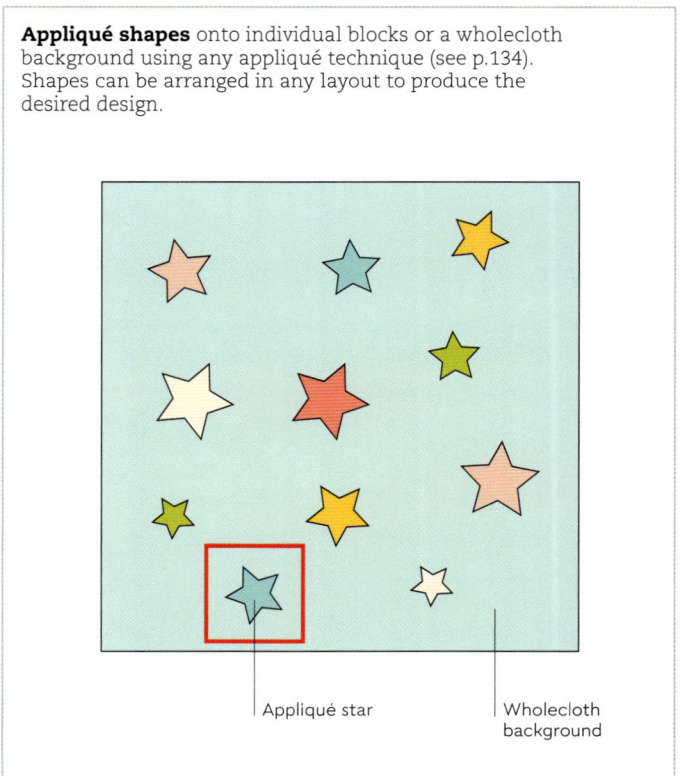

Appliqué star | Wholecloth background

FINISHING

Assembling a quilt sandwich

A quilt sandwich is made up of three layers: a quilt top, wadding, and backing. The layers of the sandwich are first prepared, then basted together using pins, adhesive, or thread to prevent shifting or puckering during the quilting process. Before assembling a quilt sandwich, refer to wadding (see p.42) for guidance on selecting the appropriate type for your project and quilt maths (see p.54) to calculate the required backing amounts.

Preparing a quilt top

Before layering a quilt sandwich, prepare the quilt top by pressing, stay stitching, and trimming loose threads. If a quilt top was assembled using EPP (see p.124) or FPP (see p.114), remove all papers before preparing.

PRESSING, STAY STITCHING, AND TRIMMING THREADS

Press the quilt top from the front and back, add a stay stitch, and trim loose threads from the back of the quilt top.

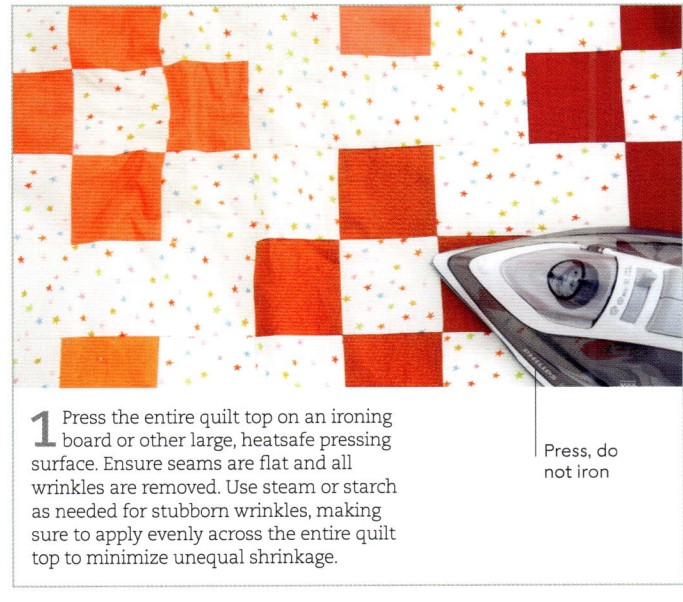

1 Press the entire quilt top on an ironing board or other large, heatsafe pressing surface. Ensure seams are flat and all wrinkles are removed. Use steam or starch as needed for stubborn wrinkles, making sure to apply evenly across the entire quilt top to minimize unequal shrinkage.

Press, do not iron

2 Sew around the perimeter of the quilt top, 3.2mm (⅛in) from the edge, using a piecing or quilting stitch length (see p.72) to make a stay stitch. This secures seams that intersect the quilt edge and prevents bias edges from stretching.

Stay stitch

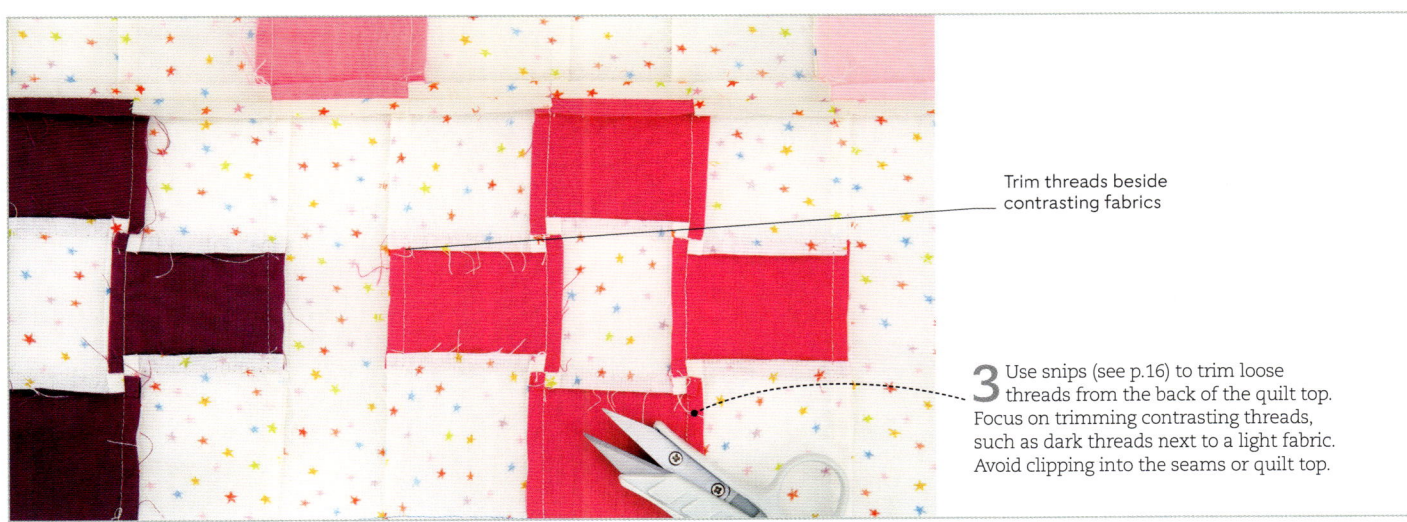

Trim threads beside contrasting fabrics

3 Use snips (see p.16) to trim loose threads from the back of the quilt top. Focus on trimming contrasting threads, such as dark threads next to a light fabric. Avoid clipping into the seams or quilt top.

Preparing wadding and backing

Before assembling a quilt sandwich, measure the quilt top and determine the required wadding and backing sizes. Wadding should be at least 10.2cm (4in) larger than the quilt top in both width and length to account for overage, while backing should be at least 15.2cm (6in) larger.

PIECING WADDING

Join wadding pieces of the same type to make wadding pieces larger, such as when using scrap wadding. Square the wadding edges (see p.67) before piecing, and join the pieces with the same side facing up.

ZIGZAG STITCH

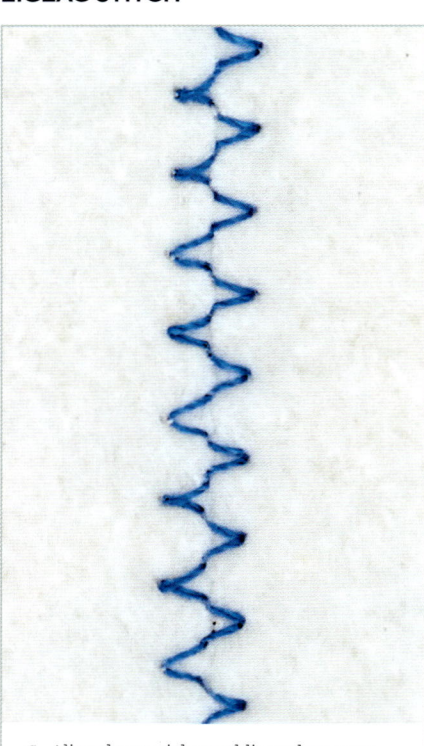

1 Align the straight wadding edges next to each other without any overlap.

2 Sew a large zigzag stitch using a neutral thread to join the wadding pieces. This technique works best for low to medium loft wadding.

FUSIBLE INTERFACING

1 Align the straight wadding edges next to each other without any overlap.

2 Place a 3.8cm (1½in) strip of fusible interfacing over the aligned edges and press according to the interfacing and wadding instructions. This technique works best for waddings that can withstand heat.

WHIPSTITCH

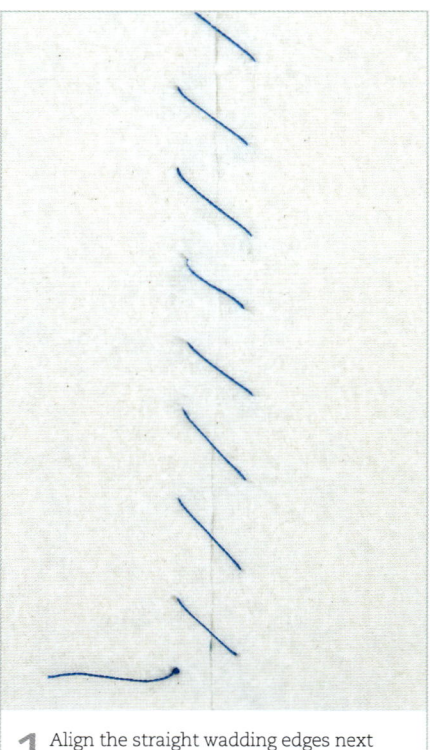

1 Align the straight wadding edges next to each other without any overlap.

2 Sew a whipstitch (see p.130) with a neutral thread, being careful to keep the joined seam flat. This technique works for all wadding types and is recommended for high loft waddings.

QUILT BACKING

Quilt backings must be pieced for quilts wider than 91cm (36in), unless using a wide back fabric (see p.40). Determine the required backing size (see p.290), then consider the number of seams and seam placement. Consider pattern matching (see p.154) the backing fabric for a seamless look or piecing a patchwork-style backing to use scraps or smaller cuts of fabric. Use a 1.3cm (½in) seam allowance to piece backing fabrics.

SEAM PLACEMENT

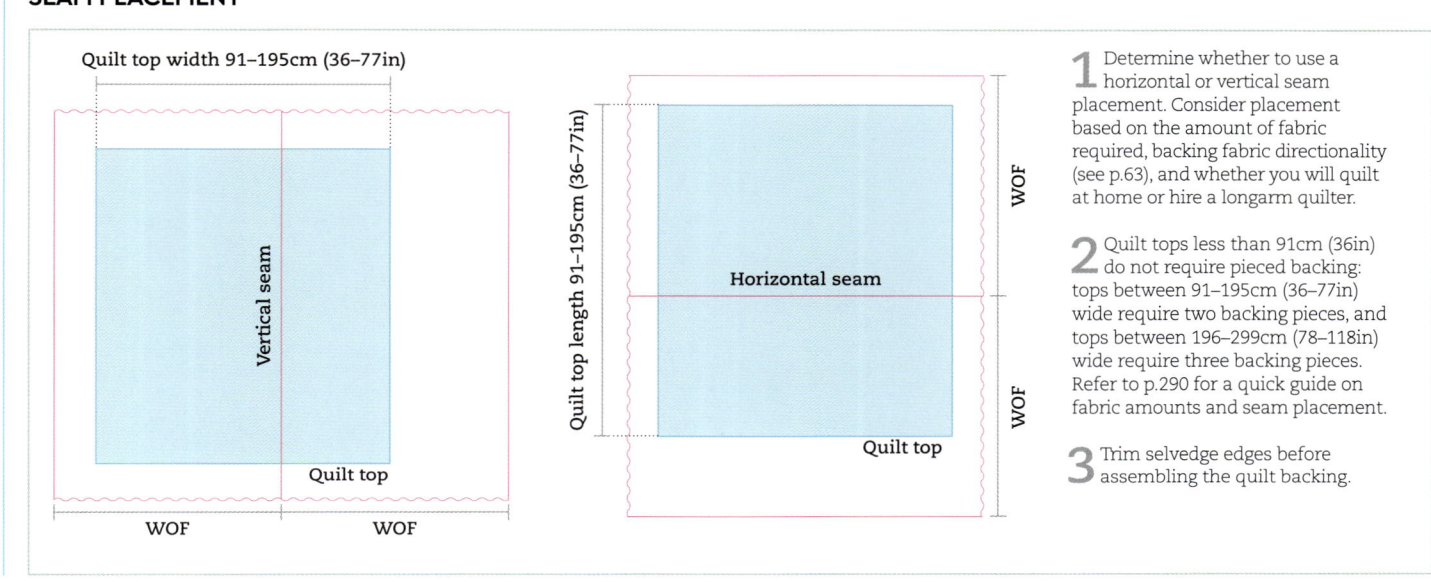

1. Determine whether to use a horizontal or vertical seam placement. Consider placement based on the amount of fabric required, backing fabric directionality (see p.63), and whether you will quilt at home or hire a longarm quilter.

2. Quilt tops less than 91cm (36in) do not require pieced backing: tops between 91–195cm (36–77in) wide require two backing pieces, and tops between 196–299cm (78–118in) wide require three backing pieces. Refer to p.290 for a quick guide on fabric amounts and seam placement.

3. Trim selvedge edges before assembling the quilt backing.

PATCHWORK BACKING

1. Determine the required quilt backing size, making sure to account for overage.

2. Make a patchwork backing to utilize scraps or increase the size of a quilt backing without purchasing more yardage or meterage.

3. Use any combination of piecing techniques (see pp.82–145) and assembly layouts (see p.146) to make the required quilt backing size.

4. Experiment with techniques you may not typically use, such as improv piecing (see p.108).

PATTERN MATCHING

When joining backing pieces of the same printed fabric, consider matching the designs and motifs to produce a seamless look. Due to varying pattern scale and repeat distances (see p.62), more backing fabric may be needed than calculated (see p.57).

1 Trim the selvedge edges from all backing fabric pieces, keeping cuts straight and square (see p.67).

2 On the wrong side of one backing piece, mark two lines 1.3cm (½in) and 2.5cm (1in) from the edge to be joined.

3 Fold the fabric WST along the 1.3cm (½in) marked line to align the fabric edge with the 2.5cm (1in) marked line to make a hem. Press.

4 Place the hemmed piece on the non-hemmed piece, both right-side up. Position the hemmed edge so the printed pattern repeats and continues across both pieces.

5 Apply a thin line of glue on the underside of the hemmed edge, then reposition the hem, keeping the pattern aligned. Press to set the glue.

6 Open the hemmed backing piece to be RST with the other, exposing the marked lines. Align the needle with the 1.3cm (½in) marked line, and sew. Check that the pattern is matched; seam rip (see p.79) and adjust as necessary.

7 Trim excess backing fabric 1.3cm (½in) away from the seam.

Stitched seam line

8 Press the seam open, flip the backing, and press again from the right side.

Pattern matches along seam

ENVELOPE BACKING

Turn any small quilt into a removable pillow cover by using an envelope-style backing (see Quilts to go, p.256). Finish the edges of two backing pieces by making a hem, attach the hemmed pieces to a quilted pillow front, and bind the raw edges. The hem placement may vary by pillow shape.

1. Measure the pillow front. Divide the length in half, then add 12.7cm (5in) to determine the length of each backing piece. The backing piece width matches the pillow front width.

2. Cut two backing pieces using the measurements from step 1.

3. Fold the long edge of one backing piece 1.3cm (½in), WST, and press. Fold 1.3cm (½in) again and press, creating a hem. Repeat on the remaining backing piece. Stitch 3.2mm (⅛in) from the folded edges to secure the hems.

4. Place the pillow front and both envelope backing pieces WST, aligning the outside edges and overlapping the hems at the centre.

5. Place clips (see p.78) around the edges of the layered pieces, then sew 3.2mm (⅛in) inside the perimeter to secure the pieces.

6. Bind as desired (see p.172).

SQUARING UP BACKING

After assembling the quilt backing, square all edges to remove excess fabric and make basting and quilting more manageable.

1. Fold the pieced backing in half horizontally, then in half horizontally again.

2. Square both raw edges (see p.67), then unfold.

3. Fold the backing in half vertically, then in half vertically again, and square both raw edges.

Layering

The three layers of a quilt are referred to as the "quilt sandwich." Gather the quilt top, wadding, and backing, and ensure the wadding and backing extend beyond all quilt top edges. Review the wadding manufacturer's guidelines to find wrinkle removal and preparation instructions.

MAKING A QUILT SANDWICH

Use a large, flat surface when layering a quilt sandwich. Place layers WST so the right side of the quilt top and backing will remain visible.

1 Place the backing right-side down on a large surface, then secure the backing edges to the surface using masking tape (see p.23).

2 Start at the centre of each side and work outward to the corners, smoothing wrinkles as you go. If working on a carpeted surface, use curved safety pins (see p.29) rather than tape.

3 Centre wadding on top of the secured backing. Smooth the wadding carefully to avoid disturbing the backing.

4 If using a needle punched wadding or wadding with scrim (see p.42), ensure the correct side is facing up.

5 Position the quilt top right-side up on top of the wadding. Check the orientation of the quilt top in relation to the directionality of the backing as needed.

6 Be sure both wadding and backing extend beyond the edges of the quilt top on all four sides. Check for stray threads showing through the quilt top; lift the quilt top and remove threads as needed.

Basting

After layering a quilt sandwich, basting is necessary before moving on to quilting (see p.160). Basting temporarily secures all three layers of the quilt sandwich to prevent shifting and can be done using pins, glue, thread, or fusible wadding.

USING PINS

Speciality curved safety pins (see p.29), are effective for short- and long-term hand or domestic machine quilting projects. Consider placing a cutting mat under the quilt sandwich while pinning to avoid scratching surfaces.

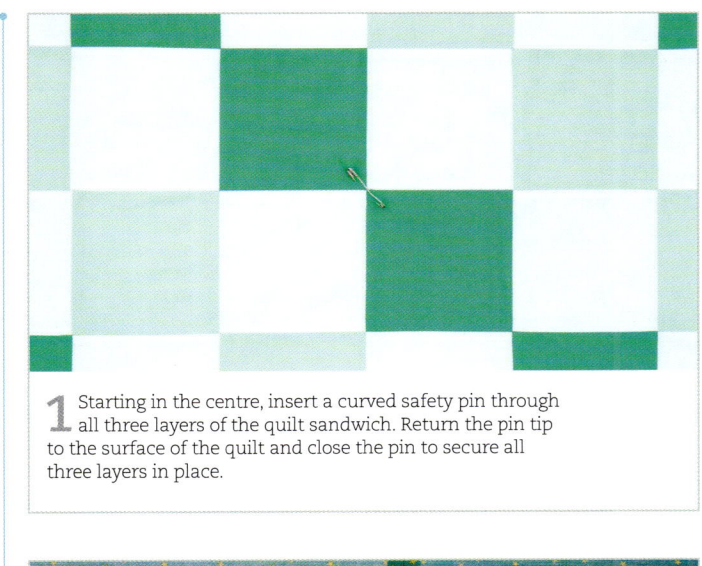

1 Starting in the centre, insert a curved safety pin through all three layers of the quilt sandwich. Return the pin tip to the surface of the quilt and close the pin to secure all three layers in place.

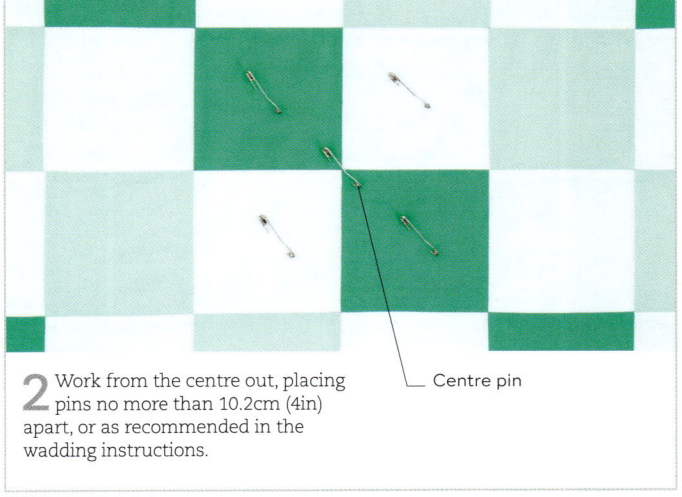

2 Work from the centre out, placing pins no more than 10.2cm (4in) apart, or as recommended in the wadding instructions.

Centre pin

3 Continue pinning out to the edges, working in a grid-like pattern.

Centre pin

4 Pin along the perimeter of the quilt top to ensure that the outside edges stay secured.

USING SPRAY ADHESIVE

Spray adhesive may save time and is appropriate for domestic machine and hand quilting. Glue using a spray designed for fabric, following the manufacturer's instructions. Work in a well-ventilated area, protect surfaces with a drop cloth, and clean up overspray.

1 After layering to ensure proper wadding and backing overage, set the quilt top aside.

2 Fold the wadding back to expose a quarter of the backing, then fold the wadding in half again, exposing approximately half of the backing.

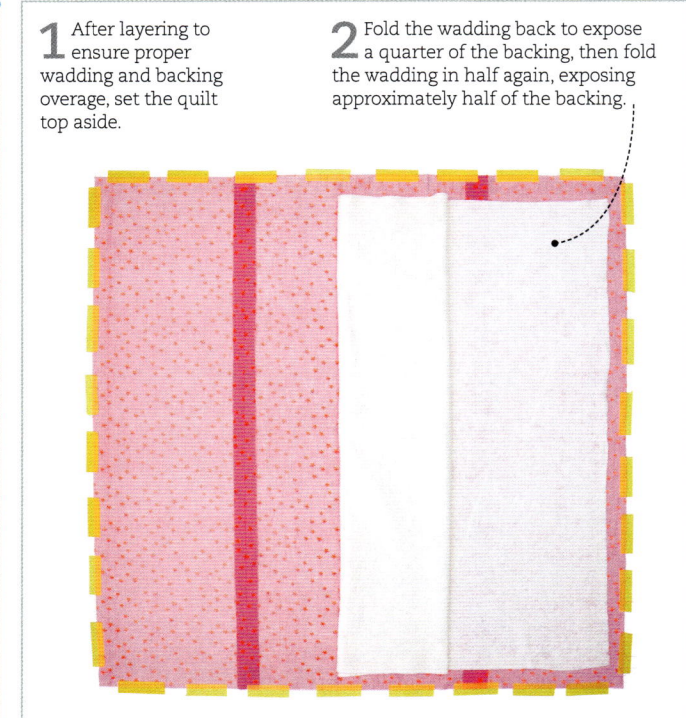

3 Spray a light, even layer on the folded wadding; avoid spraying directly on backing. Unfold the sprayed wadding back onto the quilt backing and smooth.

4 Repeat on the remaining folded wadding to adhere the first wadding half to the backing. Repeat steps 2–4 to secure the remaining wadding to the backing.

5 Return the quilt top to the wadding and repeat steps 2–4 with the quilt top.

6 Secure the entire quilt top to the wadding, repositioning as needed to avoid creating any wrinkles.

7 If the wadding can withstand heat, press with a dry iron to set the spray adhesive.

USING THREAD

Make running stitches (see p.122) using a large needle (see p.28) and contrasting thread to secure the layers of a quilt sandwich. Thread basting is ideal for long-term hand quilting projects.

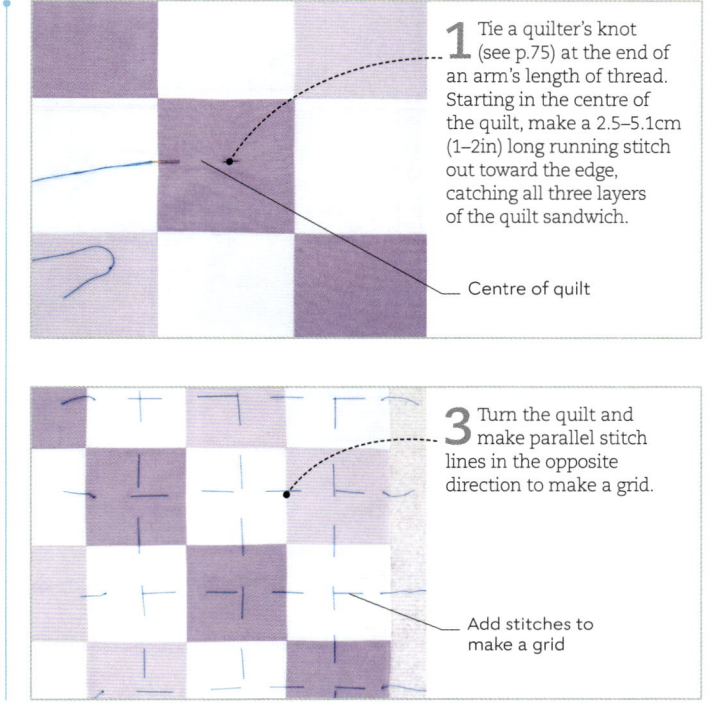

1 Tie a quilter's knot (see p.75) at the end of an arm's length of thread. Starting in the centre of the quilt, make a 2.5–5.1cm (1–2in) long running stitch out toward the edge, catching all three layers of the quilt sandwich.

Centre of quilt

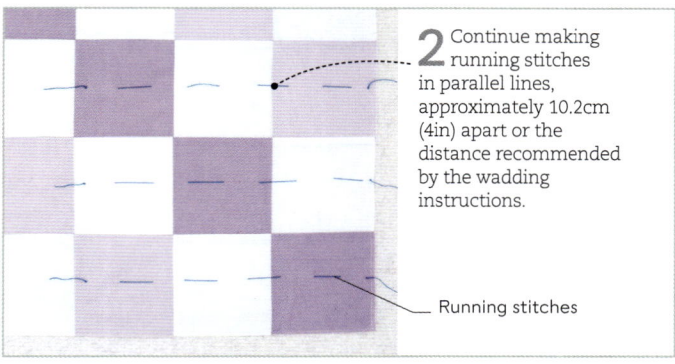

2 Continue making running stitches in parallel lines, approximately 10.2cm (4in) apart or the distance recommended by the wadding instructions.

Running stitches

3 Turn the quilt and make parallel stitch lines in the opposite direction to make a grid.

Add stitches to make a grid

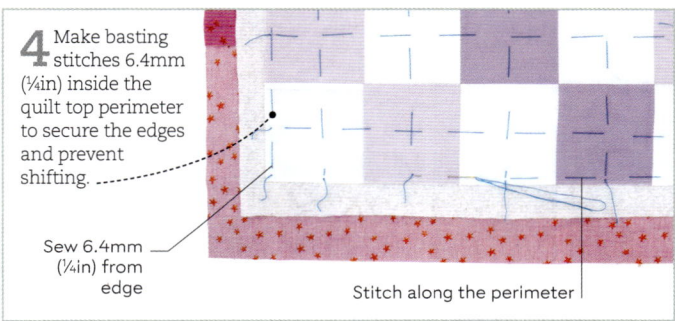

4 Make basting stitches 6.4mm (¼in) inside the quilt top perimeter to secure the edges and prevent shifting.

Sew 6.4mm (¼in) from edge

Stitch along the perimeter

USING FUSIBLE WADDING

Fusible wadding, which has a thin layer of heat-activated glue on each side, is best for smaller domestic machine quilting projects.

1 Starting in the centre of a quilt sandwich, press the quilt top to the wadding to activate the adhesive.

2 Press the entire quilt top to the wadding, working from the centre out to the edges.

3 Flip the quilt sandwich so the backing is right-side up. Repeat.

REMOVING BASTING

All basting is temporary and can be removed during or after the quilting process.

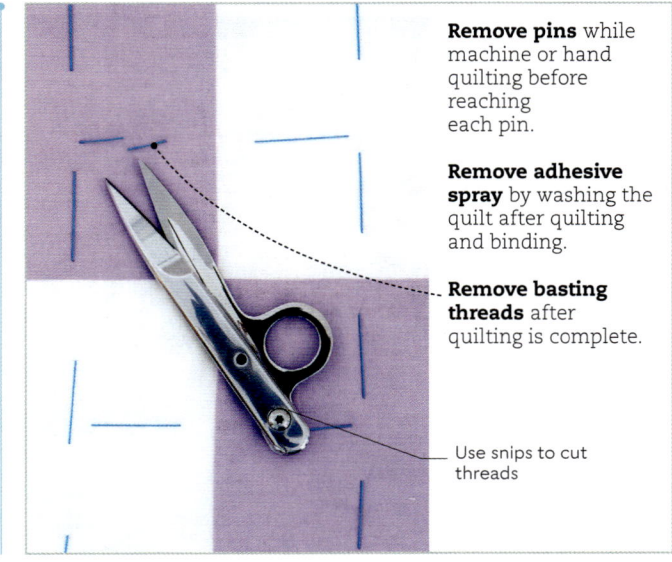

Remove pins while machine or hand quilting before reaching each pin.

Remove adhesive spray by washing the quilt after quilting and binding.

Remove basting threads after quilting is complete.

Use snips to cut threads

Quilting

Quilting involves stitching through the three layers of a quilt – quilt top, wadding, and backing – following a specific pattern or design. This stitching secures the layers together while adding texture that typically complements or contrasts the quilt design. Quilting can be done using a domestic or longarm machine (see pp.30–33) or by hand.

Preparing for quilting

Assemble and baste (see p.157) a quilt sandwich, then choose a quilting method and design. Mark quilting lines as needed to use as a guide while quilting. Consider how thread colour and weight (see p.26) will enhance a design or allow it to blend into the quilt top.

CHOOSE A QUILTING METHOD

Various quilting methods can be used to produce different effects: choose an all-over, edge-to-edge design or stitch intentionally in specific areas to highlight certain aspects of the quilt top design. Determine the desired quilting effect, drawing focus to particular areas, or blending into the background so the quilt top design can stand out.

WALKING FOOT

Walking foot quilting, done using a domestic machine, is appropriate for creating linear geometric designs, such as straight lines, standard or diagonal grids, and point-to-point quilting (see p.164). A walking foot can also be used to quilt gentle curved lines.

FREE MOTION AND RULER WORK

Free motion quilting is guided by hand, and ruler work quilting is guided by hand using speciality rulers. Free motion quilting is used to create shapes, such as meandering lines or flowers. Ruler work quilting is used to highlight certain areas or to create an all-over design.

Free motion
Ruler work

LONGARM QUILTING

Longarm machine quilting often uses computerized designs, called pantographs, that repeat across the entire quilt. Pantographs are available in a variety of designs suitable for any quilt, from geometric linear designs to organic floral or leaf-inspired motifs, to whimsical or novelty shapes.

HAND QUILTING

Hand quilting is accomplished using a needle and thread and can add character to a quilt for a more "handmade" effect. Make quilting stitches by hand to produce any quilting design, most commonly all-over motifs or echo quilting to highlight pieced shapes.

MARKING QUILTING LINES

Mark quilt tops with guidelines or registration lines (see p.143) to assist with achieving a desired quilting motif. Choose a non-permanent marking tool suitable for the fabrics used in the quilt top to draw freehand motifs or use rulers or stencils to mark specific designs.

MARKING TOOLS

A hera marker produces creased lines that do not require removal. Use a hera marker to mark straight or curved lines when working with solid or blender fabrics, as the creased lines may be difficult to see within busy prints.

Water-/air-soluble pens allow for precise markings that disappear with water or over time with air. Use these pens when connecting point-to-point markings or detailed quilting motifs. Test removal on scraps of fabric before use.

Chalk provides a temporary mark that brushes off easily. Use chalk when sketching out ideas for quilting lines, using stencils, working with dark fabrics, or for smaller quilting projects that do not require a lot of handling.

Masking tape can be used to avoid making marks on fabrics. Place masking tape directly on the quilt top and use the edge as a guide to stitch along for straight line quilting.

PREPARING FOR QUILTING **163**

USING RULERS

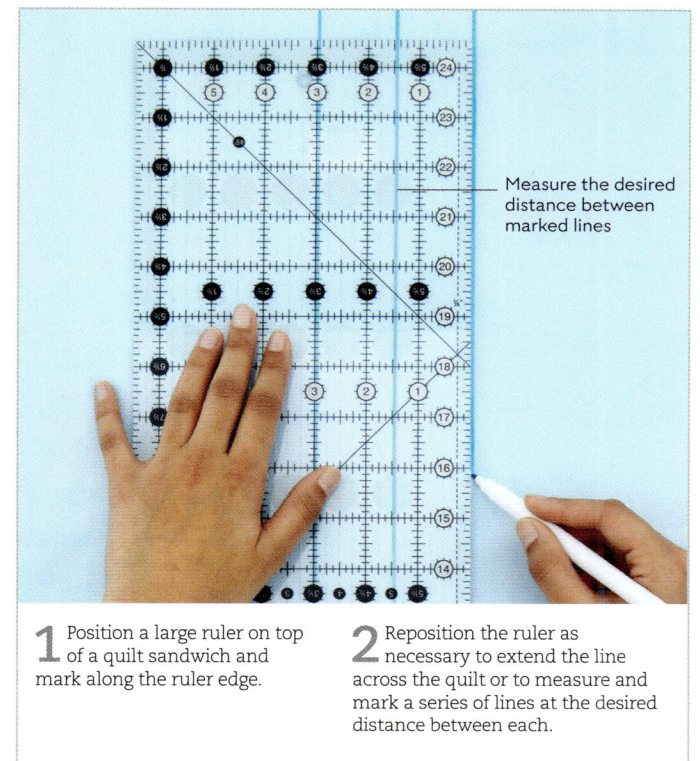
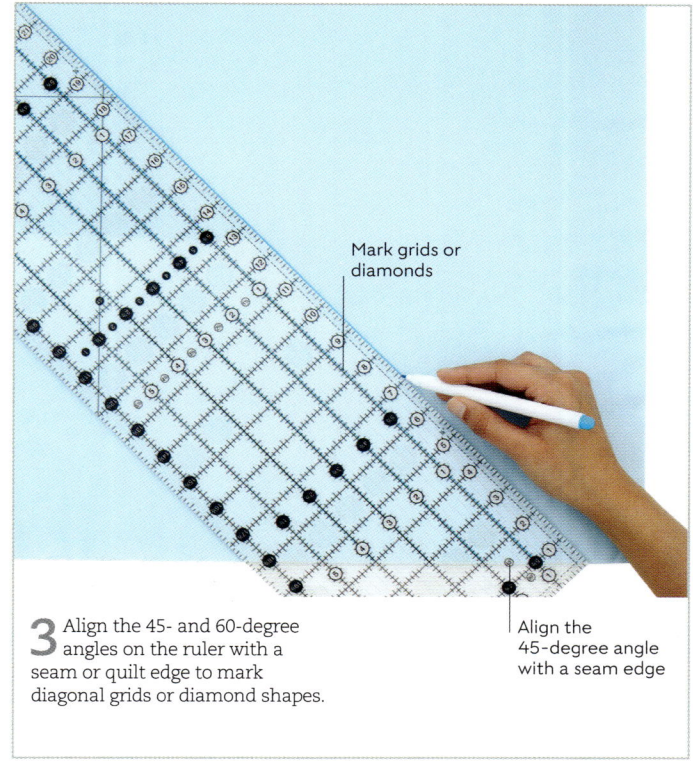

Measure the desired distance between marked lines

Mark grids or diamonds

Align the 45-degree angle with a seam edge

1 Position a large ruler on top of a quilt sandwich and mark along the ruler edge.

2 Reposition the ruler as necessary to extend the line across the quilt or to measure and mark a series of lines at the desired distance between each.

3 Align the 45- and 60-degree angles on the ruler with a seam or quilt edge to mark diagonal grids or diamond shapes.

USING STENCILS

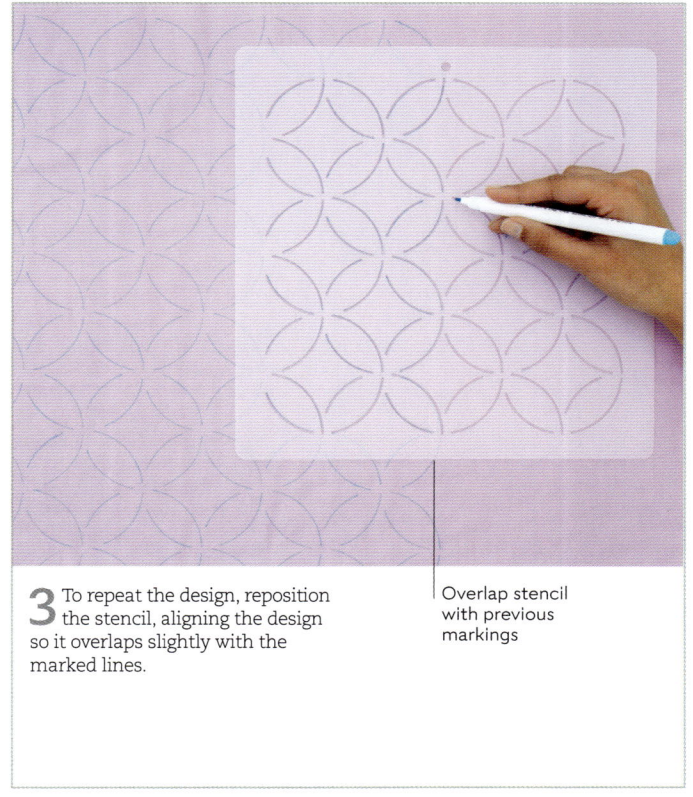

Overlap stencil with previous markings

1 Position a stencil on a quilt in the desired location, holding or taping the stencil in place so it does not shift while marking.

2 Trace the stencil motif using a water-soluble pen or chalk.

3 To repeat the design, reposition the stencil, aligning the design so it overlaps slightly with the marked lines.

Machine quilting

Machine quilting produces stitches able to withstand regular use and washing. Use walking foot, free motion, or ruler work quilting to achieve a variety of designs and textures. Mark guidelines before beginning to keep lines consistent.

WALKING FOOT QUILTING

The most common type of quilting is walking foot quilting, which is used to quilt straight or gently curved lines. A walking foot features upper feed dogs, which "walk" over the quilt top and work in tandem with the machine's lower feed dogs to guide the quilt layers evenly under the needle.

PREPARING FOR WALKING FOOT QUILTING

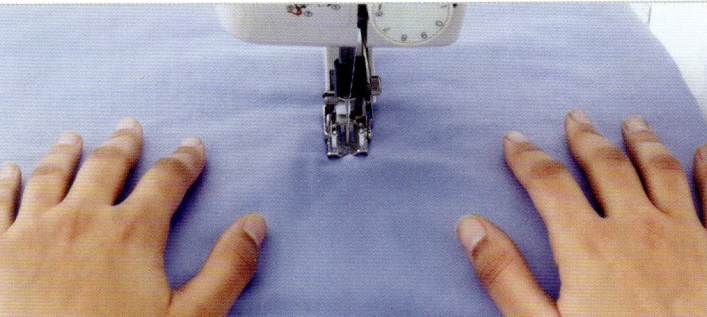

1 Attach a walking foot to your sewing machine and reference your manual for proper settings. Make a practice quilt sandwich using wadding and fabric scraps to test speed, stitch length, and tension (see p.72). Stitch slowly and use a 3.0–4.0mm stitch length to minimize puckering and ensure the quilt feeds evenly.

2 Position hands 15–20cm (6–8in) apart on either side of the walking foot. Allow the walking foot to feed the quilt under the needle while using your hands to guide the quilt forward. Stop with the needle down to reposition hands and adjust the bulk of the quilt as needed.

USING GUIDES

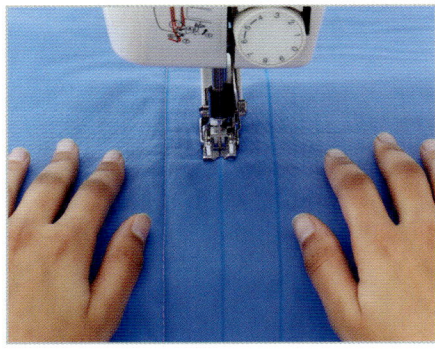

Marked lines Align the needle directly on each marked guideline. Stitch on the marked line, keeping your eyes focused on the guideline in front of the needle.

Guide foot Attach a guide bar to your walking foot so the bar is the desired distance from the needle. Stitch the first line of quilting. Align the guide bar with the quilting line, then stitch across the quilt.

QUILTING FROM POINT-TO-POINT

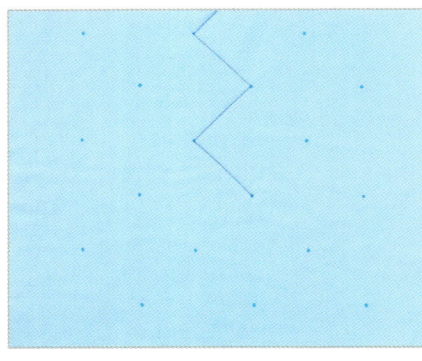

1 Point-to-point quilting is achieved by stitching between two reference points, whether marked points or seam intersections, with straight or gently curved lines. Determine the desired design and mark reference points, measuring as needed.

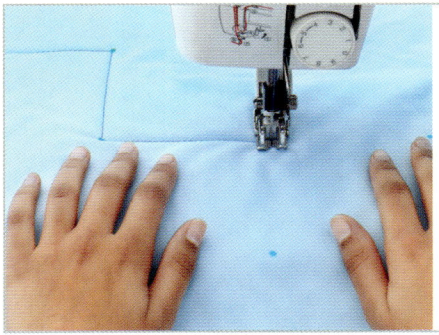

2 Begin stitching at one reference point and slowly quilt toward the next, focusing on the upcoming point rather than the needle. Stop with the needle down at the second point, lift the foot, then pivot the quilt to continue.

WALKING FOOT DESIGNS

Straight lines: Mark a guideline to use for quilting the first line, then begin quilting in the centre of one quilt edge. Stitch across the quilt, stopping to reposition the quilt and your hands as necessary. To quilt subsequent lines, return to the initial quilt edge. Stitch across the quilt, using marked lines, the walking foot edge, or a guide bar to ensure even spacing.

Grid: To quilt a grid design, stitch a set of parallel lines across the quilt. Rotate the quilt 90 degrees and quilt another set of parallel lines. Some machines have decorative quilting stitches, such as multipoint zigzag or serpentine stitches, that can be quilted along straight lines.

Curves: Quilt all-over curves by marking a centre guideline curve across the quilt. Common designs include equidistant curvy lines or arced shapes. Quilt slowly along each marked guideline, starting in the centre as you would with straight lines, stopping with the needle down to reposition as necessary.

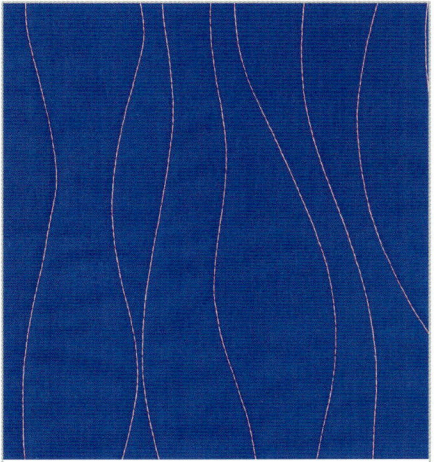

Organic lines: To quilt organic wavy lines, mark a centre guideline. Slowly move the quilt side to side under the needle to quilt gentle curves, varying the distance and depth of each curved line. Continue adding wavy lines to produce the desired density.

Point-to-point quilting: Follow the steps from the quilting from point-to-point technique (see opposite). Mark reference points across the entire quilt top to guide quilting an all-over design. Mark points within certain areas, such as a pieced shape, or use seam intersections as reference points. Experiment with connecting different points to produce various quilting designs.

Echo quilting: Quilt a line equidistant from a pieced shape or a quilted motif to make an echo, using a marked line, walking foot edge, or guide bar to assist with maintaining equal spacing. Echo quilting can be straight or curved, within or outside of a shape. Continue adding evenly spaced echo quilting lines around the shape as desired.

FREE MOTION QUILTING

When free motion quilting (FMQ), disengage all feed dogs to allow you to move the quilt sandwich freely under the needle. The needle moves directly up and down as you guide the quilt to make stitches, creating designs consisting of curves, loops, and echoes (see p.165). Begin with a simple design, such as a meander, to learn the speed at which to move your hands and the quilt, then graduate to more involved designs such as feathers.

PREPARING FOR FMQ

1 Attach a FMQ foot (see p.32), sometimes called a darning foot, to your sewing machine. Disengage the lower feed dogs and set stitch length to zero (see p.72) or refer to your manual instructions.

2 Make a practice quilt sandwich (see p.156) using wadding and fabric scraps to test the machine speed, hand movement speed, and tension. Position hands 15–20cm (6–8in) apart on either side of the FMQ foot. Use your hands to move the quilt, and stop with the needle down to reposition hands and adjust the bulk of the quilt as needed.

CREATING DESIGNS

1 Position the centre of the quilt or quilt edge under the needle.

2 Begin stitching at a steady speed while applying even pressure with your hands to gently move the quilt.

3 Practise moving smoothly and with control, experimenting with different speeds to produce even stitches.

4 Incorporate curves, loops, and echoes to produce your desired design.

RULER WORK QUILTING

Use quilting rulers (see p.19), designed specifically to use alongside a ruler foot (see p.32). Similar to FMQ, ensure all feed dogs are disengaged and move the quilt sandwich while ruler work quilting.

PREPARING FOR RULER WORK

1 Attach a ruler foot to your sewing machine. Be sure the ruler foot wall and quilting ruler are at least 6.4mm (¼in) tall. Disengage the lower feed dogs and set stitch length to zero or refer to your manual instructions. Make a practice quilt sandwich using wadding and fabric scraps to test the machine speed, hand movement speed, and tension.

2 Position one hand firmly on top of the ruler and the other on the quilt. Move the quilt using your hands, and stop with the needle down to reposition hands and adjust the bulk of the quilt as needed.

USING QUILTING RULERS

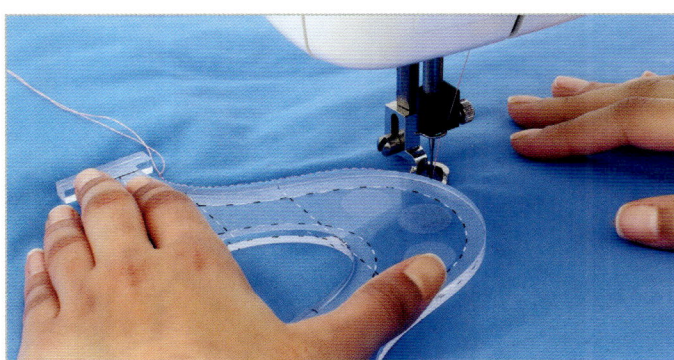

1 Position the centre of the quilt or quilt edge under the needle and place the ruler against the wall of the ruler foot. Mark reference points as needed to assist with ruler position.

2 Begin stitching at a steady speed, moving the quilt and ruler as one and guiding the ruler foot wall to trace the shape of the ruler.

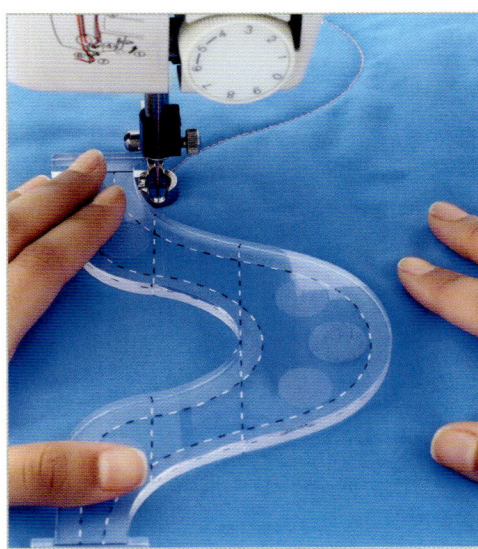

3 Some rulers include stopping points and alignment guidelines to help with repositioning.

4 After tracing the entire ruler shape, stop with the needle down, then pick up and reposition the ruler to the starting point, aligning with previous quilting.

5 Practise moving smoothly and with control, experimenting with different speeds to produce even stitches. Always keep the ruler edge against the ruler foot.

Ruler work quilting

Hand quilting

Hand quilting is the oldest technique of securing the layers of a quilt sandwich using a simple running stitch, needle, and any weight thread. All quilting motifs that can be accomplished by machine can be quilted by hand.

HANDLING A QUILT

After basting a quilt sandwich, determine the handling method most comfortable for you, whether holding the quilt in your lap or securing it in a hoop. Ensure both hands have access to the quilt: position the dominant hand on top of the quilt to make stitches, and the non-dominant hand underneath the quilt to assist with guiding the needle.

WITHOUT A HOOP

1. Hold the quilt on your lap or lay it on a table, keeping the immediate quilting area mostly flat.

2. Make quilting stitches (see opposite), repositioning the quilting area as needed, and maintaining consistent tension across stitches.

Consider marking lines to use as a guide for quilting

WITH A HOOP

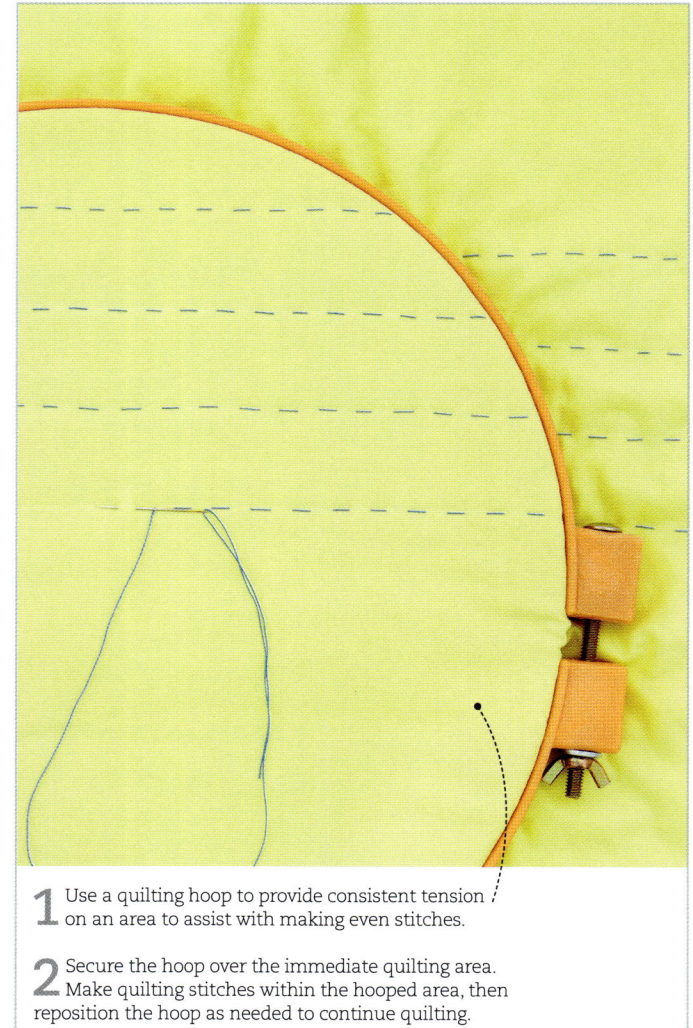

1. Use a quilting hoop to provide consistent tension on an area to assist with making even stitches.

2. Secure the hoop over the immediate quilting area. Make quilting stitches within the hooped area, then reposition the hoop as needed to continue quilting.

STITCHING

Use a stab stitch to make stitches one at a time or a rocking stitch to make many stitches at once. Smaller stitches are considered more traditional, while longer are more modern. Choose the appropriate thread and needle, mark quilting lines, and tie and bury a quilter's knot (see p.75).

STAB STITCH

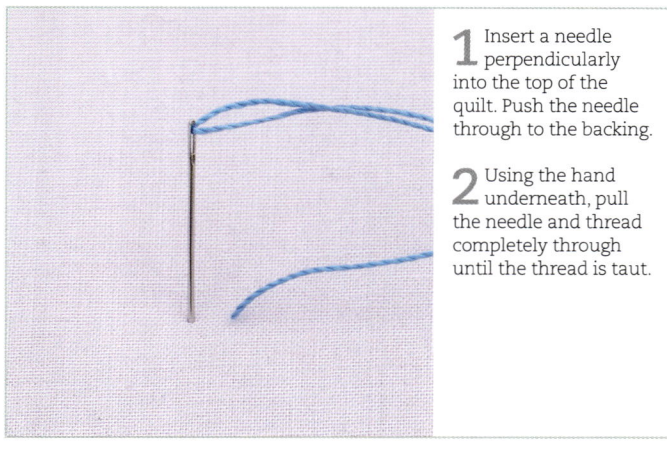

1 Insert a needle perpendicularly into the top of the quilt. Push the needle through to the backing.

2 Using the hand underneath, pull the needle and thread completely through until the thread is taut.

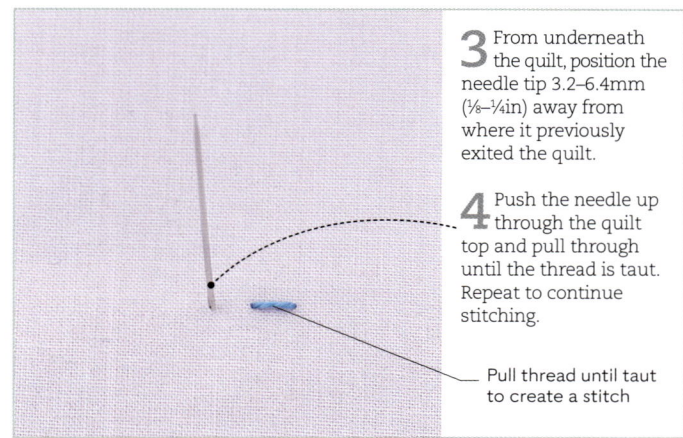

3 From underneath the quilt, position the needle tip 3.2–6.4mm (⅛–¼in) away from where it previously exited the quilt.

4 Push the needle up through the quilt top and pull through until the thread is taut. Repeat to continue stitching.

Pull thread until taut to create a stitch

ROCKING THE NEEDLE

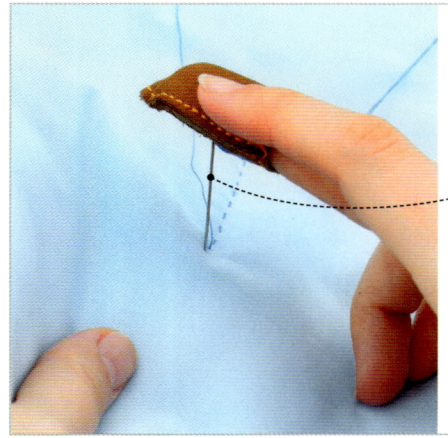

1 Insert the needle perpendicularly into the top of the quilt, pushing the needle just far enough through the quilt for the needle tip to exit the backing.

2 Stop pushing when the needle tip can be felt underneath the quilt.

3 From the top of the quilt, push the quilt toward the needle with your thumb, while pushing the end of the needle forward.

4 Guide the needle tip through the quilt. Stop pushing when the length of the needle showing on top is the same as the desired stitch length.

5 From the top of the quilt, use a rocking motion to guide the needle tip back down, while using your thumb to push the quilt toward the needle.

6 Continue rocking the needle back and forth to load the needle with 3–5 stitches.

7 Pull the loaded needle and thread completely through the quilt until the stitches are taut.

8 Repeat steps 1–7 to continue making stitches.

TRAVELLING THROUGH WADDING

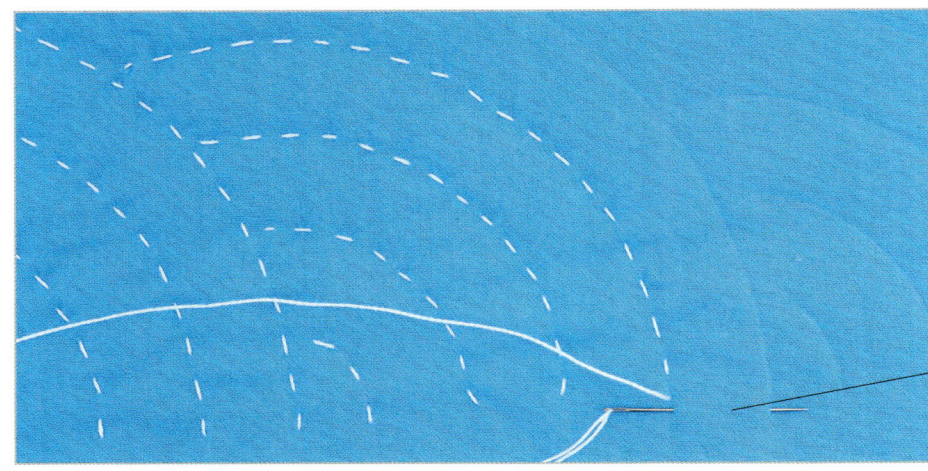

1. To move your needle and thread to a different area without stopping and knotting, insert the needle at the last desired stitch into only the wadding. Do not go through the backing fabric.

2. Glide the needle under the quilt top, through the wadding, to travel. Exit the needle tip at the desired point to begin the next stitches.

Travelling is not recommended when quilting light fabric with dark thread, as the thread may be visible under the fabric

TYPES OF HAND QUILTING

Hand quilting stitches require practice; focus first on making stitches of even length on both sides of the quilt.

TRADITIONAL HAND QUILTING

Traditional hand quilting stitches are quite small, 1.6–3.2mm (1/16–1/8in) long, and ideal for intricate quilting motifs. Use a medium-weight thread, such as 60, 50, or 40 weight, and a betweens, sharps, or milliner's needle. Use a finer thread and thinner needle to assist with making smaller stitches. Historically, traditional hand quilting stitches are made using a rocking stitch (see p.169).

BIG STITCH QUILTING

Big stitch hand quilting stitches are a modern take on hand quilting, with stitches approximately 6.4mm (1/4in) long. Use a heavy-weight thread, such as 28, 12, or 8 weight, and a milliner's, embroidery, or sashiko needle. Big stitches are most like the running stitch (see p.122). A rocking stitch can be used when big stitch quilting, but only a few stitches can be loaded onto the needle at one time.

HAND TYING

Hand tying is a classic technique of securing quilt layers with simple square knots rather than running stitches. Hand tying is versatile, working well with all wadding types. A heavy-weight thread, such as 8 weight, is recommended, though 5 weight thread or yarn may also be used. Choose a needle with a large eye in the size appropriate for the thread.

1 Make a mark where each tie will be placed. Thread a needle with approximately 41cm (16in) of thread, and bring the ends together without making a knot.

2 Insert the needle into the quilt 1–2mm (1/16in) away from a registration mark and pass the needle through all layers.

3 Rock the needle back and bring the needle tip up through the quilt top, forming a stitch. Pull the needle and thread halfway through.

4 For added security, make a second stitch, entering and exiting the needle in the same place as the first stitch.

5 Make a square knot (see p.77) securely against the quilt top. Trim thread tails, leaving at least 1.3cm (½in) beyond the knot.

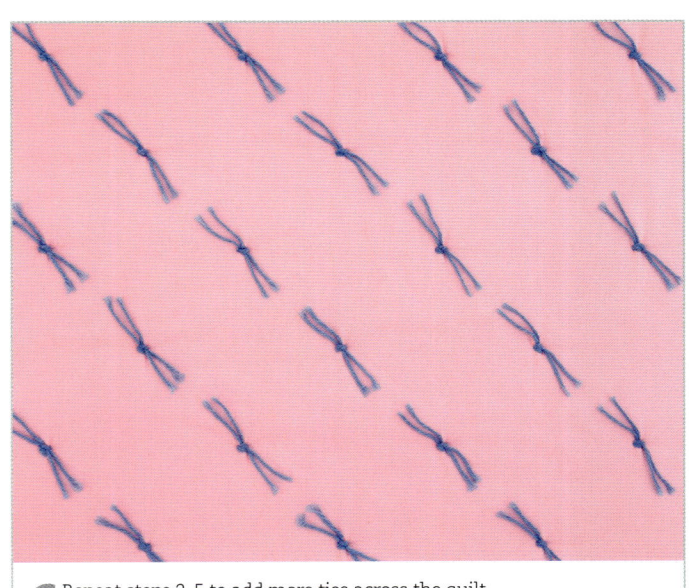

6 Repeat steps 2–5 to add more ties across the quilt. Place ties no more than 12.7cm (5in) apart, or as recommended by the wadding manufacturer.

Binding

Binding encloses the raw edges of a quilt sandwich, securing quilting stitches and fabric edges, and can be seamlessly incorporated into a quilt top design or create a contrasting frame. Binding is made of straight grain or bias strips that are joined to make a continuous binding strip. Calculate the number of binding strips needed (see p.58), or refer to Binding fabric requirements (see p.291) for a quick guide.

Preparing for binding

Before binding a quilt, trim excess wadding and backing to make straight edges and square corners. To hang small quilts or wall hangings, add corner pockets before attaching the binding.

TRIMMING A QUILT

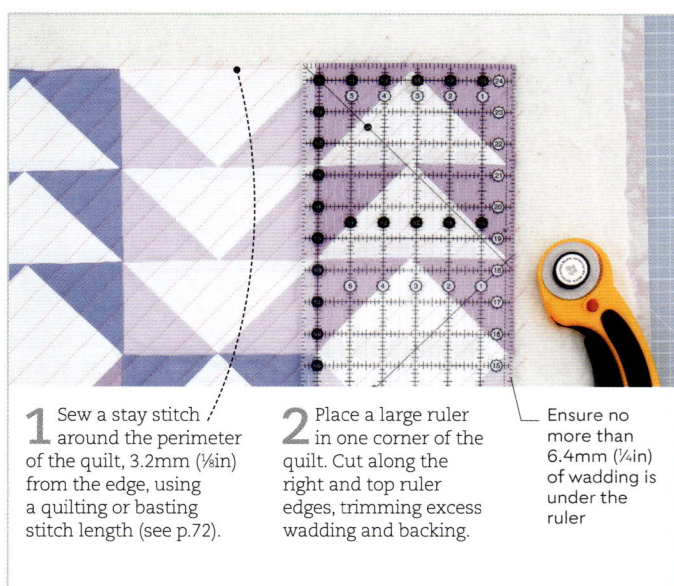

1 Sew a stay stitch around the perimeter of the quilt, 3.2mm (⅛in) from the edge, using a quilting or basting stitch length (see p.72).

2 Place a large ruler in one corner of the quilt. Cut along the right and top ruler edges, trimming excess wadding and backing.

Ensure no more than 6.4mm (¼in) of wadding is under the ruler

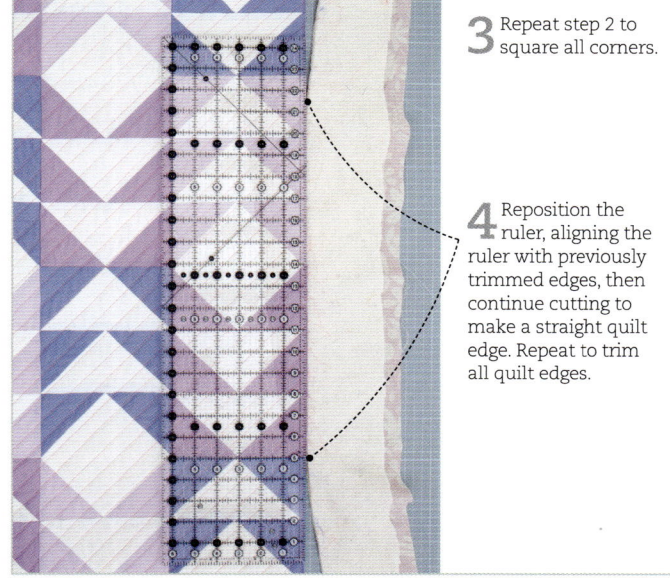

3 Repeat step 2 to square all corners.

4 Reposition the ruler, aligning the ruler with previously trimmed edges, then continue cutting to make a straight quilt edge. Repeat to trim all quilt edges.

ADDING CORNER POCKETS

1 Cut out two 11.4 x 11.4cm (4½ x 4½in) squares of neutral or coordinating backing fabric.

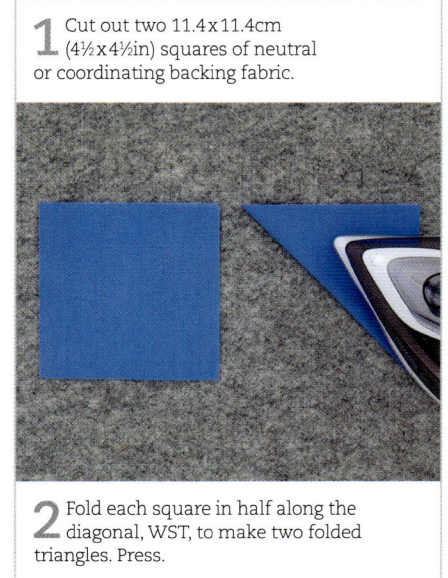

2 Fold each square in half along the diagonal, WST, to make two folded triangles. Press.

3 Place a folded triangle in the top right corner of the back of the quilt, aligning the raw edges. Pin.

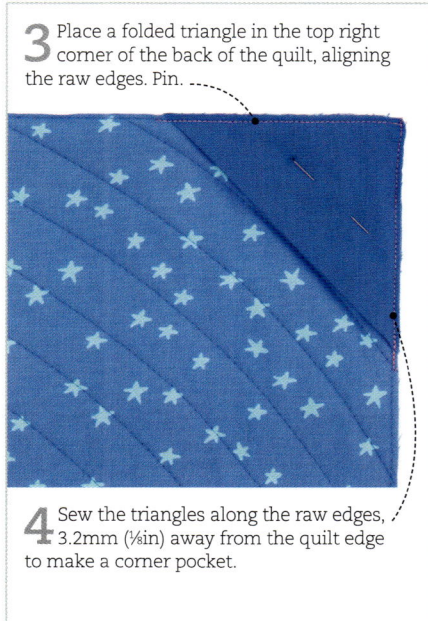

4 Sew the triangles along the raw edges, 3.2mm (⅛in) away from the quilt edge to make a corner pocket.

5 Repeat steps 3–4 on the top left corner with the remaining folded triangle.

6 Bind and finish the quilt as desired (see p.178). Insert a dowel as shown, then hang to display.

Making binding

Binding can be made using WOF strips, bias strips, or scraps of leftover fabric. Binding is typically made of narrow strips of fabric, between 5.1–6.4cm (2–2½in) wide. Join fabric strips using diagonal seams to reduce bulk and strain across the seams.

STRAIGHT GRAIN BINDING
This type of binding is made of strips cut along the cross grain, which are joined to make a stable binding that resists stretching. This type of binding works well for quilts with straight edges and those that will be heavily used.

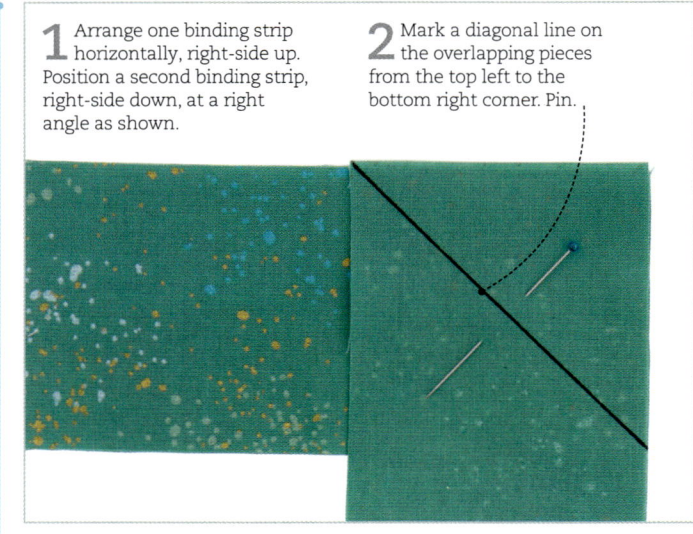

1. Arrange one binding strip horizontally, right-side up. Position a second binding strip, right-side down, at a right angle as shown.

2. Mark a diagonal line on the overlapping pieces from the top left to the bottom right corner. Pin.

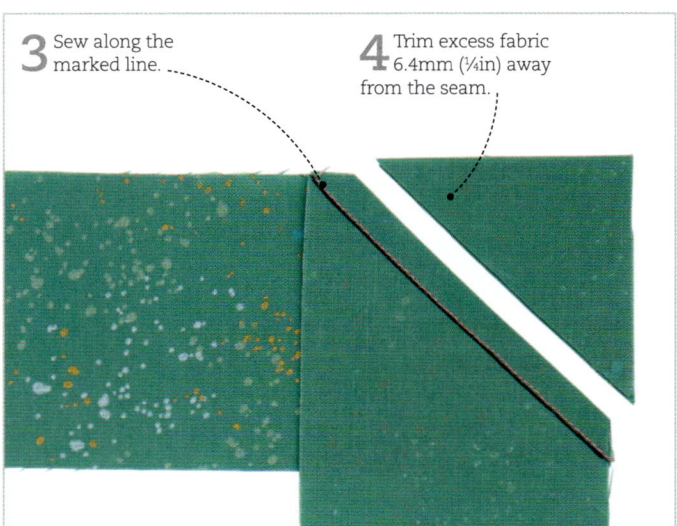

3. Sew along the marked line.

4. Trim excess fabric 6.4mm (¼in) away from the seam.

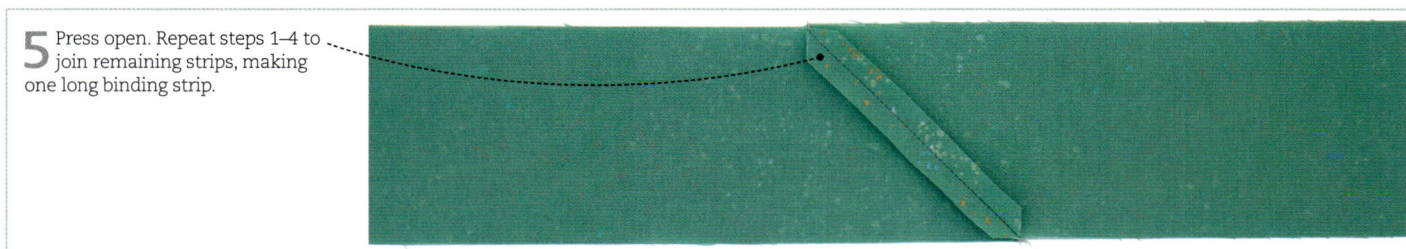

5. Press open. Repeat steps 1–4 to join remaining strips, making one long binding strip.

6. Fold the binding in half, WST, aligning the raw edges. Press.

BIAS BINDING

This binding, made of strips cut along the bias (see p.45), is stretchy and used for quilts with curved edges. Refer to p.291 to determine the starting square size.

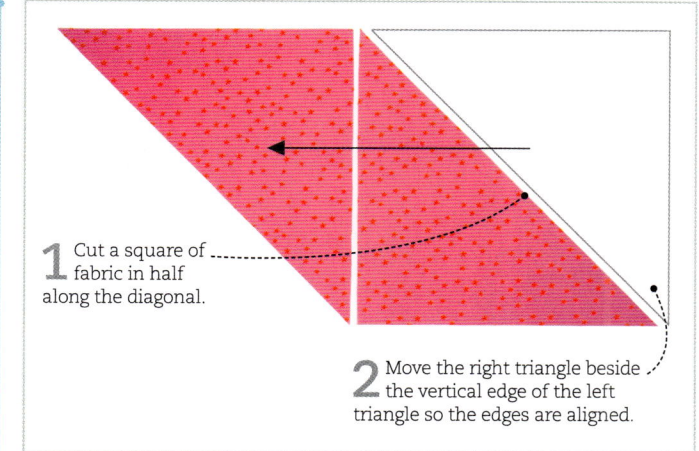

1 Cut a square of fabric in half along the diagonal.

2 Move the right triangle beside the vertical edge of the left triangle so the edges are aligned.

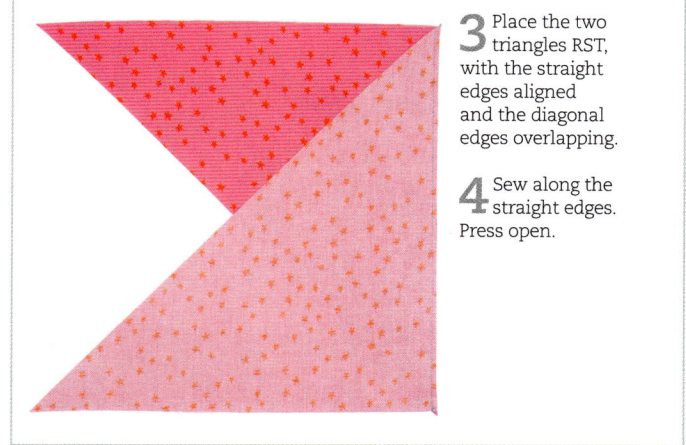

3 Place the two triangles RST, with the straight edges aligned and the diagonal edges overlapping.

4 Sew along the straight edges. Press open.

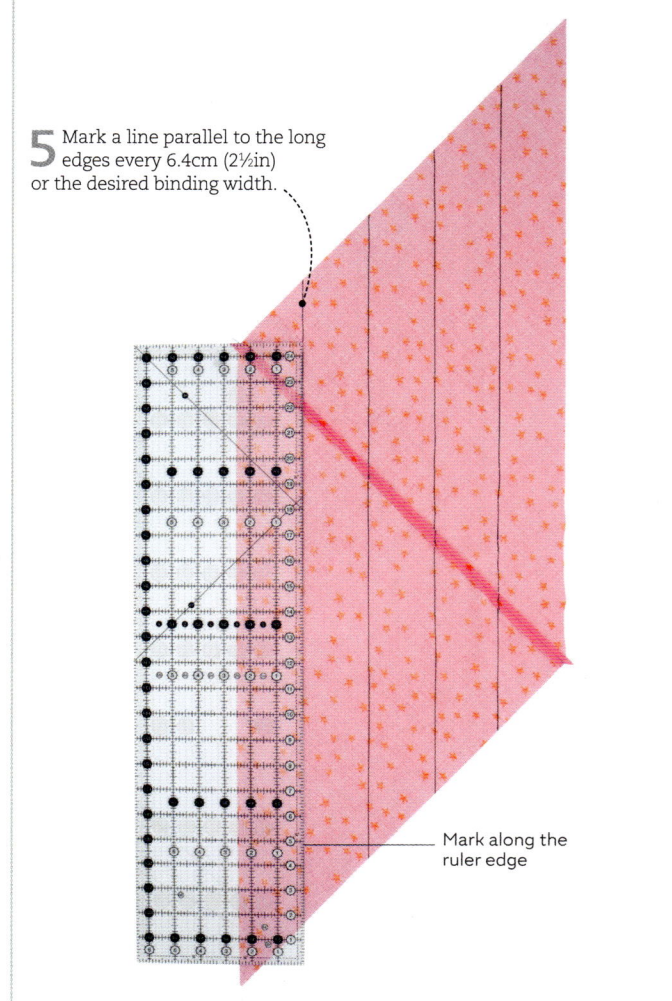

5 Mark a line parallel to the long edges every 6.4cm (2½in) or the desired binding width.

Mark along the ruler edge

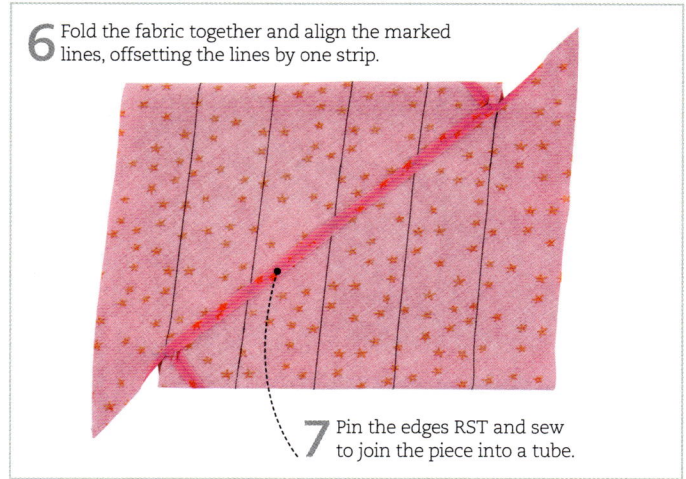

6 Fold the fabric together and align the marked lines, offsetting the lines by one strip.

7 Pin the edges RST and sew to join the piece into a tube.

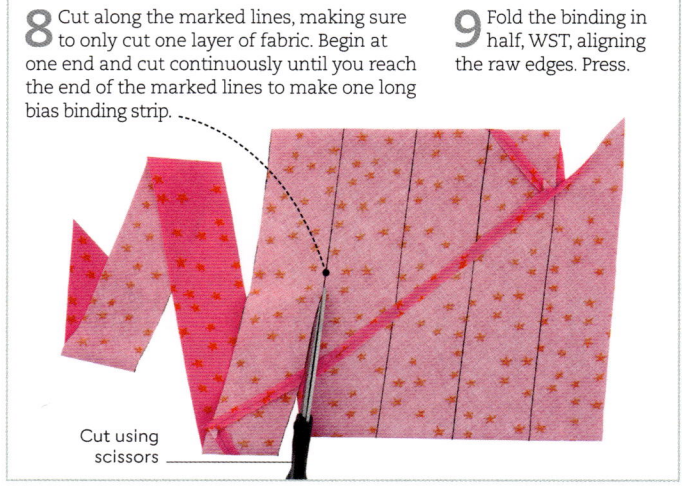

8 Cut along the marked lines, making sure to only cut one layer of fabric. Begin at one end and cut continuously until you reach the end of the marked lines to make one long bias binding strip.

9 Fold the binding in half, WST, aligning the raw edges. Press.

Cut using scissors

Attaching binding

When attaching binding to the front of a quilt, keep in mind that the binding will be wrapped around to the opposite side for finishing. Use a 6.4mm (¼in) seam allowance and a walking foot (see p.32) to ensure even stitches.

BEGINNING

1. Position one end of the binding on the quilt, aligning the raw edges.
2. Place a pin or clip approximately 25cm (10in) from the binding end to mark where to begin sewing. Backstitch to secure the stitches.
3. Sew along the edge of the binding and quilt, stopping with the needle down to realign the binding as needed.

Begin sewing here

NAVIGATING CORNERS

1. Stop sewing 6.4mm (¼in) from the corner of the quilt.
2. With the needle down, raise the walking foot, then rotate the quilt 45 degrees. Lower the foot and continue sewing to the corner of the quilt.
3. Fold the binding away from the quilt, overlapping at the corner, so the raw edge of the binding is now parallel to the horizontal quilt edge. The folded binding edge should form a 45-degree angle.
4. Fold the binding back towards the quilt top to align the raw binding edges with the horizontal quilt edge. The binding should overlap at the corner, with the newest folded edge aligning with the vertical quilt edge. Pin or clip.
5. Reposition the quilt under the foot. Backstitch to secure the stitches, then continue sewing along the quilt edge.
6. Repeat steps 1–5 at each corner.

JOINING ENDS

1. Attach the binding around all four sides of the quilt, stopping approximately 25cm (10in) away from the starting point. Backstitch.

2. Lay the binding ends on top of one another so they overlap along the edge of the quilt.

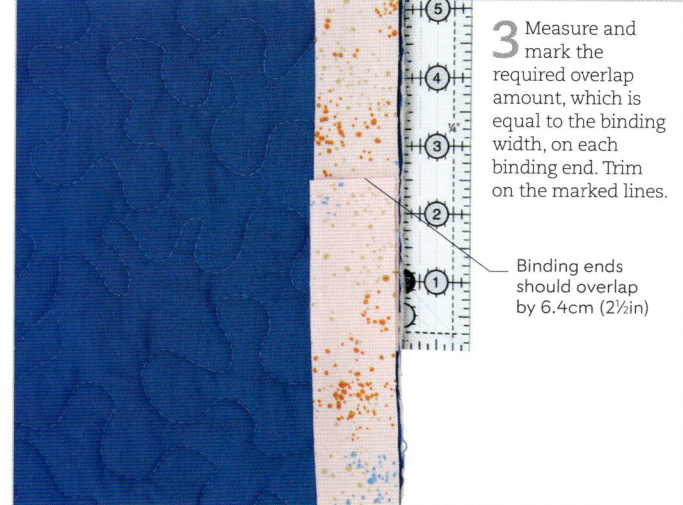

3. Measure and mark the required overlap amount, which is equal to the binding width, on each binding end. Trim on the marked lines.

Binding ends should overlap by 6.4cm (2½in)

4. Open the binding strips, then place the binding strips RST, with the top piece wrong-side up. Align the corners to form a right angle.

5. Mark a diagonal line from corner to corner. Pin.

6. Sew along the marked line. Trim excess fabric 6.4mm (¼in) away.

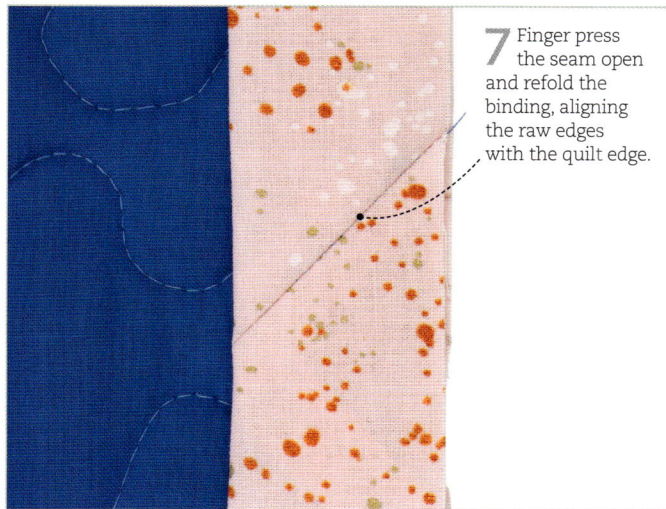

7. Finger press the seam open and refold the binding, aligning the raw edges with the quilt edge.

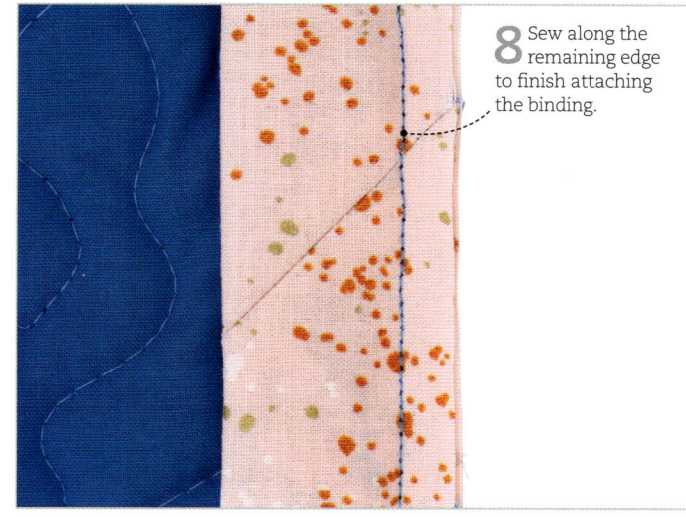

8. Sew along the remaining edge to finish attaching the binding.

Finishing binding

After attaching binding (see p.176) to one side of the quilt, fold the binding edges over to the other side. Secure the binding by machine or hand to achieve your preferred finished look.

FOLDING OVER

1 Press the binding away from the edge of the quilt to make a crisp fold.

2 Wrap the binding to the other side of the quilt to cover the raw edges.

3 Secure the folded binding edge to the quilt, making sure the fold extends slightly beyond the initial binding stitches.

MITRING CORNERS

1 Fold the binding toward the quilt on one side of the corner. Clip the binding approximately 2.5cm (1in) away from the corner.

2 Fold the binding down along the adjacent quilt edge, overlapping the first fold, to produce a 45-degree mitred corner. Clip in place.

Hold mitred corner in place

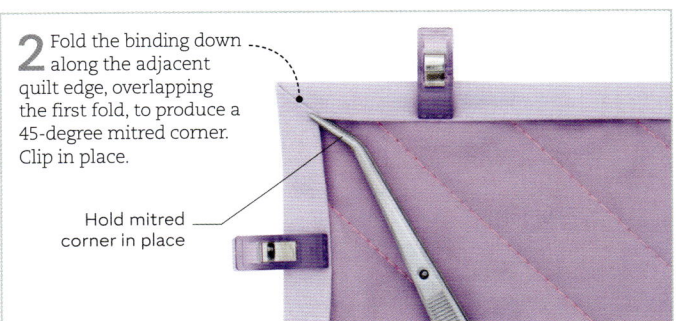

MACHINE STITCHING

1 Align the needle approximately 3.2mm (⅛in) to the right of the folded edge of the binding.

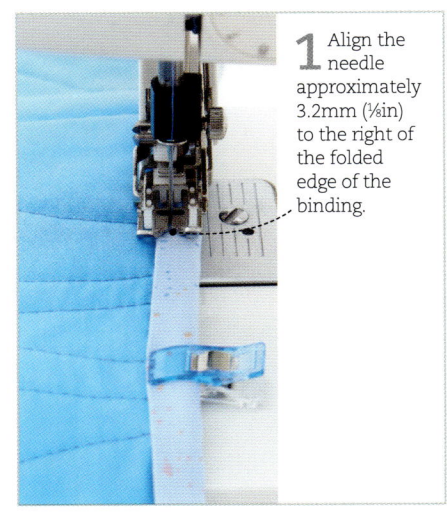

2 Sew along the binding edge, stopping, with the needle down, at the mitred corner. Ensure the needle pierces through both layers of binding.

3 Raise the foot, pivot the quilt 45-degrees, lower the foot, then continue sewing along the binding edge.

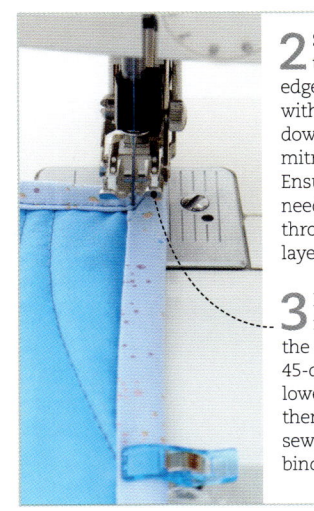

4 Backstitch at the end or knot and bury threads (see p.76) for an invisible finish.

FINISHING BINDING 179

BIG STITCHING

1 Tie and bury a knot or hide a knot under the binding.

2 Make a running stitch (see p.137) along the edge of the binding. Avoid exiting the needle through the other side of the quilt; the needle should only travel through the wadding.

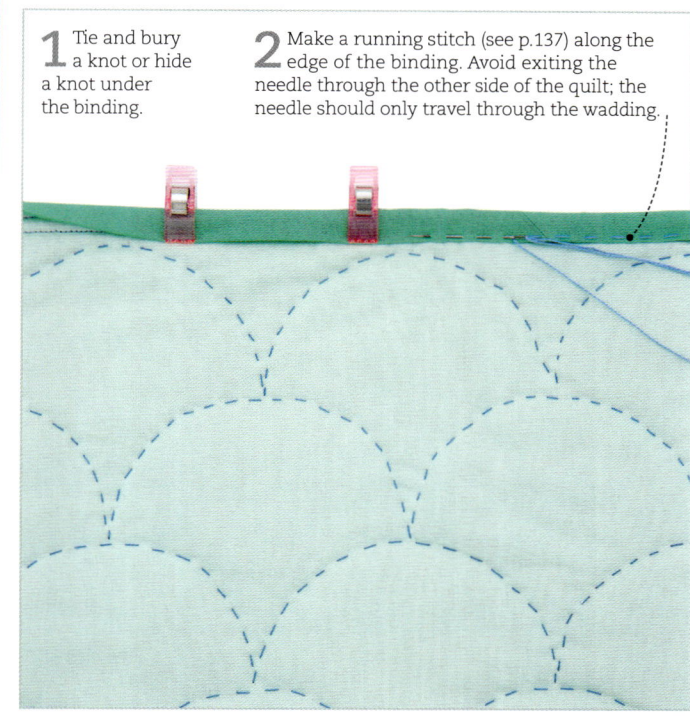

3 Mitre corners (see opposite). Be sure to stitch through both layers of binding to secure corners.

4 When you run out of thread, tie an overhand knot (see p.76) and bury the knot in the quilt sandwich. Repeat to secure all binding edges.

INVISIBLE STITCHING

1 Use a whipstitch or ladder stitch (see p.137) to secure the binding; avoid stitching through the other side.

Hide the knot under the binding

2 Mitre corners (see opposite). Stitch along the folded edges of the mitred corners for added security.

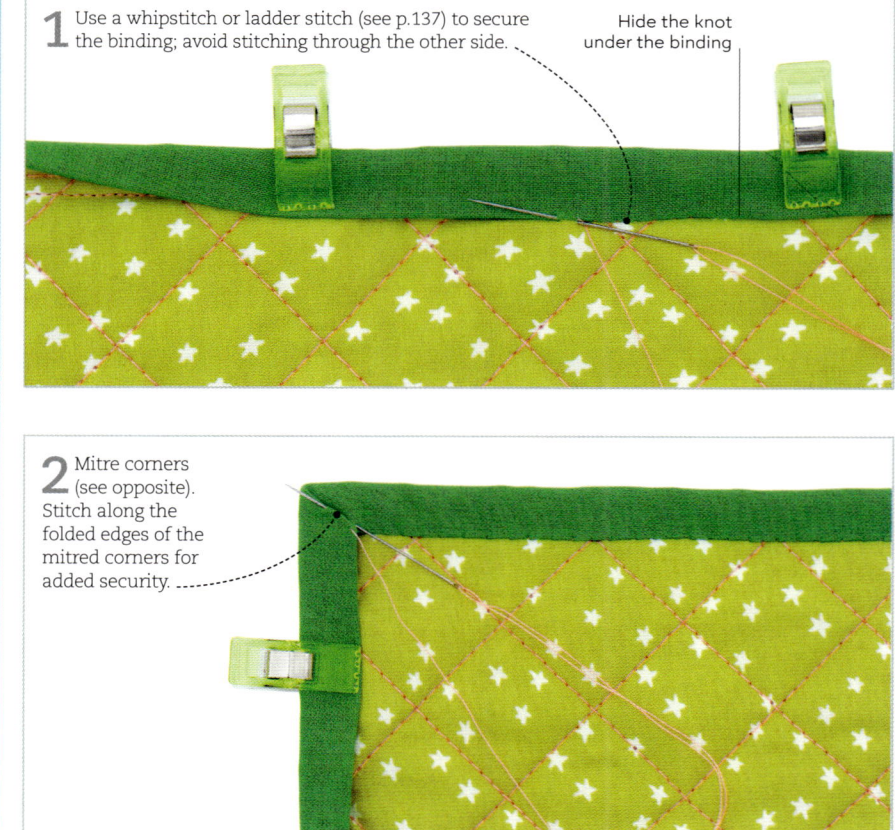

3 When you run out of thread, tie an overhand knot and bury the knot in the quilt sandwich.

4 Repeat to secure all binding edges.

Facing

Facing is an alternative binding technique that encloses quilt edges without visible binding on the front for a frameless finish. This technique creates the illusion that the piecing or quilting designs extend beyond the quilt edges.

MAKING FACING STRIPS

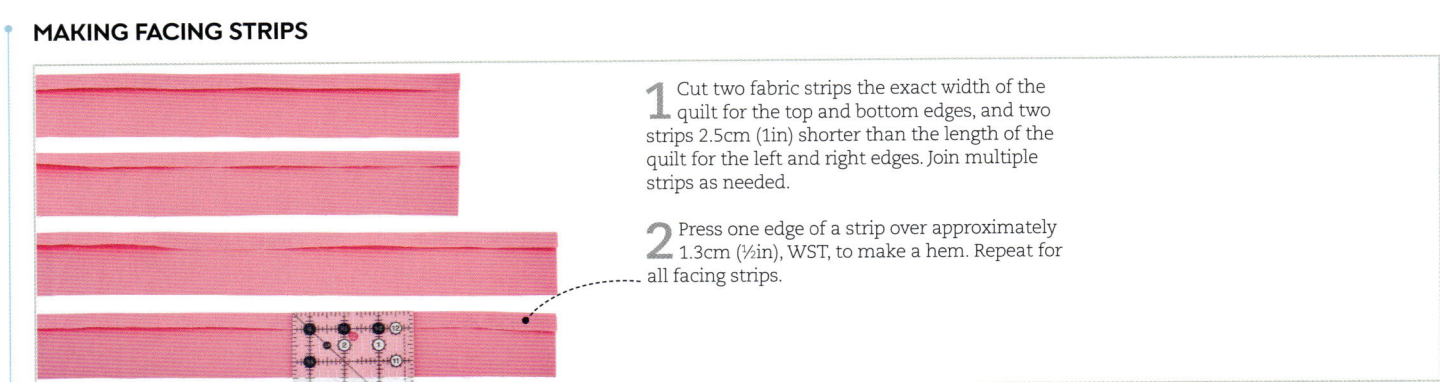

1. Cut two fabric strips the exact width of the quilt for the top and bottom edges, and two strips 2.5cm (1in) shorter than the length of the quilt for the left and right edges. Join multiple strips as needed.

2. Press one edge of a strip over approximately 1.3cm (½in), WST, to make a hem. Repeat for all facing strips.

ATTACHING FACING

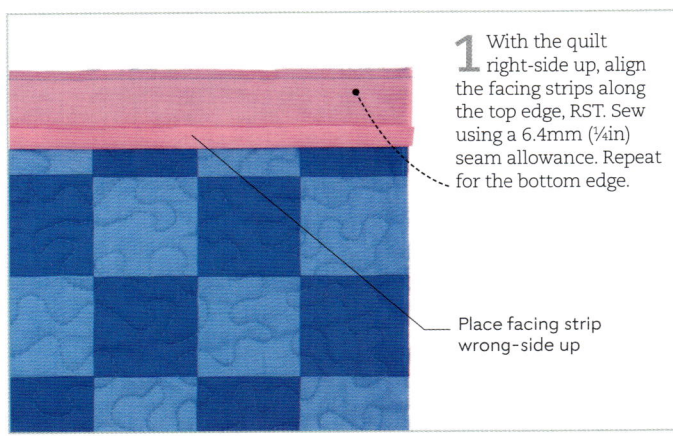

1. With the quilt right-side up, align the facing strips along the top edge, RST. Sew using a 6.4mm (¼in) seam allowance. Repeat for the bottom edge.

Place facing strip wrong-side up

2. Press the facing strips away from the quilt top.

3. Reposition the facing strips back down against the front of the quilt, RST. Pin. Repeat steps 1–3 for the bottom edge.

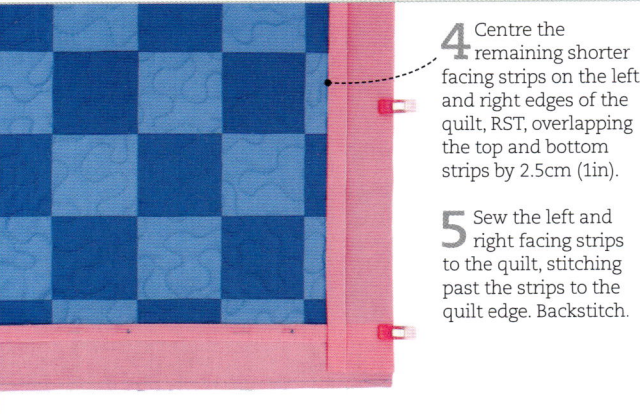

4. Centre the remaining shorter facing strips on the left and right edges of the quilt, RST, overlapping the top and bottom strips by 2.5cm (1in).

5. Sew the left and right facing strips to the quilt, stitching past the strips to the quilt edge. Backstitch.

6. Stitch diagonally across each corner of the quilt, crossing the seam allowance intersections to reinforce the corners. Repeat at least twice.

7. Trim excess fabric to the right of the stitch line.

8 Press both left and right facing strips away from the quilt top.

9 Wrap the left and right facing strips over the quilt edges, folding the facing and seam allowances toward the back. Press, then pin.

10 Place clips along the folded edges, pinching the seam allowance bulk flat against the quilt back.

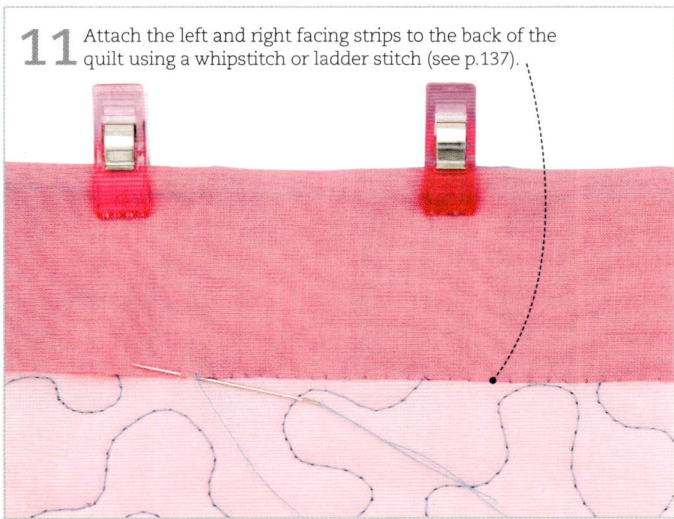

11 Attach the left and right facing strips to the back of the quilt using a whipstitch or ladder stitch (see p.137).

12 Push all four corners right-side out, allowing the top and bottom facing strips to flip to the back of the quilt.

13 Repeat steps 9–11 with the top and bottom facing strips.

14 Press the edges from the front. For added security, stitch around the entire perimeter of the quilt 3.2mm (⅛in) away from the edge using a matching thread.

Caring for quilts

Properly caring for a quilt ensures it will last a lifetime. Quilt labels act as record keepers, providing information for the next generation. Proper maintenance includes washing carefully, storing appropriately, and making timely repairs.

Labelling quilts

Add labels to quilts to preserve history and recognize the work of the maker(s). Include information such as the maker's name(s), year and location completed, and, if applicable, the name of the recipient. Purchase pre-made labels or make your own by writing or embroidering a message.

PRE-MADE LABELS

Purchase pre-made labels that have text or designs woven or screen printed onto the fabric. Pre-made labels may include information such as care instructions or when and where the quilt was made.

Personalize semi- or fully-custom labels for an easy way to add your information to quilts.

Attach pre-made labels by using any appliqué technique (see p.134) or sewing them into the binding.

HANDMADE LABELS

1 Fold a fabric square in half along the diagonal and add a message. Position it so the raw edges align with the corner of the quilt sandwich. Secure within the binding.

Triangle labels nest on the corner of a quilt and provide a large area for a message

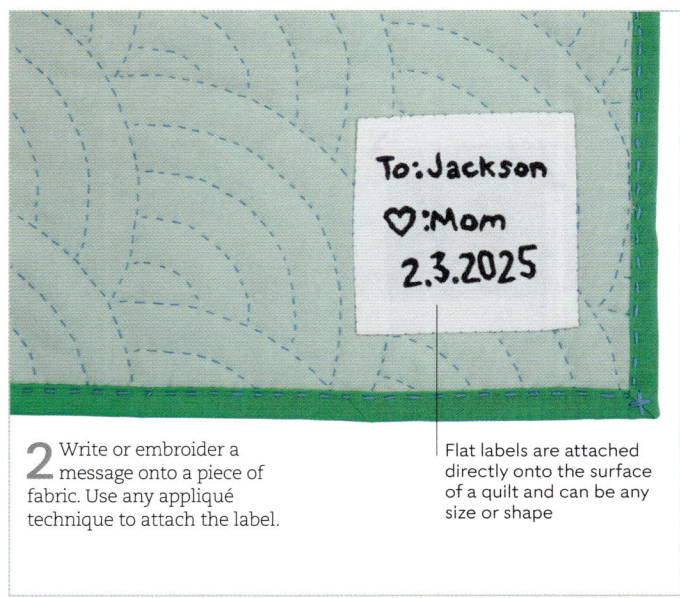

2 Write or embroider a message onto a piece of fabric. Use any appliqué technique to attach the label.

Flat labels are attached directly onto the surface of a quilt and can be any size or shape

Quilt maintenance

Maintain quilts and extend their lifespan by washing them regularly, storing properly in breathable bags or speciality boxes, and making timely repairs.

WASHING AND DRYING

For best results, follow washing instructions provided by the wadding manufacturer.

Wash quilts in a washing machine on a gentle cycle with cool water. Remove quilts promptly to help prevent bleeding.

For delicate or vintage quilts, wash by hand with a gentle soap and hang dry.

Use colour catchers (see p.23) in the first few washes to prevent fabric bleeding.

Hang quilts or tumble dry on low heat.

Due to shrinkage, quilts crinkle once washed and dried. To achieve a less crinkled texture, pre-wash fabrics, wash with cool water, and dry with no heat.

STORING

Store quilts where they will be used often or tuck them safely away from sunlight for long-term storage.

Store quilts in a dry, temperature-controlled space away from sunlight to avoid mildew and bleaching.

Fold quilts on the bias or roll quilts to avoid setting deep creases. Unfold and refold quilts regularly, alternating folding patterns, to reduce creases.

REPAIRING

As quilts are used, they may become worn or damaged and require repairs. Some repairs blend seamlessly, while others may require a visible patch. Be sure to knot and bury thread ends (see p.76).

POPPED QUILTING STITCHES

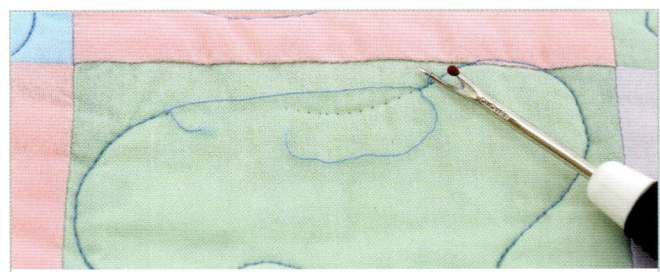

Pick popped quilting stitches (see p.79) until the top and bottom threads are long enough to knot and bury.

Machine or hand sew new quilting stitches, starting and stopping at the ends of the existing quilting or extending the new stitching over the existing quilting for extra security.

POPPED SEAMS

Fold seam allowances under and sew a ladder stitch (see p.137) by hand, in matching or neutral thread, to join the separated seam with nearly invisible stitching.

Use a machine to sew a zigzag or satin stitch (see p.136) for a durable repair. Machine stitches will be visible on both sides of the quilt.

If the seam allowances are not salvageable, treat the popped seam as a hole.

HOLES

Trim loose threads, frayed fabric, or rough wadding edges.

Appliqué (see p.134) a patch to completely cover the hole.

If the hole extends into the wadding, replace the missing wadding with a piece of the same size and type.

If the hole extends through both sides of the quilt, appliqué a patch on each side.

BINDING

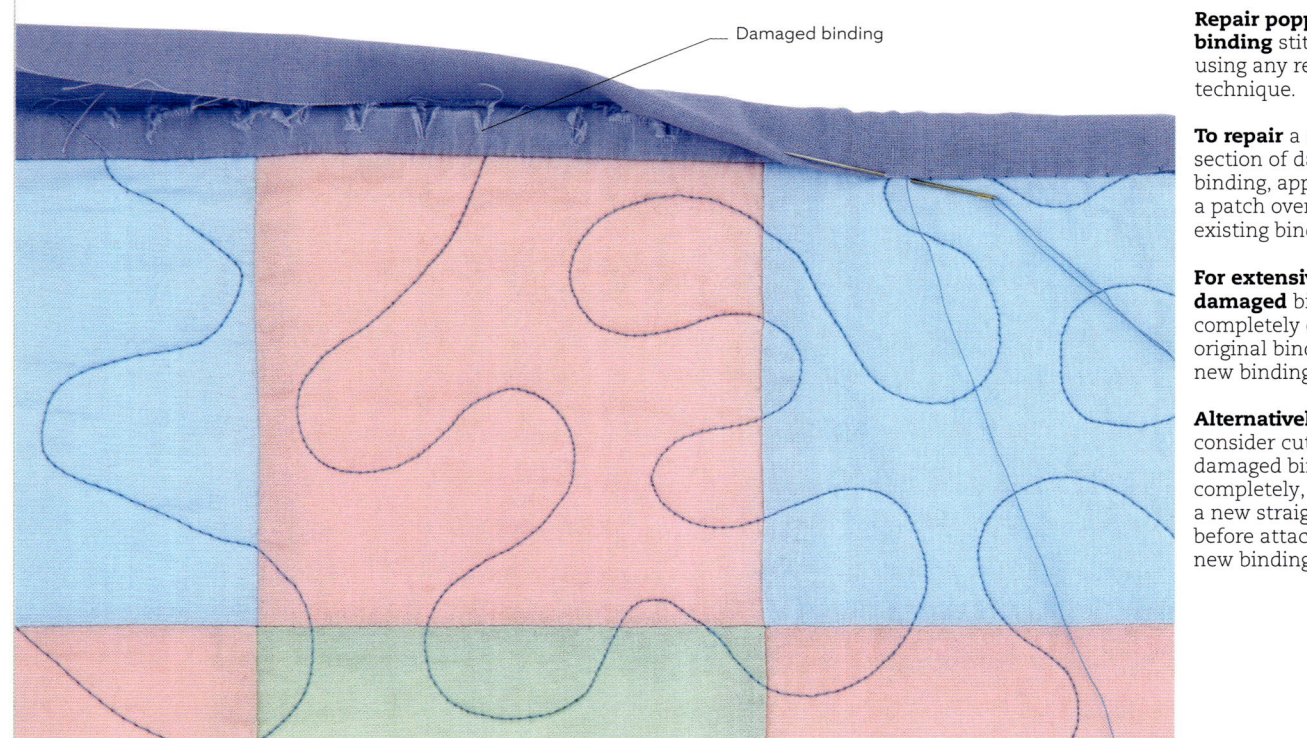

Repair popped binding stitches using any repairing technique.

To repair a small section of damaged binding, appliqué a patch over the existing binding.

For extensively damaged binding, completely cover the original binding with new binding.

Alternatively, consider cutting the damaged binding off completely, creating a new straight edge before attaching new binding.

PROJECTS

Building blocks sampler

This modern sampler pattern is designed to complement the step-by-step techniques in this book. Use the pattern as a guide alongside the in-depth instructions in the Techniques chapter (see pp.82–139) to practise making traditionally pieced, FPP, EPP, and appliquéd units.

FINISHED CRIB SIZE 99 x 114cm (39 x 45in)

TECHNIQUES USED Using templates **p.71**, Patchwork **p.83**, Common angles **p.86**, Irregular angles **p.96**, Foundation paper piecing **p.114**, English paper piecing **p.124**, Appliqué **p.134**, Matching points and seams **p.141**, Medallion quilt top layout **p.147**

MATERIALS

- Basic quilting supplies (see p.14)
- Printer, FPP template paper, and cardstock
- Tweezers (optional)
- 8.9 x 31.8cm (3½ x 12½in) ruler or FPP ruler
- Marking tools
- Washi tape
- Needle and thread for EPP
- 114 x 132cm (45 x 52in) or larger wadding

FABRIC REQUIREMENTS

Fabrics A, C, and F	(1) FE each
Fabrics B, D, E, G, and H	(1) FQ each
Background (BG)	1.25m (1½yds)
Backing*	2.5m (2½yds)
Binding	0.5m (½yd)

*Backing fabric required if using one horizontal seam.

Solids and blenders (see p.64) are recommended for this pattern due to the large variety of units, though any fabrics can be used. Consider using both warm and cool fabrics (see p.60) for a balanced design.

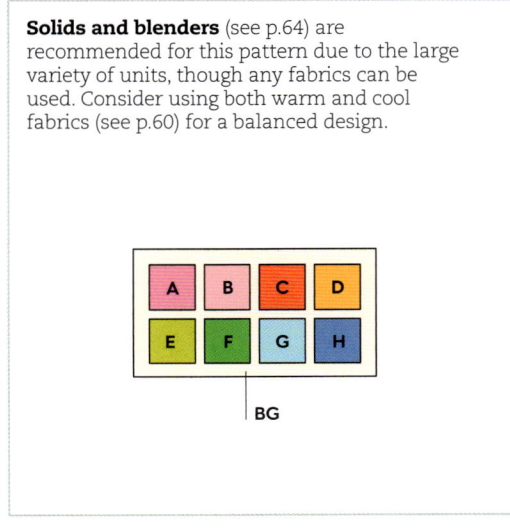

COLOUR REFERENCE

COVER QUILT DETAILS

Fabrics: Ruby and Bee Solids by Windham Fabrics in Fairy Floss (**A**), Posy (**B**), Delphinium (**C**), Pumpkin (**D**), Avocado (**E**), Pasture (**F**), Aquamarine (**G**), Provence Blue (**H**), Cream Puff (**BG**); **Quilting:** Walking foot grid; **Thread:** Aurifil 50 wt in 2405; **Wadding:** Hobbs Tuscany Unbleached 100% Cotton; **Binding:** Provence Blue

CUTTING INSTRUCTIONS

Use the fabric cutting tables and diagrams below to cut and label the pieces required from fabrics A–H and BG.
Visit *The Quilting Book* website (see p.11) to print the required QC, HC, FPP, and EPP hexagon templates.

FABRIC CUTTING TABLES AND DIAGRAMS

FABRICS A–H

A

From a FE, cut:
A1: (2) 10.2 x 20.3cm (4 x 8in)
A2: (2) 10.8 x 19.1cm (4¼ x 7½in)
A3: (1) 10.2 x 10.2cm (4 x 4in)

B

From a FQ, cut:
B1: (1) 5.1 x 5.1cm (2 x 2in)
B2: (1) 5.1 x 21.6cm (2 x 8½in)
B3: (4) 12.7 x 12.7cm (5 x 5in)
B4: (1) 8.9 x 8.9cm (3½ x 3½in)
B5: (2) 8.6 x 33cm (3⅜ x 13in)

C

From a FE, cut:
C1: (5) 5.1 x 5.1cm (2 x 2in)
C2: (1) 10.2 x 10.2cm (4 x 4in)

D

From a FQ, cut:
D1: (1) 5.1 x 8.9cm (2 x 3½in)
D2: (1) 5.1 x 25.4cm (2 x 10in)
D3: (4) 13.3 x 50.8cm (5¼ x 20in)
D4: (1) 8.9 x 8.9cm (3½ x 3½in)
D5: (1) 14.6 x 14.6cm (5¾ x 5¾in)
D6: (1) 13.3 x 48.3cm (5¼ x 19in)

E

From a FQ cut:
E1: (1) 5.1 x 11.4cm (2 x 4½in)
E2: (1) 5.1 x 15.2cm (2 x 6in)
E3: (3) 6.4 x 21.6cm (2½ x 8½in)
E4: (1) 8.9 x 8.9cm (3½ x 3½in)
E5: (2) 10.2 x 10.2cm (4 x 4in)
E6: (2) 16.5 x 16.5cm (6½ x 6½in)

F

From a FE, cut:
F1: (1) 5.1 x 15.2cm (2 x 6in)
F2: (1) 5.1 x 18.4cm (2 x 7¼in)
F3: (4) 5.1 x 38.1cm (2 x 15in)

G

From a FQ cut:
G1: (1) 5.1 x 11.4cm (2 x 4½in)
G2: (1) 5.1 x 21.6cm (2 x 8½in)
G3: (1) 20.3 x 20.3cm (8 x 8in)
G4: (5) 8.9 x 8.9cm (3½ x 3½in)
G5: (2) 14 x 16.5cm (5½ x 6½in)

H

From a FQ cut:
H1: (1) 5.1 x 8.9cm (2 x 3½in)
H2: (1) 5.1 x 18.4cm (2 x 7¼in)
H3: (4) 10.8 x 10.8cm (4¼ x 4¼in)
H4: (1) 10.2 x 10.2cm (4 x 4in)
H5: (4) 8.9 x 16.5cm (3½ x 6½in)

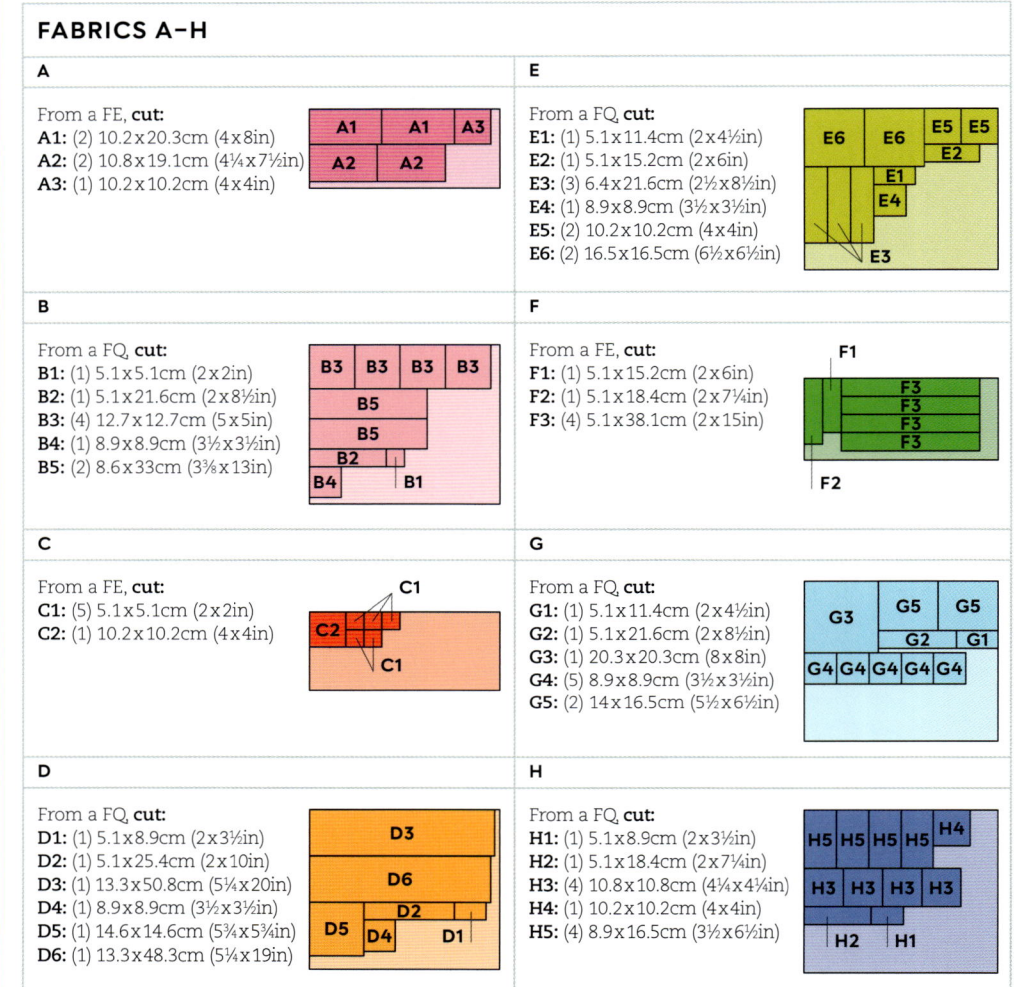

BACKGROUND (BG)

Cut (1) 38.1cm (15in) x WOF; **sub-cut:**
BG12: (1) 38.1 x 17.8cm (15 x 7in)
BG6: (1) 38.1 x 14cm (15 x 5½in)
BG1: (3) 38.1 x 3.8cm (15 x 1½in)
BG9: (2) 10.8 x 19.1cm (4¼ x 7½in)
BG10: (8) 8.9 x 8.9cm (3½ x 3½in)
BG15: (1) 24.1 x 24.1cm (9½ x 9½in)
BG2: (3) 6.4 x 21.6cm (2½ x 8½in)

Cut (1) 20.3cm (8in) x WOF; **sub-cut:**
BG7: (1) 20.3 x 20.3cm (8 x 8in)
BG5: (2) 20.3 x 10.2cm (8 x 4in)
BG4: (2) 10.2 x 10.2cm (4 x 4in)
BG8: (12) 5.1 x 5.1cm (2 x 2in)
BG3: (1) 19.7 x 19.7cm (7¾ x 7¾in)

Cut (1) 16.5cm (6½in) x WOF; **sub-cut:**
BG14: (3) 16.5 x 16.5cm (6½ x 6½in)
BG16: (2) 16.5 x 14cm (6½ x 5½in)
BG13: (1) 14.6 x 14.6cm (5¾ x 5¾in)
BG11: (1) 12.1 x 12.1cm (4¾ x 4¾in)

Cut (4) 8.9cm (3½in) x WOF; **sub-cut:**
BG17: (4) 8.9 x 100.3cm (3½ x 39½in)

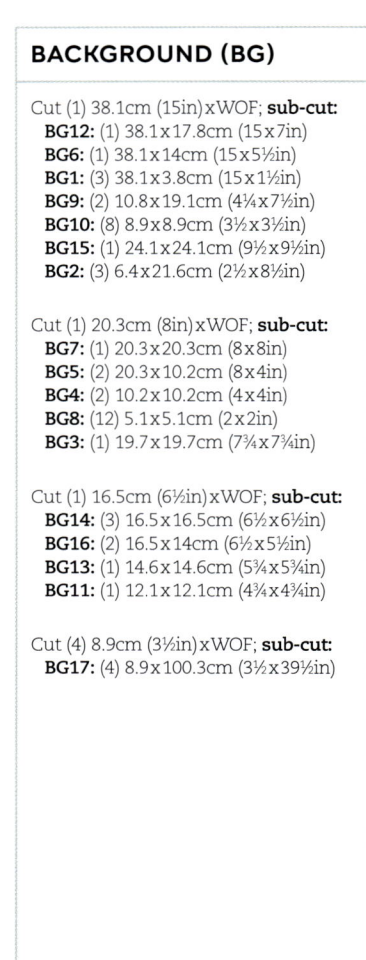

PREPARING AND CUTTING TEMPLATE SHAPES

1 Cut out four template QC-A from one D3 rectangle and four template QC-B from one BG6 rectangle as shown.

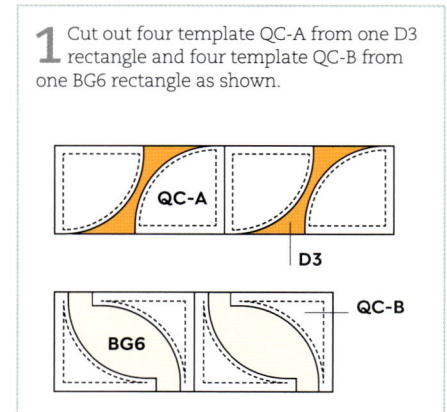

2 Cut out two template HC-A from one D6 rectangle and two template HC-B from one BG12 rectangle as shown.

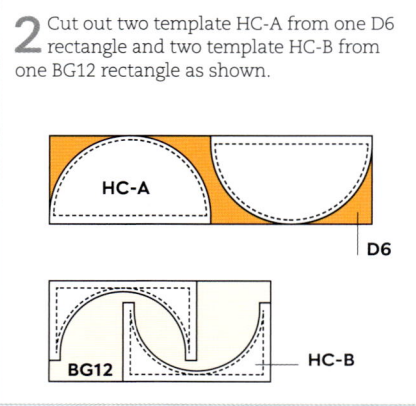

3 Purchase or cut out seven 3.8cm (1½in) hexagon paper pieces.

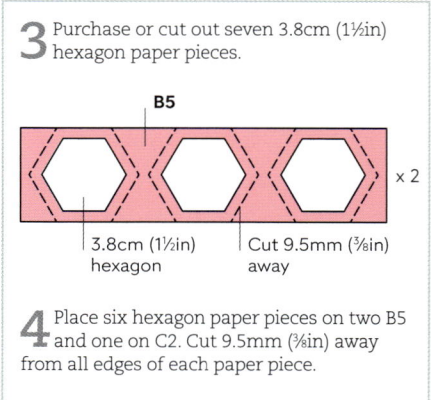

4 Place six hexagon paper pieces on two B5 and one on C2. Cut 9.5mm (⅜in) away from all edges of each paper piece.

UNIT ASSEMBLY

Refer to the pages referenced in the following steps for more detailed FPP, traditional piecing, EPP, and appliqué instructions. Example sizes in the Techniques chapter match those in this pattern.

1 Make one FPP log cabin (see p.116) using the FPP Log Cabin Template and the pieces shown in the unit 1 diagram.

2 Place and sew the pieces in order following the section numbers on the template. Label the completed template as unit 1.

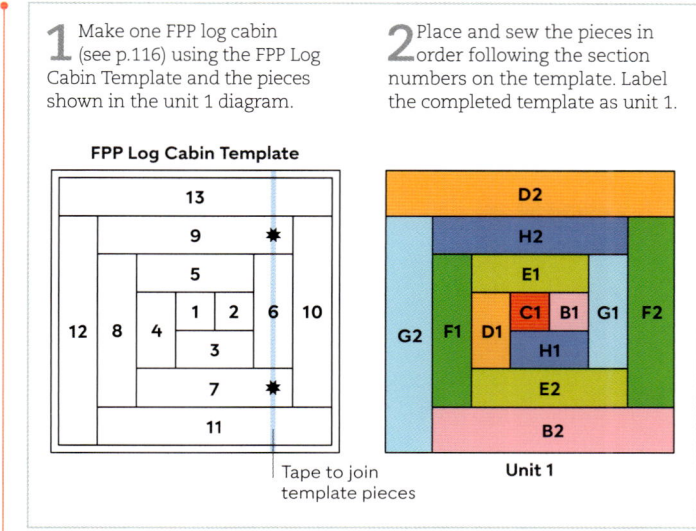

3 Make a strip set (see p.83) using four F3 and three BG1, alternating the fabrics. Press. The strip set should measure 24.1 x 38.1cm (9½ x 15in).

4 Position the strip set horizontally. Sub-cut four 8.9cm (3½in) vertical segments and label each as unit 2.

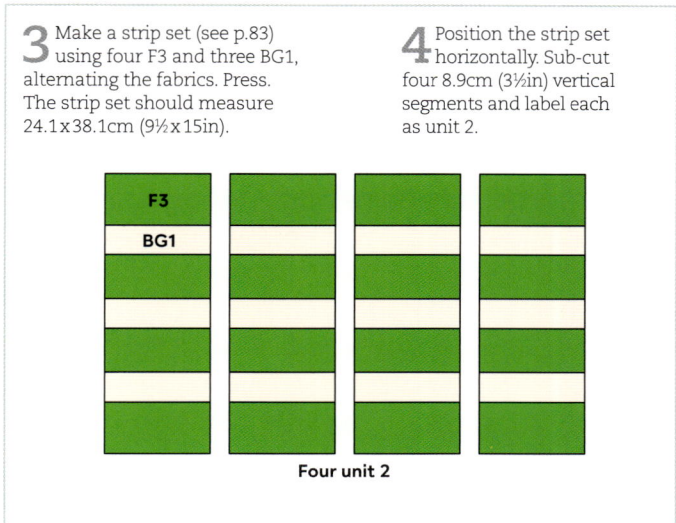

5 Make two nine patches using the odd strip piecing technique (see p.84) with three E3 and three BG2. Both nine patches should measure 16.5 x 16.5cm (6½ x 6½in).

6 Sew the nine patches RST to make a rectangular checkered unit. Press. Label as unit 3.

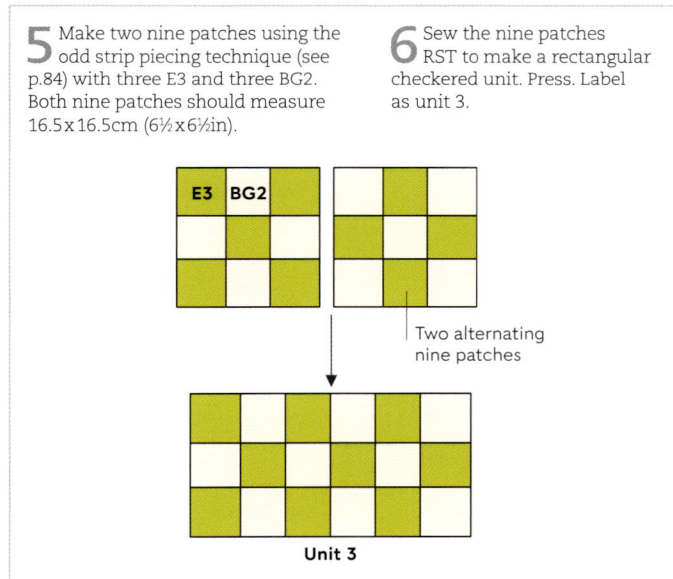

7 Make four FG using the four at a time FG technique (see p.93) with four H3 and one BG3. Press. Trim to 8.9 x 16.5cm (3½ x 6½in).

8 Arrange the FG into a column. Sew the FG RST and label as unit 4.

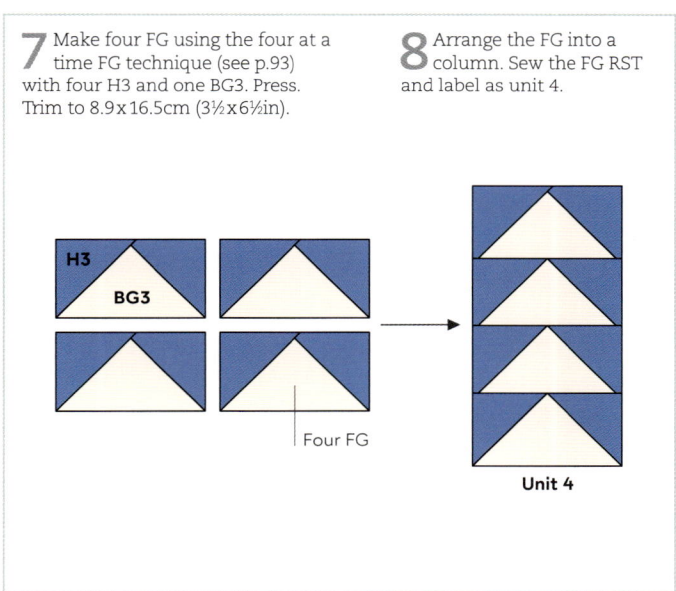

9 Make two HSTs using the one at a time HST technique (see p.86) with one H4 and one BG4. Press. Trim to 8.9 x 8.9cm (3½ x 3½in) and label each as unit 5.

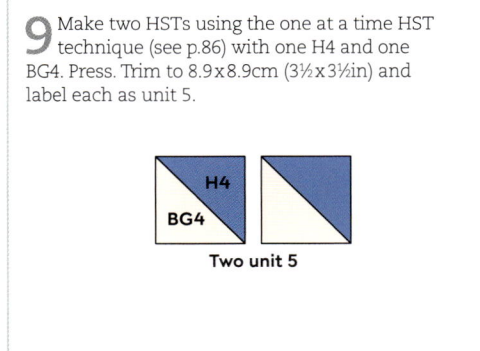

10 Make four HRTs using the one at a time HRT technique (see p.97) with two A1 and two BG5. Press. Trim to 8.9 x 16.5cm (3½ x 6½in).

11 Arrange the HRTs in a row. Sew the HRTs RST and label as unit 6.

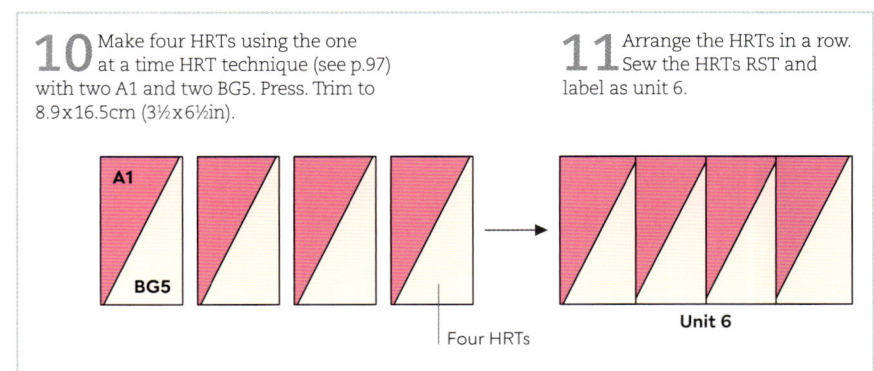

12 Make four QCs (see p.104) using four D3 convex pieces and four BG6 concave pieces. Press. Trim to 12.7 x 12.7 cm (5 x 5 in).

13 Arrange the QCs into a 2 x 2 grid, with the corners of the BG6 pieces meeting at the centre. Sew the QCs RST and label as unit 7.

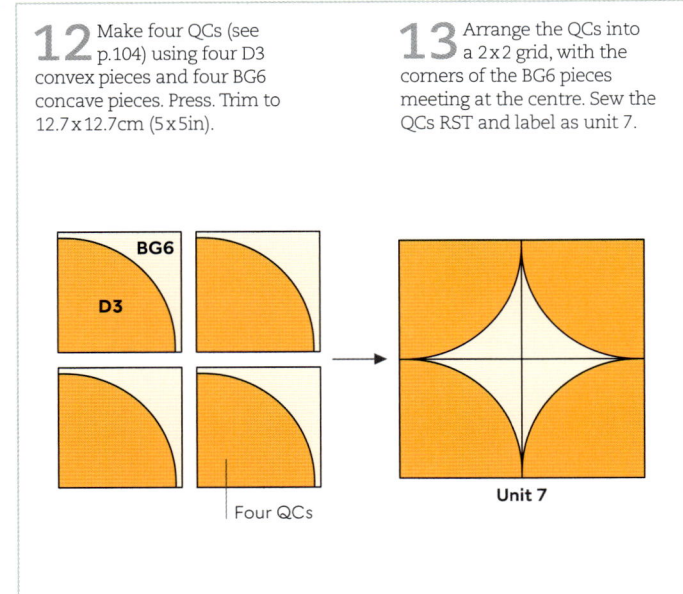

14 Make eight HSTs using the eight at a time HST technique (see p.88) with one G3 and one BG7. Press. Trim to 8.9 x 8.9 cm (3½ x 3½ in).

15 Arrange the eight HSTs, along with one unit 5 HST, into a 3 x 3 grid as shown. Sew the HSTs RST and label as unit 8.

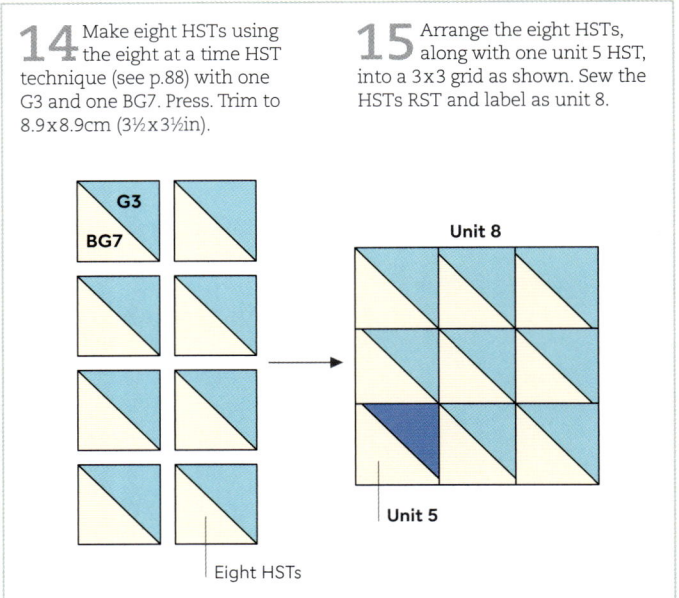

16 Make four snowball units using the stitch and flip technique (see p.89) with four B3, four C1, and twelve BG8.

17 Sew three BG8 and one C1 square to the corners of each B3 square. Press. The snowball units should measure 12.7 x 12.7 cm (5 x 5 in).

18 Arrange the units into a 2 x 2 grid with C1 corners meeting at the centre. Sew the units RST and label as unit 9.

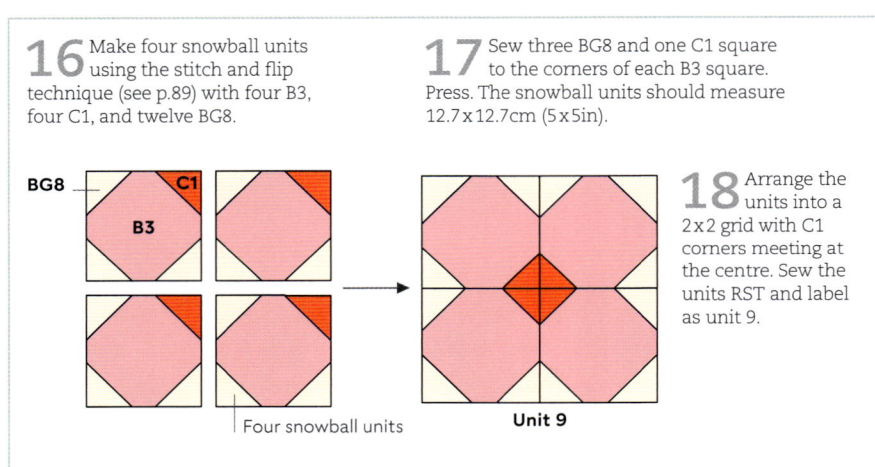

19 Make one four patch using the piece-by-piece technique (see p.84) with one B4, D4, E4, and G4 each. Press. The four patch should measure 16.5 x 16.5 cm (6½ x 6½ in) and label as unit 10.

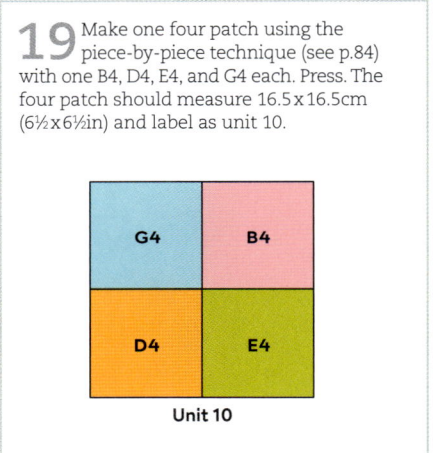

20 Make four HRTs using the two at a time HRT technique (see p.97) with two A2 and two BG9. Press. Trim to 8.9 x 16.5 cm (3½ x 6½ in). Arrange the HRTs into a row. Sew the HRTs RST and label as unit 11.

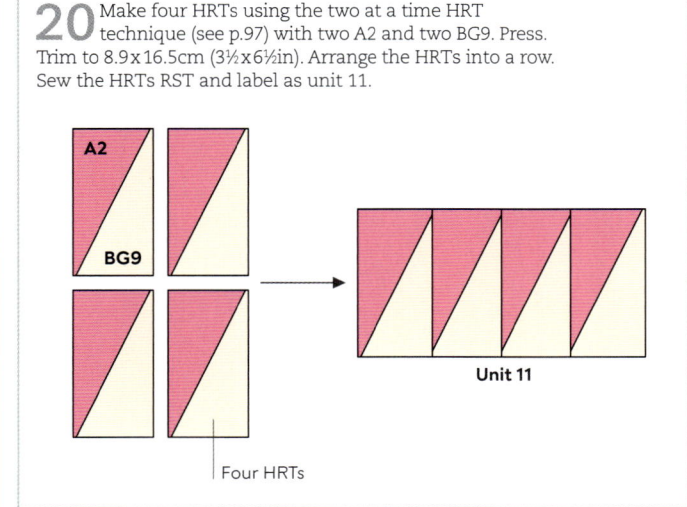

21 Make four FG using the one at a time FG technique (see p.92) with four H5 and eight BG10. Press. Trim to 8.9 x 16.5 cm (3½ x 6½ in). Arrange the FG into a column. Sew the FG RST and label as unit 12.

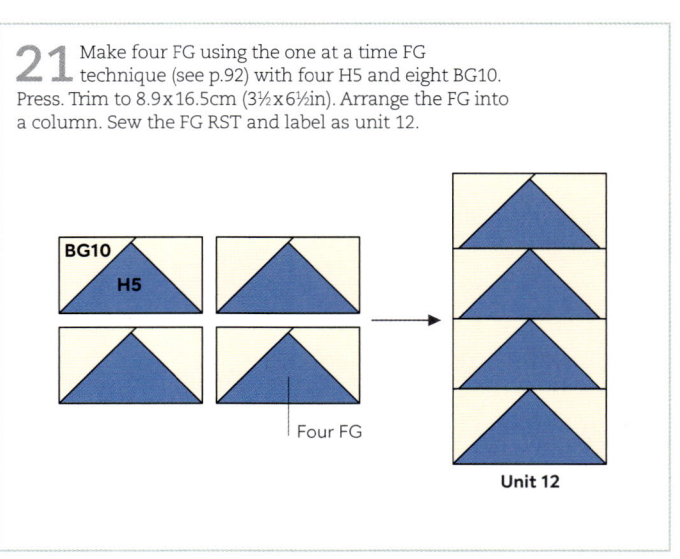

22 Make one square in a square unit using the setting triangles technique (see p.95) with two E5 and one BG11. Trim to 16.5 x 16.5cm (6½ x 6½in) and label as unit 13.

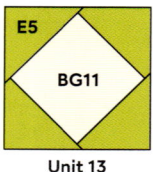
Unit 13

23 Make two HCs (see p.104) with two D6 convex pieces and two BG12 concave pieces. Press. Trim to 12.7 x 24.1cm (5 x 9½in).

24 Arrange the HCs into a column. Sew the HCs RST and label as unit 14.

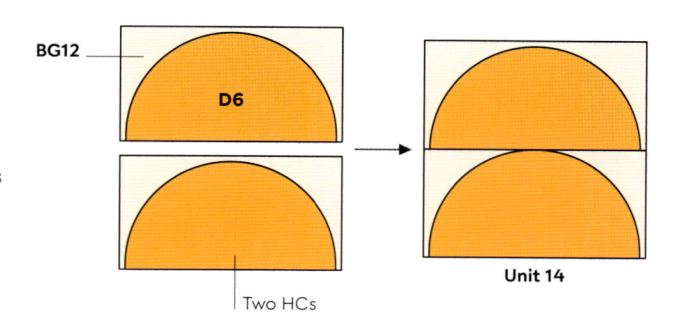
Two HCs
Unit 14

25 Make four HSTs using the four at a time piecing technique (see p.87) with one D5 and one BG13. Press. Trim to 8.9 x 8.9cm (3½ x 3½in).

26 Arrange the HSTs into a row. Sew the HSTs RST and label as unit 17.

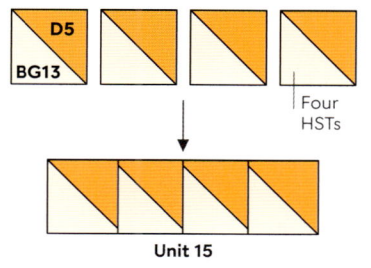
Four HSTs
Unit 15

27 Make one square in a square unit using the stitch and flip technique (see p.94) with four G4 and one BG14. Press. Trim to 16.5 x 16.5cm (6½ x 6½in) and label as unit 16.

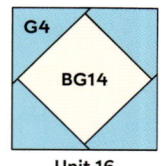
Unit 16

28 Make two HSTs using the two at a time HST technique (see p.86) with one A3 and one BG4. Press. Trim to 8.9 x 8.9cm (3½ x 3½in).

29 Arrange the HSTs into a row. Sew the HSTs RST and label as unit 17.

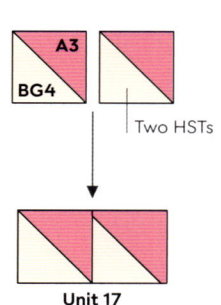
Two HSTs
Unit 17

30 Make four HSTs using the two at time HST technique (see p.86) with two E6 and two BG14. Press. Trim the HSTs to 15.2 x 15.2cm (6 x 6in).

31 Use the HSTs to make four QSTs using the two at a time QST technique (see p.90) and trim to 12.7 x 12.7cm (5 x 5in). Arrange the QSTs into a 2 x 2 grid as shown. Sew the QSTs RST and label as unit 18.

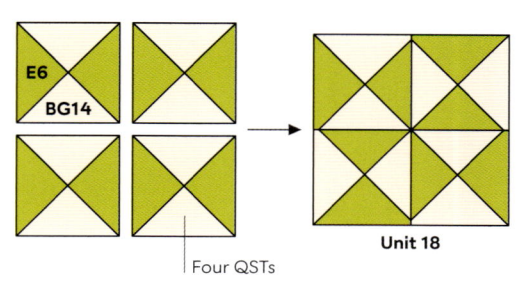
Four QSTs
Unit 18

32 Baste (see p.128) six B5 hexagon shapes and one C2 hexagon shape onto 3.8cm (1½in) hexagon paper pieces. Join the basted hexagons into a flower (see p.132) as shown.

33 Attach the hexagon flower onto the centre of one BG15 square using any appliqué technique (see p.134) and label as unit 19.

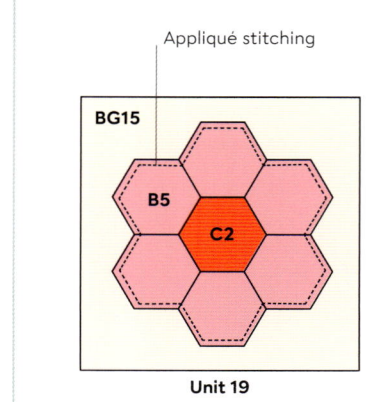
Appliqué stitching
Unit 19

34 Make four triangle in a square units (see p.99) using two G5 and two BG16. Press. Trim to 12.7 x 12.7cm (5 x 5in).

35 Arrange the units into a 2 x 2 grid with the triangle points facing out as shown. Sew units RST and label as unit 20.

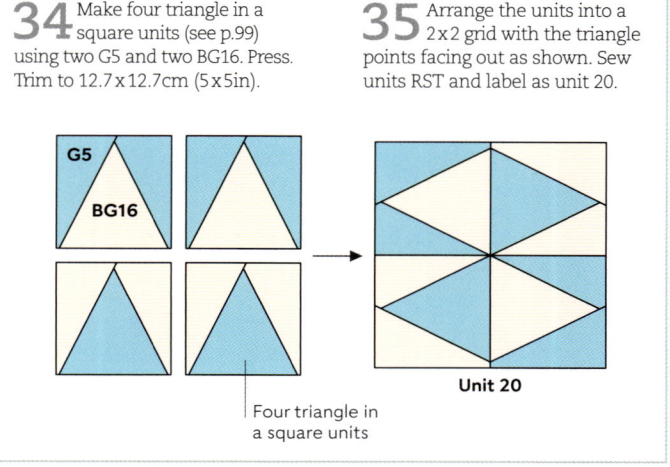
Four triangle in a square units
Unit 20

SECTION ASSEMBLY

Ensure all units are assembled and labelled correctly before beginning this section. Match all points and seams (see p.141) and press seams open (see p.80) after each step.

1 Sew unit 1 to the right of unit 2, RST, as shown.

2 Arrange the unit from step 1 and units 3 and 4 as shown. Sew the units RST and label as section 1.

3 Sew one unit 2 to the bottom of unit 5, RST, as shown.

4 Sew unit 6 to the right of the unit from step 3, RST, as shown.

5 Sew unit 7 to the top of the unit from step 4, RST, as shown. Label the unit as section 2.

8 Sew unit 10 to the top of unit 11, RST, as shown.

9 Sew unit 12 to the top of unit 13, RST, as shown.

10 Sew one unit 2 to the right of unit 14, RST, as shown.

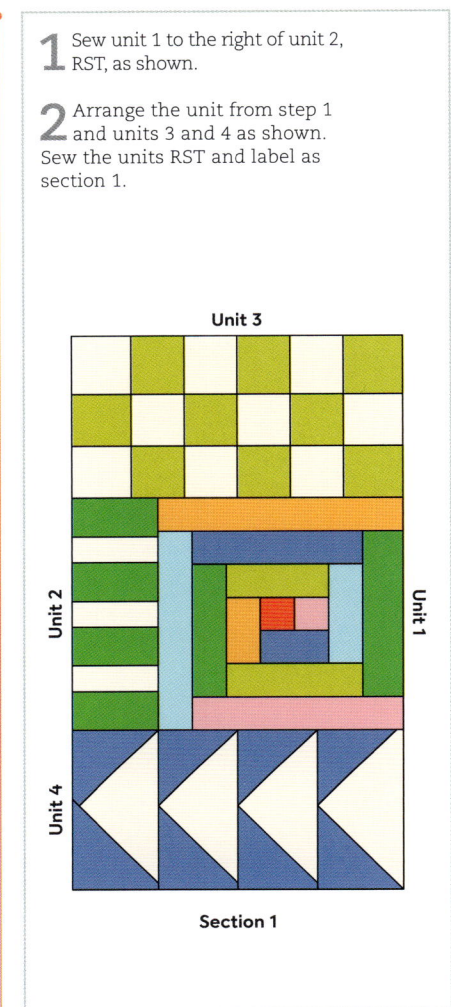

Section 1

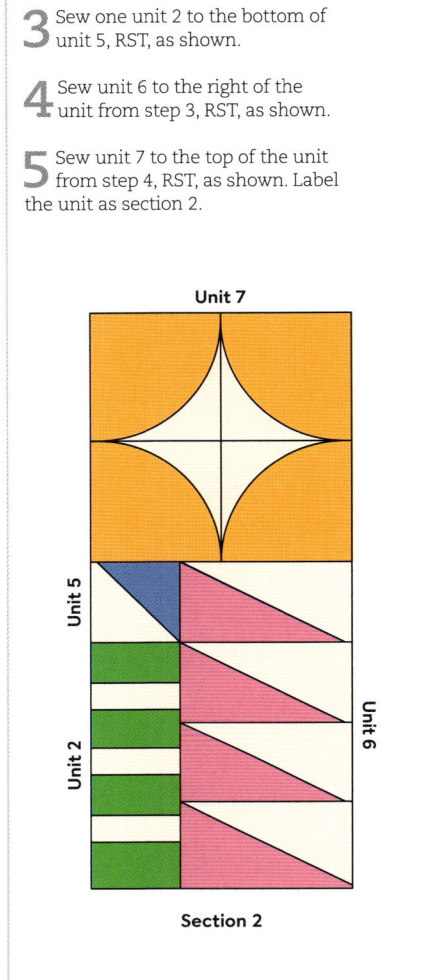

Section 2

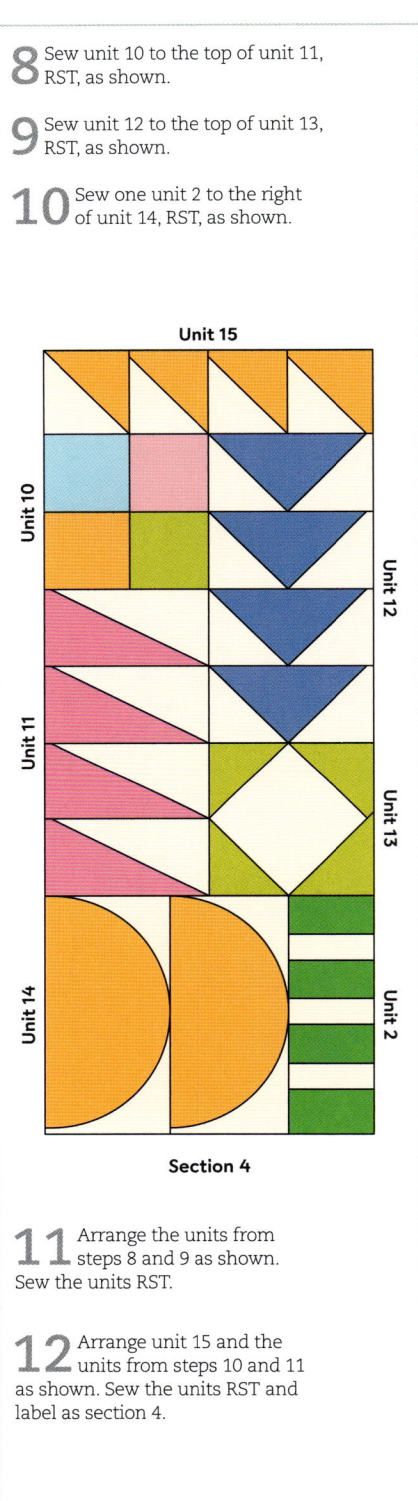

Section 4

6 Sew unit 8 to the left of unit 9, RST, as shown.

7 Sew one unit 2 to the right of the unit from step 6, RST, as shown. Label the unit as section 3.

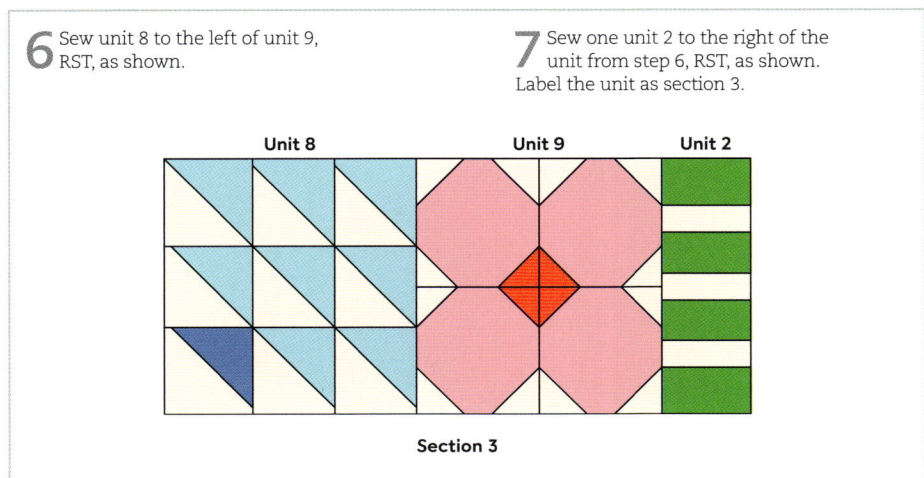

Section 3

11 Arrange the units from steps 8 and 9 as shown. Sew the units RST.

12 Arrange unit 15 and the units from steps 10 and 11 as shown. Sew the units RST and label as section 4.

BUILDING BLOCKS SAMPLER

13 Sew unit 16 to the top of unit 17, RST, as shown.

14 Arrange the unit from step 13 and units 18, 19, and 20 as shown. Sew the units RST and label as section 5.

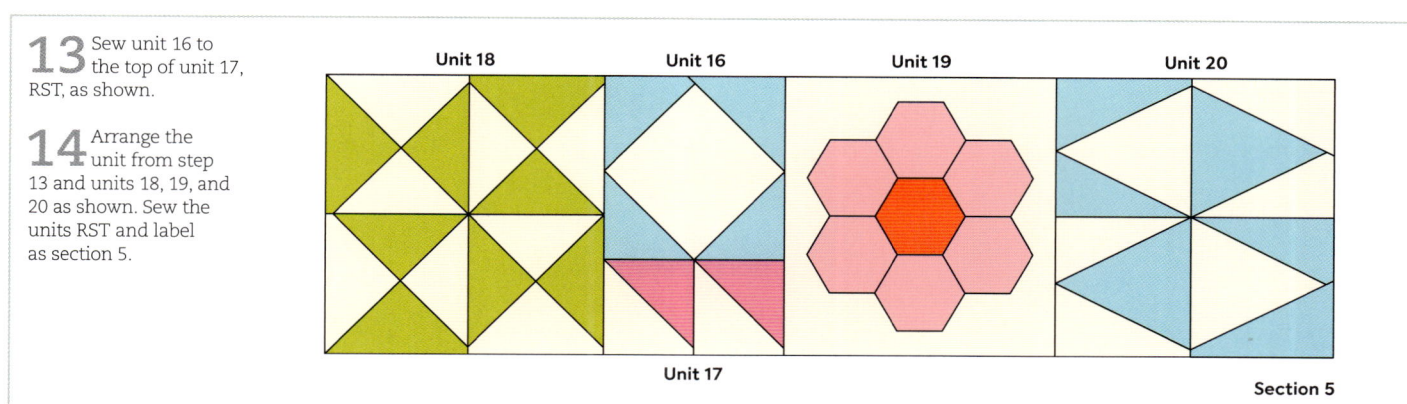

QUILT ASSEMBLY AND FINISHING

This quilt top is assembled using a medallion quilt top layout (see p.147).
Be sure to orient all sections as shown.

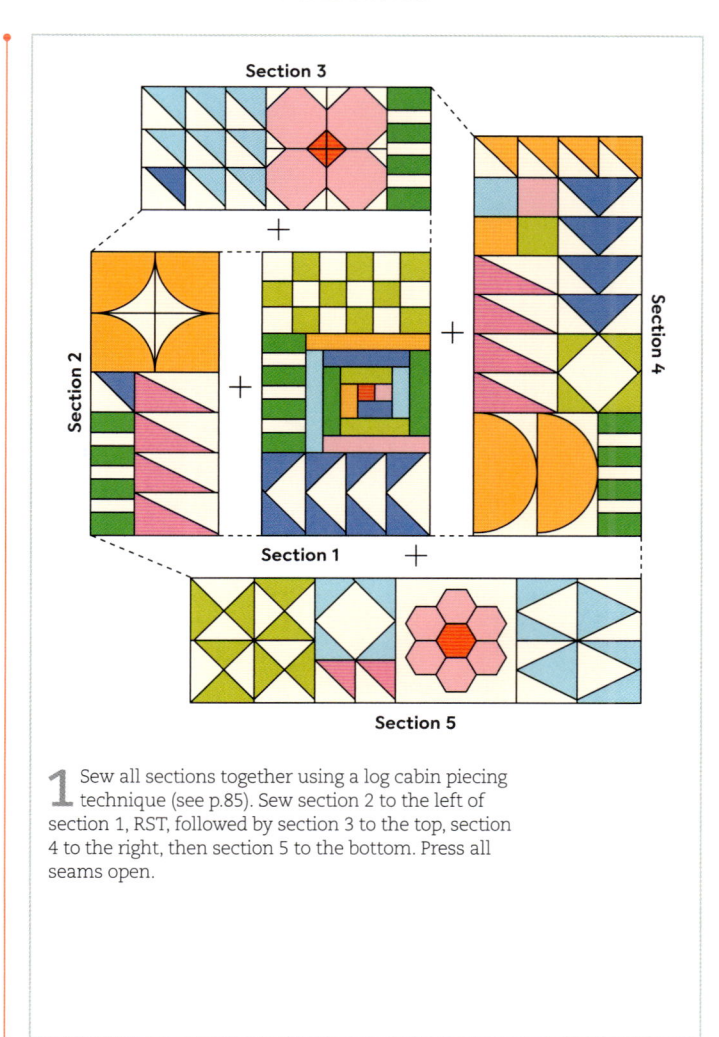

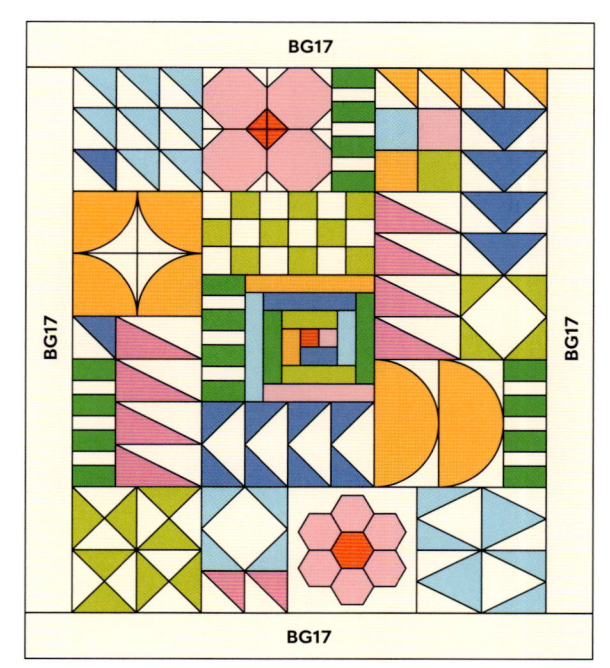

1 Sew all sections together using a log cabin piecing technique (see p.85). Sew section 2 to the left of section 1, RST, followed by section 3 to the top, section 4 to the right, then section 5 to the bottom. Press all seams open.

2 Sew two BG17 border strips to the left and right of the quilt top, RST, then sew the remaining two BG17 to the top and bottom. Press all seams toward BG17.

3 Press the entire quilt top from the front to remove wrinkles. To make binding, cut five 6.4cm (2½in) x WOF strips from the chosen binding fabric. Sew all five WOF strips, RST, to make one strip that is at least 465cm (183in) long. To finish the quilt, baste (see pp.157–159), quilt (see pp.160–171), and bind (see pp.172–181) as desired.

Cascading cabin

This quilt pattern is a modern interpretation of a traditional log cabin block. The centre log cabin is set on point, with strips extending as if they are flowing off the quilt. Experiment with colour theory to make a statement piece perfect for displaying.

FINISHED CRIB SIZE 122 x 122cm (48 x 48in)
TECHNIQUES USED Understanding colour theory **p.60**, Setting an accurate seam allowance **p.73**, Strip piecing **p.83**, Log cabin **p.85**, Setting triangles **p.95**, Registration lines **p.143**, On point quilt top layout **p.147**, Trimming a quilt **p.173**

MATERIALS

- Basic quilting supplies (see p.14)
- 24.1 x 24.1cm (9½ x 9½in) or larger square ruler
- Marking pen
- 137 x 137cm (54 x 54in) or larger wadding

FABRIC REQUIREMENTS

Fabrics A–X	(24) different 6.4cm (2½in) x WOF strips
Background (BG)	1.25m (1⅜yds)
Backing*	2.75m (3yds)
Binding	0.5m (½yd)

*Backing fabric required if using one vertical or horizontal seam.

Label and group fabrics A–X into four groups of six strips each. In the cover quilt, fabrics are grouped by hue (see p.60), and each group contains a gradient in value.

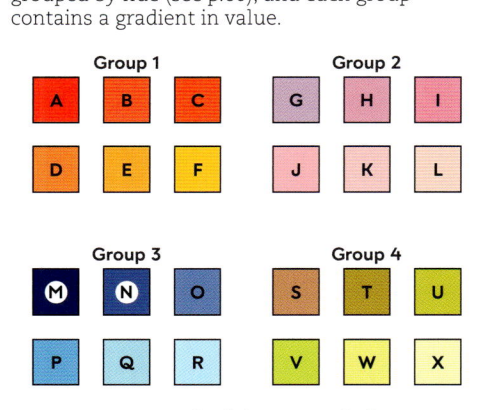

Cut out one 6.4cm (2½in) x WOF strip from each fabric when using yardage or meterage or select 24 strips from a pre-cut bundle of 6.4cm (2½in) x WOF strips.

COLOUR REFERENCE

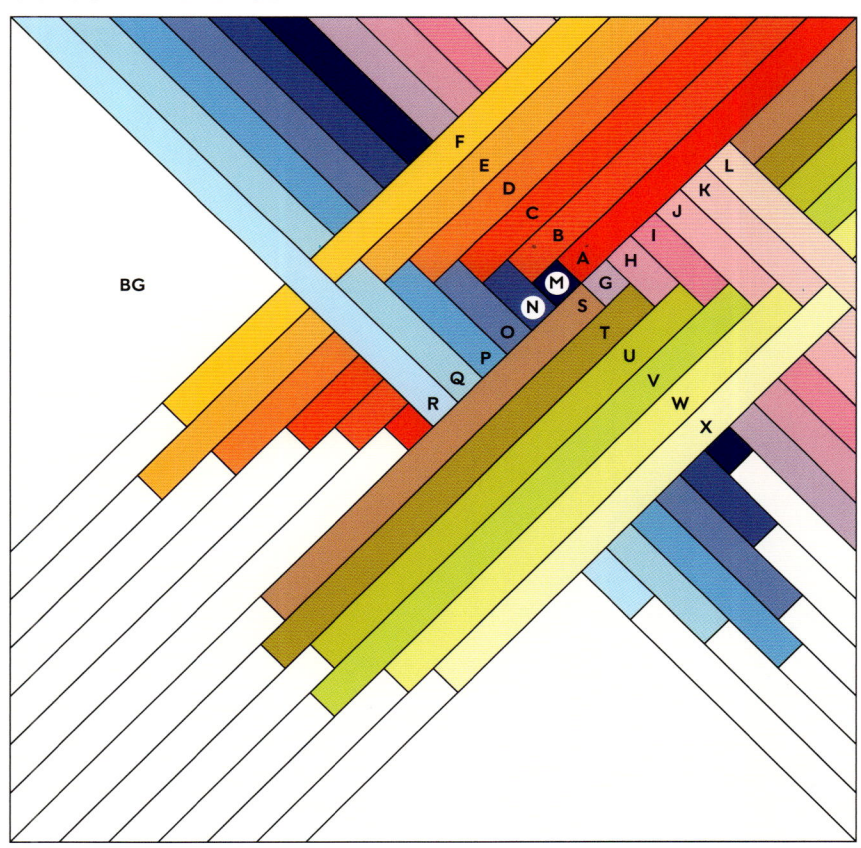

COVER QUILT DETAILS

Fabrics: Ruby and Bee Solids by Windham Fabrics in Capsicum (**A**), Delphinium (**B**), Mandarin (**C**), Marigold (**D**), Pumpkin (**E**), Mustard Seed (**F**), Vervain (**G**), Unicorn (**H**), Fairy Floss (**I**), Posy (**J**), Shell Pink (**K**), Blush (**L**), Night Sky (**M**), Majorelle Blue (**N**), Provence Blue (**O**), Sky (**P**), Aquamarine (**Q**), Marine Layer (**R**), Field Mouse (**S**), Turmeric (**T**), Avocado (**U**), Limeade (**V**), Lemonade (**W**), Sweet Cream (**X**), Wisp (**BG**); **Quilting:** Walking foot rectangular grid by Bailey of Copper and Citrus; **Thread:** Aurifil 50 wt in 2405; **Wadding:** Hobbs Tuscany Bleached 100% Cotton; **Facing:** Delphinium

CUTTING INSTRUCTIONS

Use the fabric cutting tables and diagrams below to cut out and label the pieces required from fabrics A–X and BG.

FABRIC CUTTING TABLES

FABRICS A–X
From each 6.4cm (2½in) x WOF strip, **sub-cut:**

A	**A1:** (1) 6.4x6.4cm (2½x2½in) **A2:** (1) 6.4x61cm (2½x24in)	M	**M1:** (1) 6.4x6.4cm (2½x2½in) **M2:** (1) 6.4x6.4cm (2½x2½in) **M3:** (1) 6.4x35.6cm (2½x14in)
B	**B1:** (1) 6.4x11.4cm (2½x4½in) **B2:** (1) 6.4x61cm (2½x24in)	N	**N1:** (1) 6.4x16.5cm (2½x6½in) **N2:** (1) 6.4x11.4cm (2½x4½in) **N3:** (1) 6.4x40.6cm (2½x16in)
C	**C1:** (1) 6.4x16.5cm (2½x6½in) **C2:** (1) 6.4x61cm (2½x24in)	O	**O1:** (1) 6.4x26.7cm (2½x10½in) **O2:** (1) 6.4x16.5cm (2½x6½in) **O3:** (1) 6.4x45.7cm (2½x18in)
D	**D1:** (1) 6.4x26.7cm (2½x10½in) **D2:** (1) 6.4x61cm (2½x24in)	P	**P1:** (1) 6.4x31.8cm (2½x12½in) **P2:** (1) 6.4x21.6cm (2½x8½in) **P3:** (1) 6.4x50.8cm (2½x20in)
E	**E1:** (1) 6.4x36.8cm (2½x14½in) **E2:** (1) 6.4x61cm (2½x24in)	Q	**Q1:** (1) 6.4x21.6cm (2½x8½in) **Q2:** (1) 6.4x26.7cm (2½x10½in) **Q3:** (1) 6.4x55.9cm (2½x22in)
F	**F1:** (1) 6.4x26.7cm (2½x10½in) **F2:** (1) 6.4x61cm (2½x24in)	R	**R1:** (1) 6.4x11.4cm (2½x4½in) **R2:** (1) 6.4x91.4cm (2½x36in)
G	**G1:** (1) 6.4x30.5cm (2½x12in) **G2:** (1) 6.4x6.4cm (2½x2½in) **G3:** (1) 6.4x30.5cm (2½x12in)	S	**S1:** (1) 6.4x30.5cm (2½x12in) **S2:** (1) 6.4x67.3cm (2½x26½in)
H	**H1:** (1) 6.4x25.4cm (2½x10in) **H2:** (1) 6.4x11.4cm (2½x4½in) **H3:** (1) 6.4x25.4cm (2½x10in)	T	**T1:** (1) 6.4x25.4cm (2½x10in) **T2:** (1) 6.4x77.5cm (2½x30½in)
I	**I1:** (1) 6.4x20.3cm (2½x8in) **I2:** (1) 6.4x16.5cm (2½x6½in) **I3:** (1) 6.4x20.3cm (2½x8in)	U	**U1:** (1) 6.4x20.3cm (2½x8in) **U2:** (1) 6.4x77.5cm (2½x30½in)
J	**J1:** (1) 6.4x15.2cm (2½x6in) **J2:** (1) 6.4x21.6cm (2½x8½in) **J3:** (1) 6.4x15.2cm (2½x6in)	V	**V1:** (1) 6.4x15.2cm (2½x6in) **V2:** (1) 6.4x87.6cm (2½x34½in)
K	**K1:** (1) 6.4x10.2cm (2½x4in) **K2:** (1) 6.4x25.4cm (2½x10½in) **K3:** (1) 6.4x10.2cm (2½x4in)	W	**W1:** (1) 6.4x10.2cm (2½x4in) **W2:** (1) 6.4x82.6cm (2½x32½in)
L	**L1:** (1) 6.4x35.6cm (2½x14in) **L2:** (1) 6.4x6.4cm (2½x2½in)	X	**X1:** (1) 6.4x6.4cm (2½x2½in) **X2:** (1) 6.4x82.6cm (2½x32½in)

FABRIC BG (BACKGROUND)

Cut (1) 63.5cm (25in) x WOF; **sub-cut:**
 BG-Y: (1) 63.5x63.5cm (25x25in)
 BG-S2: (1) 6.4x55.9cm (2½x22in)
 BG-D1: (1) 6.4x50.8cm (2½x20in)
 BG-R1: (1) 6.4x50.8cm (2½x20in)
 BG-U2: (1) 6.4x45.7cm (2½x18in)
 BG-W2: (1) 6.4x40.6cm (2½x16in)
 BG-X2: (1) 6.4x40.6cm (2½x16in)

Cut (5) 6.4cm (2½in) x WOF;
From the first strip, **sub-cut:**
 BG-A1: (1) 6.4x86.4cm (2½x34in)
 BG-O1: (1) 6.4x20.3cm (2½x8in)
From the second strip, **sub-cut:**
 BG-B1: (1) 6.4x76.2cm (2½x30in)
 BG-M1: (1) 6.4x30.5cm (2½x12in)
From the third strip, **sub-cut:**
 BG-C1: (1) 6.4x66cm (2½x26in)
 BG-F1: (1) 6.4x40.6cm (2½x16in)
From the fourth strip, **sub-cut:**
 BG-T2: (1) 6.4x45.7cm (2½x18in)
 BG-N1: (1) 6.4x25.4cm (2½x10in)
 BG-P1: (1) 6.4x20.3cm (2½x8in)
From the fifth strip, **sub-cut:**
 BG-E1: (1) 6.4x35.6cm (2½x14in)
 BG-Q1: (1) 6.4x35.6cm (2½x14in)
 BG-V2: (1) 6.4x35.6cm (2½x14in))

SUB-CUTTING FABRICS A–X

1 Lay each fabric strip horizontally, and sub-cut (see p.70) vertical segments according to the fabric cutting tables. Some strips may have excess fabric that is not needed.

2 Label all pieces to stay organized.

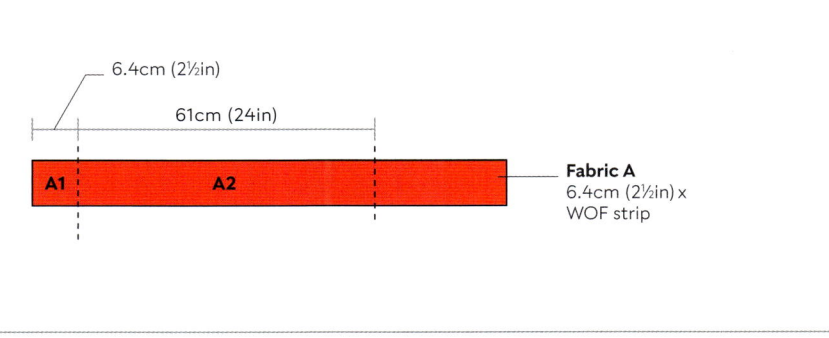

BLOCK ASSEMBLY

Some of the pieces used in this section are joined to corresponding background pieces; for example, A1 corresponds to BG-A1. Ensure all pieces are labelled correctly before beginning.

1 Mark a diagonal line from corner to corner on BG-Y. Sew a stay stitch (see p.151) 3.2mm (⅛in) away from either side of the marked line.

2 Cut directly on the marked diagonal line to make two BG-Y setting triangles. Set aside.

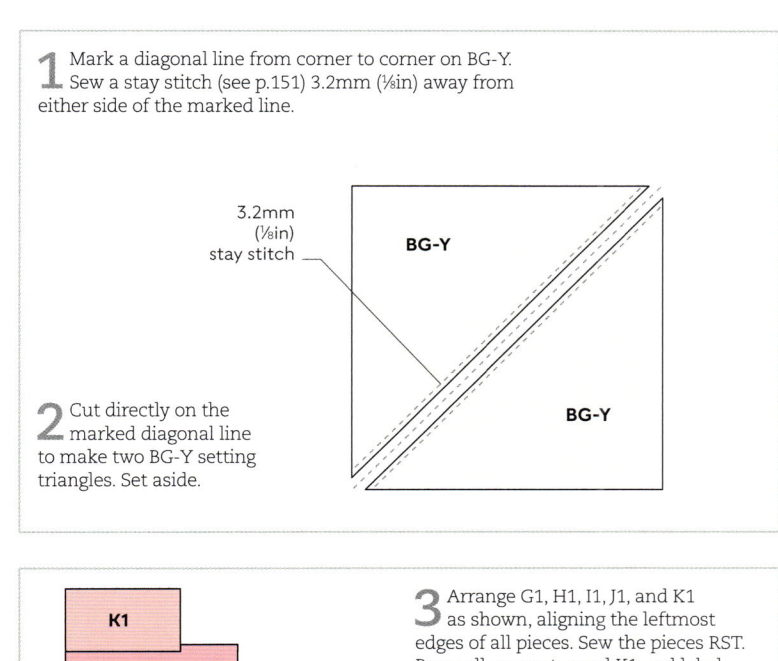

3 Arrange G1, H1, I1, J1, and K1 as shown, aligning the leftmost edges of all pieces. Sew the pieces RST. Press all seams toward K1 and label the block as block 1.

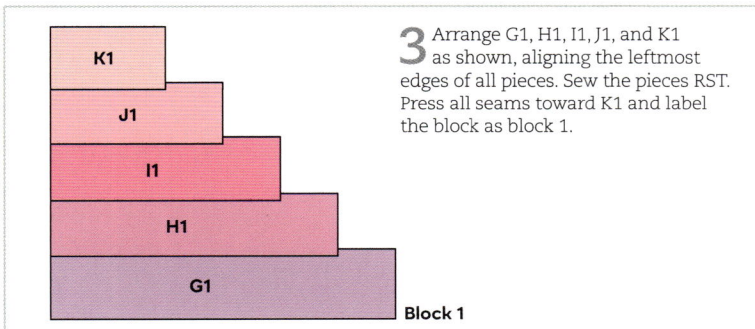

4 Sew M1 RST with its corresponding background piece, BG-M1, to make a strip. Repeat to sew N1, O1, P1, Q1, and R1 to their corresponding background pieces. Press all seams open.

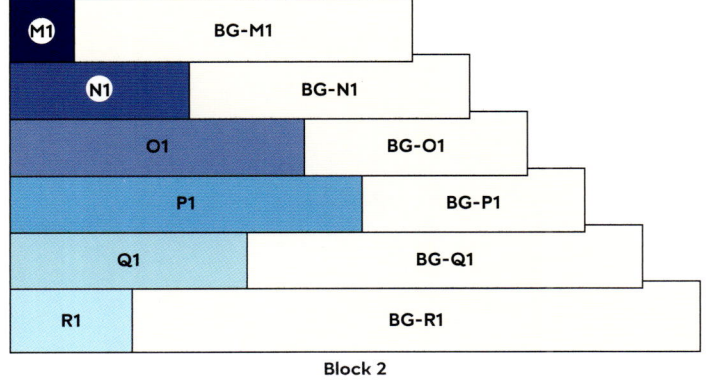

5 Arrange the strips from step 4 as shown, aligning the leftmost edges. Sew the strips RST. Press all seams toward M1 and label the block as block 2.

6 Sew S2 RST with its corresponding background piece, BG-S2, to make a strip. Repeat to sew T2, U2, V2, W2, and X2 to their corresponding background pieces. Press all seams open.

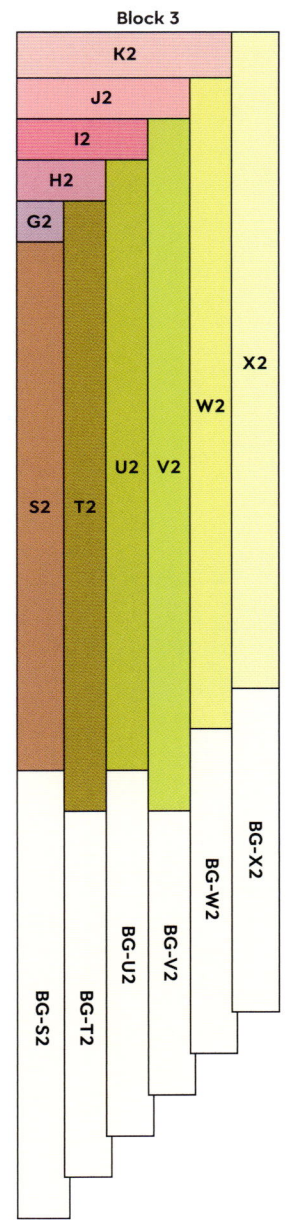

7 Using a log cabin piecing technique (see p.85), sew G2 to the top of the S2 strip. Sew the T2 strip to the right of the unit, then H2 to the top. Continue adding pieces one at a time to the right and top of the unit as shown to complete the block. Press all seams away from G2 and label the block as block 3.

8 Arrange S1, T1, U1, V1, W1, and X1 as shown, aligning the bottom edges. Sew the pieces RST. Press all seams toward X1.

9 Sew L1 to the bottom of the unit from step 8, RST, aligning the leftmost edges. Press away from L1 and label the block as block 4.

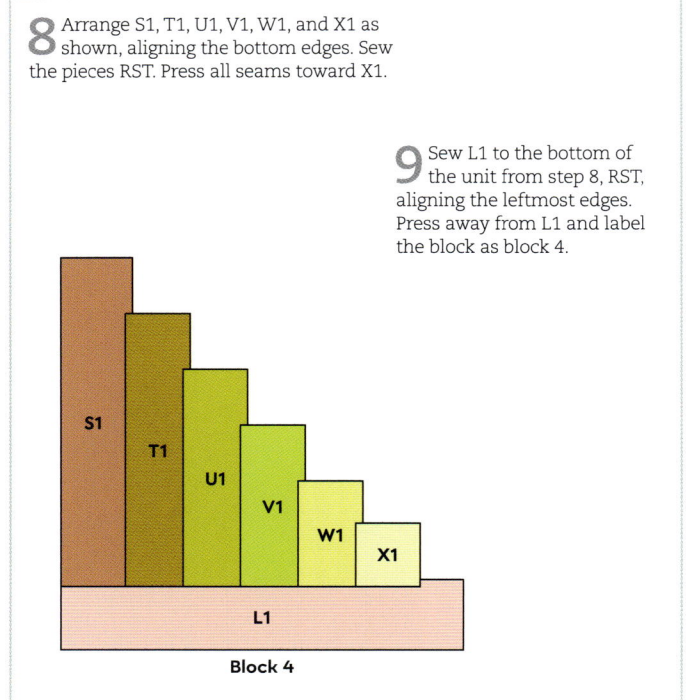

Block 4

10 Arrange G3, H3, I3, J3, K3, L2, M3, N3, O3, P3, and Q3 as shown, aligning the rightmost edges. Sew the pieces RST. Press all seams toward L2 and label the block as block 5.

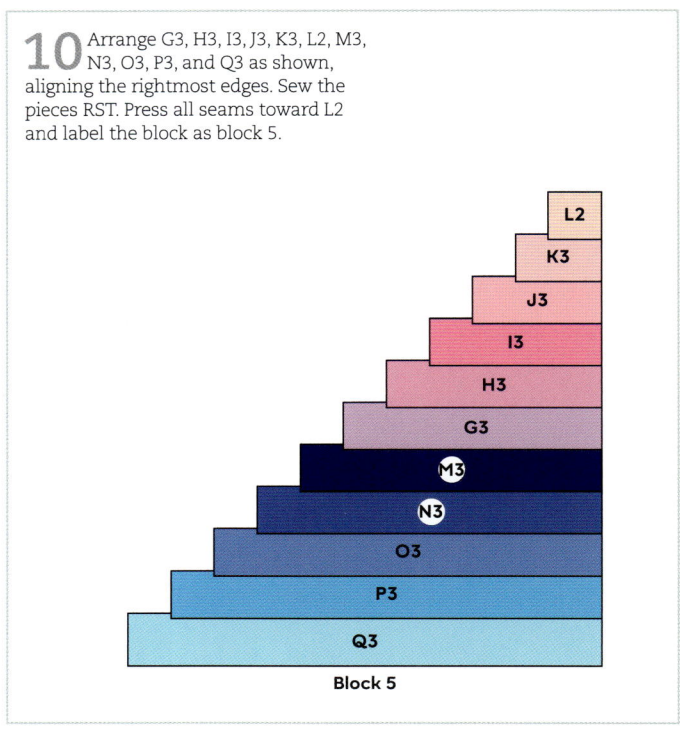

Block 5

11 Using a log cabin piecing technique (see p.85), sew M2 to the bottom of A2. Sew B2 to the left of the unit, then N2 to the bottom. Continue adding pieces one at a time to the left and bottom of the unit as shown to complete the block. Press all seams away from M2 and label the block as block 6.

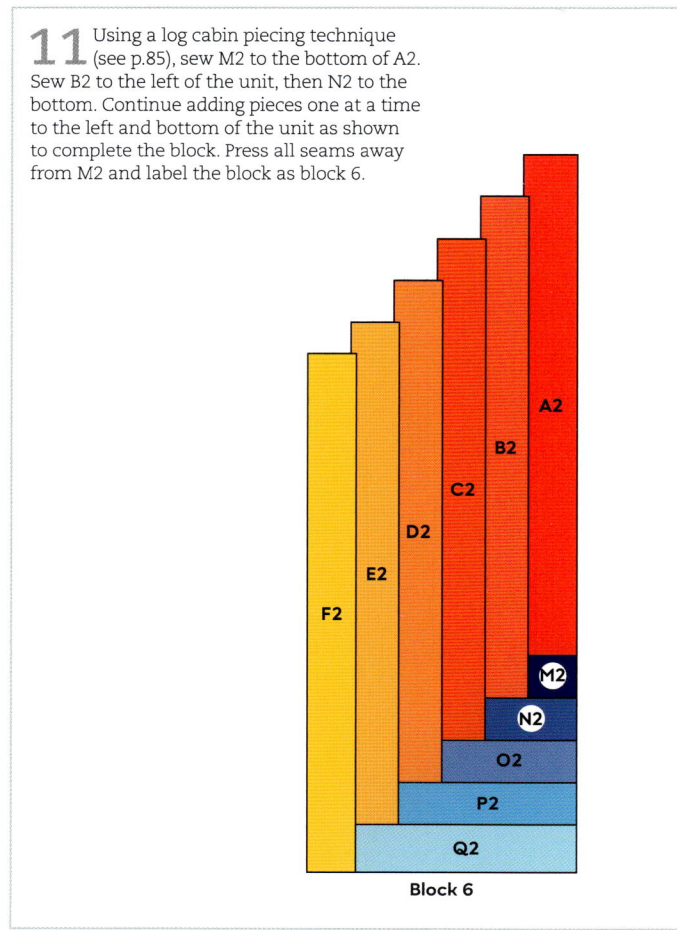

Block 6

12 Sew A1 RST with its corresponding background piece, BG-A1, to make a strip. Repeat to sew B1, C1, D1, E1, and F1 to their corresponding background pieces. Press all seams open.

13 Arrange the strips from step 12 as shown, aligning the top edges. Sew the strips RST. Press all seams toward F1 and label the block as block 7.

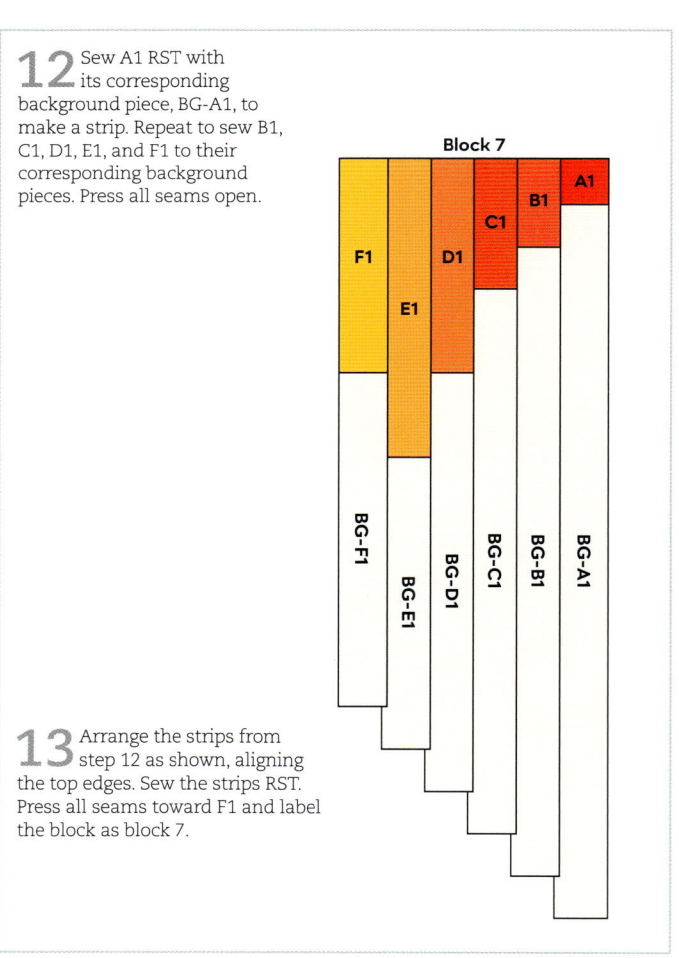

SECTION 1 ASSEMBLY

Ensure all blocks are assembled and labelled correctly before beginning this section.
Use registration lines (see p.143) to align pieces across strips when joining blocks.

1 Arrange block 1, block 2, and one BG-Y triangle as shown, aligning the bottom edges. Sew the blocks RST. Press the seams toward block 1.

2 Sew block 3 to the bottom of the unit from step 1, aligning the leftmost edges. Press the seam away from block 3.

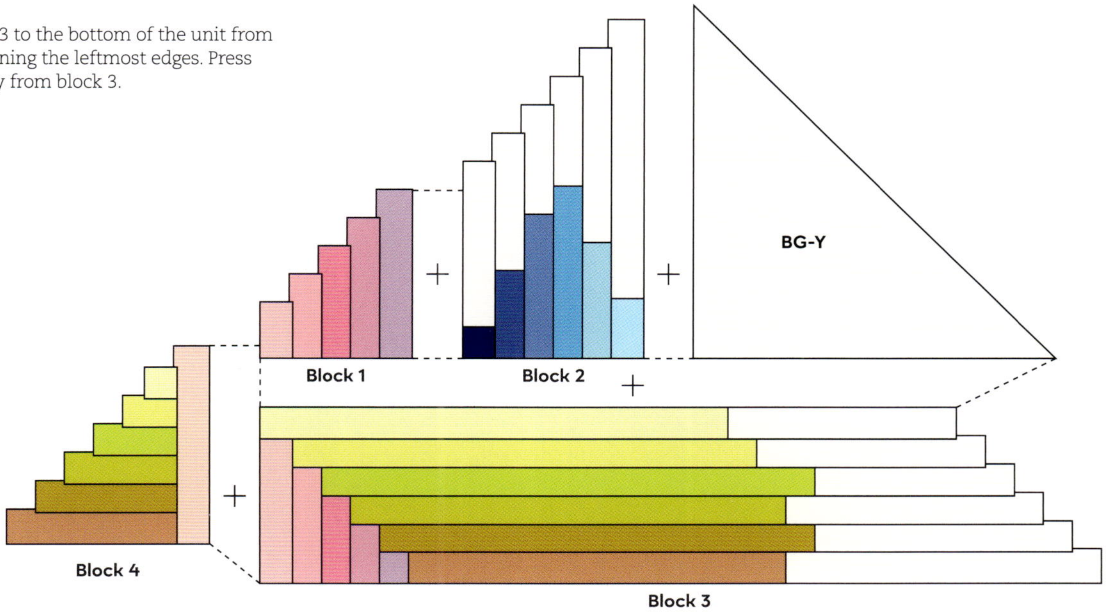

3 Sew block 4 to the left of the unit from step 2, aligning the bottom edges. Press the seam toward block 4 and label as section 1.

4 Sew a stay stitch (see p.151) around the outside edges of section 1 to prevent the bias edges from stretching. Stitch no more than 3.2mm (⅛in) away from the edges. Do not trim uneven edges.

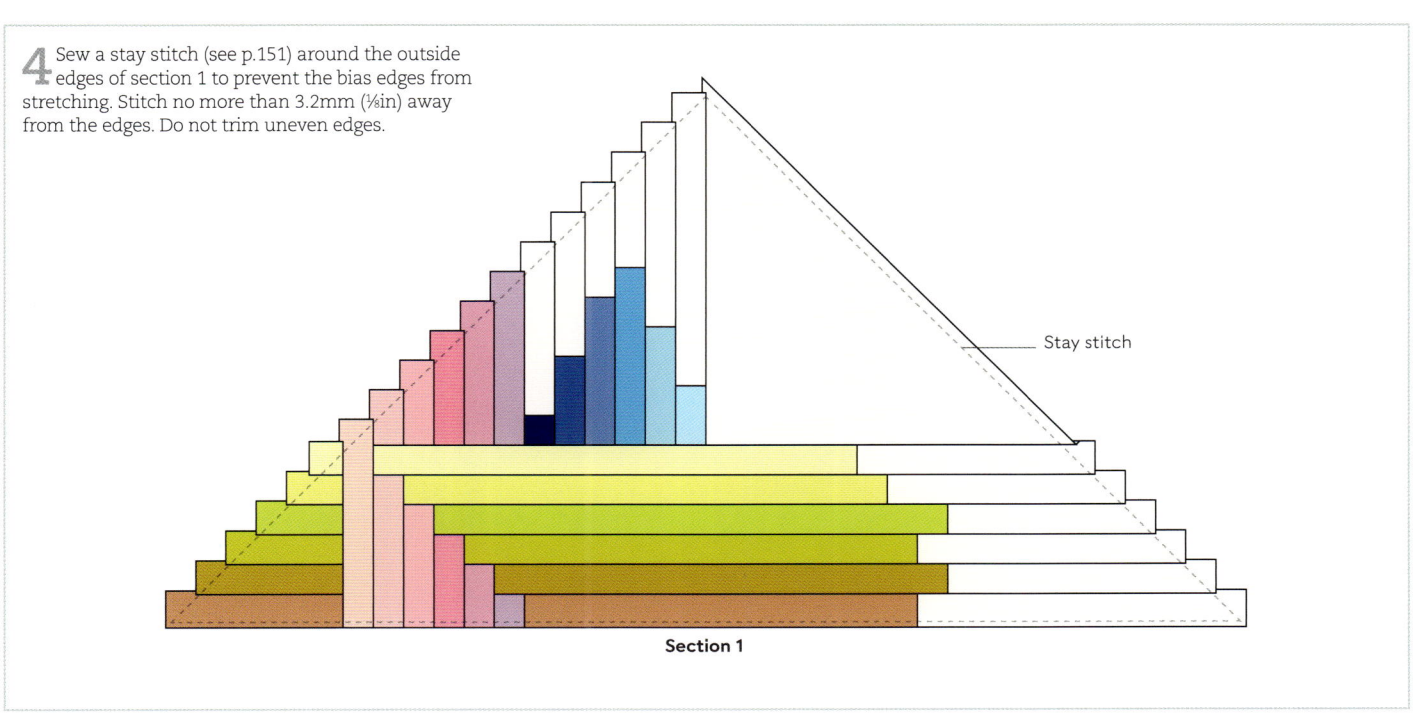

SECTION 2 ASSEMBLY

Ensure all blocks are assembled and labelled correctly before beginning this section.
Use registration lines (see p.143) to align pieces across strips when joining blocks.

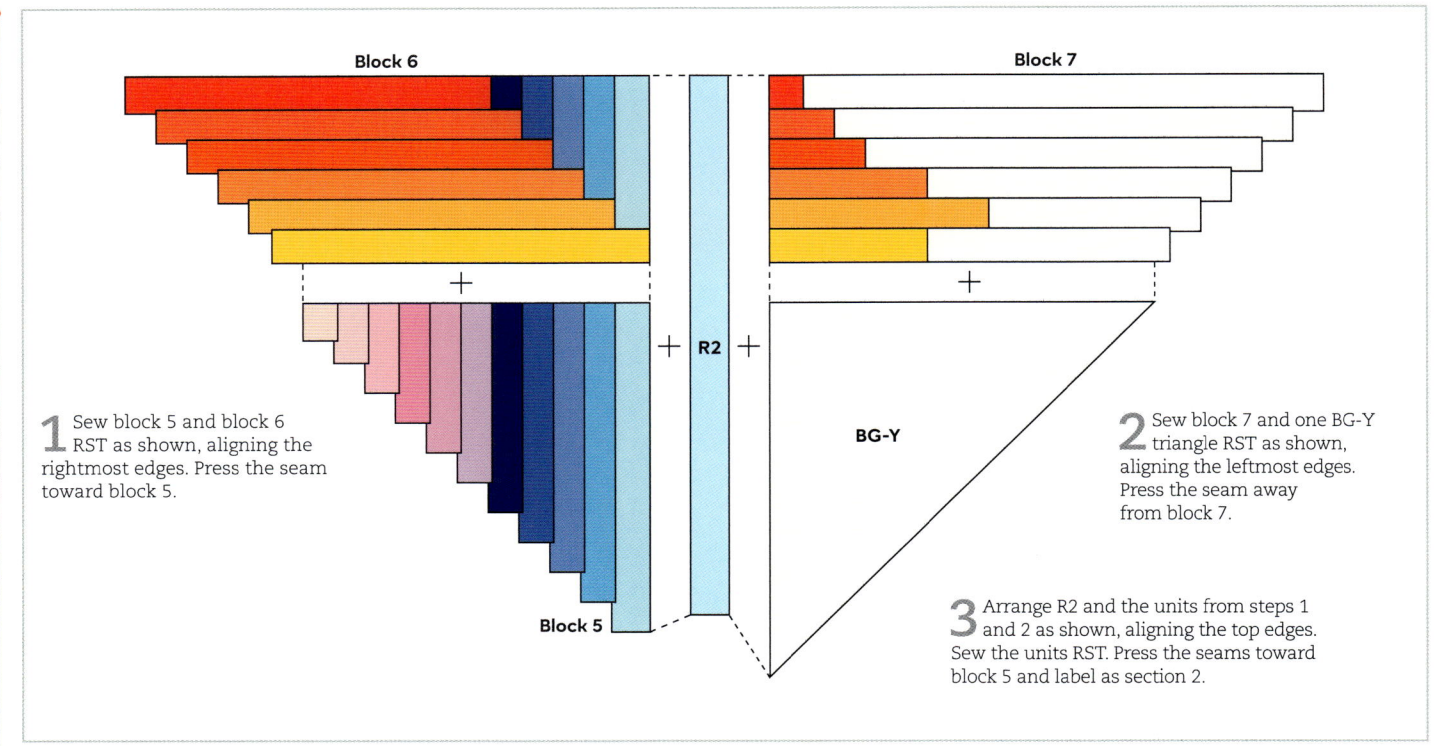

1 Sew block 5 and block 6 RST as shown, aligning the rightmost edges. Press the seam toward block 5.

2 Sew block 7 and one BG-Y triangle RST as shown, aligning the leftmost edges. Press the seam away from block 7.

3 Arrange R2 and the units from steps 1 and 2 as shown, aligning the top edges. Sew the units RST. Press the seams toward block 5 and label as section 2.

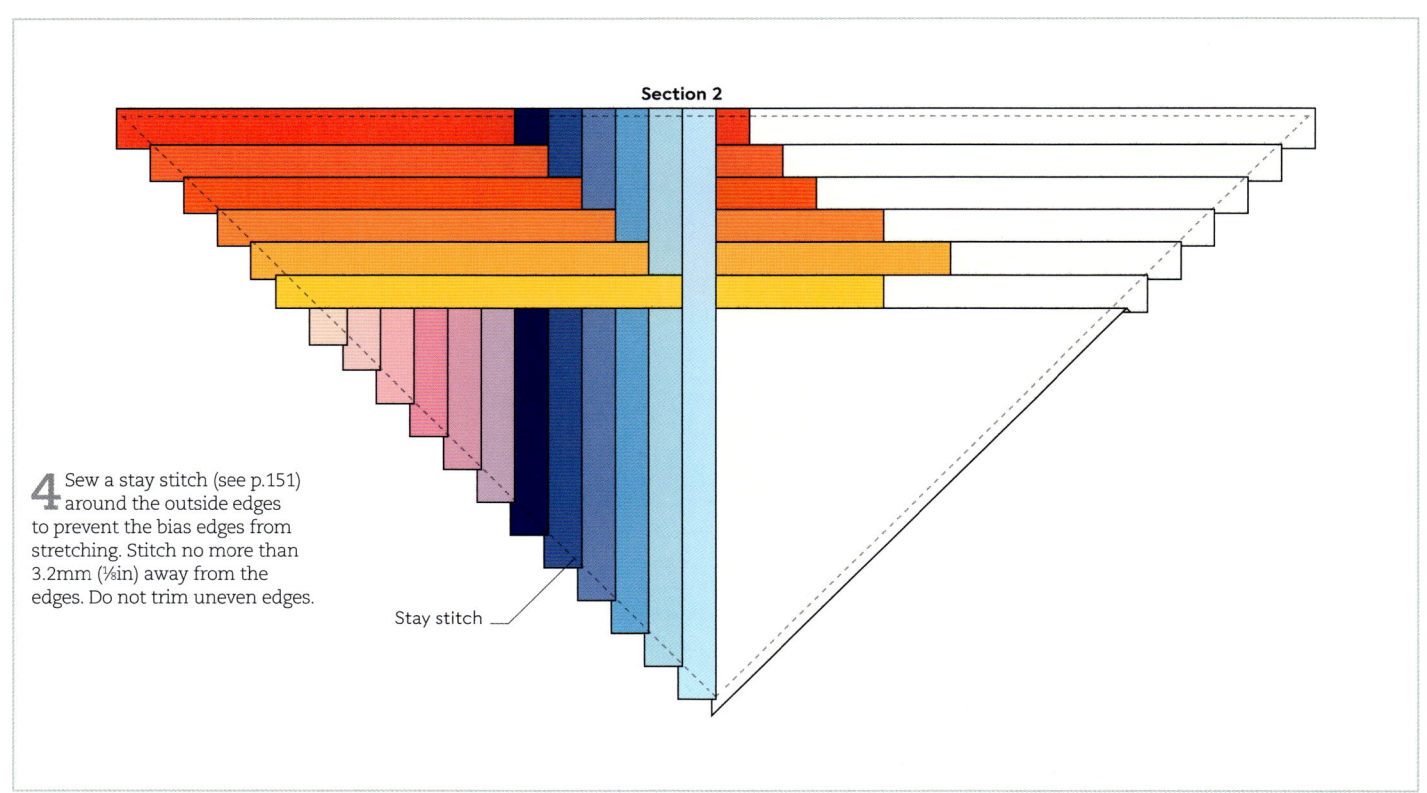

4 Sew a stay stitch (see p.151) around the outside edges to prevent the bias edges from stretching. Stitch no more than 3.2mm (⅛in) away from the edges. Do not trim uneven edges.

QUILT ASSEMBLY AND FINISHING

This pattern is assembled using an on point quilt top layout (see p.147). Mark registration lines to assist with aligning seams across both sections, and sew carefully to avoid stretching bias edges.

1. Sew section 1 and section 2 RST along their long edges as shown. Align the sections carefully, nesting the M2 and G2 seams at the centre. Press the seam open.

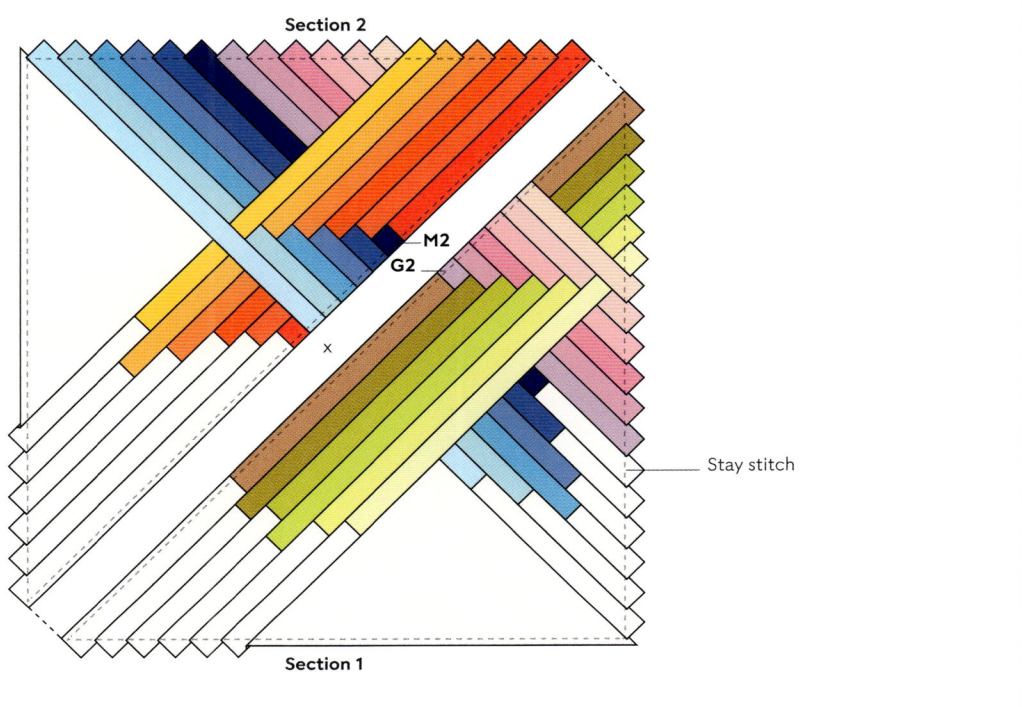

2. Trim the uneven edges to square the quilt top (see p.173), leaving at least 6.4mm (¼in) seam allowance at the three areas where seams intersect one another to preserve points. Use the centre diagonal seams to assist with ruler alignment when trimming the corners square.

3. Press the entire quilt top to remove all wrinkles. Sew a stay stitch 3.2mm (⅛in) around the outside edge of the trimmed quilt to prevent bias edges from stretching.

4. To make binding, cut six 6.4cm (2½in) x WOF strips from the chosen binding fabric. Sew all six WOF strips, RST, to make one strip that is at least 526cm (207in) long.

5. Baste (see pp.157–159), quilt (see pp.160–171), and bind (see pp.172–181) as desired.

Stellar prism

This quilt pattern is inspired by the angled shapes visible in a kaleidoscope. The design features EPP diamond stars centred within a hexagonal frame, providing practice with irregular angles, EPP, and appliqué techniques.

FINISHED THROW SIZE 165 x 178cm (65 x 70in)
TECHNIQUES USED Setting triangles **p.95**, Equilateral triangles **p.100**, Half hexagons **p.101**, English paper piecing **p.124**, Appliqué, **p.134**, Row quilt top layout **p.146**

MATERIALS

- Basic quilting supplies (see p.14)
- Tweezers (optional)
- 8.9 x 31.8cm (3½ x 12½in) or larger rectangular ruler with 60-degree lines
- Equilateral triangle ruler and half hexagon ruler (optional)
- Marking pen
- Printer and EPP template paper or 138 pre-cut 3.8cm (1½in) EPP diamond paper pieces
- 3.8cm (1½in) EPP diamond acrylic template (optional)
- Needle and thread for EPP
- 180 x 196cm (71 x 77in) or larger wadding

FABRIC REQUIREMENTS

Fabrics A–F	0.5m (½yd)
Fabric G	0.5m (¾yd)
Background (BG)	3.25m (3½yds)
Backing*	3.75m (4yds)
Binding	0.75m (¾yd)

*Backing fabric required when using one horizontal seam.

Choose fabrics that form a gradient effect for fabrics A–F, a contrasting (see p.61) fabric for fabric G, and a BG fabric that allows the design to stand out. Directional fabrics are not recommended.

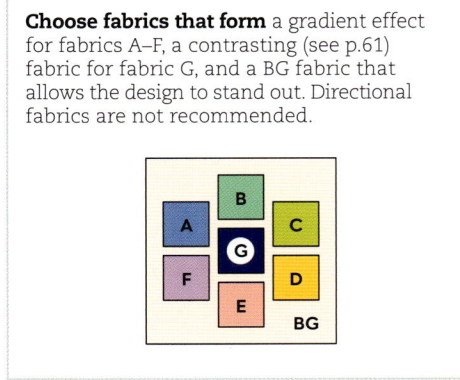

COLOUR REFERENCE

COVER QUILT DETAILS

Fabrics: Ruby and Bee Solids by Windham Fabrics in Provence Blue (**A**), Minty (**B**), Avocado (**C**), Mustard Seed (**D**), Peachy Keen (**E**), Vervain (**F**), Night Sky (**G**), Cream Puff (**BG**); **Quilting:** Ruler work and free motion; **Thread:** Aurifil 50 wt in 2311; **Wadding:** Hobbs Heirloom 100% Wool; **Binding:** Night Sky

CUTTING INSTRUCTIONS

Use the fabric cutting tables below to cut out and label the pieces required from fabrics A–G and BG. Refer to the half hexagon (see p.101), EPP diamond (see p.127), and equilateral triangle (see p.100) cutting techniques for more detailed instructions. Visit *The Quilting Book* website (see p.11) to print the required EPP diamond templates.

FABRIC CUTTING TABLES

FABRICS A–F

From each fabric:
Cut (4) 8.9cm (3½in) x WOF; **sub-cut:**
  A1–F1: (19) 8.9cm (3½in) half hexagons (19 for each fabric)

FABRIC G

Cut (9) 5.1cm (2in) x WOF; **sub-cut:**
  G1: (138) diamonds to use with 3.8cm (1½in) diamond paper pieces

BACKGROUND (BG)

Cut (6) 19.1cm (7½in) x WOF; **sub-cut:**
  BG3: (36) 19.1cm (7½in) equilateral triangles
  BG4: (20) 19.1cm (7½in) edge triangles

Cut (8) 8.9cm (3½in) x WOF; **sub-cut:**
  BG2: (114) 8.9cm (3½in) equilateral triangles
  BG1: (2) 3.8 x 25.4cm (1½in x 10in)

Cut (4) 25.4cm (10in) x WOF; **sub-cut:**
  BG1: (112) 3.8 x 25.4cm (1½in x 10in) (114 total **BG1**)

FABRIC CUTTING DIAGRAMS

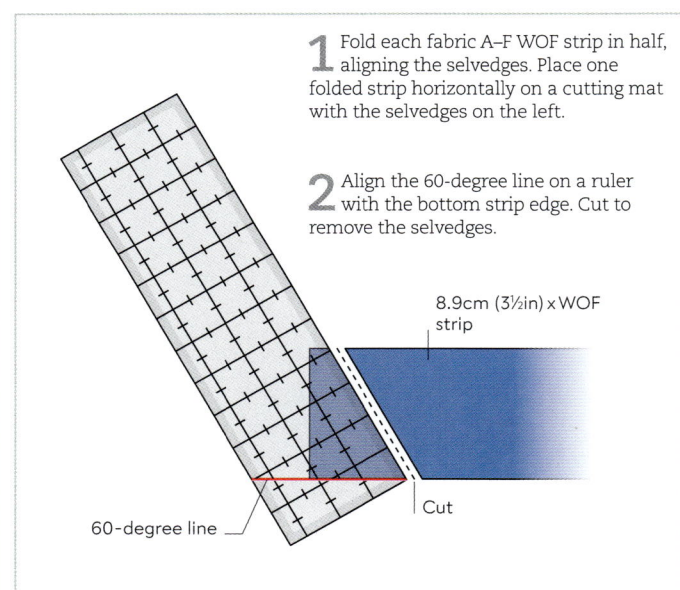

1 Fold each fabric A–F WOF strip in half, aligning the selvedges. Place one folded strip horizontally on a cutting mat with the selvedges on the left.

2 Align the 60-degree line on a ruler with the bottom strip edge. Cut to remove the selvedges.

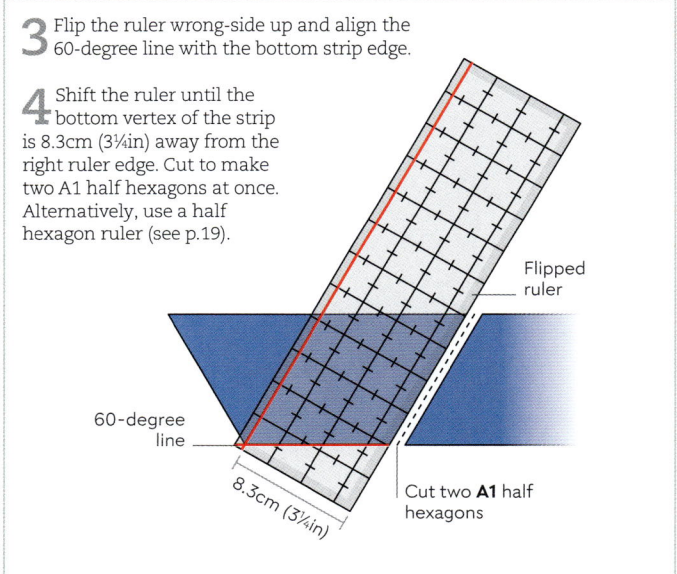

3 Flip the ruler wrong-side up and align the 60-degree line with the bottom strip edge.

4 Shift the ruler until the bottom vertex of the strip is 8.3cm (3¼in) away from the right ruler edge. Cut to make two A1 half hexagons at once. Alternatively, use a half hexagon ruler (see p.19).

5 Flip the ruler right-side up. Repeat step 4 to cut another A1, measuring away from the *top* vertex of the strip. Continue, flipping the ruler to make each cut, for a total of six A1 per WOF strip.

6 Repeat steps 1–5 to cut a total of 19 half hexagons for each fabric A–F. Label each half hexagon to match its corresponding fabric (A1, B1, C1, etc.).

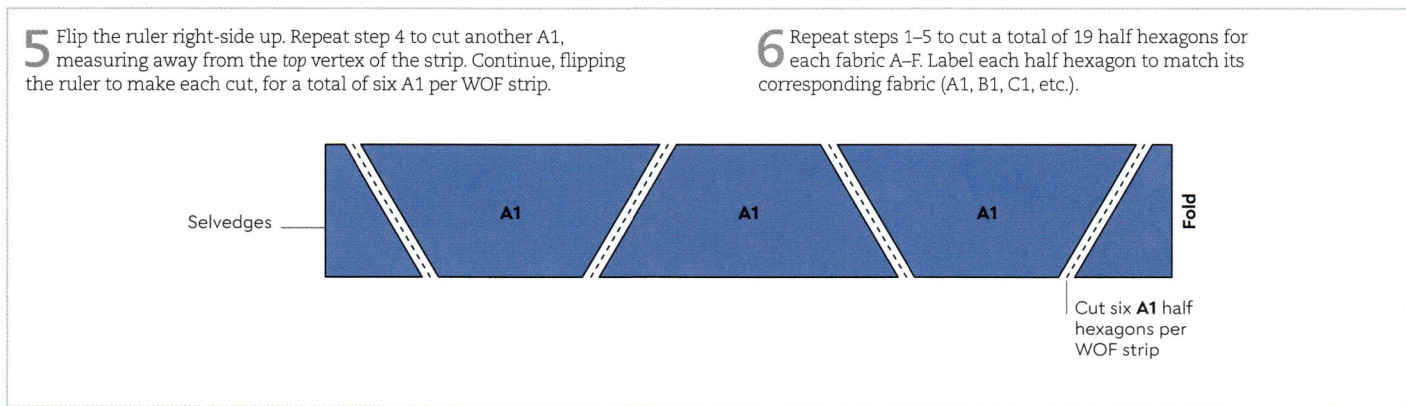

7 Fold each fabric G WOF strip in half, aligning the selvedges. Place one folded strip horizontally on a cutting mat with the selvedges on the left.

8 Place one EPP diamond paper piece on the left end of the strip. Use a ruler to cut 9.5mm (⅜in) away from all four sides of the diamond to make two G1 diamonds at once. Alternatively, use an EPP diamond acrylic template.

9 Repeat steps 7–8 to cut 16 diamonds per WOF strip for a total 138 G1.

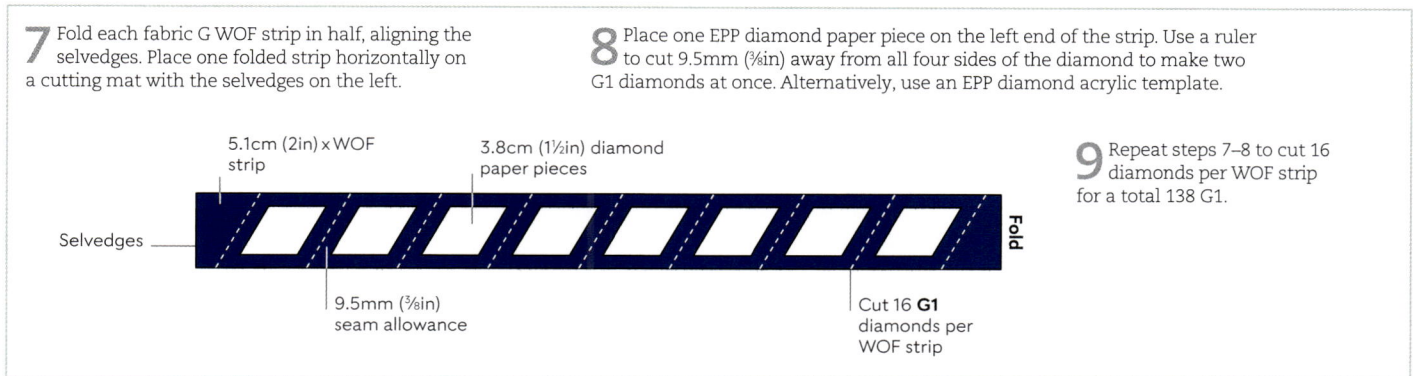

10 Fold each BG 19.1cm (7½in) x WOF strip in half, aligning the selvedges. Place one folded strip horizontally on a cutting mat with the selvedges on the left. Remove the selvedges.

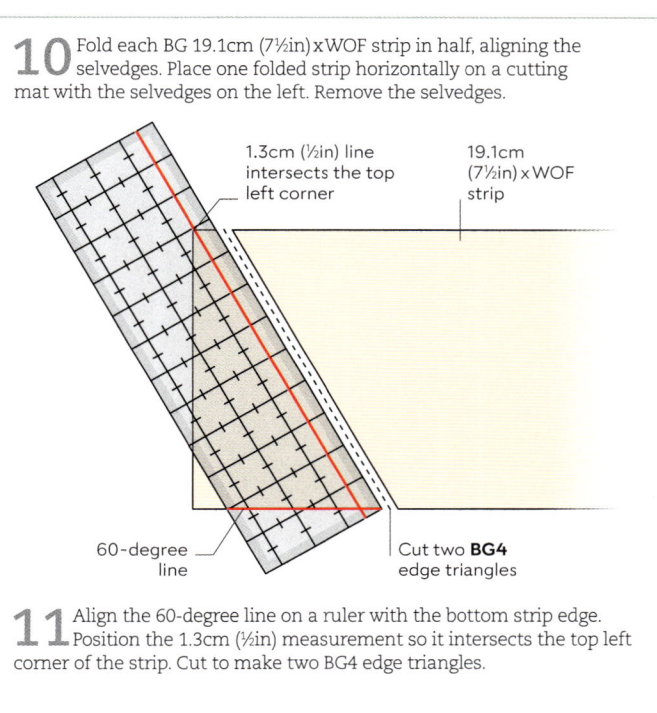

11 Align the 60-degree line on a ruler with the bottom strip edge. Position the 1.3cm (½in) measurement so it intersects the top left corner of the strip. Cut to make two BG4 edge triangles.

12 Rotate the ruler clockwise, aligning the 60-degree line with the previously cut angled edge. Ensure the 6.4mm (¼in) measurement intersects the bottom vertex. Cut to make two BG3 equilateral triangles with a blunted tip. Alternatively, use an equilateral triangle ruler (see p.19).

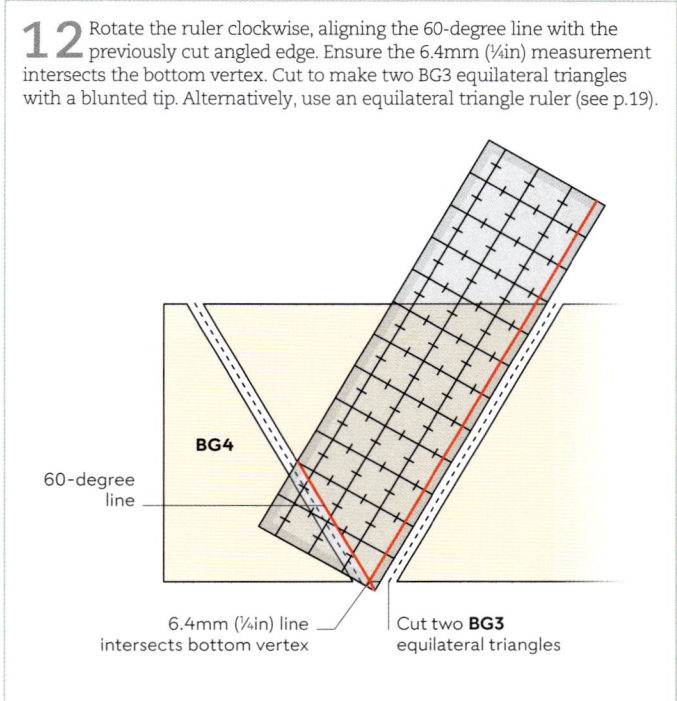

13 Rotate the ruler anticlockwise and align the 60-degree line with the bottom strip edge. Repeat step 12 to cut two more BG3, aligning the 6.4mm (¼in) measurement along the *top* vertex of the strip. Continue, rotating the ruler back and forth to make each cut, for a total of six BG3 per WOF strip.

14 Place the ruler vertically over the strip so the 1.6cm (⅝in) measurement intersects the top vertex of the strip. Cut to make two additional BG4 edge triangles for a total of four BG4 per WOF strip.

15 Repeat steps 10–14 to cut a total of 36 BG3 and 20 BG4.

16 Repeat steps 10–14 using BG 8.9cm (3½in) x WOF strips to cut a total of 114 BG2 equilateral triangles.

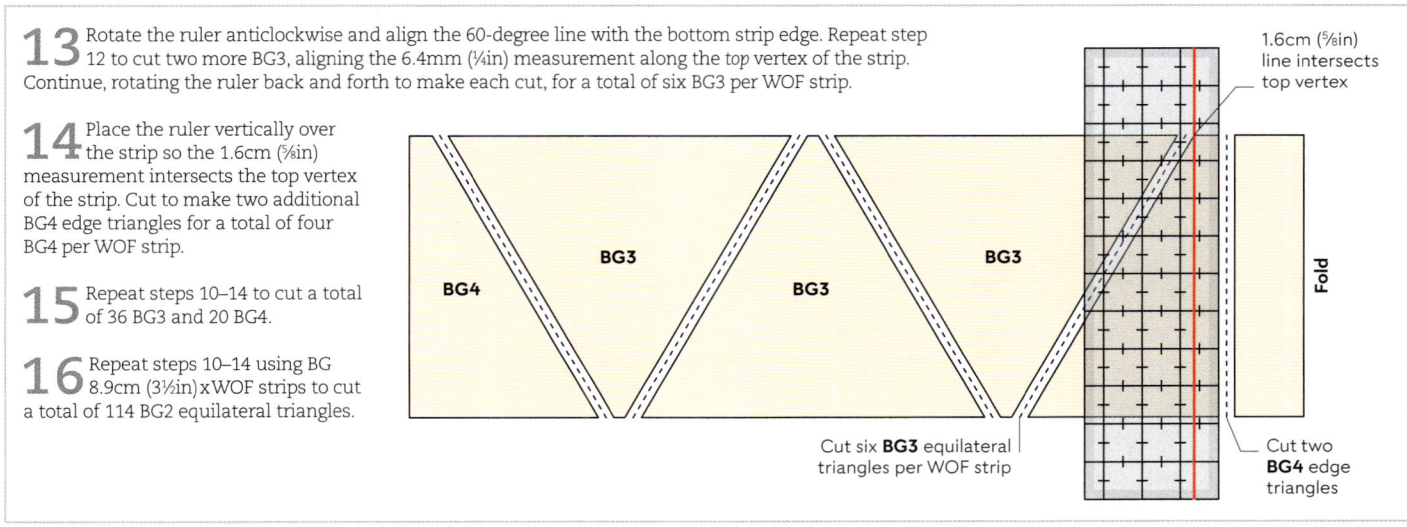

UNIT ASSEMBLY

When sewing angled units together, offset (see p.96) the edges to ensure proper alignment. Press all seams open to reduce bulk, and label all completed units to stay organized.

1. Mark the centre of one A1 half hexagon and one BG1 with a crease or removable marking tool. Sew BG1 to the bottom of A1 RST, aligning the centre marks. Press.

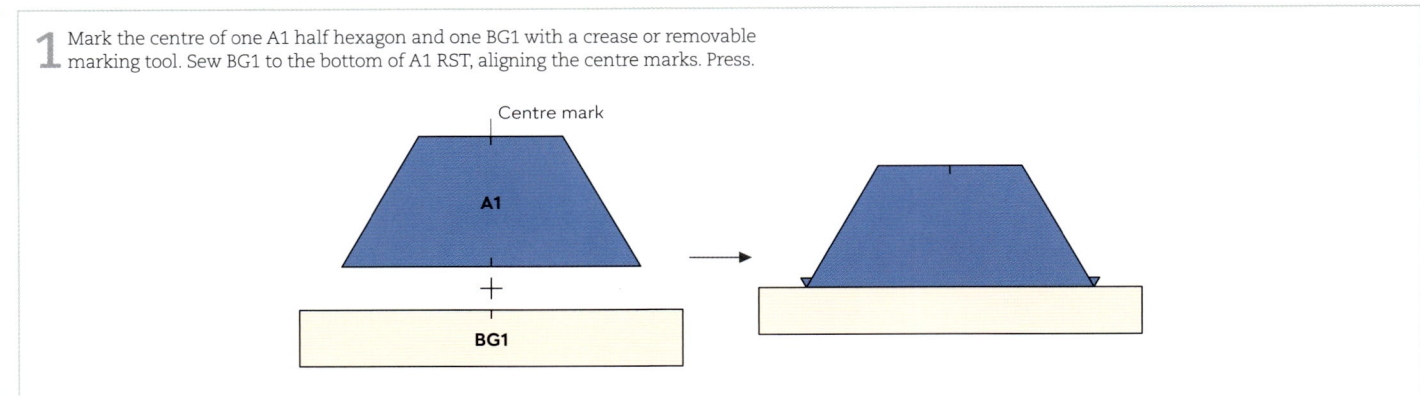

2. Mark the centre of one BG2. Align the centre marks of BG2 and the unit from step 1, RST.

3. Offset the edges of BG2 so the points extend slightly beyond the edges of the unit underneath. Sew along the aligned edges, with the stitch line intersecting exactly where the angled edges meet. Press.

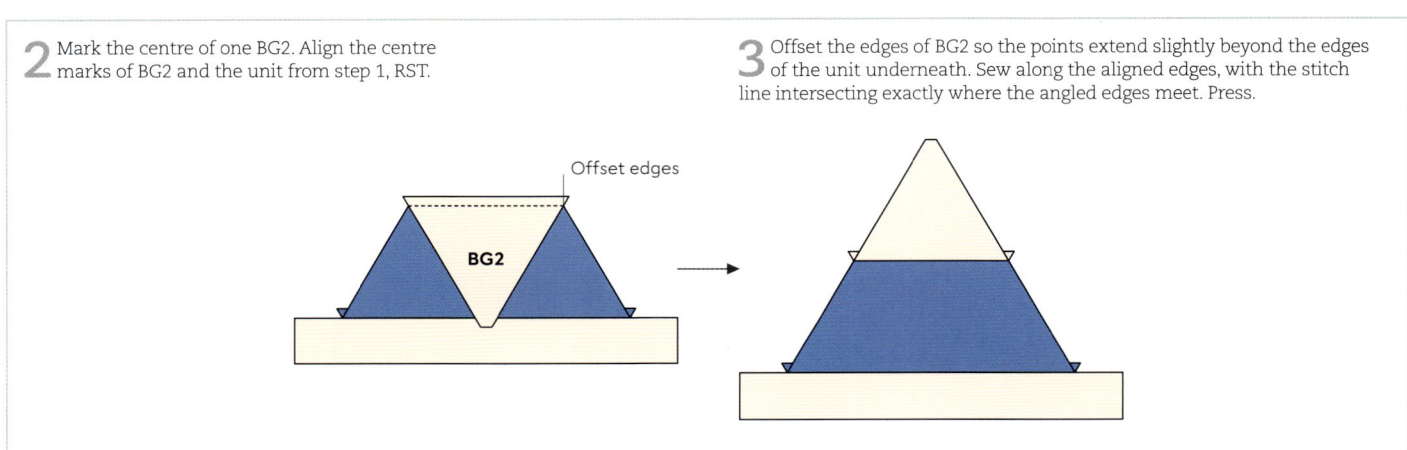

4. Trim the unit along the angled edges to remove excess seam allowance and BG1 fabric. Alternatively, use a triangle ruler to trim the edges. Label the unit as unit A.

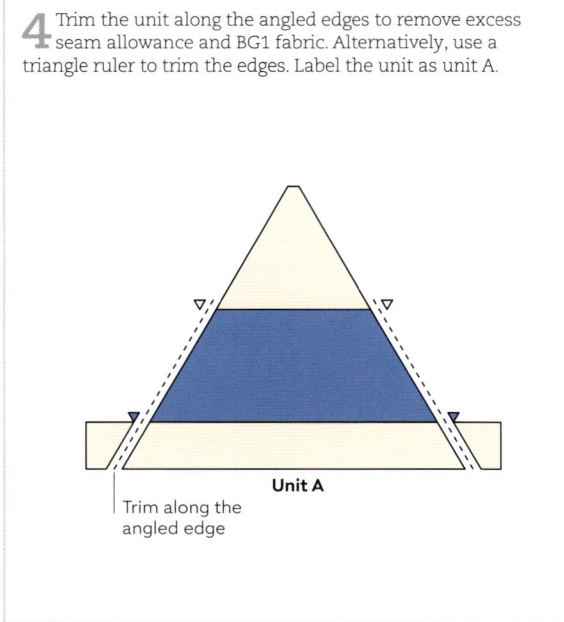

5. Repeat steps 1–4 using the remaining A1, B1, C1, D1, E1, and F1 half hexagons, BG1 rectangles, and BG2 equilateral triangles to make 19 units from each fabric A–F. Label each completed unit to match its corresponding fabric.

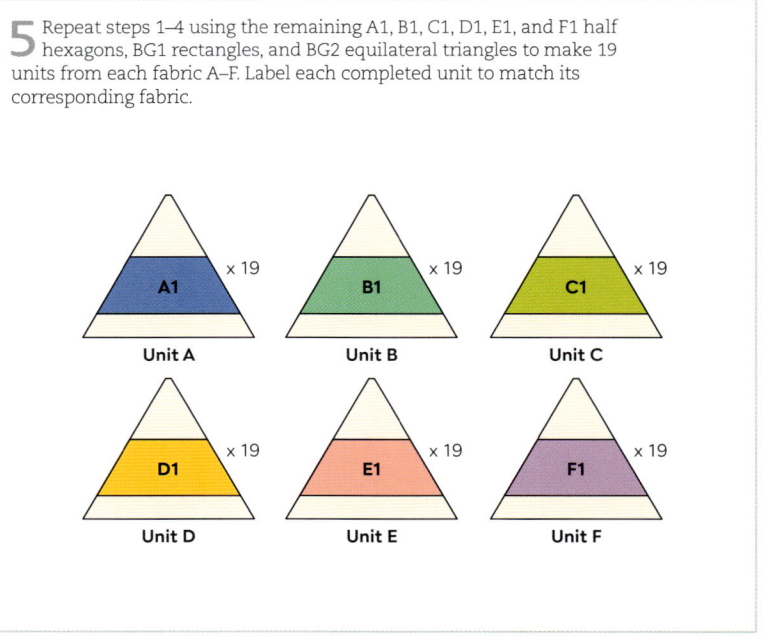

BLOCK ASSEMBLY

In this section, sew units into three different blocks: block ABC, block DEF, and block G. Align seams carefully and press seams open after every step. Refer to Basting EPP (see p.128) and Joining EPP pieces (see p.133) for more detailed instructions on how to make block G.

1 Position one unit A right-side up, with the blunted tip on the bottom. Place one unit B on top of unit A, RST, aligning the blunted tips.

2 Sew along the rightmost angled edge, ensuring the stitch line intersects the left corner of the blunted tip. Press.

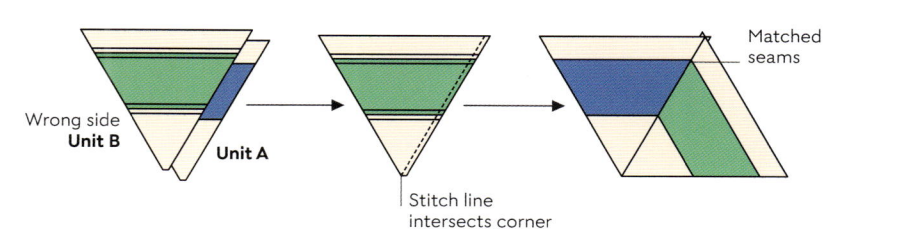

3 Place one unit C on top of the unit from step 2, RST, aligning the rightmost edges. Sew the units together to complete the block and label as block ABC.

4 Repeat steps 1–3 using the remaining units A, B, and C to make a total of 19 block ABC.

5 Repeat steps 1–4 using units D, E, and F to make 19 blocks and label each as block DEF.

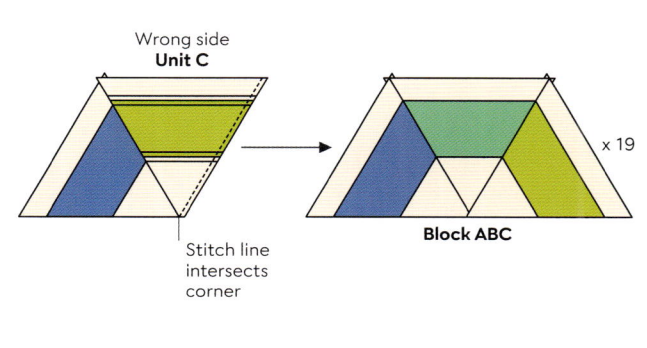

6 Centre one 3.8cm (1½in) diamond paper piece on the wrong side of one G1 diamond. Baste the top point straight down, securing it to the paper piece.

7 Baste the bottom right edge first, then the bottom left, folding the fabric tail to the right. Baste the remaining edges in a clockwise direction. Label as unit G.

9 Arrange three unit G into a row, with the fabric tails meeting at the centre. Sew two unit G RST, stitching toward the nested tails. Sew a third unit G to the unit to make a diamond row. Repeat with another three unit G to make a total of two diamond rows.

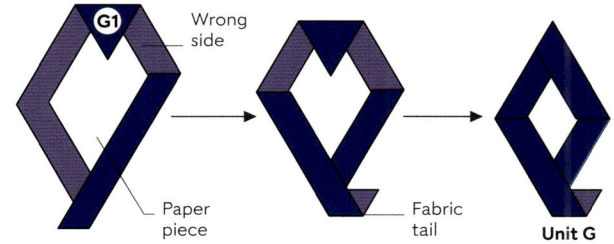

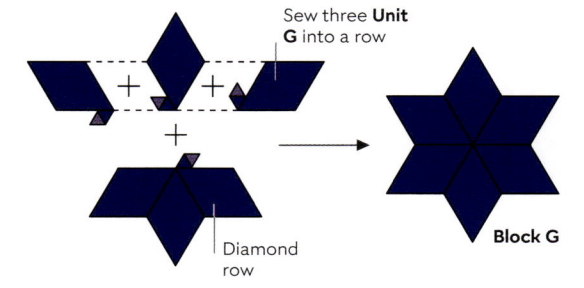

8 Repeat steps 6–7 with the remaining G1 diamonds and paper pieces to make a total of 138 unit G.

10 Align the two rows RST, nesting the tails, and sew along the straight edge to make one diamond star. Label the star as block G.

11 Repeat steps 9–10 to make a total of 23 block G.

ROW ASSEMBLY

Refer to Equilateral triangles (see p.100) and Half hexagons (see p.101) for more detailed instructions on how to assemble triangles and half hexagons into rows. Align seams carefully and press seams open after every step.

1 Arrange all blocks ABC and DEF with BG3 equilateral triangles into rows as shown.
- Make one row 1 using 12 BG3, two BG4, and one block ABC.
- Make one row 2 using six BG3, two BG4, two block ABC, and one block DEF.
- Make three row 3 using two BG4, three block ABC, and two block DEF for each row.
- Make three row 4 using two BG4, two block ABC, and three block DEF for each row.
- Make one row 5 using six BG3, two BG4, one block ABC, and two block DEF.
- Make one row 6 using 12 BG3, two BG4, and one block DEF.

2 Sew the pieces in each row into pairs first to efficiently chain piece (see p.144). Press seams, then join the pairs, adding the BG4 edge triangles last to complete each row. Ensure all pieces are oriented correctly while piecing to maintain the design.

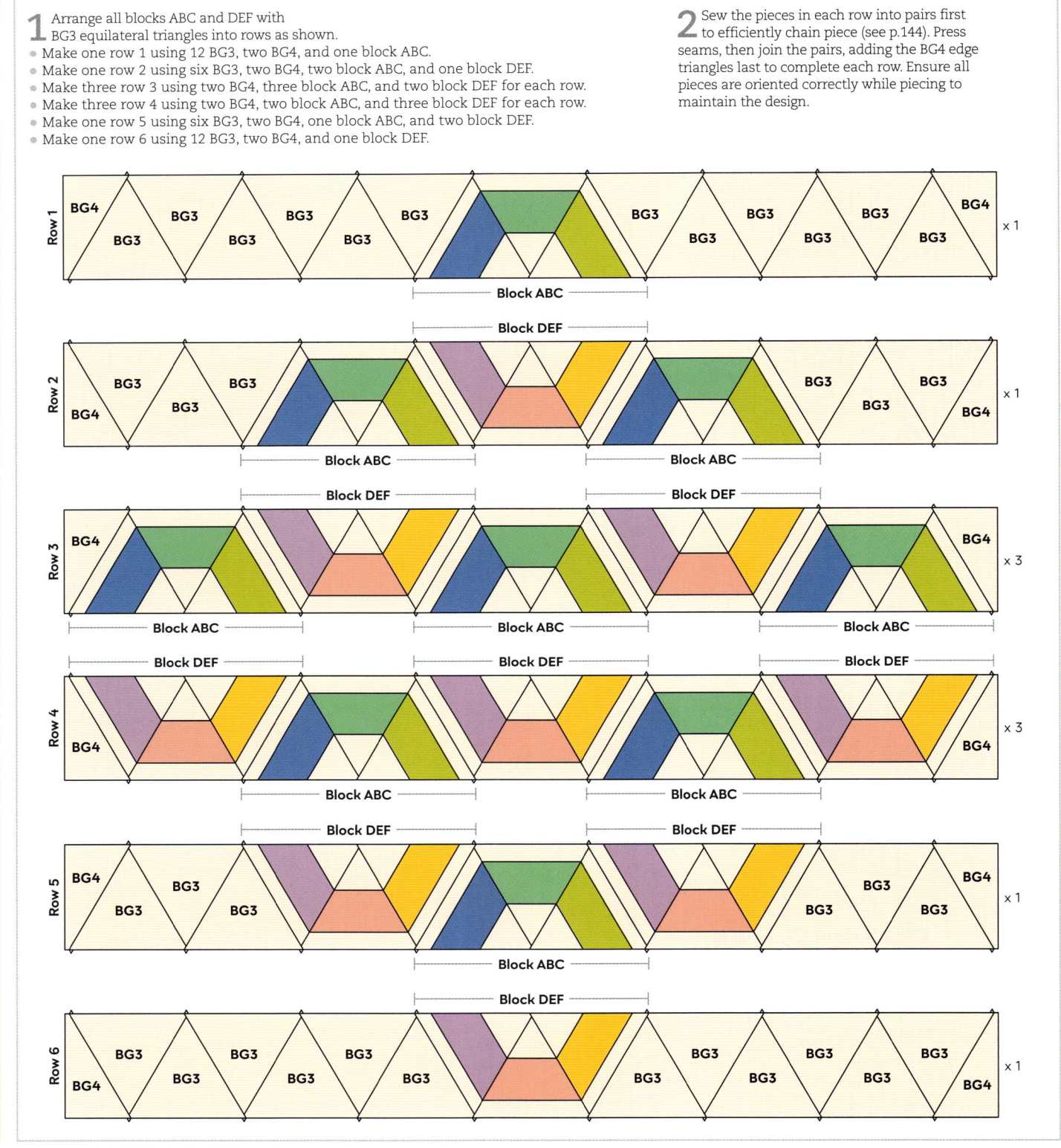

QUILT ASSEMBLY AND FINISHING

When joining rows of triangles together, pin and align seams at each triangle intersection. Take care to avoid stretching bias edges. Refer to the Appliqué section (see pp.134–139) for more detailed instructions on how to appliqué block G diamond stars to the quilt top.

1. Arrange all rows 1–6 as shown, ensuring each row is oriented correctly. Sew the rows RST, pinning at every triangle point intersection. Press.

2. Press the entire quilt top from the front to remove all wrinkles. Sew a stay stitch (see p.151) 3.2mm (⅛in) around the perimeter of the quilt to secure seams.

3. Appliqué all block G diamond stars as shown, following the appliqué instructions below for the correct placement.

4. To make binding, cut seven 6.4cm (2½in) x WOF strips from the chosen binding fabric. Sew all seven WOF strips, RST, to make one strip that is at least 724cm (285in) long.

5. To finish the quilt, baste (see pp.157–159), quilt (see pp.160–171), and bind (see pp.172–181) as desired.

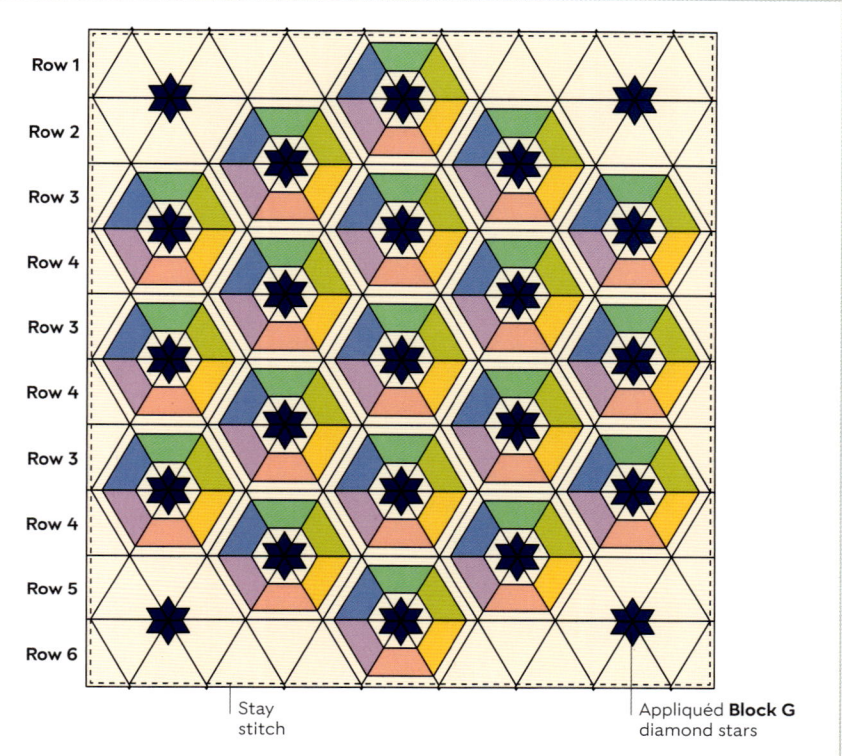

APPLIQUÉ INSTRUCTIONS

Prepare the block G diamond stars for appliqué by removing the paper pieces and pressing the block from both sides. Centre one block G in each hexagon "frame," aligning the seams of the block with the quilt top seams. Attach using any appliqué technique, tucking stray threads or excess fabric under the blocks before stitching.

Attach one block G to each corner of the quilt top, centring each diamond star where the triangles meet to form a hexagon.

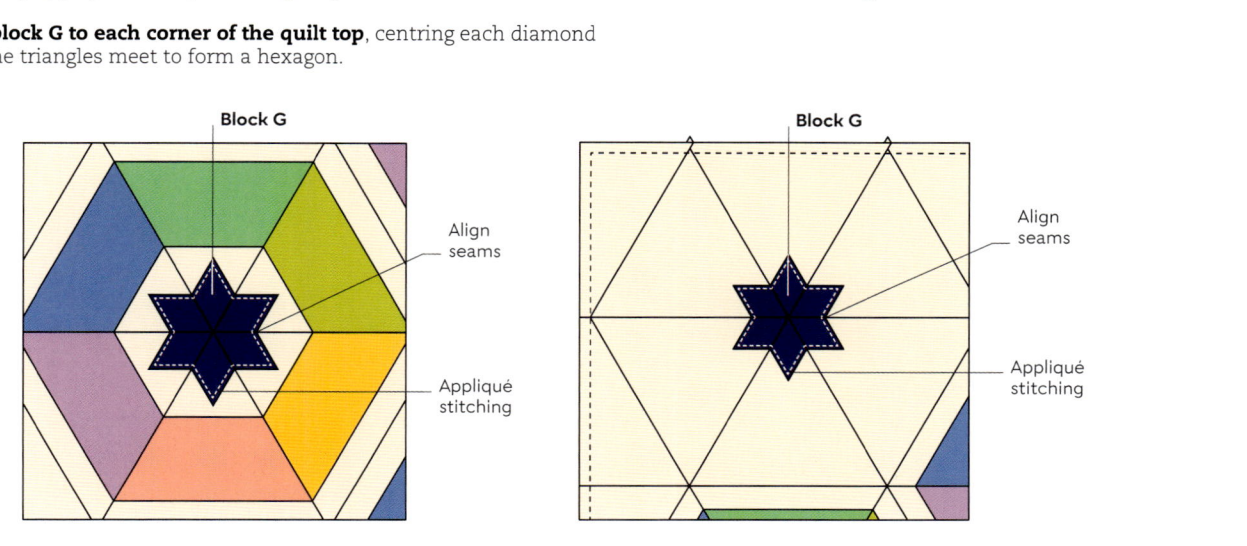

Nexus shift

This pattern is a modern interpretation of a classic Irish Chain block, incorporating HRTs to add dimension and negative space to produce the illusion that the chain is shifting. The minimalist design is ideal for practising HRTs and matching points and seams.

FINISHED THROW SIZE 165 x 165cm (65 x 65in)
TECHNIQUES USED Understanding colour theory **p.60**, Four and nine patches **p.84**, HRTs **p.97**, Matching points and seams **p.141**, Column quilt top layout **p.146**

MATERIALS
- Basic quilting supplies (see p.14)
- Marking tools
- Washi tape
- 180 x 180cm (71 x 71in) or larger wadding

FABRIC REQUIREMENTS

Fabric A	0.5m (½yd)
Fabric B	0.75m (¾yd)
Background (BG)	3.25m (3½yds)
Backing*	3.75m (4yds)
Binding	0.75m (¾yd)

*Backing fabric required when using one vertical or horizontal seam.

Choose three fabrics for fabrics A, B, and background (BG). Quilt designs using three fabrics offer an opportunity to experiment with split complementary or monochrome colour schemes (see p.61). Choose fabrics with enough contrast to showcase the design. Directional prints are not recommended for fabrics A and background (BG).

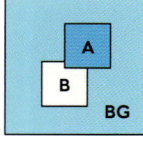

COLOUR REFERENCE

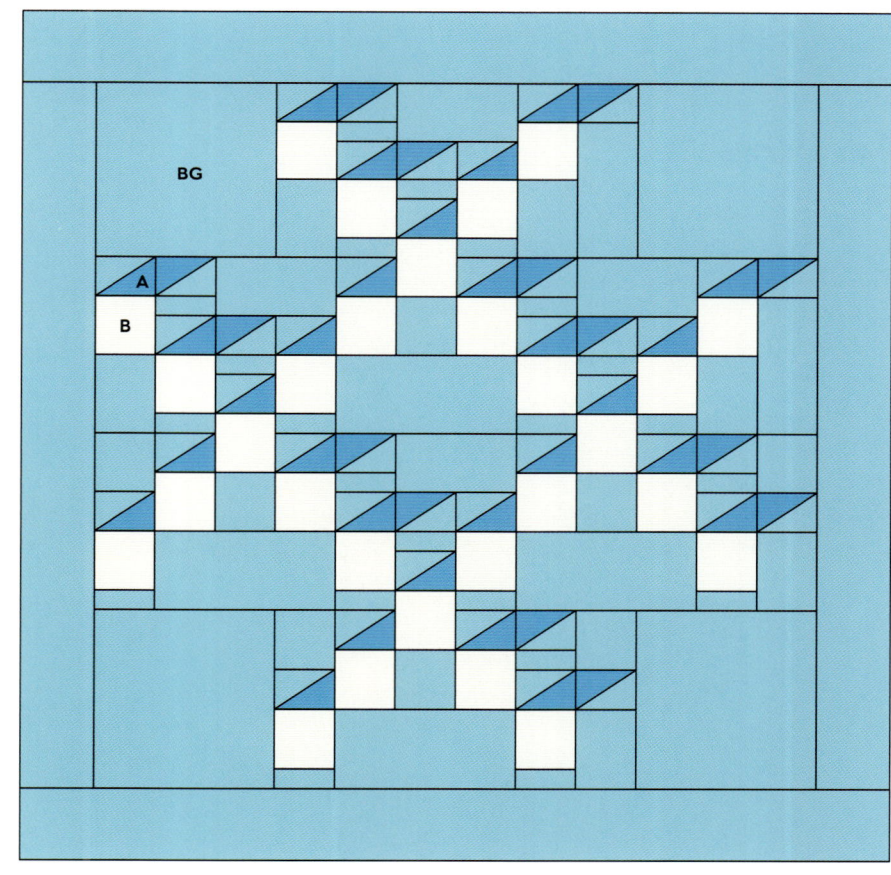

COVER QUILT DETAILS
Fabrics: Ruby and Bee Solids by Windham Fabrics in Sky (**A**), Wisp (**B**), Aquamarine (**BG**); **Quilting:** Walking foot curves; **Thread:** Aurifil 50 wt in 2805; **Wadding:** Hobbs Heirloom Natural 100% Cotton; **Binding:** Sky

CUTTING INSTRUCTIONS

Use the fabric cutting tables and diagrams below to cut out and label the pieces required from fabrics A, B, and BG.

FABRIC CUTTING TABLES

FABRICS A AND B	
A	Cut (3) 11.4cm (4½in) x WOF; **sub-cut:** **A1:** (21) 11.4 x 15.2cm (4½ x 6in)
B	Cut (4) 12.7cm (5in) x WOF; **sub-cut:** **B1:** (28) 12.7 x 12.7cm (5 x 5in)

BACKGROUND (BG)

Cut (2) 35.6cm (14in) x WOF; **sub-cut:**
 BG8: (4) 35.6 x 35.6cm (14 x 14in)
 BG5: (4) 35.6 x 16.5cm (14 x 6½in)

Cut (8) 15.2cm (6in) x WOF; label as **BG9** and set aside for borders.

Cut (5) 12.7cm (5in) x WOF; **sub-cut:**
 BG7: (2) 12.7 x 27.9cm (5 x 11in)
 BG3: (4) 12.7 x 24.1cm (5 x 9½in)
 BG6: (6) 12.7 x 16.5cm (5 x 6½in)
 BG4: (8) 12.7 x 12.7cm (5 x 5in)
 BG2: (22) 12.7 x 5.1cm (5 x 2in)

Cut (3) 11.4cm (4½in) x WOF; **sub-cut:**
 BG1: (21) 11.4 x 15.2cm (4½ x 6in)

MARKING DIAGRAMS

1 On the wrong side of one A1 rectangle, mark one registration line (see p.143) on the top edge, 6.4mm (¼in) away from the right edge. Mark a second registration line on the bottom edge of the rectangle, 6.4mm (¼in) away from the left edge.

2 Mark a diagonal line to connect the two registration lines. Repeat steps 1–2 with all A1 and BG1 rectangles.

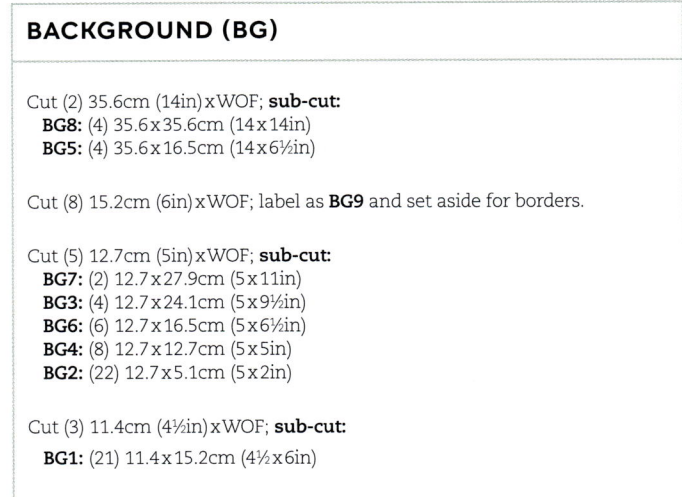

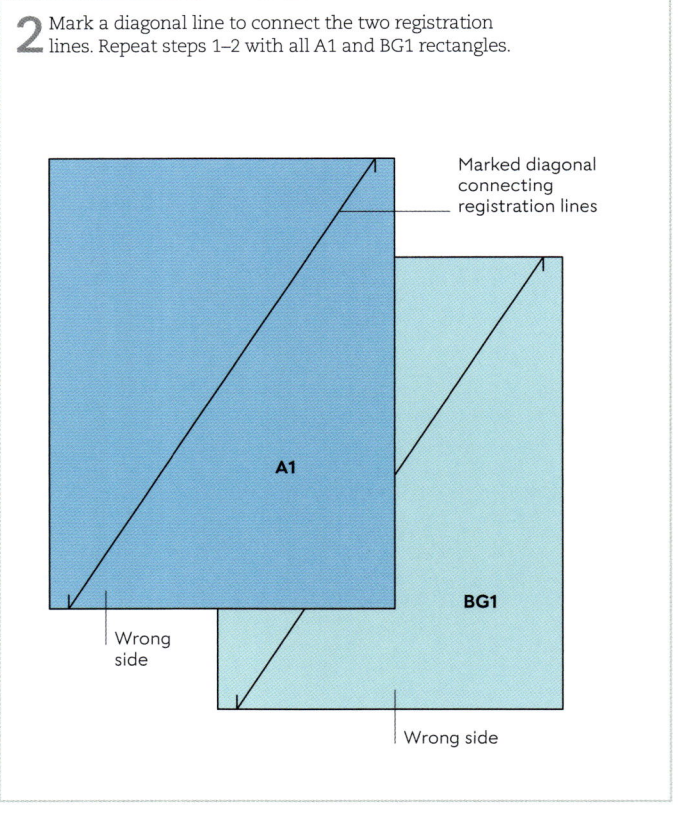

UNIT ASSEMBLY

Refer to the two at a time HRT technique (see p.97) for more detailed instructions on how to piece and trim HRTs. Press all seams open (see p.80) to reduce bulk.

1 Place one A1 and one BG1 RST. Rotate the top rectangle anticlockwise to align the registration lines on both pieces. Pin.

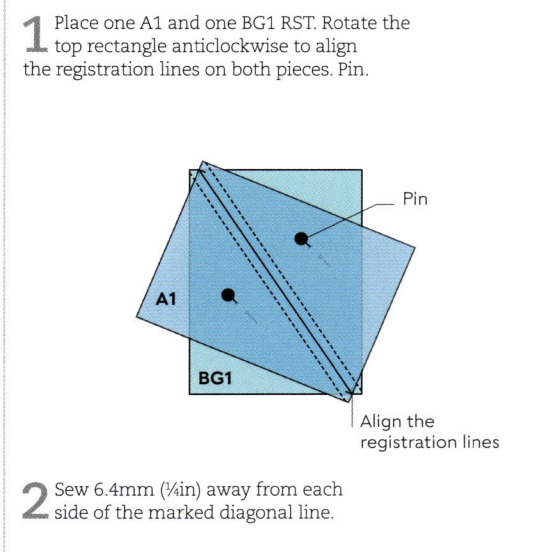

2 Sew 6.4mm (¼in) away from each side of the marked diagonal line.

3 Cut directly on the marked diagonal line to make two HRTs. Press.

4 Repeat steps 1–3 with the remaining A1 and BG1 to make a total of 42 HRTs.

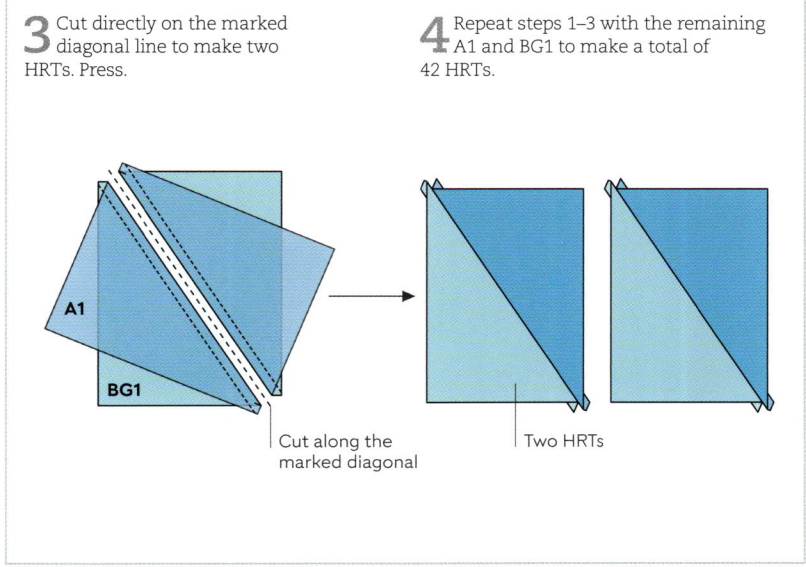

5 Place washi tape on a ruler along the 8.9cm (3½in) vertical and 12.7cm (5in) horizontal measurements to make a trimming window.

6 Mark 6.4mm (¼in) inside the top left and bottom right corners of the window with a dry erase marker. Align these marks along the seams of the HRTs while trimming.

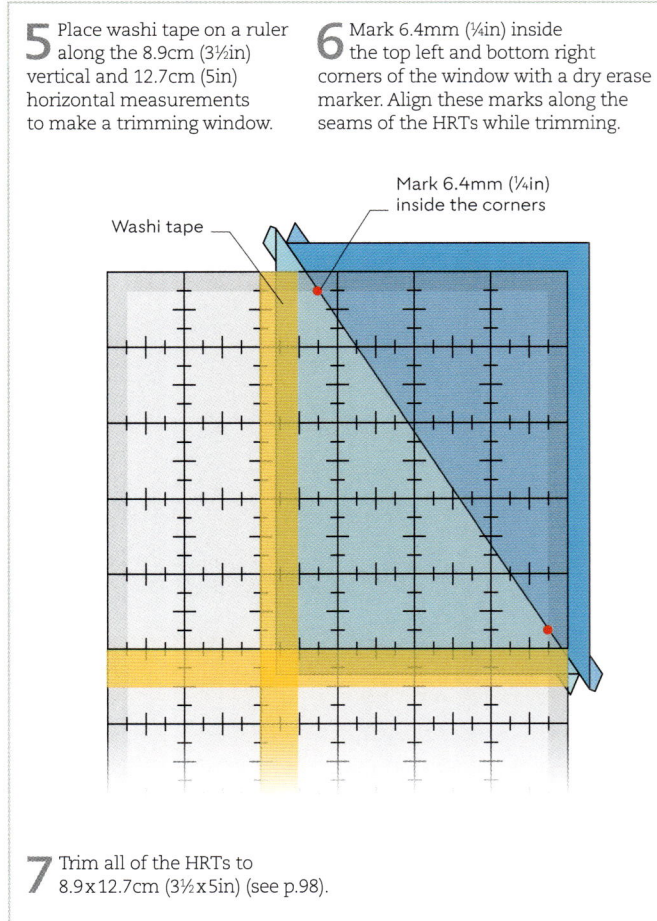

7 Trim all of the HRTs to 8.9 x 12.7cm (3½ x 5in) (see p.98).

8 Position 16 of the trimmed HRTs as shown and label them as unit 1. Set the remaining trimmed HRTs aside for steps 9–12.

Unit 1

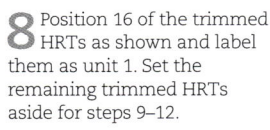

x 16

9 Pair 18 BG2 with 18 trimmed HRTs and arrange them as shown.

10 Sew one BG2 RST to one trimmed HRT to make a second unit. Press. Label the unit as unit 2. Repeat to make a total of 18 unit 2.

Unit 2

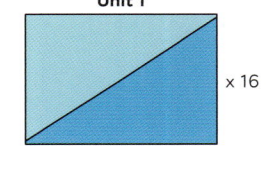

x 18

11 Pair eight trimmed HRTs with eight B1 and arrange them as shown.

12 Sew one trimmed HRT to one B1 RST to make a third unit. Press. Label the unit as unit 3. Repeat to make a total of eight unit 3.

Unit 3

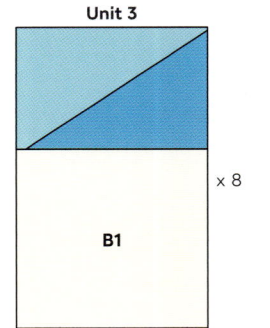

x 8

BLOCK ASSEMBLY

Assemble pieces and unit into blocks, taking care to position all pieces correctly. Align points and seams (see p.141) carefully, pin as needed, and press seams open after every step.

1 Arrange one unit 2 to the left of one BG3 as shown. Sew the pieces RST to make a horizontal strip. Press. Repeat to make a total of four strips.

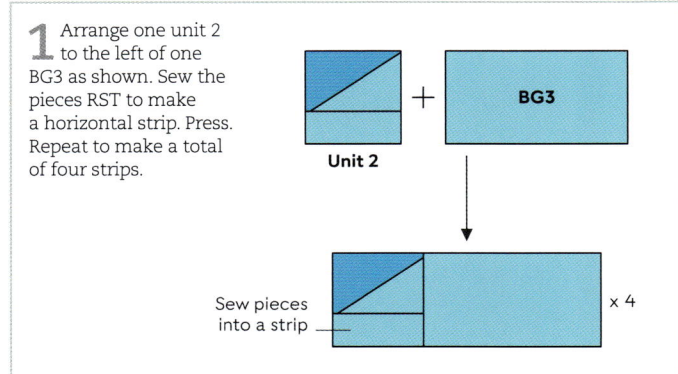

2 Arrange three unit 1 as shown. Sew the units RST to make an HRT strip. Press. Repeat to make a total of four HRT strips.

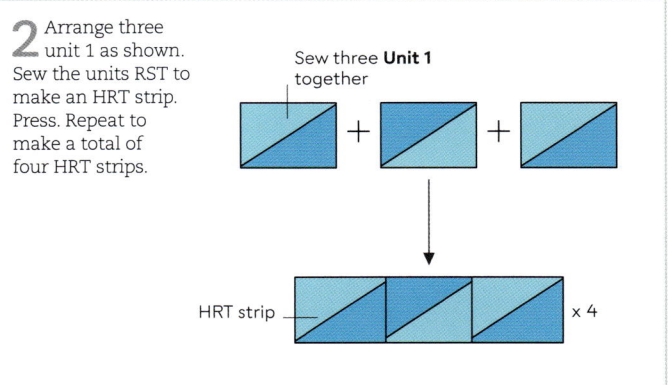

3 Arrange four B1, one BG4, and four unit 2 into a 3x3 grid, placing B1 at the centre and each corner, BG4 at the bottom centre, and unit 2 in the remaining edge positions as shown.

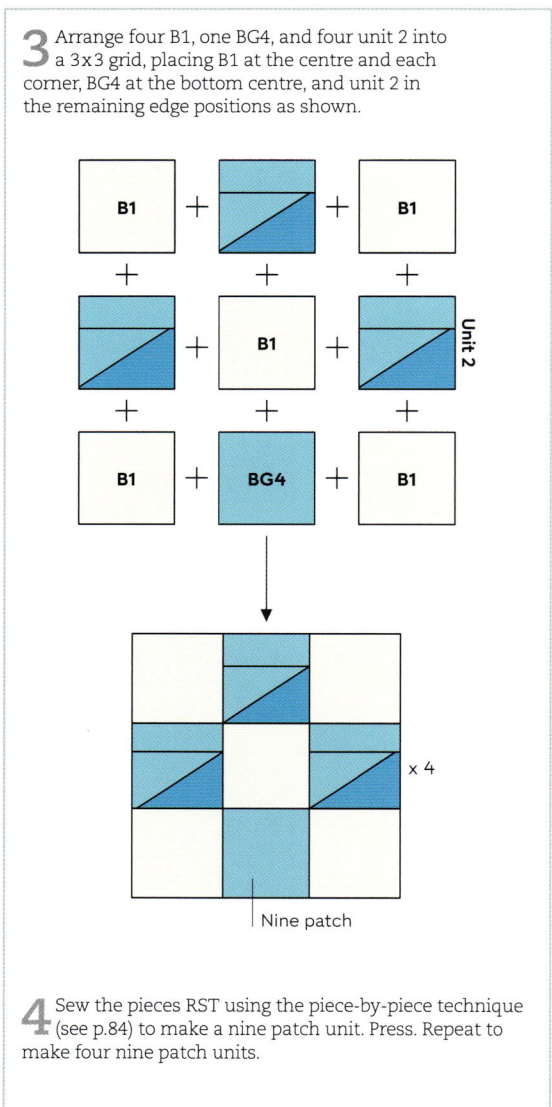

4 Sew the pieces RST using the piece-by-piece technique (see p.84) to make a nine patch unit. Press. Repeat to make four nine patch units.

5 Arrange one strip from step 1, one HRT strip from step 2, one nine patch, and one BG5 as shown.

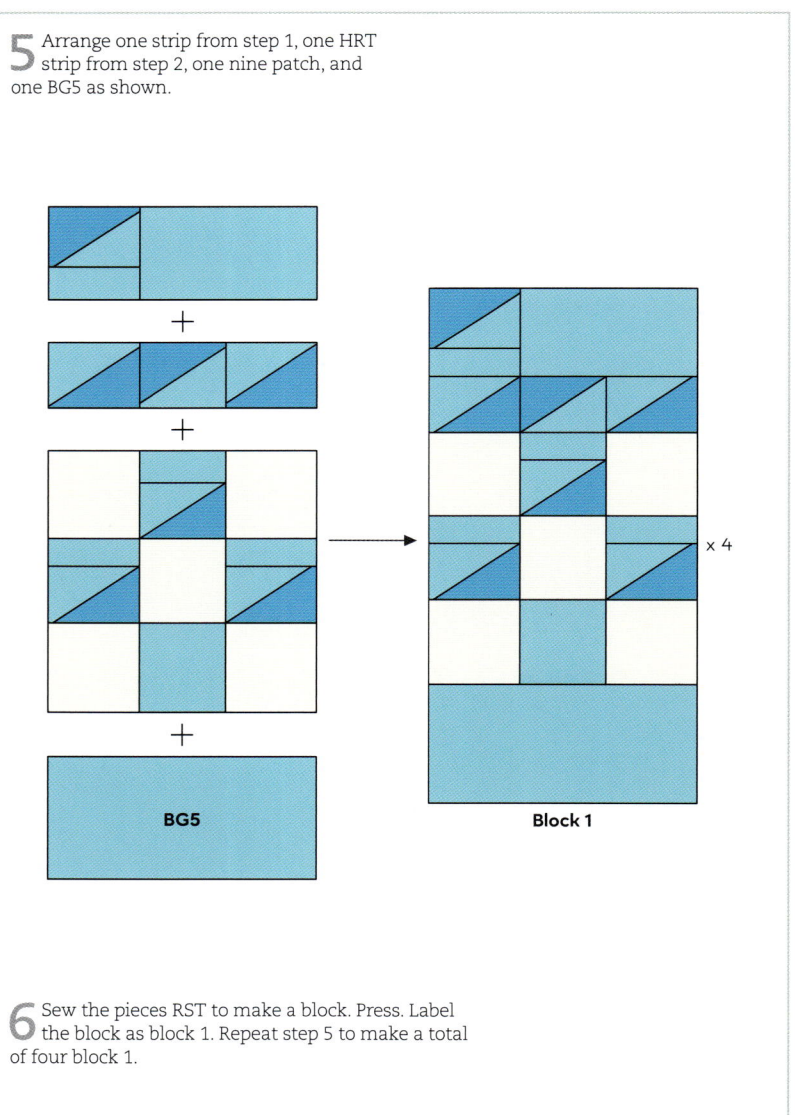

6 Sew the pieces RST to make a block. Press. Label the block as block 1. Repeat step 5 to make a total of four block 1.

NEXUS SHIFT

7 Arrange one unit 3 at the top of one BG6 as shown. Sew the pieces RST to make a vertical strip. Press. Label the strip as block 2. Repeat to make a total of four block 2.

8 Arrange one BG4, one unit 3, and one BG2 as shown. Sew the pieces RST to make a vertical strip. Press. Label the strip as block 3. Repeat to make a total of two block 3.

9 Arrange one unit 1 at the top of one BG7 as shown. Sew the pieces RST to make a vertical strip. Press. Repeat to make a total of two strips.

10 Arrange one block 2 to the left of one strip from step 9 as shown. Sew the pieces RST to make a block. Press. Label the block as block 4. Repeat to make a total of two block 4.

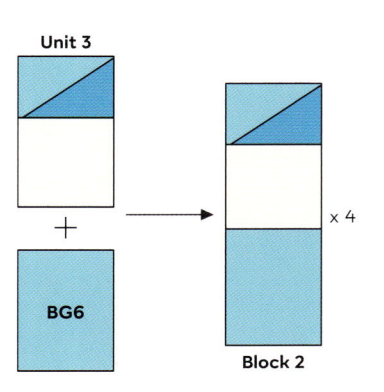

11 Arrange one unit 2, one unit 3, and one BG2 as shown. Sew the pieces RST to make a vertical strip. Press. Repeat to make a total of two strips.

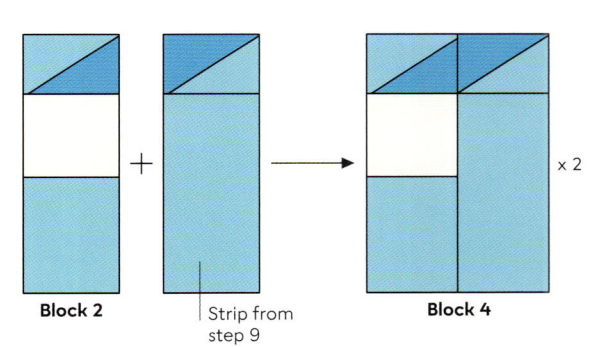

12 Arrange one BG4, one unit 1, and one BG6 as shown. Sew the pieces RST to make a vertical strip. Press. Repeat to make a total of two strips.

13 Arrange one strip from step 11 to the left of one strip from step 12 as shown. Sew the pieces RST to make a block. Press. Label the completed block as block 5. Repeat to make a total of two block 5.

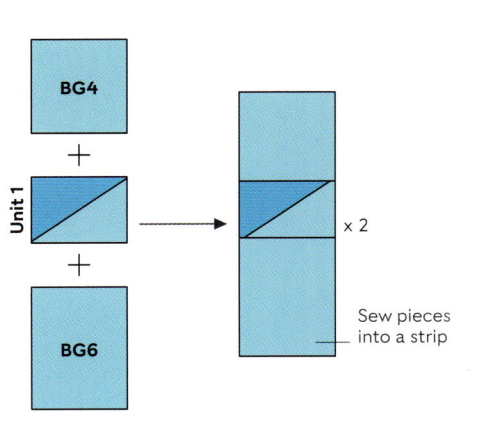

COLUMN ASSEMBLY

Ensure all blocks are assembled and labelled correctly before beginning this section. Align points and seams carefully and press seams open after every step.

1 Arrange one BG8 to the left of one block 2 as shown. Sew the pieces RST to make a unit. Press.

2 Arrange one block 2 at the top of block 3 as shown. Sew the blocks RST, then sew these joined blocks to the left of block 1 to make a second unit. Press.

3 Arrange one BG8 to the left of block 3 as shown. Sew the pieces RST to make a third unit. Press.

4 Sew the three units from steps 1–3 as shown, RST, to make a column. Press. Label the completed column as left column.

5 Arrange two block 1 as shown. Sew the blocks RST to make a column. Press. Label the column as centre column.

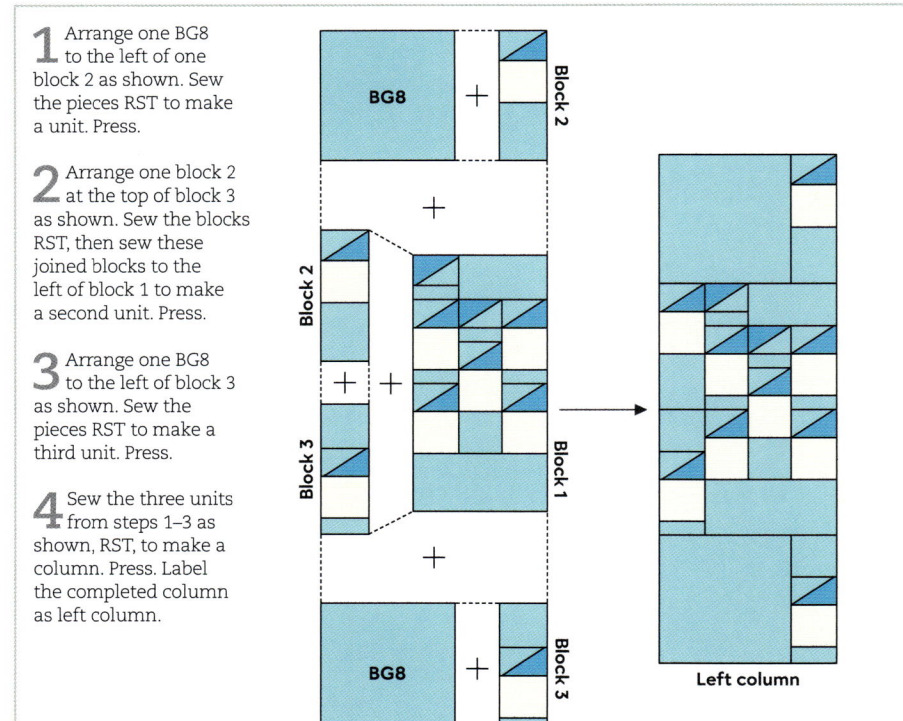

6 Arrange one block 4 to the left of one BG8 as shown. Sew the pieces RST to make a unit. Press.

7 Arrange one block 4 at the top of block 5 as shown. Sew the blocks RST, then sew these joined blocks to the right of block 1 to make a second unit. Press.

8 Arrange one block 5 to the left of one BG8 as shown. Sew the pieces RST to make a third unit. Press.

9 Sew the three units from steps 6–8 as shown, RST, to make a column. Press. Label the completed column as right column.

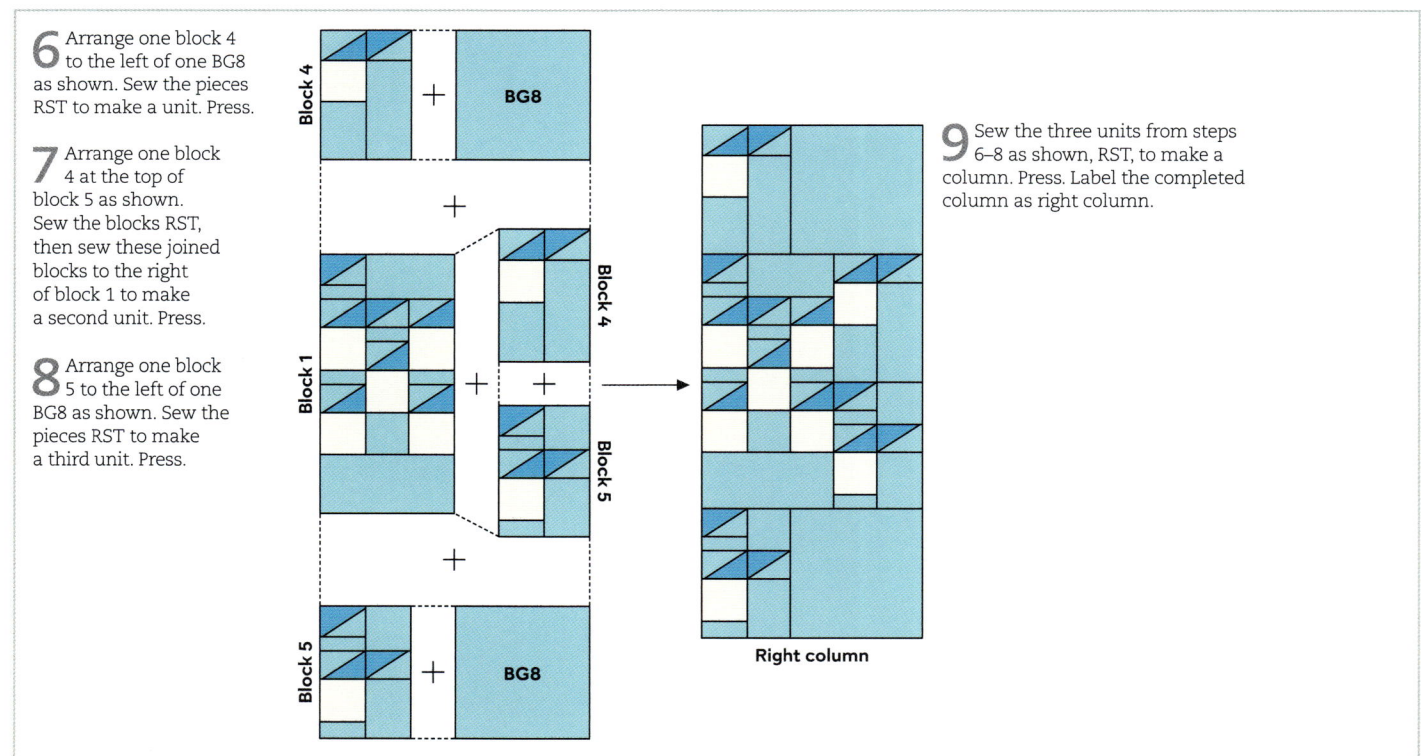

QUILT ASSEMBLY AND FINISHING

Make the border strips, then sew columns together before adding the border strips to the quilt top. Align points and seams carefully, pin as needed, and press seams open after every step.

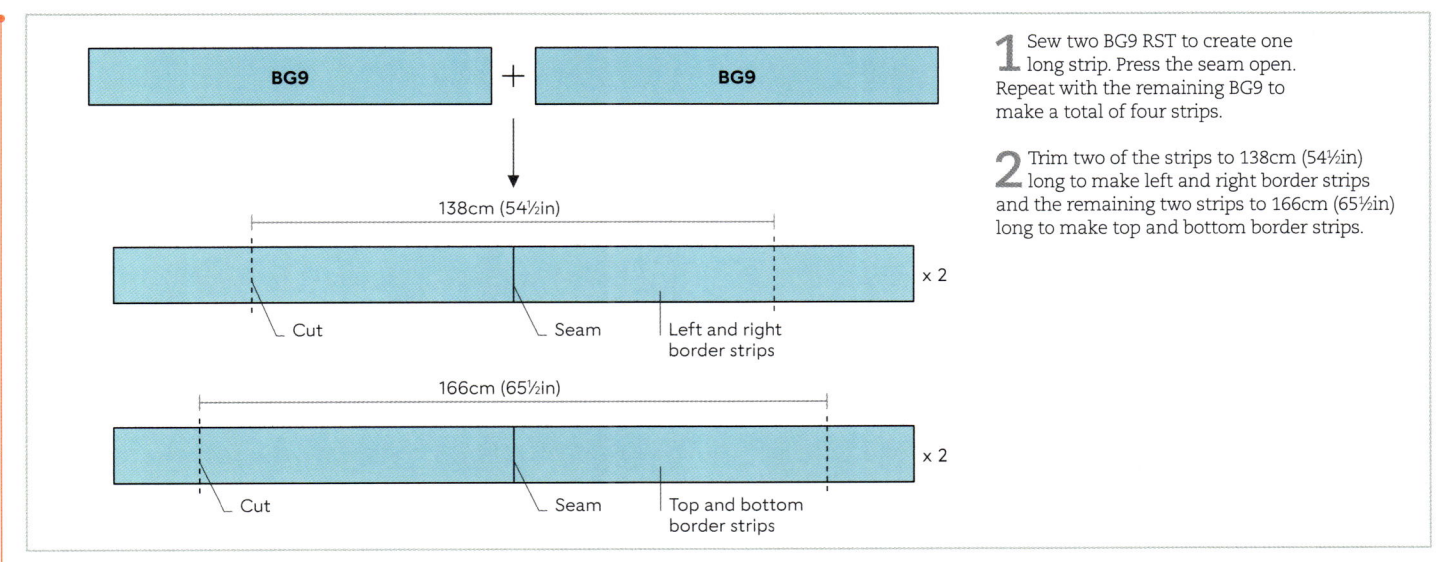

1 Sew two BG9 RST to create one long strip. Press the seam open. Repeat with the remaining BG9 to make a total of four strips.

2 Trim two of the strips to 138cm (54½in) long to make left and right border strips and the remaining two strips to 166cm (65½in) long to make top and bottom border strips.

3 Arrange the left, centre, and right columns as shown. Sew the columns RST from left to right to make the quilt top.

4 Sew the left and right border strips RST to the corresponding sides of the quilt top, then repeat with the top and bottom border strips. Press all seams toward the border strips.

5 Press the entire quilt top from the front to remove all wrinkles. Sew a stay stitch (see p.151) 3.2mm (⅛in) around the perimeter of the quilt to secure seams.

6 To make binding, cut seven 6.4cm (2½in) x WOF strips from the chosen binding fabric. Sew all seven WOF strips, RST, to make one strip that is at least 699cm (275in) long.

7 To finish the quilt, baste (see pp.157–159), quilt (see pp.160–171), and bind (pp.172–181) as desired.

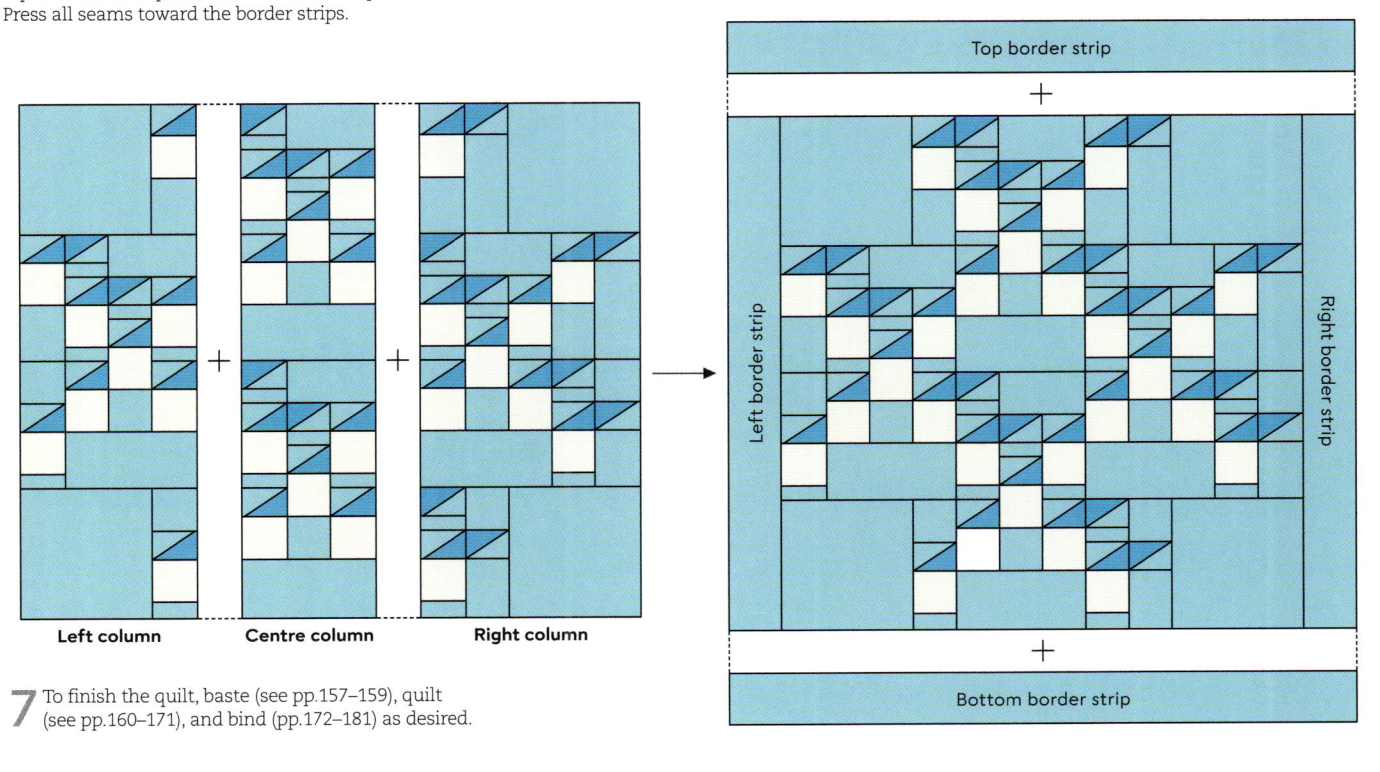

Happy patch

The playful design of this quilt pattern is inspired by a blooming flower patch. Classic nine patch centres surrounded by half circles form flower-like shapes. This pattern is ideal for applying colour theory and practising sewing curves.

FINISHED FULL SIZE 206 x 229cm (81 x 90in)

TECHNIQUES USED Understanding colour theory **p.60,** Using templates **p.71,** Four and nine patches **p.84,** Curves **p.104,** Matching points and seams **p.141,** Sashing **p.143,** Column quilt top layout **p.146**

MATERIALS

- Basic quilting supplies (see p.14)
- Paper and fabric scissors
- Printer and template paper or cardstock
- Tweezers (optional)
- 24.1 x 24.1cm (9½ x 9½in) or larger square ruler
- Marking pen
- 221 x 244cm (87 x 96in) or larger wadding

FABRIC REQUIREMENTS

Fabrics A–R	(1) FQ each
Fabric S	(1) FQ
Background (BG)	4.3m (4¾yds)
Backing*	6.75m (7.25yds)
Binding	0.75m (¾yd)

*Backing fabric required when using two horizontal seams.

Group 18 feature fabrics (fabrics A–R) into nine pairs: A with B, C with D, etc. Each pair is used together throughout the pattern to form all units and make two alternating flower shapes.

Select a complementary fabric S for the centres of each flower block and a background fabric (BG) that contrasts with the feature fabrics.

COLOUR REFERENCE

COVER QUILT DETAILS

Fabrics: Ruby and Bee Solids by Windham Fabrics in Sky (**A**), Aquamarine (**B**), Starling (**C**), Sea Glass (**D**), Minty (**E**), Matcha (**F**), Pasture (**G**), Limeade (**H**), Avocado (**I**), Lemonade (**J**), Pumpkin (**K**), Mustard Seed (**L**), Perfect Pink (**M**), Shell (**N**), Fairy Floss (**O**), Posy (**P**), Wisteria (**Q**), Dusk (**R**), Wisp (**S**), Provence Blue (**BG**); **Quilting:** Cartwheels pantograph quilted by Aimee of Sewing Scientist; **Thread:** Superior Threads So Fine! 50 wt in 524; **Wadding:** Hobbs Heirloom 80/20 Blend; **Binding:** Wisteria

CUTTING INSTRUCTIONS

Use the fabric cutting tables and diagrams below to cut out and label the pieces required from fabrics A–R, fabric S, and BG. Visit *The Quilting Book* website (see p.11) to print the required half circle templates.

FABRIC CUTTING TABLES

FABRICS A–R

From each FQ:

Cut (2) 13.3cm (5¼in) x WOF; **sub-cut:**
  A1–R1: (4) **template HC-A** convex half circle pieces (4 for each fabric)

Cut (2) 8.9cm (3½in) x WOF; **sub-cut:**
  A2–R2: (8) 8.9 x 8.9cm (3½ x 3½in) (8 for each fabric)

FABRIC S

From a FQ:

Cut (3) 8.9cm (3½in) x WOF; **sub-cut:**
  S1: (18) 8.9 x 8.9cm (3½ x 3½in)

BACKGROUND (BG)

Cut (1) 27.9cm (11in) x WOF; **sub-cut:**
  BG6: (4) 27.9 x 24.1cm (11 x 9½in)
  BG4: (1) 24.1 x 8.9cm (9½ x 3½in)

Cut (1) 24.1cm (9½in) x WOF; **sub-cut:**
  BG4: (12) 24.1 x 8.9cm (9½ x 3½in) (13 total **BG4**)

Cut (11) 17.8cm (7in) x WOF; **sub-cut:**
  BG1: (72) **template HC-B** concave half circle pieces

Cut (13) 12.7cm (5in) x WOF. Set (8) strips aside and label as **BG7**; **sub-cut:**
  BG2: (6) 12.7 x 31.8cm (5 x 12½in)
  BG3: (12) 12.7 x 12.7cm (5 x 5in)
  BG5: (24) 12.7 x 5.1cm (5 x 2in)

FABRIC CUTTING DIAGRAMS

1 From the fabric A FQ use template HC-A to cut two A1 convex pieces from each 14 x 53.3cm (5½ x 21in) strip as shown for a total of four A1. Cut eight A2 squares from the 8.9 x 53.3cm (3½ x 21in) strips. Repeat with each fabric B–R to cut all B1–R1 convex pieces and B2–R2 squares.

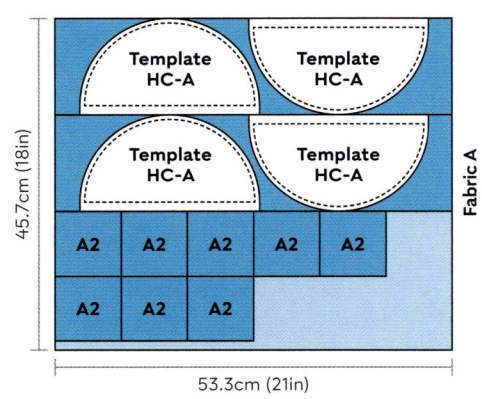

2 From the fabric S FQ, cut six S1 squares from each 8.9 x 53.3cm (3½ x 21in) strip for a total of 18 S1 squares.

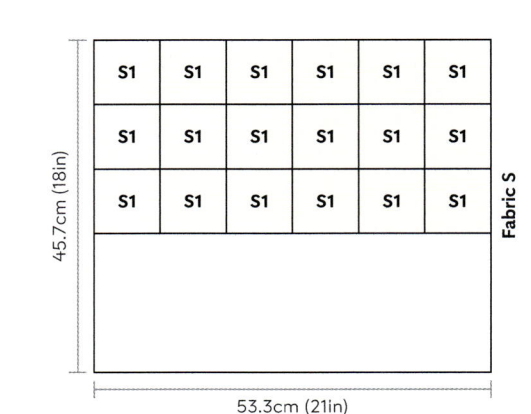

3 From each fabric BG 17.8cm (7in) x WOF strip, cut seven BG1 concave pieces using template HC-B as shown for a total of 72 BG1 concave pieces.

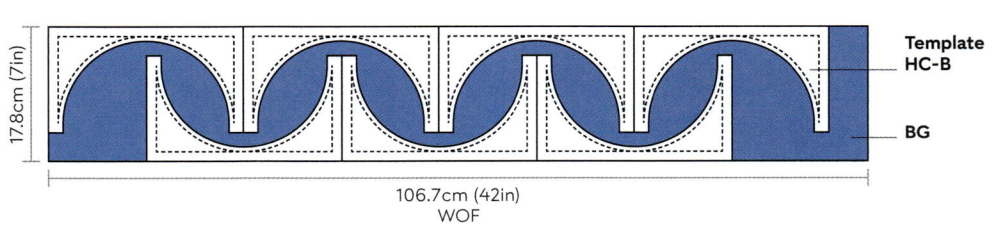

UNIT ASSEMBLY

Follow steps 1–8 to assemble units 1 and 2. Keep each fabric pair (A/B, C/D, E/F, G/H, I/J, K/L, M/N, O/P, and Q/R) together while piecing.

1. Prepare four A1 convex pieces and four BG1 concave pieces by marking the centre and quarters of the curved edges (see p.104).

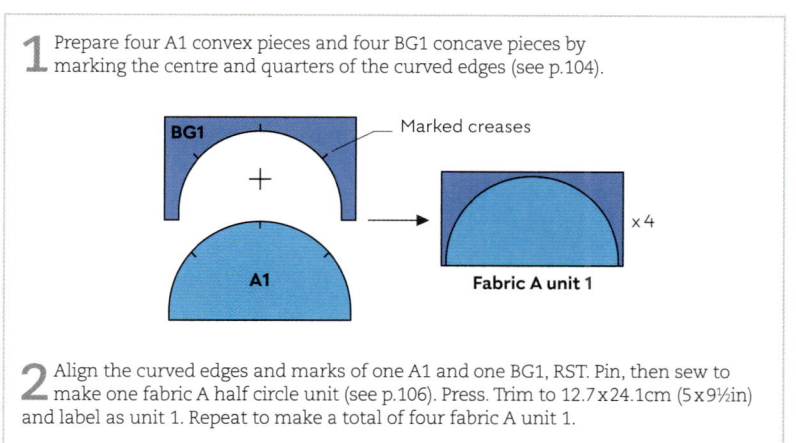

2. Align the curved edges and marks of one A1 and one BG1, RST. Pin, then sew to make one fabric A half circle unit (see p.106). Press. Trim to 12.7 x 24.1cm (5 x 9½in) and label as unit 1. Repeat to make a total of four fabric A unit 1.

3. Repeat steps 1–2 with four B1 convex pieces and four BG1 concave pieces to make four fabric B unit 1.

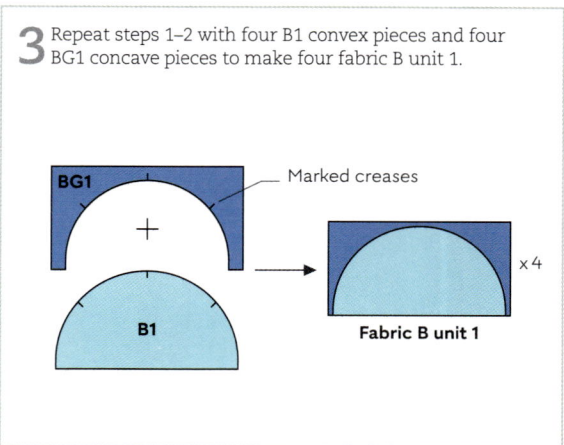

4. Arrange four A2, four B2, and one S1 into a 3x3 grid, placing A2 in each corner, S1 in the centre, and B2 in the remaining edge positions. Sew the squares RST into rows using the piece-by-piece technique (see p.84). Press.

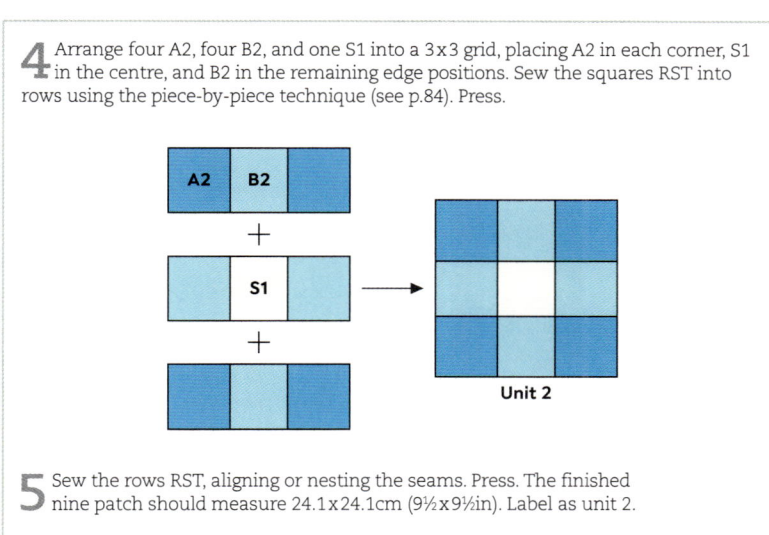

5. Sew the rows RST, aligning or nesting the seams. Press. The finished nine patch should measure 24.1 x 24.1cm (9½ x 9½in). Label as unit 2.

6. Repeat steps 4–5, alternating the fabric placements, placing B2 in each corner, S1 in the centre, and A2 in the remaining edge positions to make a second unit 2.

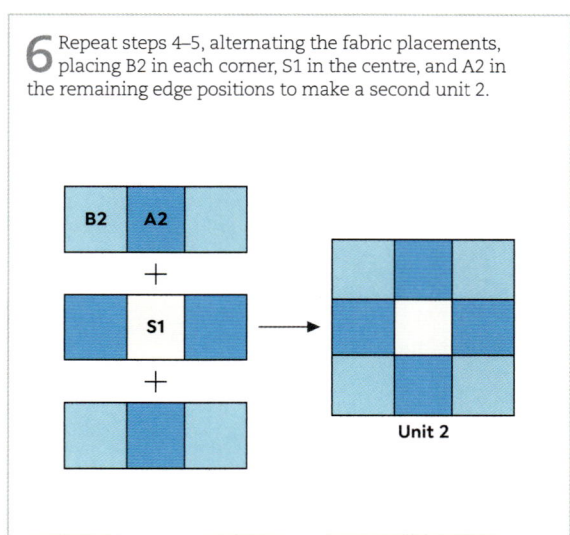

7. Repeat steps 1–6 with the remaining fabric pairs: C/D, E/F, G/H, I/J, K/L, M/N, O/P, and Q/R.

8. Group four unit 1 with one unit 2 by matching the unit 2 corner square fabric with the unit 1 fabric. Repeat to group all remaining units.

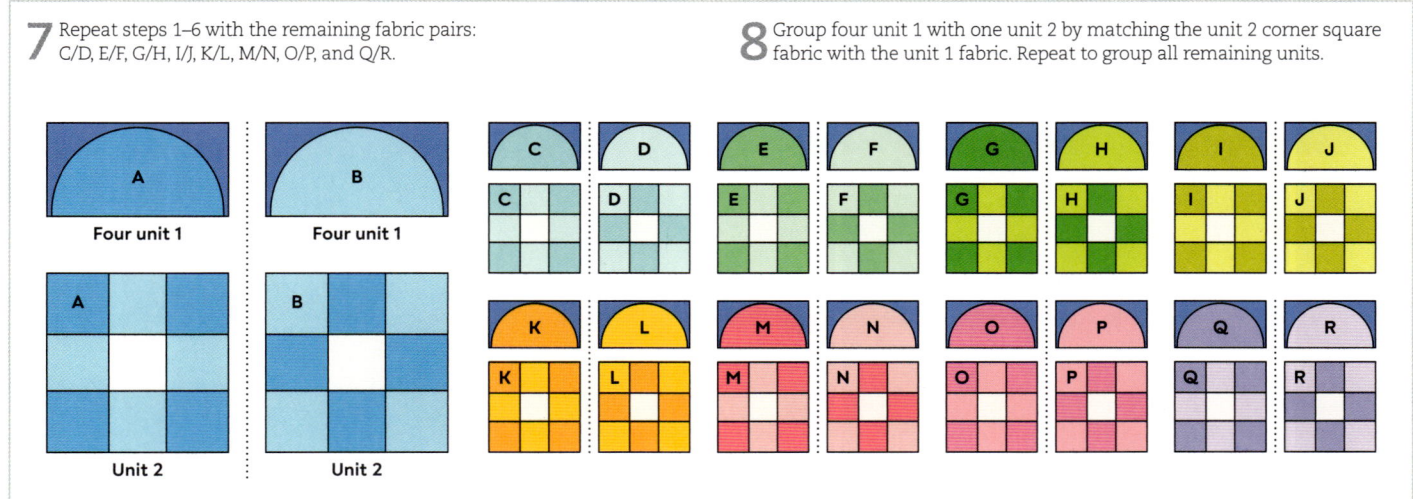

COLUMN ASSEMBLY

Before assembling columns, lay out all units and pieces to determine the desired fabric A–R placement. Be sure to keep matching units 1 and 2 grouped together.

1 Arrange all units 1 and 2 and BG2, BG3, BG4, BG5, and BG6 pieces into columns as shown. Adjust the placement of the grouped units until you are satisfied with the distribution of fabric and colour.
- Columns 1 and 11 each contain four unit 1, three BG2, and two BG3.
- Columns 2, 6, and 10 each contain eight unit 1, four unit 2, and three BG4.
- Columns 3, 5, and 7 each contain seven unit 1, two BG3, and six BG5.
- Columns 4 and 8 each contain six unit 1, three unit 2, two BG4, and two BG6.

2 Sew the pieces in each column RST. Ensure pieces are oriented correctly while sewing.

QUILT ASSEMBLY AND FINISHING

Use the strip piecing technique (see p.83) to join columns one at a time or in pairs. Match all points and seams (see p.141) carefully, pin as needed, and press seams open after every step.

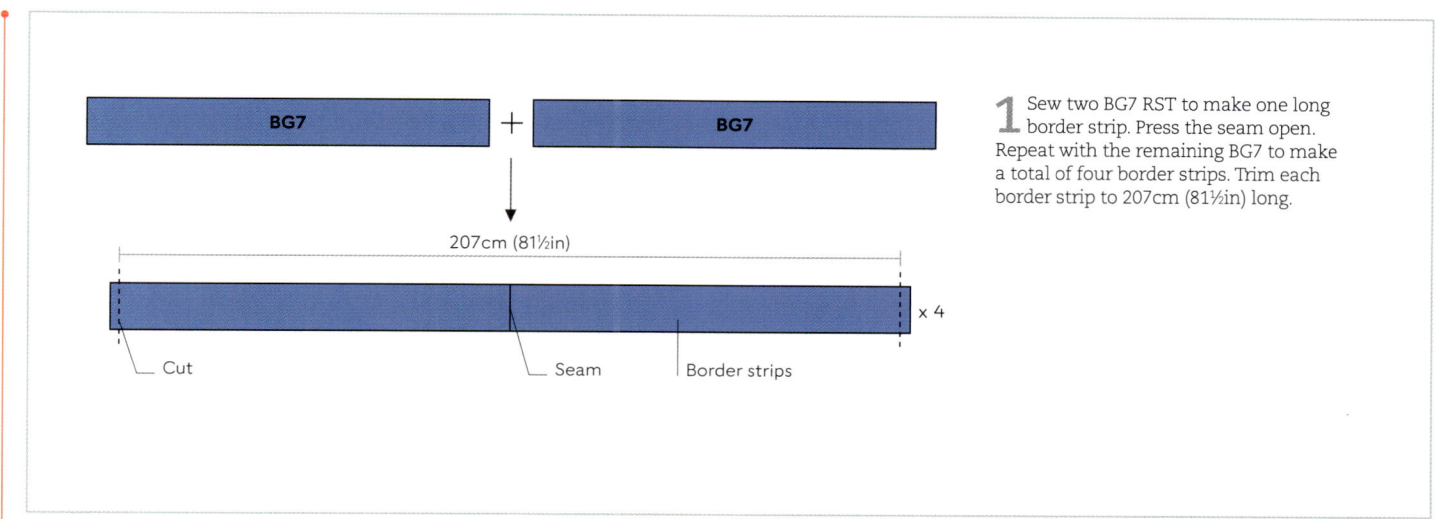

1 Sew two BG7 RST to make one long border strip. Press the seam open. Repeat with the remaining BG7 to make a total of four border strips. Trim each border strip to 207cm (81½in) long.

2 Sew columns 1–11 RST in order from left to right, taking care to match all points and seams. Press.

3 Sew one border strip to each the left and right of the quilt top, then sew the remaining border strips to the top and bottom. Press all seams toward the border strips.

4 Press the entire quilt top from the front to remove all wrinkles. Sew a stay stitch (see p.151) 3.2mm (⅛in) around the perimeter of the quilt to secure seams.

5 To make binding, cut nine 6.4cm (2½in) x WOF strips from binding fabric. Sew all nine WOF strips, RST, to make one strip that is at least 907cm (357in) long.

6 Baste (see pp.157–159), quilt (see pp.160–171), and bind (see pp.172–181) as desired.

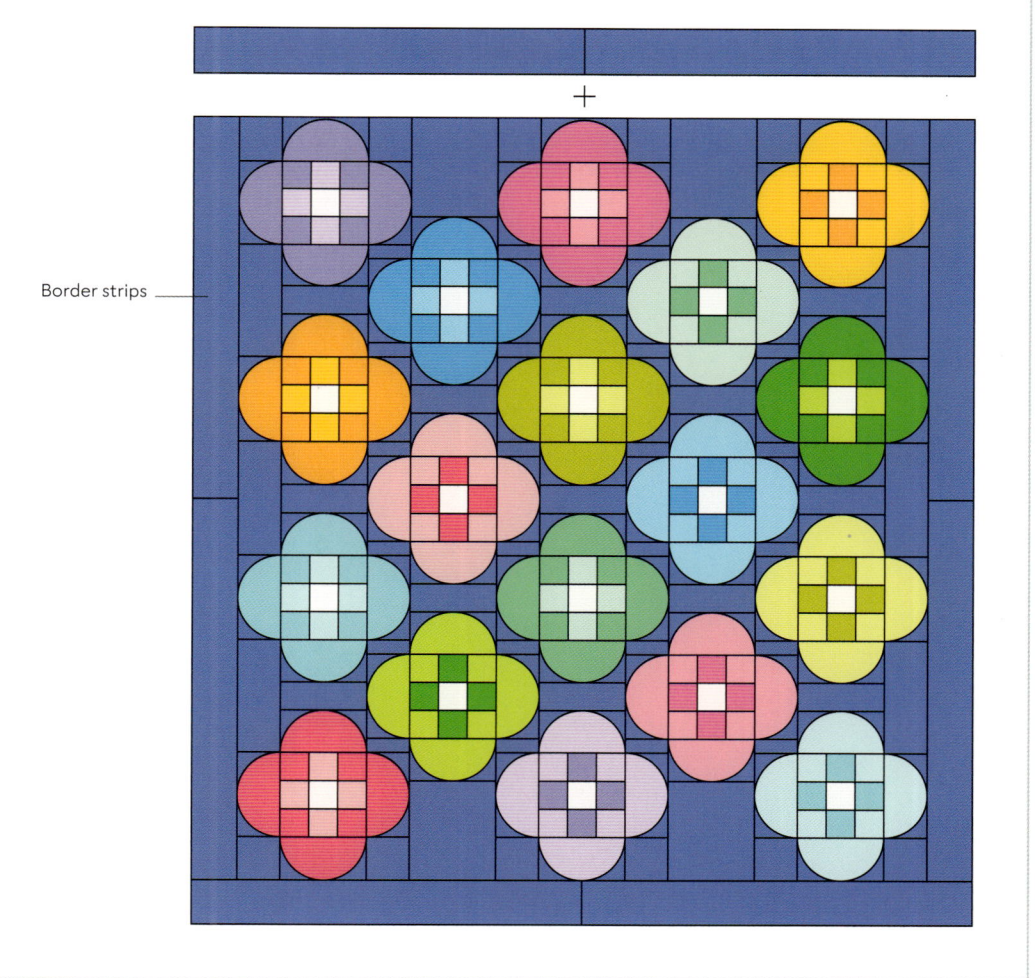

Primrose crown

This quilt pattern is a bold, quadrant-based design inspired by Texas Evening Primrose flowers. A mix of angular and curved piecing techniques, along with a symmetrical layout and large-scale units, produces a quilt that is both striking and approachable to make.

FINISHED THROW SIZE 152 x 152cm (60 x 60in)
TECHNIQUES USED Using templates **p.71**, Setting an accurate seam allowance **p.73**, HSTs **p.86**, QSTs **p.90**, FG **p.92**, Square in a square units **p.94**, Curves **p.104**, Matching points and seams **p.141**, Sashing **p.143**, Quadrant quilt top layout **p.146**

MATERIALS

- Basic quilting supplies (see p.14)
- Paper and fabric scissors
- Printer and template paper
- Tweezers (optional)
- 24.1 x 24.1cm (9½ x 9½in) or larger square ruler
- Marking pen
- 168 x 168cm (66 x 66in) or larger wadding

FABRIC REQUIREMENTS

Fabric A	0.5m (½yd)
Fabric B	0.75m (¾yd)
Fabric C	0.75m (¾yd)
Fabric D	1.5m (1½yds)
Fabric E	1.75m (1¾yds)
Backing*	3.5m (3¾yds)
Binding	0.75m (¾yd)

*Backing fabric required when using one vertical or horizontal seam.

Consider choosing fabrics with contrasting hues or a balanced mix of warm and cool tones (see p.60) to create depth. To ensure each design element stands out, select fabrics with a mix of light, medium, and dark values.

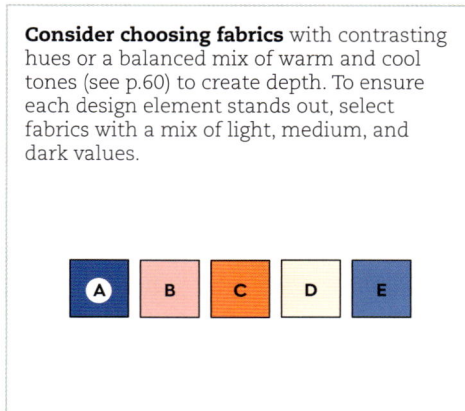

COLOUR REFERENCE

COVER QUILT DETAILS

Fabrics: Ruby and Bee Solids by Windham Fabrics in Majorelle Blue (**A**), Shell (**B**), Marigold (**C**), Cream Puff (**D**), Provence Blue (**E**); **Quilting:** Dissent pantograph quilted by Stephanie of Hillside Stitches; **Thread:** Superior Threads King Tut 40 wt in 904; **Wadding:** Hobbs Heirloom Supreme 100% Cotton; **Binding:** Marigold

CUTTING INSTRUCTIONS

Use the fabric cutting tables and diagrams below to cut and label the pieces required from fabrics A–E and BG. Visit *The Quilting Book* website (see p.11) to print the required quarter circle templates.

FABRIC CUTTING TABLES

FABRICS A–E

A	Cut (2) 16.5cm (6½in) x WOF; **sub-cut:** **A2:** (2) 16.5 x 16.5cm (6½ x 6½in) **A1:** (8) 14 x 14cm (5½ x 5½in) **A3:** (4) **template QC-B** concave quarter circle pieces
B	Cut (1) 27.9cm (11in) x WOF; **sub-cut:** **B2:** (1) 27.3 x 27.3cm (10¾ x 10¾in) **B1:** (8) 14 x 14cm (5½ x 5½in) Cut (1) 14cm (5½in) x WOF; **sub-cut:** **B4:** (8) **template QC-B** concave quarter circle pieces Cut (1) 13.3cm (5¼in) x WOF; **sub-cut:** **B3:** (4) **template QC-A** convex quarter circle pieces
C	Cut (1) 27.9cm (11in) x WOF; **sub-cut:** **C2:** (1) 27.3 x 27.3cm (10¾ x 10¾in) **C1:** (8) 14 x 14cm (5½ x 5½in) Cut (1) 14cm (5½in) x WOF; **sub-cut:** **C4:** (8) **template QC-B** concave quarter circle pieces Cut (1) 13.3cm (5¼in) x WOF; **sub-cut:** **C3:** (4) **template QC-A** convex quarter circle pieces
D	Cut (1) 27.9cm (11in) x WOF; **sub-cut:** **D4:** (1) 27.3 x 27.3cm (10¾ x 10¾in) **D1:** (8) 14 x 14cm (5½ x 5½in) Cut (1) 16.5cm (6½in) x WOF; **sub-cut:** **D2:** (2) 16.5 x 16.5cm (6½ x 6½in) **D5:** (4) 12.7 x 12.7cm (5 x 5in) Cut (2) 14.6cm (5¾in) x WOF; **sub-cut:** **D3:** (8) 14.6 x 14.6cm (5¾ x 5¾in) **D7:** (8) **template QC-B** concave quarter circle pieces Cut (4) 13.3cm (5¼in) x WOF; **sub-cut:** **D6:** (20) **template QC-A** convex quarter circle pieces **D8:** (8) **template QC-A** convex quarter circle pieces **D9:** (8) 7 x 12.7cm (2¾ x 5in)
E	Cut (1) 14.6cm (5¾in) x WOF; **sub-cut:** **E2:** (4) 14.6 x 14.6cm (5¾ x 5¾in) **E3:** (12) 7 x 7cm (2¾ x 2¾in) Cut (2) 14cm (5½in) x WOF; **sub-cut:** **E4:** (16) **template QC-B** concave quarter circle pieces **E1:** (4) 14 x 14cm (5½ x 5½in) **E3:** (4) 7 x 7cm (2¾ x 2¾in) (16 total **E3**) Cut (4) 12.7cm (5in) x WOF; **sub-cut:** **E6:** (8) 12.7 x 47cm (5 x 18½in) **E5:** (4) 12.7 x 12.7cm (5 x 5in) Cut (6) 8.9cm (3½in) x WOF; label as **E8** and set aside for borders.

FABRIC CUTTING DIAGRAMS

1 To cut B3, C3, D6, and D8 convex quarter circle pieces, fold each 13.3cm (5¼in) x WOF strip in half, aligning the selvedges. Remove the selvedges and position the QC-A template as shown.

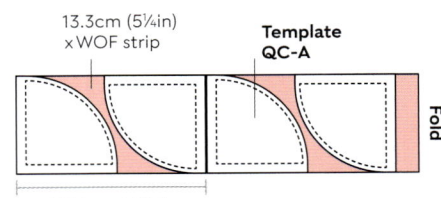

2 Cut around the template to make two QC-A pieces at once. Cut the required number of B3, C3, D6, and D8 convex pieces from the WOF strips based on the cutting table; each strip yields a total of eight pieces.

3 To cut A3, B4, C4, D7, and E4 concave quarter circle pieces, fold each respective WOF strip in half, aligning the selvedges. Remove the selvedges and position the QC-B template as shown.

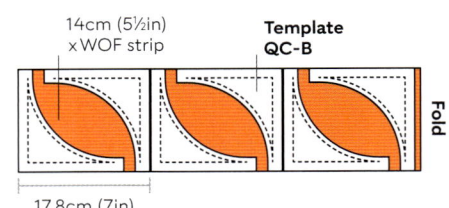

4 Cut around the template to make two QC-B pieces at once. Cut the required number of A3, B4, C4, D7, and E4 concave pieces from the WOF strips based on the cutting table; each strip yields a total of 12 pieces.

UNIT ASSEMBLY

Refer to the techniques in the traditional piecing chapter (see pp.82–107) for more detailed instructions on how to piece and trim HSTs, QSTs, FG, square in a square, and quarter circle units. Press all seams open to reduce bulk and label all completed units to stay organized.

1 Place one A1 and one B1 RST. Mark a diagonal line on the wrong side of B1.

2 Sew a 6.4mm (¼in) seam on each side of the marked line. Cut directly on the marked line to make two HSTs. Press. Trim the HSTs to 12.7 x 12.7cm (5 x 5in); label as HST A/B.

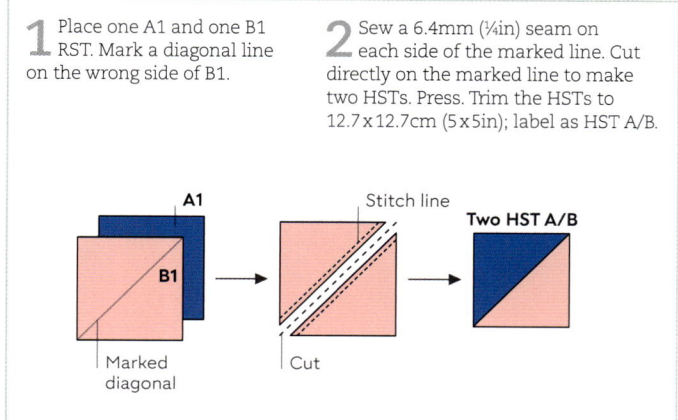

3 Repeat steps 1–2 using all A1, B1, C1, D1, and E1 to make the required number of HSTs in the following fabric combinations: four A/B, four A/C, eight A/D, four B/C, four B/D, four B/E, four C/D, and four C/E.

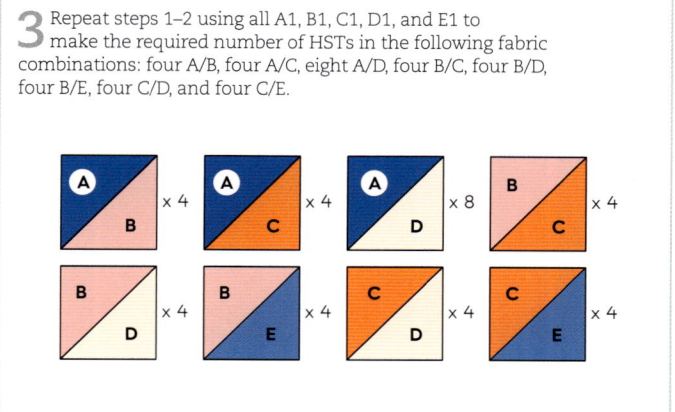

4 Follow steps 1–2 to make two HSTs with one A2 and one D2. Trim the HSTs to 15.2 x 15.2cm (6 x 6in). Place the HSTs RST, alternating the fabrics and aligning the seams. Mark a diagonal line from corner to corner on the wrong side of the top HST, perpendicular to the seam.

5 Sew a 6.4mm (¼in) seam on each side of the marked line. Cut directly on the marked line to make two QSTs. Press. Trim the QST to 12.7 x 12.7cm (5 x 5in) and label as QST A/D.

6 Repeat steps 4–5 with the remaining A2 and D2 to make a total of four QST A/D.

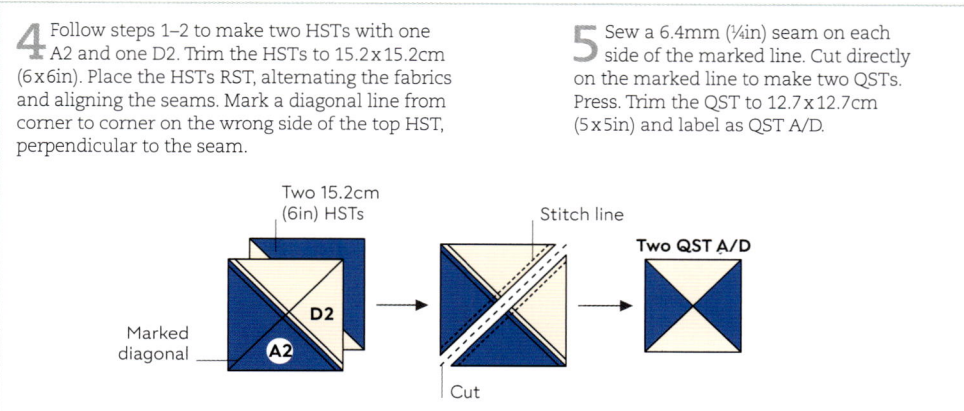

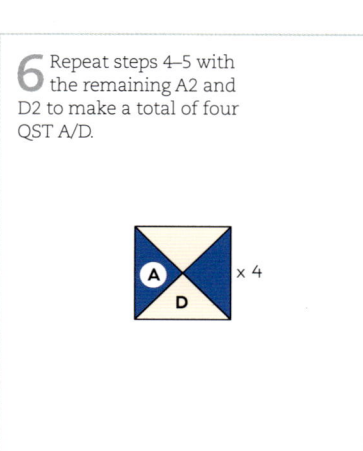

7 Mark a diagonal line on the wrong side of four D3. Place two D3 on opposite corners of one B2, RST, with the diagonal lines overlapping at the centre.

8 Sew a 6.4mm (¼in) seam on each side of the marked line. Cut directly on the marked line to make two units. Press.

9 Place one D3 on the corner of one unit from step 8 with the marked line running through the centre. Sew a 6.4mm (¼in) seam on each side of the marked line. Repeat with the second unit and remaining D3. Cut directly on the marked lines to make four FG. Press. Trim the FG to 12.7 x 24.1cm (5 x 9½in) and label as FG B/D.

10 Repeat steps 7–9 to make the required number of FG in the following fabric combinations: four C2/D3 and four D4/E2.

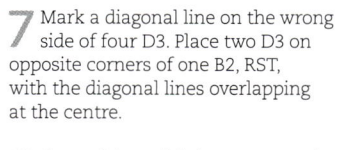
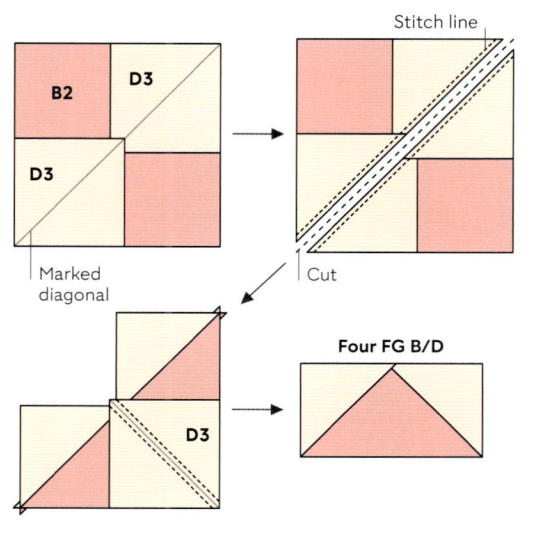
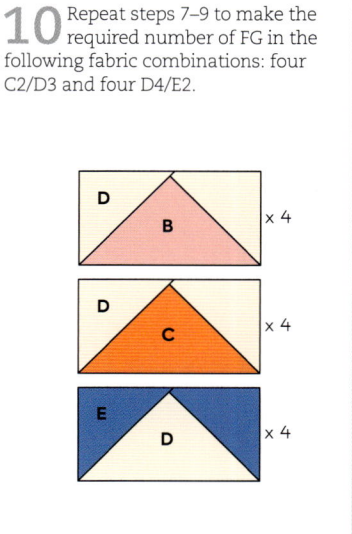

11. Mark a diagonal line on the wrong side of four E3. Place two E3 on opposite corners of one D5, RST.

12. Sew directly on the marked lines. Cut 6.4mm (¼in) away from the seams. Press.

14. Repeat steps 11–13 with the remaining D5 and E3 to make a total of four SQ D/E.

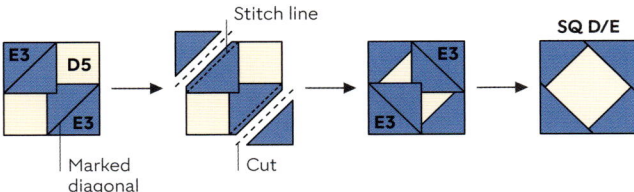

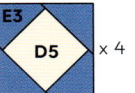

13. Repeat step 11–12 with the remaining two E3 on the remaining corners of the D5 to make a square in a square unit. Trim the unit to 12.7 x 12.7cm (5 x 5in) and label as SQ D/E.

15. Mark the centre of the curved edges (see p.104) of one A3 and one D6.

17. Repeat steps 15–16 to make the required number of QCs in the following fabric combinations: four A3/D6, four D7/B3, four D7/C3, and sixteen E4/D6.

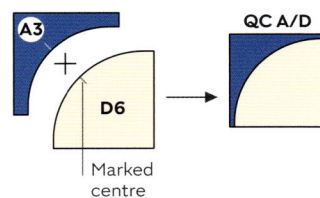

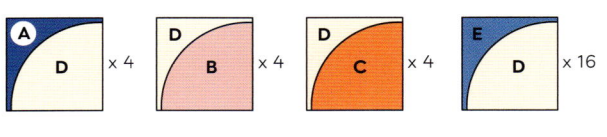

16. Align the curved edges and centre marks RST. Pin. Sew to make one quarter circle unit. Press. Trim the QC to 12.7 x 12.7cm (5 x 5in) and label as QC A/D.

18. Follow steps 15–16 to make eight QCs with eight B4 and eight D8. Do not trim.

19. Place template QC-A on top of one QC from step 18, aligning the corner of the template with the corner of the B4 concave piece. Cut along the template to make a new convex edge.

21. Repeat steps 19–20 to make a total of eight OP B/D/C.

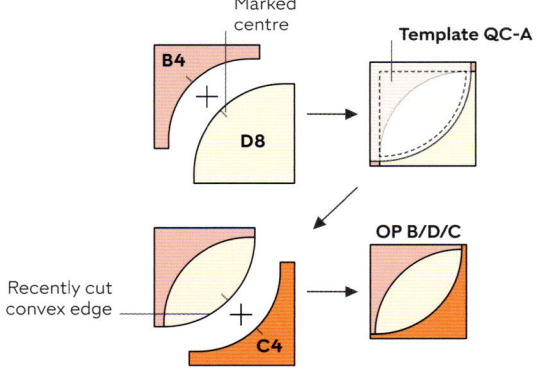

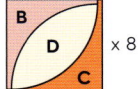

20. Pair the recently cut convex edge with one C4. Mark the centres of both pieces. Pin and sew RST to make one orange peel unit. Trim the unit to 12.7 x 12.7cm (5 x 5in) and label as OP B/D/C.

QUADRANT ASSEMBLY

This quilt is assembled using a quadrant layout (see p.146). Make two quadrant A and two quadrant B, which are mirrored versions of each other. Align seams carefully and press seams open after every step.

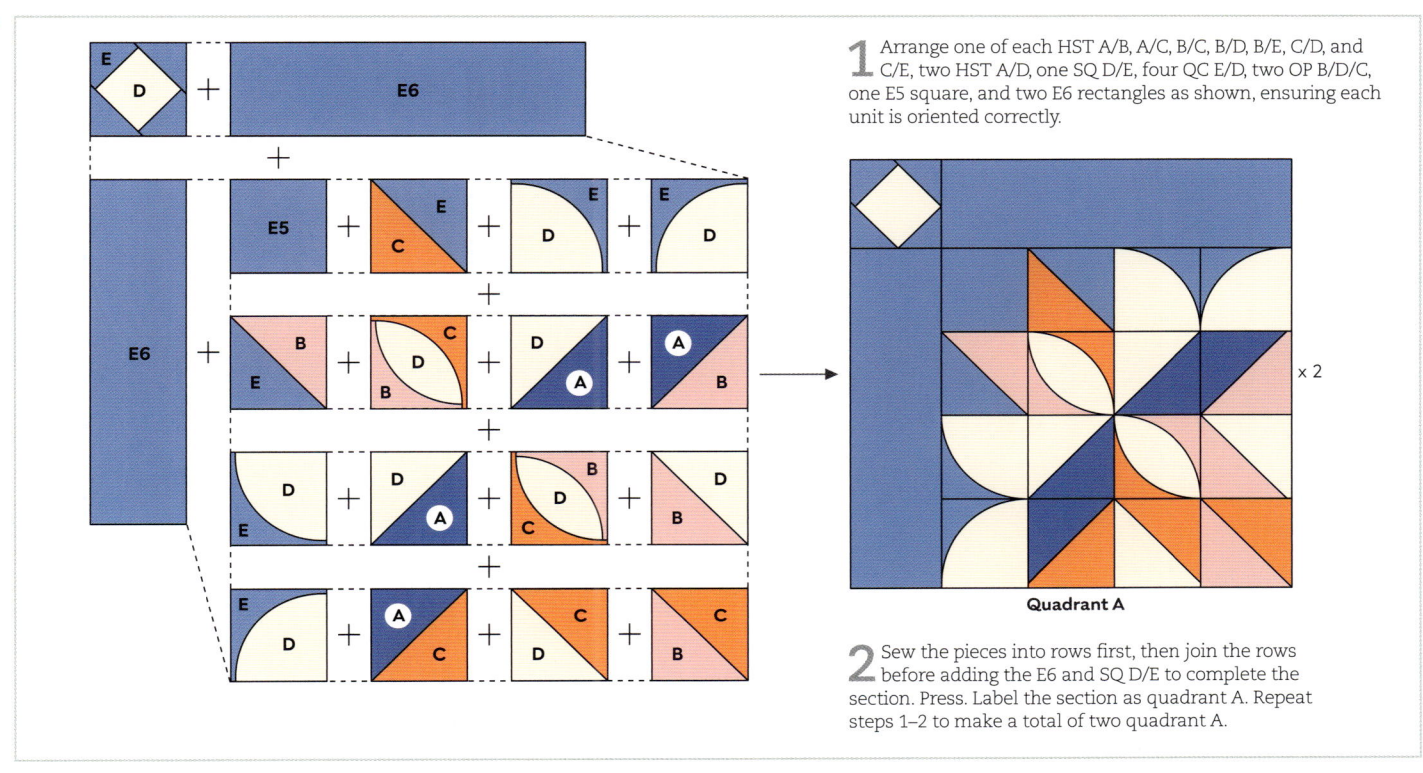

1. Arrange one of each HST A/B, A/C, B/C, B/D, B/E, C/D, and C/E, two HST A/D, one SQ D/E, four QC E/D, two OP B/D/C, one E5 square, and two E6 rectangles as shown, ensuring each unit is oriented correctly.

Quadrant A ×2

2. Sew the pieces into rows first, then join the rows before adding the E6 and SQ D/E to complete the section. Press. Label the section as quadrant A. Repeat steps 1–2 to make a total of two quadrant A.

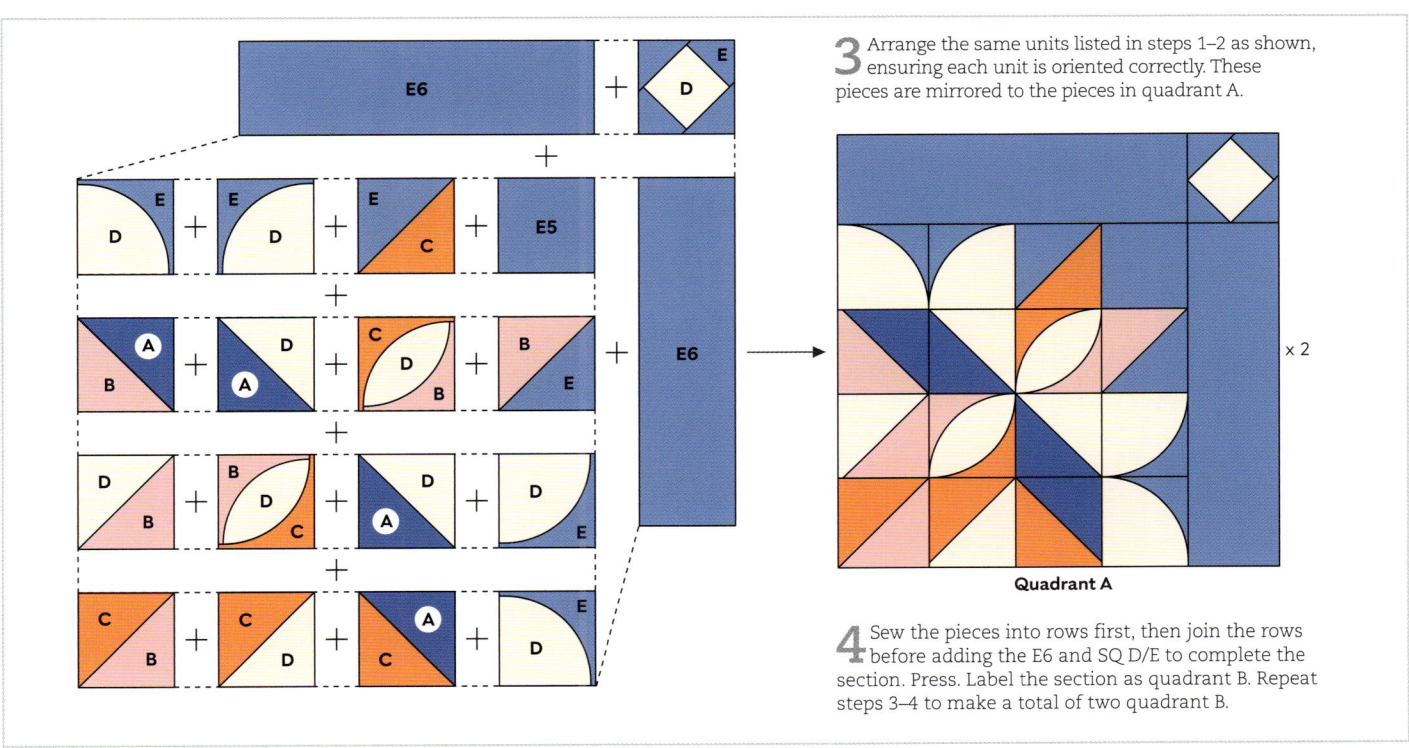

3. Arrange the same units listed in steps 1–2 as shown, ensuring each unit is oriented correctly. These pieces are mirrored to the pieces in quadrant A.

Quadrant A ×2

4. Sew the pieces into rows first, then join the rows before adding the E6 and SQ D/E to complete the section. Press. Label the section as quadrant B. Repeat steps 3–4 to make a total of two quadrant B.

SASHING ASSEMBLY

Between each quadrant are three sets of pieced sections: sashing A, sashing B, and a centre cornerstone. Align seams carefully and press seams open after every step.

1 Arrange one of each FG B/D, C/D, and D/E, one QST A/D, two QC D/B, and two D9 rectangles as shown, ensuring each unit is oriented correctly.

2 Sew the QST and D9 rectangles into a column, then sew the QCs into a second column. Join the FG and two columns as shown to complete the section. Press. Label the section as sashing A. Repeat steps 1–2 to make a total of two sashing A.

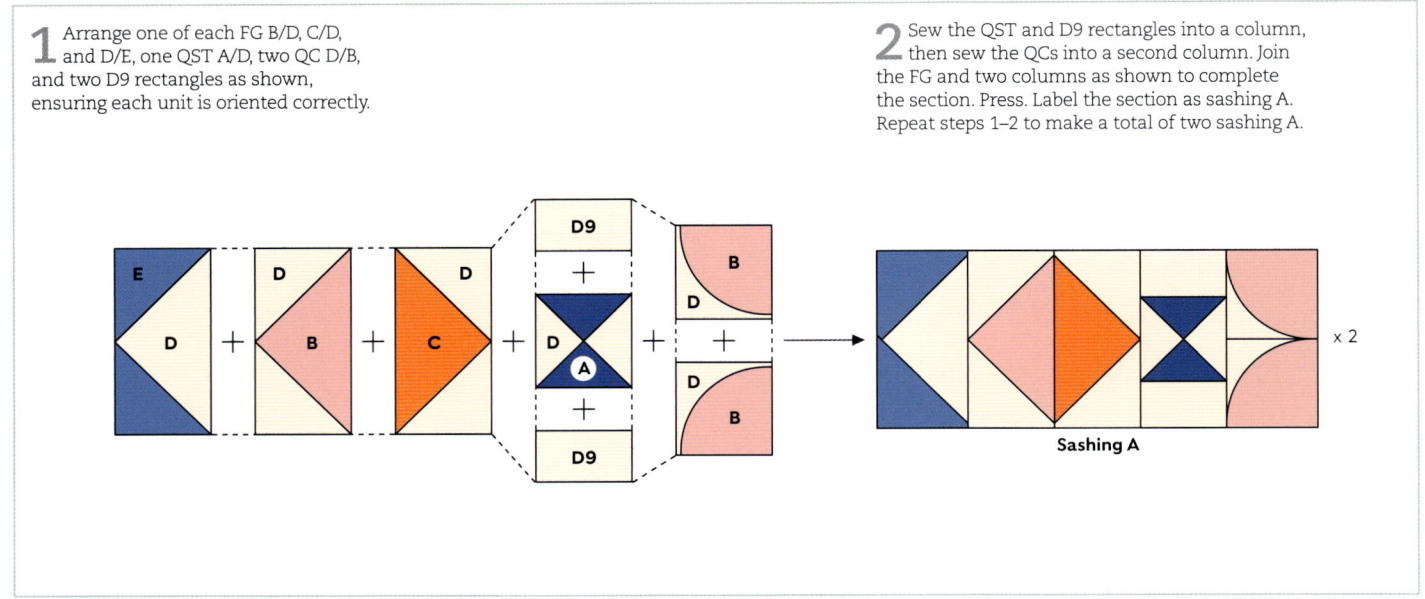

3 Arrange one of each FG B/D, C/D, and D/E, one QST A/D, two QC D/C, and two D9 rectangles as shown, ensuring each unit is oriented correctly.

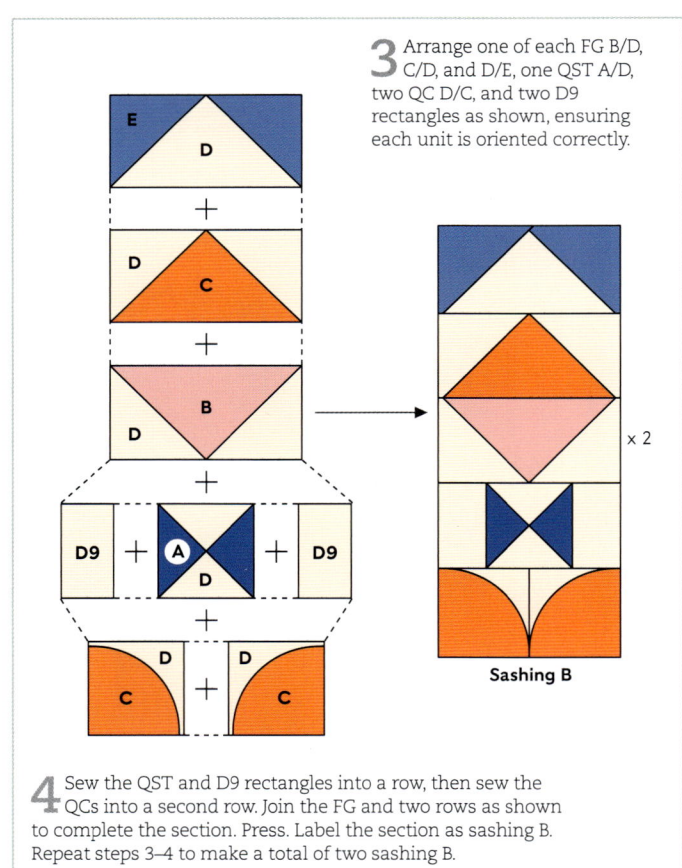

4 Sew the QST and D9 rectangles into a row, then sew the QCs into a second row. Join the FG and two rows as shown to complete the section. Press. Label the section as sashing B. Repeat steps 3–4 to make a total of two sashing B.

5 Arrange four QC A/D as shown, with the A3 concave pieces meeting at the centre.

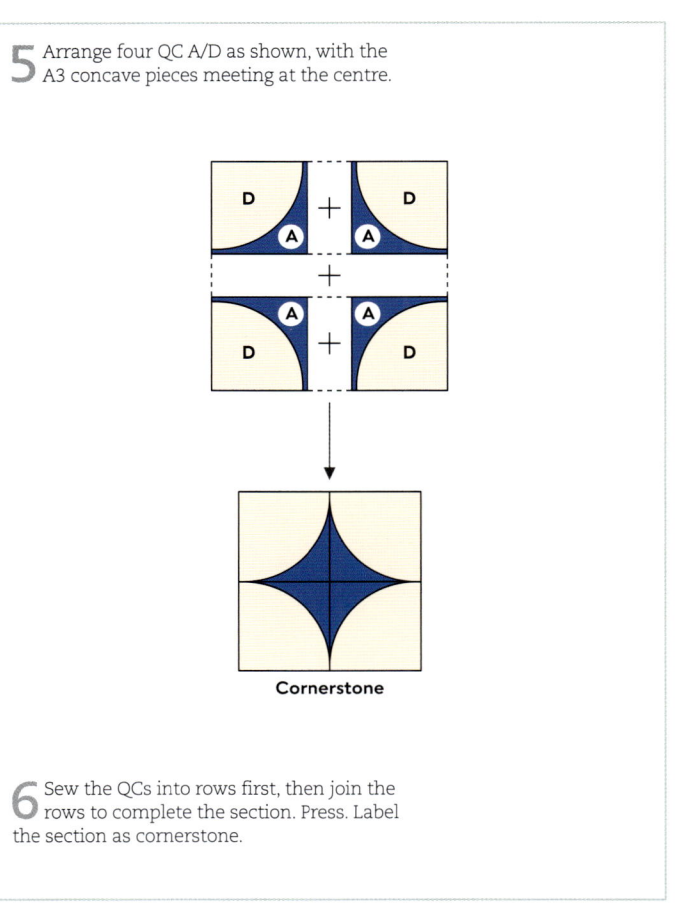

6 Sew the QCs into rows first, then join the rows to complete the section. Press. Label the section as cornerstone.

QUILT ASSEMBLY AND FINISHING

Make the border strips before piecing the sections together. Refer to the illustrations to ensure the quadrants, sashings, cornerstone, and border strips are oriented correctly. Match points and seams (see p.141) carefully and press seams open after every step.

1 Remove the selvedges from the six E8 WOF strips. Sew the strips, RST, to make one strip that is at least 584cm (230in) long.

2 Fold the strip in half, then cut two 8.9x138cm (3½x54½in) and two 8.9x154cm (3½x60½in) border strips.

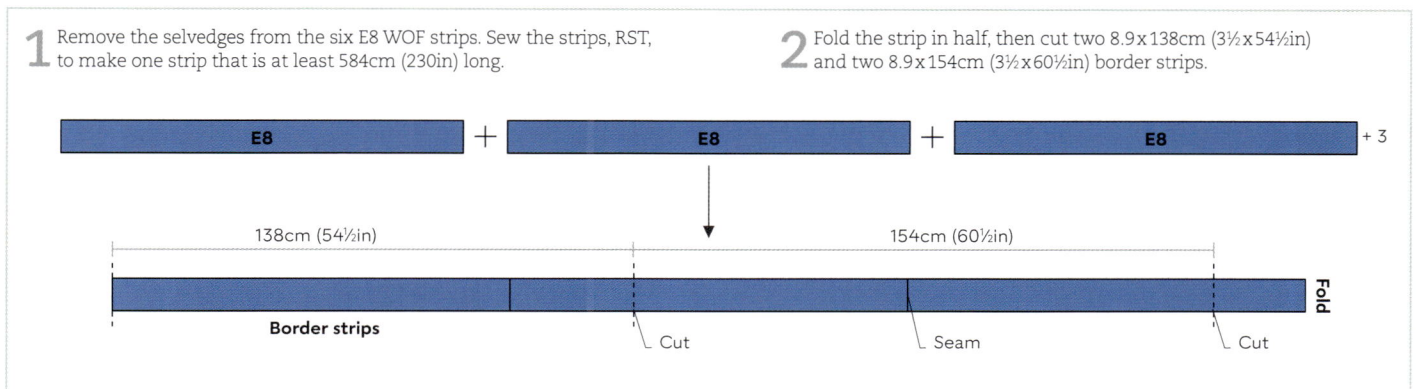

3 Arrange two quadrant A, two quadrant B, two sashing A, two sashing B, and one cornerstone as shown, ensuring each section is oriented correctly.

4 Sew quadrant A, sashing B, and quadrant B RST into a row. Press. Repeat with the second quadrant B, sashing B, and quadrant A sections to make a second row. Press.

5 Sew one sashing A to each the left and right of the cornerstone, RST, to form the centre row. Press. Sew all three rows RST. Press.

6 Sew one 138cm (54½in) border strip to each the left and right of the quilt top, then sew the 154cm (60½in) to the top and bottom. Press all seams toward the border strips.

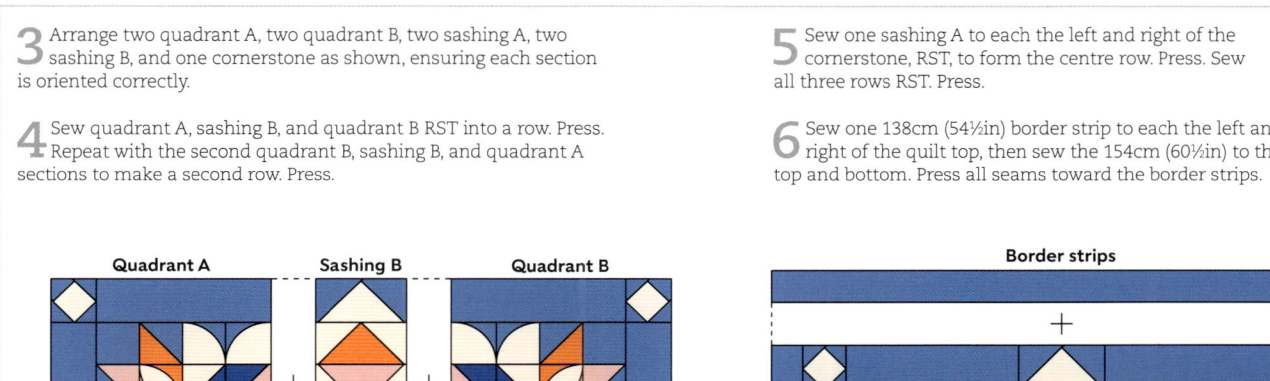
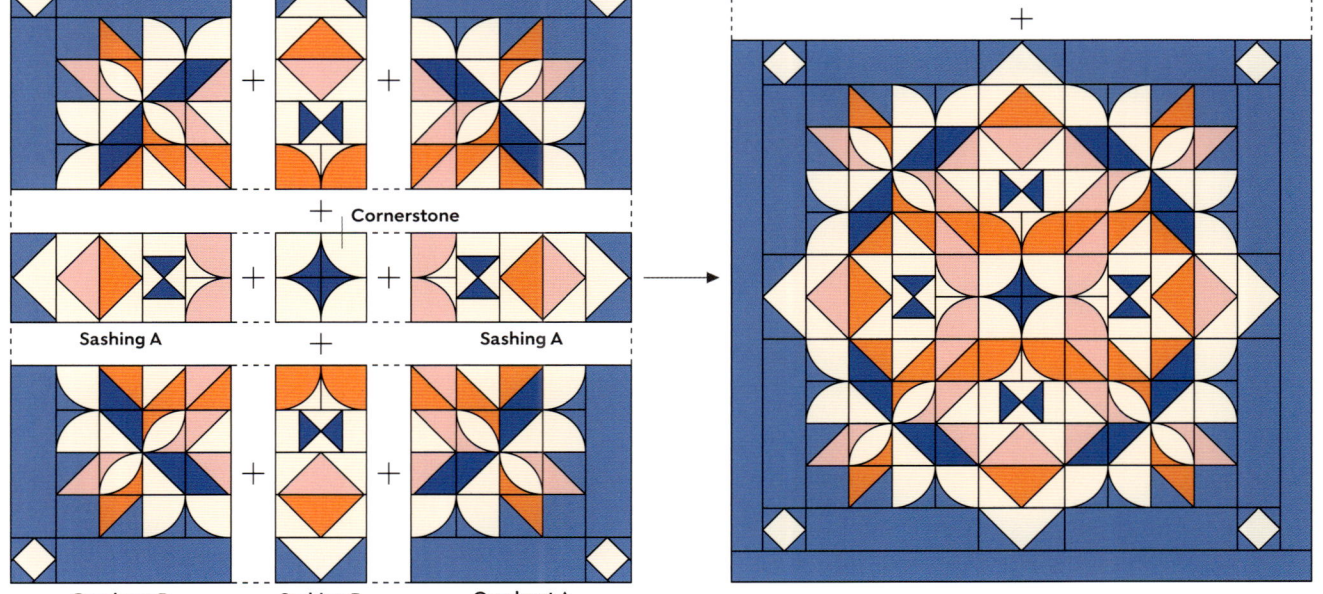

7 Press the entire quilt top from the front to remove all wrinkles. Sew a stay stitch (see p.151) 3.2mm (⅛in) around the perimeter of the quilt to secure seams.

8 To make binding, cut seven 6.4cm (2½in) x WOF strips from the chosen binding fabric. Sew all seven WOF strips, RST, to make one strip that is at least 648cm (255in) long.

9 To finish the quilt, baste (see pp.157–159), quilt (see pp.160–171), and bind (see pp.172–181) as desired.

Papered blooms

This pattern is inspired by the shifting hues of Lantana flowers, featuring central stars that radiate in bold, colourful stripes. The design is ideal for practicing FPP techniques.

FINISHED THROW SIZE 152 x 152cm (60 x 60in)
TECHNIQUES USED Understanding colour theory **p.60**, Preparing for FPP **p.115**, Piecing FPP sections **p.116**, Joining FPP templates **p.118**, Matching points and seams **p.141**, Row quilt top layout **p.146**

MATERIALS

- Basic quilting supplies (see p.14)
- Printer and FPP template paper
- Tweezers (optional)
- 8.9 x 31.8cm (3½ x 12½in) ruler or FPP ruler
- 137 x 137cm (54 x 54in) or larger wadding

FABRIC REQUIREMENTS

Fabrics A–L	(1) 0.75m (¾yd) each
Backing*	3.5m (3¾yds)
Binding	0.75m (¾yd)

*Backing fabric required when using one vertical or horizontal seam.

Choose a palette of six main hues (see p.60). Select one light value fabric and one dark value fabric for each hue, resulting in a total of 12 fabrics: six light and six dark.

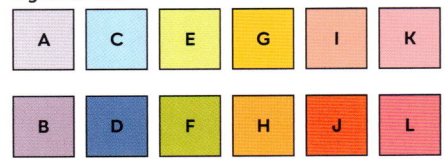

Light fabrics / Dark fabrics

Label the first hue as fabrics A and B, the second as fabrics C and D, and so on up to fabric L. Each block uses one light-dark value fabric pair; keep each pair together while cutting and piecing to stay organized.

COLOUR REFERENCE

COVER QUILT DETAILS

Fabrics: Ruby and Bee Solids by Windham Fabrics in Dusk (**A**), Vervain (**B**), Marine Layer (**C**), Provence Blue (**D**), Lemonade (**E**), Avocado (**F**), Mustard Seed (**G**), Pumpkin (**H**), Peachy Keen (**I**), Delphinium (**J**), Posy (**K**), Perfect Pink (**L**); **Quilting:** Sashiko Stars pantograph quilted by Stephanie of Hillside Stitches; **Thread:** Superior Threads King Tut 40 wt in 940; **Wadding:** Hobbs Heirloom 80/20 blend; **Binding:** Perfect Pink

CUTTING INSTRUCTIONS

Use the fabric cutting tables and diagrams below to cut out and label the pieces required from fabrics A–L. Visit *The Quilting Book* website (see p.11) to print the required FPP templates.

FABRIC CUTTING TABLES

FABRICS A–L

From each fabric:

Cut (1) 21.6cm (8½in) x WOF; **sub-cut:**
  A4–L4: (12) 21.6 x 8.9cm (8½ x 3½in) (12 for each fabric)

Cut (1) 16.5cm (6½in) x WOF; **sub-cut:**
  A2–L2: (12) 16.5 x 8.9cm (6½ x 3½in) (12 for each fabric)

Cut (2) 10.2cm (4in) x WOF; **sub-cut:** (12) 10.2 x 10.2cm (4 x 4in) squares, then cut each square in half diagonally for (24) triangles to make:
  A1–L1: (12) triangles (12 for each fabric)
  A3–L3: (12) triangles (12 for each fabric)

PREPARING FPP TEMPLATES

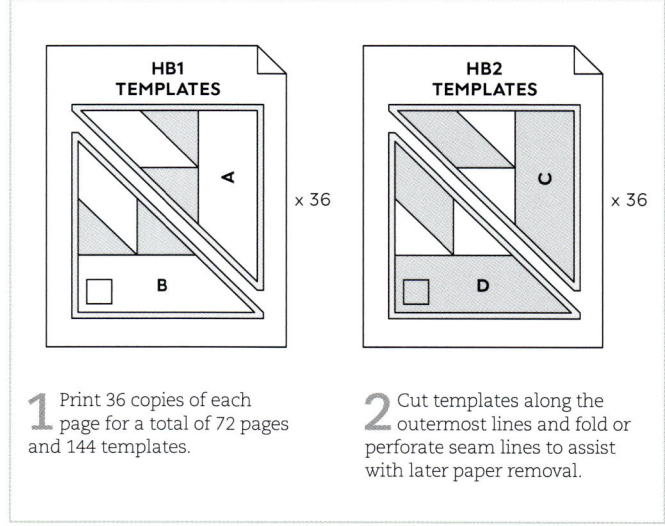

1 Print 36 copies of each page for a total of 72 pages and 144 templates.

2 Cut templates along the outermost lines and fold or perforate seam lines to assist with later paper removal.

FABRIC CUTTING DIAGRAMS

1 Cut each fabric A–L as shown, using the measurements from the fabric cutting tables. Label all pieces accordingly.

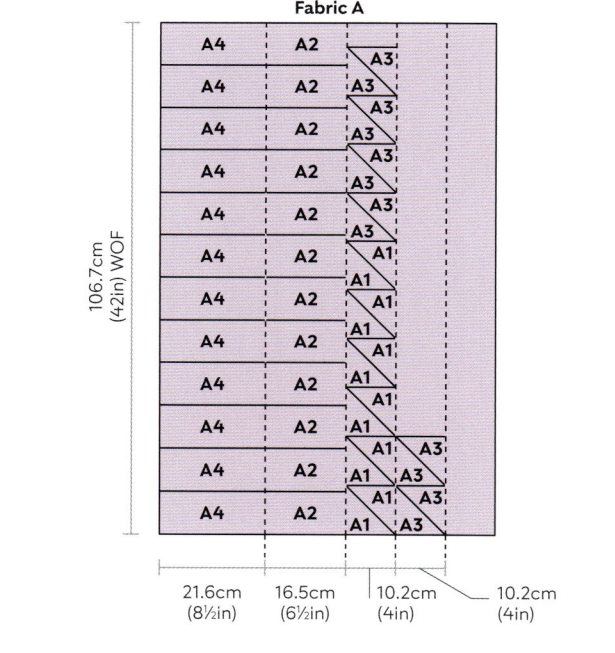

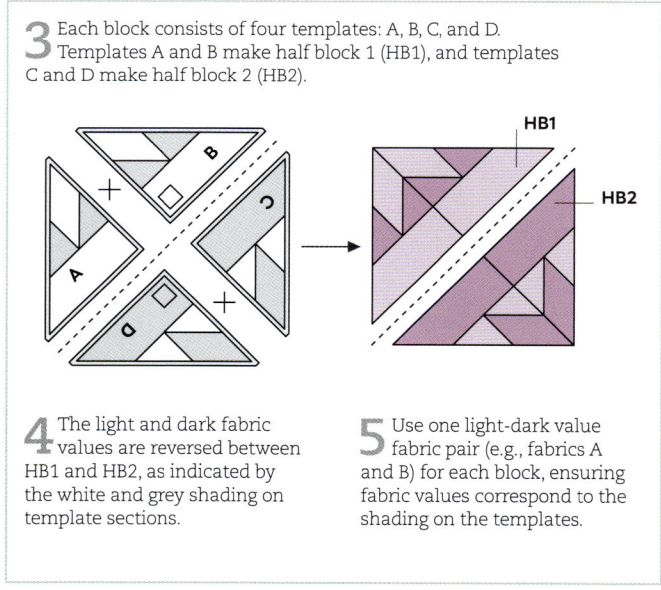

3 Each block consists of four templates: A, B, C, and D. Templates A and B make half block 1 (HB1), and templates C and D make half block 2 (HB2).

4 The light and dark fabric values are reversed between HB1 and HB2, as indicated by the white and grey shading on template sections.

5 Use one light-dark value fabric pair (e.g., fabrics A and B) for each block, ensuring fabric values correspond to the shading on the templates.

FPP BLOCK ASSEMBLY

Refer to the Piecing sections techniques (see p.116) for more detailed FPP instructions.

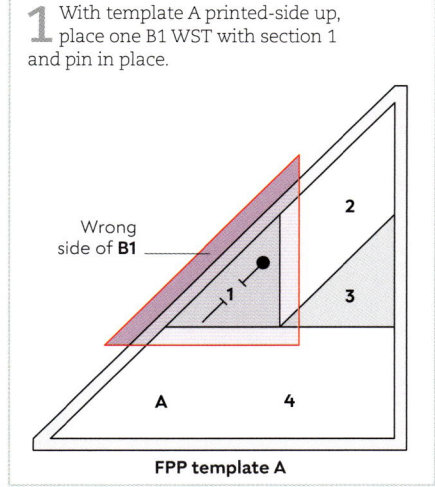

1 With template A printed-side up, place one B1 WST with section 1 and pin in place.

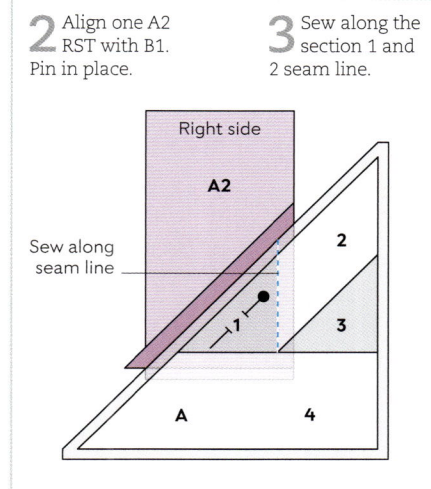

2 Align one A2 RST with B1. Pin in place.

3 Sew along the section 1 and 2 seam line.

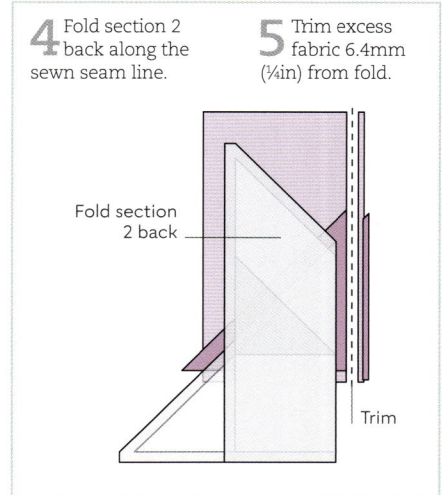

4 Fold section 2 back along the sewn seam line.

5 Trim excess fabric 6.4mm (¼in) from fold.

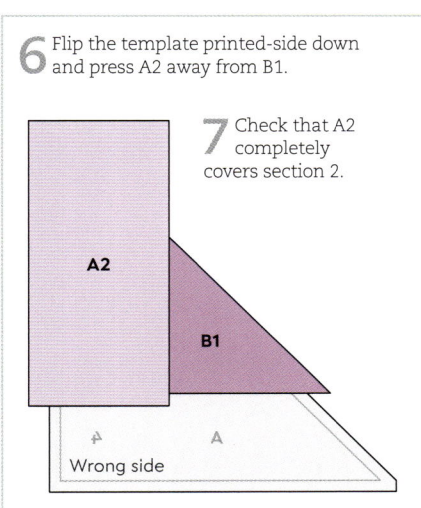

6 Flip the template printed-side down and press A2 away from B1.

7 Check that A2 completely covers section 2.

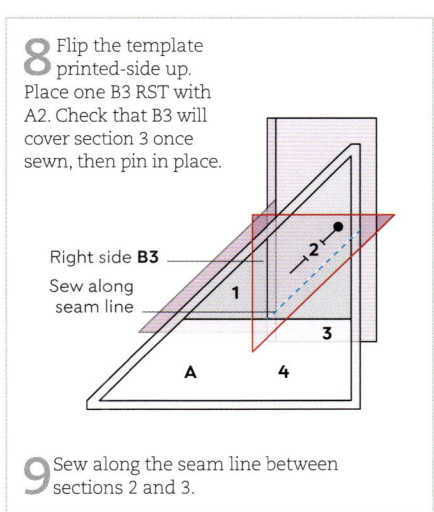

8 Flip the template printed-side up. Place one B3 RST with A2. Check that B3 will cover section 3 once sewn, then pin in place.

9 Sew along the seam line between sections 2 and 3.

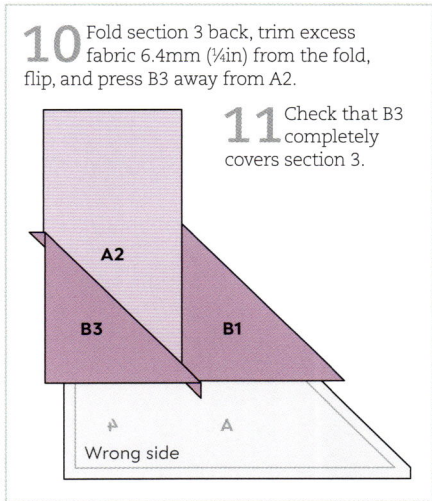

10 Fold section 3 back, trim excess fabric 6.4mm (¼in) from the fold, flip, and press B3 away from A2.

11 Check that B3 completely covers section 3.

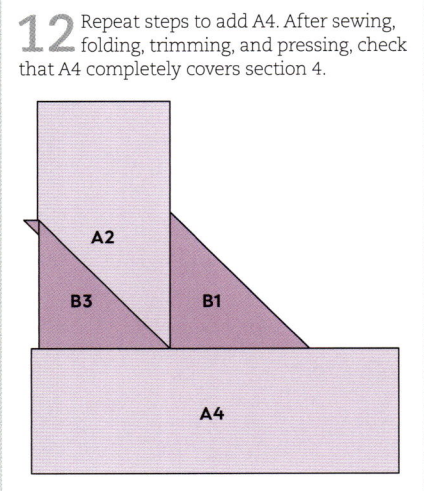

12 Repeat steps to add A4. After sewing, folding, trimming, and pressing, check that A4 completely covers section 4.

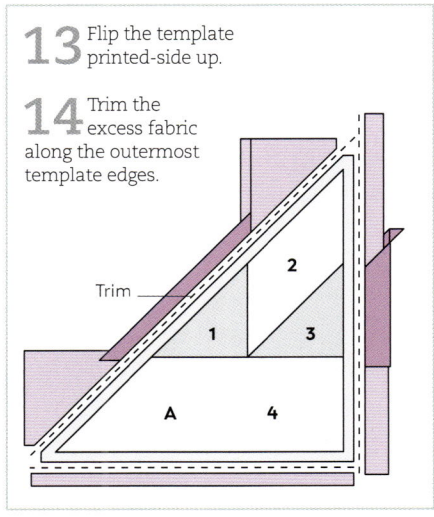

13 Flip the template printed-side up.

14 Trim the excess fabric along the outermost template edges.

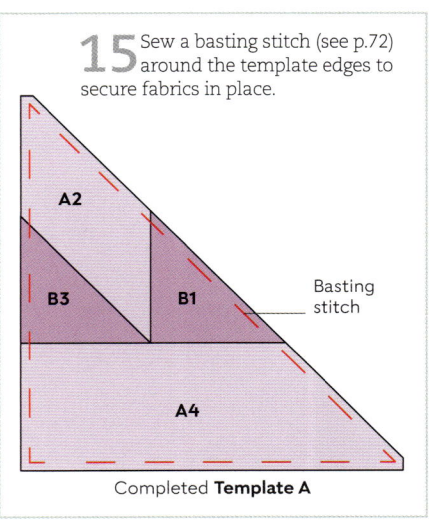

15 Sew a basting stitch (see p.72) around the template edges to secure fabrics in place.

BLOCK ASSEMBLY

Refer to Joining templates (see p.118) for more detailed instructions to assemble block A–B using fabrics A and B. Repeat to make all blocks using corresponding light-dark value fabric pairs.

1 Follow the FPP instructions on the previous page to assemble template A using B1, A2, B3, and A4.

Template A

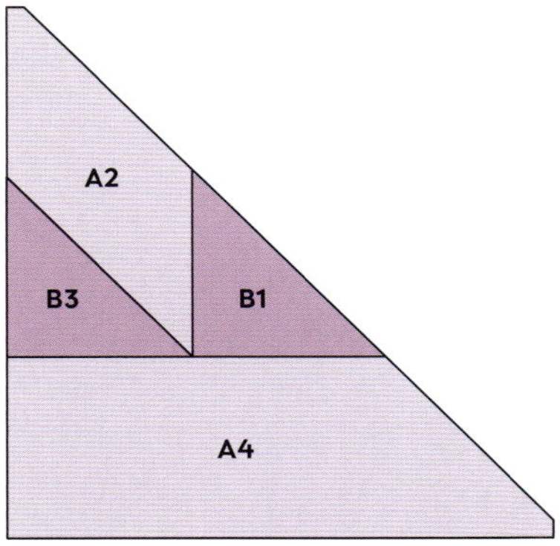

2 Repeat to assemble template B using B1, A2, B3, and A4.

Template B

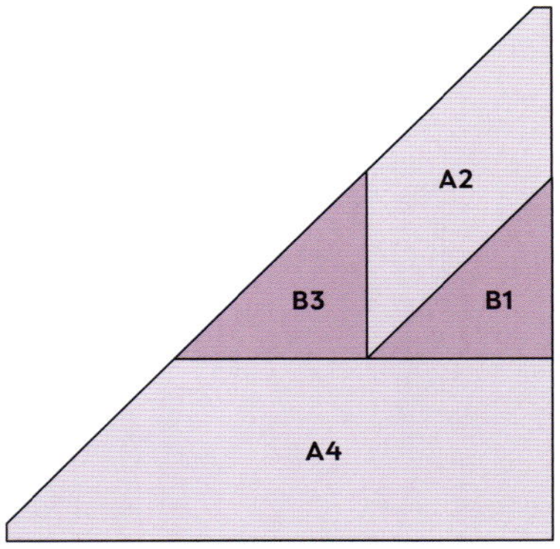

3 Follow the FPP instructions on the previous page, reversing the fabric values, to assemble template C using A1, B2, A3, and B4.

Template C

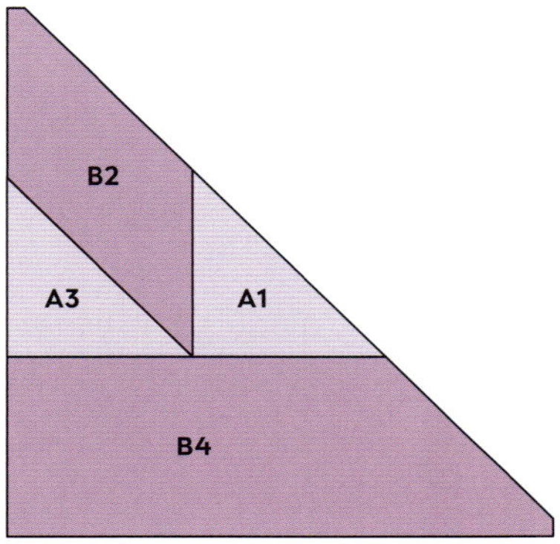

4 Repeat to assemble template D using A1, B2, A3, and B4.

Template D

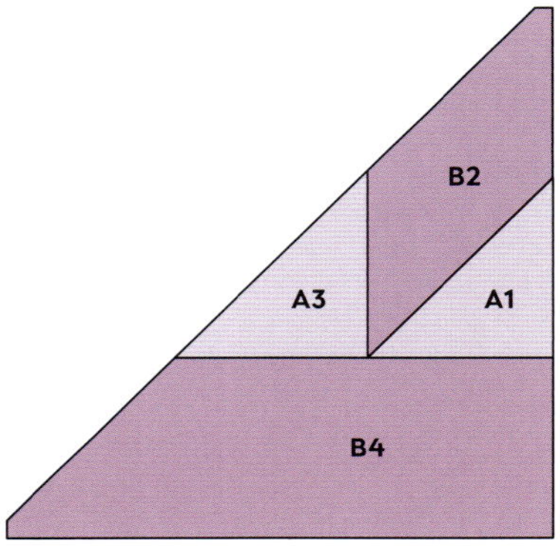

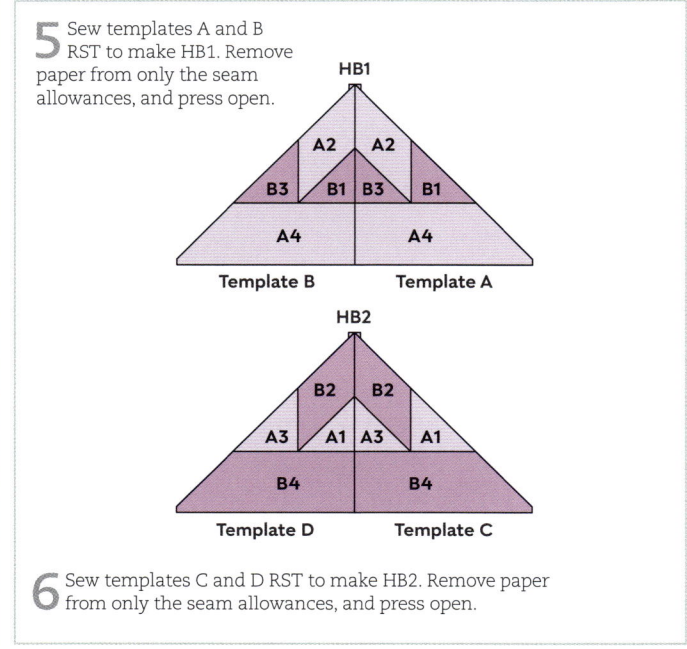

5 Sew templates A and B RST to make HB1. Remove paper from only the seam allowances, and press open.

6 Sew templates C and D RST to make HB2. Remove paper from only the seam allowances, and press open.

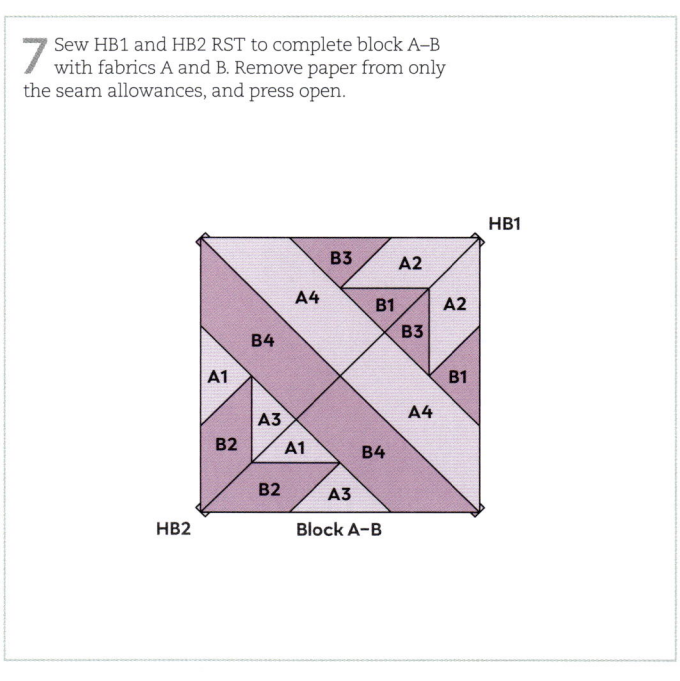

7 Sew HB1 and HB2 RST to complete block A–B with fabrics A and B. Remove paper from only the seam allowances, and press open.

Block A–B

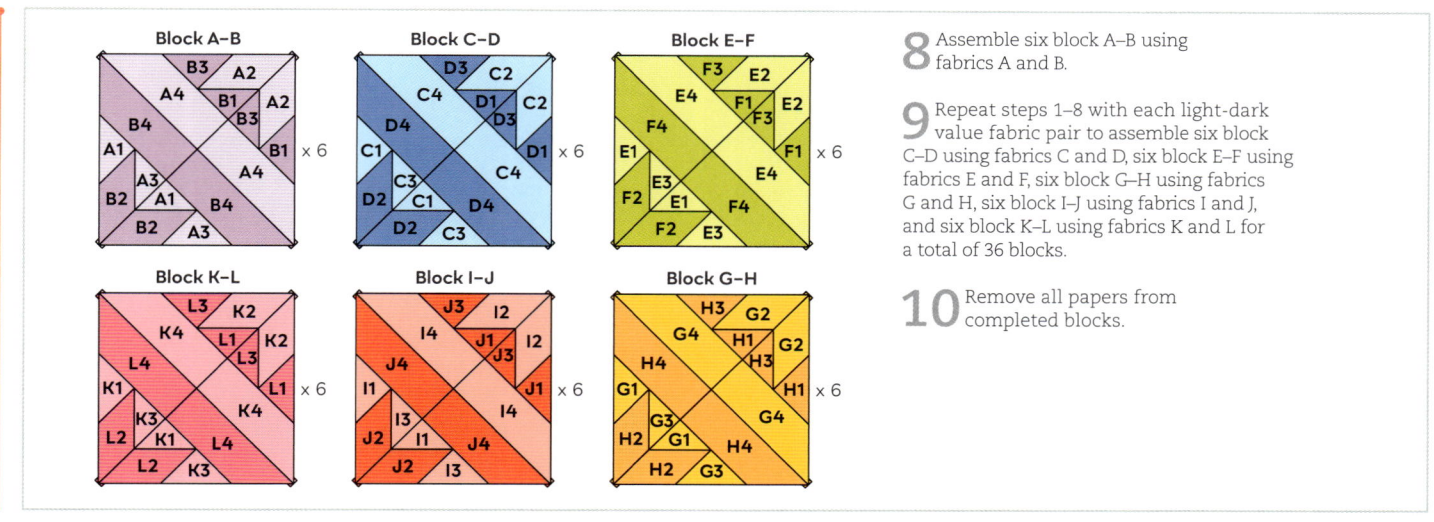

8. Assemble six block A–B using fabrics A and B.

9. Repeat steps 1–8 with each light-dark value fabric pair to assemble six block C–D using fabrics C and D, six block E–F using fabrics E and F, six block G–H using fabrics G and H, six block I–J using fabrics I and J, and six block K–L using fabrics K and L for a total of 36 blocks.

10. Remove all papers from completed blocks.

QUILT ASSEMBLY AND FINISHING

Blocks can be arranged and oriented in any way; position light value fabrics next to dark value fabrics for the most dynamic contrast.

1. Assemble the quilt by arranging quilt blocks into six rows of six blocks each. Adjust the block placement and orientation until you are satisfied with the distribution of fabric and colour.

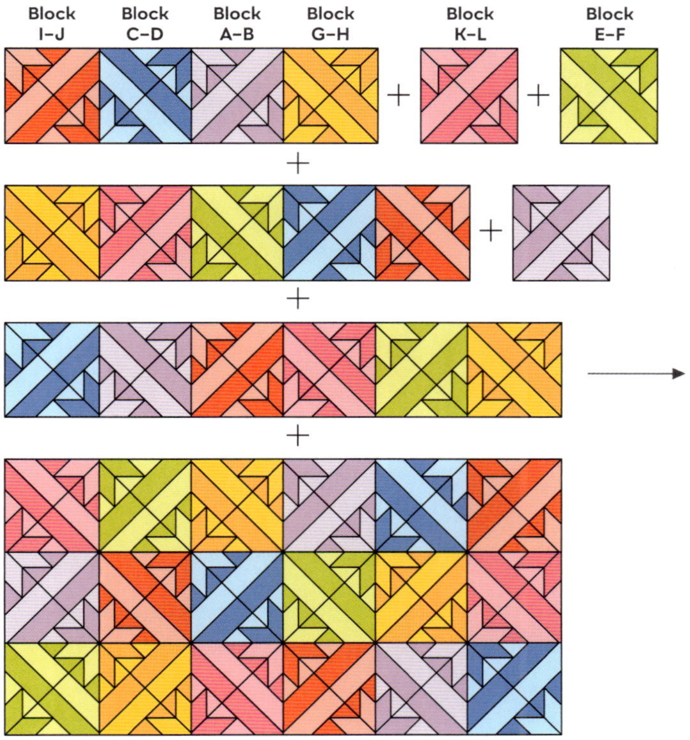

2. Sew the blocks into rows, then join the rows to complete the quilt top. Press seams open.

3. Press the entire quilt from the front to remove wrinkles. Sew a stay stitch (see p.151) 3.2mm (⅛in) around the perimeter of the quilt to secure seams.

4. To make binding, cut seven 6.4cm (2½in) x WOF strips from the chosen binding fabric. Sew all seven WOF strips, RST, to make one strip that is at least 648cm (255in) long.

5. To finish the quilt, baste (see pp.157–159), quilt (see pp.160–171), and bind (see pp.172–181) as desired.

Off script

This improv pattern is inspired by confetti shapes and the joy of celebration. Combining clear instructions with the freedom of straight edge and wavy improv piecing, this pattern is ideal for those looking for a guided approach to improvisation. The finished quilt size will vary, as each quilt will be unique to its maker.

FINISHED BABY SIZE Approximately 114 x 114cm (45 x 45in)
TECHNIQUES USED Setting triangles **p.95**, Straight edge improv **p.110**, Wavy improv **p.111**, Common improv shapes **p.112**, Registration lines **p.143**, Improv quilt top layout **p.147**

MATERIALS
- Basic quilting supplies (see p.14)
- Tweezers (optional)
- Marking pen
- 152 x 152cm (60 x 60in) or larger wadding

FABRIC REQUIREMENTS**

Fabrics A–G	(1) FQ each
Background (BG)	3m (3yds)
Backing*	3m (3yds)
Binding	0.5m (½yd)

*Backing fabric required when using one vertical or horizontal seam.

**Fabric requirements for this quilt are estimates due to the nature of improv and may need to be adjusted for your quilt.

Choose seven fat quarters (fabrics A–G) in any mix of solids, prints, or textures (see p.64). This pattern is a great opportunity to experiment with different fabrics, colours, or scraps. If using scraps, follow the cutting table to cut the required pieces from any number of fabrics. It is recommended to choose a solid or non-directional blender fabric for the background (BG).

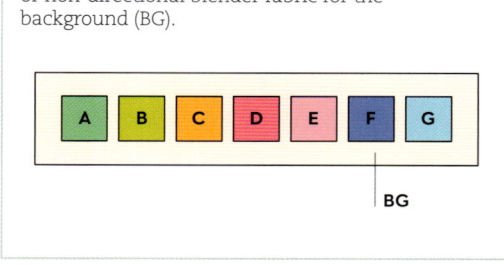

COLOUR REFERENCE

COVER QUILT DETAILS
Fabrics: Ruby and Bee Solids by Windham Fabrics in Minty (**A**), Avocado (**B**), Pumpkin (**C**), Perfect Pink (**D**), Posy (**E**), Provence Blue (**F**), Aquamarine (**G**), Cream Puff (**BG**); **Quilting:** Big stitch echo and organic lines; **Thread:** DMC 8 wt in various colours; **Wadding:** Hobbs Poly-Down Polyester; **Binding:** Minty

CUTTING INSTRUCTIONS

Use the fabric cutting tables and diagrams below to cut out and label the pieces required from fabrics A–G and BG. Keep remaining BG fabric available for filling gaps during assembly.

FABRIC CUTTING TABLES

FABRICS A–G

From each FQ:

Cut (1) 17.8cm (7in) x WOF; **sub-cut:**
  A1–G1: (1) 17.8 x 53.3cm (7 x 21in) (1 for each fabric)

Cut (1) 10.2cm (4in) x WOF; **sub-cut:**
  A2–G2: (1) 10.2 x 12.7cm (4 x 5in) (1 for each fabric)
  A3–G3: (6) 10.2 x 5.1cm (4 x 2in) (6 for each fabric)

BACKGROUND (BG)

Cut (5) 15.2cm (6in) x WOF; **sub-cut:**
  BG1: (7) 15.2 x 53.3cm (6 x 21in)
  BG2: (4) 15.2 x 10.2cm (6 x 4in)
  BG3: (4) 15.2 x 10.2cm (6 x 4in)

Set aside remaining fabric and cut additional **BG** pieces as needed to fill gaps during assembly.

FABRIC CUTTING DIAGRAMS

1. Cut the pieces from each fabric A–G as shown. Reserve excess fabric to use if a unit needs to be remade or to make additional units.

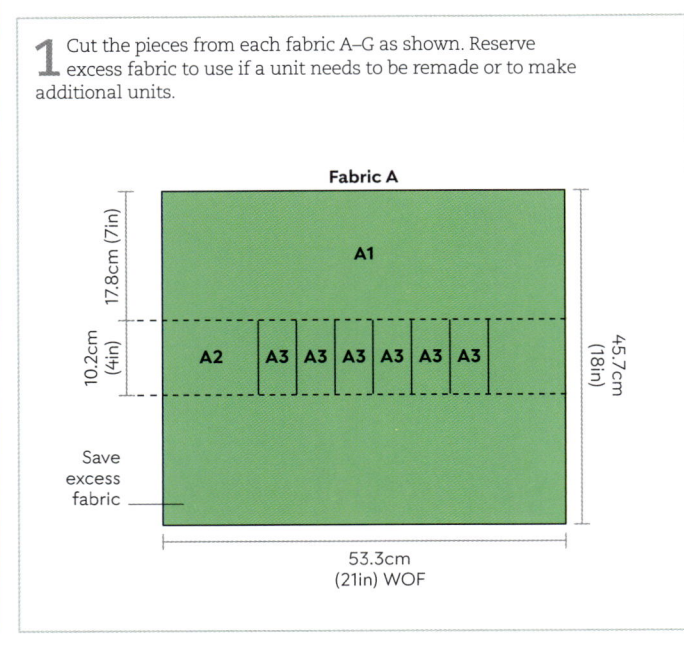

2. Cut four BG2 rectangles in half diagonally from the top left corner to the bottom right to make eight BG2 triangles. Seven triangles are needed; discard one.

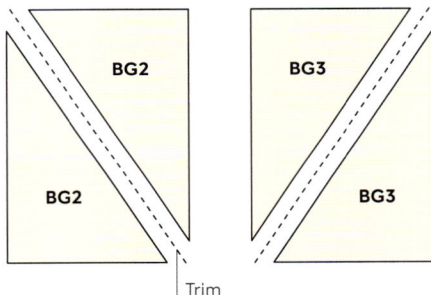

3. Cut four BG3 rectangles in half diagonally from the top right corner to the bottom left to make eight BG3 triangles. Seven triangles are needed; discard one.

UNIT ASSEMBLY

Refer to Improv piecing (see p.108) for more detailed instructions on making improv units. Use the steps below as guidance while embracing the freedom of improvisation. Align and join pieces as desired, maintaining or trimming to a 6.4mm (¼in) seam allowance (see p.73).

1 Arrange one A1 on top of one BG1, both right-sides up, with A1 overlapping BG1 by approximately 8cm (3in).

2 Cut a gentle wavy line (see step 3) within the overlap through both pieces. Mark registration lines (see p.143) at the peaks and valleys.

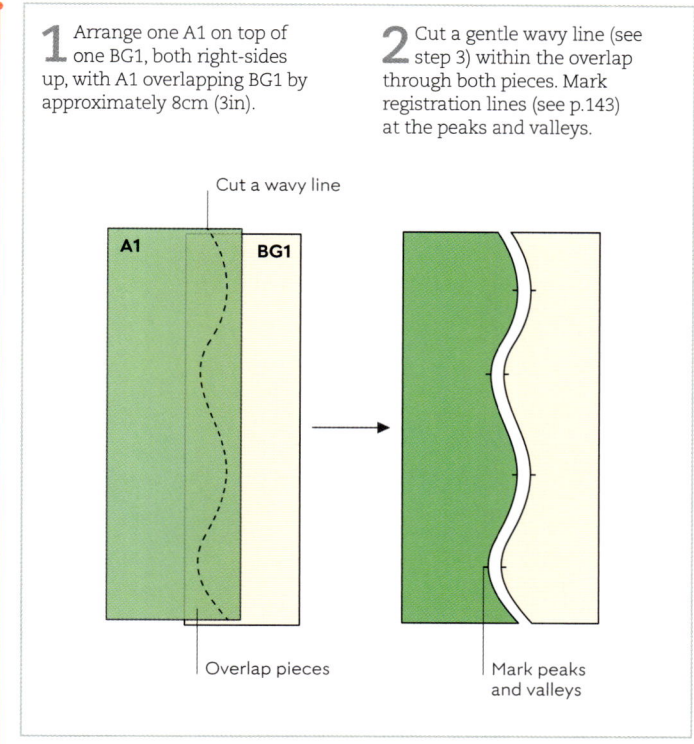

3 Cut smooth, gentle curves to make wavy edges. Avoid cutting sharp curves, as they may distort the fabrics and make joining more difficult.

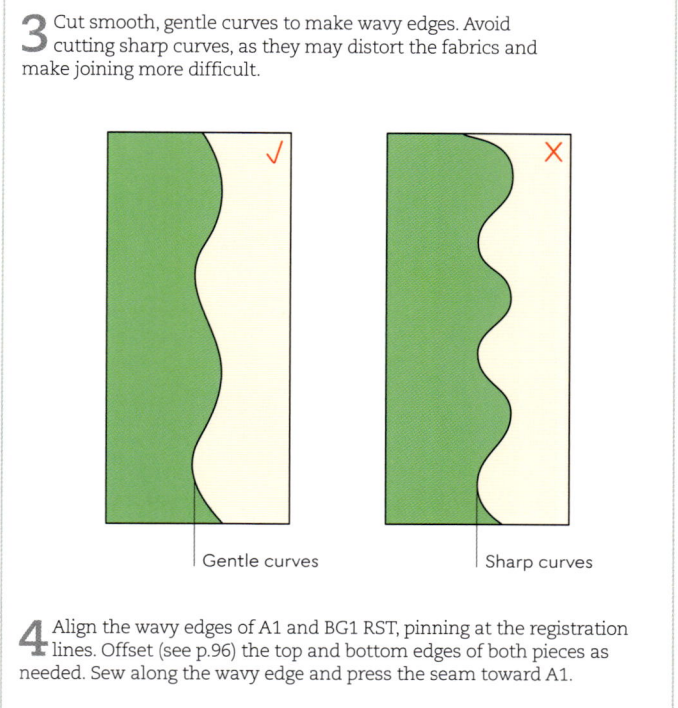

4 Align the wavy edges of A1 and BG1 RST, pinning at the registration lines. Offset (see p.96) the top and bottom edges of both pieces as needed. Sew along the wavy edge and press the seam toward A1.

5 Arrange the wavy unit on top of a second BG1, both right-sides up, with the unit overlapping BG1 by approximately 10cm (4in).

6 Cut a second gentle wavy line through A1 and BG1, echoing the first, to make a wavy shape approximately 6cm (2½in) wide. Mark registration lines at the peaks and valleys.

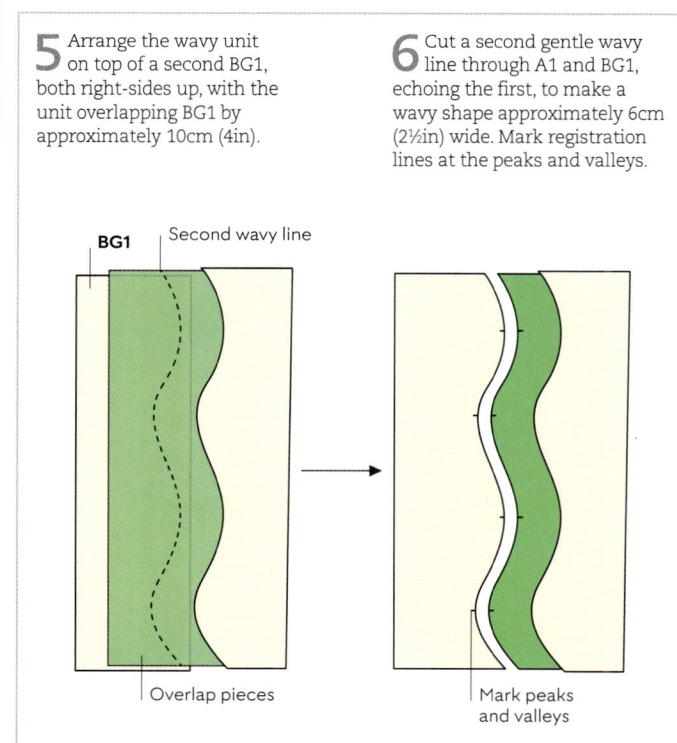

7 Align the newly cut wavy edge of A1 with BG1 RST, pin at the registration lines, and sew. Press the seam toward A1 to complete the wavy unit.

8 Trim and square (see p.67) any uneven edges of the unit, preserving as much BG fabric as possible.

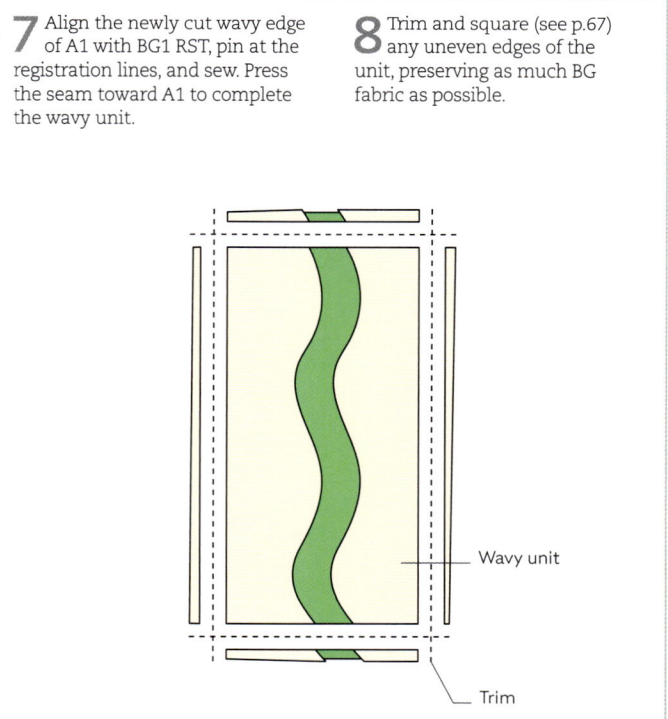

244 PROJECTS

9 Repeat steps 1–8 with B1, C1, D1, E1, F1, G1, and the remaining BG1 to make one wavy unit each from fabrics A–G. Experiment with the shape of each gentle wave. The fabric requirements include enough overage for a second attempt if needed.

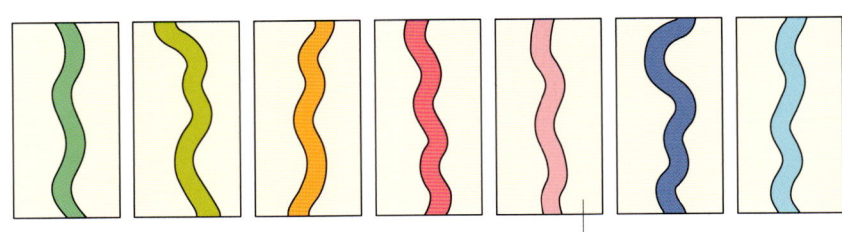

Make one wavy unit from each **fabrics A-G**

10 Select any three completed wavy units and set them aside to be used as large wave units. Each unit should measure approximately 43–51cm (17–20in) long.

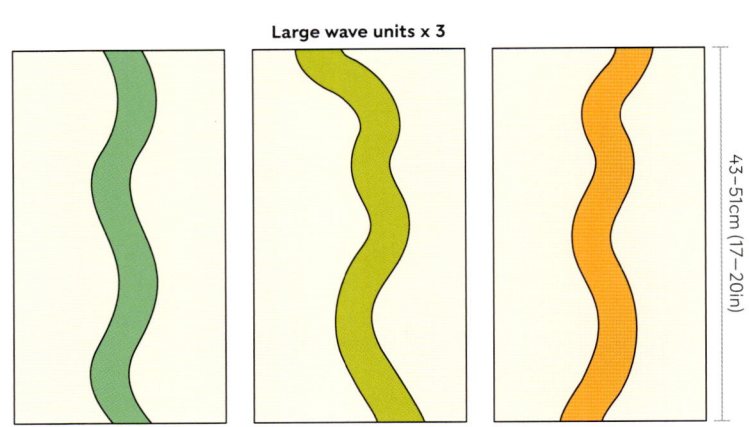

Large wave units x 3

43–51cm (17–20in)

11 Select any two completed wavy units and trim both down to approximately 30–41cm (12–16in) long. Set these units aside to be used as medium wave units.

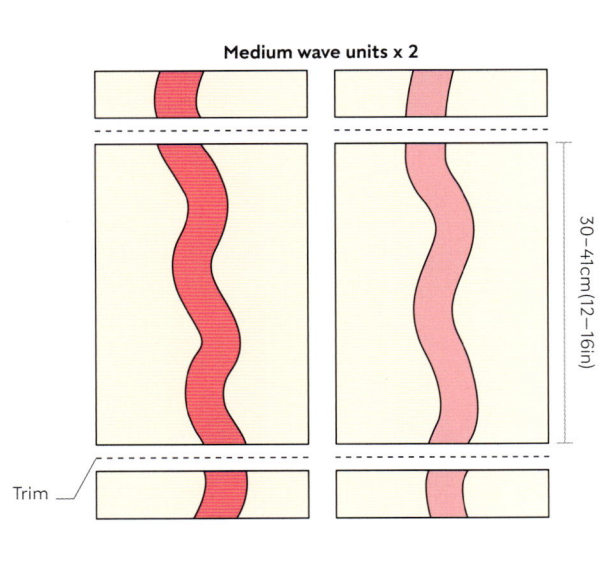

Medium wave units x 2

Trim

30–41cm (12–16in)

12 Cut the remaining two completed wavy units in half to make four units, each measuring approximately 20–28cm (8–11in) long. Set these units aside to be used as small wave units.

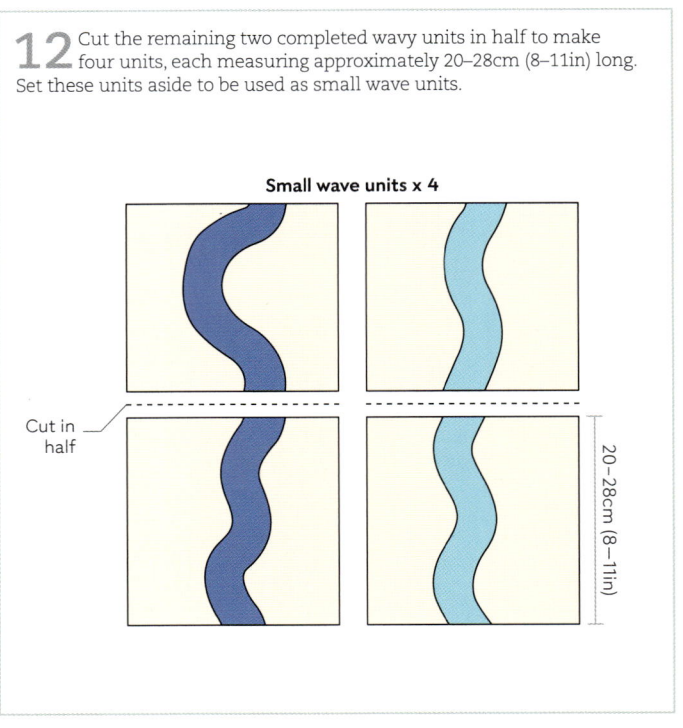

Small wave units x 4

Cut in half

20–28cm (8–11in)

13 Place one BG2 triangle RST with one A2, aligning the angled edge of BG2 with the top centre and the bottom right corner of the rectangle. Exact placement is not necessary.

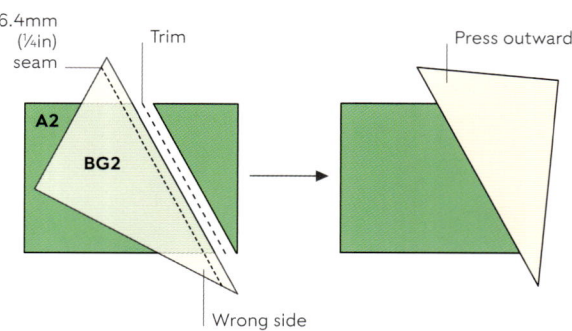

14 Sew along the angled edge with a 6.4mm (¼in) seam allowance. Trim the excess A2 fabric 6.4mm (¼in) away from the seam, and press away from the centre.

15 Place one BG3 triangle RST with the unit, aligning the angled edge of BG3 with the top centre and bottom left corner of the unit, overlapping the previously sewn seam.

16 Sew along the angled edge, trim the excess fabric, and press away from the centre to complete the triangle unit.

17 Trim and square the triangle unit, preserving as much BG fabric as possible.

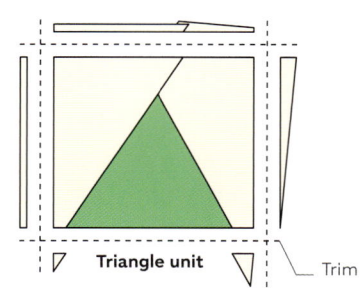

18 Repeat steps 13–17 with B2, C2, D2, E2, F2, G2, and the remaining BG2 and BG3 to make one triangle unit from each fabrics A–G. Experiment with the placement of the BG2 and BG3 triangles to make different shapes.

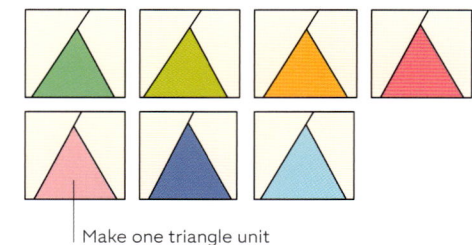

Make one triangle unit from each **fabrics A–G**

19 Gather all A3–G3. Randomly select seven rectangles and sew them together into a strip unit, using the straight edge improv technique (see p.110). Be sure to maintain a 6.4mm (¼in) seam allowance when joining pieces, but vary the seam angles and misalign the edges as desired. Press seams open and trim the strip unit to approximately 6cm (2½in) wide.

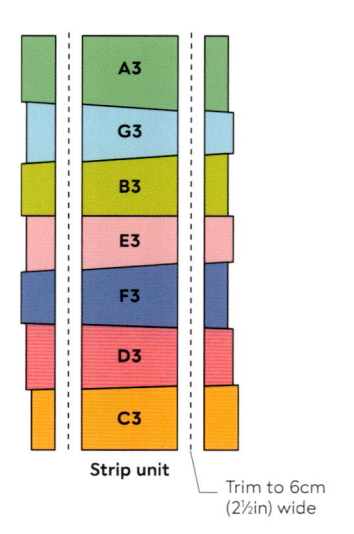

20 Repeat step 19 to make the following strip units: two strip units using seven rectangles each; two using six rectangles each; two using five rectangles each; and two using three rectangles each.

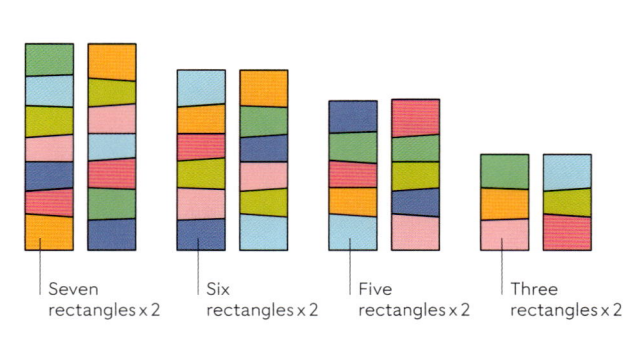

SECTION ASSEMBLY

Arrange all completed units into the desired layout, then join units and BG pieces into manageable sections. This pattern uses an example layout to show assembly steps.

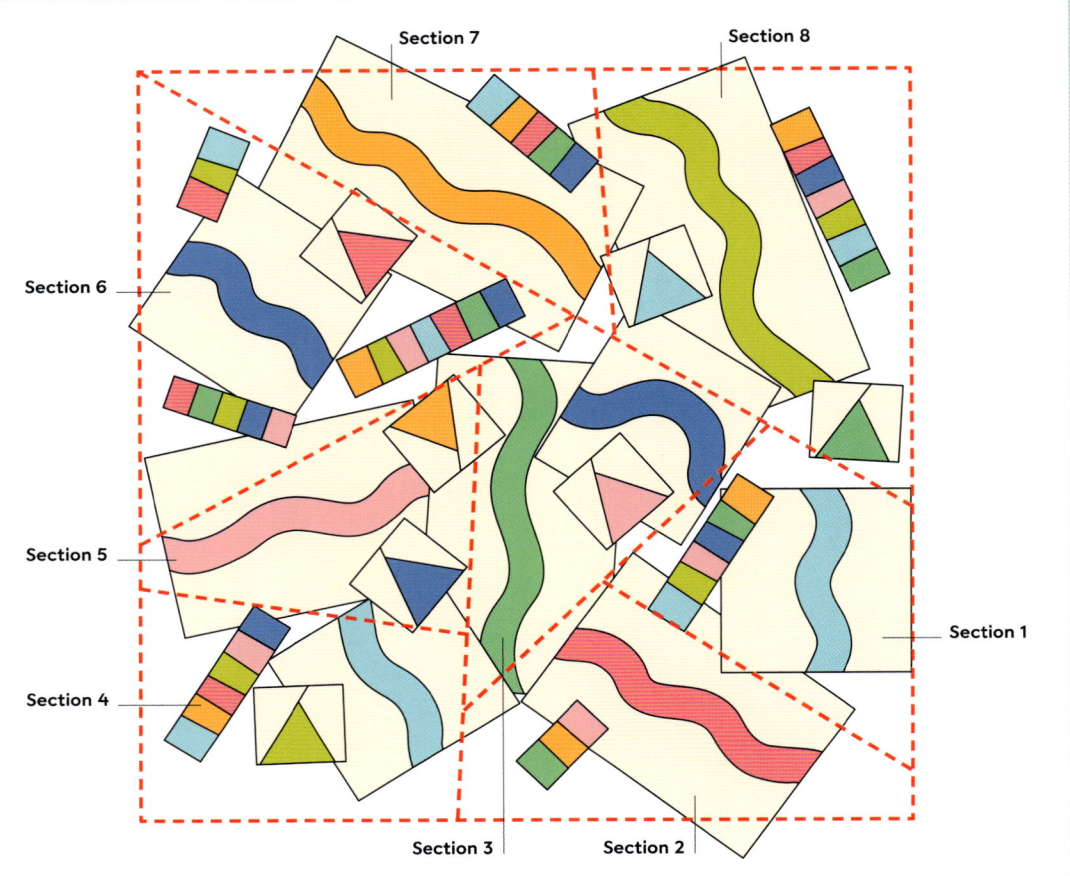

1 Arrange all completed units on a flat surface that is at least 114 x 114cm (45 x 45in). Adjust the placement of the units until you are satisfied with the distribution of shapes, fabrics, and colours. Overlapping edges and gaps will be addressed later during assembly.

2 Evaluate how units may be joined into large sections containing 2–4 units each. Ensure sections can later be joined with others using straight seams. Determine the assembly order of units in each section, then plan how sections may be joined together to form the quilt top.

3 Refer to the proposed assembly order in the example diagram: first join sections 1 and 2, then add section 3. Next, join section 4 and section 5, then sew these two joined sections to sections 1, 2, and 3. Add section 6. Join section 7 and section 8, and finally sew these two joined sections to the rest to complete the top.

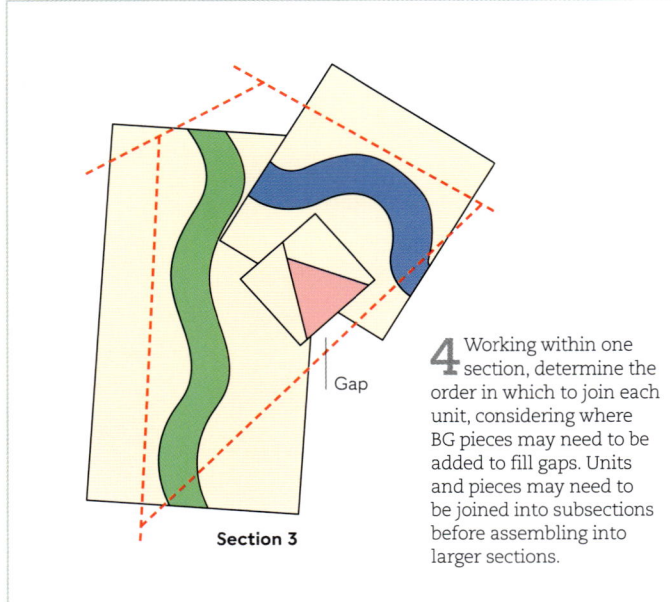

4 Working within one section, determine the order in which to join each unit, considering where BG pieces may need to be added to fill gaps. Units and pieces may need to be joined into subsections before assembling into larger sections.

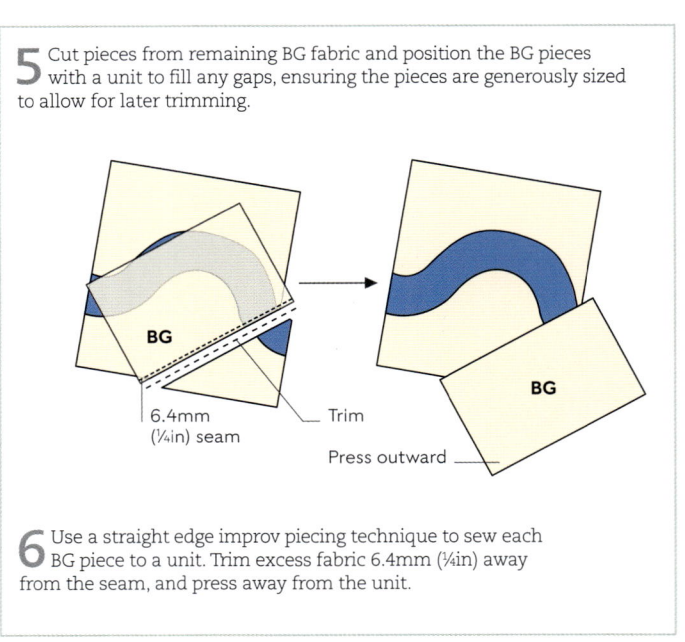

5 Cut pieces from remaining BG fabric and position the BG pieces with a unit to fill any gaps, ensuring the pieces are generously sized to allow for later trimming.

6 Use a straight edge improv piecing technique to sew each BG piece to a unit. Trim excess fabric 6.4mm (¼in) away from the seam, and press away from the unit.

7 Continue adding BG pieces one at a time, trimming the excess fabric and pressing between steps.

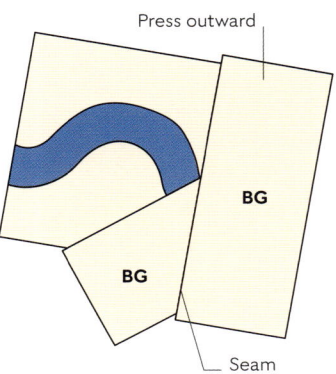

8 Periodically check the overall shape of the unit to ensure the unit will fit within and extend slightly beyond the desired section area. If a BG piece does not fully cover the intended gap, replace it with a slightly larger piece or add another BG piece before continuing.

9 Repeat steps 4–8 with the remaining units in the section. Do not trim uneven edges.

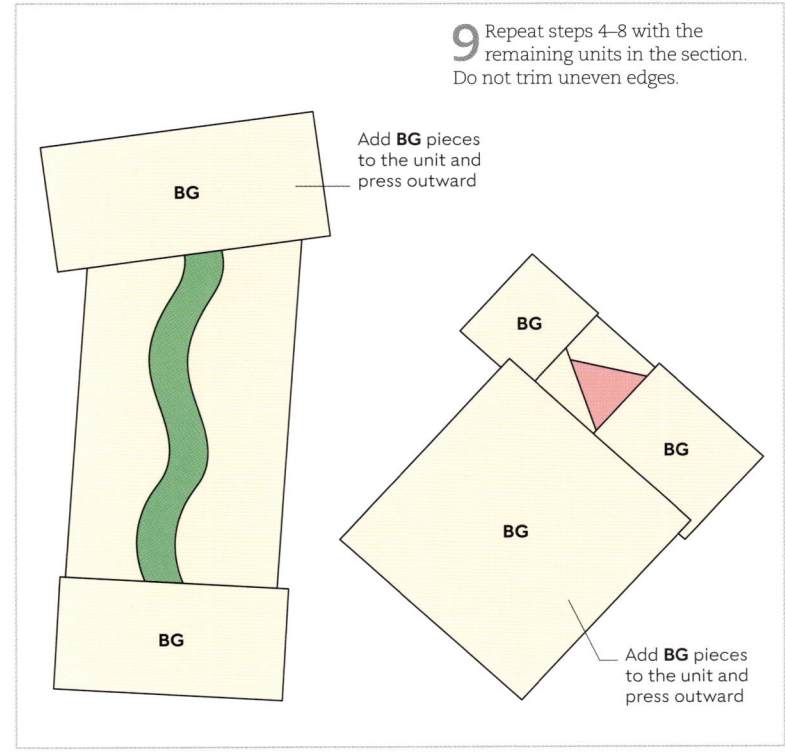

10 Position two units as planned, overlapping the edges as needed. Determine where the best seam placement would be for joining the units, then fold both pieces along the desired seam placement to form a crease. Mark registration lines across both units to assist with proper alignment.

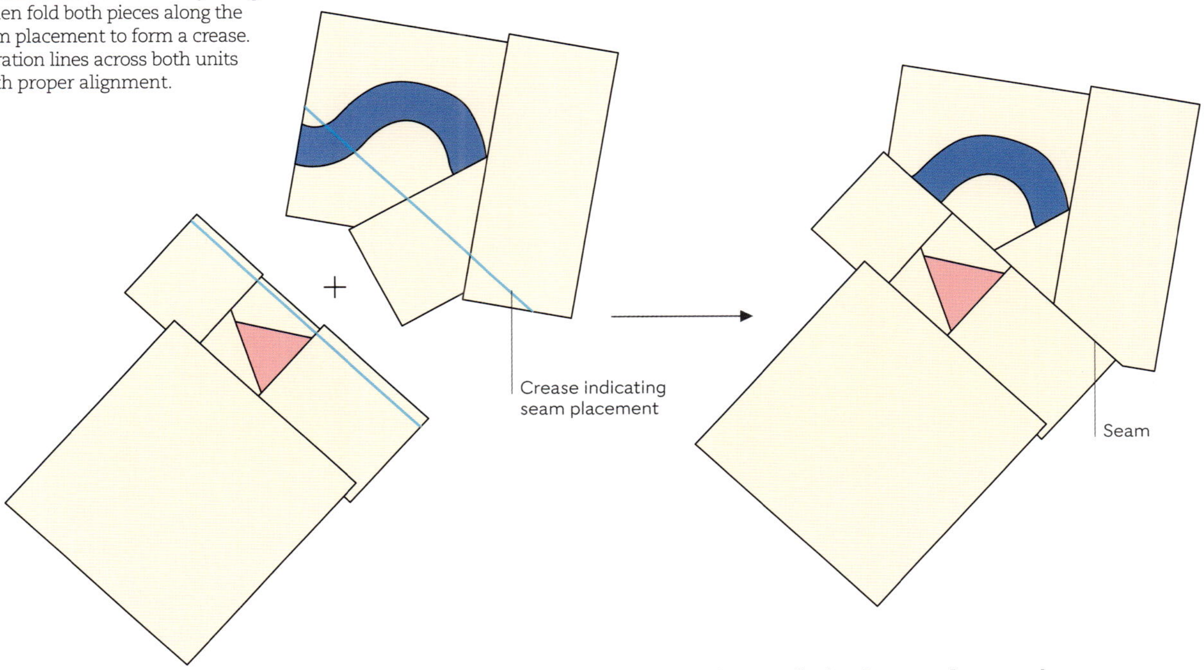

11 Place both units RST, aligning the creased seam and registration lines. Sew directly on the crease, trim the excess fabric 6.4mm (¼in) away from the seam, and press.

12 Repeat steps 10–11 to attach the remaining units and complete the section. Ensure the overall shape fits within and extends slightly beyond the desired section area. If adjustments are needed, add BG fabric or seam rip (see p.79), and resew the seams.

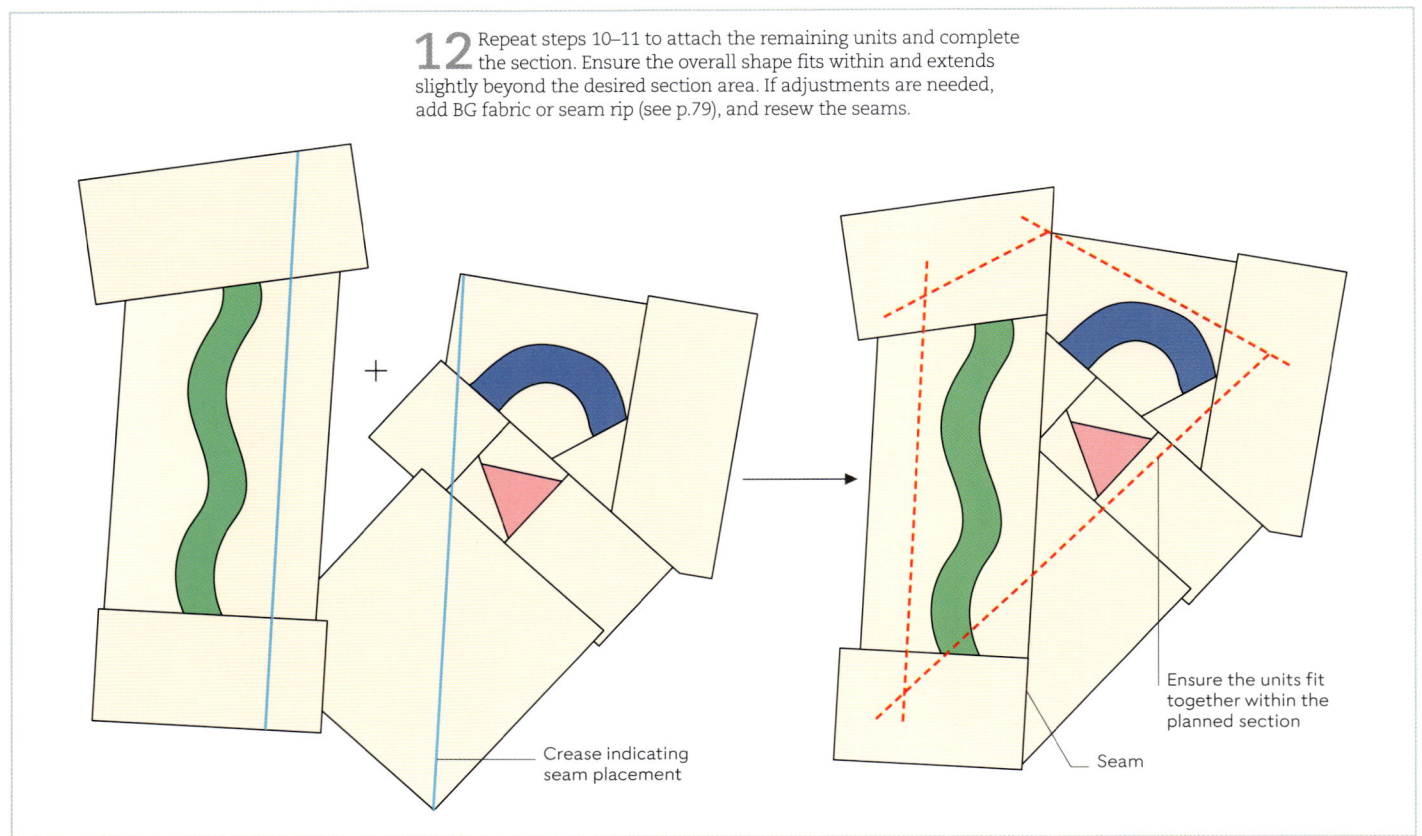

Crease indicating seam placement

Ensure the units fit together within the planned section

Seam

13 Repeat steps 4–12 to complete one section at a time, ensuring all pieces align properly and fit within the desired area.

14 As each section takes shape, periodically lay out all sections to confirm they will fit with the others as planned.

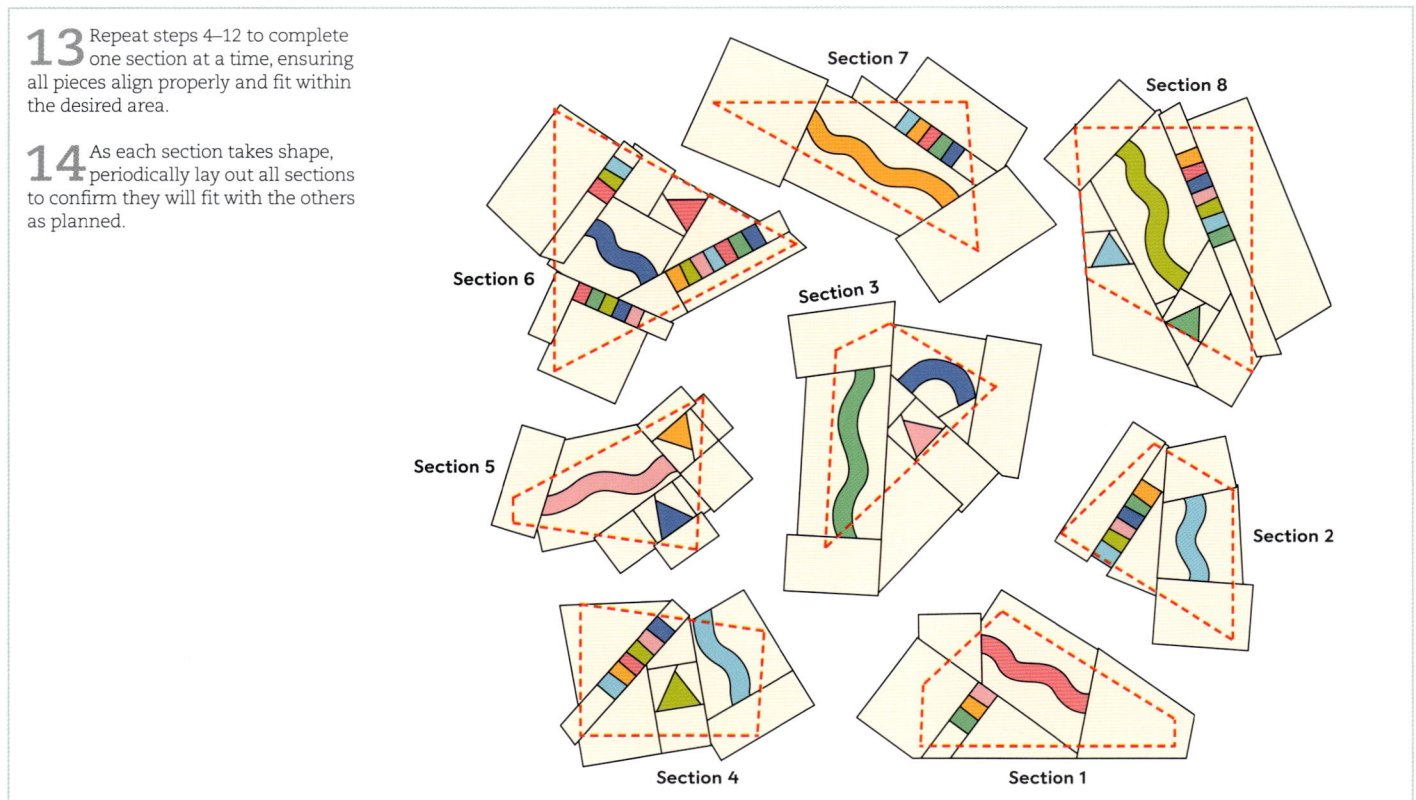

QUILT ASSEMBLY AND FINISHING

Assemble the quilt top using techniques similar to those used in section assembly. Join sections in the planned order, trimming excess fabric and filling any remaining gaps as needed.

1. Position the first two sections to be joined, overlapping the edges as needed. Determine where the best seam placement would be for joining the sections, then fold both pieces along the desired seam placement to form a crease. Mark registration lines across both units to ensure proper alignment.

2. Place both units RST, aligning the creased seam and registration lines. Sew directly on the crease, trim the excess fabric 6.4mm (¼in) away from the seam, and press. Confirm the overall shape of the joined sections fits within the desired area and adjust as needed.

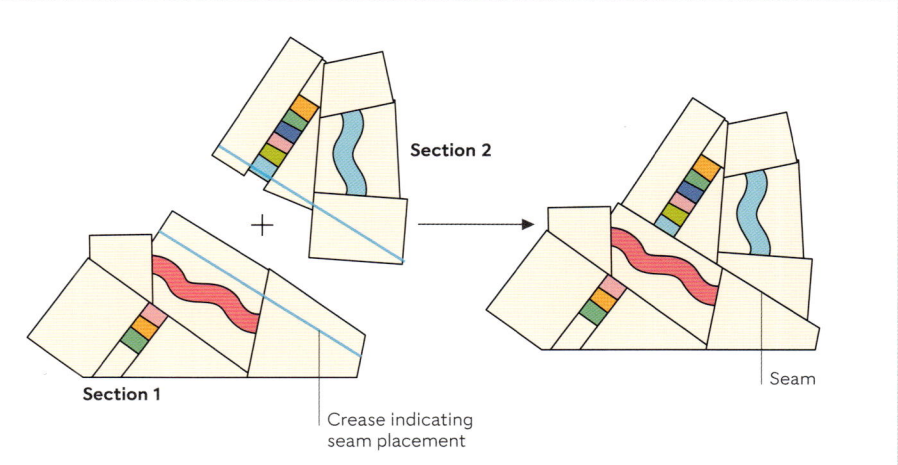

3. Continue joining sections in the planned order until the quilt top is complete. Add BG pieces as needed to fill any gaps.

4. Square (see p.67) the quilt top to remove uneven edges. Add borders as desired.

5. Press the entire quilt top from the front to remove all wrinkles. Sew a stay stitch (see p.151) 3.2mm (⅛in) around the perimeter of the quilt to secure seams and bias edges.

6. To make binding, cut six 6.4cm (2½in) x WOF strips from the chosen binding fabric. Sew all six WOF strips, RST, to make one strip that is at least 597cm (235in) long.

7. To finish the quilt, baste (see pp.157–159), quilt (see pp.160–171), and bind (see pp.172–181) as desired.

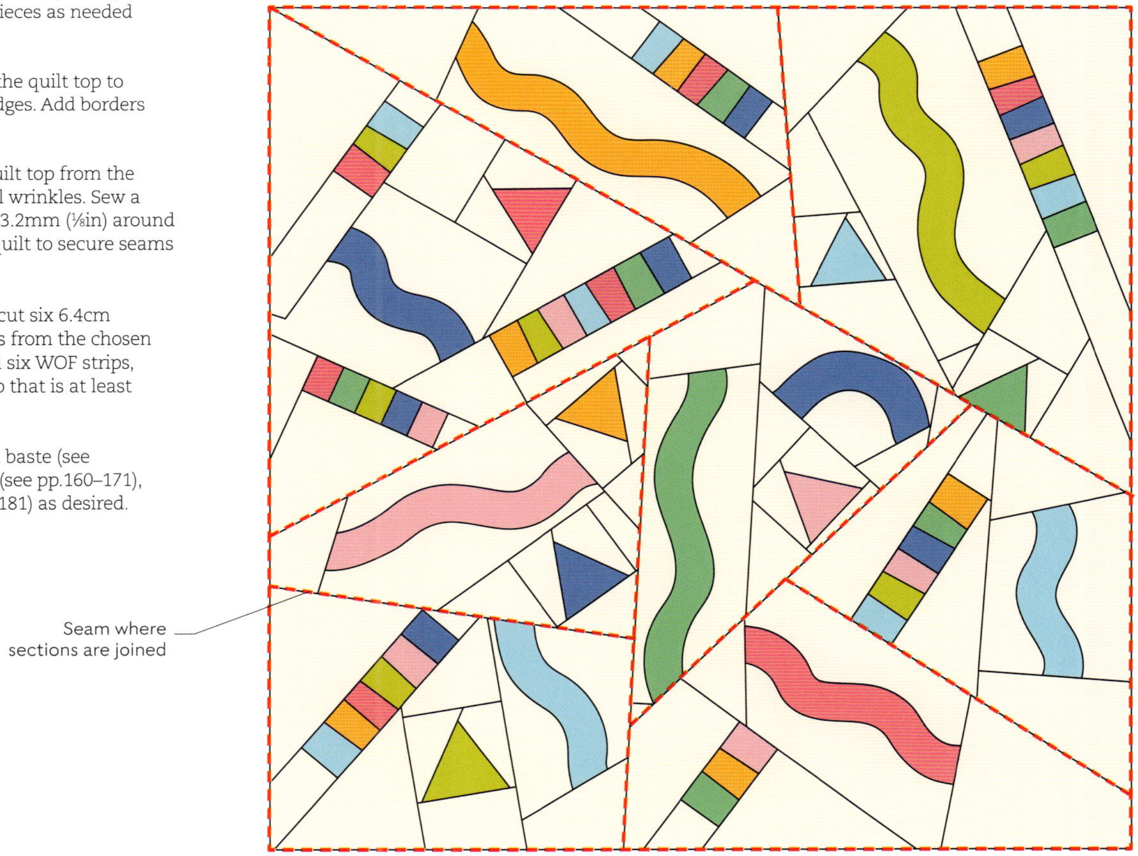

Iridian puff

This modern take on a traditional puff quilt is inspired by the gentle gradient of a rainbow. Fill fabric pockets with loose filling to make puffy, raised squares. Follow the pattern exactly, or scale to your desired size (see p.252).

FINISHED THROW SIZE 132 x 152cm (52 x 60in)
TECHNIQUES USED Quilt maths **p.54**, Understanding colour theory **p.60**, Setting an accurate seam allowance **p.73**, Nesting seams **p.81**, Matching points and seams **p.141**, Column quilt top layout **p.146**, Hand tying **p.171**

MATERIALS

- Basic quilting supplies (see p.14)
- Tweezers (optional)
- Two to three 567g (20oz) bags of loose polyester filling
- Scale for measuring loose filling (optional)
- Large needle for hand tying
- 68.6m (75yds) of heavy weight thread or yarn
- 147 x 168cm (58 x 66in) or larger wadding

FABRIC REQUIREMENTS

Fabrics A–M	(1) 0.5m (½yd) each
Puff backing (PB)	2.75m (3yds)
Backing*	3.5m (3¾yds)
Binding	0.5m (½yd)

*Backing fabric required when using one vertical seam.

Experiment with value and contrast when selecting fabrics A–M (see p.61). Alternate dark and light values for a chequerboard effect or arrange by colour for a gradient. This quilt is designed and written for 0.5m (½yd) cuts, but it also works well with pre-cuts (see p.41) or scraps. If using pre-cuts, gather 12.7cm (5in) squares and group them by colour. Each puff is sewn onto a puff backing square (PB) that will not be visible; use neutral fabric or scraps for the puff backing fabric.

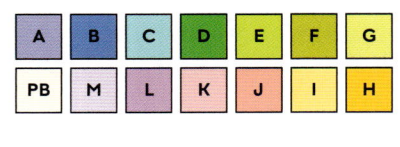

COLOUR REFERENCE

COVER QUILT DETAILS

Fabrics: Ruby and Bee Solids by Windham Fabrics in Wisteria (**A**), Provence Blue (**B**), Starling (**C**), Pasture (**D**), Limeade (**E**), Avocado (**F**), Lemonade (**G**), Mustard Seed (**H**), Daffodil (**I**), Peachy Keen (**J**), Posy (**K**), Vervain (**L**), Dusk (**M**); **Quilting:** Hand tied **Thread:** DMC 3 wt in 743; **Wadding:** Hobbs Polyester Fiberfill and Tuscany Silk; **Binding:** Mustard Seed

CUTTING INSTRUCTIONS

Use the fabric cutting tables below to cut out and label the pieces required from fabrics A–M and puff backing (PB). Refer to Quilt maths (see p.54) to calculate new wadding, backing, and binding fabric requirements if adjusting the quilt size.

FABRIC CUTTING TABLES

FABRICS A–M

From each fabric:
Cut (2) 12.7cm (5in) x WOF; **sub-cut:**
  A1–M1: (15) 12.7 x 12.7cm (5 x 5in) (15 for each fabric)

PUFF BACKING (PB)

Cut (22) 11.4cm (4½in) x WOF; **sub-cut:**
  PB1: (195) 11.4 x 11.4cm (4½ x 4½in)

TEST PUFF

From scrap fabric, **cut:**
T1: (1) 12.7 x 12.7cm (5 x 5in)
T2: (1) 11.4 x 11.4cm (4½ x 4½in)

INCREASING QUILT DIMENSIONS

1. This pattern calls for thirteen 0.5m (½yd) cuts to make 13 columns, resulting in a 132cm (52in) wide quilt. Each additional 0.5m (½yd) cut of fabric adds one column, increasing the width of the quilt by 10.2cm (4in).

2. This pattern calls for cutting 15 squares per fabric, with enough left over to make extra cuts. Cutting one additional square each from fabrics A–M adds one row, increasing the quilt length by 10.2cm (4in). The fabric requirements allow for up to nine additional rows, making the maximum possible length 243.8cm (96in) when cutting 24 squares from each fabric.

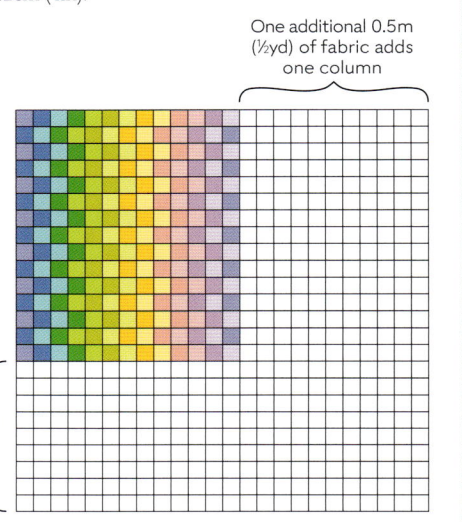

One additional 0.5m (½yd) of fabric adds one column

One additional 12.7 x 12.7cm (5 x 5in) square from each fabric adds one row

MAKING A TEST PUFF

Use approximately 4g (0.14oz) of loose polyester filling per puff to fill the pocket while leaving room for seam allowance. Approximately 1.7kg (60oz) of stuffing is required for a 132 x 152cm (52 x 60in) quilt; using more filling or increasing the quilt size may require additional packages. Make a test puff to determine the desired amount of filling before beginning. Filling density and loft vary by type (polyester, cotton, wool), so portion and purchase accordingly.

1. Follow the puff pocket assembly (see opposite) to make one pocket using one T1 square and one T2 square cut from scraps. Leave an opening on one side.

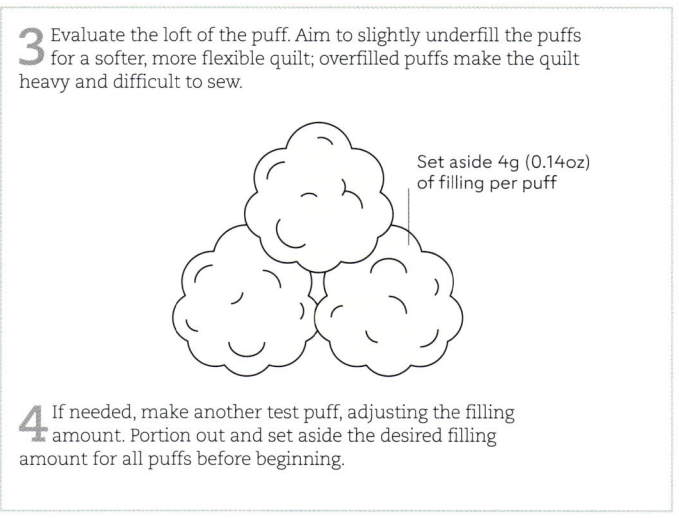

T1 — Add 4g (0.14oz) of filling
Pleat — T2 — Stitch puff pocket closed

Set aside 4g (0.14oz) of filling per puff

2. Use a scale to measure approximately 4g (0.14oz) of loose filling (about a handful). Add the filling to the pocket. Sew the opening closed with a 6.4mm (¼in) seam allowance to complete the test puff.

3. Evaluate the loft of the puff. Aim to slightly underfill the puffs for a softer, more flexible quilt; overfilled puffs make the quilt heavy and difficult to sew.

4. If needed, make another test puff, adjusting the filling amount. Portion out and set aside the desired filling amount for all puffs before beginning.

PUFF POCKET ASSEMBLY

Form each pocket by pleating the edges of a larger fabric square while sewing it to a smaller puff backing square. Use a 3.2mm (⅛in) seam allowance during this step so the seams will be hidden once the quilt is assembled.

1 Place one A1 12.7 x 12.7cm (5 x 5in) square, right-side up, on top of one PB1 11.4 x 11.4cm (4½ x 4½in) square, aligning the top right corners. Do not pin. The remaining corners of both squares will not align.

2 Sew approximately 2.5cm (1in) along the aligned edges using a 3.2mm (⅛in) seam allowance. Stop with the needle down.

3 Align the bottom right corners of both pieces. Fold the excess A1 fabric edge over itself by approximately 6.4mm (¼in), making a pleat near the centre.

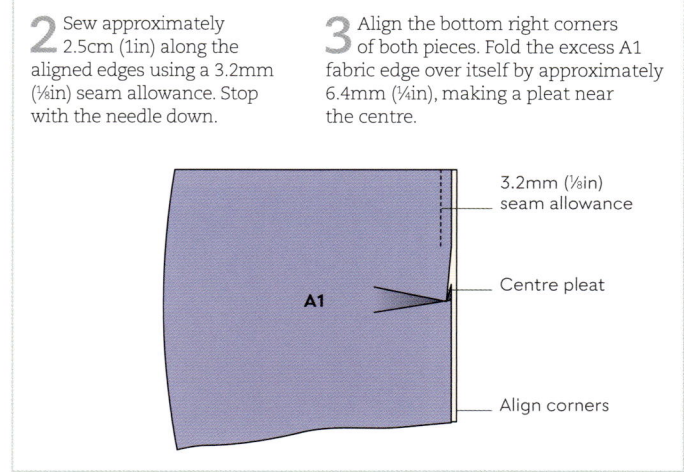

4 Continue sewing straight down to the bottom edge, keeping the bottom right corners aligned.

5 Rotate the unit anticlockwise so the pleated seam is positioned on top.

6 Align the new set of edges and sew along the seam, stopping to make a second pleat near the centre before continuing to the bottom edge.

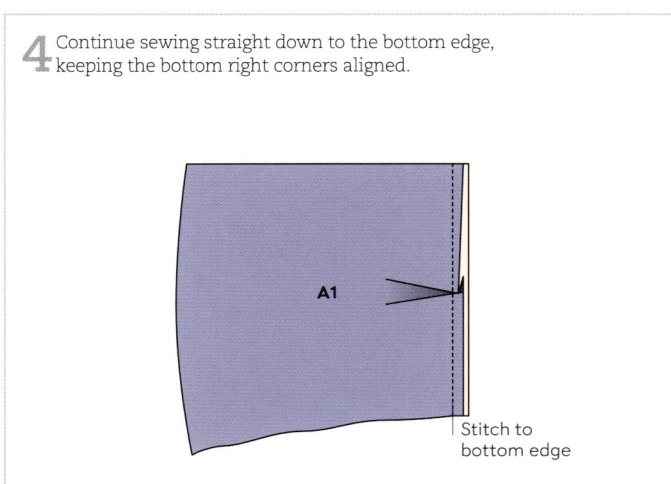

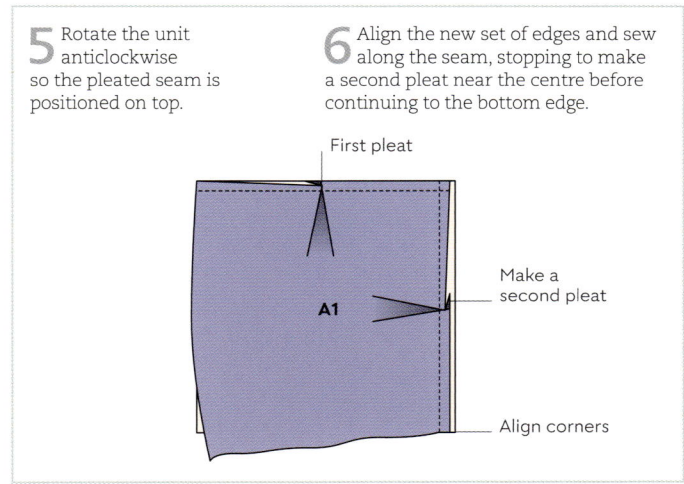

7 Rotate the unit anticlockwise so the pleated seams are positioned on the left and top.

9 Repeat steps 1–8 using the remaining A1, B1, C1, etc., and PB1 to make 15 puff pockets from each fabric A–M. Label each completed puff pocket to match its corresponding fabric.

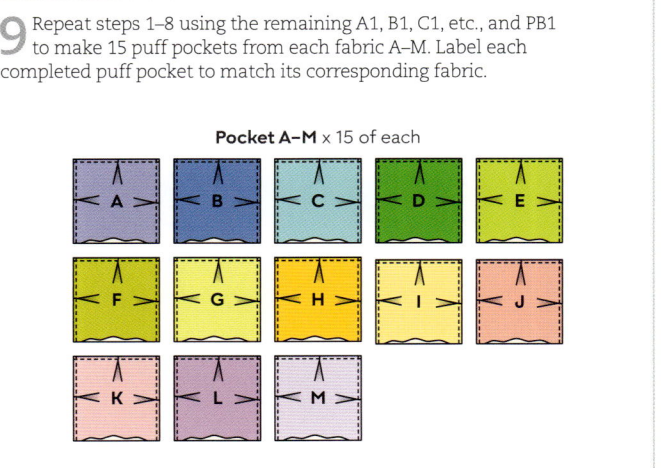

8 Align the new set of edges and sew along the seam, stopping to make a third pleat before continuing to the bottom edge. Leave the fourth edge open and unsewn. Label the unit as pocket A.

COLUMN ASSEMBLY

Alternating fabrics in each column creates a gradient effect. While assembling the columns, orient the pockets with the openings on the right to allow for filling the puff pockets.

1 Arrange pockets A–M into 13 columns as shown, with each column containing a total of 15 puff pockets. Alternate between two pockets in each column: pockets A/B in column 1, B/C in column 2, C/D in column 3, and so on, with the final column, column 13, alternating between pockets M/A. Ensure that no two pockets of the same fabric are placed side by side when arranging the columns.

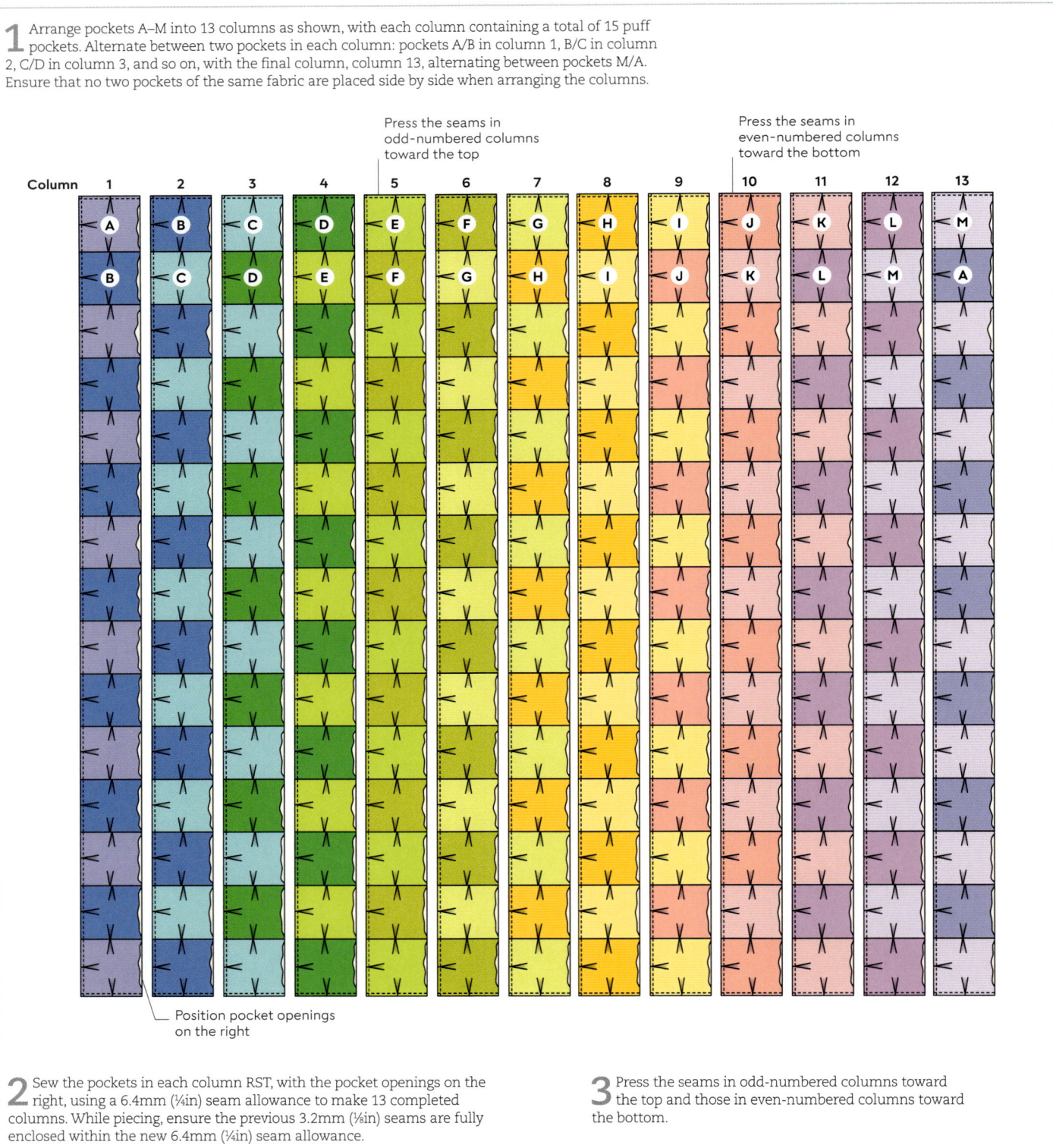

Press the seams in odd-numbered columns toward the top

Press the seams in even-numbered columns toward the bottom

Position pocket openings on the right

2 Sew the pockets in each column RST, with the pocket openings on the right, using a 6.4mm (¼in) seam allowance to make 13 completed columns. While piecing, ensure the previous 3.2mm (⅛in) seams are fully enclosed within the new 6.4mm (¼in) seam allowance.

3 Press the seams in odd-numbered columns toward the top and those in even-numbered columns toward the bottom.

QUILT ASSEMBLY AND FINISHING

Fill and enclose puffs one column at a time before attaching the next unfilled column for easier handling. When joining columns, nest seams (see p.81) and place a clip at each intersection to keep seams aligned and secure. Hand tie (see p.171) at seam intersections to quilt the puff quilt, as machine and hand quilting are not recommended due to bulk.

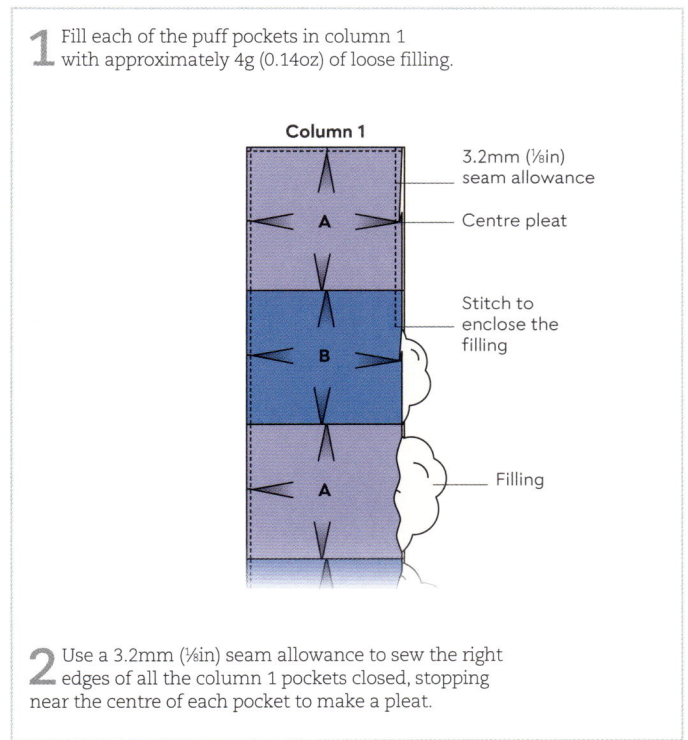

1 Fill each of the puff pockets in column 1 with approximately 4g (0.14oz) of loose filling.

2 Use a 3.2mm (⅛in) seam allowance to sew the right edges of all the column 1 pockets closed, stopping near the centre of each pocket to make a pleat.

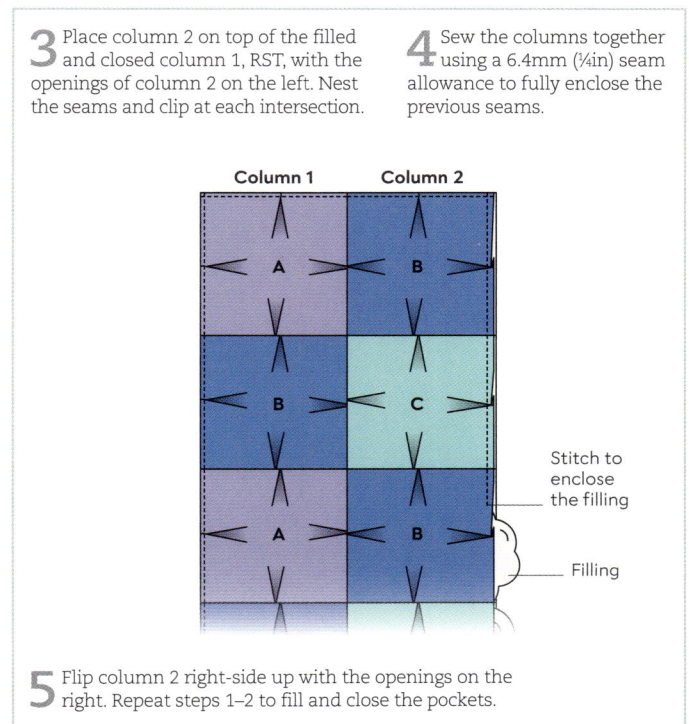

3 Place column 2 on top of the filled and closed column 1, RST, with the openings of column 2 on the left. Nest the seams and clip at each intersection.

4 Sew the columns together using a 6.4mm (¼in) seam allowance to fully enclose the previous seams.

5 Flip column 2 right-side up with the openings on the right. Repeat steps 1–2 to fill and close the pockets.

6 Continue joining each new column, filling the pockets and closing the puffs, one column at a time, until the quilt top is complete.

7 Sew a stay stitch (see p.151) 3.2mm (⅛in) around the perimeter of the quilt to secure seams.

8 Place basting pins at each seam intersection to baste. Take care not to pull the quilt too taut, as the puffs will shrink back and cause the backing fabric to pucker.

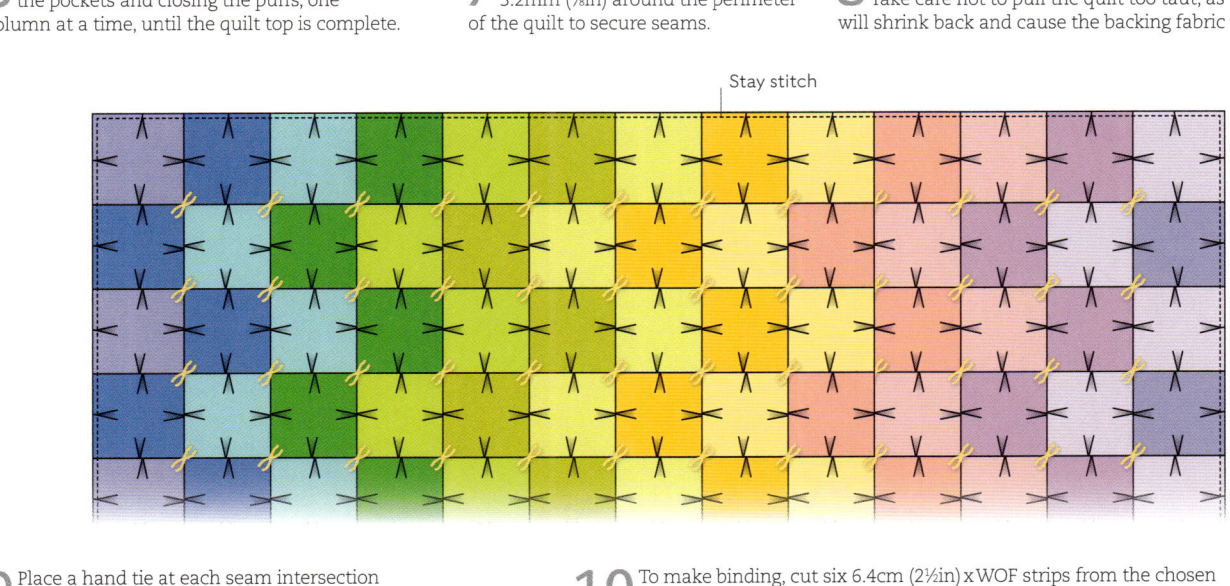

9 Place a hand tie at each seam intersection to hold the layers together between all puffs.

10 To make binding, cut six 6.4cm (2½in) x WOF strips from the chosen binding fabric. Sew all six WOF strips, RST, to make one strip that is at least 607cm (239in) long. Bind (see pp.172–181) as desired.

Quilts to go

This collection is inspired by the non-traditional ways to complete a quilt top. Display your favourite quilt block as a wall hanging or pillow cover, or take it on the go as a tote or back patch.

FINISHED SIZE Wall hanging: 71 x 71cm (28 x 28in); tote bag: 39 x 46 x 13cm (15½ x 18 x 5in); pillow cover: 46 x 46cm (18 x 18in); back patch: 36 x 36cm (14 x 14in)

TECHNIQUES USED HSTs **p.86**, FG **p.92**, Square in a square units **p.94**, Appliqué **p.134**, Matching points and seams **p.141**, Envelope backing **p.155**, Adding corner pockets **p.173**

MATERIALS
- Basic quilting supplies (see p.14)
- 24.1 x 24.1cm (9½ x 9½in) or larger square ruler

PILLOW COVER
- 56 x 56cm (22 x 22in) or larger wadding
- 46 x 46cm (18 x 18in) pillow insert

WALL HANGING
- 81 x 81cm (32 x 32in) or larger wadding
- 66cm (26in) dowel for hanging (optional)

BACK PATCH
- Jacket in preferred size
- 35.6 x 35.6cm (14 x 14in) square of fusible interfacing

TOTE BAG
- (2) 61 x 61cm (24 x 24in) or larger wadding
- (2) 3.2 x 88.9cm (1¼ x 35in) strip of wadding

COLOUR REFERENCE

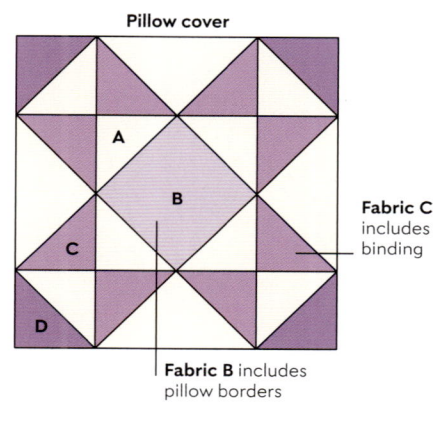

Pillow cover — Fabric C includes binding; Fabric B includes pillow borders

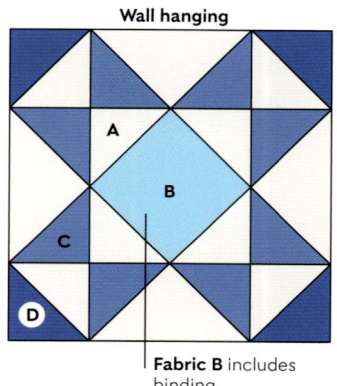

Wall hanging — Fabric B includes binding

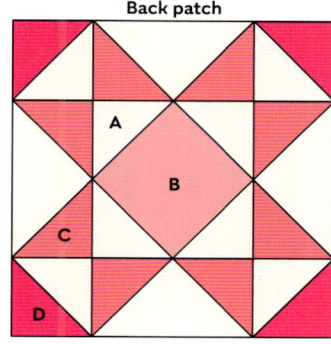

Back patch

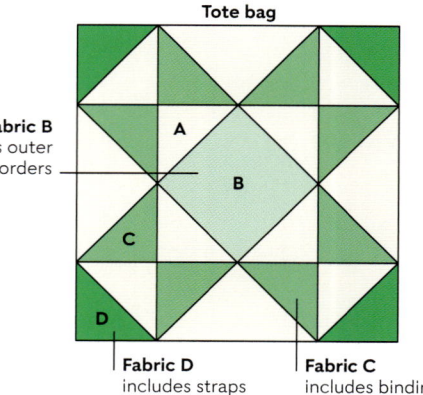

Tote bag — Fabric B includes outer tote borders; Fabric D includes straps; Fabric C includes binding

FABRIC REQUIREMENTS

PILLOW COVER	
Fabrics A, B, and C*	(1) FQ each
Fabric D	(2) 11.4 x 11.4cm (4½ x 4½in)
Lining**	(1) 61 x 61cm (24 x 24in)
Envelope backing	0.5m (½yd)
WALL HANGING	
Fabrics A*, B, and C	(1) 0.5m (½yd) each
Fabric D	(1) FQ
Backing	1m (1yd)
BACK PATCH	
Fabric A	(1) FQ
Fabric B	(1) 14 x 14cm (5½ x 5½in)
Fabric C	(4) 12.1 x 12.1cm (4¾ x 4¾in)
Fabric D	(2) 11.4 x 11.4cm (4½ x 4½in)
TOTE BAG	
Fabrics A* and C*	(1) FQ each
Fabrics B* and D	(1) 0.5m (½yd) each
Lining	(2) 68.6 x 68.6cm** (27 x 27in) / (2) 54.6 x 53.3cm (21½ x 21in)

COVER QUILT DETAILS
Pillow cover fabrics: Wisp (**A**), Dusk (**B**), Vervain (**C**), Salvia (**D**); **Wall hanging fabrics:** Ruby and Bee Solids by Windham Fabrics in Wisp (**A**), Marine Layer (**B**), Provence Blue (**C**), Majorelle Blue (**D**); **Back patch fabrics:** Wisp (**A**), Posy (**B**), Perfect Pink (**C**), Dragonfruit (**D**); **Tote bag fabrics:** Wisp (**A**), Matcha (**B**), Minty (**C**), Evergreen (**D**), Flicker in Moss by Ruby Star Society (**Lining**); **Quilting:** Walking foot and big stitch; **Thread:** Aurifil 50 wt and DMC 8 wt in various colours; **Wadding:** Hobbs Heirloom Fusible Cotton; **Binding:** Various fabrics

*Fabric requirement does not account for overage.
**Use a neutral or scrap fabric, as this lining will be hidden.

CUTTING INSTRUCTIONS
Use the fabric cutting tables and diagrams below to cut out and label the pieces required for your chosen project.

FABRIC CUTTING TABLES

PILLOW COVER

A	From a FQ: Cut (1) 22.2cm (8¾in) x WOF; **sub-cut:** 　**A2:** (1) 22.2 x 22.2cm (8¾ x 8¾in) Cut (1) 11.4cm (4½in) x WOF; **sub-cut:** 　**A1:** (4) 11.4 x 11.4cm (4½ x 4½in)
B	From a FQ: Cut (1) 14cm (5½in) x WOF; **sub-cut:** 　**B1:** (1) 14 x 14cm (5½ x 5½in) Cut (4) 6.4cm (2½in) x WOF; **sub-cut:** 　**B3:** (2) 6.4 x 47cm (2½ x 18½in) 　**B2:** (2) 6.4 x 36.8cm (2½ x 14½in)
C	From a FQ: Cut (1) 12.1cm (4¾in) x WOF; **sub-cut:** 　**C1:** (4) 12.1 x 12.1cm (4¾ x 4¾in) Cut (5) 6.4cm (2½in) x WOF; label as **C2** and set aside for binding.
D	From scrap fabric, **cut:** 　**D1:** (2) 11.4 x 11.4cm (4½ x 4½in)
Lining	From scrap fabric, **cut:** 　**L1:** (1) 61 x 61cm (24 x 24in); set aside for pillow front backing. This fabric will be hidden.
Envelope backing	Cut (1) 36.8cm (14½in) x WOF; **sub-cut:** 　**E1:** (2) 36.8 x 46.4cm (14½ x 18¼in); set aside for envelope backing.

WALL HANGING

A	Cut (1) 22.2cm (8¾in) x WOF strip; **sub-cut:** 　**A2:** (4) 22.2 x 22.2cm (8¾ x 8¾in) Cut (2) 11.4cm (4½in) x WOF strip; **sub-cut:** 　**A1:** (16) 11.4 x 11.4cm (4½ x 4½in)
B	Cut (1) 14cm (5½in) x WOF; **sub-cut:** 　**B1:** (4) 14 x 14cm (5½ x 5½in) Cut (4) 6.4cm (2½in) x WOF; label as **B2** and set aside for binding.
C	Cut (2) 12.1cm (4¾in) x WOF; **sub-cut:** 　**C1:** (16) 12.1 x 12.1cm (4¾ x 4¾in)
D	From a FQ: Cut (3) 11.4cm (4½in) x WOF; **sub-cut:** 　**D1:** (10) 11.4 x 11.4cm (4½ x 4½in); set (2) **D1** aside for corner pockets.
Backing	Cut (1) 88.9 x 88.9cm (35 x 35in); set aside for backing.

BACK PATCH

A	From a FQ: Cut (1) 22.2cm (8¾in) x WOF; **sub-cut:** 　**A2:** (1) 22.2 x 22.2cm (8¾ x 8¾in) Cut (1) 11.4cm (4½in) x WOF; **sub-cut:** 　**A1:** (4) 11.4 x 11.4cm (4½ x 4½in)
B	From scrap fabric, **cut:** 　**B1:** (1) 14 x 14cm (5½ x 5½in)
C	From scrap fabric, **cut:** 　**C1:** (4) 12.1 x 12.1cm (4¾ x 4¾in)
D	From scrap fabric, **cut:** 　**D1:** (2) 11.4 x 11.4cm (4½ x 4½in)

TOTE BAG

A	From a FQ: Cut (1) 22.2cm (8¾in) x WOF; **sub-cut:** 　**A2:** (2) 22.2 x 22.2cm (8¾ x 8¾in) Cut (2) 11.4cm (4½in) x WOF; **sub-cut:** 　**A1:** (8) 11.4 x 11.4cm (4½ x 4½in)
B	Cut (1) 14cm (5½in) x WOF; **sub-cut:** 　**B1:** (2) 14 x 14cm (5½ x 5½in) 　**B3:** (2) 10.2 x 36.8cm (4 x 14½in) Cut (2) 10.2cm (4in) x WOF; **sub-cut:** 　**B4:** (4) 10.2 x 53.3cm (4 x 21in) Cut (1) 8.9cm (3½in) x WOF; **sub-cut:** 　**B2:** (2) 8.9 x 36.8cm (3½ x 14½in)
C	From a FQ: Cut (2) 12.1cm (4¾in) x WOF; **sub-cut:** 　**C1:** (8) 12.1 x 12.1cm (4¾ x 4¾in) Cut (3) 6.4cm (2½in) x WOF; label as **C2** and set aside for binding.
D	Cut (2) 12.7cm (5in) x WOF; **sub-cut:** 　**D2:** (2) 12.7 x 86.4cm (5 x 34in); set aside for straps. Cut (1) 11.4cm (4½in) x WOF; **sub-cut:** 　**D1:** (4) 11.4 x 11.4cm (4½ x 4½in)
Lining	From scrap fabric, **cut:** 　**L1:** (2) 68.6 x 68.6cm (27 x 27in); set aside for panel backings. These will be hidden. 　**L2:** (2) 54.6 x 53.3cm (21½ x 21in); set aside for tote lining. This fabric will be visible.

BLOCK ASSEMBLY

Follow these instructions to make one envelope star block. Repeat to make additional blocks as needed.

1 Cut two A1 in half diagonally to make four setting triangles. Fold each triangle and one B1 in half to make centre creases.

2 Place two setting triangles on opposite edges of B1, RST, aligning the centre creases, and sew. Press.

3 Repeat step 2, placing the remaining two triangles RST on the remaining B1 edges, to complete the square in a square unit. Press. Trim the unit to 19.1 x 19.1cm (7½ x 7½in).

4 Place one A1 and one D1 RST. Mark a diagonal line on the wrong side of the lighter square.

5 Sew 6.4mm (¼in) away from each side of the marked line. Cut directly on the marked line to make two HSTs. Press. Trim the HSTs to 10.2 x 10.2cm (4 x 4in).

6 Repeat steps 4–5 using the remaining A1 and D1 to make a total of four HSTs.

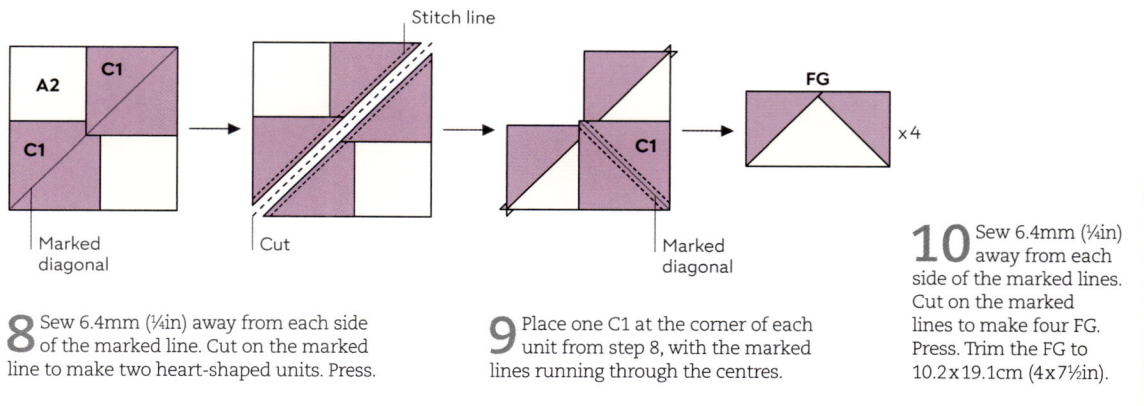

7 Mark a diagonal line on the wrong side of four C1. Place two C1 on opposite corners of one A2, RST, with the diagonal lines overlapping at the centre.

8 Sew 6.4mm (¼in) away from each side of the marked line. Cut on the marked line to make two heart-shaped units. Press.

9 Place one C1 at the corner of each unit from step 8, with the marked lines running through the centres.

10 Sew 6.4mm (¼in) away from each side of the marked lines. Cut on the marked lines to make four FG. Press. Trim the FG to 10.2 x 19.1cm (4 x 7½in).

11 Arrange the HSTs, FG, and square in a square unit as shown. Sew the pieces RST into rows. Press.

12 Sew the rows RST, aligning or nesting the seams, to complete the envelope star block. Press. The block should measure 36.8 x 36.8cm (14½ x 14½in).

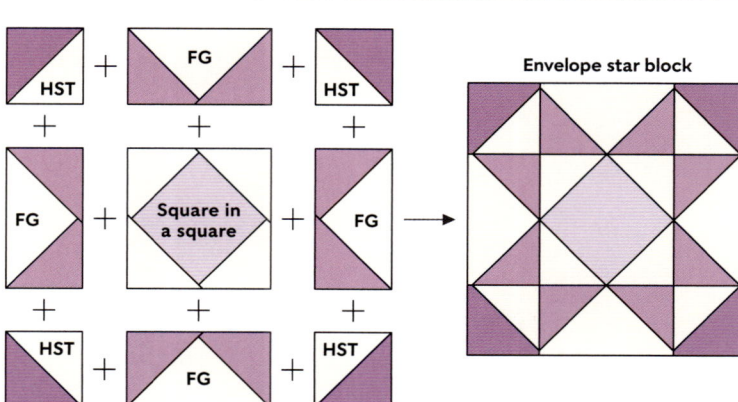

PILLOW COVER ASSEMBLY

Refer to p.155 for more detailed instructions on how to make an envelope backing for a pillow cover.

1 Follow the block assembly instructions (see p.259) to make one envelope star block.

2 Sew one B2 each to the top and bottom of the block. Press. Sew one B3 each to the left and right of the block to complete the pillow cover front. Press.

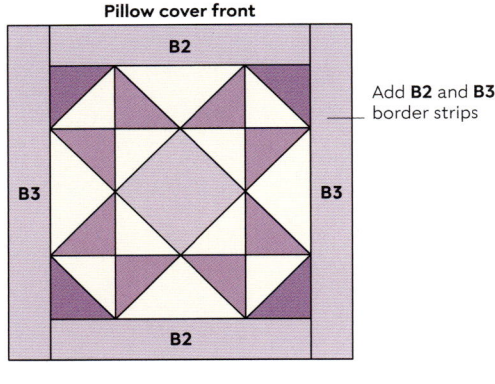

3 Baste (see pp.157–159) and quilt (see pp.160–171) the pillow cover front as desired, using L1 as the backing. Trim to 47 x 47cm (18½ x 18½in).

4 Fold the long edge of one E1 over 1.3cm (½in), WST, and press. Fold the edge over another 1.3cm (½in), then press to make a hem. Repeat with the second E1.

5 Stitch 3.2mm (⅛in) away from the hemmed edge of each E1 to secure and complete the backing pieces.

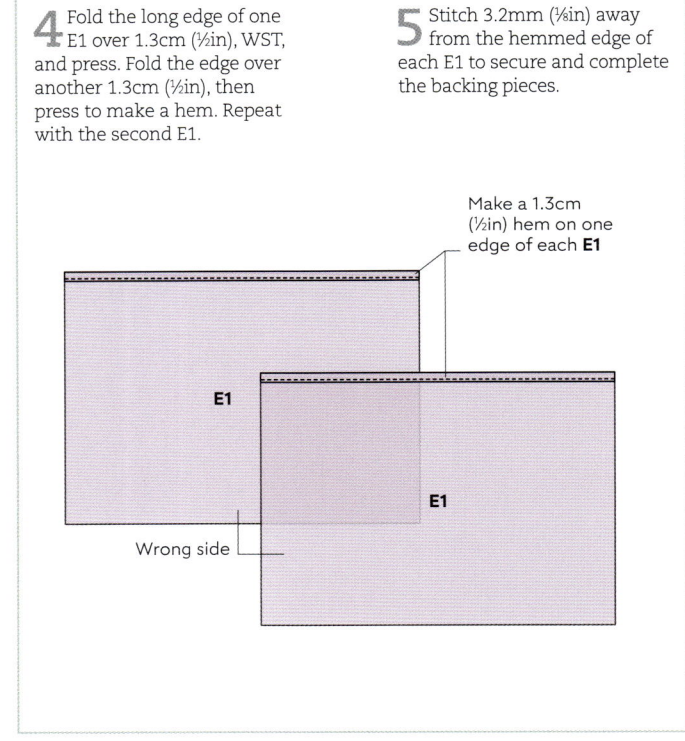

6 Place the pillow cover front and both hemmed backing pieces WST, aligning the outside edges and overlapping the hemmed edges at the centre. Place clips (see p.78) around the perimeter.

7 Sew 3.2mm (⅛in) away from the edge around the perimeter to secure the pillow front and backing.

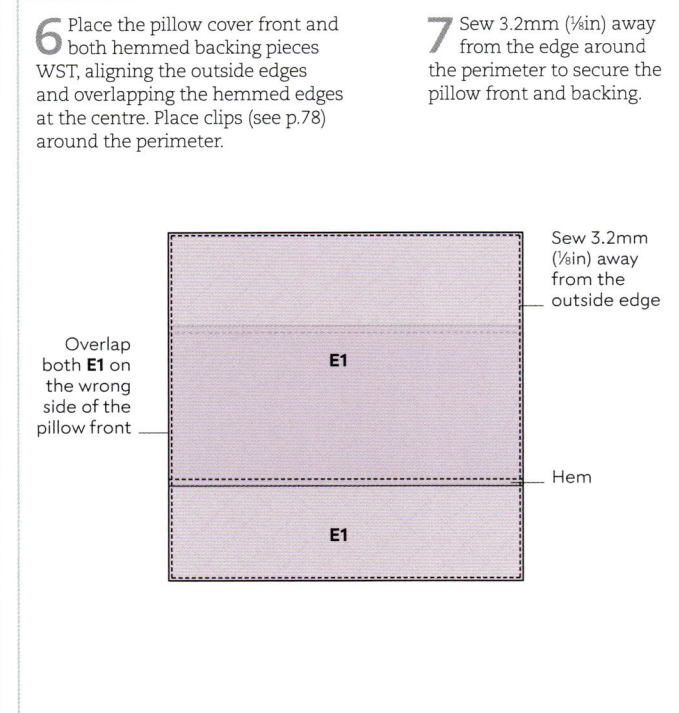

8 To make binding, sew five C2 RST to make one strip that is at least 221cm (87in) long. Bind (see pp.172–181) as desired to complete the pillow cover. Insert an 45.7 x 45.7cm (18 x 18in) pillow form.

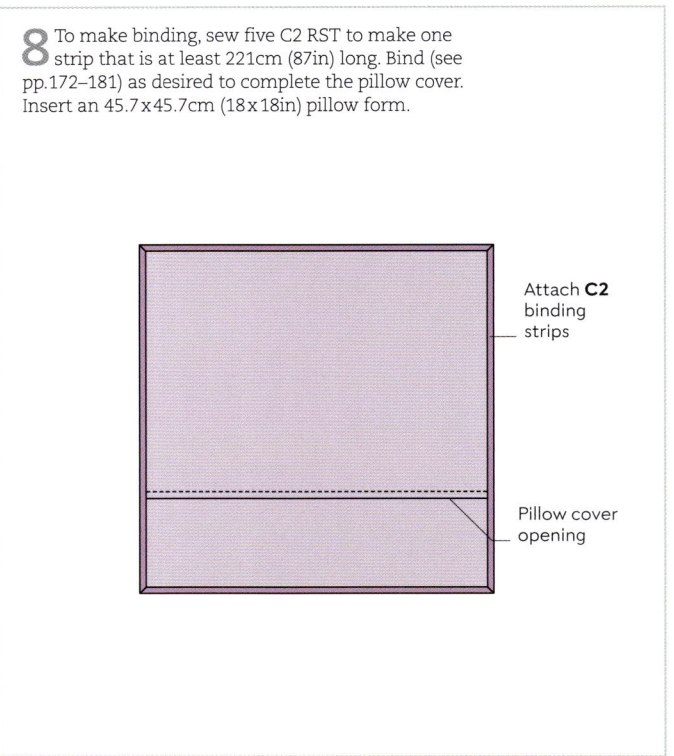

WALL HANGING ASSEMBLY

Refer to p.173 for more detailed instructions on how to attach corner pockets.

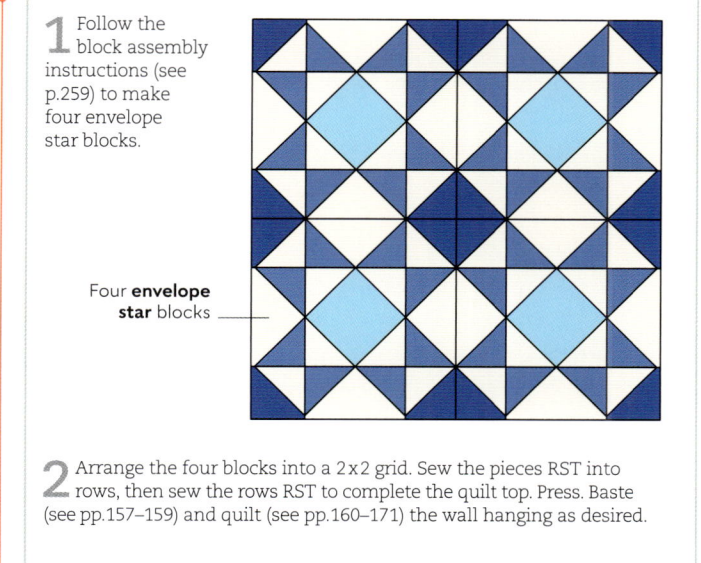

1 Follow the block assembly instructions (see p.259) to make four envelope star blocks.

Four **envelope star** blocks

2 Arrange the four blocks into a 2x2 grid. Sew the pieces RST into rows, then sew the rows RST to complete the quilt top. Press. Baste (see pp.157–159) and quilt (see pp.160–171) the wall hanging as desired.

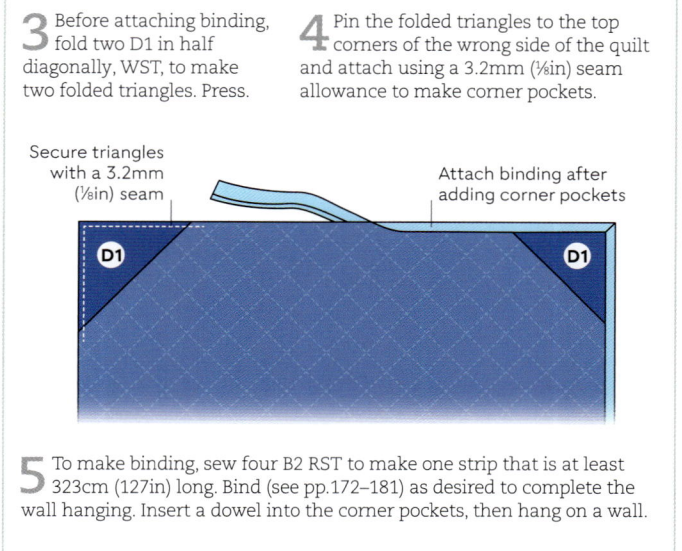

3 Before attaching binding, fold two D1 in half diagonally, WST, to make two folded triangles. Press.

4 Pin the folded triangles to the top corners of the wrong side of the quilt and attach using a 3.2mm (⅛in) seam allowance to make corner pockets.

Secure triangles with a 3.2mm (⅛in) seam

Attach binding after adding corner pockets

5 To make binding, sew four B2 RST to make one strip that is at least 323cm (127in) long. Bind (see pp.172–181) as desired to complete the wall hanging. Insert a dowel into the corner pockets, then hang on a wall.

BACK PATCH ASSEMBLY

Refer to p.134 for detailed instructions on various appliqué techniques and how to prepare block edges.

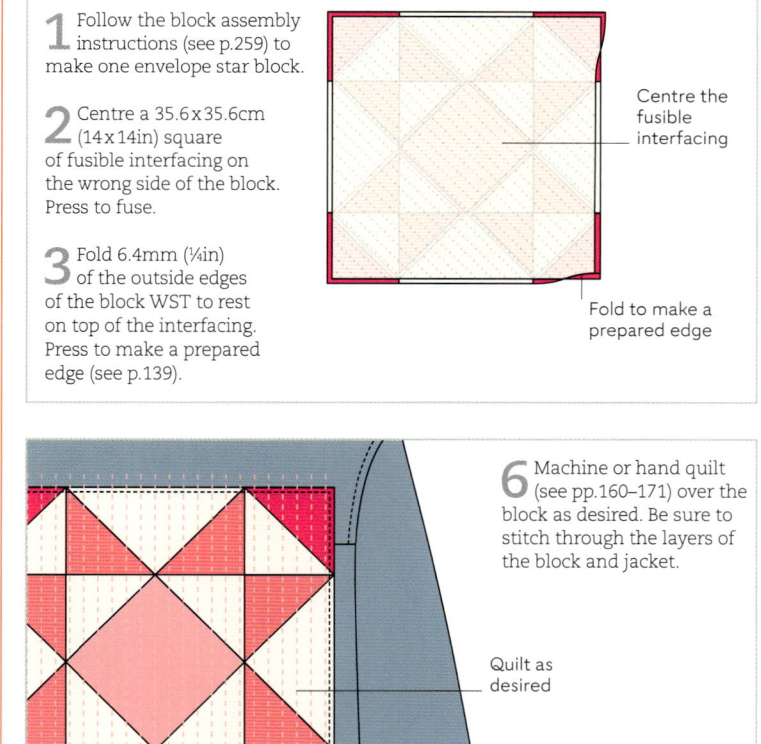

1 Follow the block assembly instructions (see p.259) to make one envelope star block.

2 Centre a 35.6x35.6cm (14x14in) square of fusible interfacing on the wrong side of the block. Press to fuse.

3 Fold 6.4mm (¼in) of the outside edges of the block WST to rest on top of the interfacing. Press to make a prepared edge (see p.139).

Centre the fusible interfacing

Fold to make a prepared edge

6 Machine or hand quilt (see pp.160–171) over the block as desired. Be sure to stitch through the layers of the block and jacket.

Quilt as desired

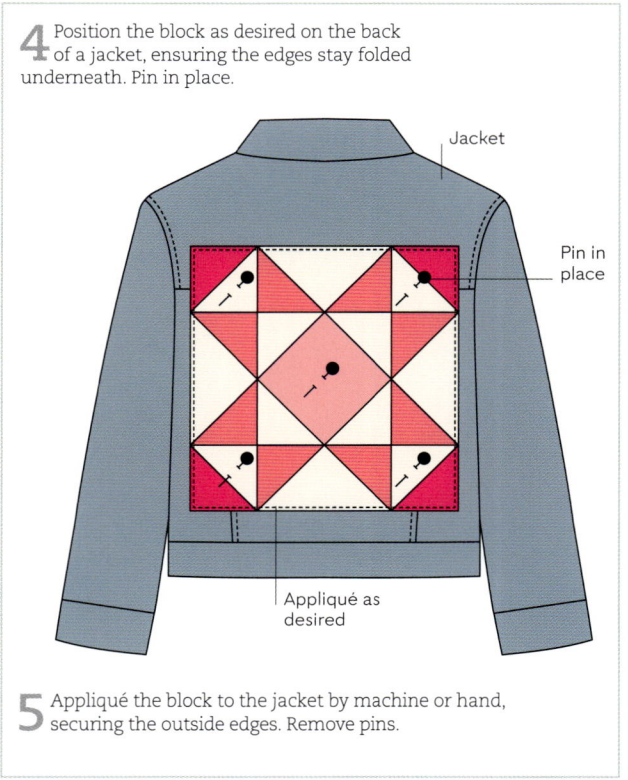

4 Position the block as desired on the back of a jacket, ensuring the edges stay folded underneath. Pin in place.

Jacket

Pin in place

Appliqué as desired

5 Appliqué the block to the jacket by machine or hand, securing the outside edges. Remove pins.

TOTE BAG ASSEMBLY

Make an outer tote, lining, and straps, then finish the tote bag with binding.
Use a 12.7mm (½in) seam allowance (see p.73) to assemble the tote bag.

1 Follow the block assembly instructions to make two envelope star blocks.

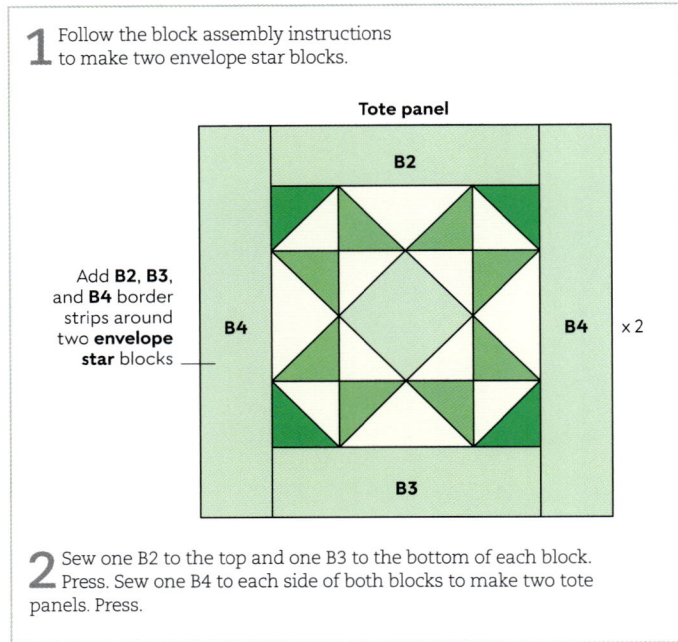

2 Sew one B2 to the top and one B3 to the bottom of each block. Press. Sew one B4 to each side of both blocks to make two tote panels. Press.

3 Baste (see pp.157–159) and quilt (see pp.160–171) the tote panels as desired, using one L1 as the backing for each.

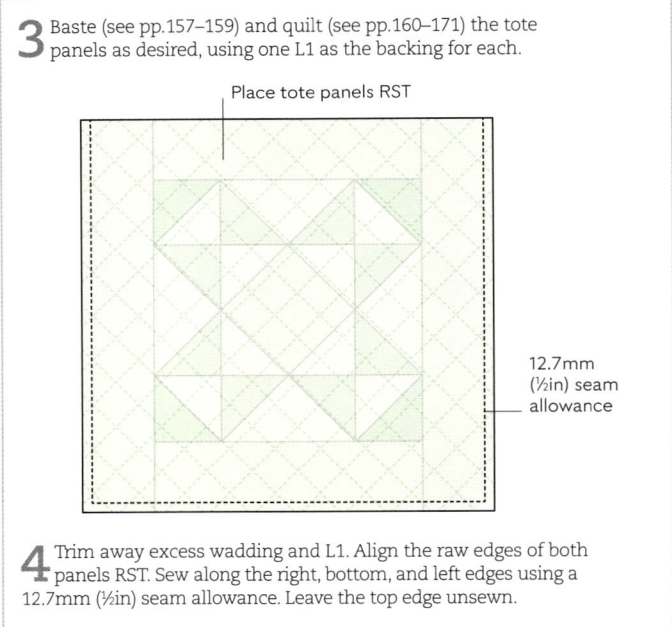

4 Trim away excess wadding and L1. Align the raw edges of both panels RST. Sew along the right, bottom, and left edges using a 12.7mm (½in) seam allowance. Leave the top edge unsewn.

5 Mark a 6.4x6.4cm (2½x2½in) square on each bottom corner of the joined panels. Use scissors to cut directly on the marked lines to remove both squares.

6 Press all seams of the joined panels open.

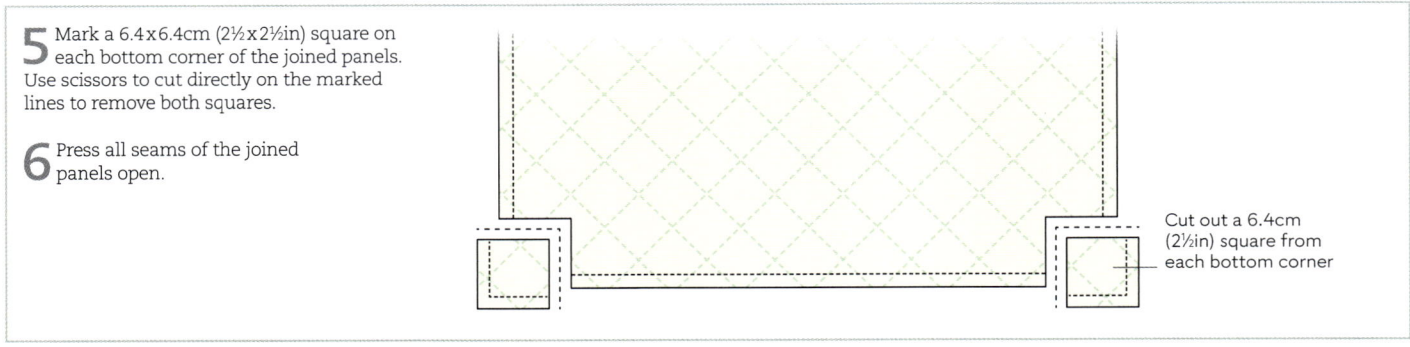

7 Align and pinch the bottom and right seams RST at the bottom right corner to form a diagonal edge. Clip (see p.78) in place.

8 Sew along the diagonal edge using a 12.7mm (½in) seam allowance, backstitching at the beginning and end. Repeat steps 7–8 with the left corner.

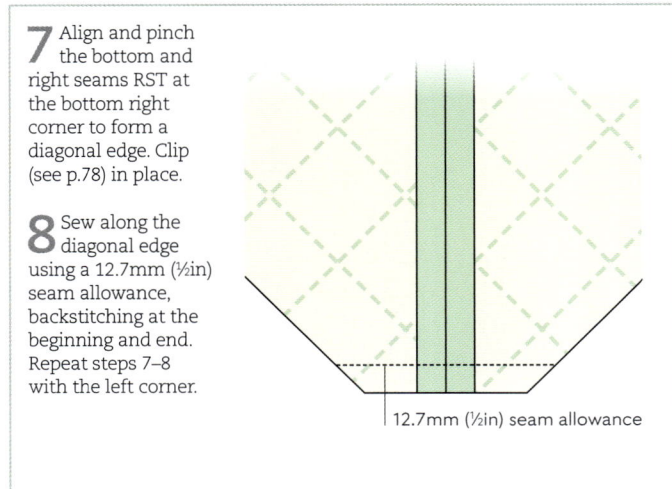

9 Flip the joined panels right-side out to form the outer tote.

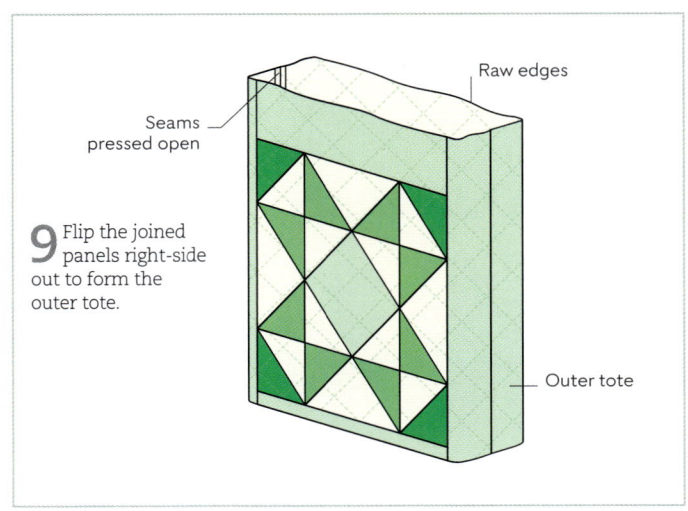

10. Fold one D2 in half lengthways, WST. Press to make a centre crease. Unfold the strip, then fold each long edge inward to meet at the crease. Press.

11. Place one 3.2x88.9cm (1¼x35in) wadding strip inside the folded strip, under the leftmost fold.

12. Fold the strip in half lengthways along the crease to align the two folded edges. The folded strip should measure 3.2cm (1¼in) wide.

13. Sew 3.2mm (⅛in) away from each edge to make the strap. Stitch additional quilting lines on the middle of the strap as desired. Trim the strap to 86.4cm (34in) long.

3.2cm (1¼in) wadding strip

Fold **D2** in half, then fold the edges in to meet at the centre

Add quilting lines for durability

14. Fold each end of the strap under 1.3cm (½in), then again 2.5cm (1in) to hem the ends. Ensure the hemmed edges are on the same side of the strap so they will rest against the outer tote.

Hemmed edge

Ensure hems are folded on the same side of the straps

15. Repeat steps 10–14 with the remaining D2 to make a second strap.

16. Pin one strap to each side of the outer tote, positioning the ends 2.5cm (1in) above the envelope star block within the top B2 piece. Use the seam lines of the envelope star block to ensure both straps are evenly aligned.

Attach strap ends with a 2.5x2.5cm (1x1in) square

2.5cm (1in)

17. Secure each strap end to the outer tote by stitching a 2.5x2.5cm (1x1in) square on the bottom of each strap. Backstitch at the beginning and end for durability.

18. Follow steps 4–8 using two L2 to make the tote lining. Keep the lining wrong-sides out. Press all seams open.

19. Place the lining inside the outer tote, WST. Align the top edges and side seams of the outer tote and lining. Pin or clip in place.

Insert the lining inside the outer tote

Align the top edges and side seams

20. Sew a 3.2mm (⅛in) basting stitch (see p.72) along the top edge to secure the layers.

21. To make binding, sew three C2 RST to make one strip that is at least 142cm (56in) long. Attach the binding to the top edge and finish as desired (see pp.172–181) to complete the tote bag.

Attach binding to the top edge

BLOCK GALLERY

Classic quilt block gallery

Many quilt blocks have become well known for their timeless design and continued use throughout the history of quilting. This gallery offers a detailed look at some of the most popular classic quilt blocks and their construction techniques.

CATEGORIZING QUILT BLOCKS

From the simplicity of a four patch to the complexity of a foundation paper-pieced New York Beauty, understanding block categorization fosters appreciation of the techniques and variations that make each block unique.

FOUR PATCH BLOCKS
The most traditional and fundamental block categories in quilting, the four patch block is ideal for creating repeating patterns or seamlessly integrating with all other block types. Blocks of this construction include:

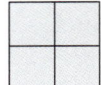
◀ **Equal four patch**
Blocks divided into four equal parts by horizontal and vertical seams.

◀ **Unequal four patch**
Blocks divided into four unequal parts by horizontal and vertical seams.

◀ **Four cross**
Blocks divided by two diagonal seams to make four major shapes.

NINE PATCH BLOCKS
The nine patch block is accessible to quilters of all skill levels. Its versatility and adaptability offers boundless variations, including popular star motifs. Blocks of this construction include:

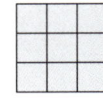
◀ **Equal nine patch**
Blocks divided into nine equal parts by two horizontal and two vertical seams.

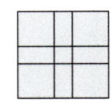
◀ **Unequal nine patch**
Blocks divided into nine unequal parts by two horizontal and two vertical seams.

◀ **Nine cross**
Blocks divided by diagonal seams to make nine major shapes.

SQUARE IN A SQUARE
Featuring a smaller square or diamond nested within a large square, square in a square blocks utilize a framed effect to highlight the centre motif. Blocks of this construction include:

◀ **Set square**
Blocks made by placing a square on point and adding triangles around it.

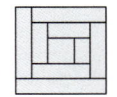
◀ **Log cabin**
Blocks made by framing a centre square or rectangle with strips or various units.

MULTI-PATCH BLOCKS

These blocks are composed of various shapes, a large number of units, or pieces arranged in non-repetitive patterns. This category includes quilt blocks that extend beyond the traditional four and nine patch structures.

CURVED BLOCKS

Deviating from the straight lines of traditional patchwork, curved blocks often add a dynamic and fluid element to quilt designs. These blocks often feature partial curves, complete circles, or combinations of multiple curves within a single unit.

FOUNDATION PAPER PIECING BLOCKS

FPP blocks are machine pieced using a foundation of paper. FPP is often used for making quilts with intricate designs or irregular angles, allowing for more precise piecing than traditional means.

HAND-PIECED BLOCKS

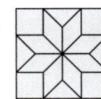

Hand piecing offers control and precision using minimal tools. This category includes quilt blocks that are historically hand pieced due to their heritage or construction technique, such as Y-seams, though any block can be pieced by hand.

ENGLISH PAPER PIECING BLOCKS

Utilizing paper templates to support the structure of complex angled shapes during the piecing process, EPP allows for unique designs that would not typically be achievable through other means.

FOUR PATCH BLOCKS

ANNIE'S CHOICE
HSTs (see p.86)

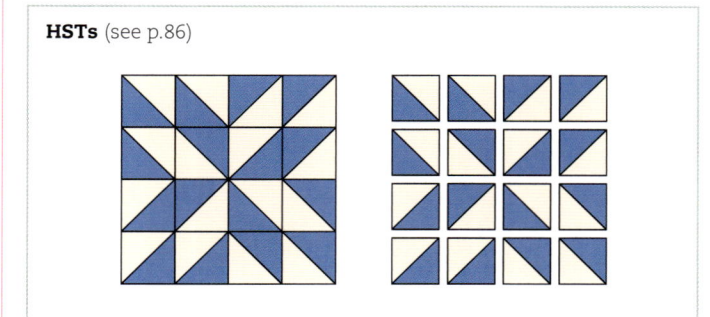

BEAR CLAW
HSTs (see p.86)

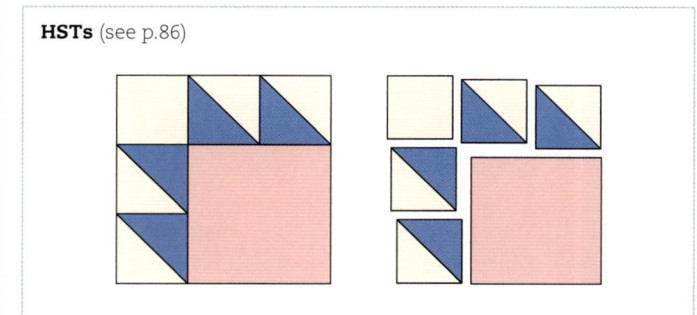

CHECKERBOARD
QSTs (see p.90); **Setting Triangles** (see p.95)

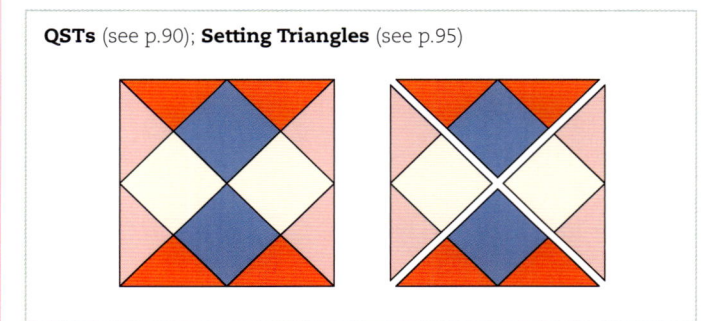

FLOCK OF GEESE
HSTs (see p.86)

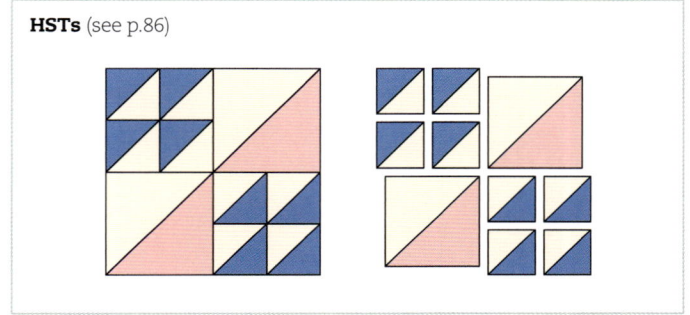

FLOWER BASKET
HSTs (see p.86)

RIBBON STAR
HSTs (see p.86)

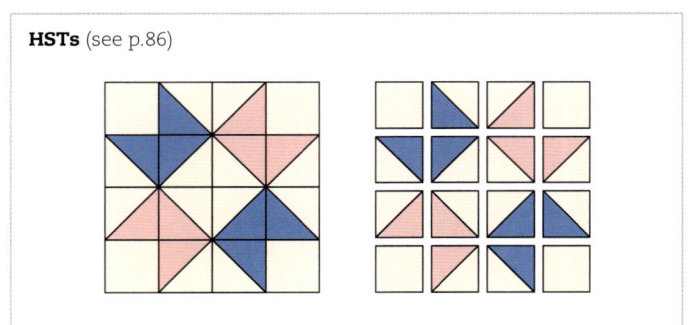

SNOWBALL FLOWER
Stitch and flip (see p.89)

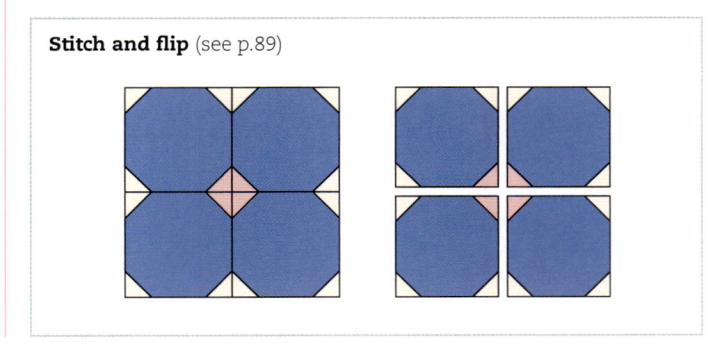

X'S AND O'S
Stitch and flip (see p.89)

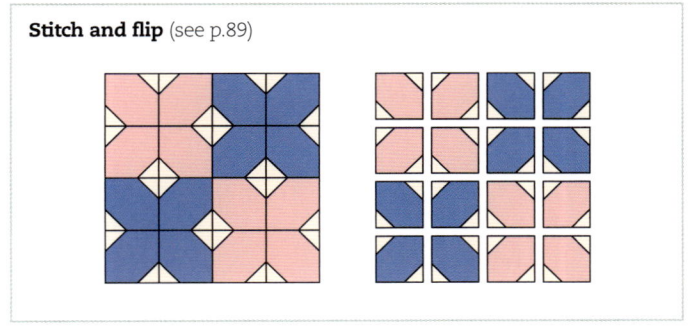

NINE PATCH BLOCKS

BEAR PAW

HSTs (see p.86); **Sashing** (see p.143)

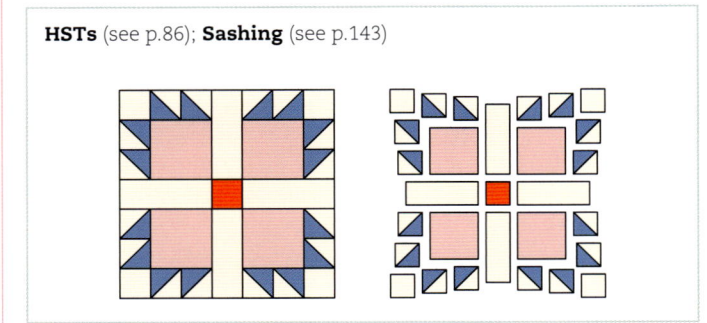

CAT'S CRADLE

HSTs (see p.86)

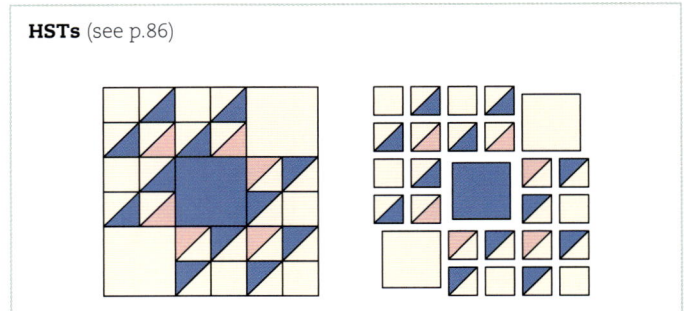

CHURN DASH

Strip piecing (see p.83); **HSTs** (see p.86)

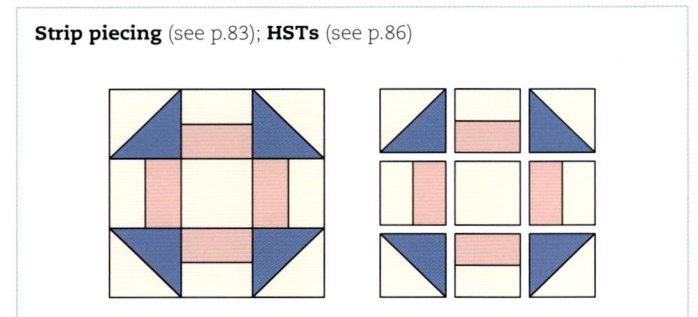

ENVELOPE STAR

HSTs (see p.86); **FG** (see p.92); **Square in a square** (see p.94)

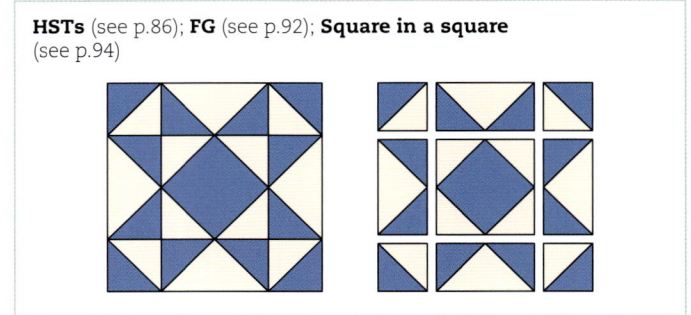

GRANNY SQUARE

Nine patch (see p.84); **Setting triangles** (see p.95)

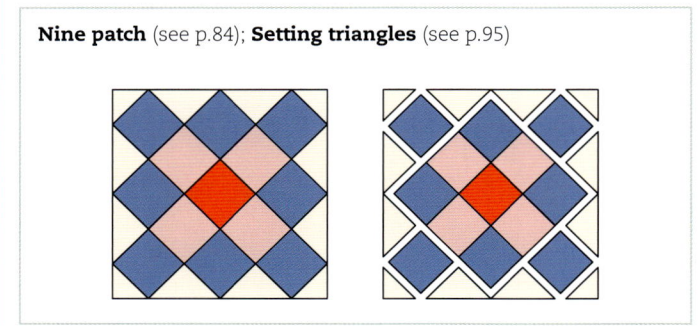

MAPLE LEAF

HSTs (see p.86); **Stitch and flip** (see p.89)

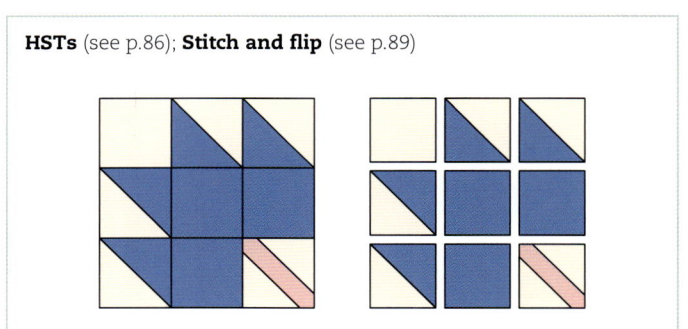

OHIO STAR

QSTs (see p.90)

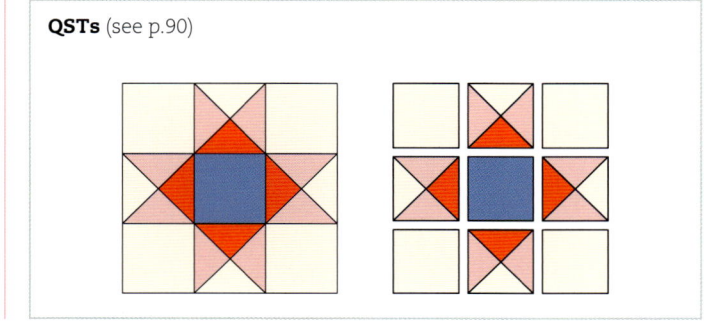

PLUS

Strip piecing (see p.83)

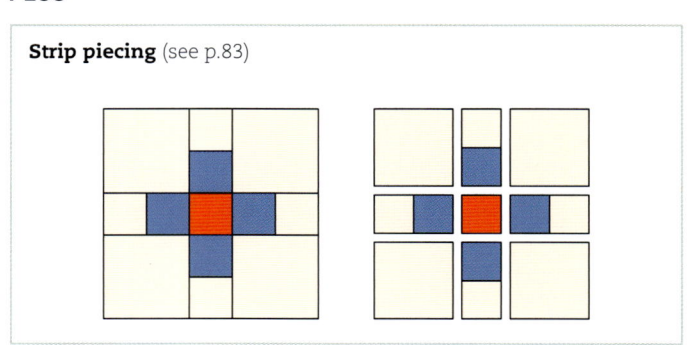

CLASSIC QUILT BLOCK GALLERY **269**

ROAD TO CALIFORNIA

Four patch (see p.84); **HSTs** (see p.86)

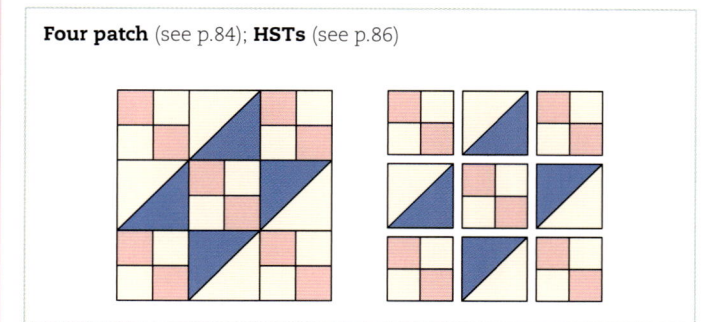

ROLLING STONE

Strip piecing (see p.83); **Square in a square** (see p.94)

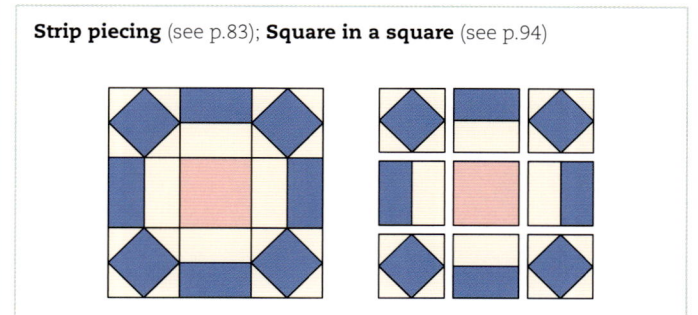

SAWTOOTH STAR

FG (see p.92)

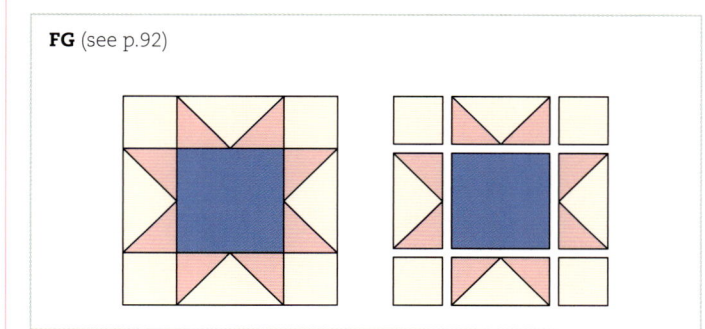

SHOO FLY

HSTs (see p.86)

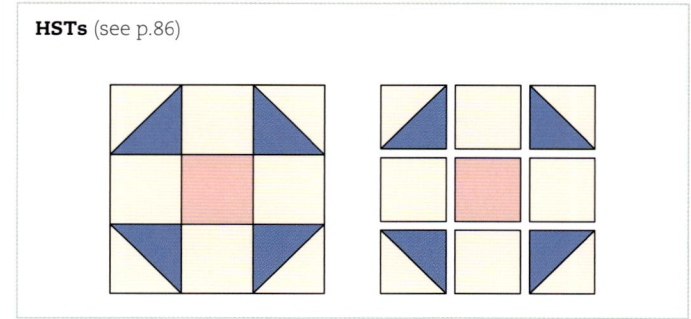

WEATHERVANE

HSTs (see p.86); **Stitch and flip** (see p.89)

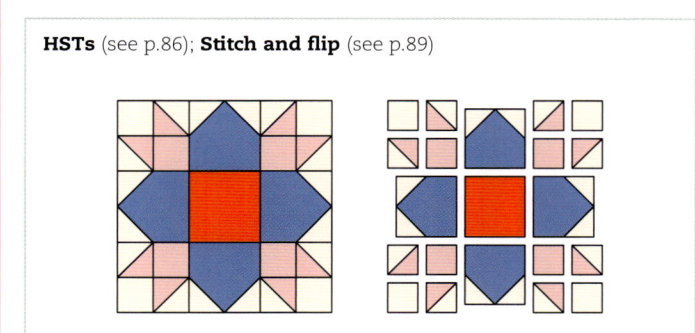

WINGED SQUARE

HSTs (see p.86)

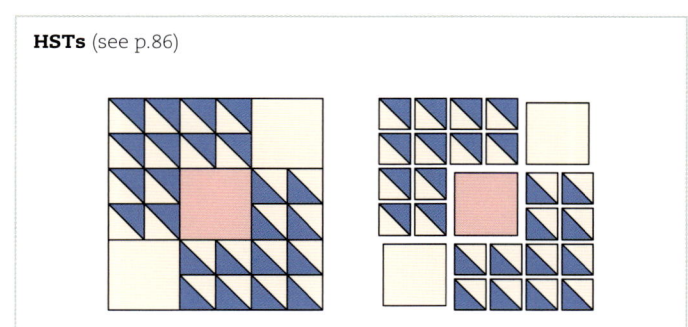

X PLUS

Strip piecing (see p.83); **Stitch and flip** (see p.89); **Sashing** (see p.143)

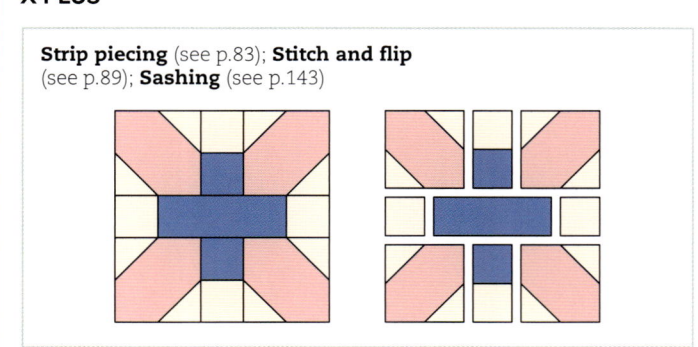

WONKY STAR

Stitch and flip (see p.89); **Improv** (see p.108)

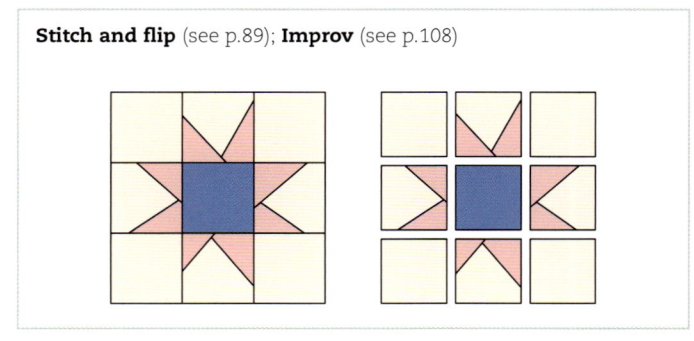

SQUARE IN A SQUARE BLOCKS

ALBUM QUILT BLOCK

Strip piecing (see p.83); **Setting triangles** (see p.95)

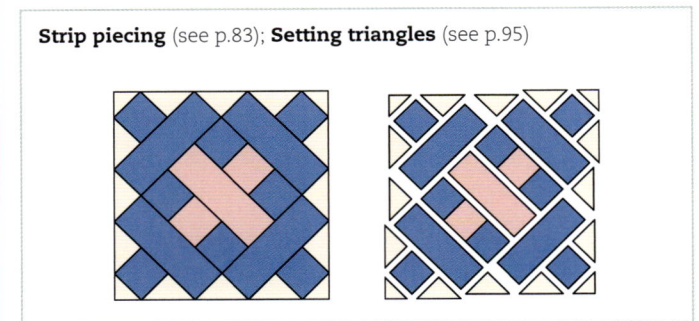

ANVIL

HSTs (see p.86)

BOX

Log cabin (see p.85); **HSTs** (see p.86)

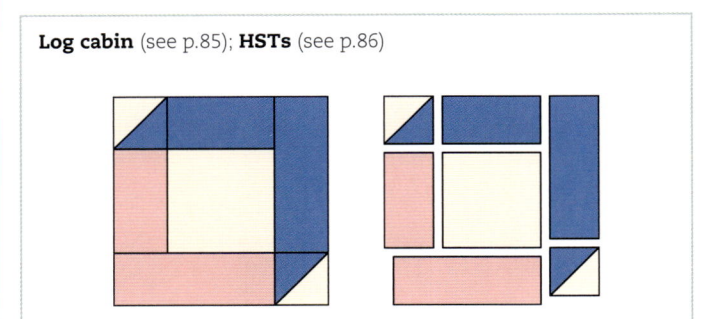

CAROL'S SCRAP TIME

HSTs (see p.86); **Setting triangles** (see p.95)

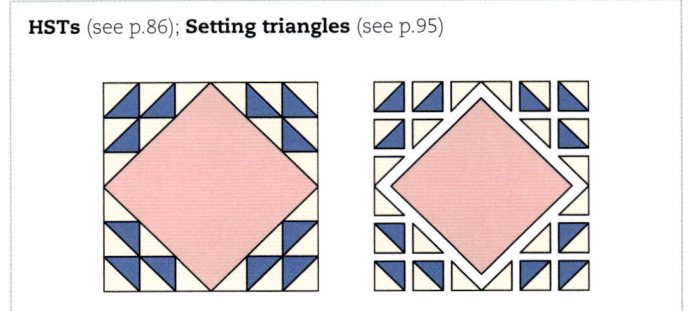

COFFIN STAR

Four patch (see p.84); **Setting triangles** (see p.95)

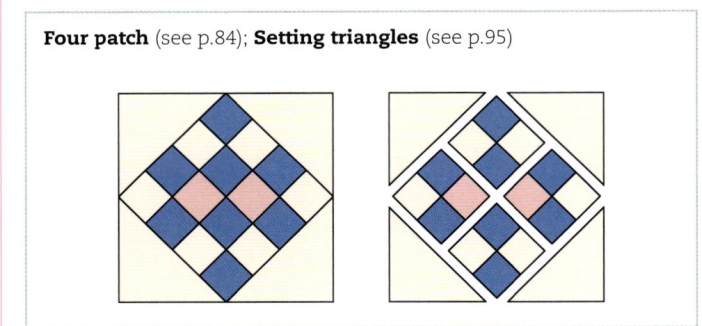

COURTHOUSE STEPS

Log cabin (see p.85)

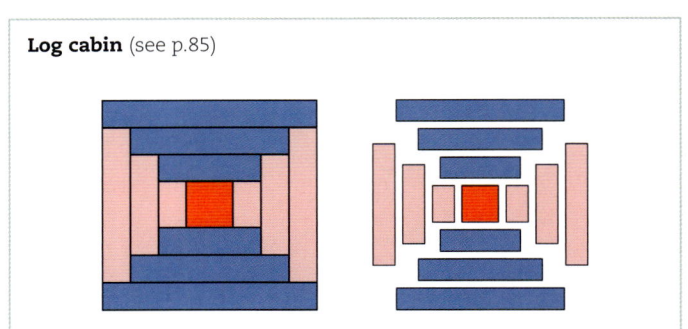

ECONOMY

Setting triangles (see p.95)

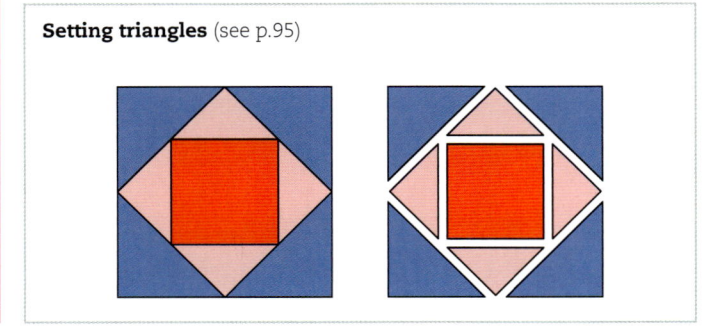

FOLLOW THE LEADER

Log cabin (see p.85); **FG** (see p.92)

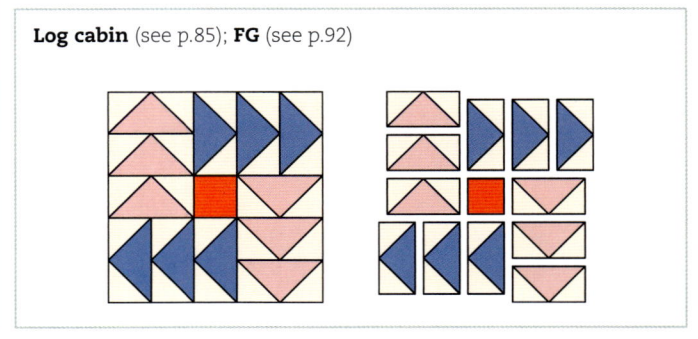

CLASSIC QUILT BLOCK GALLERY

GENTLEMAN'S FANCY

FG (see p.92); **Square in a square** (see p.94); **Setting triangles** (see p.95)

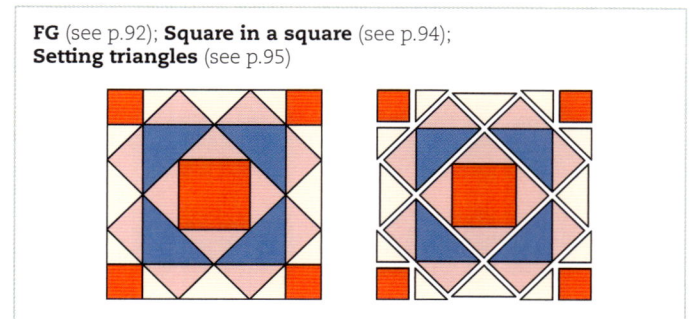

LADY OF THE LAKE

Log cabin (see p.85); **HSTs** (see p.86)

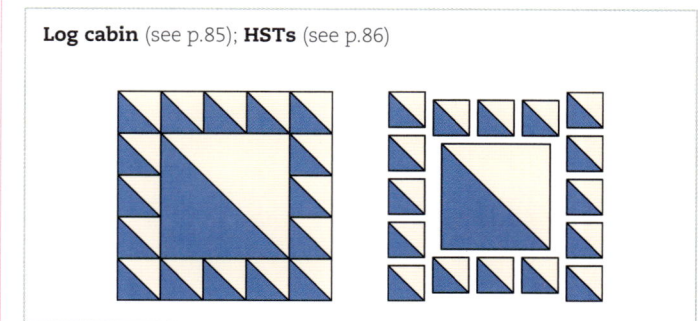

LOG CABIN

Log cabin (see p.85)

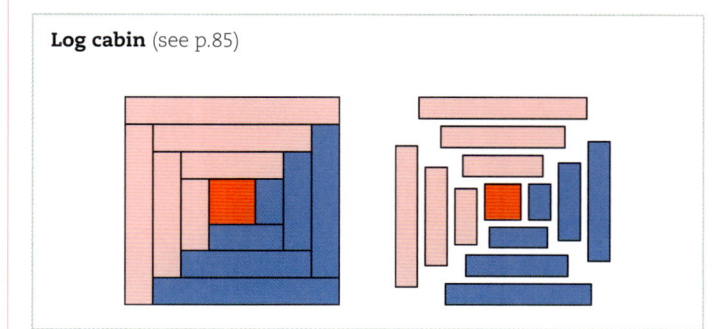

MODERN FLAME

Log cabin (see p.85); **HSTs** (see p.86)

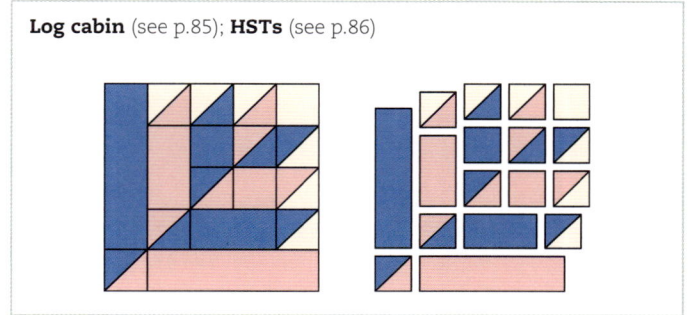

MOSAIC #21

Log cabin (see p.85); **HSTs** (see p.86); **Square in a square** (see p.94)

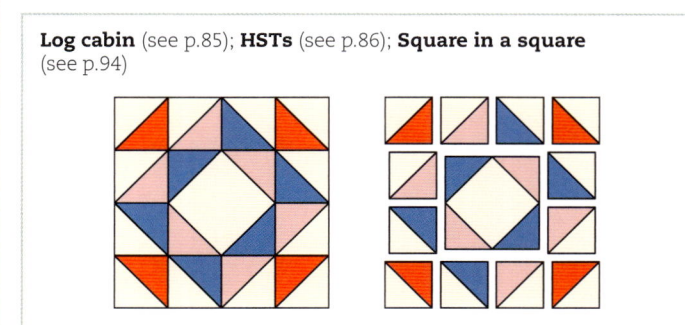

OCEAN WAVES

HSTs (see p.86); **Setting triangles** (see p.95)

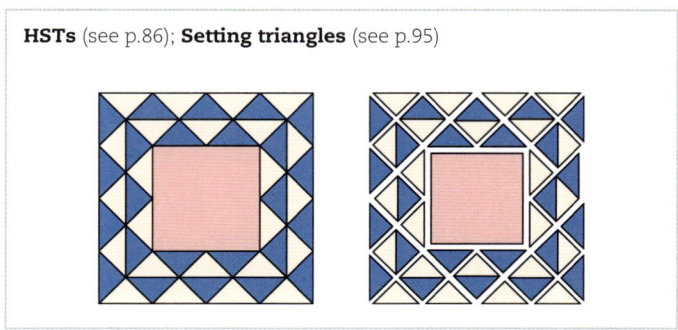

RISING STAR

FG (see p.92)

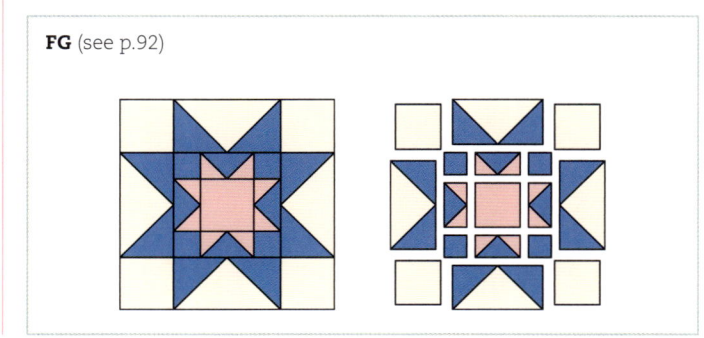

UNION SQUARE

HSTs (see p.86); **Square in a square** (see p.94); **Setting triangles** (see p.95)

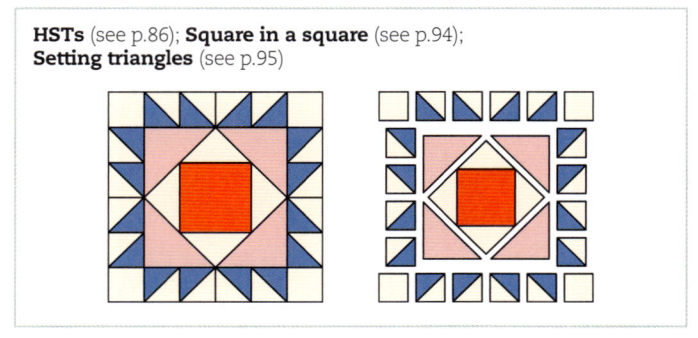

MULTI-PATCH BLOCKS

BASKET WEAVE

Strip piecing (see p.83)

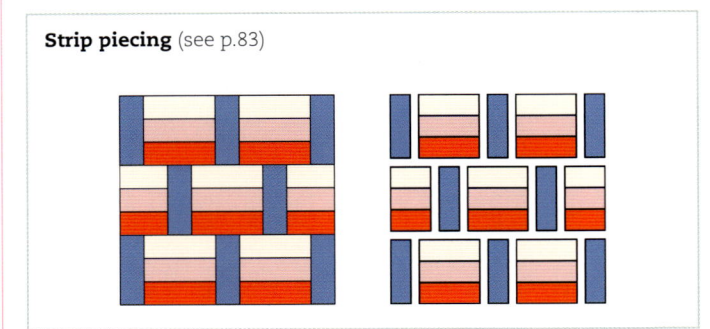

BLACKFORD'S BEAUTY

Four patch (see p.84); **FG** (see p.92)

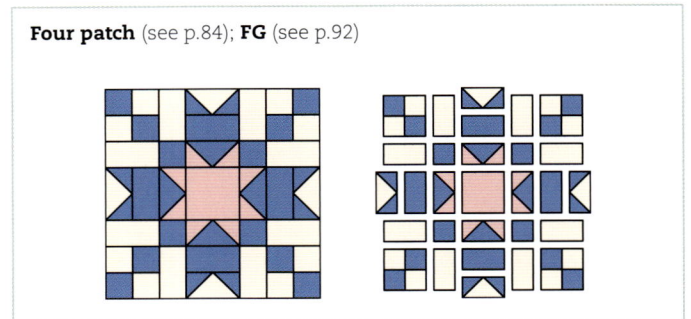

BROKEN WINDOW

HSTs (see p.86); **FG** (see p.92)

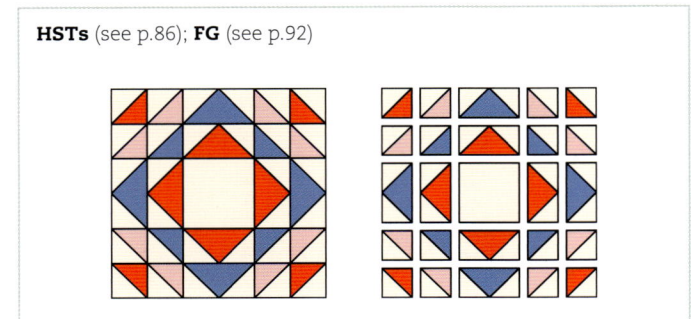

ENGLISH WEDDING RING

HSTs (see p.86)

FANNY'S FAVORITE

FG (see p.92); **Setting triangles** (see p.95)

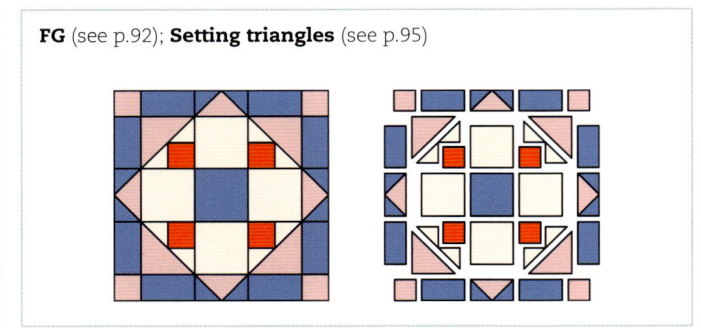

GOOSE IN THE POND

Strip piecing (see p.83); **Nine patch** (see p.84); **HSTs** (see p.86)

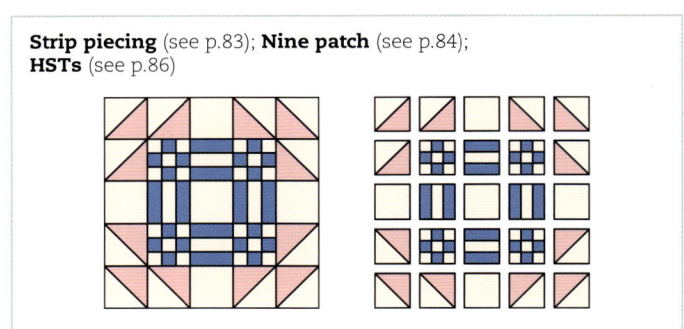

GREEN MOUNTAIN STAR

HSTs (see p.86); **QSTs** (see p.90); **FG** (see p.92)

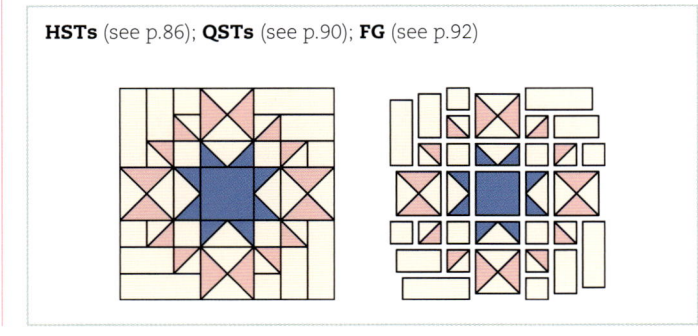

HEART

Stitch and flip (see p.89)

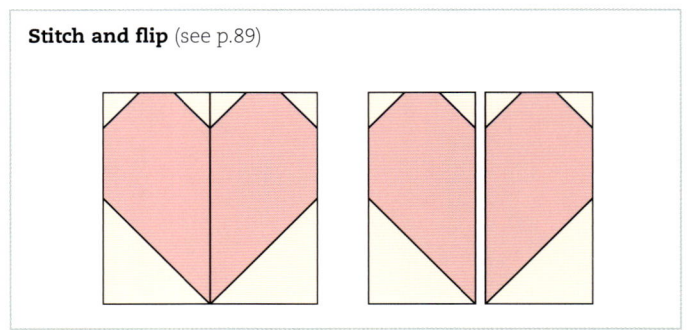

CLASSIC QUILT BLOCK GALLERY

HOUSE

Strip piecing (see p.83); **Log cabin** (see p.85); **HSTs** (see p.86)

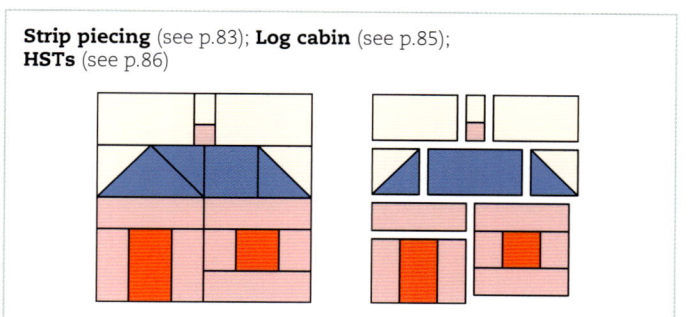

IDAHO BEAUTY

FG (see p.92); **Square in a square** (see p.94)

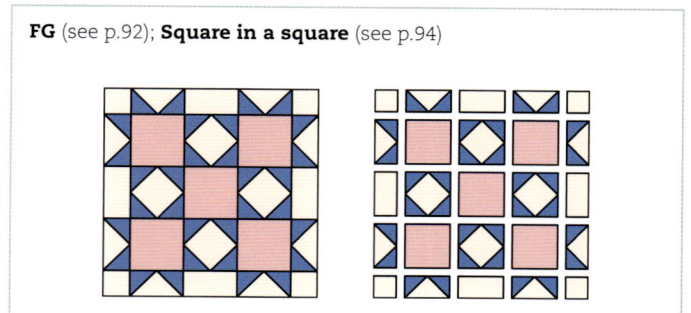

IRISH CHAIN

Strip piecing (see p.83); **Odd strip piecing** (see p.84)

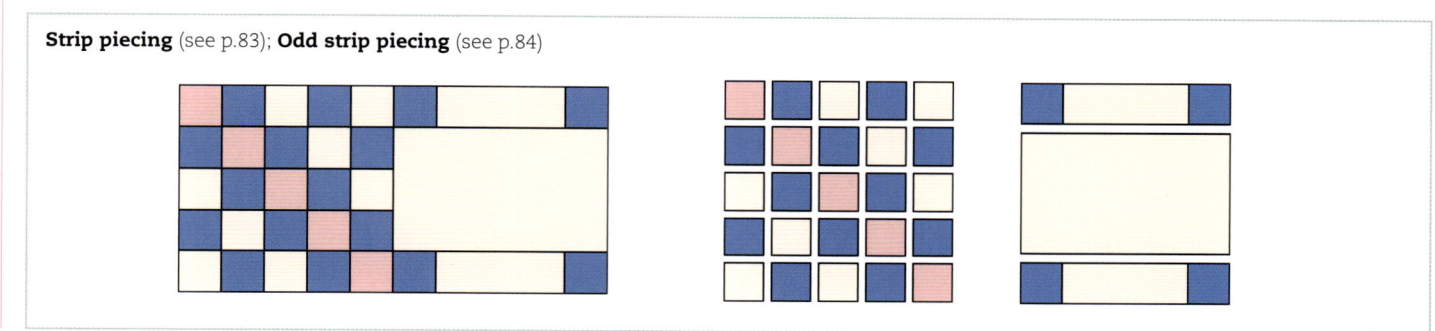

LONE STAR

Diamonds (see p.102)

MEMORY STAR

HSTs (see p.86); **FG** (see p.92)

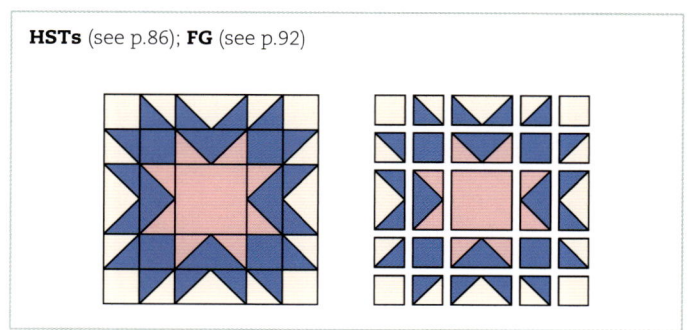

MOTHER'S CHOICE

HSTs (see p.86); **FG** (see p.92)

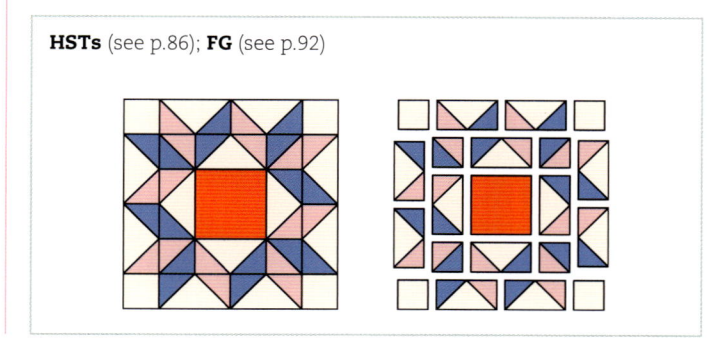

SISTER'S CHOICE

HSTs (see p.86)

CURVES

CURVED STAR
QCs (see p.104)

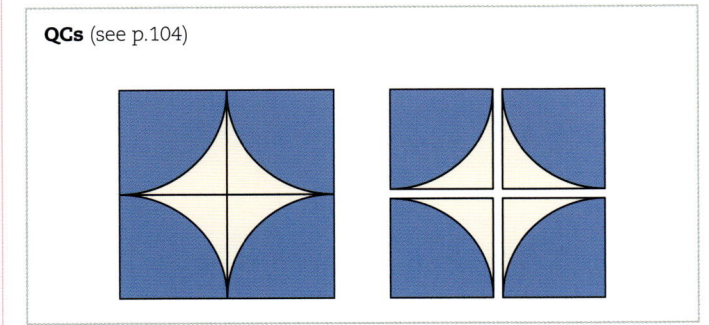

DRUNKARD'S PATH CIRCLE
QCs (see p.104)

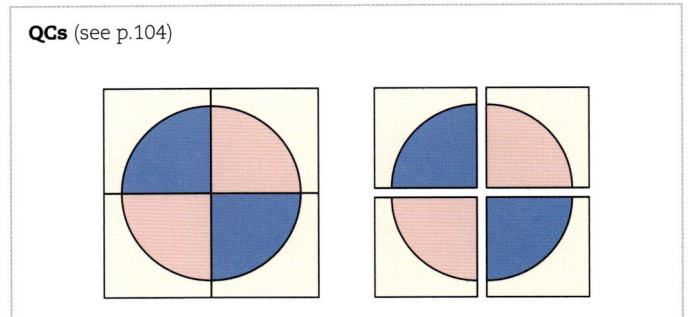

DRUNKARD'S PATH FLOWER
QCs (see p.104)

GRANDMOTHER'S FAN
Strip piecing (see p.83); **QCs** (see p.104)

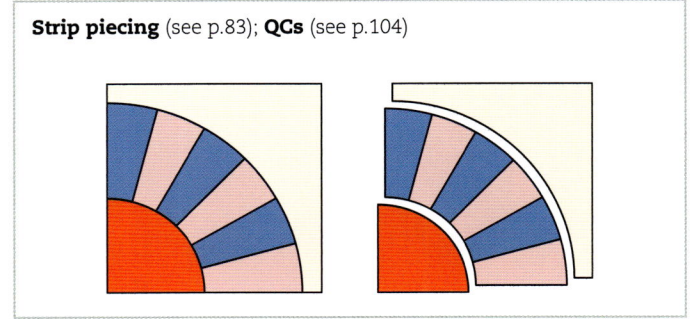

ORANGE PEEL
QCs (see p.104)

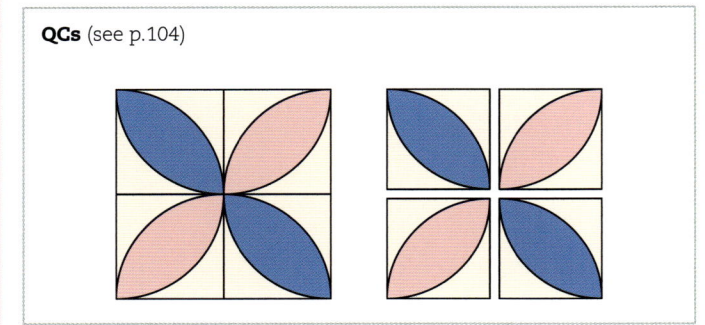

PEELED ORANGE
Curves (see p.104)

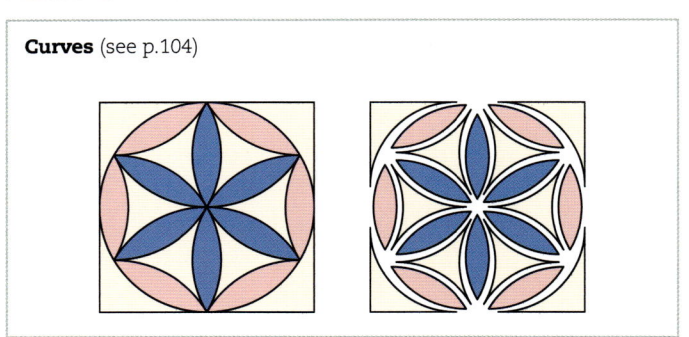

RAINBOW
QCs (see p.104)

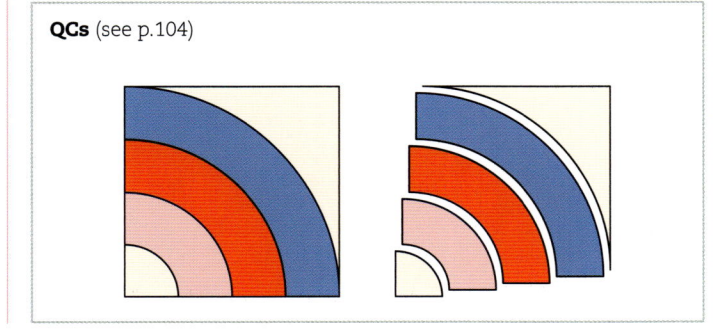

WINDING WAYS
Curves (see p.104)

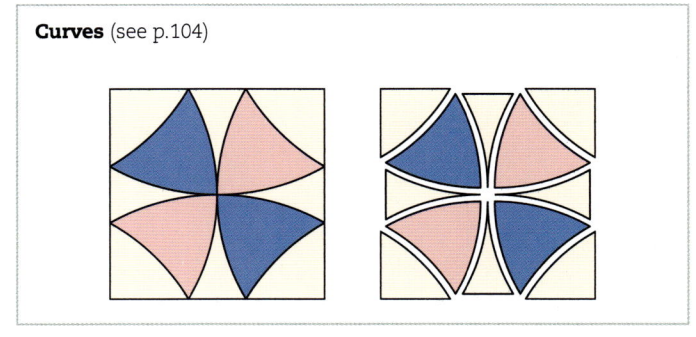

FOUNDATION PAPER PIECING

BIRDS OF PARADISE

Four patch (see p.84); **FPP** (see p.114)

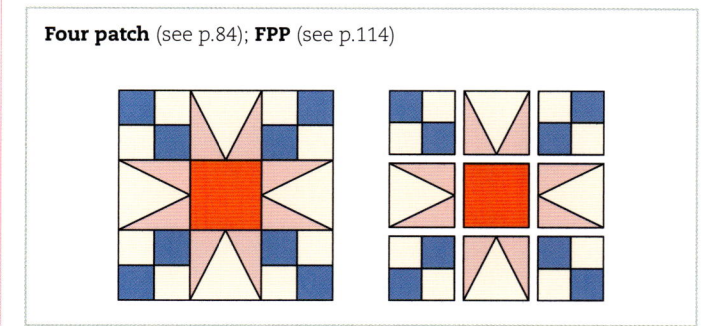

CORNER BEAM

FPP (see p.114)

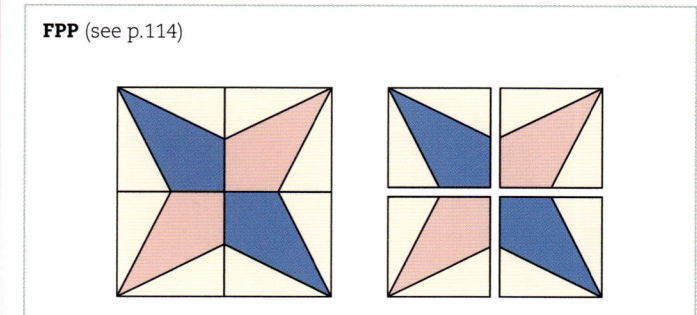

FIVE POINT STAR

FPP (see p.114)

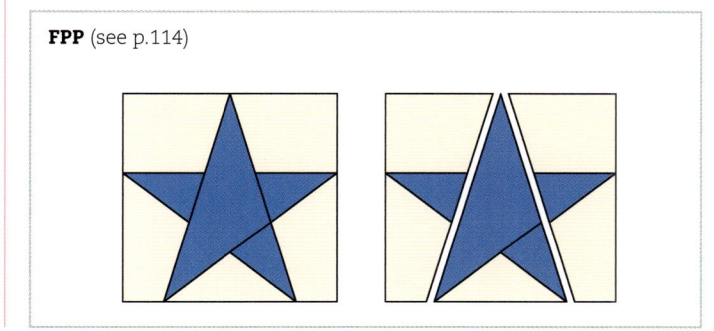

NEW YORK BEAUTY

QCs (see p.104); **FPP** (see p.114)

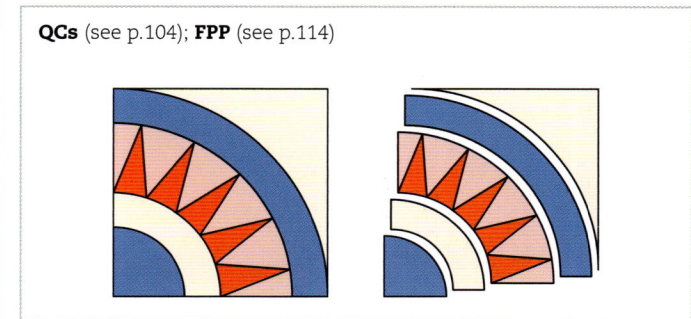

PALM LEAF

HSTs (see p.86); **FPP** (see p.114)

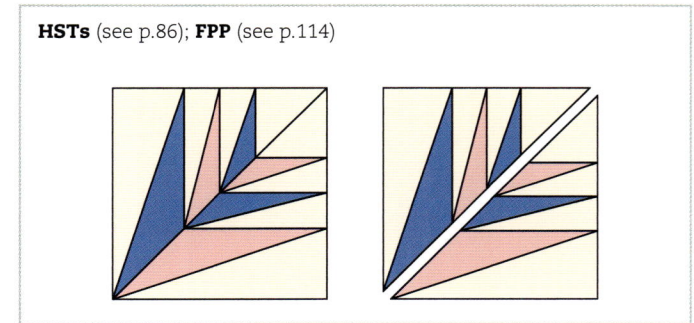

PINEAPPLE

FPP (see p.114)

STORM AT SEA

FPP (see p.114)

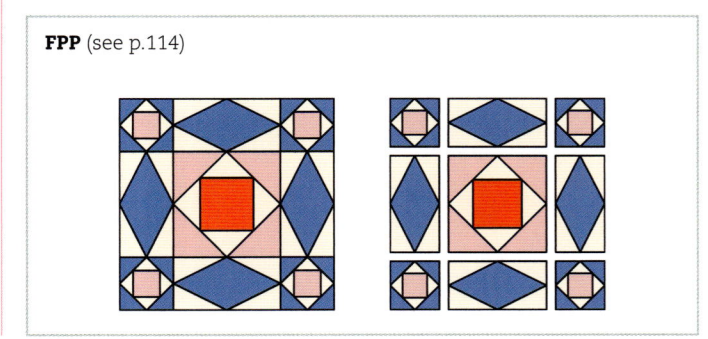

STRING

HSTs (see p.86); **FPP** (see p.114)

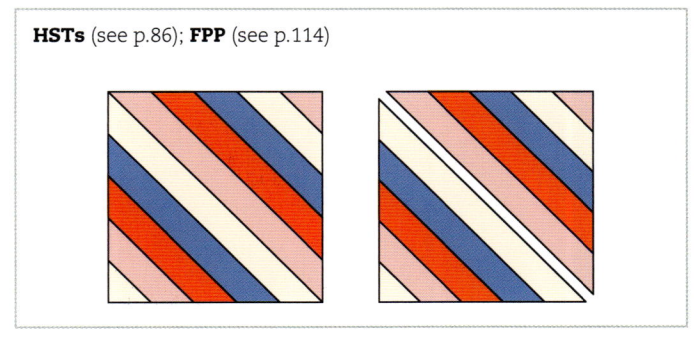

HAND-PIECED BLOCKS

CLAMSHELL

Curved seams (see p.123)

GOOSE TRACKS

Setting triangles (see p.95); **Diamonds** (see p.102); **Y-seams** (see p.123); **Sashing** (see p.143)

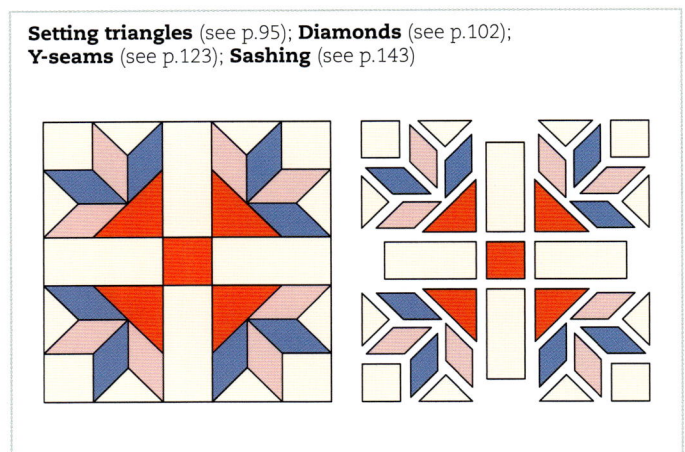

HEARTS AND GIZZARDS

HSTs (see p.86); **Appliqué** (see p.134)

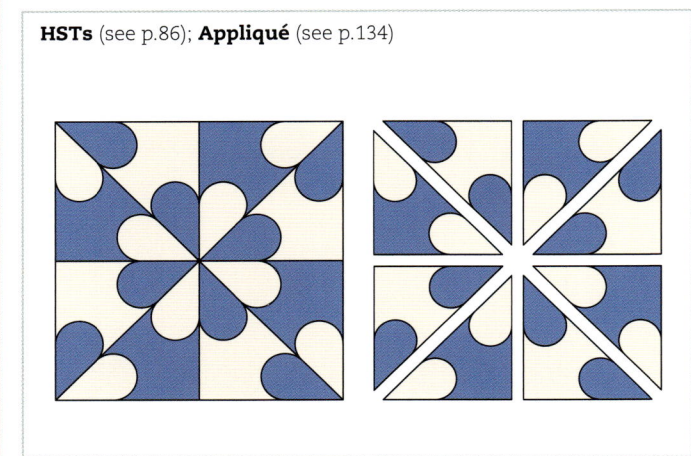

IDAHO STAR

Curved seams (see p.123); **Y-seams** (see p.123)

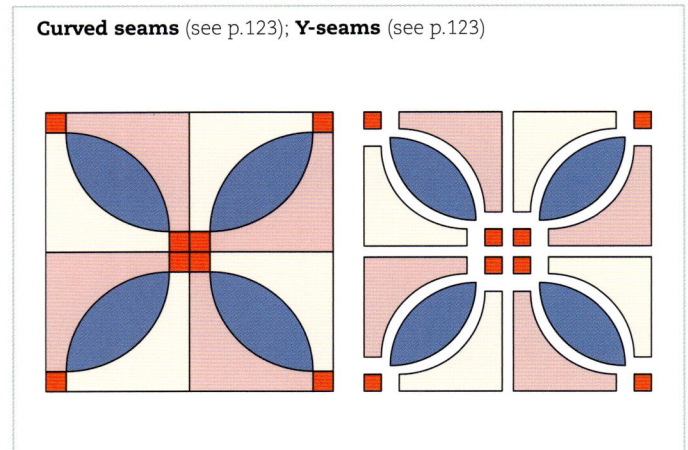

LEMOYNE STAR

Setting triangles (see p.95); **Diamonds** (see p.102); **Y-seams** (see p.123)

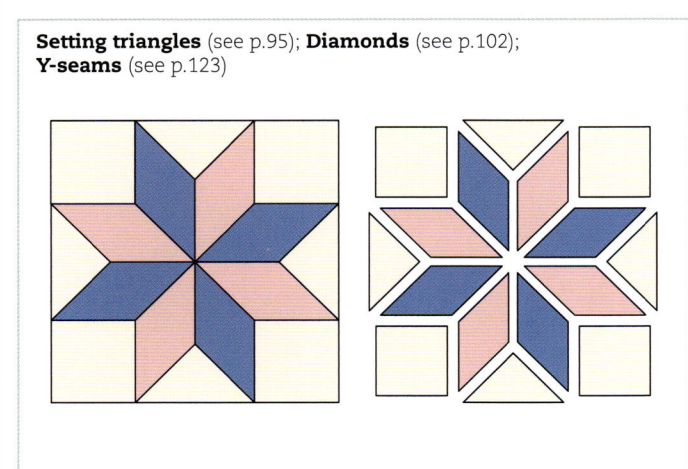

WEDDING RING

Curved seams (see p.123); **Y-seams** (see p.123)

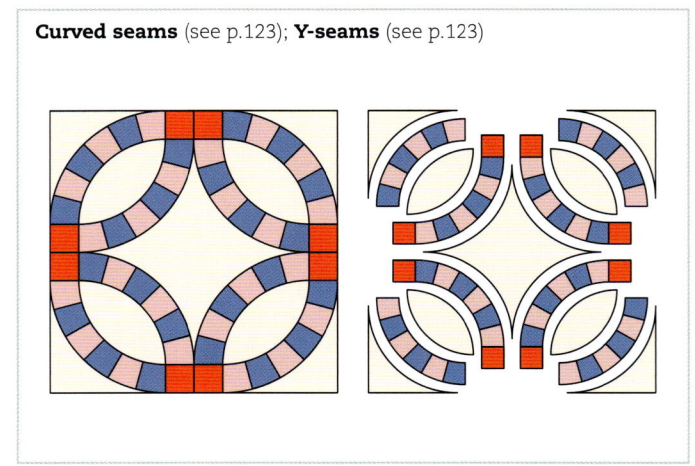

CLASSIC QUILT BLOCK GALLERY 277

ENGLISH PAPER PIECING

DRESDEN PLATE

EPP (see p.124); **Appliqué** (see p.134)

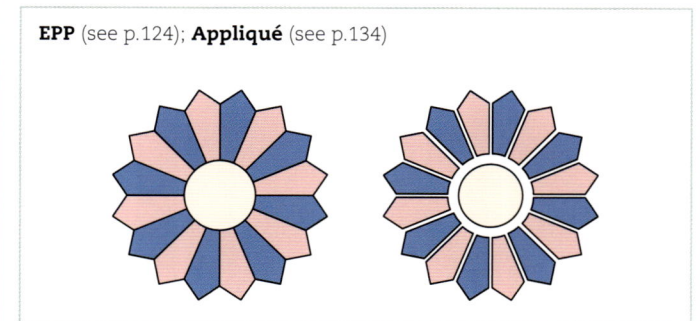

GRANDMOTHER'S FLOWER GARDEN

EPP (see p.124); **Hexagon** (see p.125)

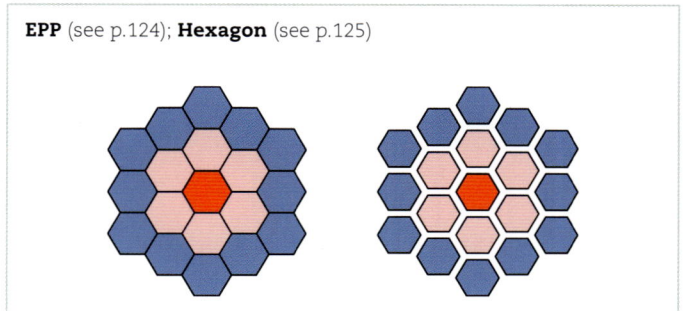

HALF HEXAGONS

EPP (see p.124); **Hexagon** (see p.125)

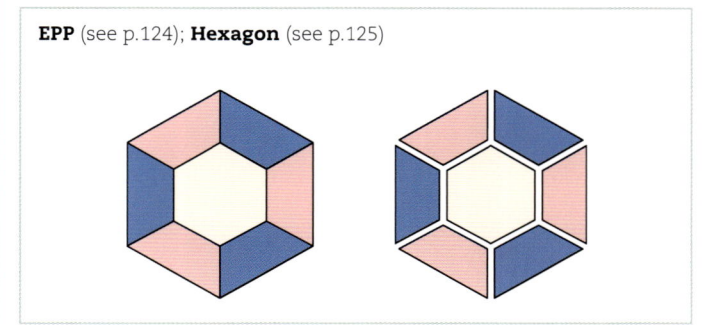

HEXAGON STAR

EPP (see p.124); **Hexagon** (see p.125); **Triangle** (see p.125)

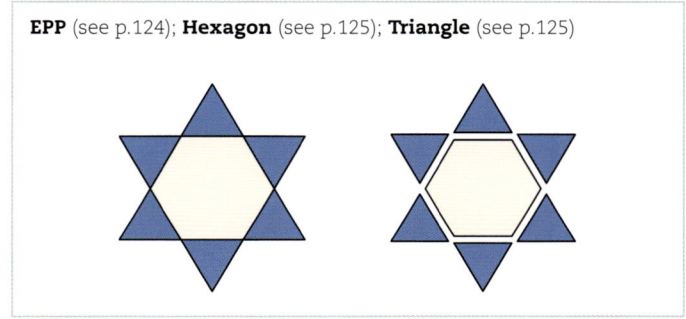

JEWEL HEART

EPP (see p.124); **Jewel** (see p.125)

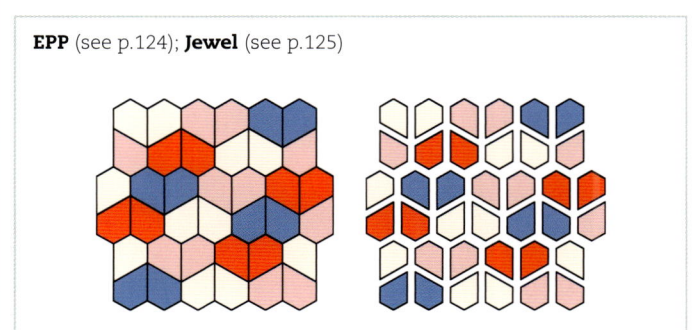

SIX POINTED STAR

EPP (see p.124); **Diamond** (see p.125)

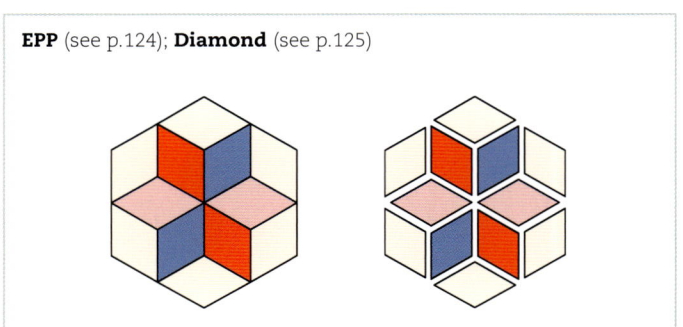

STAR BOUQUET

EPP (see p.124); **Hexagon** (see p.125); **Diamond** (see p.125); **Jewel** (see p.125)

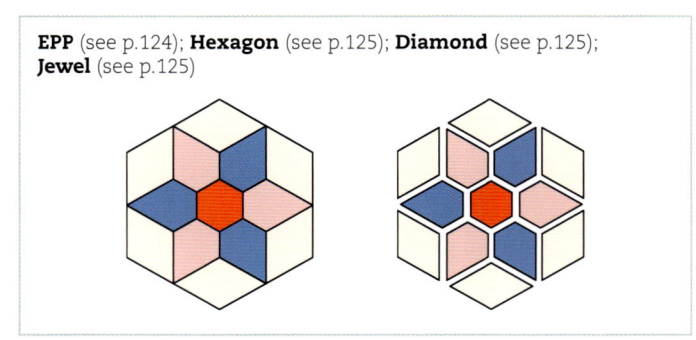

TUMBLING BLOCKS

EPP (see p.124); **Diamond** (see p.125)

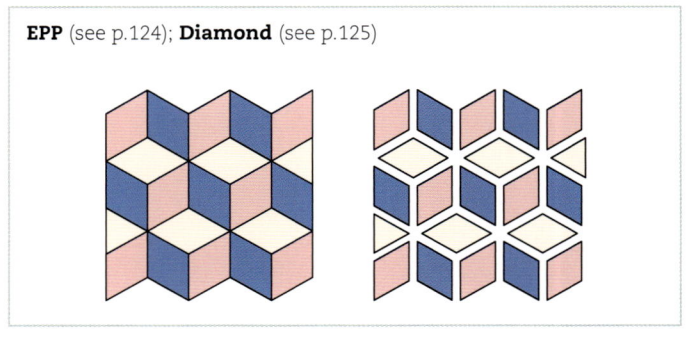

RESOURCES

Quilting charts

This section is designed to serve as a quick reference for essential conversions and calculations. Whether cutting pieces for common units, determining backing amounts, or calculating binding requirements, this collection of charts provides all of the information you need at a glance – saving time and reducing guesswork.

CONVERSIONS

Use these conversion charts to quickly convert between imperial and metric measurements as well as common fractions and decimals.

INCHES TO YARDAGE, CENTIMETRES, AND METRES			
Inches (in)	Yards (yd)	Centimetres (cm)	Metres (m)
4½	⅛	11.4	0.11
9	¼	22.9	0.23
12	⅓	30.5	0.30
13½	⅜	34.3	0.34
18	½	45.7	0.46
22½	⅝	57.2	0.57
24	⅔	61	0.61
27	¾	68.6	0.69
31½	⅞	80	0.80
36	1	91.4	0.91
54	1½	137.2	1.37
72	2	182.9	1.83
90	2½	228.6	2.29
108	3	274.3	2.74
126	3½	320	3.20
144	4	365.8	3.66
162	4½	411.5	4.11
180	5	457.2	4.57
216	6	548.6	5.49
252	7	640.1	6.40
288	8	731.5	7.32
324	9	823	8.23
360	10	914.4	9.14

Basic conversions: 1in = 2.5cm; 1cm = 0.01m.

FRACTIONS TO DECIMALS	
Fraction	Decimal
⅛	0.125
¼	0.25
⅓	0.33
⅜	0.375
½	0.50
⅝	0.625
⅔	0.67
¾	0.75
⅞	0.875

SEAM ALLOWANCE: INCHES TO MILLIMETRES	
Seam Allowance (in)	Millimetres (mm)
⅛	3.2
¼	6.4
⅜	9.5
½	12.7

CHOOSING A QUILT SIZE

Use this chart to quickly compare various quilt, wadding, and mattress sizes.

QUILT, WADDING, AND MATTRESS SIZES	Cot (US crib)	Single (US twin)	Double (US full)	King (US queen)	Super king (US king)
Suggested quilt size cm (in)	91 x 137cm (36 x 54in)	157 x 221cm* (62 x 87in)*	198 x 221cm* (78 x 87in)*	213 x 264cm** (84 x 104in)**	254 x 264cm** (100 x 104in)**
Quilt size range cm (in)	69–114 x 132–152cm (27–45 x 52–60in)	137–183 x 211–229cm (54–72 x 83–90in)	178–206 x 211–244cm (70–81 x 83–96in)	193–229 x 224–274cm (76–90 x 88–108in)	234–305 x 224–305cm (92–120 x 88–120in)
Packaged wadding size cm (in)	114 x 152cm (45 x 60in)	183 x 229cm (72 x 90in)	206 x 244cm (81 x 96in)	229 x 274cm (90 x 108in)	305 x 305cm (120 x 120in)
Mattress size cm (in)	70 x 140cm (27 x 52in)	90 x 190cm (38 x 75in)	137 x 191cm (54 x 75in)	150 x 200cm (60 x 80in)	180 x 200cm (76 x 80in)

***Suggested quilt size** allows for a 30.5cm (12in) drop on three sides.
****Suggested quilt size** allows for a 30.5cm (12in) drop on four sides.

CUTTING FROM A WOF STRIP

Use these charts to determine how many pieces of equal lengths can be sub-cut (see p.70) from a single WOF strip.

CUTS FROM A WOF STRIP (WHOLE MEASUREMENTS)		
Piece length cm (in)	# of pieces per WOF strip	Total length of pieces cm (in)
2.5 (1)	42	106.7 (42)
5.1 (2)	21	106.7 (42)
7.6 (3)	14	106.7 (42)
10.2 (4)	10	101.6 (40)
12.7 (5)	8	101.6 (40)
15.2 (6)	7	106.7 (42)
17.8 (7)	6	106.7 (42)
20.3 (8)	5	101.6 (40)
22.9 (9)	4	91.4 (36)
25.4 (10)	4	101.6 (40)
27.9 (11)	3	83.8 (33)
30.5 (12)	3	91.4 (36)
33 (13)	3	99.1 (39)
35.6 (14)	3	106.7 (42)
38.1 (15)	2	76.2 (30)
40.6 (16)	2	81.3 (32)
43.2 (17)	2	86.4 (34)
45.7 (18)	2	91.4 (36)
48.3 (19)	2	96.5 (38)
50.8 (20)	2	101.6 (40)
53.3 (21)	2	106.7 (42)

CUTS FROM A WOF STRIP (HALF MEASUREMENTS)		
Piece length cm (in)	# of pieces per WOF strip	Total length of pieces cm (in)
1.3 (½)	84	106.7 (42)
3.8 (1½)	28	106.7 (42)
6.4 (2½)	16	101.6 (40)
8.9 (3½)	12	106.7 (42)
11.4 (4½)	9	102.9 (40½)
14 (5½)	7	97.8 (38½)
16.5 (6½)	6	99.1 (39)
19.1 (7½)	5	95.3 (37½)
21.6 (8½)	4	86.4 (34)
24.1 (9½)	4	96.5 (38)
26.7 (10½)	4	106.7 (42)
29.2 (11½)	3	87.6 (34½)
31.8 (12½)	3	95.3 (37½)
34.3 (13½)	3	102.9 (40½)
36.8 (14½)	2	73.7 (29)
39.4 (15½)	2	78.7 (31)
41.9 (16½)	2	83.8 (33)
44.5 (17½)	2	88.9 (35)
47 (18½)	2	94 (37)
49.5 (19½)	2	99.1 (39)
52.1 (20½)	2	104.1 (41)

Piece width: Equal to the size of the WOF strip. **Piece length:** The measurement of a piece along the WOF.
# of pieces per WOF strip: The maximum number of **piece lengths** that can be cut from a single WOF strip. **WOF** is assumed to be 106.7cm (42in) wide.
Total length of pieces: Total *length* of the maximum number of **piece lengths** that can be cut from a single WOF strip.

CUTTING FROM YARDAGE AND METERAGE

Use this chart to determine the number of WOF strips that can be cut from a yard, metre, or fat quarter. For the maximum number of squares per yard, metre, or FQ, cut the maximum number of strips, then sub-cut (see p.70) each strip into squares.

STRIPS AND SQUARES IN A YARD, METRE, AND FQ						
	IN A YARD		IN A METRE		IN A FQ	
WOF strip cm (in)	Total # of strips	Total # of squares	Total # of strips	Total # of squares	Total # of strips	Total # of squares
1.3 (½)	72	6048	78	6552	42	1512
2.5 (1)	36	1512	39	1638	21	378
3.8 (1½)	24	672	26	728	14	168
5.1 (2)	18	378	19	399	10	90
6.4 (2½)	14	224	15	240	8	56
7.6 (3)	12	168	13	182	7	42
8.9 (3½)	10	120	11	132	6	30
10.2 (4)	9	90	9	90	5	20
11.4 (4½)	8	72	8	72	4	16
12.7 (5)	7	56	7	56	4	12
14 (5½)	6	42	7	49	3	9
15.2 (6)	6	42	6	42	3	9
16.5 (6½)	5	30	6	36	3	6
17.8 (7)	5	30	5	30	3	6
19.1 (7½)	4	20	5	25	2	4
20.3 (8)	4	20	4	20	2	4
21.6 (8½)	4	16	4	16	2	4
22.9 (9)	4	16	4	16	2	4
24.1 (9½)	3	12	4	16	2	2
25.4 (10)	3	12	3	12	2	2
26.7 (10½)	3	12	3	12	2	2
27.9 (11)	3	9	3	9	1	1
29.2 (11½)	3	9	3	9	1	1
30.5 (12)	3	9	3	9	1	1

WOF: Assumed to be 106.7cm (42in) wide.
Yard: 91.4cm (36in) long.
Metre: 100cm (39⅜in) long.
Fat quarter (FQ): Assumed to be 45.7 x 53.3cm (18 x 21in), with a **WOF** of 53.3cm (21in).

HALF-SQUARE TRIANGLES

Use this chart to determine the size of pieces to cut for making HSTs using the one, two, four, or eight at a time or strip tube techniques. For unit sizes not listed in this chart, use the provided formulas to calculate the required piece sizes.

TECHNIQUE		ONE AND TWO AT A TIME p.86	FOUR AT A TIME p.87	EIGHT AT A TIME p.88	STRIP TUBE* p.88	
FORMULA		Squares = finished size + 2.5cm (1in)	Squares = (unfinished size x 1.5) + 1.3cm (½in)	Squares = [finished size + 2.5cm (1in)] x 2	Strip width = (unfinished size ÷ √2) + 1.3cm (½in); round up to the nearest 6.4mm (¼in)	
Finished size cm (in)	Unfinished size cm (in)	Cut (2) squares cm (in)	Cut (2) squares cm (in)	Cut (2) squares cm (in)	Cut (2) WOF strips cm (in)	HSTs per strip tube
5.1 x 5.1 (2 x 2)	6.4 x 6.4 (2½ x 2½)	7.6 x 7.6 (3 x 3)	10.8 x 10.8 (4¼ x 4¼)	15.2 x 15.2 (6 x 6)	6.4 (2½)	20
6.4 x 6.4 (2½ x 2½)	7.6 x 7.6 (3 x 3)	8.9 x 8.9 (3½ x 3½)	12.7 x 12.7 (5 x 5)	17.8 x 17.8 (7 x 7)	7 (2¾)	16
7.6 x 7.6 (3 x 3)	8.9 x 8.9 (3½ x 3½)	10.2 x 10.2 (4 x 4)	14.6 x 14.6 (5¾ x 5¾)	20.3 x 20.3 (8 x 8)	8.3 (3¼)	14
8.9 x 8.9 (3½ x 3½)	10.2 x 10.2 (4 x 4)	11.4 x 11.4 (4½ x 4½)	16.5 x 16.5 (6½ x 6½)	22.9 x 22.9 (9 x 9)	8.9 (3½)	12
10.2 x 10.2 (4 x 4)	11.4 x 11.4 (4½ x 4½)	12.7 x 12.7 (5 x 5)	18.4 x 18.4 (7¼ x 7¼)	25.4 x 25.4 (10 x 10)	9.5 (3¾)	11
11.4 x 11.4 (4½ x 4½)	12.7 x 12.7 (5 x 5)	14 x 14 (5½ x 5½)	20.3 x 20.3 (8 x 8)	27.9 x 27.9 (11 x 11)	10.8 (4¼)	10
12.7 x 12.7 (5 x 5)	14 x 14 (5½ x 5½)	15.2 x 15.2 (6 x 6)	22.2 x 22.2 (8¾ x 8¾)	30.5 x 30.5 (12 x 12)	11.4 (4½)	9
14 x 14 (5½ x 5½)	15.2 x 15.2 (6 x 6)	16.5 x 16.5 (6½ x 6½)	24.1 x 24.1 (9½ x 9½)	33 x 33 (13 x 13)	12.7 (5)	8
15.2 x 15.2 (6 x 6)	16.5 x 16.5 (6½ x 6½)	17.8 x 17.8 (7 x 7)	26 x 26 (10¼ x 10¼)	35.6 x 35.6 (14 x 14)	13.3 (5¼)	7
16.5 x 16.5 (6½ x 6½)	17.8 x 17.8 (7 x 7)	19.1 x 19.1 (7½ x 7½)	27.9 x 27.9 (11 x 11)	38.1 x 38.1 (15 x 15)	14.6 (5¾)	7
17.8 x 17.8 (7 x 7)	19.1 x 19.1 (7½ x 7½)	20.3 x 20.3 (8 x 8)	29.8 x 29.8 (11¾ x 11¾)	40.6 x 40.6 (16 x 16)	15.2 (6)	6
19.1 x 19.1 (7½ x 7½)	20.3 x 20.3 (8 x 8)	21.6 x 21.6 (8½ x 8½)	31.8 x 31.8 (12½ x 12½)	43.2 x 43.2 (17 x 17)	16.5 (6½)	6
20.3 x 20.3 (8 x 8)	21.6 x 21.6 (8½ x 8½)	22.9 x 22.9 (9 x 9)	33.7 x 33.7 (13¼ x 13¼)	45.7 x 45.7 (18 x 18)	17.2 (6¾)	5
21.6 x 21.6 (8½ x 8½)	22.9 x 22.9 (9 x 9)	24.1 x 24.1 (9½ x 9½)	35.6 x 35.6 (14 x 14)	48.3 x 48.3 (19 x 19)	17.8 (7)	5
22.9 x 22.9 (9 x 9)	24.1 x 24.1 (9½ x 9½)	25.4 x 25.4 (10 x 10)	37.5 x 37.5 (14¾ x 14¾)	50.8 x 50.8 (20 x 20)	19.1 (7½)	5
24.1 x 24.1 (9½ x 9½)	25.4 x 25.4 (10 x 10)	26.7 x 26.7 (10½ x 10½)	39.4 x 39.4 (15½ x 15½)	53.3 x 53.3 (21 x 21)	19.7 (7¾)	4
25.4 x 25.4 (10 x 10)	26.7 x 26.7 (10½ x 10½)	27.9 x 27.9 (11 x 11)	41.3 x 41.3 (16¼ x 16¼)	55.9 x 55.9 (22 x 22)	20.3 (8)	4

*The strip tube technique does not require trimming.
Finished size: The size of the HST after it has been sewn into the quilt top.
Unfinished size: The size of the HST plus 6.4mm (¼in) seam allowance on all sides. HSTs must be trimmed to this size unless otherwise noted.
Squares: The size of the pieces before assembly.
WOF strips: The size of the WOF strips before cutting. **WOF** is assumed to be 106.7cm (42in) wide.

QUARTER-SQUARE TRIANGLES

Use this chart to determine the size of pieces to cut for making QSTs using the one or two at a time techniques or for making split QSTs. For unit sizes not listed in this chart, use the provided formulas to calculate the required piece sizes.

TECHNIQUE			ONE AT A TIME p.90	TWO AT A TIME* p.90		SPLIT QSTs* p.91	
FORMULA		Centre point = unfinished size ÷ 2	Squares = finished size + 3.8cm (1½in)	Use the **starting squares** to make two HSTs. Trim the HSTs to the size listed. **Squares** = finished size + 5.1cm (2in)		Use the two at a time **starting squares** to make one unfinished HST. Trim the HST to the size listed. **Unfinished HST** and **square** = unfinished size + 2.5cm (1in)	
Finished size cm (in)	Unfinished size cm (in)	Centre point cm (in)	Cut (4) squares cm (in)	Cut (2) starting squares* cm (in)	HST trimming size* cm (in)	Make (1) unfinished HST* cm (in)	Cut (1) square cm (in)
5.1 x 5.1 (2 x 2)	6.4 x 6.4 (2½ x 2½)	3.2 (1¼)	8.9 x 8.9 (3½ x 3½)	10.2 x 10.2 (4 x 4)	8.9 x 8.9 (3½ x 3½)	8.9 x 8.9 (3½ x 3½)	8.9 x 8.9 (3½ x 3½)
6.4 x 6.4 (2½ x 2½)	7.6 x 7.6 (3 x 3)	3.8 (1½)	10.2 x 10.2 (4 x 4)	11.4 x 11.4 (4½ x 4½)	10.2 x 10.2 (4 x 4)	10.2 x 10.2 (4 x 4)	10.2 x 10.2 (4 x 4)
7.6 x 7.6 (3 x 3)	8.9 x 8.9 (3½ x 3½)	4.4 (1¾)	11.4 x 11.4 (4½ x 4½)	12.7 x 12.7 (5 x 5)	11.4 x 11.4 (4½ x 4½)	11.4 x 11.4 (4½ x 4½)	11.4 x 11.4 (4½ x 4½)
8.9 x 8.9 (3½ x 3½)	10.2 x 10.2 (4 x 4)	5.1 (2)	12.7 x 12.7 (5 x 5)	14 x 14 (5½ x 5½)	12.7 x 12.7 (5 x 5)	12.7 x 12.7 (5 x 5)	12.7 x 12.7 (5 x 5)
10.2 x 10.2 (4 x 4)	11.4 x 11.4 (4½ x 4½)	5.7 (2¼)	14 x 14 (5½ x 5½)	15.2 x 15.2 (6 x 6)	14 x 14 (5½ x 5½)	14 x 14 (5½ x 5½)	14 x 14 (5½ x 5½)
11.4 x 11.4 (4½ x 4½)	12.7 x 12.7 (5 x 5)	6.4 (2½)	15.2 x 15.2 (6 x 6)	16.5 x 16.5 (6½ x 6½)	15.2 x 15.2 (6 x 6)	15.2 x 15.2 (6 x 6)	15.2 x 15.2 (6 x 6)
12.7 x 12.7 (5 x 5)	14 x 14 (5½ x 5½)	7 (2¾)	16.5 x 16.5 (6½ x 6½)	17.8 x 17.8 (7 x 7)	16.5 x 16.5 (6½ x 6½)	16.5 x 16.5 (6½ x 6½)	16.5 x 16.5 (6½ x 6½)
14 x 14 (5½ x 5½)	15.2 x 15.2 (6 x 6)	7.6 (3)	17.8 x 17.8 (7 x 7)	19.1 x 19.1 (7½ x 7½)	17.8 x 17.8 (7 x 7)	17.8 x 17.8 (7 x 7)	17.8 x 17.8 (7 x 7)
15.2 x 15.2 (6 x 6)	16.5 x 16.5 (6½ x 6½)	8.3 (3¼)	19.1 x 19.1 (7½ x 7½)	20.3 x 20.3 (8 x 8)	19.1 x 19.1 (7½ x 7½)	19.1 x 19.1 (7½ x 7½)	19.1 x 19.1 (7½ x 7½)
16.5 x 16.5 (6½ x 6½)	17.8 x 17.8 (7 x 7)	8.9 (3½)	20.3 x 20.3 (8 x 8)	21.6 x 21.6 (8½ x 8½)	20.3 x 20.3 (8 x 8)	20.3 x 20.3 (8 x 8)	20.3 x 20.3 (8 x 8)
17.8 x 17.8 (7 x 7)	19.1 x 19.1 (7½ x 7½)	9.5 (3¾)	21.6 x 21.6 (8½ x 8½)	22.9 x 22.9 (9 x 9)	21.6 x 21.6 (8½ x 8½)	21.6 x 21.6 (8½ x 8½)	21.6 x 21.6 (8½ x 8½)
19.1 x 19.1 (7½ x 7½)	20.3 x 20.3 (8 x 8)	10.2 (4)	22.9 x 22.9 (9 x 9)	24.1 x 24.1 (9½ x 9½)	22.9 x 22.9 (9 x 9)	22.9 x 22.9 (9 x 9)	22.9 x 22.9 (9 x 9)
20.3 x 20.3 (8 x 8)	21.6 x 21.6 (8½ x 8½)	10.8 (4¼)	24.1 x 24.1 (9½ x 9½)	25.4 x 25.4 (10 x 10)	24.1 x 24.1 (9½ x 9½)	24.1 x 24.1 (9½ x 9½)	24.1 x 24.1 (9½ x 9½)
21.6 x 21.6 (8½ x 8½)	22.9 x 22.9 (9 x 9)	11.4 (4½)	25.4 x 25.4 (10 x 10)	26.7 x 26.7 (10½ x 10½)	25.4 x 25.4 (10 x 10)	25.4 x 25.4 (10 x 10)	25.4 x 25.4 (10 x 10)
22.9 x 22.9 (9 x 9)	24.1 x 24.1 (9½ x 9½)	12.1 (4¾)	26.7 x 26.7 (10½ x 10½)	27.9 x 27.9 (11 x 11)	26.7 x 26.7 (10½ x 10½)	26.7 x 26.7 (10½ x 10½)	26.7 x 26.7 (10½ x 10½)
24.1 x 24.1 (9½ x 9½)	25.4 x 25.4 (10 x 10)	12.7 (5)	27.9 x 27.9 (11 x 11)	29.2 x 29.2 (11½ x 11½)	27.9 x 27.9 (11 x 11)	27.9 x 27.9 (11 x 11)	27.9 x 27.9 (11 x 11)
25.4 x 25.4 (10 x 10)	26.7 x 26.7 (10½ x 10½)	13.3 (5¼)	29.2 x 29.2 (11½ x 11½)	30.5 x 30.5 (12 x 12)	29.2 x 29.2 (11½ x 11½)	29.2 x 29.2 (11½ x 11½)	29.2 x 29.2 (11½ x 11½)

*Use **starting squares** to make HSTs first before making QSTs. The HSTs must be trimmed to the listed size.
Finished size: The size of the QST after it has been sewn into the quilt top.
Unfinished size: The size of the QST plus 6.4mm (¼in) seam allowance on all sides. QSTs must be trimmed to this size.
Centre point: A measurement to mark the centre of the QST for trimming.
Square(s): The size of the piece(s) before assembly.

FLYING GEESE

Use this chart to determine the size of pieces to cut for making FG using either the one or four at a time technique. For unit sizes not listed in this chart, use the provided formulas to calculate the required piece sizes.

TECHNIQUE			ONE AT A TIME* p.92		FOUR AT A TIME p.93	
FORMULA		Vertical centre = unfinished *length* ÷ 2	Rectangle = unfinished *width* by unfinished *length* Small squares = unfinished *width*		Large square = unfinished *length* + 3.8cm (1¼in) Small squares = unfinished *width* + 1.9cm (¾in)	
Finished size cm (in)	Unfinished size cm (in)	Vertical centre cm (in)	Cut (1) rectangle cm (in)	Cut (2) small squares cm (in)	Cut (1) large square cm (in)	Cut (4) small squares cm (in)
2.5 x 5.1 (1 x 2)	3.8 x 6.4 (1½ x 2½)	3.2 (1¼)	3.8 x 6.4 (1½ x 2½)	3.8 x 3.8 (1½ x 1½)	9.5 x 9.5 (3¾ x 3¾)	5.7 x 5.7 (2¼ x 2¼)
3.8 x 7.6 (1½ x 3)	5.1 x 8.9 (2 x 3½)	4.4 (1¾)	5.1 x 8.9 (2 x 3½)	5.1 x 5.1 (2 x 2)	12.1 x 12.1 (4¾ x 4¾)	7 x 7 (2¾ x 2¾)
5.1 x 10.2 (2 x 4)	6.4 x 11.4 (2½ x 4½)	5.7 (2¼)	6.4 x 11.4 (2½ x 4½)	6.4 x 6.4 (2½ x 2½)	14.6 x 14.6 (5¾ x 5¾)	8.3 x 8.3 (3¼ x 3¼)
6.4 x 12.7 (2½ x 5)	7.6 x 14 (3 x 5½)	7.1 (2¾)	7.6 x 14 (3 x 5½)	7.6 x 7.6 (3 x 3)	17.1 x 17.1 (6¾ x 6¾)	9.5 x 9.5 (3¾ x 3¾)
7.6 x 15.2 (3 x 6)	8.9 x 16.5 (3½ x 6½)	8.3 (3¼)	8.9 x 16.5 (3½ x 6½)	8.9 x 8.9 (3½ x 3½)	19.7 x 19.7 (7¾ x 7¾)	10.8 x 10.8 (4¼ x 4¼)
8.9 x 17.8 (3½ x 7)	10.2 x 19.1 (4 x 7½)	9.5 (3¾)	10.2 x 19.1 (4 x 7½)	10.2 x 10.2 (4 x 4)	22.2 x 22.2 (8¾ x 8¾)	12.1 x 12.1 (4¾ x 4¾)
10.2 x 20.3 (4 x 8)	11.4 x 21.6 (4½ x 8½)	10.8 (4¼)	11.4 x 21.6 (4½ x 8½)	11.4 x 11.4 (4½ x 4½)	24.8 x 24.8 (9¾ x 9¾)	13.3 x 13.3 (5¼ x 5¼)
11.4 x 22.9 (4½ x 9)	12.7 x 24.1 (5 x 9½)	12.1 (4¾)	12.7 x 24.1 (5 x 9½)	12.7 x 12.7 (5 x 5)	27.3 x 27.3 (10¾ x 10¾)	14.6 x 14.6 (5¾ x 5¾)
12.7 x 25.4 (5 x 10)	14 x 26.7 (5½ x 10½)	13.3 (5¼)	14 x 26.7 (5½ x 10½)	14 x 14 (5½ x 5½)	29.8 x 29.8 (11¾ x 11¾)	15.9 x 15.9 (6¼ x 6¼)
14 x 27.9 (5½ x 11)	15.2 x 29.2 (6 x 11½)	14.6 (5¾)	15.2 x 29.2 (6 x 11½)	15.2 x 15.2 (6 x 6)	32.4 x 32.4 (12¾ x 12¾)	17.1 x 17.1 (6¾ x 6¾)
15.2 x 30.5 (6 x 12)	16.5 x 31.8 (6½ x 12½)	15.9 (6¼)	16.5 x 31.8 (6½ x 12½)	16.5 x 16.5 (6½ x 6½)	34.9 x 34.9 (13¾ x 13¾)	18.4 x 18.4 (7¼ x 7¼)
16.5 x 33 (6½ x 13)	17.8 x 34.3 (7 x 13½)	17.1 (6¾)	17.8 x 34.3 (7 x 13½)	17.8 x 17.8 (7 x 7)	37.5 x 37.5 (14¾ x 14¾)	19.7 x 19.7 (7¾ x 7¾)
17.8 x 35.6 (7 x 14)	19.1 x 36.8 (7½ x 14½)	18.4 (7¼)	19.1 x 36.8 (7½ x 14½)	19.1 x 19.1 (7½ x 7½)	40 x 40 (15¾ x 15¾)	21 x 21 (8¼ x 8¼)
19 x 38.1 7½ x 15	20.3 x 39.4 (8 x 15½)	19.7 (7¾)	20.3 x 39.4 (8 x 15½)	20.3 x 20.3 (8 x 8)	42.5 x 42.5 (16¾ x 16¾)	22.2 x 22.2 (8¾ x 8¾)
20.3 x 40.6 (8 x 16)	21.6 x 41.2 (8½ x 16½)	21 (8¼)	21.6 x 41.2 (8½ x 16½)	21.6 x 21.6 (8½ x 8½)	45.1 x 45.1 (17¾ x 17¾)	23.5 x 23.5 (9¼ x 9¼)

*The one at a time technique does not require trimming.
Finished size: The size of the FG after it has been sewn into the quilt top.
Unfinished size: The size of the FG plus 6.4mm (¼in) seam allowance on all sides. FG must be trimmed to this size unless otherwise noted.
Vertical centre: A measurement to mark the centre point of the FG for trimming.
Rectangles and **squares:** The size of the pieces before assembly.

SQUARE IN A SQUARE

Use this chart to determine the size of pieces to cut for making square in a square units using either the stitch and flip or setting triangles technique. For unit sizes not listed in this chart, use the provided formulas to calculate the required piece sizes.

TECHNIQUE			STITCH AND FLIP* p.94		SETTING TRIANGLES p.95	
FORMULA		Centre measurement = unfinished size ÷ 2	Large square = unfinished size Small squares = (unfinished size ÷ 2) + 6.4mm (¼in)		Cut two **small squares** in half diagonally to make four total triangles.	
Finished size cm (in)	**Unfinished size** cm (in)	Centre measurement cm (in)	Cut (1) large square cm (in)	Cut (4) small squares cm (in)	Cut (1) centre square cm (in)	Cut (2) small squares cm (in)
5.1 x 5.1 (2 x 2)	6.4 x 6.4 (2½ x 2½)	3.2 (1¼)	6.4 x 6.4 (2½ x 2½)	3.8 x 3.8 (1½ x 1½)	4.8 x 4.8 (1⅞ x 1⅞)	5.1 x 5.1 (2 x 2)
6.4 x 6.4 (2½ x 2½)	7.6 x 7.6 (3 x 3)	3.8 (1½)	7.6 x 7.6 (3 x 3)	4.4 x 4.4 (1¾ x 1¾)	5.4 x 5.4 (2⅛ x 2⅛)	5.7 x 5.7 (2¼ x 2¼)
7.6 x 7.6 (3 x 3)	8.9 x 8.9 (3½ x 3½)	4.4 (1¾)	8.9 x 8.9 (3½ x 3½)	5.1 x 5.1 (2 x 2)	6.7 x 6.7 (2⅝ x 2⅝)	6.4 x 6.4 (2½ x 2½)
8.9 x 8.9 (3½ x 3½)	10.2 x 10.2 (4 x 4)	5.1 (2)	10.2 x 10.2 (4 x 4)	5.7 x 5.7 (2¼ x 2¼)	7.6 x 7.6 (3 x 3)	7 x 7 (2¾ x 2¾)
10.2 x 10.2 (4 x 4)	11.4 x 11.4 (4½ x 4½)	5.7 (2¼)	11.4 x 11.4 (4½ x 4½)	6.4 x 6.4 (2½ x 2½)	8.6 x 8.6 (3⅜ x 3⅜)	7.6 x 7.6 (3 x 3)
11.4 x 11.4 (4½ x 4½)	12.7 x 12.7 (5 x 5)	6.4 (2½)	12.7 x 12.7 (5 x 5)	7 x 7 (2¾ x 2¾)	9.2 x 9.2 (3⅝ x 3⅝)	8.3 x 8.3 (3¼ x 3¼)
12.7 x 12.7 (5 x 5)	14 x 14 (5½ x 5½)	7 (2¾)	14 x 14 (5½ x 5½)	7.6 x 7.6 (3 x 3)	10.2 x 10.2 (4 x 4)	8.9 x 8.9 (3½ x 3½)
14 x 14 (5½ x 5½)	15.2 x 15.2 (6 x 6)	7.6 (3)	15.2 x 15.2 (6 x 6)	8.3 x 8.3 (3¼ x 3¼)	11.1 x 11.1 (4⅜ x 4⅜)	9.5 x 9.5 (3¾ x 3¾)
15.2 x 15.2 (6 x 6)	16.5 x 16.5 (6½ x 6½)	8.3 (3¼)	16.5 x 16.5 (6½ x 6½)	8.9 x 8.9 (3½ x 3½)	12.1 x 12.1 (4¾ x 4¾)	10.2 x 10.2 (4 x 4)
16.5 x 16.5 (6½ x 6½)	17.8 x 17.8 (7 x 7)	8.9 (3½)	17.8 x 17.8 (7 x 7)	9.5 x 9.5 (3¾ x 3¾)	13 x 13 (5⅛ x 5⅛)	10.8 x 10.8 (4¼ x 4¼)
17.8 x 17.8 (7 x 7)	19.1 x 19.1 (7½ x 7½)	9.5 (3¾)	19.1 x 19.1 (7½ x 7½)	10.2 x 10.2 (4 x 4)	14 x 14 (5½ x 5½)	11.4 x 11.4 (4½ x 4½)
19.1 x 19.1 (7½ x 7½)	20.3 x 20.3 (8 x 8)	10.2 (4)	20.3 x 20.3 (8 x 8)	10.8 x 10.8 (4¼ x 4¼)	14.6 x 14.6 (5¾ x 5¾)	12.1 x 12.1 (4¾ x 4¾)
20.3 x 20.3 (8 x 8)	21.6 x 21.6 (8½ x 8½)	10.8 (4¼)	21.6 x 21.6 (8½ x 8½)	11.4 x 11.4 (4½ x 4½)	15.6 x 15.6 (6⅛ x 6⅛)	12.7 x 12.7 (5 x 5)
21.6 x 21.6 (8½ x 8½)	22.9 x 22.9 (9 x 9)	11.4 (4½)	22.9 x 22.9 (9 x 9)	12.1 x 12.1 (4¾ x 4¾)	16.5 x 16.5 (6½ x 6½)	13.3 x 13.3 (5¼ x 5¼)
22.9 x 22.9 (9 x 9)	24.1 x 24.1 (9½ x 9½)	12.1 (4¾)	24.1 x 24.1 (9½ x 9½)	12.7 x 12.7 (5 x 5)	17.5 x 17.5 (6⅞ x 6⅞)	14 x 14 (5½ x 5½)
24.1 x 24.1 (9½ x 9½)	25.4 x 25.4 (10 x 10)	12.7 (5)	25.4 x 25.4 (10 x 10)	13.3 x 13.3 (5¼ x 5¼)	18.4 x 18.4 (7¼ x 7¼)	14.6 x 14.6 (5¾ x 5¾)
25.4 x 25.4 (10 x 10)	26.7 x 26.7 (10½ x 10½)	13.3 (5¼)	26.7 x 26.7 (10½ x 10½)	14 x 14 (5½ x 5½)	19.4 x 19.4 (7⅝ x 7⅝)	15.2 x 15.2 (6 x 6)

*The stitch and flip technique does not require trimming.
Finished size: The size of the square in a square unit after it has been sewn into the quilt top.
Unfinished size: The size of the square in a square unit plus 6.4mm (¼in) seam allowance on all sides. Units must be trimmed to this size unless otherwise noted.
Centre measurement: A measurement to mark the vertical and horizontal centre of the square in a square unit for trimming.
Squares: The size of the pieces before assembly.

HALF-RECTANGLE TRIANGLES

Use this chart to determine the size of pieces to cut for making HRTs using either the one or two at a time technique. Keep in mind that HRTs either have a 1:2 or 2:3 width-to-length ratio. For unit sizes not listed in this chart, use the provided formulas to calculate the required piece sizes.

HALF-RECTANGLE TRIANGLES WITH A 1:2 RATIO

TECHNIQUE		ONE AT A TIME p.97	TWO AT A TIME p.97
FORMULA		Rectangles = [finished *width* + 2.5cm (1in)] by [finished *length* + 5.1cm (2in)]	Rectangles = [finished *width* + 3.2cm (1¼in)] by [finished *length* + 3.8cm (1½in)]
Finished size cm (in)	Unfinished size cm (in)	Cut (2) rectangles cm (in)	Cut (2) rectangles cm (in)
2.5 x 5.1 (1 x 2)	3.8 x 6.4 (1½ x 2½)	5.1 x 10.2 (2 x 4)	5.7 x 8.9 (2¼ x 3½)
3.8 x 7.6 (1½ x 3)	5.1 x 8.9 (2 x 3½)	6.4 x 12.7 (2½ x 5)	7 x 11.4 (2¾ x 4½)
5.1 x 10.2 (2 x 4)	6.4 x 11.4 (2½ x 4½)	7.6 x 15.2 (3 x 6)	8.3 x 14 (3¼ x 5½)
6.4 x 12.7 (2½ x 5)	7.6 x 14 (3 x 5½)	8.9 x 17.8 (3½ x 7)	9.5 x 16.5 (3¾ x 6½)
7.6 x 15.2 (3 x 6)	8.9 x 16.5 (3½ x 6½)	10.2 x 20.3 (4 x 8)	10.8 x 19.1 (4¼ x 7½)
8.9 x 17.8 (3½ x 7)	10.2 x 19.1 (4 x 7½)	11.4 x 22.9 (4½ x 9)	12.1 x 21.6 (4¾ x 8½)
10.2 x 20.3 (4 x 8)	11.4 x 21.6 (4½ x 8½)	12.7 x 25.4 (5 x 10)	13.3 x 24.1 (5¼ x 9½)
11.4 x 22.9 (4½ x 9)	12.7 x 24.1 (5 x 9½)	14 x 27.9 (5½ x 11)	14.6 x 26.7 (5¾ x 10½)
12.7 x 25.4 (5 x 10)	14 x 26.7 (5½ x 10½)	15.2 x 30.5 (6 x 12)	15.9 x 29.2 (6¼ x 11½)
14 x 27.9 (5½ x 11)	15.2 x 29.2 (6 x 11½)	16.5 x 33 (6½ x 13)	17.1 x 31.8 (6¾ x 12½)
15.2 x 30.5 (6 x 12)	16.5 x 31.8 (6½ x 12½)	17.8 x 35.6 (7 x 14)	18.4 x 34.3 (7¼ x 13½)
16.5 x 33 (6½ x 13)	17.8 x 34.3 (7 x 13½)	19.1 x 38.1 (7½ x 15)	19.7 x 36.7 (7¾ x 14½)
17.8 x 35.6 (7 x 14)	19.1 x 36.8 (7½ x 14½)	20.3 x 40.6 (8 x 16)	21 x 39.4 (8¼ x 15½)
19 x 38.1 (7½ x 15)	20.3 x 39.4 (8 x 15½)	21.6 x 43.2 (8½ x 17)	22.2 x 41.9 (8¾ x 16½)
20.3 x 40.6 (8 x 16)	21.6 x 41.2 (8½ x 16½)	22.9 x 45.7 (9 x 18)	23.5 x 44.5 (9¼ x 17½)

HALF-RECTANGLE TRIANGLES WITH A 2:3 RATIO

TECHNIQUE		ONE AT A TIME p.97	TWO AT A TIME p.97
FORMULA		Rectangles = [finished *width* + 3.2cm (1¼in)] by [finished *length* + 5.1cm (2in)]	Rectangles = [finished *width* + 3.8cm (1½in)] by [finished *length* + 3.8cm (1½in)]
Finished size cm (in)	Unfinished size cm (in)	Cut (2) rectangles cm (in)	Cut (2) rectangles cm (in)
2.5 x 3.8 (1 x 1½)	3.8 x 5.1 (1½ x 2)	5.7 x 8.9 (2¼ x 3½)	6.4 x 7.6 (2½ x 3)
3.8 x 5.7 (1½ x 2¼)	5.1 x 7 (2 x 2¾)	7 x 10.8 (2¾ x 4¼)	7.6 x 9.5 (3 x 3¾)
5.1 x 7.6 (2 x 3)	6.4 x 8.9 (2½ x 3½)	8.3 x 12.7 (3¼ x 5)	8.3 x 11.4 (3¼ x 4½)
6.4 x 9.5 (2½ x 3¾)	7.6 x 10.8 (3 x 4¼)	9.5 x 14.6 (3¾ x 5¾)	9.5 x 13.3 (3¾ x 5¼)
7.6 x 11.4 (3 x 4½)	8.9 x 12.7 (3½ x 5)	10.8 x 16.5 (4¼ x 6½)	11.4 x 15.2 (4½ x 6)
8.9 x 13.3 (3½ x 5¼)	10.2 x 14.6 (4 x 5¾)	12.1 x 18.4 (4¾ x 7¼)	12.7 x 17.1 (5 x 6¾)
10.2 x 15.2 (4 x 6)	11.4 x 16.5 (4½ x 6½)	13.3 x 20.3 (5¼ x 8)	14 x 19.1 (8.9 x 12.7)
11.4 x 17.1 (4½ x 6¾)	12.7 x 18.4 (5 x 7¼)	14.6 x 22.2 (5¾ x 8¾)	15.2 x 21 (6 x 8¼)
12.7 x 19.1 (5 x 7½)	14 x 20.3 (5½ x 8)	15.9 x 24.1 (6¼ x 9½)	16.5 x 22.9 (6½ x 9)
14 x 21 (5½ x 8¼)	15.2 x 22.2 (6 x 8¾)	17.1 x 26 (6¾ x 10¼)	17.8 x 24.8 (7 x 9¾)
15.2 x 22.9 (6 x 9)	16.5 x 24.1 (6½ x 9½)	18.4 x 27.9 (7¼ x 11)	19.1 x 26.7 (7½ x 10½)
16.5 x 24.8 (6½ x 9¾)	17.8 x 26 (7 x 10¼)	19.7 x 29.9 (7¾ x 11¾)	20.32 x 26 (8 x 10¼)
17.8 x 26.7 (7 x 10½)	19.1 x 27.9 (7½ x 11)	21 x 31.8 (8½ x 12½)	21.6 x 31 (8½ x 12¼)
19.1 x 28.6 (7½ x 11¼)	20.32 x 29.9 (8 x 11¾)	22.2 x 33.7 (8¾ x 13¼)	22.9 x 32.4 (9 x 12¾)
20.32 x 30.5 (8 x 12)	21.6 x 31.8 (8½ x 12½)	23.5 x 35.6 (9¼ x 14)	24.1 x 34.3 (9½ x 13½)

Ratio: The *width*-to-*length* proportion of the HRT.
Finished size: The size of the HRT after it has been sewn into the quilt top.
Unfinished size: The size of the HRT plus 6.4mm (¼in) seam allowance on all sides. HRTs must be trimmed to this size.
Rectangles: The size of the pieces before assembly.

TRIANGLE IN A SQUARE

Use this chart to determine the size of pieces to cut for making triangle in a square units. For unit sizes not listed in this chart, use the provided formulas to calculate the required piece sizes.

TECHNIQUE			TRIANGLE IN A SQUARE p.99
FORMULA		Vertical centre = unfinished *width* ÷ 2	Rectangles = [unfinished *width* + 1.3cm (½in)] by [unfinished *length* + 3.8cm (1½in)]
Finished size cm (in)	**Unfinished size** cm (in)	**Vertical centre** cm (in)	**Cut (2) rectangles** cm (in)
5.1 x 5.1 (2 x 2)	6.4 x 6.4 (2½ x 2½)	3.2 (1¼)	7.6 x 10.2 (3 x 4)
6.4 x 6.4 (2½ x 2½)	7.6 x 7.6 (3 x 3)	3.8 (1½)	8.9 x 11.4 (3½ x 4½)
7.6 x 7.6 (3 x 3)	8.9 x 8.9 (3½ x 3½)	4.4 (1¾)	10.2 x 12.7 (4 x 5)
8.9 x 8.9 (3½ x 3½)	10.2 x 10.2 (4 x 4)	5.1 (2)	11.4 x 14 (4½ x 5½)
10.2 x 10.2 (4 x 4)	11.4 x 11.4 (4½ x 4½)	5.7 (2¼)	12.7 x 15.2 (5 x 6)
11.4 x 11.4 (4½ x 4½)	12.7 x 12.7 (5 x 5)	6.4 (2½)	14 x 16.5 (5½ x 6½)
12.7 x 12.7 (5 x 5)	14 x 14 (5½ x 5½)	7 (2¾)	15.2 x 17.8 (6 x 7)
14 x 14 (5½ x 5½)	15.2 x 15.2 (6 x 6)	7.6 (3)	16.5 x 19.1 (6½ x 7½)
15.2 x 15.2 (6 x 6)	16.5 x 16.5 (6½ x 6½)	8.3 (3¼)	17.8 x 20.3 (7 x 8)
16.5 x 16.5 (6½ x 6½)	17.8 x 17.8 (7 x 7)	8.9 (3½)	19.1 x 21.6 (7½ x 8½)
17.8 x 17.8 (7 x 7)	19.1 x 19.1 (7½ x 7½)	9.5 (3¾)	20.3 x 22.9 (8 x 9)
19.1 x 19.1 (7½ x 7½)	20.3 x 20.3 (8 x 8)	10.2 (4)	21.6 x 24.1 (8½ x 9½)
20.3 x 20.3 (8 x 8)	21.6 x 21.6 (8½ x 8½)	10.8 (4¼)	22.9 x 25.4 (9 x 10)
21.6 x 21.6 (8½ x 8½)	22.9 x 22.9 (9 x 9)	11.4 (4½)	24.1 x 26.7 (9½ x 10½)
22.9 x 22.9 (9 x 9)	24.1 x 24.1 (9½ x 9½)	12.1 (4¾)	25.4 x 27.9 (10 x 11)
24.1 x 24.1 (9½ x 9½)	25.4 x 25.4 (10 x 10)	12.7 (5)	26.7 x 39.5 (10½ x 12)
25.4 x 25.4 (10 x 10)	26.7 x 26.7 (10½ x 10½)	13.3 (5¼)	27.9 x 31.8 (11 x 12½)

Finished size: The size of the triangle in a square unit after it has been sewn into the quilt top.
Unfinished size: The size of the triangle in a square unit plus 6.4mm (¼in) seam allowance on all sides. Units must be trimmed to this size.
Vertical centre: A measurement to mark the centre point of the triangle in a square unit for trimming.
Rectangles: The size of the pieces before assembly.

CUTTING IRREGULAR ANGLE UNITS

Use this chart to determine the WOF strip size and the number of equilateral triangles, half hexagons, or diamonds that can be cut from a single strip.

TECHNIQUE			EQUILATERAL TRIANGLES p.100		HALF HEXAGONS p.101		60° AND 45° DIAMONDS p.102		
FORMULA		Strip width = unfinished height			Distance from vertex = strip width − 6.4mm (¼in)		Distance from angled edge = strip width		
Finished height cm (in)	Unfinished height cm (in)	Cut (1) WOF strip cm (in)	Triangles per WOF strip		Distance from vertex cm (in)	Half hexagons per WOF strip	Distance from angled edge cm (in)	60° diamonds per WOF strip	45° diamonds per WOF strip
3.8 (1½)	5.1 (2)	5.1 (2)	35		4.4 (1¾)	12	5.1 (2)	17	14
5.1 (2)	6.4 (2½)	6.4 (2½)	23		5.7 (2¼)	10	6.4 (2½)	14	11
6.4 (2½)	7.6 (3)	7.6 (3)	19		7 (2¾)	8	7.6 (3)	11	9
7.6 (3)	8.9 (3½)	8.9 (3½)	17		8.3 (3¼)	6	8.9 (3½)	9	7
8.9 (3½)	10.2 (4)	10.2 (4)	15		9.5 (3¾)	5	10.2 (4)	8	6
10.2 (4)	11.4 (4½)	11.4 (4½)	13		10.8 (4¼)	5	11.4 (4½)	7	5
11.4 (4½)	12.7 (5)	12.7 (5)	12		12.1 (4¾)	4	12.7 (5)	6	5
12.7 (5)	14 (5½)	14 (5½)	11		13.3 (5¼)	4	14 (5½)	6	4
14 (5½)	15.2 (6)	15.2 (6)	10		15 (5¾)	3	15.2 (6)	5	4
15.2 (6)	16.5 (6½)	16.5 (6½)	9		16.5 (6¼)	3	16.5 (6½)	5	3
16.5 (6½)	17.8 (7)	17.8 (7)	8		17.1 (6¾)	3	17.8 (7)	4	3
17.8 (7)	19.1 (7½)	19.1 (7½)	8		18.9 (7¼)	2	19.1 (7½)	4	3
19.1 (7½)	20.3 (8)	20.3 (8)	7		19.7 (7¾)	2	20.3 (8)	4	3
20.3 (8)	21.6 (8½)	21.6 (8½)	7		21 (8¼)	2	21.6 (8½)	3	2
21.6 (8½)	22.9 (9)	22.9 (9)	6		22.2 (8¾)	2	22.9 (9)	3	2
22.9 (9)	24.1 (9½)	24.1 (9½)	6		23.5 (9¼)	2	24.1 (9½)	3	2
24.1 (9½)	25.4 (10)	25.4 (10)	5		24.8 (9¾)	2	25.4 (10)	3	2
25.4 (10)	26.7 (10½)	26.7 (10½)	5		26 (10¼)	2	26.7 (10½)	3	2

Finished height: The vertical measurement of an equilateral triangle, half hexagon, or diamond after it has been sewn into a quilt top.
Unfinished height: The vertical measurement of an equilateral triangle, half hexagon, or diamond plus 1.3cm (½in) to account for seam allowance.
WOF strip: The size of the WOF strip before cutting. This is always equal to the unfinished height of an equilateral triangle, half hexagon, or diamond. **WOF** is assumed to be 106.7cm (42in) wide.

BACKING FABRIC REQUIREMENTS

Use these charts to determine the yardage or meterage needed for backing (see p.57). The chart assumes vertical seams; for horizontal seams, use the length of the quilt top as the width.

CALCULATING YARDAGE p.57

Backing size = (**quilt top** *width* + 6in) by (**quilt top** *length* + 6in)

# of backing pieces = **backing** *width* ÷ (WOF − ½in), *rounded up to the nearest whole number*

Backing yardage = (**backing** *length* x **# of backing pieces**) ÷ 36in, *rounded up to the nearest ¼yd*

QUILT TOP LENGTH (in)	QUILT TOP WIDTH (in)		
	< 36 (1) Backing piece	37–77 (2) Backing pieces	78–118 (3) Backing pieces
20	¾yd	1½yds	2¼yds
24	1yd	1¾yds	2½yds
28	1yd	2yds	3yds
32	1¼yds	2¼yds	3¼yds
36	1¼yds	2½yds	3½yds
40	1¼yds	2¾yds	4yds
44	1½yds	3yds	4¼yds
48	1½yds	3yds	4½yds
52	1¾yds	3¼yds	5yds
56	1¾yds	3½yds	5¼yds
60	2yds	3¾yds	5½yds
64	2yds	4yds	6yds
68	2¼yds	4¼yds	6¼yds
72	2¼yds	4½yds	6½yds
76	2½yds	4¾yds	7yds
80	2½yds	5yds	7¼yds
84	2½yds	5yds	7½yds
88	2¾yds	5¼yds	8yds
92	2¾yds	5½yds	8¼yds
96	3yds	5¾yds	8½yds
100	3yds	6yds	9yds
104	3¼yds	6¼yds	9¼yds
108	3¼yds	6½yds	9½yds
112	3½yds	6¾yds	10yds
116	3½yds	7yds	10¼yds
120	3½yds	7yds	10½yds

CALCULATING METERAGE p.57

Backing size = (**quilt top** *width* + 15.2cm) by (**quilt top** *length* + 15.2cm)

# of backing pieces = **backing** *width* ÷ (WOF − 1.3cm), *rounded up to the nearest whole number*

Backing meterage = (**backing** *length* x **# of backing pieces**) ÷ 100cm, *rounded up to the nearest 0.25m*

QUILT TOP LENGTH (cm)	QUILT TOP WIDTH (cm)		
	< 91 (1) Backing piece	92–195 (2) Backing pieces	196–299 (3) Backing pieces
51	0.75m	1.5m	2m
61	1m	1.75m	2.5m
71	1m	1.75m	2.75m
81	1m	2m	3m
91	1.25m	2.25m	3.25m
102	1.25m	2.5m	3.75m
112	1.5m	2.75m	4m
122	1.5m	2.75m	4.25m
132	1.5m	3m	4.5m
142	1.75m	3.25m	4.75m
152	1.75m	3.5m	5.25m
163	2m	3.75m	5.5m
173	2m	4m	5.75m
183	2m	4m	6m
193	2.25m	4.25m	6.25m
203	2.25m	4.5m	6.75m
213	2.5m	4.75m	7m
224	2.5m	5m	7.25m
234	2.5m	5m	7.5m
244	2.75m	5.25m	8m
254	2.75m	5.5m	8.25m
264	3m	5.75m	8.5m
274	3m	6m	8.75m
284	3m	6m	9m
295	3.25m	6.25m	9.5m
305	3.25m	6.5m	9.75m

WOF: Assumed to be 106.7cm (42in) wide.
Overage: All meterage/yardage amounts include 7.6cm (3in) overage and are rounded up to the nearest quarter increment.
(1) Backing piece: Sufficient for quilt top widths ≥ 91cm (36in). **(2) Backing pieces:** Sufficient for quilt top widths 92–155cm (37–77in) when using one vertical seam.
(3) Backing pieces: Sufficient for quilt top widths 196–299cm (78–118in) when using two vertical seams. **Seam allowance** is assumed to be 12.7mm (½in).

BINDING FABRIC REQUIREMENTS

Use these charts to determine the yardage or meterage needed for 6.4cm (2½in) straight grain and bias binding (see p.58).

STRAIGHT GRAIN BINDING p.174

FORMULA	Binding *length* = perimeter of quilt + 38.1cm (15in)
	# of WOF strips = binding *length* ÷ WOF, *rounded up to the nearest whole number*
	Fabric needed = # of WOF strips x binding *width*

Perimeter of quilt cm (in)	Binding length cm (in)	# of WOF strips	Fabric needed cm (in)	Meterage (yardage) needed*
0–69 (0–27)	0–107 (0–42)	1	6.4 (2½)	0.25m (¼yd)
69–175 (27–69)	107–213 (42–84)	2	12.8 (5)	0.25m (¼yd)
175–282 (69–111)	213–320 (84–126)	3	19.2 (7½)	0.25m (¼yd)
282–389 (111–153)	320–427 (126–168)	4	25.6 (10)	0.25m (⅓yd)
389–496 (153–195)	427–533 (168–210)	5	32 (12½)	0.33m (½yd)
496–602 (195–237)	533–640 (210–252)	6	38.4 (15)	0.50m (½yd)
602–709 (237–279)	640–747 (252–294)	7	44.8 (17)	0.50m (½yd)
709–816 (279–321)	747–854 (294–336)	8	51.2 (20)	0.67m (⅔yd)
816–922 (321–363)	854–960 (336–378)	9	57.6 (22)	0.67m (⅔yd)
922–1029 (363–405)	960–1067 (378–420)	10	64 (25)	0.67m (¾yd)
1029–1136 (405–447)	1067–1173 (420–462)	11	70.4 (27)	0.75m (1yd)
1136–1243 (447–489)	1173–1280 (462–504)	12	76.8 (30)	1m (1yd)

*Meterage and yardage needed are rounded up to the nearest quarter increment.
Binding width: Assumed to be 6.4cm (2½in) wide.
WOF: Assumed to be 106.7cm (42in) wide.
Perimeter of quilt: The total added length of all sides of a quilt.
# of WOF strips: Number of WOF strips to cut and piece.

BIAS BINDING LENGTH FROM A SINGLE SQUARE p.175

Cut (1) square cm (in)	Meterage (yardage) needed*	# of 6.4cm (2½in) lines drawn	Approx. length of bias binding cm (in)
20.3 x 20.3 (8 x 8)	0.25m (¼yd)	2	58 (23)
25.4 x 25.4 (10 x 10)	0.33m (⅓yd)	2	73 (29)
30.5 x 30.5 (12 x 12)	0.33m (⅓yd)	3	127 (50)
35.6 x 35.6 (14 x 14)	0.5m (½yd)	3	150 (59)
40.6 x 40.6 (16 x 16)	0.5m (½yd)	4	226 (89)
45.7 x 45.7 (18 x 18)	0.5m (½yd)	5	318 (125)
50.8 x 50.8 (20 x 20)	0.67m (⅔yd)	5	353 (139)
55.9 x 55.9 (22 x 22)	0.67m (⅔yd)	6	465 (183)
61 x 61 (24 x 24)	0.67m (⅔yd)	6	508 (200)
66 x 66 (26 x 26)	0.75m (¾yd)	7	643 (253)
71.1 x 71.1 (28 x 28)	0.75m (1yd)	7	694 (273)
76.2 x 76.2 (30 x 30)	1m (1yd)	8	848 (334)
81.3 x 81.3 (32 x 32)	1m (1yd)	8	904 (356)
86.4 x 86.4 (34 x 34)	1m (1yd)	9	1082 (426)
91.4 x 91.4 (36 x 36)	1m (1yd)	10	1272 (501)

*Meterage and yardage needed are rounded up to the nearest quarter increment.
Binding width: Assumed to be 6.4cm (2½in) wide.
Square: The size of the square before cutting and assembly.

Glossary

Acute angle A narrow angle measuring less than 90 degrees.

Appliqué The process of attaching fabric pieces onto a background.

Backing The layer of fabric on the back of a quilt.

Backstitch A reverse stitch made to overlap and lock previous stitches in place.

Basting A temporary method of securing fabric to another material using pins, glue, or thread.

Bias The fabric direction that runs diagonally to the grain lines or selvedge.

Binding A strip of fabric, cut on either the bias or straight grain, sewn around the quilt perimeter to finish the raw edges.

Blender A fabric with subtle, small scale patterns designed to read as nearly solid.

Block (quilt block) A section of a quilt made by joining fabric pieces or units into a specific design.

Border Fabric pieces sewn to the edges of a quilt top to frame the design or increase the quilt size.

Chain piecing A technique used to continuously sew pieces together in pairs.

Colour scheme Common ways colours interact with each other on the colour wheel.

Contrast The difference between fabric colours, patterns, and textures.

Cornerstone Pieces or units sewn between sashing strips.

Directionality The orientation of designs on fabric, including one-way, two-way, and multi-directional.

English paper piecing (EPP) A hand sewing technique in which fabric is tacked around paper pieces, which are later removed, to make intricate geometric designs.

Envelope backing Type of backing made of two overlapping pieces of fabric; often used for pillow covers.

Equilateral triangle Triangles with equal sides and 60-degree angles; measured by their height.

Facing An alternative binding technique that produces a frameless finish.

Fat eighth (FE) An eighth of a yard measuring 22.9 x 53.3cm (9 x 21in); sold as a pre-cut.

Fat quarter (FQ) A quarter of a yard measuring 45.7 x 53.3cm (18 x 21in); sold as a pre-cut.

Feed dogs Metal teeth that grip the bottom fabric and move it through a sewing machine.

Finished size The final measurements after outside edges have been sewn.

Flying geese (FG) A rectangular unit consisting of one large triangle and two smaller triangles that finishes twice as wide as it is long.

Foundation paper piecing A machine piecing technique in which fabric is sewn onto a printed paper foundation, which is later removed, to make complex designs.

Fussy cutting A cutting technique in which specific designs are carefully cut from fabric.

Glue baste A type of basting, often used in EPP, in which fabric is secured to another material using glue.

Grain The direction of the weave in fabric; the warp (straight grain), runs parallel to the selvedge, and weft (cross grain), runs perpendicular to the selvedge.

Half-rectangle triangle (HRT) A rectangular unit consisting of two elongated triangles.

Half-square triangle (HST) A square unit consisting of two right-angled triangles.

Hand quilting A quilting technique involving sewing through the layers of a quilt sandwich by hand using a needle and thread.

Hem A finished fabric edge that is folded under twice and stitched to prevent fraying.

Hera marker A plastic or wood tool used to make temporary creased lines in fabric.

Improvisational (improv) An organic piecing technique involving experimentation and creativity; does not rely on a predetermined pattern or measurements.

Irregular angle In this book, an irregular angle is any angle other than 45 degrees.

Leaders and enders A small piece of fabric used to prevent fabric bunching when beginning and finishing machine sewing.

Loft The thickness, or height, of wadding.

Low volume A fabric with mini or small scale designs and light or neutral background.

Mitre/mitred corner A technique used when attaching binding to form 45-degree angles at the corners of a quilt.

Nested seams Seams pressed in alternating directions to rest against each other.

Non-directional A fabric that can be oriented in any direction without changing the overall design.

Offsetting angles Intentionally misaligning the edges of pieces so they align properly once sewn.

On point The process of sewing pieces or blocks together on the diagonal.

Overhand knot A knot made by forming a loop, then crossing one thread end through the loop.

Paper piece A reusable piece of specially cut paper used to provide stability and shape to fabric during EPP.

Patchwork Individual pieces sewn together in a simple geometric layout.

Pattern matching The process of aligning the designs on two pieces of fabric before joining them to produce a seamless appearance.

Pattern repeat The distance between identical sections of a design on fabric.

Picking Using a seam ripper to remove one stitch at a time.

Piece A single fabric segment that is sewn into a unit, block, or quilt top.

Piecing The process of sewing fabric pieces together.

Pin Temporarily securing two or more fabrics together using a sharp, straight pin.

Pre-cut Fabric pieces cut into standard sizes by a manufacturer or fabric store; typically sold as a set.

Prepared edge An appliqué technique in which the raw edges of fabric are folded under to produce a finished edge.

Presser foot An interchangeable sewing machine attachment that holds fabric flat against the feed dogs.

Pressing Flattening fabric by placing a hot iron straight down, holding for a few seconds, then lifting it straight up.

Pressing seams The process of flattening seam allowances after they have been sewn; often directed to one side or open.

Quarter-square triangle (QST) A square unit consisting of four right triangles which meet in the centre.

Quilt Three layers of material secured with stitches and binding around the perimeter.

Quilt sandwich The quilt top, wadding, and backing, layered WST.

Quilt top The top layer of a quilt; typically the focal point showcasing a pieced pattern or design.

Quilter's knot A multipurpose knot used to secure thread ends before sewing by hand.

Quilting The process of stitching through all three layers of a quilt sandwich to secure them together.

Raw edge The cut, unfinished edge of fabric or wadding.

Registration line A small mark used to assist with alignment.

Right side (RS) The side meant to be visible; "RST" refers to placing the right sides of two fabrics together.

Rock the needle The process of moving the needle up and down to form multiple stitches at once while hand sewing.

Rotary cutter A cutting tool with a circular blade used for cutting fabric accurately; used alongside a cutting mat and ruler.

Running stitch A stitch made by weaving a single length of thread through two pieces of fabric by hand.

Sashing Strips of fabric that separate elements within a block or quilt top.

Scale The size of designs on fabric.

Scoring Perforating or creasing fabric or paper to assist with folding, piecing, and cutting.

Scrim A thin layer of stabilizer added to wadding.

Seam The stitch line where two pieces of fabric are sewn together.

Seam allowance The space between the seam and fabric edge; typically 6.4mm (¼in) in quilting.

Seam ripping The process of removing a line of stitches using a seam ripper.

Selvedge The woven, outer edge of fabric that runs parallel to the lengthways grain.

Set seam The process of pressing a seam before opening the unit to set the stitches and produce a flatter seam.

Setting triangle Triangles used to fill gaps on the outer edges of a piece or quilt top oriented on point.

Spinning seams The process of pressing multiple seams in a circular direction to nest and evenly distribute bulk.

Square in a square A square unit consisting of an on point centre square surrounded by four setting triangles.

Square knot A knot made with two lengths of thread when burying machine quilting thread ends.

Squaring The process of trimming fabric, units, blocks, or quilt tops to produce straight edges and 90-degree corners.

Starch A liquid used to stabilize fabrics before cutting or after quilt top assembly.

Stay stitch A line of stitches sewn 3.2mm ($^1/_8$in) away from the perimeter of a quilt block or top to secure seams and bias edges.

Stitch and flip The process of sewing a square onto the corner of a larger piece, trimming excess fabric beyond the seam, then pressing it over to fill the corner.

Stitch length The length of a single stitch.

Strip set A group of strips sewn together to make a larger unit.

Sub-cut The process of cutting smaller pieces from larger, typically WOF strips.

Tacking corners An EPP thread basting technique in which the corners of a piece are secured in place with small stitches.

Template A paper or acrylic shape used to cut shapes out of fabric.

Tension The balance between interlocking top and bobbin threads.

Thread baste A type of basting in which fabric is secured to another material using thread.

Triangle in a square A square unit consisting of a centre triangle with a setting triangle on either side.

Unfinished size The measurements before outside edges have been sewn.

Unit Fabric pieces joined together to form a larger piece.

Vertex The point at which two angled edges meet.

Wadding The layer between the quilt top and the backing that provides loft and warmth (also known as batting).

Whipstitch A stitch used to join two straight finished edges by hand.

Width of fabric (WOF) The measurement of fabric from selvedge to selvedge; typically 106.7cm (42in) in quilting.

Wrong side (WS) The side meant to be hidden; "WST" refers to placing the wrong sides of two fabrics together.

Y-seam A type of seam formed where three pieces meet at a single point.

Index

A
acrylic templates 19, 71, 127
activist quilts 9
acute angles, basting 129
air-soluble pens 22, 162
album quilt block 270–71
analogous colour schemes 61
angles
   common angles 86–95
   diamonds 102–103
   equilateral triangles 100
   flying geese (FG) 92–93
   half hexagons 101
   half-rectangle triangles (HRT) 97–98
   half-square triangles (HST) 86–89
   irregular angles 96–103, 289
   offsetting angles 96
   quarter-square triangles (QST) 90–91
   square in a square units 94–95
   stitch and flip units 89
   triangles in a square unit 99
Annie's choice block 267
anvil block 270
appliqué 134–39
   attaching by hand 137
   attaching by machine 136
   attaching interfacing 135
   back patch 257–63
   clipping corners 135
   cutting shapes 135
   needle turn appliqué 139
   prepared edge appliqué 139
   preparing for appliqué 135
   quilt top layout 147
   raw edge appliqué 138
   transferring to fabric 135
   types of appliqué 136–39
appliqué scissors 16
art quilts 9

B
back patch 257–63
backing 50
   calculating 57, 290
   envelope backing 155
   patchwork backing 153
   pattern matching 154
   preparing 152
   seam placement 153
   squaring up backing 155
bag, tote 257–63
bamboo wadding 44
basket weave block 272
basting 157
   acute angles (EPP) 129
   basting pins 15, 29, 157
   English paper piecing 128–29
   fusible wadding 159
   glue basting (EPP) 129
   removing basting 159
   spray adhesive 23, 158
   stitching through papers (EPP) 128
   tacking corners (EPP) 128
   thread basting (EPP) 128
   thread basting (quilts) 159
batik 39
bear claw block 267
bear paw block 268
betweens 28
bias 36
bias binding 45, 175
binding 45, 50, 172–79
   adding corner pockets 173
   attaching binding 176–77
   bias binding 45, 175
   big stitching 179
   calculating 58, 291
   finishing binding 178–79
   folding over 178
   invisible stitching 179
   joining ends 177
   machine stitching 178
   making binding 174–75
   mitring corners 178
   navigating corners 176
   preparing for binding 173
   repairing 185
   straight grain binding 45, 174
   trimming a quilt 173
birds of paradise block 275
black wadding 43
Blackford's beauty block 272
blades, rotary 17
blanket stitch 136, 138
blenders 65
blocks
   block gallery 264–77
   calculating block sizes 55
   categorizing quilt blocks 266
   classic quilt blocks 266
   curved blocks 266
   English paper piecing blocks (EPP) 266
   foundation paper piecing blocks (FPP) 266
   four patch blocks 266, 267
   hand pieced blocks 266
   multipatch blocks 266
   nine patch blocks 266, 268–69
   pressing 81
   sashing between blocks 143
   scaling block size 59
   sewing units into blocks 142
   square in a square blocks 266
bobbins 32
borders 147
box block 270
broken window block 272
building block sampler 188–95
burying knots 76–77

C
caring for quilts 182–85
Carol's scrap time 270
cascading cabin 196–203
cat's cradle block 268
chain piecing 144
chalk 22, 162
chambray 38
charts, quilting 280–91
chequerboard block 267
churn dash block 268
clamshell block 276
clipping curves 105
clips, quilting 29, 78
coffin star block 270
colour catchers 23
colour
   colour theory 60–61
  conditioner, thread 25
contrast 61
conversions 280
corners
   adding corner pockets 173
   clipping 135
   corner beam block 275
   mitring binding corners 178
   tacking corners (EPP) 128
cornerstones, sashing with 143
cotton
   cotton/polyester blend wadding 43
   cotton threads 24
   cotton wadding 43
   quilting 37
   shot cotton 37
courthouse steps block 270
curved needles 28
curves 104–107
   basting curved edges (EPP) 129
   blocks 274
   clipping curves 104
   curved blocks 266
   curved EPP shapes 125
   curved star block 274

INDEX **297**

cutting curves 104
drunkard's path circle block 274
drunkard's path flower block 274
gluing curves 105
grandmother's fan 274
orange peel block 274
peeled orange block 274
pinning curves 105
preparing curves 104
pressing curves 104
rainbow block 274
sewing curves 106–107
walking foot quilting 165
winding ways block 274
cutting fabrics 68–71
cutting against a ruler 69
cutting fabric accurately 70–71
for EPP 127
using rotary cutters 68–69
using templates 71
width of fabric (WOF) strips 70
cutting instructions, pattern 53
cutting mat 15, 17
cutting tools 14, 15, 16–17

D

designs, fabric
pattern matching 154
selecting 64–65
understanding scale 62–63
diamonds 102–103
cutting 102
diamond EPP shapes 125
joining diamond segments or rows 103
piecing diamonds into rows 102
sub-cutting diamond strip sets 102–103
directional prints 63
dobby 38
domestic sewing machines 30–33
double gauze 38
Dresden plate block 277
drunkard's path circle block 274
drunkard's path flower block 274
dry-erase marker 22
drying quilts 184

E

echo quilting 165
economy block 270
edges, preparing for pre-washing 66
embroidery needles 28
English paper piecing (EPP) 124–33
acrylic templates 23
basting English paper piecing 128–29
blocks 266, 277
centre holes 126
common EPP shapes 125
cutting fabric 127
Dresden plate block 277
grandmother's flower garden block 277
half hexagons block 277
hexagon star block 277
jewel heart block 277
joining pieces 130–31
joining shapes 132
paper punch 126
papers 23
piecing curved edges 133
piecing one-by-one 132
piecing rows 133
pre-cut pieces 126
preparing paper pieces 126
print and cut 126
removing papers 133
six-pointed star block 277
star bouquet block 277
tools 15, 23
tumbling blocks 277
English wedding ring block 272
envelope backing 155
envelope star block 268
equilateral triangles 100

F

fabric shears 16
fabrics 36–41
adjusting fabric requirements 59
bias 36
blenders 65
calculating fabric requirements 52, 56–58
choosing 60–61
colour schemes and contrast 61
common quilting fabrics 37
cutting fabric for EPP 127
fabric scale sizes 62
grain 36
measuring and cutting 68–71
positioning fabric for machine sewing 72
pre-cuts 41
preparing fabrics 66–67
pressing 67
pre-washing 66
printed fabrics 62–63, 65
scraps 41, 65
selecting fabric designs 64–65
solid colours 64
squaring 67
standard cuts of fabric 40–41
starching 67
textures 64
thread count and weight 36
transferring shapes to fabric 135
uncommon quilting fabrics 38–39
understanding colour theory 60
yardage and meterage 40
facing 180–81
Fanny's favourite block 272
finished sizes 54
finishing 148–81
assembling a quilt sandwich 150–59
binding 172–79
facing 180–81
quilting 160–71
finishing tools 15, 23
five-point star block 275
flannel 38
flat back stitch 131
flock of geese block 267
flower basket block 267
flower head pins 29
flying geese (FG) 92–93
charts 285
four at a time 93
improv piecing 113
one at a time 92
trimming 93
flying geese ruler 19
folding quilts 184
follow the leader 270
foundation paper piecing (FPP) 114–19
birds of paradise block 275
blocks 266, 275
corner beam block 275
cutting fabrics 115
five-point star block 275
folding and trimming 117
joining templates 118–19
matching points 118
New York beauty block 275
palm leaf block 275
piecing sections 116–17
pineapple block 275
placing fabric 115
preparing FPP templates 115
pressing seams 119
removing papers 119
scoring seam lines 115
stitching seam lines 116
storm at sea block 275
string block 275
trimming completed templates 117
four patches 84
Annie's choice block 267
bear claw block 267
blocks 266, 267
chequerboard block 267
even strip piecing 84
flock of geese block 267
flower basket block 267
odd strip piecing 84
piece by piece 84
ribbon star block 267

snowball flower block 267
    X's and O's block 267
four-way designs 63
free motion quilting (FMQ) 161, 166
friendship quilts 9
functional quilts 9
fusible interfacing 45, 135, 152
fusible wadding 44
fussy cutting 127

G

gauze, double 38
gentleman's fancy block 271
glass head pins 15, 29
gloves, quilting 23
glue 29
    glue basting 23, 129
    gluing curves 105
    matching points and seams 141
goose in the pond block 272
goose tracks block 276
grain 36
grandmother's fan block 274
grandmother's flower garden block 277
granny square block 268
green mountain star block 272
grids, walking foot quilting 165

H

half circles (HC)
    improv piecing 113
    sewing 106
    trimming 107
half hexagons 101, 277
    cutting 101
    piecing half hexagon rows 101
half-rectangle triangles (HRT) 97–98
    charts 287
    improv piecing 112
    one at a time 97
    trimming 98
    two at a time 97
half-square triangles (HST) 86–89
    charts 283
    eight at a time 88
    four at a time 87
    improv piecing 112
    one at a time 86
    strip tube technique 88
    trimming 89
    two at a time 86
half-square triangle (HST) trimming ruler 19
hand dyed fabric 39
hand needles 28
hand piecing 120–23
    blocks 266, 276

clamshell block 276
goose tracks 276
hearts and gizzards block 276
Idaho star block 276
joining pieces 122–23
Lemoyne star block 276
marking seam allowance 121
preparing for hand piecing 121
running stitch 122
seam types 122
using pins 121
wedding ring block 276
hand quilting 161, 168–71
    big stitch quilting 170
    hand tying 171
    handling a quilt 168
    rocking the needle 169
    stab stitch 169
    stitching 169–70
    traditional hand quilting 170
    travelling through wadding 170
    types of hand quilting 170
hand quilting hoops 23, 168
happy patch 220–25
heart block 272
hearts and gizzards block 276
heirloom quilts 9
hera markers 14, 22, 162
hexagon ruler 19
hexagons
    half hexagons 101
    hexagon EPP shapes 125
    hexagon star 277
hole punches 23, 126
holes, repairing 185
hoops 23, 168
house block 273
hue 60

I

Idaho beauty 273
Idaho star 276
improv piecing 108–13, 147
    common improv shapes 112
    curved improv 111
    flying geese (FG) and triangle in a square 113
    guidelines 109
    half-rectangle triangles 112
    half-square triangles 112
    log cabin 112
    off script pattern 241–49
    patchwork 112
    QCs and HCs 113
    quarter-square triangles 113
    square in a square 113
    straight edge improv 110
    strips 112

techniques 110–13
wavy improv 111
interfacing 45
    attaching 135
    fusible 45, 135, 152
    sew-in 45, 135
    web piecing with interfacing 145
iridian puff 250–55
Irish chain block 273
ironing boards 14, 20
irons 14, 21

J K

jewel EPP shapes 125
jewel heart 277
knots 75, 76–77

L

labelling quilts 183
ladder stitch 137
lady of the lake block 271
lawn 37
layering 156
Lemoyne star block 276
light box/board 22
linen 37
loft 42
log cabin 85, 112, 271
lone star block 273
longarm quilting 33, 161
low volume prints 65

M

machine quilting 164–67
    free motion quilting (FMQ) 166
    ruler work quilting 167
    walking foot quilting 164–65
magnetic pin holder 29
magnets 23
maintenance, quilt 184
maple leaf block 268
marker pens 22
marking quilting lines 162–63
marking tools 14, 15, 22, 162
masking tape 23, 162
materials 34–45
math, quilt 54–59
measuring fabrics 68
measuring tools 15, 18–19
medallion quilts 147
medical tape 19
memory quilts 9
memory star block 273
metallic threads 24
meterage 40
    calculating 56

cutting from 282
milestone quilts 9
milliner's needles 28
modern flame block 271
monochromatic colour schemes 61
monofilament threads 24
mosaic #21 block 271
mother's choice block 273
motifs, understanding scale 62–63
multipatch blocks 266, 272–73
   basket weave 272
   Blackford's beauty 272
   broken window 272
   English wedding ring 272
   Fanny's favourite 272
   goose in the pond 272
   green mountain star 272
   heart 272
   house 273
   Idaho beauty 273
   Irish chain 273
   lone star 273
   memory star 273
   mother's choice 273
   sister's choice 273
muslin 39

N

needle minder 28
needle-punched wadding 42
needle threaders 28, 74
needles 15
   hand needles 28
   holding a needle 74
   machine needles 33
   rocking the needle 169
   threading a needle 74
   types of 28–29
   using 74–77
nesting seams 81
New York Beauty 275
nexus shift 212–19
nine patches 84
   bear paw block 268
   blocks 266, 268–69
   cat's cradle block 268
   churn dash block 268
   envelope star block 268
   even strip piecing 84
   granny square block 268
   maple leaf block 268
   odd strip piecing 84
   Ohio star block 268
   piece by piece 84
   plus block 268
   road to California block 269
   rolling stone block 269
   sawtooth star block 269
   shoo fly block 269
   weathervane block 269
   winged square block 269
   wonky star block 269
   X plus block 269
non-directional designs 63
non-slip ruler grips 19

O

ocean waves block 271
off script pattern 241–49
offsetting angles 96
Ohio star block 268
one-way designs 63
orange peel block 274
organic lines 165
organizers, thread 25
overhand knot 76

P

palm leaf block 275
paper punches 23, 126
paper scissors 16
paper templates, using 71
papered blooms 234–39
patchwork 83–85
   back patch 257–63
   four patches 84
   improv piecing 112
   log cabin 85
   nine patches 84
   patchwork backing 153
   strip piecing 83
patterns, paper
   altering 59
   understanding 52–53
peeled orange block 274
pencils 22
pens 22
picking seams 79
piecing
   chain piecing 144
   continuous piecing 144
   English paper piecing (EPP) 124–33
   foundation paper piecing (FPP) 114–19
   four and nine patches 84
   hand piecing 120–23
   improv piecing 108–13
   log cabin 85
   piecing wadding 152
   strip piecing 83
   traditional piecing 82–107
   web piecing 144–45
   web piecing with interfacing 145
pillow cover 257–63

pin cushion 29
pineapple block 275
pinking shears 16
pins and pinning 15
   basting with pins 157
   matching points and seams 141
   pinning curves 105
   preparing for hand piecing 121
   types of 28–29
   using pins 78
plus block 268
points
   matching points 141
   point-to-point quilting 165
polyester
   cotton/polyester blend wadding 43
   loose polyester filling 44
   polyester threads 24
   polyester wadding 43
pre-cuts 41
pressing
   fabrics 67
   nesting seams 81
   pressing blocks 81
   pressing curves 104
   pressing seams 80–81
   pressing seams to the side 80
   pressing seams open 80
   quilt tops 151
   setting seams 80
   spinning seams 81
pressing surface 14
pressing tools 15, 20–21
pre-washing 66
primrose crown 226–33
printed fabrics 65
   directional prints 63
   pattern matching 154
   selecting fabric designs 64–65
   understanding scale 62–63
projects 186–263
puff quilt, iridian 250–55

Q

quarter circles (QCs)
   improv piecing 113
   sewing 106
   trimming 107
quarter-square triangles (QST) 90–91
   charts 284
   improv piecing 113
   one at a time 90
   split QSTs 91
   trimming 91
   two at a time 90
quilt backing 153
   envelope backing 155

patchwork backing 153
pattern matching 154
seam placement 153
squaring up backing 155
quilt sandwiches 50
   assembling 150–59
   basting 157
   layering 156
   preparing wadding and backing 152–55
quilt tops 50
   appliqué layouts 147
   borders layouts 147
   chain piecing 144
   construction 140–47
   improv layouts 147
   layouts 146
   matching points and seams 141
   medallion layouts 147
   on point layouts 146
   preparing 151
   preparing wadding and backing 152–55
   quadrant layouts 146
   registration lines 143
   rows and columns layouts 146
   sashing 143, 146
   sewing units into blocks 142
quilter's knot 75, 76
quilting 160–67
   choosing quilting methods 161
   hand 168–71
   machine 164–67
   what it is 8–9
quilting bees 8
quilting charts 280–91
quilting clips 29, 78
quilting cotton 37
quilting guilds 8
quilting needles 28
quilting pins 29
quilting ruler 15
quilting templates 23
quilts
   activist quilts 9
   art quilts 9
   caring for 182–85
   choosing quilt sizes 49, 281
   five components of 50–51
   functional quilts 9
   heirloom quilts 9
   labelling 183
   maintenance 184
   quilt maths 54–59
   quilts to go 257–63

R

rainbow block 274
reclaimed fabric 39
rectangular rulers 18
registration lines 143
repairing quilts 184–85
repeat, measuring 63
ribbon star block 267
ripping seams 79
rising star block 271
road to California block 269
rolling stone block 269
rotary cutters 14, 17
   anatomy of 68
   holding 69
   safety tips 68
   using 68–69
ruler handle 19
ruler quilting 161
rules and ruler work quilting 71, 161, 167
   accessories 19
   cutting against a ruler 69
   holding 69
   preparing for 167
   quilting ruler 15
   speciality rulers 19
   standard rulers 18
   using 162, 167
running stitch 122, 137

S

sampler, building block 188–95
sashiko needles 28
sashing 143, 146
satin stitch 136
sawtooth star block 269
scale
   fabric scale sizes 62
   measuring scale and repeat 63
   understanding 62–63
scissors 16, 71
scoring seam lines 115
scraps 41, 65
scrim 42
seam allowances
   accounting for 54
   marking seam allowance 121
   setting accurate seam allowance 73
   testing 73
seam guides 32
seam rippers 14, 17
   anatomy of 79
seam rollers 20
seams
   curved seams 123
   matching seams 141
   nesting seams 81
   popped seams 185
   pressing seams 80–81, 119
   seam placement, backing 153

seam ripping 79
seam types 122
setting seams 80
spinning seams 81
stitching seam lines (FPP) 116
straight seams 122
Y-seams 123
see also seam allowance
self-healing cutting mat 15
self-threading needles 28
sewing machines 15
   accessories 32
   domestic sewing machines 30–33
   feet 32
   longarm quilting machines 33
   needles 33
   positioning fabric 72
   preparing machine settings 72–73
   setting accurate seam allowance 73
   stitch length 72
   tension 72
   testing seam allowance 73
   see also longarm quilting; machine quilting
sharps 28
shears 16
shoo fly block 269
shot cotton 37
sister's choice block 273
six-pointed star block 277
size
   adjusting fabric requirements 59
   calculating block or quilt size 49, 55
   calculating fabric requirements 56–58
   comparing quilt sizes 49, 281
   finished size 54
   scaling block size 59
   unfinished size 54
snips 14, 16
snowball flower block 267
solid fabrics 64
speciality rulers 19
spinning seams 81
split-complementary colour schemes 61
spray adhesive, basting with 23, 158
square knot 77
square rulers 18
square in a square
   album quilt block 270
   anvil block 270
   blocks 266, 270–71
   box block 270
   Carol's scrap time block 270
   charts 286
   coffin star block 270
   courthouse steps block 270
   economy block block 270
   follow the leader block 270

gentleman's fancy block 271
improv piecing 113
lady of the lake block 271
log cabin block 271
modern flame block 271
mosaic #21 block 271
ocean waves block 271
rising star block 271
setting triangles technique 95
square in a square units 94–95
stitch and flip technique 94
trimming 95
union square block 271
squaring fabrics 67
  squaring up backing 155
stab stitch 169
standard rulers 18
stands, thread 25
star bouquet block 277
starching fabrics 21, 67
stay stitching quilt tops 151
stellar prism 204–11
stencils 23, 163
stitch and flip units 89
stitches and stitching
  blanket stitch 136, 138
  flat back stitch 131
  joining EPP pieces 130–31
  ladder stitch 137
  popped quilting stitches 184
  running stitch 122, 137
  satin stitch 136
  stab stitch 169
  stitch length 72
  straight stitch 136
  whipstitch 130, 137, 152
  zigzag stitch 136, 152
storing quilts 184
storm at sea block 275
straight grain binding 174
straight lines 165
straight seams 122–23
straight stitch 136
straw needles 28
string block 275
strip piecing 83
strip tube technique 88
strips
  improv piecing 112
  strip piecing 83
  width of fabric (WOF) strips 70
sub-cutting 70

T

tailor's clapper 20
tape, masking 23
tape measures 18
techniques 46–185
temperature, colour 60
templates 17, 23, 71
  acrylic templates 19, 71, 127
  EPP acrylic templates 23
  FPP templates 115, 118–19
tension 72
tetradic colour schemes 61
textures 64
thimbles 14, 29, 77
thread count and weight, fabric 36
threads 15, 24–27
  8 weight 26, 27
  12 weight 26, 27
  28 weight 27
  40 weight 26, 27
  60 weight and 50 weight 26, 27
  100 weight and 80 weight 26, 27
  accessories 25
  basting with 159
  burying knots 76–77
  heavier weight threads 15
  light to medium-value threads 15
  overhand knot 76
  quilter's knot 75, 76
  spool sizes 25
  square knot 77
  thread basting (EPP) 128
  thread types 24
  trimming 151
  weights 26–27
tools 12–33
tote bag 257–63
tracing wheel 22
traditional piecing 82–107
triadic colour schemes 61
triangle ruler 19
triangles
  equilateral triangles 100
  half-rectangle triangles (HRT) 97–98, 287
  half-square triangles (HST) 86–89, 283
  quarter-square triangles (QST) 90–91, 284
  setting triangles technique 95
  triangle EPP shapes 125
triangle in a square
  charts 288
  improv piecing 113
  unit 99
trimming
  flying geese (FG) 93
  half circles (HC) 107
  half-rectangle triangles (HRT) 98
  half-square triangles (HST) 89
  quarter circles (QC) 107
  quarter-square triangles (QST) 91
  square in a square units 95
  threads 151
triangle in a square units 99
trimming a quilt 173
tumbler EPP shapes 125
tumbling blocks 277
tweezers 17
two-way designs 63

U V

unfinished sizes 54
union square 271
value, colour 60
variegated threads 24

W

wadding 42–44, 50
  basting using fusible wadding 159
  dimensions 42
  loft 42
  needle-punched 42
  piecing wadding 152
  preparing 152
  properties of 42
  scrim 42
  travelling through wadding 170
  types of 43–44
walking foot quilting 161, 164–65
  designs 165
  preparing for 164
  quilting from point-to-point 164
  using guides 164
wall hanging 257–63
washi tape 22, 32
washing fabrics and quilts 66, 184
water-soluble pens 22, 162
weathervane block 269
wedding ring block 276
whipstitch 130, 137, 152
width of fabric (WOF) strips 70
  cutting from 281
  grouping pieces into 56
winding ways block 274
winged square block 269
wonky star block 269
wool pressing mat 21
wool wadding 44

X Y Z

X plus block 269
X's and O's block 267
Y-seams 123
yardage 40
  calculating 56, 68
  cutting from 282
zigzag stitch 136, 152

ACKNOWLEDGMENTS

AUTHORS' ACKNOWLEDGMENTS This book would not have been possible without each other: we may not have understood the scale of the project we were taking on, but we knew we could do it together. We kept each other accountable, pushed one another to grow, and took turns navigating the highs and lows. Having a coauthor to challenge, cheer, and celebrate with has been an incredible gift. By the end, we were telling each other daily – we could not have done this alone.

To our families, Mitch, Jackson, and JD: thank you for your endless encouragement, unwavering support, and for keeping us caffeinated and fed. We could not have written this book without you in our corner. We love you!

Thank you to Bailey for your precise piecing and quilting on *Cascading Cabin*, and Stephanie and Aimee for quilting *Papered Blooms*, *Primrose Crown*, and *Happy Patch*. Amy, Anna, Alex, Ashelyn, and Vickeidy – your enthusiasm and quick turnaround in testing the charts were invaluable. To the group chats (you know who you are); thank you for keeping our secrets, being last-minute tie-breakers, and cheering us on every step of the way.

We are so grateful to Windham Fabrics, Ruby Star Society, Creative Grids, Hobbs Bonded Fibers, and Grace Company for supplying fabrics, materials, and images. Thank you to Jessie and Annie at Moda Fabrics for the crucial last-minute fabric pick-ups from the warehouse. A special thank you to Taz at Camberville Threads: we literally could not have made deadlines without your support and quick shipping.

Other shout-outs go to our pets for their constant companionship in early mornings and late nights, even when our attention was more focused on writing and sewing than on belly rubs and playtime; our local coffee shop for unknowingly hosting countless brainstorming sessions; and to our faithful sewing machines for limping through to the finish line with us, never giving up even when we thought we might.

Finally, thank you to the DK team: Amy, thank you for giving us the opportunity to write this book. Emma, Tom, and Glenda, your beautiful photography, design, and attention to detail brought our vision to life. And Kathy, thank you for your patience with our endless edits and rewrites. We appreciate you all so much.

PUBLISHER'S ACKNOWLEDGMENTS: DK would like to thank Alexandra Muir for acting as photoshoot technical assistant, Noor Ali for hand modelling, Katie Hardwicke and Athena Stacey for proofreading, Vanessa Bird for indexing, and Kate Reeves-Brown for anglicising.

The publisher would like to thank the following for supplying materials and images featured in this book:

Ruby + Bee Fabrics
Designed by Heather Ross and Annabel Wrigley for Windham Fabrics
windhamfabrics.com

Ruby Star Society
Fabrics designed by Melody Miller, Alexia Marcelle Abegg, Rashida Coleman Hale, Kimberly Kight, and Sarah Watts
rubystarsociety.com

Creative Grids®
Made in the USA and Home of the Original Non-Slip Grip
creativegridsusa.com
creativegrids.com

Hobbs Bonded Fibers
Makers of high-quality Hobbs batting and craft products since 1978
hobbsbatting.com/products

Grace Company
graceframe.com

Janome
janome.com

DK LONDON
Acquisitions Editor Amy Slack
Senior Designer Glenda Fisher
Production Editor Tony Phipps
Production Controller Luca Bazzoli
Sales Material and Jackets Co-ordinator Emily Cannings
Art Director Maxine Pedliham
Publishing Director Stephanie Jackson

DK DELHI
Art Editors Devina Pagay, Rajoshi Chakraborty
Senior Art Editor Ira Sharma
Project Editor Ankita Gupta
Managing Art Editor Neha Ahuja Chowdhry
Managing Editor Saloni Singh
Pre-Production Designer Manish Upreti
Pre-Production Coordinator Pushpak Tyagi
Pre-Production Manager Balwant Singh
Pre-Production Image Coordinator Jagtar Singh
Pre-Production Image Manager Pankaj Sharma
Creative Head Malavika Talukder

Design Emma Forge, Tom Forge
Editorial Kathy Steer
Photography Ruth Jenkinson
Jacket Design Eleanor Ridsdale
Illustration Christina West and Kacey Crutchfield

First published in Great Britain in 2025 by
Dorling Kindersley Limited, 20 Vauxhall Bridge Road,
London SW1V 2SA

The authorised representative in the EEA is
Dorling Kindersley Verlag GmbH. Arnulfstr. 124, 80636
Munich, Germany
Copyright © 2025 Dorling Kindersley Limited

Text and illustration copyright © Christina West and
Kacey Crutchfield 2025

Christina West and Kacey Crutchfield have asserted their right
to be identified as the authors of this work.

10 9 8 7 6 5 4 3 2 1
001–345506–Aug/2025
All rights reserved.

All rights reserved. No part of this publication may be
reproduced, stored in or introduced into a retrieval system, or
transmitted, in any form, or by any means (electronic, mechanical,
photocopying, recording, or otherwise), without the prior written
permission of the copyright owner.

DK values and supports copyright. Thank you for respecting
intellectual property laws by not reproducing, scanning or
distributing any part of this publication by any means without
permission. By purchasing an authorised edition, you are
supporting writers and artists and enabling DK to continue
to publish books that inform and inspire readers.
No part of this publication may be used or reproduced in
any manner for the purpose of training artificial intelligence
technologies or systems. In accordance with Article 4③
of the DSM Directive 2019/790, DK expressly reserves this work
from the text and data mining exception.

A CIP catalogue record for this book is available
from the British Library.
ISBN 978-0-2417-2806-2

Printed and bound in China

www.dk.com

This book was made with Forest Stewardship Council™ certified paper – one small step in DK's commitment to a sustainable future. Learn more at www.dk.com/uk/information/sustainability

ABOUT THE AUTHORS

CHRISTINA WEST is the founder and designer behind Kindred Quilt Co., an online modern quilt pattern company. What began as a mission to make personalized nursery bedding for her son has blossomed into a full-time passion for quilting and pattern design. *The Quilting Book* marks her debut as an author.

Over the past 11 years, Christina has refined her quilting skills and contributed as a pattern tester for numerous designers, magazines, and other published works. In 2020, she ventured into publishing her own quilt patterns to grow what is now her company today. Known for her vibrant colour choices and modern geometric designs, Christina is deeply influenced by childhood memories growing up in the stunning landscapes of central Texas.

Beyond her design work, Christina has collaborated with fabric companies to curate her own fat quarter bundles and has taught colour theory and quilting techniques at local guilds and quilt shops – experiences that reflect her dedication to teaching and fostering creativity within the quilting community. When she is not quilting, Christina is sharing her latest projects, tips, and inspirations with her followers on social media, coaching youth baseball, and spending time with her husband, son, and three pets in the North Texas area.

www.kindredquiltco.com
www.kindredquiltco.etsy.com

KACEY CRUTCHFIELD is a technical editor at Kacey Crutchfield Consulting, where she collaborates with quilt pattern designers to refine their patterns for publication, ensuring clarity, consistency, and accessibility. She is a former junior high English Language Arts teacher, university instructor, and academic in the field of Educational Psychology and Gifted and Talented Education. She has published in academic journals and textbooks, and *The Quilting Book* is her first venture into publishing in the quilting industry.

Kacey learned to sew as a young child in the sewing rooms of her grandmother and great-grandmother, and taught herself to quilt when experiencing burnout from academia. She quickly threw herself into applying her background in education to quilt pattern testing, then transitioned to tech editing at the encouragement of her friends and clients. She has since tech edited hundreds of quilt patterns, including prose and patterns for other quilting books, and is known for her attention to detail. She specializes in working with new quilt pattern designers by offering an accessible pricing model.

When Kacey is not editing or quilting, she is sharing about her quilting projects on social media, reading, or spending time with her husband and puppy in the North Texas area.

www.kaceycrutchfield.com